PERGAMON
INTERNATIONAL
LIBRARY
of Science, Technology
Engineering &
Social Studies

PERGAMON GENERAL PSYCHOLOGY SERIES

Editors: Arnold P. Goldstein, *Syracuse University*
Leonard Krasner, *SUNY, Stony Brook*

BEHAVIOR THERAPY AND HEALTH CARE

PGPS-43

BEHAVIOR THERAPY AND HEALTH CARE

Principles and Applications

Edited by

Roger C. Katz and Steven Zlutnick

University of Utah College of Medicine

PERGAMON PRESS INC.

New York · Toronto · Oxford · Sydney · Braunschweig

PERGAMON PRESS INC.
Maxwell House, Fairview Park, Elmsford, N.Y. 10523

PERGAMON OF CANADA LTD.
207 Queen's Quay West, Toronto 117, Ontario

PERGAMON PRESS LTD.
Headington Hill Hall, Oxford

PERGAMON PRESS (AUST.) PTY. LTD.
Rushcutters Bay, Sydney, N.S.W.

PERGAMON GmbH
Burgplatz 1, Braunschweig

Library of Congress Cataloging in Publication Data

Katz, Roger C.
    Behavior therapy and health care.

    (Pergamon general psychology series, 43)
    1. Medicine, Psychosomatic. 2. Behavior therapy.
I. Zlutnick, Steven, joint author. II. Title.
[DNLM: 1. Behavior therapy—Essays. WM420 K19b
1975]
RC49.K36 1975   615'.85   74-7331
ISBN 0-08-017829-4
ISBN 0-08-017828-6 (pbk.)

Printed in the United States of America

To Our Parents and Wives

Contents

Foreword

The fact that behavior affects both disease and the maintenance of health has long been known, and for just as long has been minimized or overlooked both by medical research workers and clinicians. One reason for this minimization of the importance of behavior and even the behavioral sciences in medicine has been the lack of procedures derived from these sciences which change behavior in a clinically useful way.

The development of behavior therapy has begun to alter this undesirable state of affairs. First, by introducing innovative and effective treatment procedures, and second, by acting as a vehicle for the application of the research methods and findings of experimental psychology to the health field. For example, the experimental analysis of behavior that was first used to examine a narrow range of animal behavior in very controlled settings has proven particularly useful in solving human problems. This method involves studying the behavior of individuals; each subject serves as his own control, and problem behavior is objectively specified and continuously measured. The variable under investigation is then introduced, removed, and reintroduced so that its effect upon the problem behavior is demonstrated. Such research has shown that behavior is determined by events in the external environment. Since many of these environmental events are modifiable, and in turn modify behavior, a number of new therapeutic procedures, usually referred to as behavior therapy, have been developed.

Behavior therapy was first applied to those organic and behavioral disorders classified as psychiatric, and over a decade ago the first book of readings appeared. For a long time this newcomer, so vigorously introduced by skillful proponents, was viewed suspiciously by the majority of psychiatrists, but over the years empirical demonstrations of effectiveness have modified this view. Remarkable progress has been made, and the treatment of many of the behavior disorders of adults and children has been much enhanced. Now this book of readings, the first of its kind, sets the scene for the application of behavior therapy to the entire health field.

Behavior therapy is particularly suited for such an application for it follows many of the best traditions of medical research. The research sequence begins with the identification of a clinical problem, and proceeds from uncontrolled clinical observation to precise clinical experiment. Alternatively, empirically tested treatment procedures are analyzed experimentally to determine which ingredients are responsible for the therapeutic effect. Since this book presents the beginnings of a new field of inquiry, the levels of experimental sophistication are quite varied, but all point the way toward further experiment and improved patient care.

Like the first applications to psychiatry, the main focus is on the treatment of particular entities, and some impressive achievements are documented. Noteworthy is the work on disorders of eating such as obesity and anorexia nervosa, and procedures that improve the management of common clinical problems, for example, enuresis and encopresis. In addition, useful approaches to the treatment of psychophysiologic disorders such as asthma and certain cardiovascular disorders are brought together in one place for the first time.

As with the application of behavior therapy to psychiatric problems, a second area of innovative experimentation exists, devoted to developing environments that facilitate therapeutic behavior change. One environment is the hospital ward where troublesome behavior is often intensified by misdirected attention. An experimental analysis of the effects of training staff to implement contingency management programs with varying patient populations should much enhance patient care. Similarly, contingency management has a place in rehabilitation and occupational and physical therapy, although the applications here are only beginning.

Finally, there is a strong possibility that an experimental analysis of behavior will lead to interventions that will diminish the risk of pathophysiologic changes. Controlled studies suggest that behavior modification approaches are more effective than other methods, such as counseling and prescribing diets, in weight reduction and point the way to programs that will change eating, smoking, and exercise patterns, to reduce the risk of developing coronary artery disease.

At this point, a few words of caution seem indicated. New therapeutic approaches tend to be oversold. Indeed, the work on cardiovascular conditioning may already be an example of this tendency. The first reports that blood pressure and heart rate could be altered by manipulating environmental contingencies was a major scientific development. But amid the publicity generated by these discoveries, rather extravagant claims were made which suggested that the control of problems such as essential hypertension was at hand. A reading of the literature reveals that most of the achieved changes in the modification of cardiac rate and blood pressure have been in normal subjects, with a magnitude of change of statistical, but not clinical significance. Very few clinically significant changes have been reported, and, when they have, the experimental analysis has been less satisfactory than in the better controlled, but clinically insignificant, studies. An important function of this book is to highlight such issues and to place recent developments in perspective.

These new research endeavors, management, and treatment programs call for increased attention to the principles and procedures of the experimental behavioral sciences in the initial and continuing education of workers in the health field. This book should prove useful to such workers and their students, and its organization by organ system seems particularly appropriate for such an audience. Moreover, up to now the application of behavior therapy to health care has proceeded in a somewhat haphazard way. Hopefully, this book will give a sense of both the achievements and the possibilities of this new endeavor and will stimulate the development of a more cohesive approach to teaching, research, and practice.

W. Stewart Agras, MD FRCP (C)
Professor of Psychiatry
Stanford University School of Medicine

The Editors

Roger C. Katz (Ph.D., University of Utah) is a clinical psychologist and was affiliated with the Department of Family and Community Medicine at the University of Utah when this book was written. His research and teaching interests are in applied behavioral analysis as well as in the use of paraprofessionals in the delivery of mental health services. Dr. Katz has published articles in such journals as *Child Development, Behavior Therapy,* and *Journal of Child Psychology and Psychiatry* on various aspects of behavioral intervention and treatment. He is currently with the Department of Psychology at the University of the Pacific.

Steven Zlutnick (Ph.D., University of Utah) is with the Division of Postgraduate Education in the Department of Psychiatry, University of Utah College of Medicine, and holds a joint faculty appointment in Psychiatry and Psychology. His primary professional interests include training and consultation in behavior modification and the application of behavior therapy to health care and social problems. Currently he is investigating the effects of operant conditioning techniques on epilepsy and chronic pain. Dr. Zlutnick has also had extensive experience in direct service activities and has developed programs for emotionally disturbed children and adult psychiatric populations. His published works are in the areas of crowding, patient care, and educational technology.

Preface

During the past decade, an emerging technology of applied behavioral science has produced important innovations in health care. This learning-theory based technology has led to an array of therapeutic procedures collectively known as behavior therapy. In mental health, the success of behavior therapy has been amply documented by Bandura (1969), Franks (1969), Ullmann and Krasner (1965, 1969), and others (Agras, 1972). Only very recently, however, have investigators begun to apply the same technology to resolve the problems of patients who require non-psychiatric medical assistance. This book attempts to bring together this growing body of literature.

The central purposes of this text are to highlight important interactions between illness and the environment, and to describe significant contributions to health care provided by behavior therapists. In conjunction with already established medical technology, behavioral techniques allow for a more comprehensive approach to patient care. In contrast, lack of attention to the environmental, behavioral, and social components of health problems may result in a less than satisfactory treatment outcome. Clearly, the patient profits from the collaboration between medical practitioners and behavioral scientists. The selected papers presented here support this premise by illustrating the means by which behavioral technology can be successfully incorporated into the general framework of health care delivery.

Many readers will be well versed in behavioral science, perhaps from having taken courses in learning theory, abnormal psychology, or behavior modification but other readers will have had little exposure in these areas. For this latter group, the introductory chapter should be especially helpful. In this chapter we have attempted to describe fundamental principles of behavior that form the basis of behavior therapy approaches to patient care. To make the introduction as informative as possible, examples of selected principles are provided as they might operate in common patient care situations. A list of references is also provided at the end of the chapter for readers who elect to pursue particular topics in greater detail.

To provide a format that is familiar to those in the health care field, chapters are generally organized according to organ system headings. For example, Chapters 2 through 7 deal with applications of behavior therapy to health problems involving the genitourinary system, gastrointestinal system, cardiovascular system, musculoskeletal system, nervous system, and respiratory system, respectively. Patient management problems and pain control are described in Chapter 8, while Chapter 9 is concerned with two additional health problems, alcoholism and obesity. Each of these chapters begins with an editors' introduction to provide appropriate context and a review of forthcoming selections. At the conclusion of each chapter introduction, points of key importance are outlined to insure that they are not overlooked.

Selection of individual papers was not an easy task, and undoubtedly there were many which, though not included, would have made valuable contributions. Generally, however, we were strongly influenced by the following criteria: (1) that entries describe practical and effective methods of patient care; (2) that they be based on experimental rather than anecdotal evidence; and (3) that they be relevant to the health problems dealt with by today's student or practicing health professional. The reader is encouraged to make full use of the references each author provides at the end of his paper. In this manner he can achieve a more complete view of the state of the field.

The book is intended for student and professional groups in health education, physical rehabilitation, clinical medicine, psychology, psychiatry, and nursing. The text is appropriate for students at either the advanced undergraduate or graduate level. Instructors may utilize the book as a primary text or as supplementary reading to present relevant material that is not reviewed in lecture or discussion group meetings. Organization of the book by organ system should facilitate integration of the material with other textbooks and classroom presentations. As a resource for students in medicine or nursing, the book reviews contemporary developments in behavioral science that will both reinforce their existing clinical knowledge and broaden their conceptual understanding of health and illness. Finally, for both students and practicing health professionals, the book describes a general problem-solving methodology for biological and behavioral disorders. This methodology and the case study examples should suggest specific treatments for health problems that are frequently encountered in clinical practice.

At this time we should like to pay special thanks to the people who assisted us in preparing this book. Among them, first and foremost, are Drs. Donna Gelfand and Lincoln Clark, both of whom contributed many valuable ideas, editorial comments, and helpful criticism throughout the course of our writing. To them our deepest appreciation is extended. Others who assisted us include Drs. Fred Kolouch, Charles Uhl, Ross Woolley, and Len Schmidt. For their many constructive suggestions we are also indebted. Finally, thanks go to LaRue Dignan and Patti Kanegae in appreciation of their outstanding secretarial assistance.

R.C.K.

S.I.Z.

CHAPTER 1

Behavior and Health Care: Review and Perspective

> On a teaching hospital's clinical research unit, one nurse identified a complex patient care problem . . . . Billy, (age 5), who had recently passed through a period of crisis, was grunting, whining, and pointing instead of talking. He was also refusing to walk, reach for anything, or eat or drink fluids well, and he was continually putting on his call light. The nurse knew that, according to current medical reports, Billy was capable of more physical activity. She attempted to solve the problem of Billy's negativism by providing him with support, encouragement, frequent visits, and explanation of his improvement in health and capabilities. But, she failed. None of his behavior changed (Berni, Dressler, & Baxter, 1971, **71**, 2180).[1]

Problems of health and illness are inextricably related to physical, behavioral, and environmental factors. Each of these factors contributes to the kinds of problems encountered in medical management. Each deserves careful attention if the needs of the patient are to be properly met. As physicians, nurses, and other health professionals face complex patient care problems that cannot be resolved by traditional medical techniques alone, the concepts and skills of other disciplines may suggest solutions. In this respect, an integrated model of health care that combines medical and behavioral science holds considerable promise.

There is a common tendency to equate health problems solely with organic illness. While organic disorders frequently form the basis of the patient's illness, it is equally true that not all of his complaints can be explained by an identifiable disease state, nor treated exclusively by medical or surgical means. On the contrary, medical assistance is often requested for problems that have significant behavioral components.

---

[1]From *American Journal of Nursing.* Copyright © by the American Journal of Nursing Company. Reprinted by permission.

Among them are various emotional problems such as depression, anxiety, lethargy, and in some cases, pain; interpersonal problems, including family and marital discord; addiction problems; obesity; psychosomatic diseases such as gastric ulcers, bronchial asthma, and ulcerative colitis; suicide; child abuse; and patient education problems which, unless resolved, may render preventive medicine an elusive goal. In each of these cases, modifying behavior is an integral part of clinical management and bears directly on improving the health status of the patient.

In discussing the relationship of behavior to health, it is important to realize that the nature of this relationship is neither static nor unidirectional. Behavior may be altered by illness as much as illness may result from behavior. All patients, regardless of their medical problems, are behaving, adjusting individuals whose past experience and present activity may dramatically affect both the rate and completeness of recovery. A basic understanding of the interaction between illness and factors that influence behavior deserves careful consideration. Some examples may help to illustrate this point.

Case No. 1   Mr. C., a 37-year-old married construction worker, came to the hospital physically unkempt, confused, terrified of hallucinated spiders, and smelling of alcohol. His physical examination revealed several minor burns about the hands, a slightly enlarged liver, and abdominal tenderness. Three days later, when he had somewhat recovered, the patient said that he had gone on a bender following an argument with his wife. He was sorry for the trouble he had caused and left the hospital promising never to drink again. One month later he was readmitted for acute alcohol intoxication.

Comment   A history of certain recurrent behaviors may contribute directly to medical problems involving structural impairment to cells and organs. Just as prolonged alcohol consumption can produce liver disease and other health hazards, cigarette smoking may lead to reduced pulmonary function or cancer, while sedentarism and overeating are often precursors to coronary artery disease, diabetes mellitus, or premature myocardial infarction. If prevention is to be an achievable goal, efforts must be undertaken to modify these precipitating behaviors.

Case No. 2   Mr. D. was a successful young accountant who had been involved in a serious automobile accident that resulted in partial hemiplegia of his right side. Physical therapy was initiated but his progress in regaining the use of his limbs was exceptionally slow. Mr. D. was described by the physical therapist as easily frustrated and lacking in both cooperation and effort.

Comment　Health problems involving brain or spinal cord injury, metabolic disease, or severe damage to bones and muscle tissue may disrupt the patient's capability in a wide variety of behavioral areas. As a consequence of these problems, activities that previously required minimal effort, such as speech, ambulation, and basic self-care skills, may be permanently impaired or regained only through extended relearning. Knowledge of the conditions under which learning most readily occurs facilitates physical therapy and hastens the acquisition of alternative coping skills.

Case No. 3　Mrs. T. had recently undergone a hysterectomy. Since then she has become periodically depressed, neglectful of her household responsibilities, and fearful of engaging in sexual activities with her husband. Mr. T. was quite concerned about these changes and sought the help of the family doctor.

Comment　The patient's emotional response to illness is another area in which behavior and health care overlap. Medical problems not only affect the patient's physical status, but also serve as a stimulus for emotional reactions such as fear, anger, resentment, or depression. Whether these reactions are temporary or become chronic behavioral problems will depend not only on the seriousness of the patient's illness, but also on the manner in which they are handled by professionals, family, and colleagues upon whom the patient must depend.

Case No. 4　Mr. G. had adult onset diabetes and was recently admitted to the hospital with diabetic acidosis. Before his discharge he was sternly admonished to restrict his carbohydrates, lose weight, engage in regular exercise, and take his diabetic medications on schedule. When followed up six weeks later, he had gained four pounds and his urine was strongly positive for sugar.

Comment　Patient management constitutes a fourth area in which behavior and health care merge. Compliance with medication, dietary or exercise regimens, attendance at follow-up visits, or cooperation with basic nursing requests all involve behavior that must be engaged in by the patient if proper management is to be realized. Noncompliance may represent either a motivational or knowledge deficit. In both cases, however, recognition of variables that control behavior should be helpful in overcoming compliance problems.

Case No. 5   Kevin had his first asthma attack when he was nine. Originally his attacks occurred only at home. Now they have begun to occur at school following the slightest provocation from his classmates. Because Kevin must often be excused from class following an attack, his school work is suffering. His teacher fears that he will have to be held back a year unless he can attend class more regularly.

Comment   The symptoms of many chronic health problems such as bronchial asthma, epilepsy, and pain syndromes are manifested behaviorally. Like other behavior these symptoms may be influenced by environmental factors. Whether or not the etiology of the problem is known, it may be possible to treat uncomfortable or potentially dangerous symptomatology by identifying the environmental conditions under which it predictably occurs. This is not to suggest that a technology of behavior can eliminate underlying physiological defects or tissue pathology. However, it may be useful in reducing certain disease related behavioral symptoms, which themselves can be a source of major concern.

The present chapter examines applied behavioral science both as a fund of knowledge and as a method of objective inquiry. Our goals in preparing this chapter are twofold: (1) to prepare the reader for subsequent chapters that require knowledge of basic principles of behavior; and, (2) to describe the technology of a therapeutic model commonly referred to as *behavior therapy*. Although this introduction is necessarily brief, a list of useful references is provided at the end of the chapter for those who would like to pursue selected topics in greater detail.

BEHAVIOR AND THE ENVIRONMENT

A discussion of behavioral principles is best introduced by providing a working definition of behavior. Thus let us begin by defining the term "behavior" as *the activity of organisms*. With specific reference to humans, this includes a broad range of activity: highly visible motor responses such as walking, speech, and the manipulation of objects; internal activity such as thinking and emotion; as well as the subtle and involuntary activity of smooth muscles and glands. As a subject matter for scientific analysis, *behavior is what organisms do*, whether it is observed directly or not, regarded as good, bad, sick, or healthy.

Although much needs to be learned about the biochemical and neurophysiological mechanisms of behavior, it is well established that behavioral phenomena are strongly influenced by both genetic and environmental factors. Generally speaking, these factors interact to determine the behavior of all animal species. Hereditary endowment is fixed at conception and provides an overall plan for subsequent development. Among higher organisms such as man, behavior itself is neither inherited nor under rigid genetic control. However, heredity gives rise to biological structures that make behavior possible and ultimately determine the range of activities that may potentially develop.

Organisms always act within the context of environmental surroundings. From the time of birth, environmental forces play a major role in influencing behavior, both present and future. We call this influencing process *learning*. We use the term to describe relatively permanent changes in behavior that result from environmental experience. Although behavior may also change as a consequence of other conditions, among them maturation, fatigue, and neural impairment, learning is an inferred construct to designate behavioral change that occurs after repeated exposure to environmental events. These events are technically known as *stimuli*. Since environments are immensely variable in the type of stimuli they provide, and higher organisms so adaptively flexible, many opportunities exist for learning diverse and unique behavior.

Just as medical science is concerned with acquiring knowledge to prevent, alleviate, or cure disease, behavioral science seeks to analyze and describe orderly relationships between environmental stimuli and behavior. By identifying stimuli capable of affecting behavior in specifiable ways, the understanding, prediction, and control of behavior become eminently more feasible. This, too, has significant therapeutic implications. A technology of human behavior based upon scientific understanding can be used to produce beneficial change.

PRINCIPLES OF RESPONDENT BEHAVIOR

Behavior may be classified as either *reflexive* or *operant* depending on whether it is elicited by preceding stimuli or maintained by the consequences it produces. From a functional standpoint, reflexive behavior is probably the less important of the two for it encompasses a limited range of activity that is unalterable in its basic form. Nevertheless, knowledge of the reflex is important to understand behavior and its relationship to the environment, as well as to serve as a starting point to introduce the subject of operant behavior.

The *unconditioned reflex* describes a relationship between stimulus and response that is usually fixed at birth and determined by the organism's inherited physiology. The pupillary response to light is one example. In this as well as other intact reflexes, all that is needed to evoke the response, pupillary constriction, is the proper eliciting stimulus, light on the eye. Whenever the stimulus is presented, the response occurs automatically in essentially the same form. Because reflexes are involuntary behaviors that occur in response to antecedent stimuli, they are frequently called *respondent behaviors*. For humans, examples of respondent behaviors that are elicited by specific stimuli include perspiration in response to warmth, salivation in response to food, vomiting in response to stimulation of the esophagus, and startle reactions in response to sudden or unexpected noise.

Respondent Conditioning

Although the structural properties of respondent behavior are determined phylogenetically, new stimuli may acquire eliciting properties through the process of *respondent conditioning.* Pavlov (1927) first described this conditioning paradigm some 50 years ago. Studying salivation and digestion in dogs, he observed that a salivary response was elicited by placing food in the dog's mouth. However, after repeated trials salivation also occurred in response to the sight of food, the feeding dish, and even the experimenter's approaching footsteps. Pavlov adopted the term *unconditioned stimulus* to refer to the food that elicited an innate or *unconditioned response,* so named because it occurs irrespective of prior learning. In a series of experiments, Pavlov showed that by associating the sound of a bell with the delivery of food, the bell alone would increase the flow of saliva. Prior to its association with food, the bell was a *neutral stimulus* since it had no affect on salivation. When it later elicited a salivary response, Pavlov designated the bell as a *conditioned stimulus,* and the corresponding change in the animal's behavior was called a *conditioned response.* One essential feature of the process by which a neutral stimulus acquires eliciting properties is its *temporal contiguity* with the unconditioned stimulus.

In respondent conditioning, new behavior is not actually acquired since the difference between the conditioned response and the unconditioned response is usually very slight. What does occur is that a new stimulus begins to elicit behavior that it previously could not. Pavlov's conditioning paradigm is shown in Fig. 1. Although conditioning occurs through paired presentations of stimuli, in actuality the conditioned stimulus precedes the unconditioned stimulus by a brief period. Both the order of stimulus presentation and the temporal delay between conditioned stimulus and unconditioned stimulus are important parameters of learning. Conditioning effects are usually not obtained if the sequence is reversed, or the interval between conditioned stimulus and unconditioned stimulus exceeds more than a few seconds (Kimble, 1961).

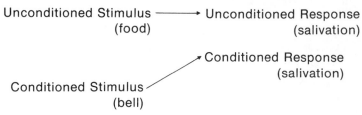

Fig. 1. Pavlov's respondent conditioning paradigm.

Respondent Extinction

At least occasional pairing of the conditioned stimulus and unconditioned stimulus are required to enable the former to evoke a conditioned response. If the conditioned stimulus is presented repeatedly without the unconditioned stimulus, *respondent extinction* will occur; that is, the conditioned stimulus will no longer elicit a conditioned response. For example, Pavlov showed that when the bell was repeatedly presented without food, the magnitude of the salivary response diminished until it no longer occurred. In a similar fashion, a young child who becomes afraid when first exposed to friendly strangers will usually show less fear with subsequent exposure. In this case the response, fear, undergoes extinction.

Both respondent conditioning and extinction illustrate a more general principle about behavior and its plasticity in relationship to the environment. Changes in behavior that result from environmental experience are not necessarily permanent, but rather they endure depending upon the permanence of the conditions that produced them. Just as extinction demonstrates the reversibility of behavioral effects, reinstating the conditioned stimulus with an unconditioned stimulus will again cause the conditioned response to occur.

Emotional Behavior

Emotional states such as fear, excitement, or depression usually involve alterations in the form and frequency of several behaviors simultaneously. Many of these altered behaviors are directly observable and include changes in facial or vocal expression, blushing or blanching, locomotor activity, postural orientation, and gestural reactions. Conversely, others are experienced internally such as increases in heart rate, blood pressure, stomach contractions, and perspiration. Because most of the behaviors that make up emotion are elicited by antecedent stimuli, emotional behaviors are generally classified as respondents.

Painful stimuli are capable of producing emotional behavior independent of prior learning. Through conditioning, however, emotional behavior may also occur in response to innocuous stimuli, thus disrupting behavior even though no real danger is present. When emotional activity is elicited by conditioned stimuli, it is called a *conditioned emotional response*. According to some investigators (Lachman, 1972), prolonged or excessive conditioned emotional responses, with accompanying physiological arousal, can produce enduring structural changes such as duodenal ulcers, ulcerative colitis, neurodermatitis, and other so-called *psychosomatic* manifestations.

Psychiatric disorders such as phobias and fetishes are also closely linked to conditioned emotional behavior. In phobias, for example, seemingly harmless objects or situations become the source of intense, oftentimes incapacitating anxiety. These events are usually avoided at all cost even though the individual may be fully aware of the irrationality of his fear. Rardin (1969) describes the reaction of one young female patient whose fear of the sight of blood seriously interfered with her desire to become a nurse.

> Her reaction to blood and possible physical injury varied from moderate discomfort to dizziness and nausea depending on the topic and circumstances. The immediate concern was her reaction to the films shown in nursing classes which vividly depicted various medical conditions. On a number of occasions, she had to put her head down or leave the room. She felt she would faint or vomit if she continued to observe the film. This reaction was interfering with her performance in the classes in which the films were shown, and the nursing faculty was beginning to question her suitability for the profession (p. 125).[2]

---

[2]From *Journal of Consulting and Clinical Psychology.* Copyright © 1969 by The American Psychological Association. Reprinted by permission.

One conditioning procedure that could be used to alter this woman's emotional reaction, and other types of phobic disorders, is known as *systematic desensitization* and is described below.

Systematic Desensitization: A Means of Modifying Conditioned Emotional Behavior The therapeutic technique of systematic desensitization has proven to be very successful in treating conditioned emotional responses having fear or anxiety as a main component. As described by Wolpe (1958, 1969), systematic desensitization is based on the premise that anxiety and relaxation are physiologically incompatible responses that cannot occur simultaneously in the presence of the same stimulus. When used as a therapeutic technique, desensitization literally involves training the patient to relax in the presence of stimuli that previously elicited anxiety.

Patients undergoing desensitization are first trained in *deep muscle relaxation* (Jacobson, 1938) through a series of muscle tensing and relaxing exercises. Following relaxation training, anxiety producing stimuli are carefully identified and arranged hierarchically from least to most fear provoking. Hierarchy items that elicit the least anxiety are then presented individually while the patient is completely relaxed. This is carried out by instructing the patient to imagine approximations to the feared stimulus, or *in vivo* by graded exposure to real stimuli. In both cases, however, progression through the hierarchy is usually gradual and dependent upon complete extinction of anxiety responses to subordinate items before succeeding items are presented. Through a series of gradual steps, the patient eventually experiences the anxiety producing stimulus with minimal subjective disturbance. As evidenced in later chapters, systematic desensitization and relaxation training have application to a wide variety of clinical disorders, including physiological disturbances linked to conditioned responses.

PRINCIPLES OF OPERANT BEHAVIOR

Respondent behaviors comprise only a small sample of the behavior of higher organisms. The remaining behavior is *operant* and controlled by stimuli that follow the response. The experimental analysis of operant behavior has resulted primarily from the research of Skinner (1938, 1953) and his colleagues at Harvard University. Skinner coined the term "operant behavior" because this type of behavior *operates* on the environment and is maintained or eliminated depending upon the *conse-quences* it produces. Buying a car, calling for help, walking, reading a book, and solving a problem are all examples of operants that occur because they alter the environment to produce specifiable outcomes. Most of our interpersonal behavior is operant in nature.

Unlike respondent behavior, operant behavior is not automatically evoked by antecedent stimuli. Because it is often impossible to identify the specific stimuli that produce operants, they are referred to as *emitted* behavior to distinguish them from the elicited quality of respondents.

Other features distinguish operant from respondent behavior. Operants are voluntary behaviors involving striated musculature and controlled by the central nervous system. Respondents more commonly entail the autonomically mediated activity of smooth muscles and glands that may not be under the organism's direct control. However, preliminary evidence from recently conducted laboratory research (Kimmel, 1967; Miller, 1969; Shapiro & Schwartz, 1972) suggests that under certain conditions this voluntary–involuntary distinction may be more artificial than real. By providing discriminable information about specific autonomic processes, a technique referred to as *biofeedback*, organisms can learn to regulate some internal activities such as galvanic skin response, blood pressure, heart rate, and brain alpha rhythm, which were previously believed to be beyond selective, voluntary control. Clinical applications of biofeedback procedures are discussed in later chapters dealing with cardiovascular and nervous system disorders.

One of the most crucial distinctions between operants and respondents is that respondents are phylogenetically determined and require only the proper stimulus to evoke them, while operants are acquired behaviors that may take any form the environment dictates within the neuroanatomical potential of the organism. Consider responses to pain inducing stimuli: pain is an unconditioned stimulus that elicits similar physiological responses in most people (e.g., increased blood pressure, rapid respiration, sweating, etc.). However, activities subsequently performed to relieve pain, such as verbally requesting medical assistance, consuming an aspirin, resting in bed, complaining, crying, or showing casual indifference, are operants that may or may not occur depending upon the person's unique conditioning history.

Although operants and respondents differ along many dimensions, in day-to-day living they interact to influence the ongoing activity of the behaving organism. In humans, for example, emotional states are usually elicited by conditioned or unconditioned stimuli. When these emotional states occur, they alter the probability that selected operant behaviors will also occur. Thus "feeling angry" increases the likelihood of operant aggression or avoidance, while "feeling love" usually results in affectionate or admiring behavior as well as continued contact with the loved person. Similarly, crying in a young child may begin as a respondent elicited in response to pain or discomfort. However, crying also produces environmental consequences (e.g., parental attention, changing a wet diaper, food, etc.). Depending on the nature of the consequences, crying may become an operant behavior as evidenced by changes in the form or frequency with which it occurs. The significance of the interaction between operants and respondents will become more apparent in discussing conditioned reinforcement and conditioned aversive stimuli in the next section.

Modifying Operant Behavior

After a decision is made to modify behavior, primary interest should be centered on the effectiveness of our treatment procedure as measured by observable alterations in the frequency or duration of the behavior in question. Has the patient spent more time in physical rehabilitation? Is he taking his medication more or less frequently than before? Are seizures occurring at a lower frequency? These are meaningful questions that reflect directly on the efficacy of clinical management.

Once agreement is reached that *outcome* as measured by overt behavioral change is of prime importance, our task is simplified considerably since only three outcomes are possible: (1) the behavior *increases* in frequency or duration; (2) the behavior *decreases* in frequency or duration; or (3) the behavior remains unaffected by our procedures. Accordingly, our objectives in discussing behavioral change are twofold: we need to specify procedures for increasing or decreasing operant behavior; and, we must devise a system to determine whether or not the desired outcome has been achieved. For the present our efforts will be directed toward techniques of altering behavior. Evaluation of behavioral change will be discussed later.

Stimulus Consequences of Behavior

As a first step in defining the principles of operant behavior modification, we need to study the kinds of stimuli that serve as behavioral consequences. Basically they fall into one of three categories: *positive, negative*, or *neutral*. For purposes of the present discussion it is best to disregard the *usual* connotations of "positive" and "negative" for they tend to be misleading within the context of an experimental analysis of behavior. As we shall see, behavior may be increased using either type of stimulus.

A *positive stimulus* is an event an organism will work to obtain. In the strictest sense it is a stimulus that increases the future probability of the response it follows. When behavior increases as a result of the stimulus it produces, the stimulus is called a *positive reinforcer*. Conversely, *a negative stimulus* is one that an organism will work to avoid. When this occurs, we label the stimulus *aversive*. Note that these definitions allow us to define stimulus effects empirically rather than subjectively. Stimulus functions should not be defined *a priori* but rather by their effects upon behavior. Masochism, where inflicting self-injury can be positively reinforcing, is a case in point. An observer might classify a beating as an aversive stimulus, but the masochistic recipient might actually work to obtain the painful event. Thus, behaviorally, the beating is a positive consequence for the person we term masochistic.

The third type of stimulus is termed *neutral* and is one that has essentially no effect upon behavior. As we shall see, however, neutral stimuli may acquire reinforcing properties under certain conditions. Similarly, reinforcing stimuli may become neutralized with respect to behavior, depending upon how they are used.

Stimuli are differentiated depending on whether they are *primary* (unconditioned) or *conditioned*. Thus we can speak of primary and conditioned reinforcing stimuli, and primary and conditioned aversive stimuli.

A *primary reinforcer* is not dependent upon conditioning to acquire its reinforcing property. Primary reinforcers are often termed "innate" or "biological" reinforcers because they are required to satisfy basic needs of the organism. Food, water, air, and sex (orgasm) are all examples of primary reinforcers for humans as well as for other animal species. In each case the reinforcing property of these events is dependent upon the amount of *deprivation* present. As deprivation is increased, the reinforcing value of the stimulus is similarly increased. For instance, the effectiveness of food as a primary reinforcer will depend on when food was last consumed. A person who has just finished a full course meal is unlikely to seek food, whereas one who has not eaten for 24 hours will go to great lengths to do so.

A *conditioned reinforcer* is a stimulus that has acquired its reinforcing property by repeated pairing with established reinforcers. Without pairing of this type, the stimulus is functionally neutral and exerts no effect upon the behavior it follows. The process by which reinforcing properties are acquired has been previously described in the section on respondent conditioning as temporal contiguity. In laboratory research the sound of a buzzer may be established as a conditioned reinforcer by presenting it just prior to the delivery of food. After repeated association of the buzzer with food, new behavior may be increased by following it with the sound of the buzzer alone. In a similar fashion, mood enhancing medications such as morphine and demerol may become conditioned reinforcers because of their close association with pleasant emotional states. More common conditioned reinforcers include attention, praise, recognition, and approval, events referred to as *social reinforcers* because they are mediated socially and indicate reinforcing aspects of social interaction. The majority of human behaviors are maintained by these social or conditioned reinforcers received through interaction with other people.

An important consideration at this point is the discrete nature of conditioned reinforcement in that most conditioned reinforcers are dependent upon a single primary reinforcer for their effects. For this reason the use of discrete conditioned reinforcers to change behavior can be somewhat precarious since they are subject to *satiation* effects. Satiation, in this instance, is to be contrasted with deprivation and refers to the decreased effectiveness of a reinforcer resulting from its excessive supply. Fortunately, another form of conditioned reinforcer may be utilized that is not sensitive to momentary satiation effects, *generalized conditioned reinforcers.* Generalized conditioned reinforcers are stimuli that allow access to more than one primary reinforcer. Money is probably the best example since it is commonly used to obtain a wide variety of other reinforcing events.

A popular therapeutic intervention based on the notion of generalized conditioned reinforcement is the *token economy* (Ayllon & Azrin, 1968), which makes use of some form of generalized conditioned reinforcer such as tokens or points. These are made contingent upon various desired behaviors and may be exchanged for "backup" reinforcers in the same fashion as money. In recent years token economy systems have been used with divergent populations such as chronic mental patients (Atthowe & Krasner, 1968; Ayllon & Azrin, 1968; Schaefer & Martin, 1966), retarded children and adults (Birnbrauer *et al.*, 1965), and normal school children (O'Leary & Becker, 1967).

Just as a primary reinforcer will increase behavior independent of prior learning, a *primary aversive stimulus* is an event an organism will work to avoid irrespective of conditioning history. Primary aversive stimuli include events capable of activating pain receptors, for example, electric shock, loud noise, extreme temperature, and other physical irritants.

Conditioned aversive stimuli are previously neutral stimuli that acquire their aversive property by repeated association with primary aversive events. When a child stops reaching for the cookie jar after his mother shouts "no," the word "no" serves as a conditioned aversive stimulus to suppress behavior since in the past it may have been associated with unconditioned aversive events such as a slap on the buttocks. In the same manner, the sight of an open wound, a dentist's drill, sick people, or medical odors can readily acquire conditioned aversive properties because of their association with unpleasant or painful experiences.

Techniques for Increasing Operant Behavior

A Table of Consequent Events is shown in Fig. 2. The rows are distinguished according to whether or not behavior results in the application or removal of a stimulus, while the columns show the corresponding behavioral outcome. Each square depicts techniques for modifying operant behavior.

Behavior Increases   Behavior Decreases

	Behavior Increases	Behavior Decreases
Apply Stimulus	POSITIVE REINFORCEMENT	PUNISHMENT
Remove Stimulus	NEGATIVE REINFORCEMENT	EXTINCTION TIME OUT FROM REINFORCEMENT RESPONSE COST

Fig. 2. Table of consequent events.

Positive Reinforcement As shown in Fig. 2, *positive reinforcement* refers to the application of a positively reinforcing stimulus (either primary or conditioned) after a response has occurred. The effect of positive reinforcement is to increase the likelihood that the reinforced response will occur again. For instance, an infant may begin to cry when he is hungry because in the past crying has been reinforced with food. If food continues to be a predictable consequence of crying, this response will probably reoccur the next time the child is hungry. Examples of conditioned positive reinforcement are also common in human affairs. For example, when we praise a patient for compliance with therapeutic plans, we increase the likelihood that he will do so again. Similarly, cultures ensure advancement in science and the arts by publicity, commendation, and monetary rewards for achievement in these areas.

Positive reinforcement can also serve to inadvertently strengthen certain undesirable behaviors. Even though we intend to influence behavior one way, the consequences of our action may cause good intentions to go astray. For example, children's tantrums are often reinforced positively by parental attention or acquiescence to the child's demands, while in adulthood various bizarre or disruptive behaviors (e.g., psychotic verbalizations, physical aggression, etc.) may be similarly maintained by the responses they produce in others (Ayllon & Michael, 1959; Liberman *et al.*, 1973). When attempting to modify behavior the effect of a particular stimulus cannot be determined by intuition or presumption, for seemingly unpleasant attention may serve to increase behavior in the same way as kindly or sympathetic attention. Just as positive reinforcement exerts its influence independent of the social acceptability of behavior, whether or not a stimulus is positively reinforcing can only be determined empirically by what it does to the individual's behavior.

One of the most important principles of behavior change is *shaping*, or the reinforcement of successive approximations to the desired response. In teaching a patient to walk using an artificial leg, we should not wait until he is actually walking before reinforcing his performance. Instead we would be wiser to make reinforcement contingent upon a more easily reached criterion, such as applying the prosthesis. Later the criteria for reinforcement could be gradually increased to include standing, balancing, or taking a single step. Shaping is based on the premise that a terminal response can be broken down into its component parts, which may then be reinforced as approximations to the final goal. The systematic use of shaping ensures that the individual meets with early and continued success rather than with repeated failure.

Positive reinforcers need not be limited to material or social events but rather may consist of opportunities to engage in certain behaviors. Using a relatively high-frequency behavior to increase behavior that occurs less frequently is called the *Premack Principle* (Premack, 1959; Homme *et al.*, 1963); less technically, it has been called "Grandma's Law" (e.g., eat your mashed potatoes and then you can ride your bicycle). A more useful example from the area of health care would be the case of a sports minded patient who is allowed to participate in recreation therapy only after compliance with required but perhaps unpleasant diagnostic procedures. Under these conditions the high-frequency behavior, engaging in recreational activities, is being used to reinforce another, less probable behavior, submitting to diagnostic tests.

Interviews as well as careful observation of the patient are often required in order to identify high-frequency behaviors that may serve as reinforcing events. Interviews alone will not always produce the desired information, since many patients are often unaware of how they spend their time, or simply will not cooperate in such an assessment.

Although positive reinforcement increases behavior, its effectiveness is dependent upon many conditions, the most important of which are the *immediacy* and *scheduling* of reinforcement. For reinforcement to be optimally useful, it must be delivered soon after the desired behavior has occurred. As the time period between response and reinforcer increases, the effective utilization of reinforcement is correspondingly reduced. In fact, inordinate delays of positive reinforcement can lead to the accidental reinforcement of other intervening behavior. In a similar fashion, behavior that coincides with the removal of unpleasant symptoms may be accidentally reinforced negatively. The application of mustard plasters for alleviation of head and chest pain is a good example of such a process. Although this procedure is often temporally correlated with symptomatic relief, few medical practitioners believe it to be causally related to improvement. Responding that results from accidental reinforcement contingencies is called *superstitious behavior*.

Schedules of reinforcement refer to the manner in which reinforcers are dispensed. The quickest way to strengthen behavior is to reinforce it continuously each time it occurs. In shaping, for example, *continuous reinforcement* is required to move from one approximation to the next. However, once behavior is occurring at an acceptable level, maintaining it at that level requires a different kind of reinforcement schedule.

When reinforcement does not occur after every response, the relationship of response to reinforcement is called an *intermittent schedule*.

Although there are many different kinds of intermittent reinforcement schedules, each of which can produce complex behavior patterns (Ferster & Skinner, 1957), generally speaking two schedules characterize the way in which reinforcement is most commonly delivered: *ratio schedules* and *interval schedules*. Ratio schedules require that a specified number of similar responses occur before reinforcement is given. This number may be *fixed* so that reinforcement occurs after every fifth, tenth, twentieth, etc., response, or it may be *variable,* occurring on the average of some number of responses, but otherwise unpredictable. On the other hand, interval schedules require that a period of time pass before a response is reinforced. With fixed interval schedules this time period is preset and constant; with variable interval schedules the length of time between reinforcement varies from one reinforcement to the next but around some average duration. These schedules operate frequently in our everyday experience. Thus the factory worker who is paid for piecework is being reinforced on a fixed ratio schedule; the employee who receives a check bi-weekly operates under fixed interval reinforcement; the gambler who wins occasionally at the slot machine experiences variable ratio reinforcement; while the mother who vigilantly watches her about-to-be toilet trained two-year-old in hopes of placing him on the potty is being reinforced for her vigilance according to a variable interval schedule.

When compared to continuous reinforcement, it is important to realize that each of these intermittent schedules represents a more efficient means of maintaining behavior. Not only do intermittent schedules require more behavior for less reinforcement, but of greater significance in promoting lasting behavioral change, the behavior they generate is more resistant to deterioration if reinforcement is subsequently withheld. For this reason, continuous reinforcement is not only unnecessary, but also unwise if maintaining behavior is regarded as a desirable goal. It is usually best to use some form of intermittent reinforcement once behavior has been established and is occurring at a reasonable frequency. The procedure used to reduce reinforcement from a continuous to an intermittent schedule is called *thinning* and entails the gradual reduction of reinforcement density without loss of performance. This procedure must be implemented carefully in order to avoid response deterioration. Thus the successful use of thinning requires careful behavioral observation as well as knowledge and experience.

A number of procedures exist that may serve to enhance the power and effectiveness of positive reinforcement; among them are imitation, instructions, and prompting.

Imitation   Most people are capable of acquiring new behavior vicariously by observing others and then *imitating* the observed performance. Several variables have been shown to influence the extent to which a model is imitated, among them being the sex, power, and social attractiveness of the model, and whether or not reinforcing outcomes are provided for the imitated behavior (Bandura, 1969). Using modeling procedures, therefore, it is possible to initiate new behavior quickly by first demonstrating the response and then reinforcing the observer for successful imitation. This should be recognized as an expeditious alternative to shaping and an extremely useful means of facilitating new behavior. For example, a nurse in a physician's office might have an older, non-fearful child receive an innoculation in the presence of a younger, more excitable one in order to alleviate the second child's fear.

Instructions   Instructions serve a dual purpose: they are a prompt for others to respond, and a means of providing information as to which behaviors are likely to produce reinforcing outcomes. Although instructions alone can be a useful way of influencing behavior, there are various ways in which they may be misused. The first and most obvious is an overreliance on instructions without providing reinforcement for the instructed activity. As most people have discovered, simply telling someone what to do may not be sufficient to produce the desired performance. Just as imitative learning is increased by provision of reinforcement, the effectiveness of instructions is similarly enhanced when reinforcement is made available for compliance with the instructions (Ayllon & Azrin, 1964; Katz, Johnson, & Gelfand, 1972). A second way in which instructions may be misused is that they serve as a consequence of some ongoing behavior. To the extent that we repeatedly instruct someone to engage or not to engage in one behavior, it may well be that our behavior, providing the instructions, inadvertently reinforces the very activity we intend to change. The critical test is whether or not the desired behavioral change takes place. For example, if a recovering hemiplegic patient is repeatedly told by the nursing staff that he should assume more independence in conducting his affairs, while his dependency continues at a steady or accelerated pace, the possibility that providing the instructions exerts a reinforcing effect for his ineffective behavior deserves close examination.

Prompting   Prompting is yet another means by which new behavior may be initiated, and this may be carried out either verbally or by physical guidance. In its verbal form, prompting is often equivalent to instructing, as when we tell a child to say "thank you." Physical prompts are often used to establish new motor responses, as in teaching a child to hold a spoon. Initially we might place his fingers around the base of the spoon and physically help him move the spoon toward his mouth. Gradually we would eliminate our prompts until the child is able to feed himself. The gradual elimination of prompts is called *fading* and is described in greater detail later in this chapter.

Negative Reinforcement Another means of increasing behavior is called *negative reinforcement.* This technique is defined as an increase in behavior following the removal or termination of an aversive stimulus, and it is based on the fact that behaviors that terminate an aversive event will tend to occur again. This procedure is depicted in the Table of Consequent Events shown in Fig. 2. Although negative reinforcement is often confused with punishment, a technique for decreasing behavior, the term "negative" refers to the kind of stimulus used and not the behavioral outcome. Like positive reinforcement, negative reinforcement is utilized to increase behavior; indeed, reinforcement always refers to an increase in behavior regardless of the valence of the stimulus used.

As noted earlier, children's tantrums are frequently maintained by positive reinforcement such as parental attention. One may ask, however, why parents reinforce their children for this annoying activity, thus helping to perpetuate it. The answer lies in a careful analysis of the consequences that maintain the parents' behavior. For most parents, a child who is visibly upset and angry constitutes an unpleasant stimulus. By intervening and attending to the child, the parent may quickly terminate the tantruming. Consequently, the parent's behavior is negatively reinforced since it is instrumental in removing or otherwise eliminating an aversive event. This mutual exchange of reinforcement whereby one party *coerces* reinforcement from the other, who in turn is negatively reinforced by capitulating, may quickly become a self-perpetuating, destructive cycle (Patterson & Reid, 1970).

Behavior maintained by negative reinforcement is often called *escape* behavior since the organism escapes from an aversive event by his response. In contrast, *avoidance* behavior is instrumental in postponing or preventing unpleasant experiences. Analgesics are often taken to escape or relieve pain. On the other hand, a patient may refuse to have a mole removed to avoid what he anticipates to be an unpleasant experience.

Techniques for Decreasing Operant Behavior

In the preceding section two ways of increasing operant behavior were described: a response may be followed by presenting a positive reinforcer or by removing an aversive stimulus. In order to decrease behavior, the converse of these operations is used; we can present an aversive stimulus or remove a positive reinforcer. Although the term "punishment" is often used generically to refer to procedures for decreasing behavior, technically this is but one of many techniques of response elimination. In the following paragraphs several of these techniques will be described. We shall pay particular attention to the relative efficacy of each, not only with respect to the immediacy and permanence of the behavioral reductions they produce, but also to their potential for eliciting undesirable side effects.

Punishment   Punishment refers to the application of an aversive stimulus after a response has occurred. As shown in Fig. 2, the effect of punishment is to decrease the behavior producing the stimulus. Within an operational framework punishment is defined according to its functional effect upon behavior. To be appropriately referred to as punishment, a stimulus presented contingent upon a response must suppress the frequency of that response (Azrin & Holz, 1966).

The effects of punishment are related to the immediacy and frequency of the punishing (aversive) stimulus as well as to the availability of alternative responses (Azrin & Holz, 1966). Like positive reinforcement, punishment is more effective when the aversive stimulus occurs immediately after the response. As punishment is delayed, its effectiveness is reduced. Inordinate delays in punishing consequences provide a partial explanation why such activities as cigarette smoking, overeating, drug abuse, and excessive drinking occur in spite of their apparent adverse effects. These behaviors provide an immediate source of positive reinforcement but often their negative effects are not experienced until long after the behavior has occurred. Greater suppression is also achieved when punishment occurs after each response rather than on an intermittent basis. To the extent that punishment occurs inconsistently, its utility in suppressing behavior is reduced.

Since many behaviors are maintained by reinforcement, it should not be surprising that reinforcement variables interact with punishment to determine punishment effectiveness. Of particular importance is the finding that more suppression occurs when punishment is used in conjunction with reinforcement for other behavior than when competing behaviors are not concurrently reinforced (Herman & Azrin, 1963; Katz, 1973). In practice, this principle amounts to using the carrot conjointly with the stick, simultaneously informing the person of what to do and also what not to do. Administering punishment just for retribution does not produce new and appropriate behavior. The latter task requires positive reinforcement.

When carefully administered and used together with other techniques of behavioral control, punishment can be a useful technique for suppressing unwanted behavior (Azrin & Holz, 1966). Nevertheless the desirability of using aversive stimuli to modify behavior has been criticized for both ethical and practical reasons. On ethical grounds it is commonly argued that to intentionally inflict pain is unfair and contrary to fundamental humanitarian values. And practical objections have centered around the often transitory effectiveness of punishment as well as its potential for eliciting undesirable behavioral byproducts (Bandura, 1962). For example, unless the punishing stimulus is severe, punishment tends to suppress behavior temporarily rather than eliminate it altogether. Furthermore, individuals often discriminate punishment conditions. When punishment is unlikely to occur, problem behaviors may quickly reappear. It is for this reason that distraught parents frequently describe their children by saying, "We hit him when he punches his little brother, but he's always doing it on the sly when he thinks we can't see him."

Punishment has also been shown to elicit aggression (Ulrich & Azrin, 1962) and other disruptive emotional activity such as crying and anger, as well as unwanted avoidance behavior, including lying and running away (Bandura, 1969). Because side effects may prove to be more undesirable than the behavior the punishment was intended to suppress, its use is probably best restricted to behaviors that require immediate suppression such as self-injurious behavior in children (Lovaas & Simmons, 1969; Risley, 1968).

Extinction   When reinforcement for a behavior is discontinued, the rate of that behavior decreases. The procedure of removing all reinforcement for a specific activity is called *operant extinction* (see Fig. 2). Extinction is based on the principle that behavior that fails to produce reinforcement is usually not repeated for very long. Referring to our example of the tantruming child, we might decrease (or *extinguish*) tantrums by instructing the parents to completely ignore them whenever they occur; that is, to place tantrums on an extinction schedule. By removing the reinforcing consequence, parental attention, the frequency of tantrums will gradually decrease. Problems associated with patients who make recurrent unreasonable demands or whose complaints can be clearly established as groundless, may be handled in a similar manner. Ignoring or withholding reinforcement (attention from staff) for these activities should eventually decrease their rate of occurrence. The selective use of extinction is an important consideration. Extinction does not mean to completely deny the patient all reinforcement, but only to withhold it consistently for certain activities deemed undesirable. If extinction is to be properly applied, it must be carried out in combination with reinforcement for appropriate behavior.

Characteristically the introduction of extinction results in a temporary increase in behavior before a decline in responding is observed. Because of these extinction "bursts," and since the majority of human activities are maintained according to intermittent schedules, the use of extinction to decrease behavior can be a slow and frustrating process. Unlike punishment, however, extinction should be recognized as a means of eliminating behavior completely without the introduction of aversive stimuli.

Resistance to extinction is commonly used as a measure of the strength of behavior. It refers to the persistence of responding after reinforcement has been discontinued. Resistance to extinction is functionally related to many variables (Kimble, 1961), but probably the most important among them is the schedule of reinforcement previously used to maintain the behavior. As indicated earlier, intermittent reinforcement generates more durable behavior than continuous reinforcement. Consequently, resistance to extinction is increased when behavior has been reinforced intermittently rather than on a continuous schedule. The persistence of intermittently reinforced behavior is clearly evidenced among people who engage in games of chance, such as lotteries, slot machines, betting, etc. In these situations, an occasional win can maintain behavior for a long period of time.

Timeout from Positive Reinforcement   Eliminating all opportunities to earn positive reinforcement can function as an aversive event to weaken the behavior it follows. This principle has given rise to a technique of decreasing behavior called *timeout from positive reinforcement.* Operationally, timeout involves removing the individual from a reinforcing environment for a brief period of time contingent upon some specified behavior. This may be accomplished by physically transferring the subject from one area to another less attractive area, such as occurs in incarceration or sending a child to his room after incidents of misbehavior. Although timeout is distinguishable from extinction, in which consequences that follow behavior are simply discontinued, both procedures decrease behavior by removing reinforcement (see Fig. 2).

Unlike extinction, timeout ordinarily suppresses behavior quickly, especially when used in conjunction with reinforcement for other desirable behavior (Holz, Azrin, & Ayllon, 1963). Nevertheless, care should be exercised in applying timeout since its termination is negatively reinforcing. For example, when a child is removed from a timeout area in the midst of a tantrum, tantruming may be inadvertently reinforced because it coincides with the removal of an aversive event. Terminating timeout should thus be made contingent upon desirable behavior.

Response Cost   The forfeiture of positive reinforcers contingent upon misbehavior is called *response cost*. Because the loss of reinforcers usually functions as an aversive stimulus, response cost decreases the behavior it follows. As a procedure of behavioral control, response cost most commonly involves the withdrawal of conditioned positive reinforcers, such as money or tokens, but it may be utilized in any setting where the control of reinforcers is possible (e.g., loss of television viewing time). For purposes of clarification, response cost, which involves the *taking away* of reinforcers, is differentiated from extinction where reinforcement is *discontinued* for a specified behavior, as well as from timeout from reinforcement where the *availability* of all reinforcement is temporarily interrupted. In common with these procedures, however, response cost entails the general operation of removing reinforcing stimuli (Fig. 2).

In order to enhance its effectiveness, response cost is best used in combination with positive reinforcement for alternative behavior (Kazdin, 1972). In token reinforcement systems, for example, response cost may involve the imposition of fines for maladaptive behavior. When used to supplement token reinforcement for appropriate behavior, this procedure can suppress activity that might otherwise interfere with rehabilitation efforts.

Differential Reinforcement of Other Behavior   Although unwanted behavior is most commonly reduced by punishment or withdrawing positive reinforcers, it is possible to achieve similar reductions without recourse to either of these operations. Behavior can also be decreased when other incompatible behaviors are positively reinforced. Since most gross motor behaviors cannot occur simultaneously, the relative strength of different behaviors will be determined by their respective success in producing reinforcement. If appropriate behavior produces more reinforcement than inappropriate behavior, it will predominate. This procedure of *differentially reinforcing other behavior* can be used alone to affect behavioral change, or in combination with alternative methods of weakening behavior. Thus, one of the most efficient ways to keep a restless cardiac patient from constantly leaving his bed, is to reinforce him when he remains in it.

Stimulus Control

Although operant behavior is controlled by consequences, stimuli that precede it may also acquire some control over responding. For example, the presence of a policeman's patrol car affects people's driving; we often slow down when one is in the vicinity and accelerate once it has passed. However, it is important to realize that the patrol car would not control our driving without differential consequences, such as the possibility of a traffic citation. When antecedent events control behavior because of consequences delivered in their presence, we refer to this as the *stimulus control of behavior*. These stimuli are called *discriminative stimuli*, since we learn to discriminate our behavior on stimulus events according to consequences associated with them.

In considering antecedent stimuli, it is possible to distinguish two ways in which they operate. One is to signal behavior, or the availability of reinforcement (these are symbolized as S^D), while the other is to signal no behavior, or the absence of reinforcement (symbolized as S^Δ). Thus seeing a friendly smile on the face of a passerby usually sets the occasion for the remark, "hello." The smile is an S^D for "hello" because we are usually reinforced for saying it under these conditions. On the other hand, a frown or look of indifference is more likely to serve as S^Δ, for we would not expect our greeting to be returned in kind.

The stimulus control of behavior assumes great importance when we consider that most behaviors are specific to certain settings; they do not occur all of the time. However, whether or not behavior does occur usually depends on the presence of discriminative stimuli that have acquired control over responding. In behavioral disorders, stimulus control variables can play a major role. For example, some forms of sexual deviancy can be conceptualized almost entirely in stimulus control terms; sexual activity occurring in the presence of stimuli that most people regard as inappropriate (e.g., fetishes, sadism, exhibitionism, etc.). The solution to the problem does not entail changing the basic response, but rather the conditions under which it occurs (see *fading*, below). It should not be surprising that stimuli associated with hospital environments also exert control over a wide variety of patient behaviors, such as statements reflecting somatic or physiological complaints and diverse forms of help-seeking activity. These behaviors occur in medical settings because it is here that they are most commonly followed by some form of desired attention.

A phenomenon related to stimulus control is *stimulus generalization.* This refers to the control of a response by events that resemble the stimulus to which the response was first acquired. For example, a patient who has had a heart attack may later overreact to any chest pain regardless of etiology. In this case generalization occurs across the dimension of chest pain and causes the patient to assume that all chest pain is the result of a serious coronary problem. In a like fashion, a patient who has had an unpleasant experience with a particular diagnostic procedure involving needle injection may generalize his fear to similar diagnostic or laboratory operations. It should be apparent that stimulus generalization and discrimination learning are reciprocal processes, for generalization implies the absence of well-defined discriminative control of behavior.

However, aspects of stimulus generalization may be used to therapeutic advantage. A procedure for accomplishing this is known as *fading,* which refers to the gradual changing of stimulus conditions under which a response occurs. Fading does not involve the manipulation of behavioral consequences, but rather the alteration of antecedent stimulus events. An example would be a child on a pediatric ward who screams and tantrums the moment his mother attempts to leave. In her presence he appears calm and able to accept the hospital routine. "Good patient behavior" is thus discriminated on mother's presence, while crying is discriminated on her absence. One therapeutic plan might be to have mother initially leave the room for a very brief period of time and quickly return before crying begins. Gradually, however, the duration of her time away from the child could be increased until the child continues to behave appropriately in her absence. Under these conditions we would have faded stimulus control by changing the stimulus conditions (mother's presence) under which a desired response (behaving calmly and cooperatively) occurs.

Chaining

Many behaviors that appear to be simple, continuous acts are in reality comprised of several discrete responses *chained* together (Ferster & Perrott, 1968). The term "chaining" essentially refers to a number of responses that occur together by virtue of their order and some terminal reinforcer delivered at the completion of the behavioral sequence. Individual behaviors in the chain are variously referred to as *components, links,* or *members.* The analysis of chained behavior holds great promise for the understanding and control of complex human behavior. There is reason to believe that interference with early components of a response chain can preclude the occurrence of the terminal link as evidenced in later chapters dealing with epileptic seizures and persistent vomiting.

CHARACTERISTICS OF BEHAVIOR THERAPY

As a conceptual model for understanding and treating behavioral disorders, *behavior therapy* has been variously described by different investigators. For example, Wolpe (1969), related behavior therapy to the general theoretical framework of learning theory. "Behavior therapy is the use of experimentally established principles of learning for the purpose of changing unadaptive behavior" (p. vii). According to Yates (1970), the essential feature of behavior therapy is its emphasis on the controlled investigation of the individual case. Bandura (1967), on the other hand, describes behavior therapy within the context of social learning theory. In so doing, he contrasts it with alternative and perhaps more traditional notions of deviant behavior:

> Most theories of maladaptive behavior are based on the disease concept, according to which abnormalities in behavior are considered symptoms of an underlying neurosis or psychic illness. Today many psychotherapists are advancing the view that behavior that is harmful to the individual or departs widely from accepted social and ethical norms should be viewed not as some kind of disease but as a way—which the person has learned—of coping with environmental demands. Treatment then becomes a problem of "social learning." The abnormal behavior can be dealt with directly, and in seeking to modify it the therapist can call on principles of learning that are based on experimentation and are subject to testing and verification (p. 78).[3]

For Krasner (1971), behavior therapy consists of the application of behavioral principles to modify human behavior labeled as deviant. In his recent review of the field he lists several essential elements of behavior therapy approaches:

---

[3]From *Scientific American.* Copyright © 1967 by Scientific American, Inc. All rights reserved.

... (a) the statement of concepts so that they can be tested experimentally; (b) the notion of "laboratory" as ranging from the animal mazes or shuttle boxes through basic human learning studies to hospitals, schoolrooms, homes, and the community; (c) research as treatment—and treatment as research; (d) an explicit strategy of therapy; (e) demonstration that the particular environmental manipulation was indeed responsible for producing the specified behavior change; (f) the goals of the modification procedure are usually determined by an initial functional analysis or assessment of the problem behavior (p. 487).[4]

An examination of these and other descriptions of behavior therapy (e.g., Bandura, 1969; Franks, 1969; Ullmann & Krasner, 1965, 1969) reveal two central characteristics. One is that its theoretical foundations derive from the study of learning. Principles of both operant and respondent behavior, many of which have been described above, form the basis of the applied technology used by contemporary behavior therapists. The other characteristic is a reliance on empirical, scientifically based methods of research and evaluation of therapy outcome. At a minimum, this entails the collection of objective data by which to measure behavioral change, and to detect the need for new procedures if the desired change is not being achieved. Additional aspects of evaluation are discussed in the next section.

DESIGN AND EVALUATION OF BEHAVIOR THERAPY PROGRAMS

In order to demonstrate cause and effect relationships between behavior and manipulated environmental events we must first specify precisely the behavior we intend to change, together with the manner in which it is to be measured. In behavioral science, *operational definitions* are used to satisfy both of these objectives. According to the doctrine of operationalism, behavior must be defined in observable terms if it is to be distinguishable from other activities and capable of objective measurement. Without well-specified operational definitions, it is unlikely that independent observers will agree whether behavioral change has occurred. To the extent that different observers cannot agree on what they have seen, attempts to measure behavior will be spurious and unreliable. This precludes meaningful evaluation of the efficacy of therapeutic interventions.

---

[4]Reproduced with permission, from "Behavior therapy," *Annual Review of Psychology*, Volume 22, page 487. Copyright © 1971 by Annual Reviews, Inc. All rights reserved.

To exemplify this point, we might consider such common patient descriptors as *depressed, irritable, angry,* or *upset.* In ordinary conversation these terms usually represent abstractions or inferences about behavior. However they do not provide much information about what the patient is actually doing. Accordingly, different observers must rely on their own subjective definitions for meaning. Observer (A) may describe the patient as depressed and upset but not hostile; observer (B) may respond to a more limited set of cues and describe the patient as irritable only, while observer (C) may see him as angry and irritable, interpreting these patterns to be the result of an underlying depression. Unless clinically descriptive terms are operationalized by enumerating the *behavioral referents* upon which they are based, there is no reliable way to communicate the nature of the patient's problems, nor to determine if therapeutic plans are producing the results for which they were intended. For example, we might operationally define "depression" by stating that the patient does not initiate spontaneous conversation, rarely makes eye contact when spoken to, and does not engage in any sort of functional activity. An increase in these activities would be expected as treatment is initiated.

Behavioral Measurement

Once target behaviors are objectively defined, behavioral measurement is accomplished by recording the frequency or duration with which these behaviors occur. Generally speaking there are three widely used procedures of behavioral measurement (Jackson *et al.,* 1971). One is to simply count each incident of behavior during a standard unit of time (e.g., a day, an hour, or work shift). A second is to record whether or not the behavior occurs during a specified time interval, irrespective of absolute frequency. The former procedure is called a *frequency tally* of behavior, and as a general rule it is best suited for measuring a single, discrete behavior of low to moderate frequency (e.g., seizures, toileting accidents in young children, etc.). The latter procedure is known as *time sampling,* and it is more appropriately used for measuring high-frequency behavior (e.g., tics, verbal behavior such as pain complaints or requests for PRN medication, etc.), or when measuring two or more behaviors concurrently. A final means of behavioral measurement is to record the *duration* of a response, or the cumulative time that it occurs during an observation period. Measures of response duration are most commonly used when each occurrence of the target behavior is relatively long, or when interest is centered on the amount of time spent on the behavior rather than the frequency with which it occurs (e.g., amount of time spent eating or in physical rehabilitation).

By way of descriptive example, let us consider a recovering cardiac patient who fails to comply with recommended care plans. For the sake of simplicity we can define noncompliance as "unauthorized getting out of bed" and measure it by the frequency with which it occurs each day. Beginning on the first day we observe ten occurrences of being out of bed, on the second day there are thirteen occurrences, on the third day eleven, on the fourth day eleven, and on the fifth day thirteen occurrences. These data are summarized graphically in Fig. 3. The frequency of behavior is shown on the vertical axis and time (days) on the horizontal axis. Figure 3 shows an average of about twelve daily occurrences of unauthorized getting out of bed. This information provides a *baseline*, or reference point against which subsequent observations can be compared.

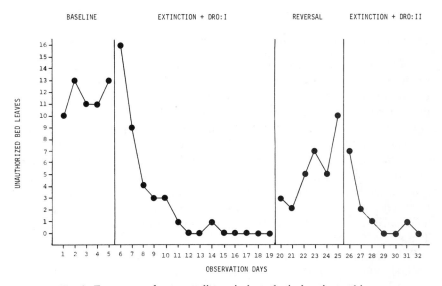

Fig. 3. Frequency of noncompliance in hypothetical patient subject.

Behavioral Analysis

After defining target behaviors and collecting baseline measurements, it is necessary to design a means of altering the troublesome activity. Treatment plans are derived from a *behavioral analysis*, which seeks to relate problem behaviors to their environmental determinants (Kanfer & Saslow, 1969; Mischel, 1968). In this analysis efforts are made to answer several important questions. Among them are: (1) what are the consequences of change for the patient and others in his social milieu—i.e., will it expedite his recovery or improve upon management of his problems; (2) under what conditions does the troublesome activity occur—i.e., what are the discriminative stimuli that occasion troublesome behavior that may be altered to affect behavioral change; (3) what are the reinforcing consequences for the behavior that might also be altered to produce corresponding change; (4) what alternative behaviors are available to the patient that might take the place of troublesome activity; and (5) what operations are needed to assist the patient to learn these appropriate behaviors. As illustrated in later papers, much of this information can be readily obtained from such sources as interviews with the patient or significant others in his social environment, questionnaires, or direct observation of the patient's behavior.

Implementing and Evaluating Treatment

On the basis of information derived from a behavioral analysis, many of the techniques described previously may be used to produce desired behavioral change. The task of the therapist is to decide which procedure(s) will be most pertinent to the needs of the patient and result in efficient resolution of the problem. Whether therapy plans are successful or unsuccessful will ultimately be determined empirically. Herein lies the significance of objectively defining behavior and collecting baseline measurements; only by comparing observations taken before, during, and after treatment can we evaluate the effectiveness of our therapeutic intervention. If the data show less than satisfactory results, renewed analysis is needed leading to corresponding alterations in treatment plans. The system is self-correcting.

Returning to our example of patient noncompliance, the results of our analysis may reveal that unauthorized bed leaves generally occur when the patient has been left alone, and that social attention from staff may be inadvertently reinforcing this activity. Equally important, we might discover that the patient receives little recognition when he does adhere to care plans. He may also tell us that he is bored and has nothing to do. Having generated some hypotheses about the kinds of events that may be maintaining the problem, we may test the validity of our interpretations by rearranging selected environmental events and contingencies. For example, we may design a treatment program incorporating extinction procedures for noncompliance and differential reinforcement of cooperative behavior (DRO). To ensure that the patient receives reinforcement for appropriate behavior, we could stipulate in the nursing care plan that he be checked at least once every 20 minutes. If the patient is in bed, a few minutes might be spent in pleasant conversation. Furthermore, discriminative stimuli for desired behaviors might also be provided, such as television, radio, interesting reading materials, or another patient with whom the patient might converse. On the other hand, if the patient is seen out of bed, he might either be ignored completely or escorted back without unnecessary attention. In this way reinforcement for noncompliance would be minimized. Data collection should continue throughout this phase.

A hypothetical outcome of this procedure is shown in Fig. 3 under the section entitled, "EXTINCTION + DRO:I." These data show a temporary increase in noncompliance (an extinction burst), followed by a gradual reduction in the number of times the behavior occurs. By the tenth day of treatment, unauthorized bed leaves are absent and do not occur again for the remainder of the two-week experimental period.

Since these data show a reduction in unauthorized bed leaves coincidental with our intervention, we may infer that the decrease was attributable to extinction and differential reinforcement. Nevertheless, it is possible that other uncontrolled events in the patient's life were instrumental in producing the change; for example, he may not have been feeling well during this period, he may have sensed that he was being closely observed and responded to these observations alone, or the change may have come about spontaneously simply as a function of time. To determine whether or not it was our intervention that produced the decrease, we might elect to use a *reversal procedure*, which entails reverting back to our earlier methods of responding to unauthorized bed leaves. We could resume attending to him while he is out of bed, refrain from attending to him when he complies, and remove television as well as other recreational paraphernalia. The effect of returning to the conditions that prevailed during baseline could then be observed. If we witness an increase in being out of bed, as shown in the section in Fig. 3 entitled REVERSAL, we would have additional evidence that our treatment procedures were in fact responsible for the reduction in noncompliant activity. To further substantiate this point, we would reinstitute our therapy plans and again bring the behavior under control (EXTINCTION + DRO:II in Fig. 3).

Another means of demonstrating behavioral control that should be mentioned is called a *multiple baseline design* (Baer, Wolf, & Risley, 1968). This design involves either the simultaneous measurement of different behaviors over time or the same behavior across different settings, so that several concurrent baselines are established. Next, the therapeutic manipulation is applied to one of the behaviors or in one of the settings until an effect is noted. These effects can then be compared against the remaining baselines for the purpose of control. Following this, the same procedure is applied to the remaining behaviors or settings. To the extent that a change in behavior occurs coincidental with these sequential manipulations, a strong case can be made for causal relationships (Hall *et al.*, 1970).

Systematically influencing behavior by reversal procedures or multiple baseline designs is necessary in applied behavioral research to validate the effectiveness of particular treatments. While these methods can be used to provide convincing demonstrations of behavior control, either for skeptical colleagues or where such demonstrations are required to establish functional relationships between behavior and a therapeutic procedure, they should not be construed as essential for each individual case. In day-to-day patient care ethical and practical considerations can override the knowledge gained from temporarily reinstating problem activities. Under these conditions the therapist's foremost concern is the attainment of therapeutic goals that either the patient or others have established. One should recognize, however, that no claims can be made about the relative efficacy of a particular treatment technique in the absence of a reversal procedure or some similar, convincing demonstration of the functional relationship between the intervention and behavioral outcome.

In this chapter we have attempted to point out some of the ways that health care involves interactions between human behavior and the environment. In so doing we have described several principles of, and attitudes about, behavior that form the basis of modern behavior therapy approaches. The following chapters deal with applications of this philosophy and technology in conceptualizing and treating various health problems. The results of these studies should speak for themselves. In so doing, however, our hope is that they not only illustrate the contributions of behavior therapy within the health care field, but also serve as a catalyst for additional research in this relatively new but promising area.

REFERENCES

Agras, S. *Behavior Modification: Principles and Clinical Applications.* Boston: Little, Brown, & Company, 1972.

Atthowe, J. and Krasner, L. Preliminary report on the application of contingent reinforcement procedures (token economy) on a "chronic" psychiatric ward. *Journal of Abnormal Psychology,* 1968, **73**, 37–43.

Ayllon, T. and Azrin, N. Reinforcement and instructions with mental patients. *Journal of the Experimental Analysis of Behavior,* 1964, **7**, 327–331.

Ayllon, T. and Michael, J. The psychiatric nurse as a behavioral engineer. *Journal of the Experimental Analysis of Behavior,* 1959, **2**, 323–334.

Ayllon, T. and Azrin, N. *The Token Economy: A Motivational System for Therapy and Rehabilitation.* New York: Appleton-Century-Crofts, 1968.

Azrin, N. and Holz, W. Punishment. In W. Honig (ed.), *Operant Behavior: Areas of Research and Application.* New York: Appleton-Century-Crofts, 1966, 380–447.

Baer, D., Wolf, M., and Risley, T. Some current dimensions of applied behavior analysis. *Journal of Applied Behavior Analysis,* 1968, **1**, 91–97.

Bandura, A. Behavioral psychotherapy. *Scientific American,* 1967, **216**, 78–86.

Bandura, A. *Principles of Behavior Modification.* New York: Holt, Rinehart, & Winston, 1969.

Bandura, A. Punishment revisited. *Journal of Consulting Psychology,* 1962, **26**, 298–301.

Berni, R., Dressler, J., and Baxter, J. Reinforcing behavior. *American Journal of Nursing,* 1971, **71**, 2180–2183.

Birnbrauer, J., Wolf, M., Kidder, J., and Tague, C. Classroom behavior of retarded pupils with token reinforcement. *Journal of Experimental Child Psychology,* 1965, **2**, 219–235.

Ferster, C. and Perrott, M. *Behavior Principles.* New York: Appleton-Century-Crofts, 1968.

Ferster, C. and Skinner, B. *Schedules of Reinforcement.* New York: Appleton-Century-Crofts, 1957.

Franks, C. (ed.). *Behavior Therapy: Appraisal and Status.* New York: McGraw-Hill, 1969.

Hall, V., Cristler, C., Cranston, S. and Tucker, B. Teachers and parents as researchers using multiple baseline designs. *Journal of Applied Behavior Analysis,* 1970, **3**, 247–260.

Herman, R. and Azrin, N. Punishment by noise in an alternative response situation. *Journal of the Experimental Analysis of Behavior,* 1964, **7**, 185–188.

Holz, W., Azrin, N., and Ayllon, T. Elimination of behavior of mental patients by response produced extinction. *Journal of the Experimental Analysis of Behavior,* 1963, **6**, 407–412.

Homme, L., deBaca, C., Devine, J., Steinhorst, R., and Rickert, E. Use of the Premack principle in controlling the behavior of nursery school children. *Journal of the Experimental Analysis of Behavior,* 1963, **6**, 544.

Jackson, D., Della-Piana, G., and Sloane, H. *Establishing a Behavior Observation System.* Utah: Bureau of Educational Research, University of Utah, 1971.

Jacobson, E. *Progressive Relaxation.* Chicago: University of Chicago Press, 1938.

Kanfer, F. and Saslow, G. Behavioral diagnosis. In C. Franks (ed.), *Behavior Therapy: Appraisal and Status.* New York: McGraw-Hill, 1969, 417–444.

Katz, R. Effects of punishment in an alternative response context as a function of relative reinforcement density. *Psychological Record,* 1973, **23**, 65–74.

Katz, R., Johnson, C., and Gelfand, S. Modifying the dispensing of reinforcers: Some implications for behavior modification with hospitalized patients. *Behavior Therapy,* 1972, **3**, 579–588.

Kazdin, A. Response cost: The removal of conditioned reinforcers for therapeutic change. *Behavior Therapy*, 1972, **3**, 533–546.

Kimble, G. *Hilgard and Marquis' Conditioning and Learning.* New York: Appleton-Century-Crofts, 1961.

Kimmel, H. Instrumental conditioning of autonomically mediated behavior. *Psychological Bulletin*, 1967, **5**, 337–345.

Lachman, S. *Psychosomatic Disorders: A Behavioristic Interpretation.* New York: John Wiley & Sons, 1972.

Liberman, R., Teigen, J., Patterson, R., and Baker, V. Reducing delusional speech in chronic paranoid schizophrenics. *Journal of Applied Behavior Analysis*, 1973, **6**, 57–64.

Lovaas, O. and Simmons, J. Manipulation of self-destruction in three retarded children. *Journal of Applied Behavior Analysis*, 1969, **2**, 143–157.

Miller, N. Learning of visceral and glandular responses. *Science*, 1969, **163**, 434–445.

Mischel, W. *Personality and Assessment.* New York: John Wiley & Sons, 1968.

O'Leary, K. and Becker, W. Behavior modification of an adjustment class: A token reinforcement program. *Exceptional Children*, 1967, **33**, 637–642.

Patterson, G. and Reid, J. Reciprocity and coercion: Two facets of social systems. In C. Neuringer and J. Michael (eds.), *Behavior Modification in Clinical Psychology.* New York: Appleton-Century-Crofts, 1970, 133–177.

Pavlov, I. *Conditioned Reflexes.* London: Oxford University Press, 1927.

Premack, D. Toward empirical behavioral laws: I. Positive reinforcement. *Psychological Review*, 1959, **66**, 219–233.

Rardin, M. Treatment of a phobia by partial self-desensitization. *Journal of Consulting and Clinical Psychology*, 1969, **33**, 125–126.

Risley, T. The effects and side effects of punishing the autistic behavior of a deviant child. *Journal of Applied Behavior Analysis*, 1968, **1**, 21–34.

Schaefer, H. and Martin, P. Behavioral therapy for "apathy" of hospitalized schizophrenics. *Psychological Reports*, 1966, **19**, 1147–1158.

Shapiro, D. and Schwartz, G. Biofeedback and visceral learning: Clinical applications. *Seminars in Psychiatry*, 1972, **4**, 171–183.

Skinner, B. *The Behavior of Organisms.* New York: Appleton-Century-Crofts, 1938.

Skinner, B. *Science and Human Behavior.* New York: Macmillan, 1953.

Ullmann, L. and Krasner, L. (eds.). *Case Studies in Behavior Modification.* New York: Holt, Rinehart, & Winston, 1965.

Ullmann, L. and Krasner, L. *A Psychological Approach to Abnormal Behavior.* New Jersey: Prentice-Hall, Inc., 1969.

Ulrich, R. and Azrin, N. Reflexive fighting in response to aversive stimulation. *Journal of the Experimental Analysis of Behavior*, 1962, **5**, 511–520.

Wolpe, J. *Psychotherapy by Reciprocal Inhibition.* Stanford: Stanford University Press, 1958.

Wolpe, J. *The Practice of Behavior Therapy.* New York: Pergamon Press, 1969.

Yates, A. *Behavior Therapy.* New York: John Wiley & Sons, 1970.

CHAPTER 2

The Genitourinary System:
Enuresis and Toilet Training

Toilet training is a significant event for young children—and for their parents as well. This is probably the first occasion for many children where sustained conformity to adult behavioral standards is strictly required. Toilet training is often viewed as a challenging but unwelcomed aspect of child rearing because achieving bladder control can be a slow and tedious process; moreover, parents may be unsure of the appropriate methods to use. Finally, toilet training can result in what appears to be intentional defiance by the child, leading to direct confrontations, scoldings, and anger. Although most parents eventually succeed in training their children, whether by trial and error, punishment, or more positive approaches, for some the frustration and embarrassment of their children's toileting accidents persists long after the age at which voluntary bladder control is usually acquired. These parents often seek professional assistance.

When nocturnal or daytime wetting occurs beyond the age of three to four years, with some degree of frequency and in the absence of organic or congenital abnormalities, the condition is clinically known as *enuresis*. By some estimates the incidence of enuresis among otherwise normal children at five years of age may be as high as twenty percent (Jones, 1960). In institutionalized retarded children this figure is considerably higher (Sugaya, 1967). Similarly, Hallgren (1957) reported a greater incidence of enuresis among children whose parents were enuretic, suggesting that hereditary factors may be important in the etiology of this disorder. The correlation is by no means perfect, however, and conflicting theories exist concerning the possible mode of genetic transmission. In an excellent review of the subject, Yates (1970) has distinguished several types of enuresis: *primary* enuresis where the child has never gained control of his urinary habits; *secondary* enuresis where control is lost following a period of dryness; *irregular* enuresis where wetting occurs sporadically; and *regular* enuresis where wetting is a daily occurrence. These distinctions are helpful for they demonstrate the many dimensions of enuresis as well as the variability among enuretic patients.

According to behavioral formulations, successful toilet training is related to both maturational and learning factors. Physiological maturation of the bladder is required to accommodate increased volume and pressure of urine. Higher nervous centers must also develop if the child is to perceive when the bladder is full, and then control bladder muscles either to start urination voluntarily or to inhibit it even though the urge to urinate may be great. This inhibitory potential must also generalize so that the urinary reflex does not occur during sleep. The development of discriminative and reinforcement control over voiding behavior is another important consideration. Some means of motivation is needed so that the response (together with its corollaries of walking to the toilet, undressing, redressing, etc.) occurs under socially appropriate conditions.

It is important to recognize that behavioral interpretations of enuresis, and indeed most of the health problems discussed in subsequent chapters, differ radically from traditional psychodynamic viewpoints. According to psychoanalytic theory (Fenichel, 1946), for example, bedwetting is regarded as the symptomatic expression of an underlying personality conflict that is usually sexual or anxiety based. This theoretical contention is important because it suggests that therapy must be directed at resolving the inferred underlying cause before reductions in the symptom can be expected. Indeed, to do otherwise—i.e., modify the overt behavior directly—is to risk precipitating new and perhaps more serious problems. The issue of "symptom substitution" whether considering enuresis or other health problems such as encopresis, anorexia nervosa, and migraine headaches, provides a clear line of demarcation between psychodynamically oriented and behavior therapists. Although this notion has been a central tenet of a variety of psychodynamic formulations, it has received little if any empirical support (Bandura, 1969; Cahoon, 1968), as indicated in the forthcoming papers on the behavioral treatment of enuresis.

The four selections contained in this chapter provide a cross section of behavioral approaches used to modify functional enuresis and to facilitate toilet training efforts. Mowrer and Mowrer's paper (Article 1), which begins the chapter, is a classic in the field. To begin with, this is the first published report in which learning principles were systematically applied to treat enuretic children. Although the authors' approach to the problem clearly reflects the influence of Pavlov's respondent conditioning model, operationally the procedure used bears close resemblance to punishment and the results might also be interpreted in terms of operant avoidance learning. Second, the long-range impact of Mowrer and Mowrer's research is significant in itself. The bell ringing alarm apparatus described by the authors has since become a familiar item to many parents and continues to be sold commercially. Third, this paper has provided one of the first theoretical rationales for the objective study of enuretic disorders. In so doing it has stimulated other investigators to perform similar research, many of whom (e.g., Baller & Schalock, 1956) have also produced impressive treatment outcomes. Finally, the paper is useful because it contains an historical overview of many different approaches that have been used to treat enuretic children and adult patients. Although Mowrer and Mowrer's paper is lengthy and subject to criticism from a methodological standpoint—e.g., for its failure to provide baseline measurements or appropriate control subjects against which comparisons could be made—the overall impact of this research, both publically and on the scientific community, far outweighs its shortcomings.

In contrast with Mowrer and Mowrer's paper, the recent work of Foxx and Azrin (Article 2) involves operant conditioning methods, and its focus is on controlling daytime rather than nocturnal wetting. According to the authors, toilet training consists of a complex set of operant behaviors, each of which must be mastered by the child if appropriate voiding and bowel elimination are to occur. Perhaps the most significant features of this research are the combined use of multiple procedures to maximize opportunities for learning, as well as the efficiency with which training was accomplished. As the authors point out, all 24 children participating in the study were successfully trained in an average of just four hours! To say the least, this is an impressive demonstration of how toilet training can be greatly facilitated through the systematic use of behavioral principles. It should also be recognized that there were several beneficial byproducts of training. In many instances control generalized to nocturnal incontinence, and both parents and children alike were almost universally pleased with the routine and results of the training program.

In analyzing human operant behavior, one activity is often found to be functionally related to another. For example, a child's performance in school reflects his ability to read, and to express himself verbally and in written form. In turn, the adequacy of these activities may depend on the child's capacity to sit quietly and attend to educational stimuli both at home and in the classroom. Similarly, a patient's alcoholic overindulgence may be related to his frustration at work, or to his inability to communicate effectively with his spouse. In both cases modifying one problem behavior may involve, if not require, corresponding changes in one or several others. This is essentially the approach taken by Nordquist (Article 3) in his work with a young oppositional child who also was a recurrent bedwetter. In this well-designed and carefully documented case study, the author instructed the child's parents how to use timeout and differential reinforcement procedures. While the thrust of the intervention was to decrease oppositional activity, it was found that as tantrums were reduced there also occurred concurrent reductions in bedwetting. In discussing these results, Nordquist raises the valid point that before parents can use expressions of approval, affection, and other social reinforcers to influence their children's behavior, these parental responses must be valued by the child and experienced as reinforcing.

Although the papers heretofore have concerned enuresis in children, toileting problems also occur in older individuals such as mentally retarded patients, chronic psychiatric patients, or the aged and infirm geriatric patient. In many cases these patients correspond to Yate's "secondary enuretic," individuals whose toileting habits were formerly appropriate but who for one reason or another lose control over voiding. Atthowe's paper (Article 4) provides a useful description of various operant conditioning procedures that were integrated within a token economy system and used to successfully eliminate nocturnal enuresis in chronic psychiatric patients. Notably, many of these patients were lobotomized or otherwise brain damaged, and had previously been assumed by staff to be incapable of reacquiring control over nighttime incontinence.

Points of key importance in this chapter include:

1. Nocturnal and daytime enuresis among children and adult patients has been successfully modified by both respondent conditioning (e.g., bell ringing or other signaling devices) and operant conditioning methods.
2. Among normal children, conditioning techniques may be applied to facilitate toilet training, although their success is clearly dependent upon maturational factors. As Foxx and Azrin caution, toilet training is best deferred until the child is 20 months old and the capabilities needed for appropriate voiding are presumed to be there.
3. Acquiring or reacquiring toileting skills requires mastery of several

complex behaviors. For this reason the use of conditioning procedures to control enuresis should be prefaced by careful instructions to individuals who will be applying them. Repeated followups are also needed to see that instructions are being carried out, and to insure that desired results are obtained.

4. Contrary to the predictions of psychodynamic therapists, modifying enuretic disorders directly has not resulted in the emergence of new symptoms. The available evidence strongly suggests that enuresis can be treated successfully without recourse to underlying personality factors, nor fear of symptom substitution. Indeed, most investigators who have used behavioral interventions report favorable rather than unfavorable collateral change.

REFERENCES

Baller, W. and Schalock, H. Conditioned response treatment of enuresis. *Exceptional Child,* 1956, **22**, 233–236 and 247–248.

Bandura, A. *Principles of Behavior Modification.* New York: Holt, Rinehart, & Winston, 1969.

Cahoon, D. Symptom substitution and the behavior therapies. *Psychological Bulletin,* 1968, **69**, 149–156.

Fenichel, O. *The Psychoanalytic Theory of Neurosis.* London: Routledge and Kegan Paul, 1946.

Hallgren, B. Enuresis, a clinical and genetic study. *Acta Psychiatrica Neurologica Scandinavia Supplement,* 1957, **114**, 1–159.

Jones, H. The behavioral treatment of enuresis nocturna. In Eysenck, H. (ed.) *Behavioral Therapy and the Neuroses.* Oxford: Pergamon Press, 1960, 377–403.

Sugaya, K. Survey of the enureses problem in an institution for the mentally retarded with emphasis on the clinical psychological aspects. *Japanese Journal of Child Psychiatry,* 1967, **8**, 142–150.

Yates, A. *Behavior Therapy.* New York: John Wiley & Sons, 1970.

ARTICLE 1

Enuresis—A Method for Its Study and Treatment*

O. H. MOWRER, Ph.D.

Department of Psychology, Institute of Human Relations, Yale University

and

WILLIE MAE MOWRER, Ph.D.†

The Children's Center, New Haven

I

Despite unremitting efforts, dating from antiquity,[1] to develop a specific form of therapy, nocturnal enuresis continues to be generally regarded as an unsolved problem. A review of the several hundred titles constituting the earlier literature on this topic reveals a remarkable array of proposed curative measures, ranging from patent superstitions and magical nostrums to a wide assortment of allegedly scientific methods. Innumerable drugs and hormones;[2] special diets (including fresh fruit,

---

*Reprinted from *American Journal of Orthopsychiatry*, Vol. 8. No. 3, July 1938, 436–459. Copyright © 1938, The American Orthopsychiatric Association, Inc. Reproduced by permission.

†The writers gratefully acknowledge encouragement and numerous courtesies extended by Professor Raymond Dodge, Professor Walter R. Miles, and Mr. Byron T. Hacker during the course of the investigation here reported.

[1]Goldman[X, p. 247] says: "The ancients were much concerned about the problem [of enuresis] as attested by Pliny, the famous historian, in his *Natural History*. He relates: 'The incontinence of urine in infants is checked by giving boiled mice in their food, in fact, this would appear to be the most common folk remedy for this condition. Other remedies are that the child should wear a clean smock at baptism, that the godparents should keep their money in their pockets, and among other remedies is the consumption of wood lice and the urine of spayed swine'."

[2]Cf. Zappert[55] and Kanner[36].

caviar, and colon bacilli); restriction of fluids; voluntary exercises in urinary control; injections of physiological saline, sterile water, paraffin and other inert substances; real and sham operations (passage of a bougie, pubic applications of cantharides plasters, cauterization of the neck of the bladder, spinal punctures, tonsillectomy, circumcision, clitoridotomy, etc.);[3] high-frequency mechanical vibration and electrical stimulation of various parts of the body; massage, bladder and rectal irrigations; Roentgen and other forms of irradiation; chemical neutralization of the urine; sealing or constriction of the urinary orifice; hydrotherapy; local "freezing" of the external genitalia with ice or "chloratyl"; elevation of the foot of the patient's bed; sleeping on the back; not sleeping on the back; and the use of a hard mattress: these are some of the methods which were commonly recommended and resorted to. In the hands of a limited number of individuals, virtually every method which was proposed seemed to produce cures; but the inability of other persons to obtain equally good results by what appeared to be precisely the same objective procedures eventually made it clear that the effectiveness of these methods was more a function of subtle psychological influences than of the particular physical praxis involved.[4] Following this realization, hypnotism and other forms of suggestion (including various kinds of placebos) were widely employed for a time; but the results were neither much better nor worse than those obtained by earlier methods, and the search for a truly rational therapeutic approach to the problem of enuresis continued.

Recent writers in this field are inclined to believe either (a) that enuresis (which can properly be said to occur only in children who are at least three years old) is merely a continuation, due to inadequate training, of the so-called physiological incontinence of infancy or (b) that it is caused by certain unconscious (or conscious) emotional needs which are not finding appropriate satisfaction during the child's waking hours.[5] Neither of these hypotheses can be lightly dismissed; each seems to provide the correct understanding of a certain class of cases, while in still other

---

[3]For an especially barbaric form of surgical mutilation, see Davis[14].

[4]Cf. Davidson[13].

[5]The present discussion is restricted to so-called "uncomplicated" enuresis, in which no organic etiology is demonstrable. Writers in this field agree that all enuretic children should have the benefit of a thorough physical examination before any form of psycho-therapy is initiated, although it is the consensus of opinion that at least 95 per cent of all children presenting this problem are medically negative.

instances of enuresis both of these causal mechanisms are probably concurrently operative.

Learning to awaken to the relatively vague and not very intense pressure created by a filling bladder, while successfully ignoring many other potentially disturbing stimuli, must be for the young child something of a feat, especially in view of the pre-existence of a strictly reflex, sub-cortical neural mechanism for the automatic relief of this need. That children do, in fact, require special assistance in the acquisition of this particular mode of control at the early age that this is demanded of them in our culture, is attested by the common practice of periodically arousing them from sleep in anticipation of the need to urinate.[6] That some

---

[6] This practice is apparently not found among primitive peoples (and to only a limited extent among the lower classes in our own culture). In the relatively few published anthropological studies which make any reference to toilet training in children, it is usually stated or implied that sphincter control during sleep is not expected of primitive children until a much later age than it is in civilized societies. Kidd[37], in writing on childhood among the Kafirs, says: "The mat on which the child has slept from infancy is burnt by the mother when the child begins to cut its second teeth. Up to that period the child has not full control of its natural functions during sleep; but as soon as the second teeth begin to appear it is supposed to have full control of itself" (p. 85). Rattray[47] reports that Ashanti children are not fully trained in this regard when they cease to be suckled (at about three or three and a half years), that it then becomes the father's responsibility, in the case of male children, to complete this training. "Should the child at first wet the sleeping-mat during the night, the father will not flog him, but will call in small boys and girls about his son's own age and tell them to come and catch this boy and make him dance a dance called *nonsua bono*. He will be tied up in his bed-mat, taken to 'the bush' and dressed in *nsansono* (a kind of nettle); water will be thrown over him and the boys will sing: 'You wash your sleeping-mat in the night; you wash your cloth in the night.' . . . Sometimes a child who has not a strong *sunsum* (spirit) will die after such ridicule . . . We have here an example at an early age of the use of the strongest of primitive sanctions, i.e. ridicule" (p. 12). It would appear from these and other reports that, although not subjected to the insistence upon cleanliness at the early age that this demand is made of children in our culture, primitive children are by no means always spared in this respect when they become somewhat older. (As an illustration of especial leniency, Whiting[54] cites an incident of bed-wetting by a Waskuk (New Guinea) girl, age eight years, in which the only adult disapproval expressed seems to have been occasioned solely by the fact that the incident occurred in the house of a stranger, being thus regarded as a mark of disrespect.)

Although regular awakening of children during the night as a method of training in bladder control is apparently rare or quite unknown among primitive peoples, it cannot be assumed, however, that specific conditioning in this respect is entirely absent. Mead[42], in describing the Arapesh, reports that "when an infant urinates or defecates, the person holding it will jerk it quickly to one side to prevent soiling his or her own person" (p. 41). The widespread practice among primitive peoples of allowing the infant to sleep until a fairly advanced age in intimate contact with the body of the mother (usually nude) would also presumably tend to

children should naturally respond more readily than others to this form of training and that the intrinsic adequacy of this training should vary from family to family seems inevitable, with a certain percentage of children consequently failing to acquire the dry-bed habit as soon as is normally expected. On the basis of this reasoning, the rational treatment of these so-called enuretic children would seem to lie, therefore, in the direction of supplementing, and if possible making more specific, the training in urinary control which has previously been given to them but without producing the desired results.[7]

The fact that methods of treatment—such as some of those mentioned at the outset of this paper—which are painful or at least disagreeable to the child, but which have no specific relationship to the real problem involved, should be capable of "curing" enuresis in some cases is not, of course, inconsistent with the assumption that enuresis is due to a specific habit deficiency. Efficient learning presupposes an adequate degree of motivation; and if in the enuretic child this has been lacking, the desire to escape an odious form of "treatment" may conceivably bring about the formation of the required habit. But, at the same time that many cases of enuresis seem analyzable in terms of defective habit formation, the understanding of other instances of this disorder appears to require a different approach. In some children a change of surroundings or the

---

insure some response of the mother and consequent disturbance of the child whenever elimination occurs in the night, although even this cannot be assumed to occur universally; for Ford[19] has observed that Fijian mothers, when themselves awake and holding sleeping children, are usually careful not to arouse them if they should urinate or defecate, instead merely removing or wiping away the excreta with leaves or bunches of grass.

That human infants, if left strictly alone as far as toilet training is concerned, would sooner or later acquire sphincter control during sleep as well as at other times seems almost certain. No healthy member of any other mammalian species, once past the stage of genuine infantile helplessness, ordinarily soils itself during sleep; it is therefore of especial interest to inquire why this practice should be so common and sometimes persist so long in human children in modern civilized societies. An attempt to account for this anomaly will be made in subsequent pages.

[7]It does not follow, however, as some writers have assumed, that the way to prevent enuresis from existing at later ages is to begin toilet training earlier and make it more intensive than is ordinarily done; probably as much or more harm is done by premature and too insistent toilet training than by delayed and lax training. Voicing the view of a large school of pediatricians and psychiatrists, Markey[39] has stated: "The longer the beginning of baby training is put off, the more fixed does a conditioning to recumbent elimination become. These joys are given up more reluctantly the longer they are allowed to last, and enuresis is prolonged as a natural result of the urge for pleasure" (p. 271). For a similar point of view, see Hamill[31].

alteration of other factors having no superficially discernible relation to enuresis will unexpectedly effect a dramatic "cure"; likewise, children in whom toilet habits have already been well established sometimes begin wetting the bed with distressing regularity for no immediately apparent reason. That enuresis in such cases is indicative of some basic frustration in the impulse life of the child and represents an attempt to obtain indirect or substitutive gratification of the thwarted needs or desires seems most likely; but it is often a difficult matter to determine precisely what these frustrated impulses are and how they can be provided with other, less devious avenues of expression.

II

Freud's dictum that "whenever enuresis nocturna does not represent an epileptic attack it corresponds to a pollution"[24, p. 51] epitomizes the view held by one group of writers.[8] As Sadger[49] has put it, urinary eroticism "is the model for all the later developing sexual acts" (p. 117) and is not distinguished by the young child from sexual feeling proper; urination, especially when it occurs during sleep and is accompanied by phantasies which would presumably be repressed during full consciousness, is thus believed to be richly charged with pleasure-giving potentialities. Marcuse[38] recalls the common observation that in boys and men a full bladder is likely to produce an erection during sleep and that in male infants the onset of urination even during waking hours is often accompanied by marked tumescence; sexual pleasure in many normal adults is said to be increased by a full bladder, and urinary sensations have been reported to replace sexual feeling proper in certain neurotic states. This functional relationship, Marcuse believes, "is to be seen as an expression of the original anatomical and physiological connection of the urinary and genital apparatus: their differentiation in the central nervous system first occurs much later, on the average at puberty,[9] although both systems remain in close interdependence" (p. 230).

---

[8]For a more recent and somewhat modified statement of this view, see Fenichel[18], who begins his discussion of enuresis with the remark that "Infantile nocturnal enuresis still offers many unsolved problems for psychoanalytic investigation" (p. 25).

[9]This assumption would seem to be more in keeping with the common folk saying, that bed-wetting will disappear spontaneously at puberty, than with careful scientific observation. According to Ackerson's data[1], obtained from "248 boys and 108 girls

Campbell[11] has reviewed a mass of evidence from children and psychotic adults suggesting that in at least some individuals urination takes on and retains—conjecturally because of unusually severe repression of genital sexuality—a definitely sex-like pleasure and meaning which may be experienced either directly or symptomatically. When urination thus becomes so highly libidinized, it can scarcely be doubted that the affected individual will tend to show extraordinarily strong resistance to the imposition of the usual urinary restraints and limitations. But urination, it must be remembered, is itself an *intrinsically pleasurable biological function*; and there seems to be no very reliable way of determining when this form of pleasure has been augmented by having been invested with substitutive capacities for sexual gratification and when it has not. So vigilant are the efforts usually made to repress genital sexuality in children in our culture that one might reasonably expect a widespread prevalence of urinary eroticism, but the writers believe that this type of libidinal displacement is actually not very common. While recognizing the difficulties of making definitive observations in this connection and at the same time acknowledging the significance of isolated cases of enuresis, such as those reported by Angel[5], and Hale[30], we do not believe that a sexual etiology can be justifiably attributed to this disorder in more than a limited portion of children who manifest it. In only one child known to the writers has enuresis seemed due to so-called urethral eroticism, and even here the facts are not entirely unequivocal.[10]

Perhaps the most significant evidence obtainable in this connection is that afforded by the dreams which commonly precede or accompany bed-wetting in children. Freud[23] has repeatedly called attention to the tendency in dreams for the sleeper to interpret potentially disturbing stimuli in such a way that they cease to be regarded, at least for the time

---

formerly enuretic (beyond their third birthday) for whom the ages at which enuresis ceased was noted" (p. 180), enuresis shows "steadily diminishing incidents from about 3 to 17 years" (p. 178). When presented in graphic form, these data give an almost perfectly straight line (with a slight tendency to become asymptotic at higher ages). There is nothing, therefore, in these or any other data known to the writers to support the common supposition concerning the advent of puberty and the spontaneous cessation of enuresis. (Addis[2] is inclined to the view that "the beginning of puberty may have a specific effect [upon enuresis] . . . and many indications suggest that enuresis is often connected with a sex factor" (p. 178); but this writer's statistics are unfortunately presented in such a way as not to show whether this actually is or is not true.)

[10]This case will be reported independently.

being, as a necessary cause for awakening. As an illustration of this process, Freud cites the case of "the sleepy [medical] student, who was awakened by his landlady with the admonition that he must go to the hospital, and then sleeps on, with the following account of his motives: "If I am already in the hospital, I shan't have to get up in order to go there. The latter is obviously a dream of convenience . . . . In a certain sense all dreams are dreams of convenience. *The dream is the guardian of sleep, not the disturber of it*" (p. 197).

As another example of a dream of convenience, Freud recalls the following personal experience: "On this occasion I became thirsty before going to bed, and emptied the glass of water which stood on the little chest next to my bed. Several hours later in the night came a new attack of thirst, accompanied by discomfort. In order to obtain water, I should have had to get up and fetch the glass which stood on the night-chest of my wife. I thus quite appropriately dreamt that my wife was giving me a drink from a vase . . . . Love of comfort is really not compatible with consideration for others . . . . Such dreams of convenience were very frequent with me in the years of my youth" (pp. 104–105).

Initially unaware of a number of earlier observations[35, 38, 44, 51, 53, 55] to the same effect (which were apparently also unfamiliar to Freud), the present writers independently discovered before proceeding far with their investigations that enuretic children very often have the most vivid "dreams of convenience" just before or during the act of urinating in bed. Under these circumstances, the sleeping child, instead of awakening to the stimulation produced by a distended bladder, fancies himself in a toilet, swimming in a pool, at the beach, alone in the forest or in some other secluded place where urination, which he now indulges in, would be allowable; in this way the child dismisses the otherwise disturbing fact that he is in bed and avoids the discomfort of awakening and really going to the toilet.[11] Adults who as children were enuretic can usually recall recurrent dreams of this kind. The writers have found that "toilet dreams" are often so convincing to children that upon being awakened immediately after the onset of urination (by a method to be

---

[11]Weissenberg[53] believes that so-called "toilet dreams" occur not as an exception but as a regular accompaniment of bed-wetting. He was able to elicit an account of dreams of this kind in a high percentage of the children whom he studied; and the fact that dreams of this kind were not reported by other children does not mean that they did not occur. English and Pearson[17] report a limited number of dreams in which urination during sleep had a more or less veiled sexual significance, but more frequently they find aggressive implications (see section IV).

described later in this paper), they can be persuaded only with the greatest difficulty that they have not already made a trip to the bathroom. Not infrequently a smaller child when aroused under these conditions and told to go to the bathroom to finish urinating will defiantly insist that he has "just been in there!"

That the child who dreams he is in the toilet and then proceeds to urinate in his bed is following what Freud has called the "pleasure principle," to the extent that he is seeking to avoid the discomfort of exertion, exposure to cold, or possible accidents while groping about in the dark, is obvious; but that there is anything specifically sexual in this act for most enuretic children seems improbable. What is more likely to be true is, that the child in whom "dreams of convenience" of this kind can successfully operate, is simply at an intermediate stage of toilet training in which a certain amount of the nervous excitation originating in the bladder goes to the cerebral hemispheres (instead of immediately discharging reflexly) and produces a disturbance there, which, however, is not yet sufficiently compelling to produce awakening. Some types of neurotic children, who are in more or less chronic flight from the reality of waking life, may be unusually sound sleepers, with resulting failure to be awakened by a degree of stimulation which would suffice to produce this reaction in a normal child. In such cases it is perhaps justifiable to refer to enuresis as a neurotic "symptom"; but in the majority of children, bed-wetting is probably to be explained along other lines.[12]

III

Another prevalent theory holds that enuresis is an hysterical manifestation, whereby deep-seated anxieties are "converted" into a physical dysfunction. According to this view, it is always dangerous to attempt to eliminate enuresis directly, lest in so doing the underlying anxieties be re-activated and freed to produce some still more serious disturbance. Although apparently valid as an explanation in isolated cases of enuresis, this theory can scarcely be upheld as universally applicable. Certain writers [13, 45, 53] have reported an increase in enuresis among children during the Great World War in countries in which there was great social

---

[12]Contrary to popular belief, enuretic children have not been found to sleep more soundly on the average than non-enuretics [12].

unrest, deprivation and general apprehension.[13] But one need not invoke the concept of conversion hysteria to account for loss of sphincter control in children under emotional stress. If excitement and nervous tension can produce lapses in this respect in children, as we know it can, even during the waking hours, how much more readily fearful dreams and nightmares might have a similar effect, when central control of the bodily functions is lessened, due to sleep. There is, however, another possible way of accounting for the fact that children seem prone to react to deprivations and thwarting with enuresis, without positing the involvement of any specific element of fright; this point will be returned to shortly.

Fearfulness has often been assumed to be a primary cause of enuresis, and it may indeed be in some cases; but what would seem to be more frequently true is that the enuresis is the primary condition and fearfulness a *consequence*, arising from the threats and punishments which are often resorted to by adults in attempting to eliminate this condition. Many children have been so harshly dealt with in connection with toilet training that they live in real terror of nocturnal lapses; and once the disgracefulness of bed-wetting, as reflected by the attitudes of adults, is accepted by the child and "internalized," a kind of vicious circle is often set up, the enuresis creating greater shame and apprehensiveness, which in turn may further aggravate the enuresis. In such cases it seems reasonable to infer that the enuresis can be eliminated or at least materially helped by relieving the child of his old anxieties; but this is usually a long tedious process. The writers have found that the simpler procedure is to give the child special training of the kind shortly to be described, which allows him to bring the urinary function under surer control and thus eliminate the cause for his previous anxiety. The stigma of being a bed-wetter weighs heavily upon a great many children; and the writers have noted that the elimination of this difficulty, when accomplished by rational, unemotional measures, comes as a distinct relief in such cases, making for better social attitudes and improved adjustment in general.[14] A "vicious circle" of the kind just described can undoubtedly be broken in some instances by attacking the emotional

---

[13]This seems to have been especially true in Germany. Post-war American tourists have reported that German hotel keepers often took it for granted that any child born between 1914 and 1918 would be a chronic bed-wetter, and acted accordingly.

[14]By the elimination of enuresis, the attitude of parents toward a previously afflicted child is often radically changed, sometimes shifting the balance from near rejection to real acceptance.

problems as basic; but this seems often to be a rather inverted method of approach, although in using other, more direct approaches the problem of motivation cannot be overlooked.

IV

Various writers [13, 25, 34, 52] have observed that enuresis seems to be unduly common among soldiers.[15] Discounting the not inconsiderable number of cases of malingering, where bed-wetting is deliberately resorted to in an attempt to obtain a disability discharge or at least to escape active service, veritable epidemics of real enuresis occur from time to time. If these outbreaks were reported only among men who are actively engaged in combat or who are in training for imminent service, the logical assumption would be that anxiety is here the prime etiological factor. The fact that enuresis may also be either recurrent or more or less chronic in barracks during times of prolonged peace suggests a different explanation, namely, that the discipline and arbitrary treatment which forms so large a part of military training may reinstate in young men attitudes of hostility and resentment which they felt as children toward parental authority but which they may have been able to express only in such a round-about way as being seemingly unable to acquire or retain the dry-bed habit.[16]

The veritable barrage of prohibitions and injunctions constituting the socialization of the growing child in our culture is inevitably frustrating; and, to make matters worse, the natural reaction to frustration [16], namely, acts of outright defiance or attack upon the frustrating person or persons, is rigorously forbidden. It is not surprising, therefore, that resentments and hostilities which are thus forced underground crop up in strange places and in weird guises. A great many instances of constipation, eating idiosyncrasies, backwardness in speech, so-called reading disabilities and other problems commonly presented by modern children, can be fully understood only when viewed in this light. Denied the luxury

---

[15]Hernaman-Johnson [32] has raised the question as to whether this may not be due to the fact that many cases of enuresis in the population at large do not ordinarily come to professional attention. No definitive data is apparently available on this point, but observations cited below suggest that this writer's supposition is not entirely correct.

[16]Cameron [10] has remarked, "In [English] schools, if punishment were meted out or other boys became critical, the disorder [enuresis] could become epidemic. Sometimes the hysterical suggestion extended to the bowel, and incontinence of faeces was added" (p. 48).

of undisguised aggression toward frustrating parents and teachers (which children in many primitive societies are encouraged to express quite openly[41, 42]), the child in our culture is driven to such devices as feigned incapacities and passive non-cooperation as the only means available of defending his individuality and warding off the too rapid encroachment of ways of life which to him seem unreasonable and foreign. Slowness in the acquisition of socially approved habits of elimination and periodic lapses in the exercise of these habits seem to be a form of self-assertion and retaliation by the infantile personality. The child who has discovered how effectively he can outrage the surrogates of the culture who are assigned to him in the form of his father and mother by the act of nocturnal enuresis, an act which is committed while he is asleep and therefore one for which he is usually not held fully accountable, has at his disposal a peculiarly effective outlet for his resentments: in this act he achieves real retaliation and at the same time tends to avoid the consequences which would follow if he committed an equally annoying act during his waking hours.[17] As McGuinness[40] has aptly said:

> Sometimes enuresis is an aggressive act in a very submissive child. It may arise from such strong emotions as fear, hatred, jealousy and inferiority. A child is at once at a disadvantage in the presence of adults in that he is physically unable to meet them on an equal ground. No matter what the adult may do, however, the child is the sole master of his function of elimination, and he can always employ this route for voicing his protest (p. 289).

In two of the thirty children on whom the present study is based, enuretic behavior had a conspicuously aggressive connotation; in various other members of the group a smaller or larger element of hostility seemed likewise to be involved. In such cases it is obviously essential that the child's attitude toward parents or parent substitutes be changed from one of ambivalence in which negative feelings predominate to one in which positive feelings are stronger.[18] Then and only then can specific

---

[17]The fact that there is a certain similarity between this and the so-called secondary gain from neurotic illnesses does not, of course, warrant the inference that, because of this, enuresis must be symptomatic of a neurosis.

[18]Goldman[28] reports that, after a negative physical examination, he routinely refers enuretic children to the psychological clinic. "Here both child and parent are studied and treated from the standpoint of functional derangement.... Enuresis is a problem of both the physician and the psychologist" (p. 293).

McGuinness says: "It is necessary to keep certain principles in mind [which are]: Making friends with the child; gaining the child's confidence and interest, and allowing him more

educational procedures be expected to produce permanently satisfactory results. In fact, it seems to be a sound generalization that in order for child training of any kind to proceed smoothly and effectively and to be enduring, the love of the child for the adult in the situation must be strong enough to counteract, or at least hold in bounds, the negative impulses which are certain to be engendered by the educative process [3]. With this principle clearly in mind one is justified in seeking for improved educational techniques as such; but without proper recognition of this basic personal equation, otherwise satisfactory methods are likely to miscarry sadly.[19]

V

The first requirement, therefore, for the establishment of satisfactory toilet habits in children is the existence of thorough confidence in, and respect and affection for the adults who are commissioned to carry out the requisite training. Moreover, the acquisition of bladder control during sleep being something of a feat for the young child, he should not be motivated to a higher level of performance than he is capable of attaining in the light of his age and specific capacities, lest anxieties be developed which will retard the real training process and perhaps lead to disturbances in other departments of the child's life. Further study of this problem is desirable, especially in the way of comparing the manner in which children react to the different total patterns of training given in various cultures, before definitive conclusions can be reached in this field; but it seems to be a safe assumption that at least one helpful step could be made toward the solution of this problem in our own culture if the training which we employ with children in order to aid them in the acquisition of bladder control during sleep could be made *more specific and precise. If*

---

chance to develop new channels of activity and self-expression. The re-education of parents is important and usually difficult" (p. 293).

[19]Not only is the establishment of a strong affectional bond between child and parent essential for the elimination of hostility as a possible cause of enuresis, but it is also known from a variety of investigations (mostly psychoanalytic) that developing love for parents (object-choice, as contrasted to the narcissism of infancy) is an important factor in suppressing infantile sexuality and bringing about the so-called latency period. To the extent, therefore, that enuresis is a form of persistent infantile eroticism, it is also important that the child-parent relationship be taken into account in enuresis therapy. (It is not without significance to note that the incidence of enuresis in orphanages, where children do not enjoy normal parental relationships, is often alleged to be exceptionally high [20, 39, 53].)

this could be done, the severity of methods used to motivate this type of learning in the child could presumably be reduced, with an improvement in the general parent-child relationship and with less emotional stress upon all concerned. This procedure, coupled with an appreciation of the aggressive implications which enuresis sometimes has, should constitute a distinct step in advance of the bungling, hit-or-miss methods which have been traditionally employed.[20]

Insofar as the most common method of training in bladder control during sleep may be said to rest upon any definite psychological theory, it would appear to be this, that if the child is repeatedly awakened at a time when the bladder is partially filled, but not so distended as to produce reflex emptying, the attendant bladder stimulation will eventually become specifically associated with the response of awakening, before the point has been reached at which voiding tends to occur automatically. On the assumption that this interpretation is substantially correct, there now arises this important question: would it not be advantageous from the point of view of most efficient habit formation if the awakening could always occur at a time when bladder distention is maximal and only at such a time, instead of at more or less arbitrarily determined intervals during the night, when bladder-filling may be at any of various stages? If some arrangement could be provided so that the sleeping child would be awakened *just after the onset of urination,* and only at this time, the resulting association of bladder distention and the response of awakening and inhibiting further urination should provide precisely the form of training which would seem to be most specifically appropriate.[21] This

---

[20]Certain writers have taken the position that enuresis has nothing to do with adequacy of habit formation, holding instead that it is *entirely* dependent upon personality dynamics. Hamill[31], for example, states that "The sleeper responds [by awakening] to the stimulus [of a full bladder] if he wants to.... The histories in all of the improved cases contain conclusive evidence of one fundamental conclusion: these children can stop [wetting the bed] if and when they wish to." It is suggestive that, using as therapy, clinical interviews based upon the foregoing assumption, Hamill obtained cures in only 40 of the 80 cases so treated.

[21]Schacter[50], one of many writers (reviewed by Anderson[4], pp. 603–604) who have expressed the view that enuresis commonly reflects a habit deficiency, believes that it "represents a weakness in the development of cortical dominance of the urinary function during sleep; more especially of a deficiency of inhibitory control over an essentially automatic function." But his proposal that the child with this difficulty be taught to set an alarm clock to awaken him at fixed intervals has the same disadvantages as periodic awakening by the parents, except that it is more convenient for the latter. For a discussion of the mechanics of habit-formation in this situation, see also Bott, Blatz, Chant, and Bott[9].

conception of an improved habit-formation sequence can be schematically represented as follows:

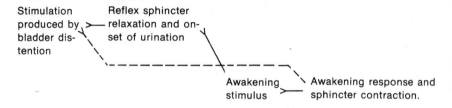

By the well-known conditioned-response principle of Pavlov, an increasingly strong functional connection (dotted line) would be expected to develop between the stimulation arising from the distention of the bladder and the responses of awakening and contracting the bladder sphincter. Soon this connection should become sufficiently well established to cause the awakening response and the contraction of the bladder sphincter to "come forward" in time and occur actually in advance of the onset of urination, instead of afterwards. The conditioned contraction of the sphincter in response to bladder distention would thus tend to inhibit the occurrence of reflex sphincter relaxation during sleep and to lead to awakening when bladder pressure finally becomes sufficiently great. We thus have a theoretical basis for the expectation that soon the subject would not only cease to urinate reflexly during sleep but would also become capable of retaining his urine longer than had previously been possible, without necessarily awakening. This, as we know, is the ideal state of affairs and the one actually attained when the conditions of "bladder training" have been favorable; not only does the successfully conditioned child refrain from urinating reflexly in bed, but he is also able to sleep through the night without having to awaken and go to the toilet more than once, if at all.

VI

If regular awakening of the enuretic child immediately after the onset of urination was to be rendered possible, it was obvious that this would have to be accomplished by means of some automatic mechanical arrangement.[22] In attempting to devise such a mechanism, four important

---

[22]Under primitive conditions, where mother and child sleep in close physical contact, with little or no clothing separating them, urination by the child is likely to produce a reaction on the part of the mother which would tend to have much the same effect as the inanimate

considerations had to be kept in mind: the child's freedom of movement should be unhampered, he should be at liberty to get out of bed at any time and go to the toilet without aid, he should be able to sleep in normal comfort, and the intensity of the awakening stimulus should be adjustable for each individual child so that it will be strong enough to arouse him yet not so strong as to produce fright or any other traumatic effect. The most satisfactory way of meeting these requirements seemed to be to take advantage of the electrolytic properties of urine so as to allow it, upon escaping from the child, to complete an electrical circuit which would then bring about the presentation of whatever stimulus might be selected to produce arousal. To this end a special type of pad has been developed, consisting of two thicknesses of heavy-absorbent cotton fabric (28 by 32 inches) which serve as a separator between two equally large pieces of # 16 bronze screening, with the top piece of the screening covered by a third thickness of the fabric. This combination is quilted together and is light in weight, durable, and not uncomfortable for the child to sleep on. As long as the pad is dry, there is no electrical contact between the two pieces of screening; but as soon as urine strikes the pad, it quickly penetrates the fabric and forms a contact. By having the two pieces of screening which are contained in the pad connected (by means of flexible, insulated wires) in series with a small battery and a sensitive relay, it is thus possible to cause the short-circuiting of the pad to activate the relay which in turn can be made to complete a second circuit which causes the waking stimulus to be presented. After some experimentation, a common electric door bell has been selected for this purpose; this, together with a rheostat for controlling its loudness, the relay, and the necessary batteries can be compactly mounted in a small metal box with a telephone jack installed at one end for insertion of a plug attached to the two wires (twisted lamp cord) communicating with the pad on which the child sleeps. A pad of the type described usually short-circuits within two or three seconds after urine strikes it, which means that the interval between onset of urination and the presentation of the waking stimulus is thus relatively brief.[23]

---

device here proposed (see Footnote 5). The present proposal is, therefore, nothing but an attempt to provide the modern civilized child with an advantage which children have doubtless enjoyed for countless ages under primitive life conditions.

[23]The construction of the pads and apparatus essential for the application of this method of treating enuresis had been described in detail elsewhere [43] and will not be considered further in the present report. It should be mentioned in passing that the electrical currents used to operate this apparatus are very weak and cannot possibly come into contact with the child so as to produce a shock.

It is possible that the accidental escape of saliva from the mouth of a sleeping child might short-circuit the pad if the saliva came into contact with it; but this is easily avoided by placing the pad under only the lower part of the child, with the head well above its upper edge. In very humid weather a pad may absorb during the day sufficient moisture from the atmosphere to render it inoperative; but a short period of drying on a radiator or over an electric lamp, before being put on the child's bed will restore its usability. If a child tends to perspire excessively during warm weather, his covering should be reduced to a minimum, and the sensitivity of the relay can be diminished somewhat so the sweat which is taken up from the child's body will not activate it and cause the presentation of the awakening stimulus. There is the further possible complication that, in the case of adolescent boys, the pad may be short-circuited by nocturnal emissions. Whether this would indeed occur and if it did occur whether it would have any untoward consequences are questions which can be answered only by empirical observations which have not as yet been made.

VII

A review of the literature on the topic of enuresis extending back two decades (which was conducted in November, 1935, at the time that the present method of treatment was first undertaken by the writers at the New Haven Children's Center) revealed no record of a similar method having previously been reported. Several references to methods of treatment were discovered which entail interference with, or obstruction of, normal urination by means of clamps, rubber sacks, and so forth;[24] and it seems likely that some of these methods—notably those which actually prevent the passage of urine—may operate somewhat like the present method of treatment in that they would conjecturally tend to produce awakening immediately after the onset of attempted urination. But they also have certain features which make them considerably less satisfactory than the present method, even though good therapeutic results have, nevertheless, been reported from their use in several instances.

Some months later (May 4, 1936), the *Baltimore Sun* published the following statement as a legend beneath an Associated Press photograph:

> Svordlovsk, U.S.S.R.—Russian science has just announced this gift to Soviet motherhood—a light which flashes when baby needs changing. Wires from batteries are

---

[24]See, for example, Glaser and Landau [27], Baretz [6], and Bonjour [8].

attached to strips of tinfoil in a special packet beneath the infant. Cloth sandwiched between the tinfoil becomes a conductor when dampened and, presto, the light goes on. The system is already in use in a hospital here.

Subsequently a survey of the literature prior to 1915 showed that in 1904, Pfaundler[46], the German pediatrician, described an arrangement very similar in principle to the one more recently developed in Russia which was originally designed for precisely the same purpose. However, instead of having a light which flashed on and signalled the infant's need of changing, Pfaundler arranged his apparatus so that an electric bell would ring. When an enuretic child was admitted to the children's ward of his hospital, Pfaundler later made a practice of having its bed equipped with one of these devices and was surprised to find that if used continuously for a month or so, the method—which he had merely hoped would serve to inform the nurses that the child was wet and needed changing—was likely to have distinct therapeutic consequences. He reports that in some cases just the knowledge that urination in bed during the night would cause a bell to ring henceforth inhibited this act (an observation which the present writers can corroborate).

Following the announcement of Pfaundler's accidental discovery of this method of treating nocturnal enuresis, Genouville[26] and Rémy-Roux[48] published, respectively in 1908 and 1910, papers dealing with the application of Pfaundler's method, which they reported as giving good results. Genouville says:

"Rapidly, at the end of a few nights, accidents become rarer and rarer. Finally they cease, due to the education of the sphincter through sudden awakening by the bell. It is nevertheless necessary, as experience has shown, to continue the use of the apparatus somewhat longer, which is a simple matter since, the accidents having ceased, the bell remains henceforth silent" (p. 101). In using this method, which he termed "suggestion without words," Genouville found, as have the present writers, that the sound of the bell will almost always inhibit further urination, even though it does not at first produce awakening; and he concluded that "It is therefore because it produces useful contractions of the sphincter and especially because it produces them at the desired physiological moment, with a precise physiological relevance, that the application of our apparatus is capable of giving good results" (p. 106).

And Rémy-Roux pertinently adds:

The effect is not the same, as Genouville has rightly said, if the parents awaken the child at fixed hours and have it urinate. We have all seen this method, commonly employed by families, fail: there is a great difference between a child's being awakened at times when the need to urinate is perhaps not even being felt and his being suddenly aroused by the bell, exactly at the instant when involuntary micturition is in the act of occurring. In the first case, it is as if one were in reality trying to habituate the child to urinating during the night, which is superfluous; in the second case, on the other hand, the child's mind is sensitized and the bell, which sounds when he is fully asleep, at the same instant that the bladder is emptying, suddenly stops the stream of urine by a vigorous contraction of the sphincter (p. 339).[25]

Although Genouville and Rémy-Roux both reported rather dramatic success with Pfaundler's method of treating enuresis, the technique apparently did not come into widespread use; but this is thoroughly understandable when one notes the cumbersome, inefficient design and construction of the Pfaundler apparatus. One major defect was that in order for the apparatus to operate, a sufficiently strong electrical current had to pass through the moistened area of the pad on which the patient slept, to ring the bell directly. This had numerous disadvantages, most serious of which were the relatively great amount of urine (Genouville says 20 to 30 c.c.) which had to be voided before an adequate contact was established and the fact that the electrical current, when it did begin to flow in sufficient amount to ring the bell, tended to produce rapid oxidation of the two metal screens contained in the pad. These difficulties are obviated by the interpolation of a sensitive relay between the pad circuit and the bell circuit. One other complication was that, with the Pfaundler method, the pad on which the child slept was not permanently quilted together, but consisted instead of two loose pieces of screening, with a removable piece of linen (Rémy-Roux used a layer of absorbent cotton) sandwiched between, the resulting combination being then placed under the bottom sheet of the child's bed. The type of pad developed by the present writers is obviously more convenient and efficient.

VIII

In using their method of treating enuresis, the writers have found it expedient to observe certain rules and principles, which have been formulated and supplied to other persons who have employed the method, as follows:

---

[25]In 1916, Uteau and Richardot [52] reported having developed a method of recording the time during the night at which bed-wetting occurred in soldiers who were under suspicion of malingering. If the wetting (which stopped a specially constructed clock) occurred just before the subject got up in the morning, instead of earlier in the night, malingering was assumed to have been established. Although their method was technically very much like that originally developed by Pfaundler, Uteau and Richardot made no attempt to apply it as a therapeutic measure.

INSTRUCTIONS

The distinctive feature of this method of treating nocturnal enuresis, or bed-wetting, is that it provides a means of causing the sleeping child to be regularly awakened immediately after the onset of urination, thus tending to establish a specific association or connection between the need to urinate and the act of awakening. With careful observation of the following rules, excellent results may be expected within four to eight weeks in children whose enuresis is not complicated by serious personality difficulties or by organic illness. In children in whom physical or serious emotional complications are suspected, this method of treatment is not recommended, except when applied under psychological or medical supervision. Neither is this method recommended, except under professional guidance, for use with children under three years of age.

Before treatment is begun the child should be fully appraised of the general nature of the method. If desired, a small amount of water (with a little table salt added) may even be poured on one of the pads on which the child is to sleep in order to indicate to him what will happen when he urinates on the pad during the night. He will see that the only thing which occurs is that the bell in the box on the floor rings and that there is no reason to be apprehensive or fearful. It should also be mentioned to older children that there is no possibility of their receiving an electrical shock.

The child should sleep in a bed that can easily be gotten into and out of, in a dimly lighted, moderately warm room from which the bathroom is conveniently accessible. Upon being put to bed each night, the child should be admonished to awaken and jump out of bed and go to the toilet the moment he hears the bell begin to ring. He should also repeatedly be urged to get up and go to the bathroom alone every time he awakens in the night, even though he feels no specific urge to do so. Once the use of this method has been commenced, all routine arousing of the child should be discontinued. In the beginning the ringing of the bell may not awaken the child. In this event the child should be aroused by the attending adult as speedily as possible *while the bell is still ringing.* After the child is on his way to the bathroom, the plug at the end of the piece of lamp cord attached to the pad should be withdrawn from the receptacle in the end of the box, a dry pad placed on the bed and connected with the box, and the wet pad dried, either on a radiator or over (but not too close to) one or two electric lamps.

It is essential that the child under treatment for enuresis by this method be required to sleep nude below the waist. He should wear only a jacket or short shirt of some kind. Otherwise a very considerable amount of urine may be voided and absorbed by the lower part of his clothing before sufficient urine reaches the pad to cause the bell to ring. The child sleeps, of course, directly on the pad, with the requisite amount of covering over him but not with a sheet or anything else between him and the pad. A rubber sheet may be used under the pad on which the child sleeps as a protection to the mattress, but this is merely a precaution rather than a necessity as there is ordinarily not enough urine voided to pass through the pad and wet anything below. Usually the ringing of the bell will inhibit further urination on the pad, even though it does not awaken the child. (If the child persistently makes a spot larger than two or three inches in diameter, it suggests that the wetting is being engaged in intentionally, after the child is already awake.) The size of the wet spot thus being ordinarily small, drying is a quick, simple process. If, after continued use, a pad becomes slightly offensive, it can be washed by immersion in a solution of warm water, soap and ammonia. After being thoroughly dried (preferably out of doors in the sunshine), it is again ready for use. With proper care a pad will give continuous service for at least two years.

Once the present method of treating enuresis has been undertaken, all other therapeutic devices, aimed specifically at the enuresis, should be discontinued. There should, for example, be no restriction of diet or fluid intake. In older children (of five years or over), we have, in fact, found it desirable to recommend the following practice. After the child has gone seven consecutive dry nights on the pad with normal fluid intake, his fluid intake is increased somewhat (by the amount of one or two cups of water) just before retiring. This practice should be continued until the child has again gone seven successive nights without wetting. The extra water and the use of the pad should then *both be discontinued.* In the case of younger children, our recommendation is that they be trained to the criterion of seven consecutive dry nights, with normal fluid intake, and the method then discontinued. No additional incentive or reward other than the privilege of ceasing to sleep on the pad should be employed in any case. Once the use of the method has been undertaken, it should not be interrupted except for the most urgent reasons until the treatment is completed. Relapses following this method of treatment are relatively rare, but if they should occur, the treatment should be resumed and continued until the child once more succeeds in having seven successive dry nights, with or without an increased fluid intake, depending upon the age of the child.

The electrical apparatus required for the use of this method is relatively simple, but the box in which it is contained is kept locked as a protection against possible damage. If the apparatus ceases to operate, the physician or psychologist who is supervising its use should be notified. Ordinarily this apparatus will give perfect service for many months without any readjustment or attention.

IX

Although careful individual records and case histories have been kept on the 30 children (ranging in age from 3 to 13 years) who have thus far been treated for enuresis by this method, it does not seem necessary to present any of these at this time. Suffice it to say that elimination of enuresis, to the criterion stated above, has been achieved *in all cases*, the maximum time required to accomplish this in any child being two months. The promptness of the therapeutic effect depends, of course, upon the age of the child, his eagerness to overcome his difficulty, and a number of other variables. We have naturally refrained from using this method with highly neurotic and psychotic children, just as one would refrain from making otherwise normal physical demands of children who are physically ill or genuinely incapacitated. One feeble-minded child, with an IQ of approximately 65, was, however, included in the group treated and responded satisfactorily. It will be interesting to determine the extent to which this method can be used to cope with enuresis in children with even lower intelligence.[26]

Personality changes, when any have occurred as a result of the application of the present method of treating enuresis, have uniformly been in a favorable direction. In no case has there been any evidence of "symptom substitution." Our results, therefore, do not support the assumption, sometimes made, that any attempt to deal directly with the problem of enuresis will necessarily result in the child's developing "something worse." Although the majority of the children with whom this therapeutic procedure has been employed were, at the time of treatment, under observation at the New Haven Children's Center and consequently living under as favorable conditions as could be provided, the method has also proved its applicability in private homes, when used by parents (under professional supervision) without any special alteration in the child's

---

[26]The method is now being tested, under the direction of Dr. Anthony J. Mitrano, with a large group of defective children at the Vineland Training School, Vineland, New Jersey. To date Dr. Mitrano reports uniformly favorable results. The method is also being successfully used under the direction of workers at the Psychological Clinic of Northwestern University.

normal surroundings. Home situations will undoubtedly be encountered in which this procedure will not work; but our findings to date suggest that there is probably a relatively large group of enuretic children who can be successfully dealt with in this way. In fact, some of the most dramatic cures of enuresis which have thus far been obtained have occurred in children treated under normal home conditions.

Relapses have sometimes occurred a few weeks or a few months after treatment, but this has usually happened in children who have had to return to an intolerable home situation, where emotional stresses are too great and newly acquired habits give way to old ones. Other children, however, have now maintained the new behavior resulting from treatment for as long as two and a half years, and the usual expectancy is that the cure will be permanent. Even if there were no therapeutic gain whatever in certain cases, the application of this method would nevertheless have some advantage, even in these instances; for the opportunity which it affords of preventing the enuretic child from urinating more than a few drops, which occurs on a pad which can be quickly exchanged and dried, and of then having the child complete the act of urination in the bathroom, is in itself an advance over the situation in which the child floods the whole bed, which then has to be completely changed.

The fact that this method of dealing with enuresis involves an automatic mechanical arrangement and is therefore less dependent upon the particular personality traits of the individuals applying it has numerous advantages, but it also has some conceivable disadvantages which should be mentioned. The method makes it possible for intimidation, physical punishment, and tense emotional tactics in general to be dispensed with, and, in effecting an eradication of enuresis, incidentally eliminates what is often a source of serious friction between parent and child. Since the method is thus relatively automatic, it gives promise of being useful in the hands of a wider percentage of persons than other less specific methods have been found to be. We must again warn against the assumption that the method can be made to function in an entirely impersonal manner in all cases; and we wish to re-emphasize the importance of its being applied only under the supervision of psychologically trained persons who are capable of detecting and dealing with emotional tensions, between the child and the surrounding adults, when these seem likely to delay or prevent the achievement of therapeutic success. In the hands of vindictive, sadistic persons this method can, to be sure, become just another means of assaulting the privacy and individuality of the enuretic child; but even in such circumstances the application of a technique from which the child is likely to obtain a specific and useful form of training seems decidedly preferable to the innumerable other procedures which are always available to brutal parents and other persons who are more intent upon obtaining gratification of displaced aggressive impulses than they are interested in helping children really overcome their difficulties.

One further point remains to be considered in this connection, namely, whether the present method of treating enuresis should be used to supplement or replace the usual methods of early toilet training. Despite certain similarities, there is this important difference between the problem of terminating the so-called physiological incontinence of infants (under three years of age) and that of eliminating the behavior which is more or less arbitrarily distinguished in older children as enuresis. In the older child, all the capacities necessary for the development of approved toilet habits are assumed to be present; here the problem appears to be primarily one of providing a specifically appropriate type of training. In the case of the infant, however, the possibility of establishing continence is directly contingent upon certain maturational factors: not only must cortical functioning have reached a relatively advanced stage of development, but the physical ability on the part of the child to get out of bed and go to the toilet unaided, or the verbal capacity to call and make his needs known, must also be taken into account. In the infant, therefore, pressure for the establishment of approved toilet habits at night must not be too insistent, and the methods used must be suited to the level of the child's physical and mental development. Since the method of treating enuresis which is described in the present paper presupposes that the child is old enough and well enough developed physically to get out of bed alone and attend to his toilet routine unassisted, it would obviously be inadvisable to try to use this method with younger children, in whom these abilities are not yet present. It may, however, prove helpful to use a pad of the kind described above, with infants merely as a means of signaling to the attending adult (e.g., by means of a light or a remotely located buzzer) that the child has urinated and is in need of attention, so that he will become accustomed to being dry instead of lying for long periods in wet clothing. Aside from this possible modified application, we do not at present recommend that the technique which we have developed for dealing with enuresis in older children be used with subjects under three years of age, except possibly in special cases where expert psychological observation and guidance can be maintained. Although we cannot afford to go too far in emulating the leniency with which children are treated in many primitive cultures, lest we undermine the very foundation of the adult type of personality which we value in civilized society, we are inclined to be unnecessarily exacting of our children and can doubtless go a long way in the direction of greater leniency in many situations, of which toilet training would appear to be one. Given the assurance of having at their disposal a reliable and effective method of dealing with the problem should it persist unduly long, parents will perhaps find it less imperative to push toilet training as feverishly as they are now inclined to do and will be able to become somewhat more casual in this connection, with salutary effect.

X

The writers anticipate that their method of dealing with enuresis will be in some quarters characterized, despite the favorable character of the results thus far obtained and the qualifications and warnings given against an over-simplified view of the problem, as "symptomatic therapy." Not so much in defense of this method—which can stand or fall on its own merits—as in an attempt to indicate some of the generally uncritical thinking which has come over into the field of child training and education in the form of careless medical analogies, we are impelled to make a few concluding remarks on this score. Illustrative of the view which has gained currency among a large group of writers regarding the meaning and management of all forms of so-called "problem" behavior in children is the following statement by Beverly [7] concerning enuresis:

> [Enuresis] must be considered as a symptom—analogous to a fever. The chief concern should be to determine the other symptoms and attempt to find the underlying cause of the difficulty. Just as we are more concerned about the cause of the fever and other symptoms, so we should primarily be concerned with the cause of the incontinence and other symptoms. Just as we no longer treat the fever primarily, but its cause, so we should no longer treat the incontinence primarily, but its cause. Just as the fever disappears when its cause has been eradicated, so the incontinence disappears if the underlying cause can be eradicated (p. 723).[27]

The common criterion as to whether a given item of child behavior is or is not a "symptom"—insofar as attention is usually given to this

---

[27] A colleague once expressed disapproval of our approach to the problem of enuresis on the grounds that if one succeeds in eliminating a child's enuresis by such direct methods, one often "loses one's barometer" and is henceforth unable to tell whether there is really anything wrong with the child, psychiatrically.

problem—seems to be whether somebody who is important in the life of the child objects to it. Let us suppose that a three-year-old child eats peas with a spoon instead of a fork and that someone does object to it; this item of behavior becomes a "symptom," and as such it must not be dealt with directly; training the child by straightforward methods to use a fork instead of a spoon would be "symptomatic therapy." What one must do is to eliminate, once and for all, the "underlying cause," which in this case is presumably the child's hunger. This reasoning is made none the less fallacious by the fact that it is implicit in the commonly recommended practice of restricting the fluid intake of enuretic children: no one can deny that a child does urinate *because* he drinks water.[28]

But let us suppose that the position now be taken that a given item of behavior, such as eating peas with a spoon instead of a fork, really becomes a "symptom" only after ordinary methods of training and disapproval have failed to eliminate it. The "underlying cause" of this behavior will now be said to be either gross stupidity or negativism, stubbornness, hostility, or some other attitude implying thwarting and frustration. Assuming that the methods employed in the situation have

---

[28]The loose way in which the term "symptom" is commonly used in the field of child conduct implies little more than that the behavior to which it refers is *caused*; such an affirmation has, of course, no significance or value. In physical diagnosis a *symptom* is usually defined as any subjectively experienceable phenomenon which a patient reports and complains of to the physician, for whom it then becomes a *sign* of a disease process. In the great majority of instances, socalled behavior problems in children are certainly not symptoms in this sense; for it is usually *other persons*, not the child himself, who reports and complains of them. In his psychoanalytic writings Freud has used the terms "symptom" and "symptom-formation" in a restricted, technically defined sense; for him they always imply anxiety, repression, and regression, occurring in a special sequence and pattern. It is the writers' impression that much would be gained if these terms were used only in this delimited and explicit manner.

It is indeed true that enuresis *may* be a symptom in the strict sense; but like so many other items of childhood behavior, it is impossible to determine from its sheer form whether it represents real psychopathology or merely reflects faulty education and training. When urinary continence has been established and maintained for some months or years and is then lost, there is a strong presumption that the resulting enuresis is, in fact, a symptom; but otherwise, in the case of children who have never ceased to show nocturnal incontinence, which is regarded as normal during infancy, how is one to know from the incontinence alone that it is a symptom rather than simply a reflection of pedagogical inadequacy on the part of nurses and parents? And when does persisting behavior of this kind suddenly cease to be normal and become a symptom? As pointed out above, the age at which bladder control during sleep is expected of children varies enormously in different cultures and can therefore scarcely be regarded as a valid criterion for judgment in this respect. The problem clearly warrants more careful consideration than has been accorded it.

been reasonably adequate (which is not always true of training for bladder control during sleep), the perverse behavior can supposedly be dealt with only by eliminating some of the basic dissatisfactions in the life of the child; punishment, while perhaps eradicating the specific behavior at which it is directed, is said only to increase the child's smoldering resentments, which will erupt sooner or later in some other form.

The writers have repeatedly stressed in this paper their belief that in a situation where an enuretic child is under the control of parents or parent substitutes whom he hates more than he loves, it will materially facilitate the treatment of his difficulty if the child's affective valences can be altered in a positive direction. But what must not be overlooked is that all education is more or less frustrating and that even the best-loved of children have periods of resentment when they show behavior which is either directly or indirectly retaliatory. If we insist, therefore, whenever behavior of this kind appears, that the only *safe* way of dealing with it is to remove the underlying frustration, we unavoidably repudiate our responsibility for the education and socialization of our children. Not only education but life itself is frustrating, and unfortunate indeed is the child who does not learn to tolerate this type of experience and to re-adjust accordingly.

The issue here involved is, in reality, a focal point of the perennial variance between clinician and educator (parent, teacher and clergyman). The specialist who is engaged exclusively in therapeutic work sees mainly the bad effects of education and is likely to reach the conclusion that education in general is mainly bad.[29] The educator, on the other hand, sensing his position as the authorized agent for perpetuating the accepted values and traditional ways of the culture, is inclined to hew close to the traditionally prescribed line, letting the chips, in the form of distorted, broken personalities, fall as they may. The charge by the clinician that the educator is "brutal" and "sadistic" and the counter-charge by the educator that the clinician is "unrealistic" are perhaps but the displaced expressions of a common dissatisfaction with the tense, ruthlessly competitive conditions of civilized life as we know it, which neither the educator nor the clinician usually cares to criticize, much less take active steps to change. Dollard[15] has brilliantly set this problem and the reader is referred to his paper for a discussion of its further implications. Present purposes will have been served if these remarks but call attention to the

---

[29]It must be said, to their great credit, that both Sigmund Freud[22] and Anna Freud[21] have carefully sought to avoid this error.

futility of the guerrilla warfare which continually occurs between the clinician and the educator, which could be so profitably turned into a joint attack upon the problems of "social engineering" and the creation of a culture giving greater promise of "maximal gratification of the instinctual life of individuals while guaranteeing the security of all in the pursuit of their aims"[15, p. 433].

SUMMARY

A survey of the literature on the topic of nocturnal enuresis shows that most modern writers in this field are inclined to believe either (a) that enuresis is merely a continuation, due to inadequate training, of the physiological incontinence of infancy or (b) that it is caused by certain emotional needs which are not finding appropriate expression during the child's waking hours. Those writers who subscribe to the latter view may be sub-divided according to whether they believe: (1) that enuresis is a substitutive form of gratification of repressed genital sexuality, (2) that it is a symptom of deep-seated anxieties and fears, or (3) that it is a disguised expression of hostility toward parents or parent substitutes which the victim of the enuresis does not dare to express more openly.

There can now be scarcely any doubt that one or more of these emotional factors are of predominant etiological significance in isolated cases of enuresis and, that they are contributing factors in a much larger group of cases; but they do not, in the opinion of the present writers, provide a fully satisfactory and comprehensive explanation of enuresis in general. On the basis of a variety of evidence which is cited, it appears that there is a relatively large group of enuretic children in whom faulty habit training is the predominant, perhaps exclusive, causal factor and that it is an important contributing factor in many instances of enuresis where emotional considerations are also involved.

In many primitive societies the young child spends much of its waking as well as sleeping life in intimate contact with the body of the mother, with little or no clothing between them. Under these circumstances, the onset of urination by the child is likely to produce an immediate response on the part of the mother, which tends to check the urination and produce awakening, thereby providing psychologically efficient conditions for the development of bladder control in the child during sleep. But conditions are very different in our own culture; and if a child in civilized societies is to have the benefit of this more specific form of conditioning, it is clear that some automatic mechanical arrangement will have to be provided. Such an arrangement is described in the present report.

The method of approach to the problem of enuresis here proposed, combined with an appreciation of the aggressive implications which this form of behavior commonly involves, has produced therapeutic success in all of the 30 children with whom it has so far been employed. In no case has there been any indication of "symptom substitution," such personality changes as have resulted from its application being uniformly in a favorable direction. It is concluded that the widespread view that enuresis is always a "symptom" and must not be dealt with directly, represents the misapplication of a concept illicitly borrowed from adult medicine and psychopathology.

REFERENCES

1. Ackerson, L. *Children's Behavior Problems.* Chicago: University of Chicago Press, 1931, 268 pp.
2. Addis, R. S. A statistical study of nocturnal enuresis. *Arch. of Disease in Children*, 1935, **10**, 169–178.
3. Aichhorn, A. *Wayward Youth.* New York: Viking Press, 1936, 236 pp.
4. Anderson, F. N. The psychiatric aspects of enuresis. *Amer. Jour. of Pediatrics*, 1930, **40**, 591–618 and 818–850.
5. Angel, A. From the analysis of a bedwetter. *The Psychoanalytic Quarterly*, 1935, **4**(1), 120–134.
6. Baretz, L. H. A new treatment of enuresis in the male. *The Urologic and Cutaneous Review*, 1936, **XL**, 5.
7. Beverly, B. I. Incontinence in children. *Jour. of Pediatrics St. Louis*, **2**(6), 718.
8. Bonjour, J. Un moyen pour quérir l'incontinence d'urine nocturne. *Rev. med. de la Suisse Rom.*, 1931, **51**, 82–83.
9. Bott, E. A., Blatz, W. E., Chant, Nellie, and Bott, Helen. Observation and training of fundamental habits in young children. *Genetic Psychology Monographs*, 1928, **4**(1), 1–161.
10. Cameron *et al.* Discussion on enuresis. *Proc. Royal Soc. Med.*, 1924, **17**, 37–40.
11. Campbell, C. N. A case of childhood conflicts with prominent reference to the urinary system; with some general considerations on urinary symptoms in the psychoneuroses and psychoses. *Psychoanalytic Review*, 1918, **5**, 269–290.
12. Courtin, W. Relations between enuresis and sleep. *Arch. Kinderh.*, 1923, **74**, 40–50.
13. Davidson, W. C. Enuresis. *Abt's Pediatrics Phila.*, 1924, **4**, 867–878.
14. Davis, G. G. Gersuny's operation for the cure of enuresis. *Ann Surg. Phila.*, 1908, **48**, 792–793.
15. Dollard, J. Mental hygiene and a "scientific culture." *The International Jour. of Ethics*, 1935, **XLV**, 4.
16. Dollard, J., Doob, L. W., Miller, N. E., Mowrer, O. H., and Sears, R. *Integrational Possibilities of the Frustration-Aggression Hypothesis for the Social Sciences.* New Haven: Yale University Press, 1939.

17. English, O. S. and Pearson, G. H. J. *Common Neuroses of Children and Adults.* New York: Norton, 1937, 320 pp.
18. Fenichel, O. *Outline of Clinical Psychoanalysis.* Albany: Psychoanalytic Quarterly Press, 1934, 492 pp.
19. Ford, C. S. Unpublished notes on the Fiji Islanders.
20. Fordyce, A. D. *et al.* Discussion on enuresis. *Proc. Royal Soc. Med.,* 1924, **17**, 37–40.
21. Freud, A. *The Technique of Child Analysis.* New York: Nervous and Mental Disease Publishing Company, 1928, 59 pp.
22. Freud, S. *A General Introduction to Psycho-Analysis.* New York: Liveright, 1935, 412 pp.
23. Freud, S. *The Interpretation of Dreams.* New York: Macmillan Company, 1920, 510 pp.
24. Freud, S. *Three Contributions to the Theory of Sex.* New York: Nervous and Mental Disease Publishing Company, 1916, 117 pp.
25. Fuchs, A. and Gross, S. Incontinentia vesicae und Enuresis nocturna bei Soldaten. *Wiener klinische Wochenschrift,* 1916, **29**, 1483–1486.
26. Genouville. Incontinence d'urine. *L'association Francaise d'urologie, Paris,* 1908, **12**, 97–107.
27. Glaser, J. and Landau, D. B. A simple mechanical method for the treatment of enuresis in male children. *Jour. of Pediatrics,* 1936, **8**, 197–199.
28. Goldman, M. R. Treatment of enuresis—past and present. *Penn. Med. Jour.* 1934–35, **38**, 247–251.
29. von Gulácsy, Z. Beiträge zur Pathologie des Bettnässens. *Arch. Kinderh.,* 1935, **105**, 81–86.
30. Hale, G. C. A case of persistent enuresis. *Canadian Med. Assn. Jour. Toronto,* 1914, **4**, 413–417.
31. Hamill, R. C. Enuresis. *Jour. of Amer. Med. Assn.,* 1929, **93**(1), 254–257.
32. Hernaman-Johnson, F. The treatment of urinary incontinence by electrical methods. *The Lancet,* 1921, 1295–1296.
33. Hernaman-Johnson, F. Urinary disturbances—incontinence and frequency: their cure by electrical methods. *The Practitioner,* 1919, **102**, 139–142.
34. Hoffman, R. L. Bladder stutterers. *Military Surgeon,* 1919, **45**, 107–109.
35. Janet, P. *Les Troubles Psychopathiques de la Miction.* Essai de Psychophysiologie Normale et Pathologique, Paris, 1890, 216 pp.
36. Kanner, L. *Child Psychiatry.* Baltimore: Charles C. Thomas, 1935, 527 pp.
37. Kidd, D. *Savage Childhood—A Study of Kafir Children.* London: Adam and Charles, 1906, 314 pp.
38. Marcuse, M. Das Bettnässen (Enuresis nocturna) als sexualneurotischen. *Symptom. Ztschr. F. Sexualwissensch.,* 1924–25, **11**, 229–237.
39. Markey, O. B. Psychiatric implications in enuresis. *Arch. Pediat.,* 1932, **49**, 269–278.
40. McGuinness, A. C. The treatment of enuresis in childhood. *Med. Clinics of N. Amer.,* 1935, **19**, 287–294.
41. Mead, M. Growing Up in New Guinea. New York: Blue Ribbon Books, Inc., 1930, 372 pp.
42. Mead, M. *Sex and Temperament in Three Primitive Societies.* New York: William Morrow & Co., 1935, 335 pp.
43. Mowrer, O. H. Apparatus for the study and treatment of enuresis. *Amer. Jour. of Psych.,* 1938, **LI**, 163–166.
44. Ochsenius, K. Auf Behandlung der Enuresis. *Müchener Medizinische Wochenschrift,* 1923, **70**(i), 432.

45. Ochsenius, K. Zur Behandlung der Enuresis. *Müchener Medizinische Wochenschrift,* 1925, **72**(ii), 1342.
46. Pfaundler, M. Demonstration eines Apparates zur Selsttätigen Singalisierung Statt-gehabter Bettnässung. *Verhandlungen der Gesellschaft Für Kinderheilkunde, Wiesba-den,* 1904, **21**, 219–220.
47. Rattray, R. S. *Ashanti Law and Constitution.* Oxford Clarendon Press, 1929, 420 pp.
48. Rémy-Roux. Nouvel appareil electrique contre l'incontinence nocturne d'urine. *Bulletin et Mémoires de la Sociéte de Médecine de Vaucluse, Avignon,* 1908–1911, **2**, 337–340.
49. Sadger, J. Ueber Urethralerotik. *Jahrb. f. psychoan. u. psychopath. Forschungen,* **2**, 409.
50. Schacter, M. Considerations generales sur l'enuresis nocturne infantile. *Jour. de Med. de Paris,* 1932, **52**, 619–621.
51. Schwarz, O. Versuch einer Analyse der Miktionson omalien nach Erkaltungen. *Wien Klin. Wchnschr.,* 1915, **28**, 1057.
52. Uteau and Richardot, I. *Appareil pour dépister la simulation dans l'incontinence nocturne d'urine. Paris Médical,* 1916, **6**(ii), 233–235.
53. Weissenberg, S. Über das Bettnässen und die Rolle der Traume in seinem Bilde. *Zeitschrift für Kinderheilkunde,* 1925–26, **40**, 343–352.
54. Whiting, J. W. M. Unpublished notes on the Waskuk peoples of New Guinea.
55. Zappert, J. Enuresis. *Ergebn. d. inn. Med. u. Kinderh.* Berlin, 1920, **18**, 109–188.

ARTICLE 2

Dry Pants: A Rapid Method of Toilet Training Children*†

R. M. FOXX and N. H. AZRIN

Anna State Hospital, Anna, Illinois, U.S.A. and Rehabilitation Institute,
Southern Illinois University, Carbondale, Illinois, U.S.A.

Abstract: Toilet training sometimes requires considerable time. An intensive learning procedure was devised for shortening this training time and tested with 34 children who were experiencing toilet training problems. The procedure had the following major characteristics: (1) a distraction-free environment, (2) an increased frequency of urination by increased fluid intake, (3) continuous practice and reinforcement of the necessary dressing skills, (4) continuous practice and reinforcement in approaching the toilet, (5) detailed and continuing instruction for each act required in toileting, (6) gradual elimination of the need for reminders to toilet, (7) immediate detection of accidents, (8) a period of required practice in toilet-approach after accidents as well as (9) negative reinforcement for the accident, (10) immediate detection of correct toileting, (11) immediacy of reinforcement for correct toiletings, (12) a multiple reinforcement system including imagined social benefits as well as actual praise, hugging and sweets, (13) continuing reinforcement for having dry pants, (14) learning by imitation, (15) gradual reduction of the need for immediate reinforcement and (16) post-training attention to cleanliness. All 34 children were trained and in an average of 4 hours; children over 26 months old required an average of 2 hours of training. After training, accidents decreased to a near-zero level and remained near zero during 4 months of follow-up. The results suggest that virtually all healthy children who have reached 20 months of age can be toilet trained and within a few hours.

Until a child has learned to toilet himself properly and without a reminder, the parent and the child must suffer problems of hygiene, skin

---

*The research was supported by the Illinois Department of Mental Health. We wish to thank Afton Jarvis and Angela Foss for serving as trainers. Reprints may be obtained from either author at the Behavior Research Laboratory, Anna State Hospital, Anna, Illinois 62906.

irritations, excessive dependence on the parent, inconvenience, expense, and, as the child matures, also social embarrassment. Although all normal children seem to learn eventually to toilet themselves, parental "common sense" procedures have resulted in no more benefit than has occurred without training. For example, Madsen, Hoffman, Thomas, Koropsak and Madsen (1969) found that parental training for 1 month reduced accidents by only 5 per cent which is about the same insignificant decrease that they obtained without any toilet training. In view of this failure of training efforts, the common attitude of permissiveness regarding toileting (Spock, 1968) is understandable and justified. One can understand why this permissive view of toilet training as an exercise in futility has recurred about every decade for the past 60 years (Wolfenstein, 1965). Some success in reducing training time has been indicated recently by special reinforcement procedures (Madsen, 1965; Madsen *et al.*, 1969; Mahoney, Van Wagenen and Meyerson, 1971; Pumroy and Pumroy, 1965). Unfortunately, all of these procedures have required at least 1 month of training, all but one (Madsen *et al.*, 1969) have been tested with only 1, 2 or 3 children and all but one (Mahoney *et al.*, 1971) still required continuous reminders to toilet at the end of training. In spite of these limitations, these results indicate that intensive training can reduce somewhat the age at which a child will toilet himself.

Recently, a method has been developed for rapidly training the retarded to toilet themselves without prompting (Azrin and Foxx, 1971; Foxx and Azrin, 1973a; Azrin, Sneed and Foxx, 1973). The success of those efforts indicated that similar and even more rapid training might be achieved with normal children by use of that general method. The present study evaluated a modification of that method with a group of nonretarded children.

METHOD

Children

Thirty-four children were selected for training, 22 boys and 12 girls. Children were recruited by a newspaper ad, by a word-of-mouth request by the authors, and by referral from mothers whose children had been trained by the procedure. Since the training procedure required the child to be capable of responding to verbal instructions, a screening test was devised for ascertaining a potential trainee's instructional responsiveness. The child was asked successively to point to his (1) nose, (2) eyes, (3) mouth, (4) hair, (5) to sit down, (6) to stand up, (7) to walk with the mother to another room, (8) to look at the mother, (9) to imitate the mother in a simple task, (10) to bring the mother a toy. Of the 43 children referred, 9 could not satisfy the test for instructional responsiveness. All but two of the nine children were under 20 months of age. The mean age for the final sample of 34 children was 25 months with a range of 20 months to 36 months. Virtually all of the parents mentioned difficulties in toilet training their child that led them to seek outside assistance and several mentioned the use of spankings and rewards. Several children, especially the younger ones, did not speak more than a few words and did not dress themselves.

General Rationale

The present method was based on the same rationale used previously to devise a rapid toilet training procedure for the retarded (Azrin and Foxx, 1971; Foxx and Azrin, 1973a). Normal testing was viewed as a governed reaction that included dressing skills, independence of action, and awareness of one's appearance as well as sensitivity to bladder and bowel pressures. The general method was to provide an intensive learning experience that maximized the factors known to be important for learning; then to fade out these factors once learning had occurred. The learning factors maximized were a distraction-free environment, a large number of trials, consideration of the component responses, operant reinforcement for correct responses, a variety of reinforcers, quality of the reinforcers, frequency of reinforcement, manual guidance, verbal instruction, immediacy of reinforcement, immediacy of detection of incorrect responses and negative reinforcement for the incorrect re-sponse. For the present application to nonretarded children, the previous reliance on manual guidance was deemphasized and greater reliance placed on verbal instructions. An imitation procedure was added as well as a procedure for verbal and symbolic rehearsal of the benefits of toileting correctly. Since children are typically more active than adults, the adult procedure (Azrin and Foxx, 1971) was changed to require more activity. A description follows of the specific procedure used to emphasize each of these learning factors.

Setting (Distraction-Free Environment)   Distractions and competing activities could be expected to interfere with the child's performance of the required toileting. Accordingly, all toys were removed and only the trainer was present. Although training was conducted in the home of the child or in the home of the trainer, the parents and family members were asked to leave for the day. The trainers were two adult female assistants. Only one assistant was used for each child.

Increased Number of Trials: Increased Urinations   In order to provide many opportunities to reinforce correct toiletings and to negatively reinforce incorrect toiletings, a high frequency of urinations would be desirable. An increased frequency was achieved by giving the child fluids to drink about every 5 min such that about two cups were consumed per hour. The drinks were selected on the basis of the mother's statement of what the child preferred and usually consisted of soft drinks, juices, punches, and milk.

Operant Reinforcement for Correct Toileting   Reinforcement for a response is known to increase the strength of that response. Consequently, reinforcers were given for the act of urinating in the "potty chair" that was provided and also for each of the component skills preceding and following the urination. Reinforcement was withheld at other times and for non-toileting acts.

Component Skills   Common sense application of reinforcement procedures is often interpreted to mean reinforcing the child after he has completed a correct urination. The present procedure considered each of the component skills such as approaching the potty-chair, grasping the pants, lowering the pants, sitting on the potty-chair, wiping onself, arising after urination, raising the pants, removing the urine-filled pot from the chair, bringing the pot to the toilet, emptying the pot, flushing the toilet, and returning the pot to the chair. Reinforcers and instructions were given for each of these component acts.

Quality of Reinforcers   Tasty edibles were used as reinforcers. In addition, an effort was made to identify for use as reinforcers many other events that were of central importance to the child's happiness by questioning the mother and child beforehand. Thus, for a given child a specific type of sweets (such as chocolates) or food (such as potato chips) was used. In addition, the reinforcement consisted of effusive verbal praise, a bodily hug, kisses, caresses, smiles, and applause. Symbolic types of reinforcers were also included (see Symbolic Rehearsal below) by telling the child how pleased his important friends, relatives, and "heroes," would be.

Variety of Reinforcers Since any single reinforcer might lose its effectiveness through constant and exclusive use, the large variety of reinforcers described above were used successively and in various simultaneous combinations.

Immediacy of Reinforcement The more immediate the reinforcement the greater is the strength of the reinforced response. Since the major response act was urinating while seated on the potty-chair, immediate detection and reinforcement at this moment was critical. Although close visual observation of the seated child would usually be sufficient for immediate detection and was used for five children, a special signaling potty-chair (Star Tinkle, Nursery Training Devices, Inc., Concord, California, approximate cost $10) assisted in this detection. The special chair sounded a musical signal when urination activated a device located in the bowl of the chair. The trainer was then alerted and immediately reinforced the child. For the component skills, such as lowering the pants and sitting on the chair, the trainer relied solely on visual observation and gave immediate reinforcement for each component.

Frequency of Reinforcement The greater the frequency of reinforcement, the greater the strength of the reinforced response. This principle dictated that the reinforcement be given for every instance of correct urination and every instance of the component skills. Only when the habit and skills were firmly established was the reinforcement frequency decreased (see Fading of Prompts and Reinforcements below).

Graduated Guidance For each of the component skills, the trainer instructed the child as to what to do, then manually guided the child through the proper movements if the child did not initiate the movement himself. The manual guidance was graduated at any given moment such that no more guidance was used than was necessary for the movement to be carried out. This Graduated Guidance technique, described in detail in Azrin and Foxx (1971), Foxx and Azrin (1972), Foxx and Azrin (1973a; 1973b), served the purpose of teaching the child the correct movements as well as motivating him to respond quickly to instructions.

Verbal Instruction The child was instructed to carry out the correct toileting in a detailed manner that specified each movement such as putting the fingers beneath the briefs and toward the back of the hips rather than simply instructing him to go to the toilet or to lower his pants. The Graduated Guidance ensured immediate completion of the skill in the rare event that the instructions were not understood or were ignored. The reinforcers at the completion of the act encouraged the child to carry out the act at the next opportunity whether that act had been carried out as a result of instructions or of the Graduated Guidance.

Imitation   Imitation is a proven method of teaching details of a skill and was used in addition to verbal description. Directed imitation was used to teach the child how to toilet and to learn the positive benefits of doing so. The child was given a hollow doll that could be filled with water through the mouth and would release the water through a hole between its legs. The trainer taught the child to perform all of the toileting skills and procedures with the doll that were being used with the child such as praising and feeding the doll, lowering and raising its pants and allowing it to urinate in the potty-chair. This directed imitation was conducted continuously between the child's own practice trials at the start of training until the child had learned the component toileting skills.

Dry Pants Check   The objective of the training was not to educate the child to urinate frequently and correctly but to do so at whatever frequency was necessary to insure dry pants. To teach this awareness of his appearance the trainer inspected the child's pants about every 5 min, having the child himself touch his pants, and reinforcing the child if the pants were dry. The fluids were given as part of this reinforcement and thereby fulfilled the double function of increasing the frequency of urination as well as being a reinforcer.

Negative Reinforcement for Accidents   To discourage accidents, the trainer reprimanded the child when he wet his pants. The trainer also omitted the reinforcers at the next dry pants check, and omitted any social interaction with the child for about 5 min (time-out from positive reinforcement). Also serving as a negative reinforcer was the requirement that the child himself change into dry pants which was done at the end of the time-out period so that wet pants would be associated with loss of social interaction. The final element of the negative reinforcement was a required period of practicing rapidly the complete act of toileting (described below under "Positive Practice"). The trainer closely observed the child's pants, expression and posture so as to detect an accident immediately and to impose the negative reinforcers immediately.

Prompted Practice Trials   To provide practice in toileting and to associate urination in the potty-chair with reinforcement, the child was instructed to toilet himself about every 10 min. He was allowed to sit on the potty-chair for about 5 min during each trial until one or two urinations occurred during the first minute after seating himself. This short latency urination was interpreted to mean that the child was bladder trained. Thereafter, he was required to be seated for only about 1 min during each trial.

Positive Practice   A period of required practice in toileting was used as an educational tool as well as a negative reinforcer. After the verbal reprimand had been given for an accident, the trainer required the child to practice going to the potty-chair from various locations in the house for a total of 10 rapidly conducted trials. During each trial, the child went to the chair, lowered his pants, seated himself for about 2 sec, stood up, raised his pants and then moved to another location. As described in detail elsewhere (Foxx and Azrin, 1972, 1973a, 1973b; and Azrin, Kaplan and Foxx, 1973), this period of Positive Practice was educative but also negatively reinforcing because of the effort required.

Verbal and Symbolic Rehearsal   An objective of the procedure was to create a desire by the child to remain dry in order to please his parents, family, and friends. Yet, the limitations of the training situation precluded the possibility of having these "significant others" actually present and participating. As a substitute, this social reinforcement was arranged symbolically by telling the child, as part of the reinforcement, that each of these persons would be delighted at his success. A list of these significant individuals was obtained prior to the training and included favored television or story-book characters as well as real persons. To insure the child's involvement, the child was asked to reply to questions about this symbolic reinforcement such as "What will Santa Claus (or Mickey Mouse, or Daddy, or Mommy, or your brother Bobby) say about your dry pants?"

Fading of Prompts and Reinforcers   The detailed instructions and continuous reinforcement for each component skill were given at the start of training but then withdrawn as the child progressed. The instructions on the practice trials were successively omitted for each component act that was conducted at least once without instructions. The instruction to initiate a practice trial was omitted entirely once the child initiated and carried out one entire practice trial without any prompts having been given. Also, after this unprompted toileting, reinforcers for correct toileting were given only intermittently, and then discontinued entirely as were also the dry-pants inspections. The critical point in training was the first occasion of toileting with no need for instructions. Typically, only an additional half-hour or hour was needed thereafter with no instructions during that time and with the reinforcement for dry pants given only once or twice. Thus, the trainer was functioning primarily as an observer after the first unprompted toileting.

Post-Training Attention   The primary motivation desired for maintaining the toileting habit was the pleasure of the child's parents and family. To insure this motivation after training, the parent inspected the child's pants before each meal or snack and at naptimes and bedtime and praised the child for having dry pants. If an accident occurred, the parent reprimanded the child, made him change his pants, and required him to practice going to the toilet (Positive Practice). No reminders to toilet were given. This scheduled attention to the child's appearance was conducted only for a few days after training and then discontinued once the child had no accidents.

RESULTS

Reduction of Accidents

Figure 2.1 shows the number of accidents before and after training for the 34 children. The mothers had recorded the number of accidents by counting the number of times the child had to be changed each day during the week preceding and following training. Following training, the parents were contacted every month for 4 months by telephone or by a personal visit from one of the trainers. Prior to training, the children averaged about 6 accidents per day per child. Within the first post-training week, accidents had decreased by 97 per cent to 0.2 accidents per day per child, or about one per week. This near-zero level of accidents endured during the entire 4-month follow-up period and applied to bowel movements as well as urinations. A within-subject comparison of the children's pre- and post-training accidents by the Wilcoxin Matched-Pairs Signed Ranks Test (Siegel, 1956) showed a significant ($p < 0.01$) reduction of accidents for the very first day after training, and for each month of the post-training period.

Training Time   The mean training time was 3.9 hr; the median time was 3.5 hr and the range was one-half hour to 14 hr. Training was considered complete when the child toileted himself completely and with no prompts. The older children, aged 26–36 months, were trained in a training time of about $2\frac{1}{4}$ hr. The 20–25 month old group had a mean training time of about 5 hr.

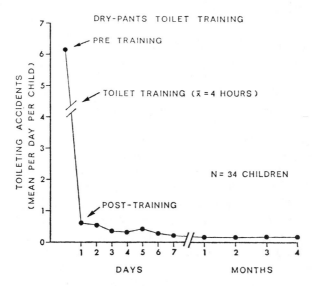

Fig. 2.1. The effect of the "Dry Pants" toilet training procedure on the frequency of toileting accidents, both bladder and bowel, of 34 normal children. The toilet training period is shown as an interruption in the curve and required an average of 4 hours per child. The "Pre-Training" data point represents the children's accident rate per day during the week prior to training. Data points are given for the first 7 days after training and monthly thereafter. Each datum point is the average number of accidents per day per child.

Parent Reaction   Most of the parents, although hopeful, were somewhat skeptical about the favorable outcome of training program, possibly because of their own unsuccessful experiences in attempting to train their children. Upon seeing their child independently toilet himself, raise and lower his own pants, carry the plastic pot into the toilet and empty the contents into the toilet stool, flush the toilet and replace the plastic pot, the parents characteristically expressed disbelieving pleasure. These parents were eager to suggest friends and relatives whose children might also benefit from the training procedure. It was found that the only parent who did not express pleasure over the rapidity with which his child was trained had bet a friend $100.00 that his child would not be trained in one day. Ironically, this child was trained in about one-half hour. Although the child did not have an accident for 2 months after training, we discovered on the 3-month follow-up that the child had been returned to diapers for no apparent reason other than the economic consideration of the wager.

Reaction of the Children   Most of the children reacted to the training program as if it were a very pleasant experience, hugging and kissing the trainer. The high density of positive reinforcement in the form of hugs, praise, candies, applause, smiles, treats, and the undivided attention of the trainer undoubtedly contributed to the children's pleasant attitude during the training program. Several features of the program seemed especially pleasurable to the children including playing with the doll, emptying the potty and flushing the toilet.

A few of the children initially reacted negatively to the attempts to toilet train them. These children were generally "problem children" who resisted most efforts by the parents and also actively resisted the toilet training attempts by their parents despite being physiologically and psychologically ready for training. Typically, these few children engaged in a temper tantrum at the start of training but cooperated thereafter when this initial reluctance was overcome by providing them with immediate Graduated Guidance whenever they failed to respond to a request. The typical comment by the mothers of these problem children was that the child had become more cooperative and pleasant in his general conduct after the toilet training.

Bedwetting   None of the children were given specific training for bedwetting (enuresis). Yet, the mothers of 10 children (about 30%) reported that their child stopped wetting at night during the entire first week immediately following the daytime training. Follow-up checks showed that all 10 of these children continued to stay dry at night during the 4-month follow-up period.

DISCUSSION

The results showed that the training program was an effective method of training normal children to toilet themselves without any prompting. All 34 children were trained. Training was accomplished rapidly requiring an average of only 4 hr per child and only about 2 hr for children older than 26 months. The accidents quickly decreased to a near zero level and remained near zero during the 4-month follow-up. Bowel training and bladder training were accomplished concurrently with no need for a differential training procedure. An incidental benefit was that bedwetting (enuresis) was also eliminated for about one-third of the children. Successful training was achieved even for children as young as 20 months, for problem children who resisted any type of training and for children who did not speak. The training program appeared to be a pleasant experience for the children.

The present results demonstrate that toilet training is not a futile exercise; training can be achieved by intensive learning procedures, as was also indicated by recent reinforcement studies (Madsen *et al.*, 1969; Mahoney *et al.*, 1971). Consequently, one can no longer defend an attitude of fatalistic permissiveness on the grounds that bladder and bowel control cannot be hastened. A permissive attitude would still be justified if the training effort produced an enduring negative emotional attitude. The results showed the converse: the children who were negative prior to training were described as more pleasant and cooperative after training. Permissiveness does seem justified for the average child under 19 months of age. The present results showed that all normally responsive children over 19 months of age could be trained in a few hours but greater difficulty should be expected with younger children as indicated by the present finding that the younger children required more training time. Since normal toileting requires locomotive skills, manual dexterity, and maturation of the bladder and bowel muscles, little gain would occur from training prior to the emergence of these skills. Also, the present method relies heavily on verbal, instructional, and symbolic procedures and should not be so rapidly effective with children who are not verbally and socially responsive. Overall, we suggest that training be deferred until a child is 20 months of age since the training effort for the average child below that age might counterbalance the convenience of having him trained.

REFERENCES

Azrin, N. H. and Foxx R. M. A rapid method of toilet training the institutionalized retarded. *J. appl. Behav. Anal.*, 1971, **4**, 89–99.

Azrin, N. H., Kaplan, S. J. and Foxx, R. M. Autism reversal: Eliminating stereotyped self-stimulation in retarded individuals. *Am. J. Men. Def.*, 1973, **78**, 241–248.

Azrin, N. H., Sneed, T. J. and Foxx, R. M. Dry bed: A rapid method of eliminating bedwetting (enuresis) of the retarded. *Behav. Res. & Therapy*, 1973, **11**, 427–434.

Foxx, R. M. and Azrin, N. H. Restitution: A method of eliminating aggressive-disruptive behavior of retarded and brain damaged patients. *Behav. Res. & Therapy*, 1972, **10**, 15–27.

Foxx, R. M. and Azrin, N. H. *Rapid Toilet Training of the Retarded*. Research Press, Champaign, Illinois, 1973a.

Foxx, R. M. and Azrin, N. H. The elimination of autistic, self-stimulatory behavior by overcorrection. *J. appl. Behav. Anal.*, 1973, **6**, 1–14.

Madsen, C. H. Positive reinforcement in the toilet training of a normal child. In *Case Studies in Behavior Modification* (edited by Ullmann, L. P. and Krasner, L.), pp. 305–307. Holt, Rinehart and Winston, New York, 1965.

Madsen, C. H., Hoffman, M., Thomas, D. R., Koropsak, E., and Madsen, C. K. Comparisons of toilet training techniques. In *Social Learning in Childhood* (edited by Gelfand, D. M.), pp. 124–132. Brooks Cole, Belmont, California, 1969.

Mahoney, K., Van Wagenen, R. K. and Meyerson, L. Toilet training of normal and retarded children. *J. appl. Behav. Anal.*, 1971, **4**, 173–181.

Pumroy, D. K. and Pumroy, S. S. Systematic observation and reinforcement technique in toilet training. *Psych. Rep.*, 1965, **16**, 467–471.

Siegel, S. *Non Parametric Statistics for the Behavioral Sciences*. McGraw-Hill, New York, 1956.

Spock, B. *Baby and Child Care*, Rev. Edn. Pocket Books, New York, 1968.

Wolfenstein, M. Trends in infant care. In *Marriage, Family and Society* (edited by Rodman, H.), pp. 116–127. Random House, New York, 1965.

ARTICLE 3

The Modification of a Child's Enuresis: Some Response-Response Relationships*

VEY MICHAEL NORDQUIST[1]

The University of Tennessee

Abstract: The present study attempted to evaluate experimentally the relationship between two response classes, enuresis and oppositional behavior. One child who had a long history of bedwetting was observed in his home setting. Parents' reports and initial observations confirmed that the child was oppositional much of the time. When a timeout operation and differential attention were presented, removed, and presented again, the frequency of oppositional behavior decreased, increased, and decreased accordingly. Fluctuations in enuretic activity also correlated with the presence and absence of the timeout and differential attention operations. The suppression of oppositional behavior and enuretic activity persisted over an 18-month treatment period. It was suggested that the parental operations performed on oppositional behavior may have led to an increase in the parents' social reward value. Cessation of enuretic activity was explained in terms of a shift in parental reinforcer effectiveness.

Yates (1969) indicated that the conditioning method for treating childhood enuresis may not be as effective as was once thought. He recently compiled results from every study that selected an initial arrest criterion of six dry nights per week and provided follow-up data over a minimum period of six months. Taking these studies as a whole, Yates reports that only 53% of the cases were successfully treated by the conditioning method. Although he suggests that this figure might be

*Reprinted from *Journal of Applied Behavior Analysis*, 1971, **4**, 241–247. Copyright © 1971 by the Society of Experimental Analysis of Behavior, Inc. With permission of the journal and Vey Michael Nordquist.

[1]I would like to express my appreciation to Dr. Robert Wahler, Department of Psychology, University of Tennessee, for his helpful comments. Thanks are also due to Michael Thomas and Norbert Reese for serving as observers. Reprints may be obtained from the author, Dept. of Child Development, University of Tennessee, Knoxville, Tenn.

somewhat higher if experimenters had more closely supervised parents in administration of the method, even the most careful instructions are no guarantee that mistakes will not be made in the home (Bostock and Shackelton, 1957).

When initial symptom arrest has been achieved, it is not clear that the treatment effect will be sustained once the conditioning apparatus is removed. Lovibond (1964) reported that the relapse rate may be as high as 35 to 40% when follow-up extends to 2 yr or more. Turner and Young (1966) reported a similar relapse figure over a 3 to 5 yr follow-up period.

There are other drawbacks to the conditioning method. Bostock and Shackelton (1957) reported a number of problems encountered in the use of the apparatus. Equipment failure is not uncommon. Parents also find the treatment process inconvenient. Furthermore, the overall cost is often very high.

The purpose of the present research was to assess the effectiveness of a new method for treating childhood enuresis, one which, if successful, would be relatively inexpensive and minimally inconvenient. Although nocturnal enuresis is not particularly amenable to direct manipulation by contingent social reinforcement, there may be a means by which parents could indirectly control enuretic activity. Wahler, Sperling, Thomas, Teeter, and Luper (1970) reported the successful treatment of two moderate stutterers by controlling secondary response classes that were functionally related to stuttered speech. Stuttering is a response class with characteristics similar to enuresis. Most conspicuously, stuttering is not particularly responsive to treatment by reinforcement therapies (see Wahler *et al.*, 1970). By modifying secondary response classes (in one case, oppositional behavior; in the other case, hyperactivity) that were responsive to social reinforcement contingencies, the therapists produced dramatic reductions in the frequency of stuttered speech. Their data clearly negated the possibility that stuttered speech had somehow been inadvertently affected by the reinforcement procedures. The results suggest that some aberrant behaviors typically inaccessible to the usual reinforcement operations might be treated effectively by controlling another response class functionally related to the target behavior.

The present study was undertaken in order (1) to identify a response class functionally related to nocturnal enuresis, (2) to manipulate this response class through the proper distribution of social reinforcement contingencies, and (3) to assess the short and long-term effects of these operations on the incidence of enuretic activity.

METHOD

Patient, Therapy Setting, and Observers

The patient was a 5.5 yr-old boy referred to the University of Tennessee Psychological Clinic because of excessive bedwetting and tantrum behavior. This was his first referral to the clinic by his parents. After the initial interview, all further contacts with the family were made in their home.

Records of patient and parent behaviors were obtained through the use of a behavioral check list (to be described later). All observers used in the study had had formal training in the use of operant principles and procedures of naturalistic observation. Inter-observer reliability checks were computed at regular intervals. In every case, a procedurally naive observer's scores were checked against the experimenter's scores.

General Procedure

During the initial interview, the parents were asked to describe their child's problem behavior and how they typically responded to it. They stated that the boy wet his bed four to five times each week. He had never gained control over nocturnal micturition. They indicated that he was capable of voiding on his own during the daytime, but it later became apparent that the mother very often reminded the boy to go to the bathroom at regular intervals during the day. The parents had also instructed the boy's teacher to remind him to use the bathroom regularly.

The parents stated they were unable to control much of their child's behavior. They said he often refused to follow instructions and was particularly difficult to handle before bedtime. They reported that he had an average of one tantrum per day, although the frequency of tantrum behavior varied considerably from one day to the next. This behavior consisted of screaming, kicking, throwing objects, hitting the parents, and occasionally hitting his 2.5-yr-old sister. Tantrums usually occurred when the parents attempted to enforce an instruction. Spanking, reasoning, threats, and isolation were methods they had used to enforce their demands, all to no avail. They stated that they rarely responded in any aversive way to bedwetting, however. Indeed they were afraid that any attention to bedwetting would only increase the problem.

After the initial interview, the parents were asked permission to observe the boy in his home environment; arrangements were subsequently made to visit them on a weekly basis to obtain records of the child's behavior. Observations were made during the 1-hr period immediately before bedtime because it was during this period that the parents felt most ineffectual.

Behavior Classification, Baseline Observations, and Reliability

After the initial home visit, it was readily apparent that most of the boy's behavior could be classified into two response categories: oppositional behavior and cooperative behavior. During the next home visit, efforts were made to obtain frequency counts for both child response classes. For a behavior to be scored oppositional, it had to satisfy one of the following criteria: (1) when a parental request or command was presented and the child did not comply within a 20-sec interval, his behavior was considered oppositional. The boy's behavior would continue to be scored oppositional during consecutive 20-sec intervals until he complied or until a new request was presented; (2) oppositional behavior was also scored when the boy clearly violated an implied command; that is, when he initiated behavior clearly unacceptable to the parents. Examples of this type of behavior would be hitting, taking something from his sister, screaming, and yelling.

A behavior was scored cooperative when the boy complied with a parental request within a 20-sec interval. Checks for cooperative behavior were entered in consecutive 20-sec intervals until the request was completed or until a new instruction was delivered. Since both child response classes were defined as a function of parental instructions, the number of parental instructions per session was also recorded.

Frequency counts for both child response classes were made by having an observer make coded checks for the occurrence of a behavior class within successive 20-sec intervals for a period of 30 min. An occurrence of a class, regardless of its duration during an interval, was scored as a single response unit so that no more than 90 units could be recorded for any one class during an observation period.

Baseline observation periods commenced on the second home visit and continued until the child response classes appeared to be stable. During these sessions, the parents were instructed to behave as though visitors were not present. The only requirement was that they initiate going-to-bed activities shortly after the observers arrived. They were not told to deliver any particular kind of instructions, nor were they told to deliver a certain number of instructions. After each baseline session, they were asked to report the number of tantrums and the number of enuretic episodes that had occurred since the last observation session. They recorded this information on a calendar provided by the experimenter. The parents were also instructed one week before the first baseline session not to make any comments to the boy about bedwetting.

Inter-observer reliability checks were computed during the last session of each baseline and treatment period. After each reliability check session, an agreement or disagreement was tallied for every 20-sec interval and the percentage of agreement was computed for each response class by subtracting total disagreements from total agreements and dividing by total agreements. Agreement percentages for oppositional behavior ranged from 83 to 90% with a mean of 87%. Agreement percentages for cooperative behavior ranged from 84 to 100% with a mean of 90%. Agreement percentages for parental instructions ranged from 80 to 100% with a mean of 92%.

Contingency Management Program

During the baseline sessions, a number of parental behaviors were identified that were felt to be related to oppositional behavior. When the boy was cooperative, the parents often retired to a place in the house where they could converse quietly or read the paper. However, they quickly responded to disruptive behavior. A long interrogation process usually ensued, typically culminating in parental threats or requests for the boy to be good.

After the last session of Baseline 1, the parents were asked to discontinue negotiating with the boy and threatening him when he was disruptive. They were told that this type of attention probably helped to maintain his undesirable behavior. They were informed they would have to start making their attention contingent upon cooperative behavior and begin using a timeout operation to suppress oppositional behavior. The latter operation consisted of placing the boy in a corner in his bedroom whenever he refused to follow a parental command or whenever he initiated disruptive behavior. For example, if the boy took a toy from his sister, yelled at his father, or refused to come to the table for dinner, the parents were told to take the boy to his bedroom, sit him in a corner, and leave the room. He remained in the corner for 10 min. If he had a tantrum during timeout, he was not removed until the tantrum had subsided for several minutes. During the first week of treatment, it was not uncommon for the boy to spend as much as 40 min in timeout. Nevertheless, he never attempted to leave the corner. When it was time for the boy to get into bed and he refused, the parents were told not to place the child in the corner. They were instructed to place him in bed and leave the room. They were asked not to return, even if the boy screamed or cried.

Before beginning the contingency management program, the experimenter and parents discussed several examples of child behavior and how they should respond to them. Particular emphasis was given to the distribution of social reinforcement. The parents were encouraged not only to tell the child that they approved of his behavior, but also show their appreciation with physical affection. It was not uncommon, therefore, for the parents to place their arms around the boy, hug him and say: "Good boy, David," or, "David, we're proud of you when you behave like that." Of course, the parents were told to continue ignoring enuretic activity. They also continued to keep daily records of tantrum behavior and enuretic episodes. During observation periods, it was necessary to dispense with the timeout operation so that a continuous 30-min record could be obtained. On all other evenings, timeout was used by the parents. The first observation session occurred three weeks after the last session of Baseline 1 because the family was out of town during weeks No. 4 and 5.

Experimental Demonstrations of Parental Control

The parents had no difficulty implementing the contingency management program. As expected, and as later data will show, the predicted changes in the boy's oppositional and bedwetting behaviors occurred. At this point, it was necessary briefly to reinstate baseline procedures in order to demonstrate clear parental control over the boy's behavior. The parents were therefore instructed to discontinue the differential attention and timeout operations. They continued to ignore bedwetting, however. After two baseline sessions, the parents were instructed to reinstate the treatment procedures. During this period, they were told once again not to make comment to the boy if he did wet his bed. They also continued keeping daily records of tantrum behavior and enuretic activity. These procedures remained in effect for the duration of the study.

RESULTS

Figure 3.1 describes frequency counts in 20-sec units of David's oppositional and cooperative behavior over baseline and treatment

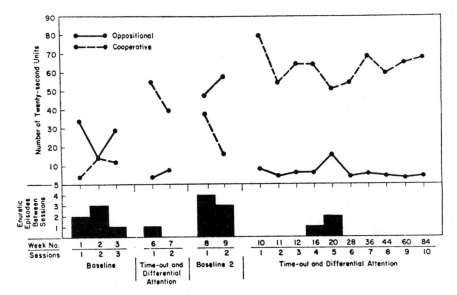

Fig. 3.1. Number of David's 20-sec oppositional and cooperative units over baseline and treatment periods and the number of enuretic episodes recorded by parents during the period between each session. All observations were made during 30-min sessions held in the home. The week numbers are listed to correspond with each observation session so that the time interval between sessions is easily determined.

sessions. Also depicted is the number of enuretic episodes that occurred between each session.

As predicted, David's behavior varied with the systematic presentation and withdrawal of parental reinforcement contingencies. Frequency counts for oppositional behavior were much lower during treatment sessions than baseline sessions. On the other hand, frequency counts for cooperative behavior were much higher during treatment sessions than baseline sessions. Of greater interest, however, is the rather strong relationship between the behaviors under direct experimental control and the frequency of enuretic activity. In Fig. 3.1, the number of enuretic episodes clearly varies with the presence and absence of the treatment program; decreases in enuretic activity occurred only at those times when the contingency management program was in effect. The number of enuretic episodes rose dramatically, however, when the program was not in effect.

The data in Fig. 3.1 lead to three conclusions: (1) social reinforcement contingencies provided by both parents were probably responsible for the

Table 3.1. Number of Parental Instructions Presented to David Each Session and the Number of Tantrums and Enuretic Episodes Recorded by Parents Between Sessions.

	Baseline			Timeout and Differential Attention				Baseline No. 2		Timeout and Differential Attention																
Weeks	1	2	3	4	5	6	7	8	9	10	11	12	13	14	15	16	17	18	19	20–	21–	28–	36–	44–	60–	84
Sessions	1	2	3	–	–	1	2	1	2	1	2	3	–	–	–	4	–	–	–	5	–	6	7	8	9	10
Number of parental instructions per session	19	17	20	–	–	15	18	31	21	21	17	18	–	–	–	18	–	–	–	21	–	20	16	18	22	19
Number of tantrums per week	7	6	8	10	3	0	0˜	1	4	2	0	0	0	0	0	0	0	0	0	3	2	0	0	0	0	0
Number of enuretic episodes per week	2	3	1	1	0	0	0	4	3	0	0	0	0	0	0	1	0	0	2	0	0	0	0	0	0	0

changes observed in oppositional and cooperative behavior; (2) the frequency of enuretic activity correlated directly with the presence and absence of parental reinforcement contingencies, and (3) treatment effects remained stable over a continuous 18-month observation period. With regard to the first conclusion, one might argue that fluctuations in David's behavior were due to fluctuations in the number of parental instructions across baseline and treatment periods. Table 3.1, however, shows that parental instructions did not vary systematically from one period to the next.

With regard to the second conclusion, it would appear that the frequency of enuretic activity was more closely associated with the operations performed on oppositional behavior. In Fig. 3.1, the first session of Baseline 2 depicts a marked rise in the frequency of oppositional behavior. The frequency of cooperative behavior, however, does not drop appreciably, even though four enuretic episodes occurred during the week immediately preceding this session. Although cooperative behavior eventually decreases during the second session of Baseline 2, enuretic activity remained fairly stable, as did the level of oppositional behavior. Again, the data suggest that enuretic activity was functionally related to oppositional behavior.

After David's parents had put the contingency management program in operation, they were able rapidly to control the frequency of oppositional and cooperative behavior. More importantly, they quickly gained control over enuretic activity. One of the primary purposes of the present research, however, was to assess the stability of the treatment effects over time. Both Fig. 3.1 and Table 3.1 describe results of the program over an 18 month treatment period. Very stable frequency levels are recorded for oppositional and cooperative behavior and enuretic activity. There was a time, though, when the parents decided to discontinue using the timeout operation. During weeks 19, 20, and 21, they discontinued administering the timeout procedure because: "We didn't think he needed it anymore. He has been so good." During this period, one can observe a slight rise in the level of oppositional behavior and enuretic episodes as depicted in Table 3.1. The close correspondence between the rise in enuretic activity and absence of the timeout operation is again quite interesting. After the parents reinstated the timeout operation (week # 22), David's behavior quickly returned to treatment level. Thereafter, no significant changes were observed in the boy's behavior.

DISCUSSION

The present findings are of particular significance for clinical practitioners and pose some interesting theoretical puzzles as well. It seems clear
that some cases of childhood enuresis might be effectively treated by
using the procedures outlined above. There is a strong indication that
enuresis may be functionally related to other aspects of a child's behavior
that are more amenable to direct parental control. The procedures
discussed above are not limited in application to oppositional and
cooperative response classes. Essentially the same operations have
already been used to modify a wide variety of aberrant behaviors (see
Sherman and Baer, 1969). Possibly, some of these behaviors may be
functionally related to enuretic activity. At any rate, the clinician has an
option available to him that may prove effective and save the parents
considerable psychological and financial discomfort.

Although the clinical implications of the present research are clear, it is
difficult to place the results into theoretical perspective. How is it possible
to control one response class (enuresis) simply by controlling a second,
and seemingly unrelated response class (oppositional behavior)? It is
virtually impossible to identify environmental stimuli that may have
contributed to the changes in enuretic activity *and* oppositional behavior.
Wahler *et al.* (1970) found exactly the same lack of stimulus commonality
between stuttering and oppositional behavior. Since the parents in the
present study were instructed not to reinforce enuretic activity, it is
unlikely that the fluctuations observed in enuretic frequency could be
attributed to systematic shifts in parental reinforcement contingencies.

Wahler (1969) published some interesting research that may offer a way
out of this theoretical dilemma. He showed that the presence or absence
of a timeout operation correlated directly with parental reinforcer effectiveness. That is to say, parents scored higher on a test of reinforcer
effectiveness during periods when a timeout operation was used as
opposed to periods when the operation was not used. If, as Wahler (1969)
has shown, parents of oppositional children tend to have low reinforcer
value, it is possible that David's parents also functioned as agents of low
social reinforcement. Of course, there is no evidence to support this
contention, but it does seem reasonable. Assuming for the moment that
the parents had little reinforcer value, any effort on their part to reinforce
self-initiated diurnal voiding would probably fail. It was noted earlier that
David's mother often reminded him to go to the bathroom at regular
intervals during the day. Indeed, it is possible that the mother had to

remind the boy because attempts to reinforce independent voiding behavior had not proved effective. Be that as it may, if the parents did not function as agents of positive social reinforcement, any efforts on their part to condition voiding behavior to the appropriate discriminative cues would fail. Detrusor muscle tension would probably not become a discriminative stimulus for independent going-to-the-bathroom behavior because parental reinforcement after the act would have little reinforcing power.

If, however, parental reinforcer value suddenly shifted—if the parents suddenly became effective agents of positive social reinforcement—one might predict an increase in independent diurnal voiding if parental reinforcement was made contingent upon the behavior. There are no empirical data to show an increase in parent reinforcer value; nor do any show an increase in independent diurnal voiding during treatment periods. It is known, however, that the parents were instructed to reinforce all cooperative behaviors during treatment periods, including self-initiated diurnal voiding behavior. Also, the timeout operation was used only when the contingency management program was operative and the timeout operation has been shown to correlate with increased parent reinforcer effectiveness (Wahler, 1969). It is known too from the parents' reports that David did not have to be reminded to urinate during treatment periods, but again, no hard data support their claims. Nevertheless, it is tentatively concluded that detrusor muscle tension probably took on new discriminative properties as a result of a shift in parent reinforcer effectiveness. David apparently learned to associate bladder tension with self-initiated diurnal voiding behavior because an effective social reinforcer was made contingent on the behavior. Through this process, one can account for the transfer from external discriminative control (mother's prompts) to internal discriminative control (detrusor muscle tension) over diurnal voiding behavior. Of course, the best evidence for the acquisition of internal cues with discriminative properties for proper voiding behavior is the cessation of nocturnal enuretic activity. David has not wet his bed once during the past 16 months. Although the results are impressive, additional time is needed to assess prolonged treatment effects.

The present research offers a new and simple means for treating childhood enuresis. The techniques described are easy for most parents to learn and are particularly amenable to a wide variety of problem behaviors, some of which may be functionally related to enuretic activity. Further research efforts should be aimed at isolating those response classes that bear a functional relationship to childhood enuresis. Whether or not the changes in enuretic activity observed in the present research were due to a shift in parent reinforcer effectiveness is an issue easily subjected to empirical test.

REFERENCES

Bostock, J. and Shackelton, M. Pitfalls in the treatment of enuresis by an electric awakening machine. *Medical Journal of Australia,* 1957, **2,** 152–154.

Lovibond, S. H. *Conditioning and Enuresis.* Oxford: Pergamon, 1964.

Sherman, J. A. and Baer, D. M. Appraisal of operant therapy techniques with children and adults. In C. M. Franks (Ed.), *Behavior Therapy: Appraisal and Status.* New York: McGraw-Hill, 1969. Pp. 192–219.

Turner, R. K. and Young, G. C. CNS stimulant drug and conditioning treatment of nocturnal enuresis: A long-term follow-up study. *Behaviour Research and Therapy,* 1966, **4,** 225–228.

Wahler, R. G. Oppositional children: A quest for parental reinforcement control. *Journal of Applied Behavior Analysis,* 1969, **2,** 159–170.

Wahler, R. G., Sperling, K. A., Thomas, M. R., Teeter, N. C., and Luper, H. L. The modification of childhood stuttering: Some response-response relationships. *Journal of Experimental Child Psychology,* 1970, **9,** 411–428.

Yates, A. J. *Behavior Therapy.* New York: John Wiley & Sons, Inc., 1969.

ARTICLE 4

Controlling Nocturnal Enuresis in Severely Disabled and Chronic Patients*[1]

JOHN M. ATTHOWE, Jr.[2]

University of Montana

Abstract: Investigations designed to control urinary incontinence among the aged, the brain damaged and the chronic patient have been few. In the present study, 12 chronic patients, half of whom were lobotomized, were assigned to a special "therapeutic" program designed to control nocturnal enuresis. The program, superimposed upon a token economy program, consisted of a 2-month non-contingent, aversive treatment (personally costly and effortful) phase followed by a 6-month contingency management phase in which positive reinforcers were made contingent upon not wetting. A more active program and the noticeable recording of infractions brought about some reduction in bedwetting. The aversive treatment resulted in the attainment of continence in all patients except those who were originally labeled severe enuretics. The addition of a contingency management program not only maintained this improvement but eventually eliminated bedwetting in even the severe enuretics. Lobotomized and severely disturbed patients required up to 7 months of continuous treatment to become continent. However, all patients remained continent through a 42-month follow-up period.

Nocturnal enuresis is considered the number one nursing problem by most hospital staffs. Nursing attendants and others who come in daily contact with patients find it hard to adopt a "therapeutic attitude" toward those who are incontinent, especially when patients are old, relatively noncommunicative and uncooperative.

Most studies dealing with enuresis involve children. However, incontinent adults constitute as great or even greater problems. It has been

---

*Reprinted from *Behavior Therapy*, 1972, **3**, 232–239. Copyright © 1972 by Academic Press, Inc. With permission from Academic Press, Inc. and John M. Atthowe, Jr.

[1]The author gratefully acknowledges the help of K. A. Welt in critically reviewing the manuscript.

[2]Requests for reprints should be sent to J. M. Atthowe, Jr., Psychology Department, University of Montana, Missoula, MT 59801.

estimated that 85% of the incontinence seen in hospitals occurs in persons 65 years of age or older (Lowenthal, 1958). The incontinent patient generally is not considered for home or community placement no matter what other positive attributes he may have. In the San Francisco Bay Area, the main difference between those chronically ill patients receiving care in their homes and those remaining in the extended care facilities is the factor of incontinence (Salmon, Atthowe, & Hallock, 1966).

Very few attempts have been made to retrain the chronically disturbed, disabled or aged enuretic patient. One of the major reasons for this lack of concern with the retraining of the chronic and older patient is the assumption that enuresis is a result of deficient cerebral and subcortical control (Yates, 1970). It has been assumed that the ability to control nocturnal enuresis is a high-level skill requiring an intact nervous system and a normally functioning brain, requisites that the chronic or process schizophrenic, the aged and the chronically ill often do not possess. The results of the present study seriously question these assumptions.

STUDIES OF ENURESIS IN THE CHRONIC PATIENT

In the past few years, a number of attempts have been made to treat the incontinent, institutionalized patient. The impetus to these studies has been the success associated with behavior therapy and behavior modification techniques (Jones, 1960; Lovibond, 1964; Yates, 1970).

A number of studies have shown that nocturnal enuresis and incontinence among chronic, psychiatric patients, who have no organic problems, can be significantly decreased. Most of these studies have utilized operant procedures rather than the traditional "bell-and-pad" device developed by Mowrer and Mowrer (1938).

Carpenter and Simon (1960) found that the contingent administration of rewards and punishments plus visits to the toilet every 2 hr produced continence at the end of 4 months. Monroe (1963) found differences between a younger and an older group of chronic patients. With the younger group, Monroe found that all of the patients reached continence within 9 weeks, and twelve of the fifteen remained dry throughout a 3-month follow-up period. Treatment involved a much more active and stimulating ward environment in which patients were encouraged to urinate before going to bed and were awakened every 3 hr and escorted to the bathroom. If a patient got up on his own and went to the bathroom, the next scheduled visit to the bathroom was omitted. With an older and more deteriorated group of patients Monroe (1963) found that only 44% of the patients became continent.

Wetzel (1969) found that using meals and snacks to reinforce daytime continence plus candy and cigarettes (accompanied by a verbal explanation) to reinforce the emission of appropriate toilet responses not only significantly reduced daytime mishaps but generalized to nighttime accidents as well. Wagner and Paul (1970) used a combination of contingent reinforcement and "bell-and-pad" sheets. They created three levels of sleeping comfort on the ward and introduced periodic checking. If a patient was not soiled, he received a reward as well as praise. In addition, meals were made contingent upon being dry. Wagner and Paul's results showed that all of the 19 patients had fewer incidents of daytime soiling at the end of the 22 weeks treatment period and 18 had fewer incidents of nocturnal soiling; nine achieved complete nocturnal continence. Thirteen months after the termination of treatment, a 3-day follow-up was conducted. Of the 13 patients remaining on the ward, none showed any instances of daytime soiling and only two showed any night soiling.

A study by Grosicki (1968), however, with quite old and deteriorated patients, many of whom had nervous system or genitourinary system impairments, found no significant reduction in incontinence from a baseline period. However, Grosicki does say that data collection was reduced to 8 weeks in the token phase because of a dramatic reduction in incontinence (45%).

From these studies it appears that incontinence can be reduced. However, extensive chronicity, advanced age, and organic involvement renders incontinent patients less susceptible to change. A further complication is the length of the treatment and follow-up periods. It also seems harder to modify nocturnal enuresis than daytime incontinence. In addition, all of these studies point to a very crucial but hard-to-control factor: staff involvement and expectation. Unless satisfactory staff participation is insured, results may be subject to many different interpretations.

THE PRESENT STUDY

The present study was carried out as a part of an intensive "total push" or token economy program (see Atthowe & Krasner, 1968). The author

met two to three times a week with the three nursing assistants[3] who
worked the 11 p.m.–7 a.m. shift. It was decided that one of the main
problems we would try to control was excessive bedwetting. The four of
us designed the following program in which the contributions of each
were included.

Eighteen of the 86 patients on the ward were selected as bedwetters by
the ward staff. During the baseline period of 2 months, five patients were
eliminated from the study for not wetting their beds at least once, and one
patient was transferred to another ward. We found, as did Wagner and
Paul (1970), that a number of institutionalized patients become labeled
"enuretic" for some happening or happenings long ago. This infraction
gets recorded in the patient's record, and he is hereafter labeled an
enuretic for all time.

Subjects

Twelve patients, all of whom had been continually hospitalized for over
20 years, were assigned to a special therapeutic program. Their ages
ranged from 42 to 77 years; five were over 65. All of the patients were
labeled chronic schizophrenics, and ten carried the additional diagnosis of
chronic brain syndrome. Six patients were lobotomized. All were
delusional, generally uncommunicative and were the chief management
problems on the ward.

The Definition and Incidence of Enuresis

What constitutes a severe or a mild enuretic is a difficult problem. With
our chronic backward population, the incidence of bedwetting varied
considerably. Some patients would not wet for 2 or 3 weeks and then wet
every night for a week. Nevertheless, some patients were considered
much more of a problem than others. Therefore, we placed patients into
one of three categories based on our baseline observations. Four patients,
including three of those lobotomized, wet their beds at least once per
night on an average of two or more times a week (at least 16 times during
the 2-month baseline period). This group was labeled *severely enuretic.*
Five patients wet at least twice a month (4–15 times) and were labeled

---

[3]The nursing assistants all of whom were especially cooperative and effective, were
Herbert Bowles, Donald Bradford and Sam Asbury.

moderately enuretic. The remaining three patients wet only once during the two month baseline period and were labeled *mildly enuretic.*

Design of the Study

The enuretic program was superimposed upon a much larger token economy program. In order to minimize the effects of recording and the newness of the token program, we established a fairly extensive and stable baseline period after the creation of the token economy. During the baseline period, the incidence of bedwetting was recorded for all patients. The baseline period was followed by a treatment period divided into two phases: a 2-month noncontingent, aversive phase during which no reinforcers were systematically present and a 6-month contingency management program in which positive reinforcements were introduced and were made contingent upon not wetting. In addition, three follow-up periods of 30 days each were carried out 2, 22 and 43 months after the termination of the treatment. Follow-up consisted of going through the nursing notes for a 30-day period.

The Therapeutic Program

The therapeutic program was divided into two phases. The first phase involved the creation of an aversive environment—a therapeutic regimen requiring a much more costly expenditure of effort on the part of each patient. Patients were informed that the "therapeutic" program was "designed to reduce bedwetting." There were four aversive features to the program. First, the enuretics were assigned to a large and crowded 30-bed wing of the ward. Secondly, lights were turned on for 10 min in this wing four times during the night, at 11 p.m., 12:30 a.m., 2 a.m. and 4 a.m. The third feature required that patients be escorted to the bathroom when the lights were turned on, whether they were wet or not, and kept there for approximately 10 min. They were not allowed to smoke. The fourth aversive feature was more subtle and less measurable but, at the same time, probably quite potent. That is, each time the lights came on other patients who were sleeping in the wing were awakened. This, in turn, generated some aversive comments. In all probability, this aversive social pressure influenced the patients to some degree. All of the enuretics were again checked at 6 a.m. upon rising.

This aversive and effortful routine was carried out for 2 months. Escape or avoidance of the routine was not possible. It was assumed that a dramatic and effortful routine would make it possible for our lobotomized and very disturbed patients to discriminate their undesirable behavior and its consequences. Furthermore, it was assumed that subsequent reduction in the aversive schedule as the patient improved would be much more reinforcing if the schedule was seen as very costly and contingent upon *their* inability to control their micturition. During the aversive phase, it was found that most instances of bedwetting occurred before 12:30 a.m. (approximately 85%). The practice of sitting a patient or a child on the toilet just before retiring and rewarding him if he urinates would seem to have considerable merit.

After 2 months of the aversive schedule, a patient who did not wet his bed during the night was immediately rewarded with a token at 6 a.m. and praised. By now the tokens had some well-established value on the ward. In addition, the 4 a.m. trip to the toilet was eliminated. After two consecutive dry nights, the 2 a.m. trip was also eliminated. Although the 4 a.m. and 2 a.m. trips were not deemed critical, in that few errors occurred after 12:30 a.m., this did not dull the reinforcing value of these omissions. Upon remaining dry for 1 week, all of the nightly trips to the bathroom were eliminated, and the patient was given the opportunity to move to "better" sleeping quarters. Whether he moved or not was contingent upon his having earned enough tokens to buy a more desirable sleeping arrangement (see Atthowe & Krasner, 1968). Throughout the program, the patient was informed when he did well and why he received or did not receive a token. In addition, by getting up on his own and going to the toilet during the night, a patient could earn an extra token. Patients were also encouraged to go the toilet before retiring. However, no token was given for this act, an error on our part. By reinforcing appropriate antagonistic responses, a more desirable behavior pattern was nurtured.

RESULTS

The results are summarized in Table 4.1. It can be seen that a more active program and the noticeable recording of infractions brought about a marked reduction in bedwetting. Eight patients were on record as having wet more than three times per week during the 6 months prior to the initiation of the token economy. Furthermore, a noncontingent, aversive program of only 2 months duration superimposed upon an active token economy eliminated incontinence in all of the chronic bedwetters except those who were originally labeled severe enuretics. The addition

Table 4.1. Incidence of Nocturnal Enuresis Before, During and After Treatment.

| | | | Treatment period | | | Follow-up period | | |
| | | | | Contingency management phase | | | | |
Type of enuresis	Before experiment	Baseline period (2 months)	Aversive phase (2 months)	(at 4 months)	(at 6 months)	2 months	22 months	43 months
Severe	8	4	2	0	0	0	0	0
Moderate	4	5	0	0	0	0	0	0
Mild	6	3	2	3	0	0	0	0
Continent	0	5[a]	13	14	16[b]	16	15[c]	13[d]

[a] One patient transferred.
[b] One severe case died.
[c] One mild case died.
[d] One severe case transferred to a medical ward. One severe case, records not up to date.

of a contingency management program not only maintained this improvement but eventually eliminated incontinence in the severe enuretics, three of whom were lobotomized, although this process required 7–8 months of treatment.

The follow-up data were not as rigorously collected and a number of patients had transferred to wards where record-keeping was less systematic. However, if we take the nursing records at face value, we have a record of remarkable persistence. Twenty-two months after the termination of treatment, all of the ten patients who were living were still continent. After 43 months, two patients had been placed in homecare programs, and one patient had been placed with relatives, but subsequently returned, and all who remained were continent. However, the records of three of the original four severe enuretics were not available at this time.

All of the major comparisons were significant. McNemar's (1969) test of change was significant ($p < 0.001$) when the baseline data were compared with the results at the end of treatment on the variable of continence vs. incontinence. When the baseline data are compared with the results of the 2-month, aversive treatment program in regard to the achievement of continence or not, the McNemar test was significant at the 0.01 level.

A binomial test was computed to assess the decrease in frequency of bedwetting from one period to another. Assuming a 50–50 likelihood of change and utilizing a one-tailed test, the difference between the baseline period and the period before the study began was significant ($p < 0.05$). The difference between the baseline period and the aversive phase was significant at the 0.02 level; the overall changes between the baseline period and the two contingency management treatment periods (4 and 6 months) were both significant ($p < 0.001$).

DISCUSSION

The results of the present study are consistent with those found by other investigators. Nocturnal enuresis is controllable, even in the very old and the neurologically disabled if the treatment phase of the study is continued long enough. All of the enuretic patients except those who were severely enuretic became continent during the carrying out of the aversive regimen. It is possible that the more stimulating token program, in and of itself, or record-keeping, per se, could have brought about much of this change. However, the severely incontinent patients were considerably more resistant to change. Half of this latter group did not change until the positively reinforcing contingencies were introduced. It took approximately 7 months before all of the severe patients were continent. The large temporal, individual differences shown among our chronic population tempted some of our staff to assume that some patients could not be changed.

One of the factors which contributed to our results was the motivation and commitment of the personnel involved. This program was the result of the joint effort of the author and three night attendants assigned to the ward. Controlling enuresis requires effort on the part of someone besides the patient.

The major problem in controlling enuresis is not its elimination but the maintenance of the newly acquired continence. Most studies of children and adolescents show a fairly high remission rate (Yates, 1970). Little work has been done to demonstrate the persistence of continence among chronic patients. The persistence of continence that we found in this study is probably related to the broader scope of our procedures as well as to the procedure, per se. Our enuresis program was part of a much larger token economy program that involved the entire lives of the patients. In addition, the program was designed to make each patient dramatically aware of the contingencies associated with wetting and not wetting. Not wetting not only earned material rewards, it also made life much less costly and effortful and brought about genuine social reinforcement from the staff and from other patients.

The past incidence of enuretic behavior is another variable to consider in any treatment program. The incidence of nocturnal enuresis not only varies considerably from person to person but also from time to time for a given person. Merely labeling the problem as a problem and showing concern can bring about some change. However, severe cases seem to demand a much more systematic and extended treatment program.

REFERENCES

Atthowe, J. M., Jr. and Krasner, L. Preliminary report on the application of contingent reinforcement procedures (token economy) on a "chronic" psychiatric ward. *Journal of Abnormal Psychology*, 1968, **73**, 37–43.

Carpenter, H. A. and Simon, R. Effect of several methods of training on long-term incontinent, behaviorally regressed hospitalized psychiatric patients. *Nursing Research*, 1960, **9**, 17–22.

Grosicki, J. P. Effect of operant conditioning on modification of incontinence in neuropsychiatric geriatric patients. *Nursing Research*, 1968, **17**, 304–311.

Jones, H. G. The behavioral treatment of enuresis nocturna. In H. J. Eysenck, (Ed.), *Behaviour Therapy and the Neuroses*. Oxford: Pergamon, 1960. Pp. 377–403.

Lovibond, S. H. *Conditioning and Enuresis*. Oxford: Pergamon, 1964.

Lowenthal, M. Nobody wants the incontinent. *R-N*, 1958, **21**, 82–85.

McNemar, Q. *Psychological Statistics* (4th Ed.) New York: Wiley, 1969.

Monroe, K. L. Treatment of nocturnal enuresis among hospitalized neuropsychiatric patients. Unpublished doctoral dissertation, Purdue University, 1963.

Mowrer, O. H. and Mowrer, W. H. Enuresis: a method for its study and treatment. *American Journal of Orthopsychiatry*, 1938, **8**, 436–459.

Salmon, P., Atthowe, J. M., Jr. and Hallock, M. R. *RAPIDS: A Method of Classifying Patients Receiving Long-Term Care*. San Mateo, CA: Department of Public Health and Welfare, 1966.

Wagner, B. R. and Paul, G. L. Reduction of incontinence in chronic mental patients: A pilot project. *Journal of Behavior Therapy and Experimental Psychiatry*, 1970, **1**, 29–38.

Wetzel, C. The effects of operant conditioning and nicometrazol on the modification of daytime incontinence of regressed chronic schizophrenics. Unpublished doctoral dissertation, University of Illinois, 1969.

Yates, A. J. *Behavior Therapy*. New York: Wiley, 1970.

CHAPTER 3

The Gastrointestinal System: Anorexia Nervosa, Chronic Vomiting, and Encopresis

The articles in this chapter focus on three gastrointestinal problems: anorexia nervosa, chronic vomiting, and encopresis, all of which appear to have significant behavioral components. Of these disorders, none poses so grave a danger to the patient than does anorexia nervosa. Characterized by refusal to consume food, this disorder carries with it a rather alarming incidence of mortality, which may run as high as 15% (Dally & Sargant, 1966). Extensive morbidity is also associated with anorexia and may include amenorrhea, and a variety of problems secondary to poor nutrition, such as electrolyte imbalance and avitaminosis. Weight loss is generally severe, and may be as great as 60% (Bachrach *et al.*, 1965).

The incidence of anorexia appears to be higher among females, many of whom were previously overweight, or *perceived* themselves to be obese as children. This is often accompanied by dieting, with unrealistically low idealized weight goals. The intensity with which these patients pursue diets often borders on the obsessive and may be accompanied by the ingestion of laxatives and self-induced vomiting. Explanations of this disorder have included conflict over sexuality (Nemiah, 1963), fantasies of pregnancy, as well as a variety of other psychodynamic hypotheses (Bliss & Branch, 1960).

In the past the treatment of anorexia has taken many forms, including intubation, high calorie diets, psychotherapy, chemotherapy (chlorpromazine) and "one-to-one" intensive nursing care. A variety of successful treatments have been reported in individual cases but none consistently so (Bliss & Branch, 1960).

Viewing the intake of food as an operant, however, behavior therapists have produced some encouraging results in the treatment of this most difficult problem. A significant characteristic of the anorexic's environment is the concern expressed by hospital staff and family. This concern usually manifests itself by a great deal of pleading, cajoling and reprimands revolving around such topics as the sanctity of life, responsibility to self and others, and the potentially fatal consequences of not eating. It should not be surprising, therefore, to discover that the predominant therapeutic strategy of most behavior therapy approaches involves strict contingency management of reinforcement for food consumption, calorie intake, or weight gain. Extinction is frequently an adjunct to reinforcement procedures, and involves the removal of all potentially reinforcing attention for not eating and subsequent weight loss.

The paper by Garfinkel *et al.* (Article 5) describes the successful treatment of five cases of anorexia nervosa with operant conditioning techniques. Utilizing a variety of reinforcing events including physical activity, off ward socializing, overnight and weekend passes, and other privileges, the authors were able to produce weight gains ranging from 23 to 46 lb.

Azerrad and Stafford (Article 6) initiated a token system of reinforcement to increase food consumption and weight gain in a 13-year-old anorexic girl. Initially, points could be earned for increases in weight only. Eventually, however, the program was modified and reinforcement made contingent upon the amount of food consumed. This paper is noteworthy because it clearly emphasizes some of the obstacles frequently encountered in the treatment of anorexia. In this case the patient had been concealing heavy objects in her robe to produce the initial weight gains and earn reinforcement surreptitiously.

Both of these studies reflect the complexities of treating the severe anorexic: criteria for reinforcement must be easy for the patient to achieve; the patient must be closely monitored in order to eliminate the reinforcement of pseudo-improvement and the potential of self-induced vomiting to offset required consumption; and finally, the ward environment must be consistent with respect to the optimal control of reinforcing events, particularly staff attention, in order to avoid the inadvertent reinforcement of anorexic behaviors.

Chronic vomiting is another example of a debilitating and potentially dangerous gastrointestinal disorder. Ruminative vomiting with an *organic* etiology is generally amenable to a variety of treatment techniques, including surgery, antinauseants, and antiemetics. However, as Hoyt and

Stickler (1960) observed in their review of 44 children with persistent vomiting, ... "the cause of the syndrome of recurrent vomiting, while possibly psychogenic, is not known definitely."

A variety of behavior therapy approaches have been shown to be effective in the treatment of vomiting and three of these are included here. Two independent investigators have used aversive conditioning techniques (punishment) to eliminate vomiting, although the problem was approached quite differently in each case. Lang and Melamed (Article 7) treated a 9-month-old child whose persistent vomiting was proving to be life threatening. Utilizing an electromyograph to monitor the child's vomiting response, they applied a brief electric shock contingent upon the first sign of reverse peristalsis. Only three sessions were required to completely suppress vomiting. Although vomiting was the only response modified directly, the nursing staff noted that the child also became more active, aware of his environment and affectionate toward others. At a one year followup he continued to thrive.

Similarly, Kohlenberg (Article 8) employed shock in an effort to eliminate vomiting in a 21-year-old severely retarded female. However, in this case shock was applied contingent upon stomach contractions, a behavior which reliably *preceded* the vomiting response. With this procedure, he was able to completely eliminate vomiting in less than a day. Furthermore, a significant weight gain was noted in the 25 days following the commencement of therapy. Both Lang and Melamed, and Kohlenberg comment on the unusually high number of shocks required (20–30) to eliminate the vomiting response, indicating an apparent higher degree of resistance to punishment than has been noted for other behaviors (Lovaas & Simmons, 1969; Tate & Baroff, 1966).

Wolf *et al.* (Article 9), describe a third approach to vomiting which involves the use of extinction procedures in a 9-year-old retarded girl for whom vomiting had become a daily occurrence. Suspecting that being excused from class after vomiting was serving to reinforce the response, the authors were able to completely eliminate vomiting by instructing the teacher to ignore it and to detain the child until class was over.

Another gastrointestinal disorder, encopresis, has been defined as a disturbance in fecal control not due to an organic etiology (Dorland, 1965; Warson *et al.*, 1954). As with enuresis, Yates (1970) distinguishes between *continuous* encopresis, in which bowel control has never been established, and *discontinuous* encopresis where control has been established and subsequently lost. This distinction is similar to primary and secondary enuresis. Yates further notes that both forms of the disorder occur more commonly in boys than in girls; however, little is known of its relative incidence.

Encopresis, particularly in its soiling form, almost always elicits strong reactions from those in the patient's environment. In spite of its social repugnance, however, encopresis in all of its forms is a rather discrete behavior. Its occurrence is easily noted and the appropriate reciprocal behavior is quite obvious—elimination in the toilet. Examined in such a context, it should not be surprising that a variety of therapy techniques have proven dramatically successful. Tomlinson (Article 10) describes the relative ease with which bowel retention of one year's duration in a 3-year-old boy was rapidly eliminated by giving him bubble gum contingent upon successful elimination in the toilet. Laxatives were required only twice to initiate the response. Normal, routine elimination had been established by the second week of therapy. A two-week interval with the child's grandparents, in which the contingency was removed, provided a natural reversal with which to show the efficacy of positive reinforcement in controlling appropriate bowel elimination patterns.

Three diverse yet successful approaches to the treatment of soiling are also included here. Barrett (Article 11) eliminated soiling in a $5\frac{1}{2}$-year-old child with a combination of reinforcement and timeout procedures. In this case the parents designed and implemented the entire therapy program. In still another example of aversive control, Ferinden and Handel (Article 12) describe a punishment procedure in which the soiling in school by a 7-year-old child resulted in his having to clean up the mess and make up lost time after class. Employing positive reinforcement in the form of a differential reinforcement procedure, Pedrini and Pedrini (Article 13) initiated a token system for an 11-year-old boy with a history of frequent soilings in school. In this case the child could earn one coupon for each class period that he abstained from soiling; the coupons could then be exchanged for books which he desired to purchase. Thus soiling was eliminated in less than one week by reinforcing behavior directly incompatible with it.

Points of key importance in this chapter include:

1. Gastrointestinal disorders, such as anorexia nervosa, chronic vomiting and encopresis have been successfully treated with operant conditioning techniques.
2. With the exception of anorexia, these disorders were successfully treated with great rapidity, frequently in periods as short as one day.
3. In the majority of cases, treatment was implemented by parents, teachers, or nursing personnel.

4. The conspicuous absence of reversals in most of these studies reflects the extreme unpleasantness of the behaviors in question. Most individuals are loathe to reinstate vomiting, encopresis, and starvation for the sake of scientific rigor.
5. Although psychodynamic formulations have been proposed (Nemiah, 1963; Sterba, 1949), there is good evidence that these disorders are responsive to contingency management techniques.

REFERENCES

Bachrach, A., Erwin, W. J., and Mohr, J. P. The control of eating behavior in an anorexic by operant conditioning techniques. In Ullmann, L. and Krasner, L. (eds.) *Case Studies in Behavior Modification.* New York: Holt, Rinehart & Winston, 1965.

Bliss, E. and Branch, C. *Anorexia Nervosa.* New York: Paul B. Hoeber, 1960.

Burns, C. Encopresis (incontinence of feces) in children. *British Medical Journal,* 1941, 2, 767–769.

Dally, P. and Sargant, W. Treatment and outcome of anorexia. *British Medical Journal,* 1966, 2, 293–295.

Dorland's Illustrated Medical Dictionary. Philadelphia: W. B. Saunders, 1965.

Hoyt, C., and Stickler, G. A study of forty-four children with the syndrome of recurrent (cyclia) vomiting. *Pediatrics,* 1960, 25, 775–779.

Lovaas, O. and Simmons, J. Manipulation of self destruction in three retarded children. *Journal of Applied Behavior Analysis,* 1969, 2, 143–158.

Nemiah, J. Emotions and gastrointestinal disease. In H. Lief, V. F. Lief, and N. R. Lief (eds.) *The Psychological Basis of Medical Practice.* New York: Paul B. Hoeber, 1963.

Sterba, E. Analysis of psychogenic constipation in a two-year-old. In Freud, A., Hartmann, H. and Krie, E. (eds.) *Psychoanalytic Study of the Child,* vols. 3–4. New York: International University Press, 1949.

Tate, B. and Baroff, G. Aversive control of self injurious behavior in a psychotic boy. *Behaviour Research & Therapy,* 1966, 4, 281–287.

Warson, S., Caldwell, M., Warriner, A., Kirk, A., and Jensen, R. The dynamics of encopresis. *American Journal of Orthopsychiatry,* 1954, 24, 402–415.

Yates, A. *Behavior Therapy.* New York: John Wiley & Sons, 1970.

Treatment of Anorexia Nervosa Using Operant Conditioning Techniques*

PAUL E. GARFINKEL, M.D., STEPHEN A. KLINE, M.D., and
HARVEY C. STANCER, Ph.D., M.D.[1]

University of Toronto, Clark Institute of Psychiatry, Toronto 2B, Canada

Abstract: This paper describes a successful operant conditioning program using a variety of reinforcers which were individualized for 5 hospitalized female anorexia nervosa patients, resulting in rapid weight gain to premorbid levels. The patients studied met the following criteria: (a) weight loss greater than 25 per cent of body weight; (b) morbid aversion to food with conscious dietary restriction; (c) absence of medical illness; and (d) amenorrhea.

A detailed medical and laboratory investigation preceded the treatment regimen.

During the initial 7 days in the hospital, the patients were observed by the medical and nursing staff. On the basis of their observations a system of rewards was tailored for each patient. Goals were set for both daily and weekly weight gains. The specific rewards included physical activity, socializing off the wards, overnight and weekend passes and progressive privileges on the ward. It was made clear that the responsibility for weight gain rested with the patient.

Weight gain was rapid. Patient discomfort was minimized. The patients experienced no side effects related to the therapy.

It is stressed that this is only the initial phase in the therapy of this disorder. Further treatment is then individualized to meet the ongoing needs of the patients.

Anorexia nervosa is described by Bruch[6] as a self-imposed starvation and relentless pursuit of thinness leading to cachexia. Female patients commonly present with amenorrhea. Medical illness which could explain the symptoms is absent. The variety of techniques reported for treatment

*From Garfinkel, P. E., Kline, S. A., Stancer, H. C. "Treatment of Anorexia Nervosa Using Operant Conditioning Techniques," *Journal of Nervous and Mental Disease*, **6**: 428–433, 1973, The Williams & Wilkins Co. Reproduced by permission.

[1]The authors thank Dr. E. Rzadki for allowing his patient to participate in this study, and are grateful for the assistance of the nursing staff of the Clinical Investigation Unit of the Clarke Institute of Psychiatry and the Burnside wing of the Toronto General Hospital. (Send reprint requests to Dr. Harvey C. Stancer.)

of anorexia nervosa indicates the difficulty of managing this disorder. Treatments for the weight loss have included tube feedings[16], drugs[7–9], and psychotherapies[3, 10, 15].

While these various methods are often useful in helping the patient put on weight, they have serious drawbacks: the risk of infection and death with tube feeding[5], the high incidence of bulimia and other undesirable effects following treatment with chlorpromazine[9], and the very slow weight gain with psychotherapy[4].

In an attempt to overcome these drawbacks, a variety of behavior therapies have been introduced by Azerrad and Stafford[1], Bachrach *et al.*[2], Hallsten[11], Lang[12], and Leitenberg *et al.*[13]. Blinder *et al.*[4] recently reported successful weight gain in 6 patients with anorexia nervosa using activity or access to activity as the paradigm for reinforcement. Four of the 6 patients also received chlorpromazine. Stunkard[14] later suggested that other reinforcements might also be considered. We have adopted this suggestion, and describe here a modified operant conditioning program using a variety of reinforcers which were individualized for 5 hospitalized female patients, resulting in rapid weight gain to premorbid levels.

SUBJECTS AND METHODS

Subjects

Five female patients were studied who met the following criteria: (a) weight loss greater than 25 per cent of body weight; (b) morbid aversion to food with conscious dietary restriction; (c) absence of medical illness; and (d) amenorrhea. Four patients were admitted to the Clinical Investigation Unit of the Clarke Institute of Psychiatry between March 31, 1971 and June 14, 1972. One patient was admitted to the psychiatric ward of the Toronto General Hospital in April, 1971, where the present treatment program was begun in July, 1971.

Medical Investigation

All patients were clinically assessed and laboratory examinations were undertaken to exclude medical illness that might explain the symptomatology. The following tests were performed in addition to the routine hematological and urinary procedures: skull X-ray, electroencephalography, serum sodium, potassium, chloride, growth hormone response to a glucose tolerance test, T_3, T_4, plasma cortisol (diurnal), follicle-stimulating hormone, luteinizing hormone (not done in patient 1) and urinary 17-keto and 17-hydroxy steroids.

Behavioral Investigation

During the patient's initial 7 days in the hospital, no visitors were allowed and the patient was restricted to the ward. A detailed psychiatric history was taken and the patient's behavioral characteristics were noted separately by the medical and nursing staff. The nursing staff was assigned to regular and constant working hours. The dietitian consulted with each patient and devised an acceptable diet with a daily intake goal of 3,000 calories.

Methods

On the basis of the findings of the medical and nursing staff, a system of rewards was tailored for each patient. Goals were set for both daily and weekly weight gain. A daily weight minimum was set at 0.15 kg and a weekly minimum at 1.0 kg. The specific rewards included physical activity, socializing off the wards, overnight and weekend passes and progressive privileges on the ward. These were discussed with each patient and a verbal contract negotiated. It was made clear that the responsibility for weight gain rested with the patient.

From admission, daily weights were recorded in the morning before breakfast with the patient in a hospital gown. Once the verbal contract was set, these recordings were used for the attainment of daily and weekly rewards. The protocol for the patient at the general hospital was similar to the above except that the nurses were not on a regular shift and visitors were allowed during the initial period.

CASE HISTORIES

Case 1

This 5-foot 3-inch, 13-year-old high school student was admitted on March 31, 1971, on referral from her family doctor. In the fall of 1970, the patient lost her appetite and voluntarily curtailed food intake. She went from 56 kg to 32 kg over a 5-month period. Menarche occurred in September, 1969, with her last menstrual period in September, 1970. She was hospitalized in a nearby city for 7 weeks in an attempt to get her to put on weight. Tube feedings increased her weight by 3 kg. She was then referred to the Clarke Institute.

She presented as a composed, mature adolescent who was excessively attentive to detail and was not hyperactive. She resented the confinement to the adult ward where there were no other adolescents.

For the first 6 weeks in the hospital, she was expected to eat three meals a day and encouraged to drink milkshakes between meals. Her weight increased only 0.5 kg during the total period. She was then placed on a reward system. These rewards included evening walks and the use of the adolescent ward during the day for a daily weight gain of 0.15 kg. A weight gain of 1 kg/week rewarded her with a weekend pass. She gained 9 kg over 6 weeks and was discharged for outpatient follow-up. Her weight increased further and has remained constant at 53 kg for 5 months. Menses resumed 10 months after discharge.

Case 2

This 5-foot 6-inch, 19-year-old high school student was admitted on May 20, 1971, on referral from her family practitioner. In June, 1970, she began a strenuous diet because she felt that her hips and thighs were too fat. At that time she weighed 56 kg. By the time she entered the hospital she weighed 38.6 kg. Menarche was at age 13. She had not had a menstrual period since May, 1970.

On the ward, she was secretive and hyperactive, standing to read the newspaper and exercising vigorously in the shower. She claimed she did not like to sit still because no energy was burnt up.

A system of positive reinforcement was instituted utilizing physical activity and off-ward privileges as a reward for weight gain. For a daily weight gain of 0.15 kg she was rewarded with exercise privileges and daily walks outside the hospital. Weekend passes plus weekly patient outings were rewards for a weekly weight gain of 1 kg. As she was depressed on admission she was placed on amitriptyline (Elavil) 50 mg t.i.d. This was discontinued midway through the behavioral treatment program.

By August, 1971, she was discharged weighing 49.4 kg. She has maintained this weight for 9 months. She has not menstruated to date. Follow-up has consisted of individual and family psychotherapy.

Case 3

This 5-foot 6-inch, 17-year-old high school student was transferred to the psychiatric wing of a general hospital on April 22, 1971, following an unsuccessful weight-gaining program on the medical service. In the fall of 1970 she developed a dysphagia for solid foods. Her weight dropped from 52 kg in June, 1970, to 32.3 kg on admission. She had been amenorrheic since June, 1970. Prior to that, menses had been regular for 3 years.

On the medical ward she was allowed to eat whatever foods she wished and was medicated with diazepam (Valium) 2 mg t.i.d. and cyproheptadine hydrochloride (Vimicon) 4 mg t.i.d. She gained 1.5 kg in 7 weeks (to 33.8 kg). For the first 2 months on the psychiatric unit she was treated with psychotherapy together with regular insulin (Toronto) 10 units t.i.d., chlorpromazine (Largactil) 100 mg q.i.d., amitriptyline 25 mg t.i.d., and the threat of tube feedings. She gained only 1.4 kg in 2 months. On June 22 she was placed on strict bed rest and allowed out of bed when she gained weight. A further 1.2 kg (to 36.4 kg) were added in 10 days.

On the psychiatric ward she was observed to be bored and lethargic. She also seemed anxious to socialize with her friends off the ward. She expressed interest in ward activities, especially occupational therapy.

On July 1, 1971, the therapy was modified using ward privileges including occupational therapy and off-ward socializing with friends and relatives as reinforcers for a weight gain of 0.15 kg/day. A gain of 1 kg/week permitted her weekend passes. On this regimen she gained 8.6 kg in 6 weeks at which time she was discharged. She has been seen weekly for individual and family therapy for 9 months and has maintained her weight at 45 kg. Regular menses returned 2 months following discharge.

Case 4

This 5-foot 2-inch, 18-year-old student was admitted on February 11, 1972, on referral from a nearby general hospital. In June, 1970, she began to diet because she felt that her weight was in the wrong places. She lost 2 kg over the summer. In September, 1970, her parents decided to move to a small town. She lost interest in food, as she put it, "to express my disappointment at the move." Her weight dropped from 50 kg to 29.2 kg by February, 1971. Menstruation, which had been regular for 4 years, ceased in August, 1970.

Two 5-week hospitalizations between February and August, 1971, managed to increase her weight by a total of 7.3 kg. During the first hospitalization she received tube feedings and during the second she was given a free choice of foods. She was transferred to the Clarke Institute after her third admission. She weighed 30.1 kg.

On admission the patient was cheerful but demanding. She insisted that she be given a wide range of ward privileges and physical activities. She did not appear hyperactive, but alluded continually to her energy excess. An interesting feature of her behavior was that she bloated herself with black coffee and then claimed she did not have room for food.

A program was structured providing ward and off-ward privileges and participation in an exercise program for a daily weight gain of 0.15 kg. Coffee-drinking privileges were included in her daily reward system, and she voluntarily reduced her intake to 3 to 4 cups per day. Weekend passes were granted for a weekly gain of 1 kg.

The patient gained 14.6 kg in 8 weeks. She was discharged weighing 44.7 kg. Menses returned 1 day prior to discharge. No follow-up is yet available.

Case 5

This 5-foot 4-inch, 16-year-old high school student was transferred from a nearby general hospital on June 14, 1972. In July, 1971, she began to diet and her weight fell from 54 kg to 43 kg by October, 1971. She was hospitalized for $6\frac{1}{2}$ months. Treatment included regular inpatient psychotherapy and tube feedings on three separate occasions. She was finally discharged in May, 1972, weighing 41 kg. She was readmitted 3 weeks later weighing 36 kg. After 2 further weeks in the hospital she was transferred to the Clarke Institute because of suicidal intent and failure to gain weight. She weighed 35.6 kg. Menarche was at age 13. She had been amenorrheic since June, 1971.

On the ward she was observed to be sullen and morose. She expressed interest in acquiring privileges off the ward and outside the hospital. She described specific interests in arts and crafts and in regular exercise.

Based on this manifest behavior we structured a system of operant reinforcement. For weight gains of 0.15 kg/day she was allowed daily exercise, walks out of hospital and participation in a pottery class. Weekly weight gains of 1 kg or more were rewarded with yoga class, patient outings, and weekend privileges outside the hospital. The patient's weight increased to 47.5 kg in 3 weeks. At discharge she was amenorrheic.

However, previously observed interpersonal family difficulties became more manifest after discharge resulting in a loss of weight. She was readmitted for further treatment including family intervention.

DISCUSSION

This paper reports a successful method for rapid weight gain in 5 patients with anorexia nervosa. Case 1 had lost 24 kg (42 per cent of her original weight) at the time of hospitalization; she gained 9 kg in the hospital and continued gaining after discharge so that at present she is 53 kg (95 per cent of her original weight). Case 2 lost 17.4 kg (30.5 per cent); at discharge she weighed 49.4 kg (87 per cent). Case 3 lost 19.7 kg (39 per cent); at discharge she weighed 45 kg (87 per cent). Case 4 had lost 19.8 kg (39.8 per cent); at discharge she weighed 44.7 kg (90 per cent). Case 5 had lost 18.4 kg (34 per cent); at discharge she weighed 47.5 kg (88 per cent).

There are several advantages to this method of treatment. The rapidity of weight gain compares favorably with other methods reported as successful[4]. Patient discomfort is minimized. We have not experienced any side effects related to the therapy. None of our patients later went on to bulimia.

One patient had no prior treatment and 4 had previously been treatment failures: case 1 with tube feedings; case 3 with insulin, major and minor tranquilizers, and the threat of tube feedings; case 4 with tube feedings and high caloric diet; case 5 with tube feedings and psychotherapy. Their subsequent weight gain in this treatment program underlines its efficacy. Case 1 gained an average of 1.5 kg/week over 6 weeks; case 2 averaged 1.1 kg over 9.5 weeks; case 3 averaged 1.4 kg over 6 weeks; case 4 averaged 1.8 kg over 8 weeks; and case 5 averaged 4.0 kg over 3 weeks (see Fig. 5.1).

Two of the patients were felt to be depressed and were treated with amitriptyline (cases 2 and 3). In case 2 this was discontinued midway through her treatment program with no effect on her rate of weight gain. Case 3 remained on the medication until she left the hospital. She was placed on amitriptyline 2 months prior to beginning the behavior modification program with no effect on her weight. The dose was then held constant throughout her hospital stay. While she was an outpatient the drug was discontinued. Her weight has not changed.

Operant conditioning techniques have been employed to restore eating

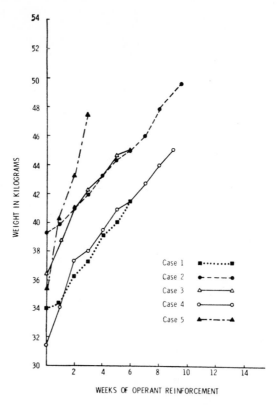

Fig. 5.1. Weight gain in 5 cases in which operant conditioning techniques were used to treat anorexia nervosa.

behavior in anorexia nervosa in a few reported cases. Bachrach *et al.*[2] reinforced eating behavior and secondarily weight gain in a single patient. The patient was placed in a barren room with all possible reinforcers removed and ate all her meals with one of the authors present. Leitenberg *et al.*[13] reported on the treatment of 2 patients using praise and the granting of various privileges to restore eating behavior. Azerrad and Stafford[1] used a token system of reinforcement to increase the rate of eating in a single patient. Tokens could be exchanged for specific items and special events. Blinder *et al.*[4] treated 6 patients using access to physical activity as a reinforcer for weight gain.

We have utilized the same basic principles as the above but with important modifications. Both goals and accruing privileges are clearly defined for the patient at the commencement of treatment. The patient is made to feel responsible for the weight gain. Power struggles between staff and patient, which may occur with other methods, are avoided. Tokens are eliminated as intermediary steps. It is unnecessary to place the patient in a barren environment stripped of all possible reinforcers. We feel that the key to the treatment is the selection of appropriate reinforcers which must be specifically related to the patient's manifest behavior.

We consider the technique described to be useful for treatment of the weight loss in anorexia nervosa. Restoration of weight is basic to the overall treatment program because of the risk of cachexia and death. This constitutes only one part of the total therapeutic program. Following discharge, treatment is modified to meet the needs of the patient.

REFERENCES

1. Azerrad, J. and Stafford, R. L. Restoration of eating behavior in anorexia nervosa through operant conditioning and environmental manipulation. *Behav. Res. Ther.*, 1969, 7, 165–171.
2. Bachrach, A. J., Erwin, W. J., and Mohr, J. P. The control of eating behavior in an anorexic by operant conditioning techniques. In Ullmann, L. P., and Krasner, L. (Eds.) *Case Studies in Behavior Modification*. Holt, Rinehart and Winston, New York, 1965.
3. Barcai, A. Family therapy in the treatment of anorexia nervosa. *Am. J. Psychiatry*, 1971, 128, 286–290.
4. Blinder, B. J., Freeman, D. M. A., and Stunkard, A. J. Behavior therapy of anorexia nervosa: Effectiveness of activity as a reinforcer of weight gain. *Am. J. Psychiatry*, 1970, 126, 1093–1098.
5. Browning, C. H. and Miller, S. I. Anorexia nervosa: A study in prognosis and management. *Am. J. Psychiatry*, 1968, 124, 1128–1132.
6. Bruch, H. Changing approaches to anorexia nervosa. *Int. Psychiatry Clin.*, 1970, 7, 3–24.
7. Crisp, A. H. Clinical and therapeutic aspects of anorexia nervosa—A study of 30 cases. *J. Psychosom. Res.*, 1965, 9, 67–78.
8. Dally, P. J. and Sargant, W. A new treatment for anorexia nervosa. *Br. Med. J.*, 1960, 1, 1770–1773.
9. Dally, P. J. and Sargant, W. Treatment and outcome of anorexia nervosa. *Br. Med. J.*, 1966, 2, 793–795.
10. Groen, J. J. and Feldman-Toledano, Z. Educative treatment of patients and parents in anorexia nervosa. *Br. J. Psychiatry*, 1966, 112, 671–681.
11. Hallsten, E. A. Adolescent anorexia nervosa treated by desensitization. *Behav. Res. Ther.*, 1965, 3, 87–91.
12. Lang, P. Behavior therapy with a case of anorexia nervosa. In Ullmann, L. P. and Krasner, L. (Eds.) *Case Studies in Behavior Modification*. Holt, Rinehart and Winston, New York, 1965.

13. Leitenberg, H., Agras, W. S., and Thomson, L. E. A sequential analysis of the effect of selective positive reinforcement in modifying anorexia nervosa. *Behav. Res. Ther.*, 1968, **6**, 211–218.

14. Stunkard, A. J. New therapies for the eating disorders. *Arch. Gen. Psychiatry*, 1972, **26**, 391–398.

15. Thomae, H. *Anorexia Nervosa.* International Universities Press, New York, 1967.

16. Williams, E. Anorexia nervosa, a somatic disorder. *Br. Med. J.*, 1958, **2**, 190–195.

Restoration of Eating Behavior in Anorexia Nervosa Through Operant Conditioning and Environmental Manipulation*

JACOB AZERRAD† and RICHARD L. STAFFORD‡

Children's Rehabilitation Center, Department of Pediatrics, University of Virginia Medical School

Abstract: A token system of reinforcement was employed to increase the rate of eating in a girl with anorexia nervosa. This token system increased eating rate when it was superimposed on the existing reinforcement-laden environment of a residential treatment center for children. In addition, during the entire course of the experiment (baseline R-1 R-2 R-3 R-4), the patient was receiving noncontingent reinforcement in the form of supportive therapy with a psychologist who allowed her to speak about current problems. No attempt was made to explore "dynamics" nor to perform what is often termed probing or depth therapy. In addition, a re-educational program for the parents assisted them in learning the methods being used at the Center and assisted them with the transition between Center and Community.

INTRODUCTION

Operant methodology has only been infrequently employed to restore eating behavior in anorexia nervosa. Bachrach, Erwin and Mohr (1965) restored eating in a woman with chronic anorexia whose weight had fallen from 120 to 47 pounds. All possible reinforcers were removed from her

*Reprinted from *Behaviour Research and Therapy*, 1969, 7, 165–171. Copyright © 1969. With permission from Pergamon Press and J. Azerrad.

†Director of Psychological Research, Community Evaluation and Rehabilitation Center, Walter E. Fernald State School, Waverly, Massachusetts.

‡Associate Professor of Psychology, Department of Psychology, University of South Alabama, Mobile, Alabama.

hospital environment (radio, T.V., books, magazines, social contacts) and, subsequently, returned to her contingent on the eating of increasingly larger amounts of food. Barlow, Agras and Leitenberg (1967) also employed positive reinforcement to restore the eating behavior in two teen-age girls. A therapist was with the patients at the dinner meal at which time the patients were asked to count mouthfuls of food eaten. In addition, social reinforcers were given (T.V. and trips downtown) for weight gain. Both Bachrach *et al.* (1965) and Barlow *et al.* (1967) removed all potential reinforcers from their patients' environments during the experimental procedures. The present research employs similar procedures in a residential treatment center for children where it was not possible to remove all potential reinforcers from the patient's environment prior to initiating the experimental procedures.

The patient, a thirteen-year-old girl, was admitted to the University of Virginia Hospital Children's Rehabilitation Center on November 6, 1967. A physical examination revealed ". . . a markedly emaciated, white female who appeared to be in no distress. When asked how she was feeling, she said, 'I guess I'm sick because I was brought here' . . . Extremities were markedly thin." A psychiatric evaluation four days after admission described her as a " . . . very emaciated looking young girl . . . extremely lethargic, sitting in her chair with her head leaning against the back of the chair, speaking in a very soft, slow fashion. My feeling was that this girl was quite disturbed, that she had great difficulties with separation and that she was concerned about growing up and the sexual maturation which was taking place." Her only previous hospitalization was at age six for appendicitis.

Her loss of weight began as a self-imposed diet during the summer of 1967. She attributed this dieting to her peers teasing her about her weight. It was at about this time that her mother recalled overhearing the patient and a girlfriend discussing dieting. It was only after the family had returned from a vacation trip during the latter part of August that they noticed her loss of weight. In addition, mother also recalls diet magazines, and brochures about dieting in the patient's room. On August 25, she was taken to her local physician. He did not consider her weight loss excessive and attributed it to puberty and adolescence. A tranquilizer and appetite stimulant were prescribed; however, she refused to take them.

In mid-October, she was examined by a physician in a neighboring town. His impression was that she ". . . presents the classical instance of anorexia nervosa and ... her illness is serious enough to demand immediate psychiatric care." It was at this point that the parents contacted the senior author. The initial interview with the parents revealed the existence of extreme manipulation within the home environment. The family's anxiety about the patient's failure to eat resulted in their allowing her to dictate grocery purchases, meal planning, and the foods which the individual members of the family were, and were not, permitted to eat. Her younger brother would often sneak ice-cream treats late at night when the patient was not looking, because this was one of the foods which was on his sister's prohibited list. The patient also saved her lunch money since she did not wish to eat lunch. She also hoarded sizeable quantities of food in her room. At mealtime, she was apt to throw away food when she believed the other members of her family were not looking, in order to give the impression that she was eating more than she actually was.

During the next three weeks, recommendations were made to help the family eliminate manipulative behaviors and reduced rate of eating. An attempt was made to establish mealtime as a discriminative stimulus, (Ferster *et al.*, 1962); socialization at mealtime was made contingent on eating, and pleasurable activities were postponed until after improved eating behaviors had occurred. Discussions of her failure to eat were to be avoided, and all manipulative behaviors were to be handled by not allowing them to control the activities of the other members of the family. Within a week, manipulative behaviors within the home were totally eliminated; however, her weight continued to fall. Two weeks later, her weight had dropped seven-and-one-half pounds. She was then admitted to the Children's Rehabilitation Center.

Hoarding was the most conspicuous behavior during the patient's first week at the Center. Among the items hoarded were food, ball pens, scissors, paper cups, napkins, and a syringe which had been disregarded in a waste paper basket. Though she was observed stealing on only one occasion, several items which were missing were found among her belongings. Subsequently, if something was missing, she was the first one to be accused and, often, was unjustly blamed for stealing. On one occasion, a nurse who had become angered by her behavior called her a "thief," and later told her that she had given up on her. A consulting psychologist diagnosed her as "obviously psychotic," and many members of the medical staff put considerable pressure on the authors to transfer her to another treatment center where they were more familiar with children who had "psychiatric problems."

METHOD

During the first week after admission, the patient was seen daily in a supportive counseling relationship. No attempt was made to explore "dynamics" and "depth therapy." She was simply allowed to talk about current problems. Sessions took place every day for the first week, and then twice weekly until she was discharged. At the beginning of the second week, the reinforcement program was initiated.

Instructions to the Staff

(1) The patient should be weighed each morning at 6:30, just prior to the breakfast meal.
(2) If the patient is observed taking food from the dining area, the nurse assigned to observe her should tell her what she had observed, and ask her to return the food with a minimum of social interaction.
(3) Discussions about the patient's failure to eat are to be avoided. If she initiates a conversation about her eating difficulties, the topic of conversation should be politely changed.
(4) The patient's parents will be allowed a 1-hr visit with her each week. No telephone calls may be made by the patient.

Initial Reward System (R-1)

(1) Reward points (3 × 4 in. white index cards with the denomination 1, 2, 3, 5, or 10 and the words "reward points" handwritten across the face of the card) were established as a token of exchange redeemable for items often used, but unavailable to the patient at the Center (hair curlers, writing paper, stamps). Special events (movies, trips) were also made contingent on the patient trading in a specified number of reward points. Later, these same reward points could be used to purchase items from local department stores or from the Sears and Roebuck catalogue.
(2) Reward points were earned by the patient each morning immediately after she had been weighed at the rate of:
    (a) one reward point for maintaining her weight of the morning before,
    (b) one reward point for each 0.1 kg of weight gain thereafter.
    (c) If weight loss occurred, reward points were withheld until weight lost had been regained.

Intermediate Reward System (R-2)

The initial reward system was terminated on day twelve. Subsequently, reward points were made contingent on amount of food eaten during the three previous meals. Kitchen personnel recorded food eaten at each meal and were advised to observe her during mealtime rather than record food eaten on the basis of food remaining on her tray. This was to insure the recording of food actually consumed rather than food hoarded or put on another child's plate.

Final Reward System (R-3) (R-4)

On day thirty-five, each food was assigned a specific reward point value as noted in Table 6.1. Reward points were administered immediately after the completion of each meal rather than after each three meals. A nurse, assigned to observe the patient at the specific meal, recorded foods consumed on a small white pad. At the completion of the meal, she showed the patient what had been recorded, and then gave her the reward points earned at that meal. Reward points were redeemable for items at local department stores or for items in the Sears and Roebuck catalogue (R-3).

Table 6.1. Mealtime Point Schedule.

Liquids		Main dishes		Desserts	
Milk (8 oz)	2	Bun	1	Cookie	1
Orange juice (6 oz)	2	Cereal	2	Ice cream	2
Soup (bowl)	2	Egg (one)	2	Pudding	2
Tomato juice (6 oz)	2	Hamburger	4	Toast and jelly	2
		Meat or fish (full portion)	4		
		Potatoes or rice	2		
		Salad	2		
		Sandwich	4		
		Serving bacon	2		
		Slice of bread	1		

On day fifty-eight, the final reward system was modified (R-4). In addition to reward points being capable of purchasing material objects, they could also be used to purchase extra days of home visit on the sliding scale noted in Table 6.2. Home visit was available in the following manner. The patient was allowed to go home every week on Saturday

Table 6.2.   Earned Home Visit Schedule.

Weight (kg)	Number of hours required to earn one day of home visit*
29.0	14
29.5	12
30.0	10
30.5	9
31.0	8
31.5	7
32.0	5
35.0	3
39.0	2

*Points earned at mealtime will be converted into extra hours of home visit at the rate of one hour for each 15 points earned. All points earned during any given week must be converted into extra hours of home visit. Hours not used because they could only be converted into a part-day of home visit can be carried over until the next week.

evening at 6 p.m., and return the following Tuesday at 9:30 a.m., regardless of the number of reward points earned. However, reward points earned at mealtime could be traded in for extra days of home visit (whole days only) which would allow her to leave on Friday evening, Thursday evening, and so on, according to the number of extra days of home visit earned. She would always return to the Center on Tuesday morning, because this was more convenient for her parents. The patient was given a copy of the schedule and the system was explained to her in detail.

Discussions with the Parents

After the patient was admitted, her parents were seen for 1 hr a week to provide them with the information necessary to modify their behavior. The discussions had a two-fold purpose: (1) To teach the parents the behavior modification program being employed at the Center; (2) To instruct them in the methods which would be most effective in making the transition between treatment center and community.

During home visits, the patient was gradually introduced to individuals and activities within the community. Initially, she made short trips to the local shopping center, and visits to relatives were of short duration. Later, visits were lengthened, and she gradually was permitted to meet with more of her friends and relatives. At a later date, she went to church with her parents, to Sunday school, and finally made visits to her public school just prior to discharge.

RESULTS

Figure 6.1 shows the effect of the reinforcement program on the patient's weight. Within one day after the implementation of the Initial Reward System (R-1), the patient's weight began to increase. However, it was soon noted that this weight gain was due to the patient stuffing heavy objects in her clothing, and the fact that she was wearing more and heavier articles of clothing. All future weighings were in the nude.

Figure 6.2 indicates the number of reward points earned for food eaten, a measure which roughly parallels the caloric value of the food eaten each day. The Intermediate Reward System (R-2) began on day twelve. After an initial plateau, both amount of food eaten (Fig. 6.2) and weight (Fig.

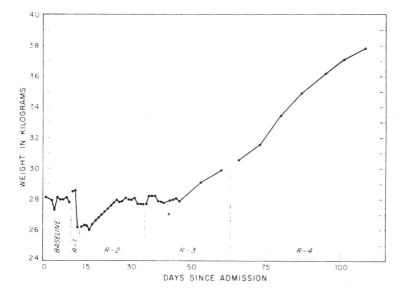

Fig. 6.1. Effect of reinforcement on weight in a case of anorexia nervosa.

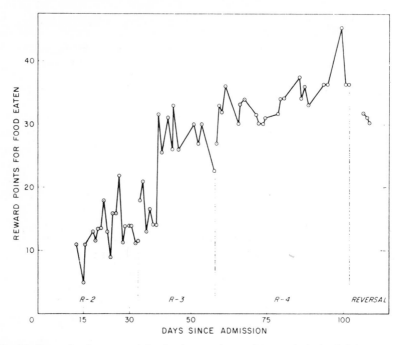

Fig. 6.2. Reward points earned for food eaten (approximate caloric intake) in a case of anorexia nervosa.

6.1) increased significantly. After ten days of steady weight gain, the patient's weight plateaued once again.

Thirty-four days after admission, the Final Reward System was put into effect (R-3). All foods were assigned reward point values on the basis of their approximate caloric value (Table 6.1), and reward points were made contingent on specific foods eaten at each meal. Within one week, there was a marked increase in amount of food eaten, followed by an increase in weight several days later. This Final Reward System was modified on day fifty-eight, at which time extra days of home visit were made contingent on reward points earned at mealtime, in addition to the material items which had been available since the beginning (Table 6.2). A significant increase in amount of food eaten was noted within two days, and this was followed by an increase in rate of subsequent weight gain. Amount of food eaten remained at this new level until day 108, at which time the patient was told that she would be discharged on the following weekend. Amount of food eaten during the next three days declined. Five months after discharge, she was continuing to gain weight at the rate of one pound per month.

DISCUSSION

The results suggest that a token system of positive reinforcement (in the form of reward points redeemable for material items and home visit) contingent on amount of food eaten is an effective method of increasing eating rate in anorexia nervosa. The initial failure to increase eating rate through the administration of reward points contingent on very small units of weight gain was due to the fact that weight gain, no matter how small, is too far removed from the behavior of eating. When reward points were subsequently administered, contingent on amount of food eaten, both food eaten and weight increased. There were three distinct levels of eating rate, each significantly higher than the preceding one; and each increase followed interventions which increased the immediacy or amount of reinforcement which followed eating behavior. Initially, amount of food eaten increased when reward points (redeemable for material items and special privileges) were administered contingent on amount of food eaten per day. Eating rate increased once again when the reward points were administered immediately after each meal, each food being assigned a specific reward point value. Finally, a significant increase in food intake was noted after reward points were given added value in that they were redeemable for extra days of home visit in addition to the material items. Though no attempt was made to reverse procedures, it was noted that eating rate did, in fact, drop immediately after the patient was told that discharge was scheduled for the following week-end (reward points would no longer be needed to earn home visit).

This study demonstrates the use of positive reinforcement to increase eating rate in anorexia nervosa when a token system of reinforcement is superimposed on existing reinforcers within the environment. Bachrach *et al.* (1965) and Leitenberg *et al.* (1968) employed positive reinforcement to increase eating rate; however, both removed all existing reinforcers from the patient's environment prior to the onset of experimental procedures. In the present study, the bulk of potentially reinforcing events at the Center were present during the course of the experiment (occupational therapy, parties, school, girl scout activities, supportive therapy, etc.).

REFERENCES

Bachrach, A. J., Erwin, W. J., and Mohr, P. J. The control of eating behavior in an anorexic by operant conditioning techniques. In *Case Studies in Behavior Modification* (Eds. Ullmann, L. P. and Krasner, L.) Holt, Rinehart & Winston, New York, 1965.

Barlow, D. H., Agras, W. S., and Leitenberg, H. Control of classic neurotic "symptoms" through reinforcement and non-reinforcement. (September, 1967). Association for Advancement of Behavioral Therapies, Washington, D.C., 1967.

Ferster, C. B., Nurnberger, J. I., and Levitt, E. B. The control of eating. *J. Mathetics*, 1962, 1, 87–110.

Leitenberg, H., Agras, W. S., and Thomson, L. A sequential analysis of the effect of selective positive reinforcement in modifying anorexia nervosa. *Behaviour Research and Therapy*, 1968, 6, 211–218.

ARTICLE 7

Case Report: Avoidance Conditioning Therapy of an Infant with Chronic Ruminative Vomiting*[1]

PETER J. LANG and BARBARA G. MELAMED[2]

University of Wisconsin

Abstract: This paper reports the treatment of a 9-month-old male infant whose life was seriously endangered by persistent vomiting and chronic rumination. An aversive conditioning paradigm, employing electric shock, significantly reduced the frequency of this maladaptive response pattern in a few, brief treatment sessions. Electromyographic records were used in assessing response characteristics of the emesis, and in determining the shock contingencies used in therapy. Cessation of vomiting and rumination was accompanied by weight gains, increased activity level, and general responsiveness to people.

A variety of techniques have been used in the treatment of persistent vomiting in infants and children. In general these therapies are tailored to the known or hypothesized causes of the disorder. Thus, the presence of functional disturbance in the intestinal tract would encourage the use of

*Reprinted from *Journal of Abnormal Psychology*, 1969, **74**, 1–8. Copyright © 1969 by the American Psychological Association. With permission of American Psychological Association and P. J. Lang.

[1]This study was supported in part by a grant (MH-10993) from the National Institute of Mental Health, United States Public Health Service.

[2]The authors wish to thank David Kass, the physician in immediate charge of the present case, for giving the authors the opportunity to explore this treatment method and for his assistance during its application. The authors are also indebted to Charles Lobeck, Chairman of the Department of Pediatrics of University Hospitals, Madison, Wisconsin, who made facilities available for use, and to the assigned nursing staff without whose help and cooperation the present result could not have been accomplished. The authors also express their appreciation to Norman Greenfield and Richard Sternbach of the Department of Psychiatry, University of Wisconsin, for the loan of a polygraph, and to Karl G. Stoedefalke of Physical Education for providing additional EMG preamplifiers.

pharmacologic agents—"tranquilizers," antinauseants, or antiemetics. If gastric, anatomical anomalies can be diagnosed, their surgical removal often proves to be the most effective treatment. Animal studies suggest that surgical manipulation of the central nervous system may also become a vehicle for emesis control (Borison, 1959).

When diagnosis excludes obvious, organic antecedents, both the etiology and treatment of the disorder appear less certain. However, clinical workers have described an apparently "psychosomatic" vomiting in children which is generally accompanied by a ruminative rechewing of the vomitus. In reviewing the syndrome, Richmond, Eddy, and Green (1958) adhere to the widely held pyschoanalytic hypothesis that it results from a disruption in the mother-infant relationship. They suggest that the condition is brought about by the inability of the mother to fulfill an adult psychosexual role which is reflected in marital inadequacy. She is unable to give up her own dependent needs and is incapable of providing warm, comfortable, and intimate physical care for the infant. This lack of comfort from without causes the infant to seek and recreate such gratification from within. Thus, in attempting to regain some satisfaction from the feeding situation, he regurgitates his food and retains it in his mouth. The recommended treatment is the interruption in the mother-infant relationship by hospitalization and the provision of a stimulating, warm environment with a substitute mother figure. This method achieved success in the four cases reviewed. Berlin, McCullough, Lisha, and Szurek (1957) offer a similar psychoanalytic interpretation in reporting a case study of a 4-yr-old child hospitalized for 8 mo. at Langley-Porter Clinic. Psychotherapy, involving concomitant counseling to improve the relationship between the parents, led to an alleviation of the child's vomiting reaction.

From the point of view espoused by learning theorists, emesis and rumination may be learned habits. In point of fact, vomiting has been clearly demonstrated as a conditioned response in at least three independent studies (Collins & Tatum, 1925; Kleitman & Crisler, 1927; Pavlov, 1927). This prompts the corollary hypothesis that such behavior could be eliminated directly by counterconditioning procedures.

A number of case reports indicate that considerable success may be achieved in modifying alimentary habits in the clinic setting. Both Bachrach, Erwin, and Mohr (1965) and Meyer[3] successfully treated adult anorexic patients by making various social and physical reinforcers

---

[3]Meyer, V. Personal communication, 1964.

contingent on eating behavior or weight gain. Lang (1965) described the therapy of a young adult patient who became nauseous and vomited under social stress. In this case, counterconditioning methods increased the patient's tolerance of formerly aversive social situations, and thus markedly reduced the frequency of nausea and emesis.

The only study reviewed, attempting to apply conditioning methods specifically in the treatment of ruminative vomiting was reported by White and Taylor (1967). Electric shock was applied to two mentally retarded patients (23-yr.-old female, 14-yr.-old male) whenever throat, eye, or coughing gestures signaled rumination. They suggest that the shock served to distract the patient and he engaged in other activities rather than ruminating. Significant improvement occurred after 1 wk. of treatment, and gains were maintained at a 1-mo. follow-up.

The following case report illustrates the efficacy of aversive conditioning in reversing the vomiting and rumination of a 9-mo.-old infant whose life was endangered by this behavior. The case is of general interest because of the extreme youth of the patient, the speed of treatment, and the fact that conditioning procedures were undertaken only after other treatments had been either ruled out by diagnostic procedures, or had been given a reasonable trial without success. These data also have further implications for the understanding of aversive conditioning procedures in clinical practice.

HISTORY OF PROBLEM AND FAMILY BACKGROUND

A. T. at the age of 9 mo. was admitted to the University Hospital for failure to retain food and chronic rumination. This infant had undergone three prior hospitalizations for his persistent vomiting after eating and failure to gain weight. Born in an eastern state after an uneventful 39-wk. pregnancy, the patient was bottle fed and gained steadily from a birth weight of 9 lb. 4 oz. to 17 lb. at 6 mo. of age. Vomiting was first noted during the fifth month, and increased in severity to the point where the patient vomited 10–15 min. after each meal. This activity was often associated with vigorous thumbsucking, placing fingers in his mouth, blotchiness of the face, and ruminating behavior. The mother remarked that the start of vomiting may have coincided with her indisposition due to a broken ankle which forced the family to live with maternal grandparents for several weeks. Some friction was reported between the patient's mother and her own adoptive mother concerning care of the child. The patient's father is a part-time college student and the family received financial assistance from the paternal grandfather, a successful dentist. At the time of the most recent hospitalization, the social worker's report suggested that the parents were making a marginal marital adjustment.

Three brief periods of hospitalization which included medical tests (gastrointestinal fluoroscopy, EEG, and neuropsychological testing) failed to find an organic basis for this persistent regurgitation. An exploratory operation was performed and a cyst on the right kidney removed, with no discernible effect on his condition. The patient had no history of head trauma. One previous incident of persistent vomiting in a paternal uncle was noted to be of very short duration. The paternal grandfather and two uncles are reported to suffer ulcers.

Several treatment approaches were applied without success. Dietary changes (Pro-Sobee, skim milk), the administration of antinauseants, and various mechanical maneuvers to improve the feeding situation (different positions, small amounts at each feeding, burping) gave short-lived, if any, relief. As thumbsucking often preceded the response, restraints were tried. However, this did little to reduce the frequency of emesis. An attempt had been made to initiate intensive nursing care "to establish and maintain a one-to-one relationship and to provide the child with warm, friendly, and secure feelings [nurse's chart]." This had to be abandoned because it was not inhibiting the vomiting and some observers felt that it increased the child's anxiety and restlessness.

At the time the present investigators were called in, the infant was in critical condition, down to a weight of 12 lb., and being fed through a nasogastric pump. The attending physician's clinical notes attest that conditioning procedures were applied as a last attempt, "in view of the fact that therapy until now has been unsuccessful and the life of the child is threatened by continuation of this behavior."

THERAPEUTIC PROCEDURE AND RESULTS

The patient was given a private room, continuous nursing care, and assigned a special graduate nurse to assist in the conditioning procedures. The authors closely observed the infant for 2 days during and after normal feeding periods. He reliably regurgitated most of his food intake within 10 min. of each feeding and continued to bring up small amounts throughout the day. Observers on the hospital staff suggested that vomiting was originally induced by thumb pressure at the back of the throat. However, at this stage thumb manipulations were not a necessary part of the vomiting sequence. He did protest, however, if hand restraint was enforced. His frail appearance and general unresponsiveness, made him a pathetic looking child as seen from a photograph taken just prior to treatment (Fig. 7.1).

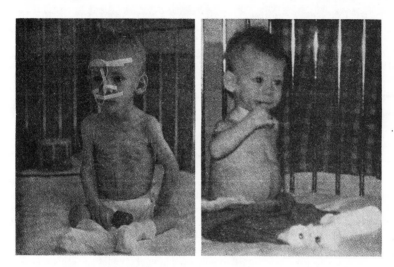

Fig. 7.1. The photograph at the left was taken during the observation period just prior to treatment. (It clearly illustrates the patient's debilitated condition—the lack of body fat, skin hanging in loose folds. The tape around the face holds tubing for the nasogastric pump. The photograph at the right was taken on the day of discharge from the hospital, 13 days after the first photo. The 26% increase in body weight already attained is easily seen in the full, more infantlike face, the rounded arms, and more substantial trunk.)

In an attempt to obtain a clearer picture of the patterning of his response, electromyograph (EMG) activity at three sites was monitored on a Gilson Polygraph. Responses leading up to and into the vomiting sequence reliably coincided with the nurse's concurrent description of the sequence of behavior. Figure 7.2 illustrates the typical response pattern. The uppermost channel of information represents muscle potentials recorded just under the chin, and shows the sucking behavior which usually preceded vomiting; the lowest channel is an integrated record taken from the throat muscles of the neck; the center channel which monitors the upper chest region is largely EKG artifact. It can be noted from this segment that the onset of vomiting is clearly accompanied by

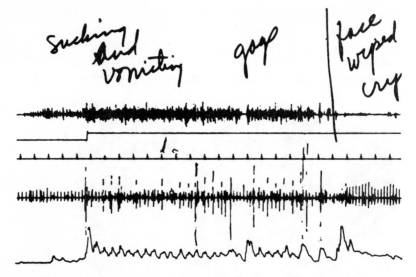

Fig. 7.2. Three channels of EMG activity are presented. (The nurse observer's comments are written just above the first channel. The intense muscle activity on this line is associated with sucking behavior, recorded from electrodes on the underside of the chin. The second channel is just below the one pulse per second, timing line, and was taken from electrodes on the upper chest, at the base of the throat. The EKG dominates this channel, with some local muscle activity. Electrodes straddling the esophagus yielded the lowest line, which in this integrated record clearly shows the rhythmic pulsing of the vomiting response.)

vigorous throat movements indicated by rhythmic, high-frequency, high-amplitude activity, in contrast with quiescent periods and periods where crying predominated.

The authors were concerned with eliminating the inappropriate vomiting, without causing any fundamental disturbance in the feeding behavior of the child. Fortunately, the child did not vomit during feeding, and the sucking and vomiting could be distinguished readily on the EMG. After 2 days of monitoring, conditioning procedures were initiated. The aversive conditioning paradigm called for brief and repeated shock (approximately 1 sec. long with a 1-sec. interpulse interval) as soon as vomiting occurred, continuing until the response was terminated. An effort was made to initiate shock at the first sign of reverse peristalsis, but not during the preceding sucking behavior. The contingency was determined from the nurse's observations of the patient and the concurrent EMG records. In general, the nurse would signal as soon as she thought an emesis was beginning. If EMG confirmed the judgment, shock was delivered. Occasionally, the EMG would initiate this sequence, with the observational judgment following.[4] Shock was delivered by means of a Harvard Inductorium to electrodes placed on the calf of the patient's leg. A 3,000-cps tone was temporally coincident with each shock presentation.[5] Sessions were chosen following feeding to insure some frequency of response. Each session lasted less than 1 hour.

After two sessions shock was rarely required. The infant would react to the shock by crying and cessation of vomiting. By the third session only one or two brief presentations of shock were necessary to cause cessation of any vomiting sequence. Figure 7.3 illustrates the typical sequence of a conditioning trial.

The course of therapy is indicated in Fig. 7.4. Few shocks were administered after the first day of treatment, and both the time spent vomiting and the average length of each vomiting period were abruptly reduced. After only two sessions it seemed that the infant was anticipating the unpleasant consequences of his behavior. He would begin to suck vigorously using his thumb, and then he would remove his thumb and cry loudly.

The data graphed (Fig. 7.4) for the second treatment session represent those reinforcers that the authors are certain were delivered. Early in this session, it became obvious that the infant was not receiving the majority of the administered shocks. The electrodes were at that time attached to the plantar surface of the foot. Observation suggested that the patient had learned to curl his foot, either coincident with emesis or at the first sensation of shock, so as to lift the electrodes off the skin and thus avoid

---

[4]Particular thanks are due to Mary Kachoyeanos, the nurse who assisted at all the therapy sessions.

[5]Shock level was first determined by applying the electrodes to the *E*s, who judged it to be quite painful and unpleasant. Intensity was incremented slightly during the first and second sessions on the basis of the patient's response, but was subsequently unchanged. The inductorium does not permit for exact or wholly reliable measures of current level. However, under the conditions of treatment described here, the average current was within a range of from 0.10 to 0.30 ma., with a cycle frequency of approximatly 50 cps. It should be borne in mind that pulses from an inductorium vary widely in amplitude, and the authors' instrument produced some spikes over 10 ma. Electrodes were first applied to the ball of the foot and then moved to the calf for reasons stated in the text. The accompanying tone was generated by a Hewlett-Packard signal generator and administered by a small oval speaker in a free field. The intensity was loud but not painful (approximately 80–95 db.), and varied considerably because of spontaneous changes in the infant's position. It was employed in order to increase the density of the reinforcer and on the possibility that the therapists might employ it alone, if shock proved to have negative side effects.

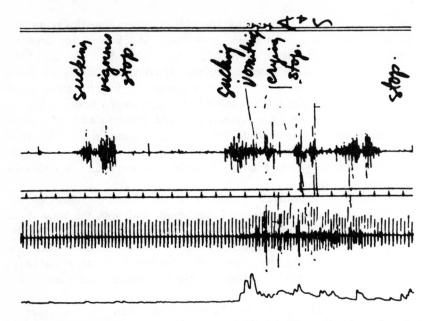

Fig. 7.3. The electrode positions are the same as in Fig. 7.2. (The top line shows the point at which two brief shocks were administered. It may be noted that they follow closely on the first pulse of the vomiting response and that the rhythmic regurgitation observed in Fig. 7.2 never gets underway.)

the painful stimulus. At this point, the electrodes were relocated on the calf, and conditioning proceeded normally. If the shock administrations prior to this procedural change are added to those on the graph, Day 3, afternoon figures for emesis period, percentage of emesis, and shock, respectively, are 11 sec., 21.6% and 77.

By the sixth session the infant no longer vomited during the testing procedures. He would usually fall asleep toward the middle of the hour. Figure 7.5 indicates the sequence of response demonstrating the replacement of vigorous sucking with what the nursing observers described as a "pacifier" use of the thumb.

To vary the conditions under which learning would take place, thereby providing for transfer of effects, the sessions were scheduled at different hours of the day, and while the infant was being held, playing on the floor, as well as lying in bed. Nursing staff reported a progressive decrease in his ruminating and vomiting behavior during the rest of the day and night, which paralleled the reduction observed across therapy sessions.

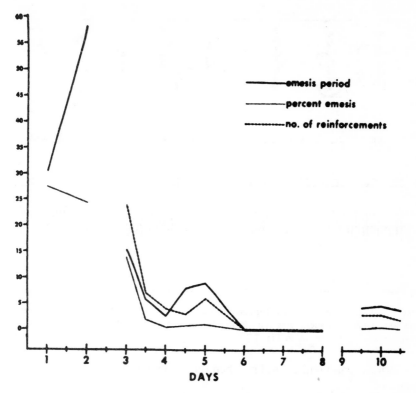

Fig. 7.4. The abscissa describes successive days (morning and afternoon) on which observation or treatment was accomplished. ("Emesis period" is the length of any continuous period of vomiting. "Percentage of emesis" is the total time spent vomiting divided by the time observed. Sessions varied from 16 min. to 60 min. Treatment began on Day 3 which included two unshocked emesis periods. In Session 10 tone alone was presented on one trial. It is of interest to note that following therapy, nursing staff reported that they could now block the very rare vomiting periods with a sharp handclap.)

After three sessions in which there was no occurrence of vomiting, the procedure was discontinued. Two days later there was some spontaneous recovery, which included some vigorous sucking, with a little vomiting and rumination. Three additional sessions were initiated to maintain the reduced frequency of the response (see Fig. 7.4). Except for a brief slackening prior to these trials, there was a steady, monotonic increase in his weight as shown in Fig. 7.6. In general, his activity level increased, he became more interested in his environment, enjoyed playroom

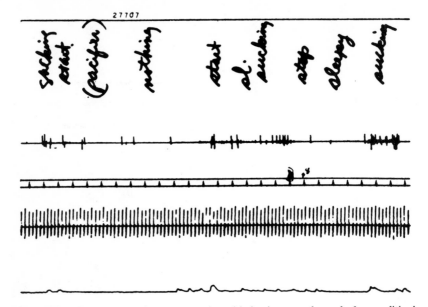

Fig. 7.5. The above segment is representative of behavior near the end of a conditioning session. (Only mild sucking activity is apparent in the upper EMG channel. The electrode positions are the same as in Fig. 7.2.)

experience, and smiled and reached out to be held by the nurse and other visitors.

The mother was reintroduced the day following the last conditioning trial. She took over some of the patient's caretaking needs, including feedings. There was no marked change in his ruminating behavior at this time. The mother responded well and her child reciprocated her attention. He was discharged from the hospital 5 days later, after exhibiting almost no ruminating behavior. The remarkable contrast in his physical appearance is noted in a photograph taken on the day of discharge (Fig. 7.1).

FOLLOW-UP

Correspondence with the mother indicated that there was no further need for treatment. A. T. was eating well and gaining weight regularly. She reported that any thumbsucking or rumination was easily arrested by providing him with other forms of stimulation. He was beginning to seek attention from other people and enjoyed the company of other children.

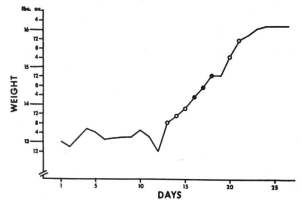

Fig. 7.6. The infant's body weight as determined from the nursing notes is plotted over time, from well before conditioning therapy was instituted to the day of discharge from the hospital. (Days on which conditioning sessions occurred are marked by circles on the curve. Reinforcers were delivered only on days marked by open circles. The decline in body weight in the few days just prior to therapy was probably occasioned by the discontinuance of the nasogastric pump, in favor of normal feeding procedures. The marked weight gain from Day 13 to 18 is coincident with the first 6 days of therapy. The temporary reduction in weight increase, associated with a resumption of emesis, is apparent at Day 19. The additional conditioning trials appear to have acted immediately to reinstate weight gain.)

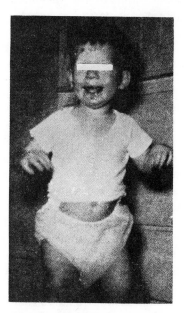

Fig. 7.7. The patient 5 mo. after treatment.

One month following discharge from the hospital, he was seen for a physical check-up. He appeared as a healthy looking 21-lb. child and, aside from a slight anemic condition, was found fully recovered by the attending physician. His local physician reported on a visit 5-mo. later when his weight was 26 lb., 1 oz. "His examinations were negative for any problems. . . . He was eating quite well . . . no vomiting had recurred. He was alert, active and attentive." A snapshot taken by the mother a few weeks before this examination is reproduced in Fig. 7.7. One year after treatment he continues to thrive. Mother and father are both pleased with his development, and no further treatment is indicated.

DISCUSSION

The rapid recovery of this 9-mo.-old male infant following brief aversive conditioning therapy, argues for the effectiveness of behavioral modification in the treatment of this type of psychosomatic disorder. The vomiting and ruminating were treated as maladaptive behavior patterns, and electric shock was used to inhibit a previously well-established response sequence. Elimination of the response was accompanied by increase in the infant's responsiveness to people, as well as substantial weight gains and physiological improvement.

Treatment was undertaken without analysis of the disorder's antecedents. Nevertheless, the family history of the infant could be construed as consistent with other cases in the literature. One clinical worker suggested that a feeling of hostility dominated this infant's home. It is true that the parents' wedding was attended by difficulties and the subsequent birth of the patient occurred before the parents were fully prepared for this responsibility. Furthermore, the mother later expressed anxiety about her marriage and complained of the problem of balancing the separate demands of father and child. She also reported her feeling that her own step-mother had not provided a good maternal model. As a consequence she felt inadequate herself and uncertain in the role.

The caseworker's notes are thus rich in "dynamics," and while one is unable to establish the relative accuracy or significance of these statements, it is clear that this case is interpretable within traditional personality theories. Nevertheless, therapies generated by this orientation were not successful in the present case. In deference, it should also be noted that "one-to-one" care was not maintained as long or as consistently as in many cases reported in the literature, and despite evidence of some marital discord, no extensive counseling of the parents was undertaken. However, like many psychiatric treatments, the above are expensive of professional personnel and prolonged in duration. The aversive conditioning procedures used here achieved success in little more than a week, and considering the developing danger to the child's life, speed was of more than usual importance.

No evidence of "symptom substitution" was observed following treatment. On the other hand, positive social behavior increased coincident with the successful conditioning therapy. The infant became more responsive to adults, smiled more frequently, and seemed to be more interested in toys and games than he had been previously. An analogous improvement in social behavior was noticed in the defective adults treated by White and Taylor (1967). Lovaas, Freitag, Gold, and Kassorla (1965) and Lovaas, Schaeffer, and Simmons (1965) have cited similar effects following the avoidance conditioning of tantrum behavior in autistic children. The latter investigators suggest that the *E*s attained secondary reinforcing value because of their association with shock reduction. This provides the basis for training the children to exhibit affectionate patterns toward adults. In the present case this contingency was very imprecise, and it is not clear that the above mechanism mediated change. What could be called normal infant behavior increased regularly, as the emesis decreased. The social environment appeared simply to replace ruminating as the infant's focus of attention.

Aversive conditioning has been applied widely in adult therapy as well as with autistic children. Eysenck and Rachman (1965) and Feldman (1966) describe its use in treating alcoholic and sexual disorders. However, one hesitates to interpret these findings in a straightforward manner. Adult patients may submit to aversive conditioning procedures from a variety of motives, and cognitive factors may blunt the impact or distort the meaning of aversive stimuli. The present case is of particular interest because these procedures were successful in treating an apparently normal child. Furthermore, the absence of language and the limited cognitive development achieved at this age permit one to interpret this change as avoidance conditioning, unmitigated by the above factors.

Finally, it should be noted that the present case represents a productive use of psychophysiologic recording in therapy. Not only did the EMG provide extensive documentation of the response, but concurrent recording was of considerable help in guiding the treatment effort. Specifically, these records confirmed in an objective manner external observations of mouth and throat movements which seemed to precede emesis. Furthermore, they extended these observations, helping the authors to specify those aspects of the response which were unique to the vomiting sequence, thus assuring that shock was never delivered following noncontingent behavior. Finally, observation of the recordings during therapy probably reduced the latency of reinforcement, particularly during the early trials when the validity of external signs seemed less certain, and provided the clearest indicator of the end of the response when shock was promptly terminated. While the importance of this information to the results obtained cannot be unequivocally established, it certainly increased the confidence of the therapists in their method, and, in turn, the speed and precision with which they proceeded. The further exploration of physiological analysis in the therapeutic setting is encouraged.

REFERENCES

Bachrach, A. J., Erwin, W. J., and Mohr, J. P. The control of eating behavior in an anorexic by operant conditioning techniques. In L. P. Ullmann and L. Krasner (Eds.) *Case Studies in Behavior Modification.* New York: Holt, Rinehart & Winston, 1965.

Berlin, I. N., McCullough, G., Lisha, E. S., and Szurek, S. Intractable episodic vomiting in a three-year old child. *Psychiatric Quarterly,* 1957, **31**, 228–249.

Borison, H. L. Effect of ablation of medullary emetic chemoreceptor trigger zone on vomiting response to cerebral intra-ventricular injection of adrenaline, apomorphine and pilocarpine in the cat. *Journal of Physiology,* 1959, **147**, 172–177.

Collins, K. H. and Tatum, A. L. A conditioned salivary reflex established by chronic morphine poisoning. *American Journal of Physiology,* 1925, **74**, 14–15.

Eysenck, H. J. and Rachman, S. *The Causes and Cures of Neurosis.* San Diego, Calif.: Knapp, 1965.

Feldman, M. P. Aversion therapy for sexual deviations: A critical review. *Psychological Bulletin,* 1966, **65**, 65–79.

Kleitman, N. and Crisler, G. A quantitative study of the conditioned salivary reflex. *American Journal of Physiology,* 1927, **79**, 571–614.

Lang, P. J. Behavior therapy with a case of nervous anorexia. In L. P. Ullmann and L. Krasner (Eds.) *Case Studies in Behavior Modification.* New York: Holt, Rinehart & Winston, 1965.

Lovaas, O. I., Freitag, G., Gold, V., and Kassorla, I. Experimental studies in childhood schizophrenia: Analysis of self-destructive behavior. *Journal of Experimental Child Psychology,* 1965, **2**, 67–84.

Lovaas, O. I., Schaeffer, B., and Simmons, J. Building social behavior in autistic children by use of electric shock. *Journal of Experimental Research in Personality,* 1965, **1**, 99–109.

Pavlov, I. P. *Conditioned Reflexes: An Investigation of the Physiological Activity of the Cerebral Cortex.* Lecture III, Oxford, England: Oxford University Press, 1927.

Richmond, J. B., Eddy, E., and Green, M. Rumination: A psychosomatic syndrome of infancy. *Pediatrics,* 1958, **22**, 49–55.

White, J. D. and Taylor, D. Noxious conditioning as a treatment for rumination. *Mental Retardation,* 1967, **5**, 30–33.

ARTICLE 8

The Punishment of Persistent Vomiting: A Case Study*[1]

ROBERT J. KOHLENBERG

University of Washington

Abstract: In an attempt to control severe vomiting in a mentally retarded patient, shock was delivered after each stomach tension, a pre-vomiting response that consisted of an overt abdominal movement. Contingent shock resulted in an initial transitory increase followed by a decrease in rate of stomach tensions. There was a decrease in emitted vomitus, which resulted in a weight gain of the patient.

There are serious dangers to physical health from persistent vomiting and its consequent weight loss. In some cases, such vomiting occurs in the absence of organic antecedents, which suggests that external variables control the behavior. Two studies on vomiting (Lang and Melamed, 1969; Luckey, Watson, and Musick, 1968) indicate that aversive stimuli can be used effectively to control this behavior.

The application of an aversive stimulus requires a well-defined, discrete response such that a contingency can be specified. In nonorganically based vomiting that is often observed among mental retardates, specification of the target response is often difficult because the vomiting behavior (projection of material from the mouth) is often a slow, continuously occurring response spanning up to 1.5 hr after meals without discrete onsets or offsets. It is also apparent that the emission of vomitus

*Reprinted from *Journal of Applied Behavior Analysis*, 1970, **3**, 241–245. Copyright © 1970 by the Society for the Experimental Analysis of Behavior, Inc. With permission from the Society and Robert J. Kohlenberg.

[1]The research was conducted at Fircrest School, Seattle, Washington. I wish to thank Dr. Sandra Belcher, Keith Jaggard, Miriam Levin, and Sue Menig for their invaluable assistance. I am also indebted to Dr. Irwin Sarason for aid in the preparation of this manuscript. Reprints may be obtained from the author, Department of Psychology, University of Washington, Seattle, Washington 98105.

from the mouth is the end result of a chain of responses that originates lower in the alimentary canal. Since behavior at the beginning of a chain tends to be weaker than later components (Findley, 1962; Kelleher and Fry, 1962; Thomas, 1964; Thomas and Stubbs, 1957), punishment effects would probably be greater when delivered early in the chain. Thus, in addition to being discrete, the response selected for the contingent aversive stimulus should also be at the beginning of the chain.

The nebulous nature of the vomiting response presents a further difficulty associated with the assessment of treatment effects. Gelfand and Hartmann (1968), in their discussion of the evaluation of behavior therapy treatment, suggest that data concerning the problem behavior should be collected during every treatment session in order to identify the precise variables controlling the subject's behavior. It would therefore be desirable to obtain continuous, within-session measures of vomiting.

In the case reported by Lang and Melamed (1969), an EMG recording apparatus was used to detect reverse peristalsis. Electric shock was applied in an avoidance paradigm; the onset and offset of the shock was contingent on the onset and offset of the EMG-defined response. Vomiting was substantially reduced as measured by a reduction in daily duration of periods during which emesis occurred.

Although Lang and Melamed's procedure was highly effective, the use of an EMG-defined response is limited by equipment availability and obfuscation of records by movement artifacts produced by active subjects. The general treatment of non-organically based vomiting would thus be facilitated if the contingency could be specified by direct observation without special apparatus. Without equipment to detect reverse peristalsis, it is especially important that a relationship is demonstrated between the response to be punished and the eventual emission of vomitus. An on-going measure of emitted vomitus could be used to establish such a relationship and facilitate the assessment of treatment effects. In the one other study on aversive control of vomiting, Luckey *et al.* (1968) reported successful treatment of vomiting through punishment. The punished response is not specified however; nor do the authors present pre-treatment baseline data or measures of vomiting.

The purpose of the present study was to control persistent vomiting in a severely retarded girl, whose life reportedly was endangered by loss of body weight. A technique for measuring the amount of emitted vomitus over time was explored as a means of obtaining continuous measures and establishing a relationship between vomiting (the referral problem) and stomach tensions, an overtly visible abdominal movement (selected as the target response). A punishment paradigm was employed and the immediate within-session effects of punishment on the target response and amount of vomitus was investigated.

METHOD

Subject

A 21-yr-old, severely retarded female who had been institutionalized since 2 yr age, served as the subject. Her diagnosis included mongolism and mild quadraplegia. She did not exhibit verbal behavior but appropriately responded to commands such as, "sit down" and "come here."

At the time of this study, the subject was not involved in ward programs or activities and spent most of her day in a chair. This general lack of behavior may have been in part a function of her physically weakened state.

Vomiting had been noted in the medical record as occurring after every meal during the preceding three months. There was a weight loss of 3, 4, and 6 pounds over the three months before treatment began; this constituted a serious medical danger in the opinion of the ward physician. At the beginning of this study the subject was 58.5 in. tall and weighed 74 lb.

Procedure

Since preliminary observations indicated that vomiting began after each meal and continued for approximately 1 hr, an 80-min aftermeal period was selected for the experimental session. There were nine such 80-min periods, one after each meal on three consecutive days.

Immediately after completion of a meal in the ward dining room, the subject was brought into an adjacent private room and seated in a chair and then given a glass of milk or juice, which facilitated the onset of vomiting. The subject was attired in briefs so that an observer seated to the side of the patient could observe surface abdominal activity. A towel was placed in a bib-like manner around the neck. This bib was replaced every 8 min with a fresh bib. At each bib change, the bib was removed and used to wipe off any remaining vomitus on the subject's hands and face and then was placed and sealed in a plastic bag. Each bib and plastic bag had been weighed and numbered before the experimental session. After completion of each session, the bags with bibs were re-weighed with the difference in the pre- and post-session weights constituting the measure of emitted vomitus.

Before the experimental sessions, the abdominal surface was observed in order to select a discrete response. The abdominal area was selected for observation because it was a likely site for an early antecedent in the chain leading to vomitus emission. A response—stomach tension—selected as a target candidate for the aversive contingency was a discrete abdominal movement that resembled an abrupt diaphragm breathing response.

It was decided that if observations during the experimental sessions revealed a substantial correlation between stomach tensions and emitted vomitus, the punishment of stomach tensions would be attempted as a means of controlling vomiting. Although a correlation between stomach tensions and vomitus would not demonstrate a causal relationship, the absence of such a correlation would preclude this response as a possible antecedent.

During the pre-experimental period, two experimenters simultaneously observed and independently signaled stomach tensions and obtained 100% agreement on the occurrence of the response. The bib-changing procedure was perfected in such a way that the entire operation was performed in several seconds.

There were two experimenters present during each session. One signaled the occurrence of a stomach tension and administered treatment. The other experimenter recorded data, timed intervals, and assisted in bib changing. Treatment was initiated on the twenty-fifth minute of Day-Two Lunch. Thereafter, every stomach tension was momentarily shocked with an electric prod (Hot Shot Products Co., Model B12) held by the observer seated at the subject's side. Punishment was delivered by placing the prod contacts on the subject's thigh and momentarily pressing the control button. Shock duration was estimated to be less than 1 sec.

After completion of the three-day experimental period, a program was instituted for control of vomiting consistent with ward routine. The subject was allowed the freedom of the ward but was casually observed by ward personnel. If vomitus was found to be present, the subject was immediately confined to a chair and observed for 1 hr. If stomach tensions occurred, they were punished by ward personnel in the same manner as during the three-day experimental sessions. At least two regular ward personnel from each shift were trained to participate in the post-experimental maintenance program described above. Training consisted of didactic lectures on the principles of operant conditioning, observation of experimental procedures, and supervised experience with program procedures.

RESULTS AND DISCUSSION

The weight of emitted vomitus and number of stomach tensions are given in Fig. 8.1. It can be seen that pre-treatment stomach tensions and emitted vomitus were present at each session and occurred for at least

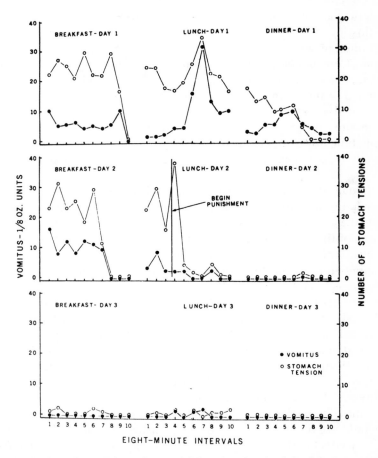

Fig. 8.1. Number of stomach tensions and $\frac{1}{8}$-oz units of emitted vomitus for each 8-min interval before and after contingent shock.

56 min after the beginning of the session. These data were consistent with the nurses' reports that vomiting occurred after each meal. Figure 8.1 also shows a similarity in shape of the curves for stomach tensions and vomitus and suggests a positive relationship between the two.

Declines in the rate of stomach tensions near the end of the session were always accompanied by declines in emitted vomitus. There appeared to be less correspondence at the beginning of sessions, which could represent a time lag between the onset of stomach tensions and the initial appearance of vomitus. The absolute levels of emitted vomitus and stomach tension varied considerably from session to session, which may reflect the variability of menus and amount of food ingested at each meal.

Following the first block of punishment on Day-Two Lunch, nine ($\frac{1}{8}$-oz) units of vomitus were emitted during the remaining 48 min of the session. Comparable amounts of vomitus in the four previous sessions were 42, 35, 70, and 43 units. As shown in Fig. 8.1, subsequent sessions continued to show substantial decreases or complete absence of stomach tension and vomitus. These data indicate that stomach tensions were an appropriate response for the aversive contingency. There is insufficient information, however, clearly to specify stomach tensions as an early link in the chain, although this would be suggested by the location (abdominal area).

Although the contingent shock did subsequently reduce rates of stomach tension, there was a paradoxical transitory increase in rate during the first 8-min block of punishment. As shown in Fig. 8.1, the addition of the punishment contingency was accompanied by 38 stomach tensions during this first block. This effect is paradoxical because punishing stimuli tend to show suppression effects within the first few applications (Azrin and Holz, 1966; Lovaas and Simmons, 1969). Similar to the present findings, both Luckey *et al.* (1968) and Lang and Melamed (1969) indicated that upward of 25 shocks were administered before substantial suppression was observed. Compared to other behavior control studies (Lovaas and Simmons, 1969; Risley, 1968; Tate and Baroff, 1966), the relatively large number of shocks delivered in vomiting-control studies could indicate that the response system involved is more resistant to punishment. Further, the unconditioned response to shock may be similar to the visceral responses that are being punished and would add to observed rates of the punished response. The transitory facilitory effect in the present study might also be the result of an initially elicited response that is subsequently suppressed through the punishing effect of the eliciting stimulus.

Data for 25 days after completion of the experimental sessions indicated that 64 out of 75 meals were emesis-free. This can be compared to records that indicated vomiting occurred after every meal in the three months before treatment. There were, however, 11 post-treatment, after-meal periods during which vomitus occurred. After confining the subject to a chair (contingent on the presence of vomitus), there were no further stomach tensions or vomitus emissions for four of the after-meal periods. One shock resulted in complete suppression in each of the remaining seven periods. It should also be pointed out that the relatively infrequent post-treatment periods, during which vomiting occurred, appeared to be considerably less severe and to involve smaller amounts of vomitus than pre-treatment periods.

The post-experimental session data given above indicate that occasional shocks were necessary to keep the vomiting behavior under control. The program did eliminate the health hazard, as evidenced by a 10.5 lb weight gain in 25 days.

Although the longer-term data were less precise than those presented to this point, it appeared from informal observations that the ward program for controlling vomiting was continued for five months and both weight gains and lower frequencies of vomiting were maintained for 10 months after treatment began. Thus, there was a five-month period during which shock was not used and vomiting was controlled.

At the time of this writing, however, 1 yr since treatment began, vomiting appears to have become a problem again. Thus, the follow-up data indicate that while punishment can be an effective procedure for controlling vomiting and eliminating the health hazard, a maintenance program involving occasional shocks may be required.

REFERENCES

Azrin, N. H. and Holz, W. C. Punishment. In W. K. Honig (Ed.) *Operant Behavior: Areas of Research and Application.* New York: Appleton-Century-Crofts, 1966. Pp. 213–270.

Findley, J. P. An experimental outline for building and exploring multi-operant behavior repertoire. *Journal of the Experimental Analysis of Behavior,* 1962, **5,** 113–166.

Gelfand, D. N. and Hartmann, D. P. Behavior therapy with children: A review and evaluation of research methodology. *Psychological Bulletin,* 1968, **69,** 204–215.

Kelleher, R. T. and Fry, W. Stimulus functions in chained fixed-interval schedules. *Journal of the Experimental Analysis of Behavior,* 1962, **5,** 167–173.

Lang, P. J. and Melamed, B. G. Case report: avoidance conditioning therapy of an infant with chronic ruminative vomiting. *Journal of Abnormal Psychology,* 1969, **74,** 1–8.

Lovaas, O. I. and Simmons, J. Q. Manipulation of self destruction in three retarded children. *Journal of Applied Behavior Analysis*, 1969, 2, 143–158.

Luckey, R. E., Watson, C. M., and Musick, J. K. Aversive conditioning as a means of inhibiting vomiting and rumination. *American Journal of Mental Deficiency*, 1968, 73, 139–142.

Risley, T. The effect and side effects of punishing the autistic behaviors of a deviant child. *Journal of Applied Behavior Analysis*, 1968, 1, 21–34.

Tate, B. G. and Baroff, G. S. Aversive control of self-injurious behavior in a psychotic boy. *Behaviour Research and Therapy*, 1966, 4, 281–287.

Thomas, J. R. Multiple baseline of stimulus functions in an FR chained schedule. *Journal of the Experimental Analysis of Behavior*, 1964, 7, 241–245.

Thomas, J. R. and Stubbs, A. Enhancement of fixed ratio performance by briefly presented conditioned reinforcing stimuli. *Psychonomic Science*, 1966, 5, 329–330.

ARTICLE 9

A Note on Apparent Extinction of the Vomiting Behavior of a Retarded Child[*][1]

MONTROSE M. WOLF, JAY S. BIRNBRAUER, TOM WILLIAMS,
and JULIA LAWLER

Vomiting is usually classified as respondent behavior that is elicited by a class of unconditioned stimuli (emetics) and presumably, given the necessary history, by conditioned stimuli. Several reports in the medical literature describing a childhood "syndrome" characterized by a high rate of vomiting behavior were reviewed by Hoyt and Stickler (1960), who concluded that "the cause of the syndrome of recurrent vomiting, while possibly psychogenic is not known definitely."

Laura was a nine-year-old girl diagnosed as suffering from mental retardation, cerebral palsy, aphasia, hyperirritability, and brain damage. She was admitted to Rainier School, an institution for the retarded, about ten months before our observations began. According to Laura's dormitory nurse, Laura vomited at a moderate rate upon admission, but within a few weeks the rate declined to its present level of "a couple of times a month."

Approximately six months after admission, Laura was enrolled in the school program in a developmental level class, which met three hours a day. After about a month, Laura began to vomit occasionally in class, and within three months, vomiting became practically an everyday occurrence. Among other consequences, the teacher returned Laura to her dormitory whenever Laura vomited on her own dress, which happened

*From *Case Studies in Behavior Modification* edited by Leonard P. Ullmann and Leonard Krasner. Copyright © 1965 by Holt, Rinehart and Winston, Inc. Reprinted by permission of Holt, Rinehart and Winston, Inc. and Montrose M. Wolf.

[1]The assistance, under aversive data-gathering conditions, of Larry Hakala and John Nonnenmacher is gratefully acknowledged. This study was supported in part by research grants (M-2232 and MH-01366) from the National Institutes of Health.

fairly frequently. Drug therapy was initiated but had no effect. At the end of the third month Laura was temporarily dropped from school because of her vomiting.

Two months later a second teacher volunteered to work with Laura and to attempt an experimental analysis of the vomiting behavior. It was our guess that the vomiting was an operant. The first step in our design was to try to decrease Laura's vomiting by operant extinction, by not allowing her access to possible reinforcers during the vomiting episodes. Our hunch was that return to the dormitory had been the reinforcing consequence responsible for maintaining the behavior.

Our planned second step was to reinstate the vomiting after the extinction rate reached a stable low level by presenting the apparent reinforcer contingent upon vomiting, that is, allowing her to return to her dormitory. The new teacher was asked to record (with the help of an observer) the number of times Laura vomited each day in class, to make every effort to continue the class as usual, and not to send Laura back to the dormitory till class had ended. The teacher also attempted to shape desirable behavior using M&M's and praise as reinforcers. These positive reinforcement procedures were discontinued during the vomiting episodes.

The course of Laura's vomiting behavior throughout the semester is presented cumulatively in Fig. 9.1. As can be seen, the rate of vomiting

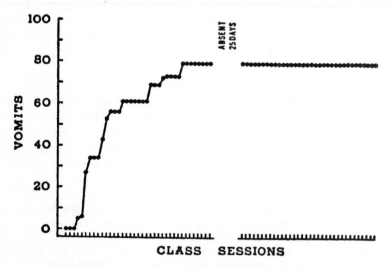

Fig. 9.1. A cumulative record showing the cessation of vomiting behavior of a retarded girl.

declined to zero in an orderly manner over a period of thirty class days, or six calendar weeks. Twenty-one vomits was the highest number recorded on any one day. Laura was absent two Fridays during the first six weeks and was later absent twenty-five days, as shown in Fig. 9.1, as a result of her dormitory's being quarantined.

The vomiting responses were not equally distributed throughout the days of the week. The total for Mondays was thirty-five, Tuesdays twenty-six, Wednesdays twelve, Thursdays five, and Fridays one. This relationship between the day of the week and the number of vomits resembles that typically described as spontaneous recovery.

Our original plan, attempting to increase the vomiting rate by positive reinforcement after a stable rate was reached during extinction, was foiled by the fact that the rate remained at zero, leaving us with no response to reinforce. Without the important step of reinstatement, the probable nature of the conditioning history, operant or respondent, cannot be accurately inferred. Although this detracts from the analytical value of the data, it is irrelevant for the practical value of the extinction technique. It is probable that the classroom procedure would have been equally effective in extinguishing the behavior regardless of the type of conditioning history.

If the vomiting had clearly been the result of respondent conditioning, the extinction procedure would have been carried out in much the same manner. The same care would have been taken not to positively reinforce the respondent behavior, since such a procedure might result in an increase in the behavior through operant control (Bijou and Baer, 1961; Skinner, 1938). Laura would still have been sent to class and forced to remain in the presence of the conditioned eliciting stimuli in order for respondent extinction to occur. The existence of certain correlated operant behavior suggested, however, that Laura's vomiting was operant or perhaps operantly controlled respondent behavior (Bijou and Baer, 1961; Skinner, 1938). Concurrent with virtually every vomiting episode, Laura screamed, tore her clothes, and destroyed property. Such behaviors in other abnormal children have succumbed to operant response controlling techniques (Wolf, Risley, and Mees, 1964; Zimmerman and Zimmerman, 1962). Frequently during these tantrums, Laura escaped from her classroom and attempted to return to her dormitory; she was returned to the classroom each time. The vomiting itself also had certain operant components, such as the selection of targets: the teacher's desk (on one occasion, a neighboring teacher's desk), the table at which the class was seated, and her own clothes when she had taken them off.

The tantrumlike behaviors decreased in frequency to zero along with the vomiting, while Laura's productive classroom behavior apparently increased. Her appearance and responsiveness to the teacher's demands improved markedly. Toward the end of the semester, we doubted that return to the dormitory was still an effective positive reinforcer, since Laura had seemingly come to "enjoy" her classroom activities.[2]

REFERENCES

Bijou, S. W. and Baer, D. M. *Child Development*. Vol. I: *A Systematic and Empirical Theory*. New York: Appleton-Century-Crofts, 1961.

Hoyt, C. S. and Stickler, G. B. A study of 44 children with the syndrome of recurrent (cyclic) vomiting. *Pediat.*, 1960, **25**, 775–779.

Skinner, B. F. *The Behavior of Organisms*. New York: Appleton-Century-Crofts, 1938.

Wolf, M. M., Risley, T., and Mees, H. Application of operant conditioning procedures to the behavior problems of an autistic child. *Behav. Res. Ther.*, 1964, **1**, 305–312.

Zimmerman, E. H. and Zimmerman, J. The alternation of behavior in a special classroom situation. *J. exp. Anal. Behav.*, 1962, **5**, 59–60.

---

[2]Editors' note. Additional information which was obtained after completion of the article was summarized by the authors as follows: We continued taking data on the subject's vomiting behavior throughout the school year following the one described above. The general class conditions were similar to the previous year's including the same teacher and many of the same students. About a month after the beginning of the fall term the subject vomited once in class and was immediately returned to her dormitory. During the next three months, each time the subject vomited she was returned to her dormitory. Vomiting occurred in over one-third of the class sessions. At that point we returned to the extinction procedure. The subject was kept in the classroom the entire session regardless of whether or not she vomited. During the next few months the vomiting decreased in an orderly manner from a high rate (twenty-nine being the most responses in any one session) to only one vomit in class during the last two months of the school year. The resulting extinction curve was similar to that of the previous year.

The Treatment of Bowel Retention by Operant Procedures: A Case Study*

J. R. TOMLINSON

Psychological Services, Board of Education, Minneapolis, Minnesota

Abstract: A long standing problem of bowel retention in a 3-year-old child was treated by an operant approach. A contingency was established in which the response of voluntary elimination was the only available instrumental response that would be followed by a bubble gum reinforcer. The sole task of the parents was to check the adequacy of the child's response and to dispense the gum. The rate of voluntary defecation increased from a base rate of once per week to six times per week by the end of the third week. The rate was maintained at this level at the end of a 2-year period, though a new reinforcer was introduced at the end of the first year. During the fourteenth week, when the contingency was removed the rate fell to its original level.

Several studies have reported the use of operant techniques in the modification of enuresis and encopresis. Madsen (1965) made candy contingent on successful bowel elimination in the toilet training of a 19-month-old child. Peterson and London (1965) used parental praise and popsicles as reinforcers for successful elimination in a 3-year-old child with a bowel retention problem. Lal and Lindsley (1968) successfully treated chronic constipation by the use of social contingencies.

In none of these studies, however, has a particular reinforcer been solely contingent upon the subject's making the desired response. The present study describes the treatment of a long-standing bowel retention problem in a child, by establishing a reinforcement contingency such that a specific desired object could be obtained only by making the response of elimination.

---

*Reprinted from *Journal of Behavior Therapy and Experimental Pyschiatry*, 1970, 1, 83–85. Copyright © 1970. With permission from Pergamon Press and J. R. Tomlinson.

CASE HISTORY

The subject of this study was the author's 3-year-old son. Beginning around age 2, approximately the time that toilet training was accomplished, the operant level of elimination without prior administration of a laxative, was averaging about once a week.

Praise for successful use of the toilet had been the primary technique employed in toilet training and minimal attention had been paid to failures in the process. For approximately 1 year following successful toilet training, the operant level of one elimination per week without a laxative remained unchanged. When asked or encouraged to eliminate, the child would report that it was painful and, although willing to spend considerable time on the toilet, he routinely denied feeling any elimination cues. Because he was capable of retention for up to 10 days, chronic constipation was continually present and elimination was, indeed, likely to be painful.

A series of physiological examinations, including barium X-rays, indicated no physiological disfunction. Changes in diet, recommended by several pediatricians, were temporarily effective but rarely for more than a week following their introduction.

METHOD

The initial task was to define the problem in behavioral terms. The target was to obtain an increase in the rate of self-initiated elimination behavior, without prior administration of a laxative, to the operant level of the average child's eliminative behavior. It was decided to accomplish this by making the elimination response the only available instrumental response that would be followed by a particular reinforcer.

Bubble gum was chosen as the object most likely to operate as a reinforcer because, at the time of the study, it was one item the child usually asked for at least once a day. Following the establishment of a base rate, the experimental procedure was initiated and he was informed that, from that day on, he could only obtain bubble gum by making an adequate defecation response. Once the response had been made in any given day, he could have as many pieces of gum he wanted for the remainder of that day, with the stipulation that he could not save any from one day to the next. To reduce the delay between response and reinforcement, the gum was placed in the bathroom where, although inaccessible, it could still be seen.

His mother was instructed to discontinue all her previous behavior relevant to this problem. Her sole task was to dispense the reinforcer whenever the response occurred. Verbal reinforcement following the desired response was to be limited to a simple statement of "good" and she was instructed that, whenever he asked for gum, she was to remind him of the new arrangement. Once he had made the defecation response during the day, he was to inform one of his parents who would dispense the gum after checking the adequacy of his stool.

Because of the presence of constipation at the time when these procedures were instituted, a mild laxative was administered daily for the first week to increase the probability that the appropriate response would occur and to reduce the likelihood that it would be difficult or painful.

RESULTS AND DISCUSSION

On the third day following institution of the training procedures, voluntary defecation occurred. The rate of voluntary defecation then increased to five times per week for the next 2 weeks and then to six times per week where it remained for the next 5 months (see Fig. 10.1).

Although removal of the reinforcement contingency was not systematically introduced as part of the study, an accidental set of circumstances during the third month of treatment provided some evidence with regard to this point. The child spent the 14th week at the home of his grandparents, who were not informed of the gum contingency and dispensed it at the child's request. At this time, the operant level of voluntary defecation dropped to the earlier rate of once per week. Upon returning home, the contingency was re-established and the rate immediately returned to its previous experimental level.

At the end of 2 months, the gum supply was moved from the bathroom to the kitchen and the child was instructed that, following defecation, he was to inform one of his parents who would then dispense the gum there. For the remaining 2 months, the operant level remained between six and seven times per week. At the end of the first year, the gum reinforcer was replaced by dessert following the evening meal if, at some time during the day, defecation had occurred. Two years following the institution of these procedures, the operant level remains at six defecations per week.

The results of this study suggest that procedures based on an operant

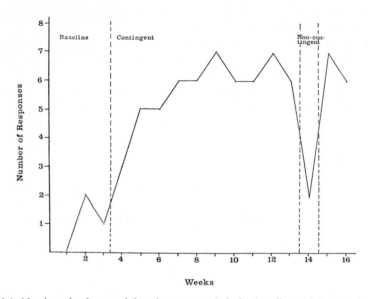

Fig. 10.1. Number of voluntary defecations per week during baseline and gum contingency conditions. About the 14th week voluntary defecations decreased when the dispensing of gum did not depend on defecation.

model were successful in eliminating a problem of long-standing in a relatively short period of time. It is also worth noting that an emotional interaction between the child and his mother that had centered on this problem, essentially disappeared once the training procedures were established.

REFERENCES

Lal, H. and Lindsley, O. R. Therapy of chronic constipation in a young child by rearranging social contingencies, *Behav. Res. & Therapy*, 1968, **6**, 484–485.

Madsen, C. H. Positive reinforcement in the toilet training of a normal child: a case report, In *Case Studies in Behavior Modification*. (Eds. L. P. Ullmann and L. Krasner), pp. 305–307. Holt, Rinehart & Winston, New York, 1965.

Peterson, D. R. and London, P. A role for cognition in the behavioral treatment of a child's eliminative disturbance, In *Case Studies in Behavior Modification*. (Eds. L. P. Ullmann and L. Krasner), pp. 289–295. Holt, Rinehart & Winston, New York, 1965.

Behavior Modification in the Home: Parents Adapt Laboratory-Developed Tactics to Bowel-Train a 5½-Year-Old[*][1]

BEATRICE H. BARRETT[2]

Behavior Research Department, Walter E. Fernald State School, Waverley, Massachusetts

Although a child may be eligible for institutionalization, parents may have to, or want to, keep him at home. The high cost of private residential schools is prohibitive for many families, and state training schools are often so overcrowded that they can offer little more than custodial care. Intensive office treatment may be precluded by its cost, and most outpatient clinics have long waiting lists. The problem persists despite increasing improvement of residential facilities, development of community mental health centers, and community support of special education programs.

The feasibility of alleviating the situation by offering parents the opportunity to train their own problem children effectively at home is just beginning to be explored (Lindsley, 1967). Yet home-treatment by parents could, potentially, capitalize on many "built-in" advantages—a low patient-to-therapist ratio, highly motivated therapists, first-hand

*Reprinted from *Psychotherapy: Theory, Research and Practice*, 1969, 6(3), 172–176. With permission from journal and Beatrice H. Barrett.

[1]This work was supported by grant MH-14880 from the Applied Research Branch, National Institute of Mental Health, U.S. Public Health Service, and by project grant MH-MA-5-67 from the Massachusetts Department of Education, Bureau of Special Education, funded by the U.S. Office of Education under Title I of the Elementary and Secondary Education Act of 1965.

[2]Linda Jarvis was primarily responsible for initiating the home treatment program, and Nabum Stiskin assisted in guiding the parents' efforts. Ruth Cohen helped to organize the data and obtain follow-up information. Judith Rosenberg edited this report. I am grateful for their capable, enthusiastic contributions to this service endeavor.

knowledge of the child's behavioral and medical history, round-the-clock opportunity to make observations and to control the child's environment, and extremely low cost. The missing ingredients are primarily procedural: what to do, when to do it, and how to assess its effectiveness.

Wahler *et al.* (1965) and Hawkins *et al.* (1966) have trained mothers to modify their children's behavior, but in both cases the parent-advisors selected the "target" behaviors, determined how these behaviors would be treated, and evaluated the effectiveness of treatment. During all observation and treatment sessions, the advisor was present to tell the mother what to do and when to do it via a series of pre-arranged signals.

In the case that we present, the parents assumed greater responsibility for their children's treatment. Our goal was to enable the parents to eliminate what they considered to be the most distressing behavior in their child. Observation and treatment were carried out by the parents at home. The choice of treatment and assessment procedures was theirs. Our contribution to their efforts was to explain to them the rudiments of behavior modification and to encourage them to maximize the contingencies existing in their home. We met with them only a few times, and for short periods, to offer suggestions and encouragement.

INITIAL CONSULTATION WITH PARENTS

After reading a newspaper article about conditioning, the parents called seeking help in bowel-training their $5\frac{1}{2}$-year-old son. Accompanied by the child, they met with us the next day. They complained that the child was hyperactive, nonverbal, and not toilet-trained, that he had a short attention span, and that he was a food-stealer as well as a fussy eater. They believe his developmental difficulties began with a febrile seizure following a smallpox vaccination at age 12 months. Subsequent seizures occurred at $1\frac{1}{2}$ years, 2 to $2\frac{1}{2}$ years (every 6 to 7 weeks), and $3\frac{1}{2}$ years. Since the second seizure, the child has been on chronic Dilantin and phenobarbital medication.

He is the second of three children. He began walking at 13 months. At 10 months he began uttering a few words, but his current vocalization is limited mainly to inarticulate sounds. He seldom cries or displays other affect. He occasionally responds to commands, and he can discriminate some objects. He can use a fork and spoon and drink from a cup without spilling, but he runs awkwardly.

When he was $3\frac{1}{2}$ his parents took him to a physician who offered the diagnosis of moderate diffuse brain damage. Patterning was prescribed and was carried out at home 12 times a day for two years. Three months before contacting us the parents terminated this treatment because they saw no evidence of improvement. They were told that the child was not progressing because he was "unwilling to please."

For $2\frac{1}{2}$ years the parents had been attempting to control the child's hyperactivity by locking him in his room most of the time. The room was stripped of everything but a bed and a few toys. The child was taken to the bathroom every three hours or so during the day, and he often urinated at these times. But bowel movements rarely occurred during the scheduled toileting—the child continued to defecate in his room or in the yard, and he often engaged in feces-smearing. With increasing years of unsuccessful treatment, the parents' anger and desperation mounted. They usually reacted to the child's defecation and smearing by screaming at him and spanking him.

The parents hoped to get the child into a summer training camp. To be eligible, he had to be bowel-trained. For this reason, they urgently sought effective training methods. They had been considering the possibility of institutionalizing the child, but they were still hopeful that he could have the advantages of living at home with his family while receiving special training.

We told the parents that our service to them would be limited to suggestions. We felt that they themselves could assume responsibility for training their child at home. We advised them to continue their usual routines for one week, except—and this was our only requirement—that they had to keep daily records of the child's disturbing behavior: when it occurred, where it occurred, who was present, and what was done about it. It was left to them to decide what behaviors to record. We gave them a supply of ordinary columnar paper on which to keep their records, and we scheduled weekly appointments at our institution to review their data and discuss whatever plans for treatment seemed indicated.

SECOND CONSULTATION

During the first week the mother recorded 15 bowel movements and 21 urinations outside the toilet. She had mentioned the child's delight with daily snacks of chocolate cookies. We suggested that she not give these to him unless he used the toilet for bowel movements. It was clear from the records that the child was capable of doing this since he occasionally moved his bowels when he was put on the toilet. We suggested that rather than attending to his misplaced bowel movements by yelling at him or slapping him, they might obtain better results by praising him and giving him chocolate cookies immediately after appropriately placed bowel movements. Other bowel movements, we advised, might be dealt with simply by taking away his favorite pillow, which he usually kept with him.

The mother also wished to extend the range of food the child would eat and to eliminate his running away from the table during meals. We suggested recording the types and amounts of food the child ate and refused and the frequency of his leaving the table.

FURTHER CONSULTATION

During the next three weeks the parents tried to modify their reactions to the child's soiling and smearing. The mother continued to keep records of bowel movements and urinations, but she abandoned the food and table-leaving records. She preferred to concentrate on toileting, which was easiest for her to define and most demanding on her time and patience.

The mother's records revealed that she was not reserving cookies only for bowel movements in the toilet. She admitted that she frequently "gave in" on other occasions, as we noticed during a brief home visit. The child continued to defecate in his room, and his smeared feces often required as much as two hours to clean up.

Our last suggestion to the mother was to restrain the boy in a chair facing a bare corner of his room for 30 to 45 minutes after every misplaced bowel movement. We furnished her with a suitable chair (which she began to use 13 days later). She was advised, also, to give him cookies and to praise him lavishly right after—and only after—every appropriately placed bowel movement. Consistency was stressed. We urged her to train her maid in the treatment procedures.

THE PARENTS' TACTICS

Figure 11.1 shows the immediate effects of the combined procedures for decelerating inappropriately placed and accelerating appropriately placed bowel movements. During 15 days, when bowel movements outside the toilet resulted in restraint and isolation, their rate dropped from an average of 2.2 to 0.9 per day. The mother reported that during his

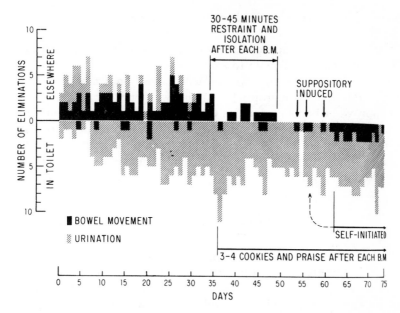

Fig. 11.1. 26-day cure of encopresis by parents in home. Parents' daily records of frequency and location of bowel movements and urinations showed (1) rapid deceleration of inappropriate bowel movements under contingent restraint and isolation, (2) subsequent episodes of fecal hoarding relieved by suppository administration, and (3) accompanying onset of self-initiated appropriate toileting (day 57) sustained by cookies and praise following each bowel movement.

second period in the chair the child cried for the first time in many months and that each subsequent use of the chair made him very upset. However, the parents were pleased with his progress.

A new development, not unexpected in encopretic children, emerged: for four days the child retained his feces. On the fifth day his parents administered a suppository and took him to the toilet. His product earned him warm praise and cookies. After two more suppository administrations, the child stopped soiling and indicated when he wished to use the toilet. He continued to receive chocolate cookies for his properly placed bowel movements.

THE PARENTS' ACHIEVEMENT

The parents called us to express their elation over the rapid results of their treatment. They had eliminated not only the child's encopresis but also his urinary "accidents." The child was attending summer camp with no difficulty.

After 15 days of appropriate toileting the parents stopped keeping records and gave their data to us.

On telephone follow-up, we learned that within a month the parents were able to sustain appropriate toileting with only occasional reminders and approval. Chocolate cookies were no longer necessary. Four months after treatment the child was enrolled in a private training school. In two months he has not had an accident at school or at home on weekends. Training opportunities from which he had previously been excluded are now available to him.

ANALYSIS OF TREATMENT

Technically, treatment of the child's encopresis began on the 35th day, when the parents first instituted *consistent* consequences for both inappropriate and appropriate bowel movements. Prior to that time they had not developed sufficient control of their own behavior to institute an effective program for controlling the child's behavior. His success in manipulating his parents was observed and pointed out during a second home visit the day before use of the chair began.

At no time did we require specific treatment procedures (*Cf.* Allen and Harris, 1966). We gave the parents a general, brief explanation of the importance of carefully selecting and timing behavioral consequences and the advisability of arranging penalties for inappropriate behavior. The final choice of consequences was theirs. Five office appointments and two home visits preceded initiation of consistent treatment by the parents. A final home visit followed their report of success. We rejoiced in their triumph, collected their data, and suggested that they gradually stop giving the child cookies for using the toilet. We never actually observed the home-treatment.

The two items we provided—recording paper and a restraining chair—helped the parents to control their own behavior. Our requirement of separate records for each behavior they wished to modify helped them to define the behaviors, to determine their relative nuisance value, and eventually to assign priority to the most readily specified and most reliably recorded act. In addition, these records permitted us to evaluate the parents' effectiveness as behavior modifiers. We have no reason to doubt the reliability of the records. The decrease in frequency of bowel movements as treatment progressed (2.2 per day before treatment, 1.4 per day after treatment) is apparently not unusual (Neale, 1963). That enuresis may end during the course of encopresis-treatment is also evident from other reports (Giles and Wolf, 1966).

The restraining chair allowed for a well-defined time-out period (Ferster and Appel, 1961) contingent on each inappropriate bowel movement. It gave the parents a way to withhold potentially rewarding consequences from the child and was a convenient substitute for their other ineffective efforts at punishing him. In addition, the chair kept the child from engaging in his long-standing repertory of hyperactive behaviors, so that bowel accidents produced not only time out from parental attention but time out from behaviors with unspecified but perhaps intrinsically reinforcing properties (Premack, 1959). Its aversiveness for the child was evident from his reaction to it.

The possibility that the child would hoard his feces had not been mentioned to the parents. Use of a suppository to reinstate and, in effect, to schedule toilet-placed, cookie-producing bowel movements was the parents' idea. Because the suppository administration elicited the child's first self-initiated toileting—the result his parents wished—its effectiveness was demonstrated. They rapidly discontinued the procedure when the child's behavior showed it was no longer necessary.

CONCLUDING COMMENTS

Parents of a retarded, hyperactive, "autistic" child rapidly eliminated his encopresis by adapting laboratory-developed procedures for behavioral control. They decelerated inappropriate bowel movements by contingent periods of isolation and restraint. They generated and sustained appropriate bowel movements by food and praise. They terminated fecal retention by scheduling bowel movements with suppositories. Their systematically recorded data showed them and us the immediate effects of procedures which they selected and applied with minimal professional guidance. Their successful treatment enabled their child to participate in training programs previously denied him because of his encopresis.

This case illustrates the ease with which simple, objective, and inexpensive methods of behavioral measurement and control can be communicated to and applied by parents to rapidly cure a symptom that often requires months of professional treatment by more traditional approaches. This is only one of a growing number of examples that clearly reveal the feasibility and practicality of parents' managing and training their own problem children (Sebastian, 1967). Lal and Lindsley (1968) recently reported a case, similar to ours, in which parents rapidly eliminated chronic constipation in their three-year-old child by rearranging social contingencies. The parents' records showed that, with a little professional guidance, they were quite capable of managing their own child's behavior. From behavior research laboratories have emerged tools which parents should have the opportunity to use.

REFERENCES

Allen, K. E. and Harris, F. R. Elimination of a child's excessive scratching by training the mother in reinforcement procedures. *Behaviour Research and Therapy*, 1966, 4, 79–84.

Ferster, C. B. and Appel, J. B. Punishment of S^Δ responding in matching-to-sample by time-out from positive reinforcement. *Journal of the Experimental Analysis of Behavior*, 1961, 4, 45–56.

Giles, D. K. and Wolf, M. M. Toilet training institutionalized, severe retardates: an application of operant behavior modification techniques. *American Journal of Mental Deficiency*, 1966, 70, 766–780.

Hawkins, R. P., Peterson, R. F., Schweid, E., and Bijou, S. W. Behavior therapy in the home: amelioration of problem parent-child relations with the parent in a therapeutic role. *Journal of Experimental Child Psychology*, 1966, 4, 99–107.

Lal, H. and Lindsley, O. R. Therapy of chronic constipation in a young child by rearranging social contingencies. *Behaviour Research and Therapy*, 1968, 6, 484–485.

Lindsley, O. R. The child knows best. Paper presented at American Association on Mental Deficiency, Denver, Colorado, 1967.

Neale, D. H., Behaviour therapy and encopresis in children. *Behaviour Research and Therapy*, 1963, 1, 139–149.

Premack, D. Toward empirical behavior laws: I. Positive reinforcement. *Psychological Review*, 1959, 66, 219–233.

Sebastian, E. B. In the home. Paper read in Symposium on Modification of Retarded Behavior, American Association on Mental Deficiency, Denver, Colorado, 1967.

Wahler, R. G., Winkel, G. H., Peterson, R. F., and Morrison, D. C. Mothers as behavior therapists for their own children. *Behaviour Research and Therapy*, 1965, 3, 113–124.

ARTICLE 12

Elimination of Soiling Behavior in an Elementary School Child Through the Application of Aversive Techniques*

WILLIAM FERINDEN, Jr. and DONALD VAN HANDEL

Linden Board of Education, Department of Special Services, Linden, New Jersey

Abstract: A case study illustrating the application of aversive techniques in a school setting was presented. Soiling behavior, which had occurred as often as three times per day before aversive procedures were initiated, was eliminated in this child with no reoccurrence in a six month follow-up. This report lends additional confirmation to the feasibility of employing aversive conditioning or punishment in modifying or eliminating socially unacceptable behavior. Also, it is another example in which amelioration of symptomatology appropriately seemed to precede a thorough investigation of etiological factors.

Although punishment is often used to shape the behavior of youngsters in school, the person dealing out the punishment (administrator, teacher, etc.) almost always feels compelled to cover its application or apologize for its use. Thus the punisher often refers to his actions as "setting limits," "expressing disapproval," "teaching the youngster respect for authority," and "taking away privileges."

Holz and Azrin (1963) defined punishment as being a consequence of responding that reduces the future rate of that response. There are two basic punishment operations: (a) the presentation of a stimulus that is usually aversive and (b) the removal of a positive reinforcing condition.

Upon analysis of recent research, Thomas (1968) concluded that in order to increase the efficiency of the punishment operations at least the following should be kept in mind:

1. The punishment should be neither so mild as to be inconsequential nor so strong as to be immobilizing or devastating.

---

*Reprinted from *Journal of School Psychology*, 1970, **8**, 267–269. With permission from journal and Donald Van Handel.

2. The punishment should be tied immediately to the response that one wishes to reduce and should be administered matter-of-factly after the response.

3. Punishment of every response to be reduced should generally be used for obtaining immediate suppressive effects under the conditions during which the punishment is applied.

4. Alternative pro-social responses incompatible with the punished response should be allowed and reinforced.

The application of aversive techniques in a school setting is illustrated in the following case:

George was born prematurely during the seventh month of pregnancy; birth weight was three pounds. He remained in incubation for two months. According to the mother, he reached the various developmental milestones on schedule with the exception of a continuation of soiling up to the present time.

At the age of seven, George was examined at a medical center upon referral by the school. The diagnosis was: psychogenic megacolon with a five to six year history of soiling underwear with fecal material and chronic constipation.

The parents were then referred to a mental health clinic at which George was evaluated by a psychiatrist. The doctor found no indications of neurological damage and considered the youngster to be an emotionally immature personality type.

Although the psychiatrist felt that collaborative psychotherapy was indicated for parents and child, this did not materialize because of a lack of parental cooperation.

At the recommendation of the classroom teacher and the psychiatrist, George was retained in second grade to give him an opportunity to catch up with his peers both emotionally and academically. However, repetition of the grade appeared to have little value in that George continued to have academic difficulties and frequent soiling.

Prior to George's referral to the psychologist, the teacher had been instructed to allow the boy to leave the room whenever necessary and to use the closest bathroom to his class. In addition, the mother was counseled regarding George's problem and possible causal factors were discussed. She was requested to be certain that the youngster attended to his bodily needs before leaving for school in the morning and before returning to school after lunch.

All of these suggestions proved ineffectual. Soiling occurred almost daily, as often as three times in one school day. With each occurrence,

George was sent home to be cleaned up and to receive a change of clothing.

At this point a behavior modification program utilizing aversive techniques was instituted.

METHOD

George was required to bring a change of clothing to school. He was made responsible for cleaning himself and for washing out his soiled clothing. He was provided with a strong soap (causing mild irritation to the skin) for cleaning purposes, and the water temperature was kept below room temperature. Furthermore, he was compelled to make up time lost from the classroom after school hours.

This procedure was employed as an aversive consequence to the soiling response of this subject.

Concurrent with the aversive consequence contingency, the child was exposed to frank discussions with the psychologist regarding the social implications of this behavior. In one of the earlier sessions, the boy admitted that he was acting like a baby and if he were a baby he could stay home all the time with his mother and watch T.V.

RESULTS AND DISCUSSION

A marked decrease in the occurrence of soiling under the aversive consequence conditions is apparent in Fig. 12.1, which depicts the frequency of soiling responses before and after the initiation of aversive procedures.

After the first application of aversive procedures, George soiled himself just nine more times. Aversive procedures were re-applied after each of these incidents.

The boy and his mother, as well as the classroom teacher, reported that he was interacting more positively with his peer group. The degree of interaction with his peers actually seemed to be inversely related to the frequency of soiling. In addition, the mother indicated that there were now no incidents of soiling in the home.

Thus soiling, which had occurred as often as three times per day before the application of aversive procedures, was eliminated in this child with no reoccurrence in a six month follow-up.

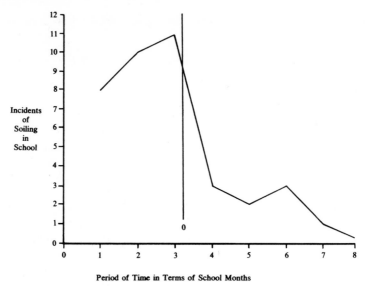

Period of Time in Terms of School Months

O = Aversive procedures initiated

Fig. 12.1. Incidence of soiling response before and after initiation of aversive procedures.

REFERENCES

Holz, W. C. and Azrin, N. H. A comparison of several procedures for eliminating behavior. *Journal of the Experimental Analysis of Behavior*, 1963, **6**, 399–406.
Thomas, E. J. Selected sociobehavioral techniques and principles: An approach to interpersonal helping. *Social Work*, 1968, **13**, 12–26.

Reinforcement Procedures in the Control of Encopresis: A Case Study*[1]

BONNIE C. PEDRINI and D. T. PEDRINI

University of Nebraska at Omaha

Abstract: A student and his problems were pin-pointed, recorded, and changed. The first 3 wk. were used to establish a base rate. S defecated in class, once every few days. After he was programmed with reinforcers (charting and coupons toward book purchases), he may have had one accident, only, for the remainder of the school year (8 wk.). Follow-up through the seventh month of the next school year (the time of this writing) indicates one accident only. During this 7-mo. period, he was not programmed with book coupons or any other specific reinforcer. He had internalized a previous external model of control.

Encopresis is a behavior which may be modified through operant conditioning or behavior modification or behavior therapy techniques (Gelber & Meyer, 1965; Keehn, 1965; Neale, 1963). John (a pseudonym, a fifth grader, 11 yr.) was referred to a school psychologist because John did not have any control over his bowels and had involuntary stools frequently in school. The referral further stated that they did not know whether this condition should be diagnosed as encopresis or whether there was an organic basis for it. The medical opinion favored an emotional problem, which was supported by the school psychologist who described John as of superior intelligence and significantly above grade level in reading and spelling and at grade level in arithmetic.

The mother said John had never been toilet trained and that he did not know when to go to the bathroom. John's mother was separated from her husband, contemplating divorce, and there were many personal and emotional problems in the home. John was seen in play therapy four times

---

*Reprinted with permission of author and publisher: Pedrini, B. C. and Pedrini, D. T. Reinforcement procedures in the control of encopresis: a case study, *Psychological Reports*, 1971, **28**, 937–938.

[1]The first author was the behavior therapist, the co-author served as advisor.

and then was abruptly terminated by the mother. His problems at school continued. The next year, John was again referred to a school psychologist, a behavior therapist. Referral was based on John's inability to control his bowels. Conferences were held by the behavior therapist and John's teachers who had agreed to cooperate—they recorded John's behavior (i.e., whether or not he had controlled his bowels during each period of the day) for three weeks (when unsure of John's behavior they recorded a question mark).

In the first week (5 school days), teachers reported John defecated in class on three occasions. In the second week (5 school days), he defecated on four occasions and possibly one other. In the third week (3 school days), he defecated on one occasion. The teacher indicated that these 3 wk. seemed typical.

During the period teachers were recording John's behavior in class, a conference was held with John's mother. She obviously had many problems—acted as though men were a necessary evil, had been divorced, and blamed most of John's problems on her husband. Given the opportunity she would have focused on her problems rather than John's. However, she did state that she was willing to help John. She said that John had never really learned to control his bowels, though various techniques and treatments were tried. She stated that the only thing John enjoyed was babysitting for money and reading. It was decided John could be reinforced with book coupons which could be used to earn books. After a certain number of book coupons were obtained, his mother would buy him a book of his choice. If he wanted to, John could order the books, at a discount price, through the school. John would receive one coupon after each class period during which he had controlled himself. He could receive as many as eight coupons in one day (he had 8 classes per day). His mother set the price limit of the books John could buy at $5.00.

It was decided that he would need the following number of coupons to obtain books: 1st book, 40 coupons; 2nd book, 55 coupons; 3rd book, 75 coupons; 4th book, 90 coupons; and 5th book, 110 coupons.

The behavior therapist then spoke to John for the first time. John said that his mother had told him a little bit about what we planned to do. He seemed pleased with the plan and quickly determined how many days it would take to get his first book. He said that he would record the times he got a coupon. According to Lindsley,[2] charting or logging is a great value in and of itself and often times all that is needed.

---

[2]O. R. Lindsley, Singing a little data song. (Unpublished paper, Special Education Research, Children's Rehabilitation Unit, Univer. of Kansas Medical Center, 1968.)

In the fourth week (5 school days), John started receiving coupons according to plan. During the fourth week, John did not defecate in class and had earned one book and by the sixth week another book. His teachers said that he seemed to have no difficulty. One teacher commented, "The kids are even starting to talk to him." In the fifth week (5 school days), John may have had an accident. The teachers were unsure, but his mother said it was obvious when he got home. His teachers did say that he seemed overly excited on that day. It is possible that he soiled himself going home or arriving at home. For the sixth, seventh, eighth, ninth, tenth, and eleventh weeks he did not defecate in class. Everyone was definite about this.

The school year was then over. John still seemed very excited about the plan. He said his mother was thinking of keeping it up during the summer. She said John still had problems at home but that he had improved slightly. It was decided that she should use techniques other than book coupons so that if there were any problems at home, they were less likely to be carried over to school. She said she was very pleased with John's progress in school. John's teachers felt that he was now being accepted by his school peers.

In the following school year, when John was a sixth grader, he had only one accident over 7 mo. of school; it occurred at the beginning of the school year. He had eaten corn during lunch and thought that he might have defecated in the physical education class because of it. Following that incident, John would cut physical education classes after being served corn for lunch. This may be an illustration of "superstitious behavior" as understood by Skinner (1948). During this seven-month period, John was not reinforced with book coupons or any specific reinforcer. He had apparently internalized the control.

REFERENCES

Gelber, H. and Meyer, V. Behavior therapy and encopresis: the complexities involved in treatment. *Behaviour Research and Therapy*, 1965, **2**, 227–231.

Keehn, J. D. Brief case-report: the reinforcement therapy of incontinence. *Behaviour Research and Therapy*, 1965, **2**, 239.

Neale, D. H. Behavior therapy and encopresis in children. *Behaviour Research and Therapy*, 1963, **1**, 139–150.

Skinner, B. F. Superstition in the pigeon. *Journal of Experimental Psychology*, 1948, **38**, 168–172.

CHAPTER 4

The Cardiovascular System: Arrhythmias and Elevated Blood Pressure

Since the pioneering work of Neal Miller and his associates (Miller, 1969), several published articles have described the control of cardiovascular processes by operant conditioning methods. As suggested by the papers in the present chapter, this area of research may have important implications for treating some cardiovascular symptoms, such as abnormalities in heart rhythm and elevated blood pressure. In addition, however, the results of cardiac conditioning studies question the accuracy of certain traditional interpretations of behavior, and for this reason they deserve special attention as well.

One of the major assumptions being challenged is that responses mediated by the autonomic nervous system are only susceptible to modification by respondent conditioning (Kimble, 1961). Because autonomic behavior does not produce discriminable consequences on the external environment, it was thought to be impossible to control by operant methods. In line with this viewpoint, operant conditioning was believed to be effective only for voluntary skeletal responses governed by the central nervous system. The controversy surrounding the mechanisms of autonomic learning has yet to be resolved, and requires continued research to control for such factors as placebo effects and instructional set (Blanchard & Young, 1973; Katkin & Murray, 1968; Schwartz, 1973). Nevertheless, an impressive body of evidence has accumulated to suggest that many autonomic behaviors are capable of voluntary regulation by reinforcement under the proper training conditions.

The critical feature of human studies on cardiac control, as well as other forms of autonomic learning, is to provide the subject with immediate information about changes in internal processes that he would ordinarily not perceive (Shapiro & Schwartz, 1972). This information about biological function may be conveyed by electronic monitoring devices and has come to be known as *biofeedback.* In the learning situation, biofeedback information is usually combined with some form of contingent reinforcement when desired changes in internal behavior are produced. Following a period of biofeedback (and reinforcement) training, response measures are compared against previously obtained baselines to determine whether stable changes in internal processes have occurred.

Most of the published articles on cardiac conditioning have dealt with heart rate changes in animals or normal human subjects (Blanchard & Young, 1973; Miller & DiCara, 1967; Schwartz, 1972). Recently, however, a few investigators have moved beyond analogue research to produce encouraging results in some patients suffering from serious cardiac disorders, such as hypertension, tachycardias, and premature ventricular contractions. In the present chapter, three of these studies are described. As an adjunct to current medical treatments, the application of behavior principles may eventually have major clinical usefulness, especially when drugs are contraindicated or for patients who have not responded favorably to medication regimens. Teaching patients how to voluntarily control potentially serious cardiac symptoms is one of the more intriguing possibilities suggested by this exciting area of research.

Scott *et al.* (Article 14) begin this chapter with a description of cardiac control by operant reinforcement in six human subjects. For four of the subjects, who were normal with respect to cardiovascular function, increases in heart rate above preset criterion levels were reinforced with television viewing in one case, and with money in the others. The effect of contingent reinforcement was to accelerate heart rate in all subjects. The remaining two subjects had lengthy histories of tachycardia and anxiety. For these patients training was directed at decelerating heart rate to within normal limits. Except for some minor modifications, the conditioning procedure was similar to that used for the normal subjects. Training resulted in decreased heart rate from 89 and 96 beats per minute (BPM) at baseline to 72 and 82 BPM, respectively, on the final six experimental trials. In both cases heart rate eventually stabilized below pathological levels. Anecdotal data suggested that other signs of clinical improvement accompanied the reductions in tachycardia, among them decreases in anxiety and a return to gainful employment. There are several notable features of this well-designed research. One is the controlled investigation of multiple variables on cardiac function. The effects of noncontingent and contingent reinforcement, as well as informing the subjects of the nature of the response to be reinforced are all carefully documented. Another feature is the shifting from a constant criterion of reinforcement, which remained unchanged throughout each experimental trial, to a variable criterion which could be changed on a minute-to-minute basis depending on the subject's performance. The latter allowed for a higher density of reinforcement to occur, produced more efficient shaping of heart rate, and generally resulted in substantial increases in the degree of cardiac control achieved by the subjects. The third feature is most significant from a clinical standpoint for it concerns the resistance to extinction of cardiac changes shown by the subjects whose heart rates were abnormally high. Why heart rate in these subjects did not return to earlier baseline levels is an intriguing question for future research.

Weiss and Engel (Article 15) describe the treatment of eight patients with documented histories of premature ventricular contractions (PVCs) who were treated by operant conditioning methods. These patients were alternately prompted to accelerate and decelerate their heart rate, and then to maintain it within a preset range of BPM that was established according to individual patient requirements. A visual feedback apparatus was used to signal the patients when desired heart rate activity was occurring. No other form of external reinforcement was applied. A final step of the training consisted of fading the external feedback source in order to bring cardiac changes under the control of internal interoceptive or cognitive stimuli. The results showed that all of the patients acquired some degree of voluntary control over heart rate activity. More important, concurrent reductions in PVCs were obtained in five of the patients. These cardiac changes not only generalized outside of the original training environment, but were maintained during followup periods of up to 21 months. Weiss and Engel conclude their paper by discussing several variables that appear to be related to successful PVC control.

In the final selection, Benson *et al.* (Article 16) describe a conditioning procedure, conceptually similar to both Scott *et al.* and Weiss and Engel's, that was used to reduce elevated systolic blood pressure in a group of seven hypertensive patients. An external feedback stimulus and monetary rewards were made contingent on reduction in systolic pressure below criterion levels. Medication regimens were unaltered during the course of the study. Although the procedure was not uniformly successful, a fact which may be related to underlying biological constraints (Schwartz, 1973), clinically significant decreases in blood pressure were obtained in five of the seven patients ranging from 16 to 34 mm Hg. Since neither the generalizability nor persistence of blood pressure changes were assessed, the therapeutic usefulness of the procedure remains questionable. Nevertheless, the results appear promising.

Points of key importance in this chapter include:

1. Specific cardiovascular processes such as heart rate and blood pressure can be modified by operant conditioning techniques. In some studies clinically significant improvements in cardiac patients have been achieved through biofeedback and reinforcement operations.
2. Although this area of research is just beginning, much of the technological groundwork has been laid and preliminary results warrant at least cautious optimism that conditioning procedures may be used as an adjunct, or in some instances even be an alternative to, current pharmacological therapy.
3. Additional experimental research is needed to determine the replicability, generalizability, and stability of cardiac changes produced by operant conditioning, as well as to better understand the mechanisms of autonomic learning in general. Without this information the practical significance of conditioning therapies will remain unknown.

REFERENCES

Blanchard, E. and Young, B. Self-control of cardiac functioning: A promise as yet unfulfilled. *Psychological Bulletin*, 1973, **79**, 145–163.

Katkin, E. and Murray, N. Instrumental conditioning of autonomically mediated behavior: Theoretical and methodological issues. *Psychological Bulletin*, 1968, **70**, 52–68.

Kimble, G. *Hilgard and Marguis' Conditioning and Learning.* New York: Appleton-Century-Crofts, 1961.

Miller, N. Learning of visceral and glandular responses. *Science,* 1969, **163**, 434–445.

Miller, N. and DiCara, L. Instrumental learning of heart rate changes in curarized rats: Shaping and specificity to discriminative stimulus. *Journal of Comparative & Physiological Psychology,* 1967, **63**, 12–19.

Schwartz, G. Biofeedback as therapy: Some theoretical and practical issues. *American Psychologist,* 1973, **28**, 666–673.

Schwartz, G. Voluntary control of human cardiovascular integration and differentiation through feedback and reward. *Science,* 1972, **175**, 90–93.

Shapiro, D. and Schwartz, G. Biofeedback and visceral learning: Clinical applications. *Seminars in Psychiatry,* 1972, **4**, 171–183.

ARTICLE 14

A Shaping Procedure for Heart-Rate Control in Chronic Tachycardia[*][1]

ROBERT W. SCOTT, EDWARD B. BLANCHARD,
EILEEN D. EDMUNSON, and LARRY D. YOUNG

University of Mississippi Medical Center

Abstract: Six experiments of single-subject design are presented in which an operant conditioning paradigm, utilizing a variable criterion shaping procedure with commercial television programs or money as reinforcement, was employed to accelerate or decelerate heart rate (HR). In the four analogue experiments in which the HR of normal Ss was accelerated, changes of 16 to 35 BPM above a stable baseline were obtained. In the two clinical experiments, involving patients with chronic tachycardia and anxiety, decelerations of HR to the normal range were obtained and other clinical improvements noted. In all cases these changes in HR were maintained over at least three successive trials (days). The results are discussed in terms of the applicability of this shaping procedure to the treatment of chronic tachycardia.

Although the fact that human heart rate (HR) can be changed through operant conditioning and/or biofeedback procedures is well established, for the most part the magnitude of change obtained has been relatively small, in the range of 1 to 6 beats per minute (BPM); the duration of the trial relatively short, usually about 1 min.; the number of training sessions few, in the range of 1 to 5; and the actual clinical application of the procedures non-existent (Blanchard & Young, 1973).

---

*Reprinted with permission of author and publisher: Scott, R. W., Blanchard, E. B., Edmunson, E. D., and Young, L. D. A shaping procedure for heart-rate control in chronic tachycardia, *Perceptual and Motor Skills*, 1973, **37**, 327–338.

[1]The authors wish to express their thanks to W. Stewart Agras for his helpful criticism of earlier versions of this manuscript. Preparation of the manuscript was supported in part by Grant No. 1R01HL149006-01 from the National Heart and Lung Institute, Robert W. Scott, Principal Investigator. Requests for reprints should be addressed to Dr. Robert W. Scott, Psychiatry Department, University of Mississippi Medical Center, 2500 N. State, Jackson, Mississippi 39216.

To be of use in treating patients with tachycardia (abnormally high HR) relatively large scale changes in HR which are maintained over both relatively long experimental trials, and more important, over several experimental sessions, or days, are necessary. In a previous report (Scott, Peters, Gillespie, Blanchard, Edmunson, & Young, 1973, a shaping procedure to obtain large scale stable changes in HR was described. That procedure called for raising or lowering S's HR by requiring S to meet a criterion HR for reinforcement. An apparent weakness in that procedure was that the criterion remained constant throughout the experimental trial and was adjusted only after S had met or exceeded the criterion on three consecutive experimental trials. In this initial procedure it was observed that Ss might initially contact the contingency early in the experimental trial but then move away from it later in the trial. Such a procedure tended to minimize the amount of reinforcement obtained by S and hence lessened the efficiency of the procedure.

The present paper reports experiments aimed at improving the former technique by substituting a more flexible shaping procedure.

STUDY 1

Overview

All of the experiments here are of the single-subject reversal, or ABA design. Basic to this design is the establishment of a stable baseline level of the target behavior (A), introduction of an experimental manipulation (B), and removal of the experimental manipulation and a return to baseline conditions (A). In some experiments several experimental manipulations might be introduced sequentially or in an additive fashion.

Two basic kinds of experiments are presented: (1) analogue experiments in which the HR of normal volunteers is accelerated and (2) clinical experiments in which the HR of patients with tachycardia is decelerated. The authors' strategy has been to try a procedure first in an analogue experiment. If it proves successful, the next step has been to attempt the procedure with a clinical case. This last point needs to be stressed because analogue experiments only have value if factors discovered in them can be shown to have relevance for a true clinical population.

In the first study three experiments are presented; in two, Ss' HR was accelerated and in the other, a clinical case, S's HR was slowed. In both experiments a new variable criterion shaping procedure was introduced after a number of trials with the original constant criterion procedure (Scott *et al.*, 1973).

Method

Subjects *S*s for the first two experiments were college women, ages 20 and 18 yr., respectively. Both were reported to be in good health, on no medications, and participated as paid volunteers.

The third *S* was a 46-yr.-old male referred by the Cardiology Department; he had a 20-yr. history of tachycardia and had not been able to work for 14 mo. prior to the beginning of the experiment. He was receiving partial Social Security disability benefits because of his condition.

Apparatus *S* was comfortably seated in a reclining chair in an air conditioned, sound-attenuated room. Facing him were a television set and a pair of running time meters. Access to the video portion of ongoing commercial television programs served as the reinforcer for the entire first experiment and part of Exp. 2. The running time meters accumulated seconds of correct and incorrect response, i.e., *S*'s HR at, or beyond, the criterion HR. Both S_2 and S_3 received 1¢ per 10 sec. of correct response.

S's HR was recorded and counted electronically. Through a series of electronic circuits it was possible to make automatic beat-to-beat decisions regarding whether *S* was to receive reinforcement.

Procedure Several aspects of the procedure were common to all experiments. Each experimental session lasted 40 min. and consisted of two 20-min. segments. The first was an "adaptation" period during which *S* sat quietly with the television set off. The second 20 min. was the "experimental" trial during which the various manipulations described below were carried out.

Each *S* was initially informed that he was participating in a research program which involved the monitoring of various aspects of his internal behavior. He was also told that the response being monitored was not related to respiration or to muscle tension and that he was therefore to relax and breathe normally during all experimental trials. As will be indicated later, some *S*s were informed of the nature of the response as part of the particular experiment in which they participated.

Two basic procedures were used to alter *S*'s HR in the desired direction. The first, described in more detail by Scott *et al.* (1973), consisted of establishing for the experimental trial a constant criterion (CC) HR which S had to achieve in order to receive reinforcement.

The second experimental procedure involved the use of a variable criterion (VC), changed on a minute-to-minute basis according to an empirically derived set of rules, which S had to achieve in order to receive reinforcement. The basic idea of this procedure was to maximize S's contact with the contingency to provide more precision and efficiency in shaping S's HR. The exact decision rules are presented in Table 14.1.

EXPERIMENT 1

Procedure

The first three conditions of this experiment are the same as reported by Scott *et al.* (1973). Initially, trials consisted of 20-min. periods during which S_1 continued to sit comfortably in the subject chamber (Baseline) until her HR showed stability. Stability was defined as three consecutive trials in which HR evidenced less than 10% variability, that is, the HR value for any trial was within $\pm 5\%$ of the mean HR for three consecutive trials. In the next condition, the reinforcer, access to the video portion of ongoing commercial television programs (the audio portion was available non-contingently throughout the experiment) was delivered to S non-contingently (NCTV). In the third condition the video portion of the television program was made contingent upon HR acceleration using the constant criterion shaping procedure (CC + CTV). In the next condition, the procedure was identical to the preceding condition except that S_1, who had been ignorant of the response under study to this point, was informed (I) of the nature of the response. In the next condition, the variable criterion shaping procedure was introduced (VC + CTV). In the final condition, the experimental analysis was completed by giving S_1 access to the reinforcer on a non-contingent basis (NCTV).

The number of trials in any condition was dependent upon S_1's performance. However, no condition was terminated until her HR achieved stability.

Results

For all of the experiments reported in this paper, the average HR for the 20-min. experimental trials is presented in two-day blocks. In

Table 14.1. Variable Criterion Shaping Procedure.

Relative to the criterion on trial N if:	The criterion for trial $N+1$ is:	
	Acceleration	Deceleration
HR surpasses by 4 or more bpm	Raised to 2 bpm below behavior	Lowered to 2 bpm above behavior
HR surpasses by 2 or 3 bpm	Raised to 1 bpm below behavior	Lowered to 1 bpm above behavior
HR equals the criterion or surpasses the criterion by 1 bpm	Held 1 min. If HR remains unchanged, raised 1 bpm on trial $N+2$	Held 1 min. If HR remains unchanged, lowered 1 bpm on trial $N+2$
HR fails by 1 bpm	Held indefinitely	Held indefinitely
HR fails by 2 or 3 bpm	Held 1 min. If HR remains unchanged, lowered to 1 bpm above behavior on trial $N+2$	Held 1 min. If HR remains unchanged, raised to 1 bpm below behavior on trial $N+2$
HR fails by 4 or more bpm	Lowered to 2 bpm above behavior	Raised to 2 bpm below behavior

conditions for which there were only three trials, the two points plotted represent the average of Trials 1 and 2 and of Trials 2 and 3.

S_1's baseline HR was 75 BPM. The presentation in Condition 2 of non-contingent reinforcement had no effect. The implementation in Condition 3 of the contingency and constant criterion shaping procedure led to an initial increase of about 5 BPM. However, 16 trials in this condition resulted in little over-all increase. Informing S of the nature of the response in Condition 4 had no effect. The introduction of the variable criterion shaping procedure resulted in an increase in HR of 16 BPM which was maintained over the final three trials. Mean HR for the final trials was 91 BPM. In the last condition (non-contingent television) S's HR returned to its baseline level.

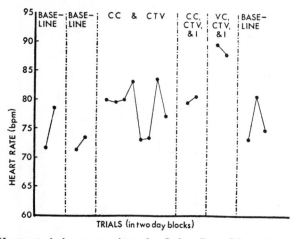

Fig. 14.1. Heart rate in beats per minute for S_1 for all conditions of the experiment.

EXPERIMENT 2

Procedure

This experiment serves as a replication of Exp. 1 with some methodological changes. The first condition of this experiment was the same as the second condition of Exp. 1, namely, baseline during which the initial reinforcer, access to the video portion of ongoing commercial television programs was available non-contingently. In addition to establishing a baseline HR, this condition also served as a control for the effect on HR of S's focusing her attention. It was felt that an adequate control in baseline would require a visual stimulus to which *S* attended. Commercial television programs were used since, *a priori*, it seemed that *S* would attend to this meaningful material more readily than to some other stimulus complex such as random movement of the meters. This condition was used as a baseline procedure for all of the other experiments reported in this paper.

In the second condition the video portion of the television program was made contingent upon S_2's emitting an accelerated HR using the constant criterion shaping procedure (CC + CTV). In the next condition the reinforcer was changed from television to money. The fourth condition was a return to baseline conditions of non-contingent access to television. In the fifth condition the variable criterion shaping procedure was employed with money as the reinforcer (VC + Money). In the final condition the experimental analysis was completed by again returning to baseline conditions.

One additional methodological change was that S_2 was informed of the nature of the response from the very beginning.

Results

S_2's baseline HR was 70 BPM. The presentation in Condition 2 of contingent reinforcement in the form of access to commercial television fare had no effect in 10 trials.

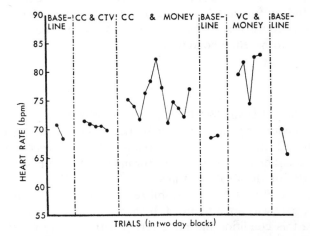

Fig. 14.2. Heart rate in beats per minute for S_2 for all conditions of the experiment.

With the change in reinforcement to money, 24 trials led to both increased variability and an over-all increase of about 5 BPM. Her HR in the second baseline condition was 68 BPM. Nine trials on the variable criterion shaping procedure led to a 16 BPM increase which was stably maintained. In the last condition S_2's HR returned to its baseline level.

EXPERIMENT 3

Encouraged by the results of our analogue experiments, a clinical experiment was conducted.

Procedure

There were several slight methodological changes employed with this experiment that differ from those used with the preceding one. Principal among these was that S_3's HR was being decelerated. Since S_3 was a clinical case and was taking part in the experiment as a form of treatment, he was informed of the response being conditioned. Also, on the basis of Exp. 2, money was used as the reinforcer from the very beginning rather than access to television.

Thus Condition 1 consisted of baseline trials during which non-contingent television was presented. In Condition 2 the attempt was made to decelerate S's HR using the constant criterion shaping procedure with money as the reinforcer (CC + Money). In the third condition, the variable criterion procedure was introduced (VC + Money). The final condition was a return to baseline condition.

Results

S_3's baseline HR was 89 BPM. Introduction of the constant criterion shaping procedure in Condition 2 for 26 trials led to essentially no change. In Condition 3, 18 trials on the variable criterion procedure led to a dramatic reduction of S_3's HR to the normal range, a drop of 17 BPM. His average HR for the final six trials was 72 BPM. During the return to baseline in Condition 4, S_3's HR stabilized at 77 BPM. For clinical reasons further reversal was not attempted. It should be noted, however, that his HR during this condition did not overlap with his rate for the final six trials of Condition 3.

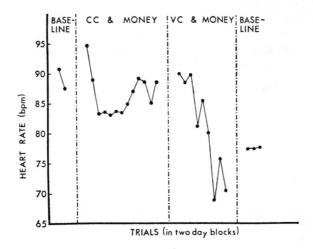

Fig. 14.3. Heart rate in beats per minute for S_3 for all conditions of the experiment.

DISCUSSION

These three experiments pointed out the obvious advantages of the variable criterion shaping procedure for changing HR over the initial constant criterion shaping procedure. Use of this procedure consistently led to changes in mean HR of 16 BPM or more for an entire 20-min. trial. Moreover, the changes were maintained over several consecutive sessions, demonstrating a stability of change not previously reported.

Although, in terms of absolute magnitude of change, the results for accelerating HR are not quite comparable to the best previously reported results (Headrick, Feather, & Wells, 1971; Stephens, Harris, & Brady, 1972); they are equivalent or better in terms of duration of trial, and they far surpass these reports in terms of stability of change coming off of a stable baseline. The results for decelerating HR surpass anything previously reported in terms of both absolute magnitude and stability of change.

Clinical Changes

One final observation from our data is worth noting. In Ss whose HR was decelerated in both this study (S_3) and in a previous study (Scott *et al.*, 1973), there were pre-experimental complaints of being "anxious, tense or nervous." There was a decrease in these verbalizations concurrent with the deceleration of HR. Furthermore, there were other anecdotal data relating to clinical improvement: S_3, whose verbal report of feeling less anxious coincided with the middle of the variable criterion shaping procedure (Condition 3), actively sought and obtained employment toward the end of treatment. This was his first gainful employment in over 16 mo. and came in spite of his already receiving Social Security disability benefits. An 18-mo. follow-up revealed him still to be regularly employed. Moreover, he spontaneously decreased his dosage of a minor tranquilizer from 40 mg per day, which he had been taking for 14 mo., to less than 10 mg per day. For the clinical S in the earlier study there were reports from the ward of improved behavior and a decrease in tricophilic behavior which had previously been observed at a high rate.

Since the variable criterion procedure was apparently more generally effective, the constant criterion procedure was abandoned and the variable criterion procedure introduced from the beginning in the next series of experiments.

STUDY 2

Method

Subjects Ss for the first two experiments (analogue) of this study were a 20-yr.-old female student (S_4) and a 22-yr.-old male student (S_5), respectively. Both were reported to be in good health and on no medication; they participated as paid volunteers. S for the third experiment (clinical) (S_6), was a 50-yr.-old male patient on the Psychiatry Department Inpatient unit with a diagnosis of anxiety neurosis. This patient had a 26-yr. history of various complaints, including tachycardia, and had not been gainfully employed for 27 mo. prior to the experiment because of tachycardia and feelings of "anxiety and weakness." S_6 was on no medication during the experiment.

Apparatus   The same apparatus used in Study 1 was used in all of these experiments.

Procedure   In all three experiments of Study 2, many of the same basic procedures of Study 1 were followed with regards to length of trials and instructions to Ss. The same experimental procedure was followed in each experiment: Condition 1 was a baseline condition during which non-contingent television was presented for the experimental trial. In

Condition 2, money was used as the reinforcer with the variable criterion shaping procedure. Condition 3 represented a return to baseline conditions.

In both Exp. 4 and Exp. 5, an exact replication of Exp. 4, HR was being accelerated. Neither S_4 nor S_5 was informed of the nature of the response being conditioned.

Results

S_4's baseline HR was 57 BPM. In six trials during Condition 2, the variable criterion procedure resulted in a rise of 30 BPM to an average of 87 BPM for the final three trials. In the reversal (Condition 3) nine trials were necessary for S to return to her resting HR and show stability.

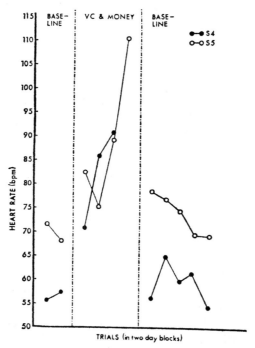

Fig. 14.4. Heart rate in beats per minute for S_4 and S_5 for all conditions of the experiment.

S_4's baseline HR was 68 BPM. Eight trials with the variable criterion shaping procedure led to an increase of over 35 BPM with an average HR for the final 3 trials of 106 BPM. Nine trials were necessary for S's HR to return to a stable level of 69 BPM.

EXPERIMENT 6

The conditions of this experiment with a clinical case were the same as those with S_4 and S_5 with two important exceptions: during the second condition S_6's HR was decelerated, and he was informed of the nature of the response from the very beginning.

Results

The clinical S's (S_6) baseline HR was 96 BPM. Nineteen trials with the shaping procedure led to a decrease of 14 BPM. In the return to baseline conditions, S_6's HR did not return to its high level. Instead over 8 trials, it remained decelerated, stabilizing at approximately 78 BPM. This failure of a decelerated HR to return to its pathologically high baseline level has been observed previously (Exp. 3 and also Scott *et al.*, 1973).

The results of Exp. 6 (S_6), the clinical case, are comparable to our previous clinical results with this procedure. Moreover, there were concomitant improvements in S_6 in terms of his reporting that he felt less anxious and stronger and that he was able to perform more household chores without tiring rapidly.

DISCUSSION

These three experiments provide additional evidence for the potency of the variable-criterion procedure in producing large magnitude changes in HR for both experimental and clinical Ss. In relation to the only chronic studies that report large magnitude changes in HR (Headrick *et al.*, 1971; Stephens *et al.*, 1972) the data from Exps. 4 and 5 are comparable or superior in terms of magnitude of HR acceleration demonstrated. Both previous reports include only within session changes with the additional minor weaknesses of 1-min. trial length (Headrick *et al.*, 1971) and no attempt to establish a stable baseline HR (Stephens *et al.*, 1972). In contrast, the present investigation found changes in absolute HR for all

*S*s that were maintained over successive days and came after establishing a stable baseline HR.

The magnitude of deceleration of HR for S_3 and S_6 exceeds the 5 BPM decreases reported by Stephens *et al.* (1972) and are further strengthened in that they also represent changes for 20-min. trials which are maintained over days. A particularly gratifying aspect of this research is that analogue studies can be justified on more than theoretical bases in that the results are replicable in clinical experiments.

An exciting clinical aspect of our work is the apparent resistance of *S*'s HR, once decelerated, to return to its previous high, pathological level. In any earlier study (Scott *et al.*, 1973) involving the deceleration of HR in a tachycardia patient, there was little acceleration of HR during an extinction phase. In fact, a large number of trials were necessary to accelerate that *S*'s HR back to his baseline level. For S_3, of the present study, this same resistance to extinction of a decelerated HR was noted. Since this was a clinical case, no attempt was made to obtain a return to his elevated baseline level. This finding was replicated in a second clinical case (S_6).

The resistance of a decelerated HR to extinction is in sharp contrast to our results in which HR has been accelerated. In these latter cases, HR readily returns to baseline level once the extinction procedure is instituted. Further replication of the present findings will have to be obtained before any final conclusion can be drawn. However, this

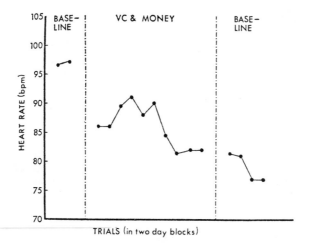

Fig. 14.5. Heart rate in beats per minute for S_6 for all conditions of the experiment.

apparent resistance to extinction of a HR decelerated to the normal range does have the clinical implication that a high degree of durability may be available from this procedure.

In contrast to the verbal reports of our patients of feeling less tense and anxious as HR is decelerated is our finding with S_4: during the final experimental trials when her HR was 94 BPM, she reported feeling tense and anxious. Headrick *et al.* (1971) reported that their S who achieved large increases in magnitude of HR also complained of feeling anxious toward the end of the experiment. These results are not consistent, however, since S_5 made no such statements.

REFERENCES

Blanchard, E. B. and Young, L. D. Self-control of cardiac functioning: a promise as yet unfulfilled. *Psychol. Bull.*, 1973, **79**, 145–163.

Headrick, M. W., Feather, B. W., and Wells, D. T. Unidirectional and large magnitude heart rate changes with augmented sensory feedback. *Psychophysiol.*, 1971, **85**, 132–142.

Scott, R. W., Peters, R. D., Gillespie, W. J., Blanchard, E. B., Edmunson, E. D., and Young, L. D. The use of shaping and reinforcement in the operant acceleration and deceleration of heart rate. *Behav. Res. & Therapy*, 1973, **11**, 179–186.

Stephens, J. J., Harris, A. H., and Brady, J. V. Large magnitude heart-rate changes in subjects instructed to change their heart rates and given exteroceptive feedback. *Psychophysiol.*, 1972, **93**, 283–285.

ARTICLE 15

Operant Conditioning of Heart Rate in Patients with Premature Ventricular Contractions*

THEODORE WEISS, MD† and BERNARD T. ENGEL, PhD

Abstract: Operant conditioning of heart rate (HR) was carried out in 8 patients with premature ventricular contractions (PVCs). All of the patients showed some degree of HR control. Five of these patients showed a decrease in PVCs in association with the learning of HR control. Four patients have shown persistence of a low PVC frequency after study, the longest followup being 21 months. Pharmacologic studies suggested that decreased PVC frequency was mediated by diminished sympathetic tone in 1 patient and increased vagal tone in another.

These findings suggest that some aspects of cardiac ventricular function can be brought under voluntary control. Once such control has been acquired, it can mediate clinically significant changes in cardiac function.

For many years, and in a multiplicity of experimental situations, the technics of operant conditioning have been employed to modify and control somatic behavior—i.e., actions involving the use of skeletal muscle[1]. In the last decade, a large volume of additional research has accumulated, indicating that visceral and other involuntary responses also

From the Section of Physiological Psychology, Laboratory of Behavioral Sciences, Gerontology Research Center, National Institute of Child Health and Human Development and Baltimore City Hospitals.

The authors would like to thank Drs. Gustav C. Voigt and Kenneth M. Lewis for permitting them to draw patients from the Clinic, and for regular consultation on the patients; Drs. Lewis A. Kolodny and Jay J. Platt for referring Patients 6 and 7, respectively; Mr. Reginald E. Quilter for assisting in the development and maintenance of various instruments used in this study; and Mr. Richard H. Mathias for assisting in the analysis of the ward telemetry data.

Address for reprint requests: Bernard T. Engel, PhD, Baltimore City Hospitals, Baltimore, Md 21224.

*Reprinted from *Psychosomatic Medicine*, Vol. 33, No. 4 (July–August 1971), 301–321. With permission from American Psychosomatic Society, Inc. and Theodore Weiss.

†Dr. Weiss is now at the Department of Psychiatry, University of Pennsylvania.

are amenable to operant control[2, 3]. Response systems studied have included heart rate[4–7], blood pressure[8, 9], rate of urine formation[10], regional blood flow[11], vasoconstriction[12], and galvanic skin potential[13–15].

In addition to reports of operant conditioning of visceral responses in normal man and in animals, there are three studies in which patients with pathologic visceral responses showed improvement after operant training. Engel and Melmon[16] conditioned more regular cardiac rhythms in patients with several kinds of cardiac arrhythmias, and White and Taylor[17] and Lang and Melamed[18] each conditioned patients to stop or decrease ruminative vomiting.

Several studies have shown the effects of neural impulses on premature ventricular contractions (PVCs)[19]. Hypothalamic lesions and stimulation[20–22], afferent vagal stimulation[20, 23], efferent cardiac sympathetic nerve impulses[20, 24], and cardiac sympathectomy[25] all have been shown to produce dramatic changes in PVC frequency. Also, both increases and decreases in PVC frequency have been reported using classic conditioning technics[26, 27].

Because of these considerations, we undertook a study of patients with PVCs to see if operant conditioning could produce clinically significant control of this arrhythmia.

MATERIALS AND METHODS

Patients

Selection   Eight patients with PVCs were obtained from Baltimore City Hospitals, and from referrals by private physicians.

Hospitalization Procedure   Patients were hospitalized for the duration of the study and given passes each weekend. After admission, they were given a complete physical examination and a standard battery of laboratory tests including a 12 lead EKG and PA and lateral chest X-rays.

Experimental Design

Laboratory   All formal cardiac training took place in the laboratory although each patient was encouraged to practice his technics outside the laboratory as well.

While in the laboratory, the patient lay in a hospital bed in a sound-deadened room. At the foot of the bed was a vertical display of three differently colored light bulbs, an intercom and a meter.

The three lights provided the patient with feedback information about his cardiac function. The top light (green) and the bottom light (red) were cue lights. The middle light (yellow) was the reinforcer; it was on when the patient was producing the correct heart rate (HR) response. Our system enabled us to feed back this information to the patient on a beat-to-beat basis.

When the fast (green) cue light was on, a relative increase in HR would turn on the reinforcer light. When the slow (red) cue light was on, a relative decrease in HR would turn on the reinforcer light.

The meter accumulated time. Whenever the patient was performing correctly, the meter arm moved, and when he performed incorrectly, it stopped.

One to three 80-minute conditioning sessions were carried out daily. A typical session began with about 10 minutes for the attaching of EKG leads, and of a strain gauge around the lower chest to monitor breathing. Then, the patient lay quietly for 20 minutes more. During the last 10 minutes of this period, a baseline HR was obtained. The feedback lights were off throughout the baseline period. Two to three minutes were allowed for setting the trigger level for heart rate (HR) conditioning. The trigger level was the HR (e.g., in a speeding session) at or above which the reinforcer light would go on. Then the patient had either one 34-minute period during which the feedback lights were on, or two such periods of 17 minutes each, separated by a 10-minute rest period.

Because this was primarily a clinical study, the patient's responses at any stage of the study always dictated the procedure. In general, however, we followed a standard sequence for conditioning. During the initial or control session, the patient simply lay in bed in the laboratory for the prescribed time period. The feedback lights were never turned on. Next, HR speeding was taught for about 10 sessions, followed by HR slowing for about 10 sessions. For about 10 further sessions, a differential contingency was taught, in which the patient alternately had to increase and decrease his HR during periods of 1–4 minutes throughout the session. During these sessions, the green and red cue lights would come on alternately so that the patient would know whether to speed or to slow.

The last training contingency usually was a range situation in which the patient had to maintain his HR between preset upper and lower limits. Only the yellow light would be on when the HR was within this range.

When the rate was too fast, the yellow light would go off and the red light would go on, cueing the patient to slow down. When the rate was too slow, the green light would come on, cueing the patient to speed up. Because a premature beat caused the HR to go above range, and the compensatory pause caused the HR to go below range, this contingency also gave the patient prompt feedback every time he had a PVC.

In the range contingency, feedback was phased out gradually. Initially, the feedback was available for 1 minute and unavailable for the next. In later sessions, it was available for 1 minute and unavailable for 3; in the final sessions, it was on for 1 minute and off for 7. By this procedure, the patient was weaned from the light feedback and made to become aware of his PVCs through his own sensations.

Each patient was told in detail about the nature of the experiment, and he was allowed to inspect all his data throughout the study.

Ward   The patient's EKG was monitored three nights per week for 10 minutes out of every hour, using a telemetry apparatus.

Pharmacologic Studies   In 3 patients, studies were carried out with the use of some or all of the following autonomically active drugs—isoproterenol, propranolol, atropine, edrophonium, phenylephrine and phentolamine—administered intravenously. This was done in the laboratory after conditioning had been completed in order to elucidate the mechanism underlying HR and rhythm changes.

Followup   Clinical follow-up was done in the Baltimore City Hospitals Cardiac Clinic by Dr. Weiss, and by the referring physicians. The visits usually included an EKG with a 1–2 minute rhythm strip.

Apparatus

Laboratory   Variations in interbeat intervals were detected by a Beckman–Offner cardiotachometer and converted into electrical signals whose magnitudes were proportional to HR. The cardiotachometer output was also fed into a BRS Electronics Schmitt trigger, which was used to control the patient's feedback. The input to the Schmitt trigger was regulated by a zero suppression circuit on the amplifier to permit adjustment of the trigger point. In order to reduce the hysteresis in the Schmitt triggers, we grounded the emitters. An EKG from a precordial lead was recorded on a Beckman–Offner dynograph, and on magnetic tape using an Ampex SP 300 tape recorder.

Ward   The EKG signal from two chest electrodes was transmitted to a Parks model 220-1 converter and a telemetry receiver in an adjacent room, where the EKG was recorded on a tape recorder for subsequent analysis.

Analytic Procedures

Laboratory   All heart beats were counted automatically, and mean HRs were calculated from these data. PVCs were counted manually, all being counted when they were less frequent (under 10/min); and two to four 1-minute samples per 10 minutes being counted when they were more frequent.

Ward   Mean HR was determined by counting five to six 10-beat samples or five 30-second samples distributed across each 10-minute epoch. All PVCs were counted.

Pharmacologic Studies   Heart rate was counted either automatically or manually from a continuous EKG record. All PVCs were counted manually from the same record.

Clinical History and Followup   Heart rate and PVC frequency generally were determined from EKGs. Some data were derived from physical examinations.

RESULTS

The results will be presented on a patient-by-patient basis. However, since the findings do suggest some general principles, these will be presented as well. Each of the tables summarizes some of the major findings for each patient; however, specific references to these data will be made in the individual patient presentations.

Patient 1

LR, a 52-year-old Caucasian female, had a history of five myocardial infarctions (MI) in the 13 years prior to study. In association with the last two, 8 months and 5 months prior to study, she had PVCs. Maintenance quinidine therapy was required to suppress them after the last MI. She had been on digoxin for 1 year. Because of persistent diarrhea, the quinidine was discontinued 2 weeks prior to study, and PVCs increased in frequency from about one to two per minute to ten per minute.

Laboratory   Table 15.1 reports the proportion of sessions during which this patient performed successfully as measured by changes in heart rate or (during the range sessions) by percentage of time heart rate

Table 15.1. Ratios of Sessions During Which Each Patient Performed Successfully to Total Number of Sessions for Each Contingency.

Patient	Speed	Slow	Differential	CRF	Range 1:1 On	Range 1:1 Off	Range 1:3 On	Range 1:3 Off	Range 1:7 On	Range 1:7 Off
1 (Study 1)	4/9	4/6	7/9	5/6	—	—	—	—	—	—
1 (Study 2)	—	—	—	8/10	3/5	4/5	2/4	3/4	2/4	2/4
2	11/14	5/7	9/9	10/10	2/2	2/2	2/2	2/2	3/3	3/3
3	5/11	9/10	8/10	2/3*	4/4*	4/4*	3/4*	3/4*	5/5*	5/5*
4	6/10	5/10	10/10	5/5	11/11	11/11	7/7	7/7	—	—
5	1/10	9/9	12/14	15/15	—	—	—	—	—	—
6	1/6	5/11	—	13/16	—	—	—	—	—	—
7	2/8	7/10	—	2/4	—	—	—	—	—	—
8	—	16/18	—	15/15	—	—	—	—	—	—

During the range sessions, successful performance was defined as maintenance of HR within the correct range for more than 50% of the time.
   *Slow.

was within the correct range. Figure 15.1 shows the absolute heart rates and the frequencies of occurrence of PVCs during the training periods of each session.

During speeding training, the patient was able consistently to increase her HR from baseline in the afternoons but not in the mornings (when she also had few PVCs). In association with these successful performances, her PVCs increased to over 23/min (Fig. 15.2). The patient said that she thought about relaxing to speed her heart. During the slowing sessions, the patient was able consistently to decrease her HR from baseline, and PVCs were consistently less frequent—1–4/min (Fig. 15.2). She said that she concentrated on breathing maneuvers.

The patient differentiated consistently although she did not increase her HR with respect to her baseline rate during the speeding phases of the sessions. PVC incidence was quite low, under 1/min. At this

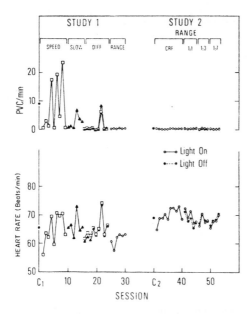

Fig. 15.1. Patient 1. PVC and HR levels during training; C1 and C2 are initial sessions during Studies 1 and 2, respectively, when no feedback was provided. Diff, differential conditioning; CRF, continuous feedback; 1:1 feedback on 1 minute, off 1 minute; 1:3 feedback on 1 minute, off 3 minutes, etc; □, speeding; ▲, slowing; ○, range.

time, the patient reported that her heart was functioning in a dysrhythmic fashion, when actually it was beating quite regularly. Her cardiograms were shown to her, and the differences between her rhythm strips during the speeding sessions and the present sessions were explained to her in detail. After her misconceptions had been clarified, she subsequently learned to recognize correctly the presence of PVCs.

During the range sessions, the patient consistently maintained her HR within the predetermined, 10-beat range (usually 60–70 beats/min) and PVCs were very infrequent, generally about 0.2/min.

After a 3-week recess, the patient's digoxin was stopped. The only discernible effect was an increase in baseline HR of about 5 beats/min to about 68. Twenty-three further range sessions were carried out. Gradually, the patient's feedback was decreased until it was present only 1 minute out of 8 by the last four sessions. PVCs remained very rare, about 0.1/min. She was discharged off all medications.

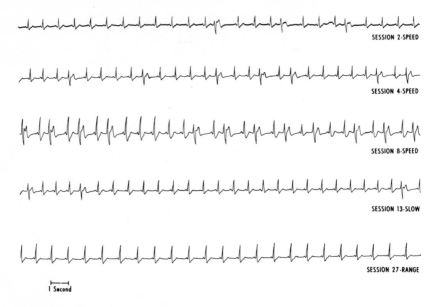

SESSION 2-SPEED

SESSION 4-SPEED

SESSION 8-SPEED

SESSION 13-SLOW

SESSION 27-RANGE

1 Second

Fig. 15.2. Patient 1. EKG rhythm strips during conditioning. These tracings show increase in PVCs during speeding conditioning, and decrease in PVCs during slowing and range conditioning.

Ward   Cardiac activity on the ward (Tables 15.2 and 15.3) paralleled events in the laboratory—i.e., her PVC incidence was highest during the period when she was speeding, and lower during the period when she was slowing.

Pharmacologic Studies   After the study, we tested the patient with pharmacologic agents. Atropine (1.0 mg) speeded her HR to 98 but did not produce PVCs. Isoproterenol (0.5–1.5 μg/min) speeded her heart rate and produced PVCs when the HR was above 90. The PVC configuration was the same as those she had spontaneously and during conditioning to speed her heart rate. This suggests that decreased sympathetic tone accounts for her diminished PVC incidence.

Followup   Twenty-one months of follow-up data have been obtained. PVCs remained quite low for 4 months, none being seen on five EKGs. Subsequently, they became more variable—commonly about 1/min, but as high as 6/min. The patient continues to be able accurately to identify PVCs. She says she rarely has significant numbers of them at home.

Table 15.2. Premature Ventricular Contraction Frequencies (PVCs/min) on Ward During Different Phases of Study.

Patient	Speeding	Slowing	Differential	Range or PVC avoidance
1	10.7	7.6	2.0	0.8
2	1.4	2.3	1.1	0.5
3	34.4	30.0	12.4	—
4	6.6	5.7	5.0	2.1
5	10.2	6.6	4.9	3.8
6	3.1	7.1	—	6.5
7	16.6	4.7	—	9.4
8	—	15.2	—	10.2

Table 15.3. Heart Rates (beats/min) on Ward During Different Phases of Study.

Patient	Speed	Slow	Differential	Range or PVC avoidance
1	66.9	67.5	66.8	67.0
2	51.7	50.9	50.7	50.4
3	82.9	83.4	69.7	—
4	61.0	57.1	56.0	53.2
5	77.3	75.0	71.5	74.0
6	62.5	79.2	—	66.8
7	74.4	76.1	—	72.7
8	—	83.4	—	88.7

When she does, she sits down and rests, and they stop within 20 minutes and do not return.

Patient 2

IW was a 62-year-old Caucasian male with a history of one MI 7 years prior to study. Thereafter, he had intermittent angina on exertion. PVCs were noted first in 1965; they were present on four of six EKGs taken thereafter, at times in a bigeminal rhythm. The average frequency was 14/min on EKG, and 3–5/min clinically. Two months prior to study, his angina worsened. An exercise tolerance test, performed to clarify the relationship between his angina and his PVCs produced bigeminy and multifocal PVCs in association with a heart rate of 95–100 beats/min. Modest exercise, raising HR from the usual level of about 55–80 beats/min, was associated with a temporary cessation of PVCs. When the HR slowed below 60, the PVCs returned. A subsequent therapeutic trial on diphenylhydantoin produced no significant change in the PVC frequency or in the patient's angina.

Laboratory   The patient performed successfully in all phases of the study as measured by changes in heart rate (Table 15.1). Figure 15.3 reports his absolute heart rates and PVC incidences during each training session.

In order to speed his heart, the patient said that he thought about "pushing or forcing" his heart to the left, and about its beating rapidly. In several of the speeding sessions, he had long periods of bigeminal rhythm, the PVCs having two configurations. One configuration was like that of the patient's usual PVCs, with the major vector in the same direction as that of the regular QRS. It will be referred to as the *usual type PVC*. The other configuration was seen in the laboratory only in association with HR speeding. Its major vector was in the opposite direction from that of the

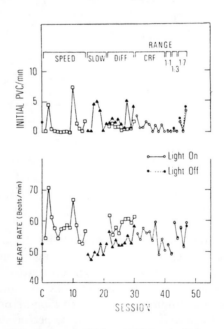

Fig. 15.3. Patient 2. PVC and HR levels during training.

normal QRS. It will be referred to as the *speeding type PVC*. Apart from the bigeminy, the patient's PVCs were infrequent during speeding, usually less than 1/min. The patient also had several prolonged episodes of bigeminy on the ward recordings of the night after speeding session 11, and on the following night. Both times, these occurred during waking hours when he said he would practice HR control. Many of the bigeminal PVCs on telemetry were of the speeding type. This type of PVC had not been seen on telemetry prior to then.

PVCs were more frequent during slowing, usually 1.5–5/min. They were of the usual type. No bigeminy was seen. He said that he concentrated on the "heart slowing down and stopping."

During the differentiation sessions, PVCs occurred more and more frequently in the slowing periods and less frequently in the speeding periods (Fig. 15.4). The PVCs were of the usual type. The patient said that he used the same technics for HR speeding and slowing described above. At comparable heart rates, PVCs were most frequent during HR slowing, least frequent during HR speeding and of intermediate frequency during the baseline periods. These findings suggest that the active processes involved in slowing and speeding the heart were more important in modulating PVC frequency than was the heart rate per se.

During range conditioning sessions, PVCs generally were infrequent, usually less than 1/min.

Ward   Telemetry data showed little variation in HR (Table 15.3). Apart from periods of bigeminy during the waking hours, PVCs were infrequent (Table 15.2). As in the laboratory, they were most frequent during the slowing contingency.

Pharmacologic Studies   Studies with autonomically active drugs were done in this patient. Isoproterenol (0.5–1.0 μg/min) led to a HR increase from the resting level of 52 beats/min to 93 beats/min, and to bigeminy and ventricular tachycardia. The PVCs were of the speeding type. The ventricular tachycardia stopped after the isoproterenol infusion was stopped. No antiarrhythmic agents were required. Atropine (1.0 mg) also speeded the HR to 86 beats/min and increased PVC frequency from zero to 8/min. These PVCs were of the usual type. Both edrophonium (1–10 mg) and propranolol (0.5 mg every 3 minutes for six times) separately slowed the heart to about 48 beats/min, but neither affected the frequency of PVCs. They generally remained below the baseline frequency of 2.5/min. When isoproterenol was readministered (same dosages) after propranolol administration, PVCs increased in frequency

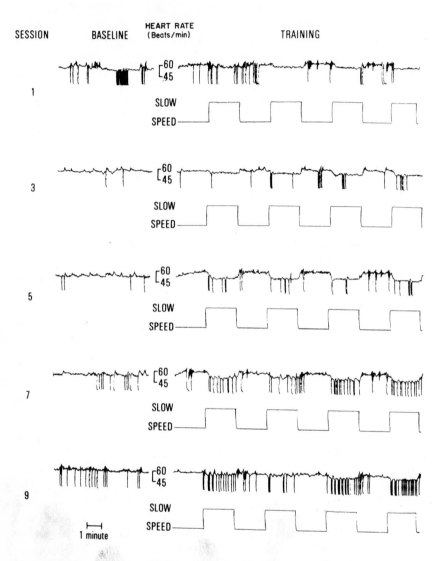

Fig. 15.4. Patient 2. Differential HR conditioning. Tracings are cardiotachometer records. PVCs are shown by long vertical lines. As differentiation proceeds, patient speeds and slows appropriately, and PVCs are progressively more concentrated in slowing periods.

to about 10/min although HR did not increase. Their configuration was of the usual type. These results suggest that PVCs of the speeding type were related to increased sympathetic tone. They do not clarify the mechanism underlying the usual type of PVCs.

Followup The patient has been followed for 10 months since the study. Initially, he continued to have very rare PVCs, averaging 0.4/min on three EKGs. When they were more frequent at home, he said he could decrease them by concentrating on a steady heart beat. His angina continued to worsen, and 4 months after discharge, he had another MI. After recovery from this, the patient's PVCs were somewhat more frequent, averaging 2.2/min in the clinic and, according to him, more at home. He said that it took 15–20 minutes to stop them with HR speeding at home. We therefore readmitted him 9 months after the first study. At that time, PVCs were rare, less than 1/min in the laboratory and on the ward. Because they originated consistently from two foci, quinidine was added to the patient's regimen. This reduced them even further, to one every 4–5 minutes.

Patient 3

MK was an obese 36-year-old Caucasian female with an 8-year history of documented PVCs. They were present on four of six EKGs taken during the 8 years prior to study. The average frequency was 12.8/min. During the last several months before the study, she had had three to four syncopal episodes. An EKG taken by her private physician shortly after one of these revealed unifocal PVCs at a frequency of 21/min. The syncopal episodes had occurred when she was angry or excited. She also reported "a big thumping feeling" in her chest in association with strong emotions and moderate physical exertion such as walking half a mile. To stop this, she said that she sat down and relaxed for half an hour or more.

Laboratory The patient did not speed consistently from baseline (Table 15.1); however, she did perform successfully in all other phases of the study. During the speeding sessions, PVC frequency was high—up to 40/min (Fig. 15.5)—and at times, coupling of PVCs occurred (Fig. 15.6). The patient said that she thought about arguments with her children and about running through a dark street during the speeding sessions.

During the slowing sessions, PVC frequency fell to about 20/min (Fig. 15.5). The patient said she thought about swinging back and forth in a swing during these sessions.

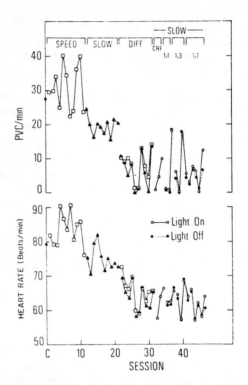

Fig. 15.5. Patient 3. PVC and HR levels during training. Slow₁ refers to first block of slowing sessions; Slow₂ to second block.

The patient differentiated well although she speeded from baseline during the speeding blocks in only one session. She slowed during the slowing blocks in all ten sessions. PVCs became much less frequent, usually under 10/min, and at times there were none for periods ranging up to 8 minutes. She said that she concentrated on the same things described above during the conditioning periods.

Because PVCs were least frequent at the lower HRs, slowing of the HR under 65 beats/min rather than range control was taught next. The patient's HR was under 65 beats/min during twelve of the sixteen sessions. She said that she thought about swinging on a see-saw and about relaxing during these sessions. PVC frequency was usually under 10/min; it was at zero for periods as long as 17 minutes (Fig. 15.6).

The patient frequently decreased her PVCs when the training portion of the session began and the feedback lights were turned on (Fig. 15.7).

OPERANT CONDITIONING

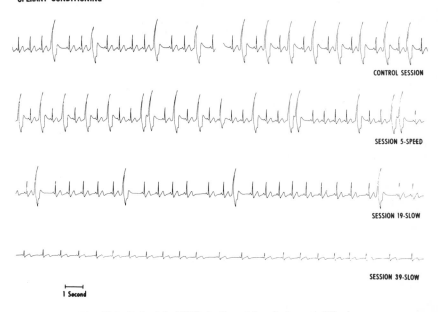

CONTROL SESSION

SESSION 5-SPEED

SESSION 19-SLOW

SESSION 39-SLOW

⊢———⊣
1 Second

Fig. 15.6. Patient 3. EKG rhythm strips during conditioning.

Also, the PVCs often returned promptly when the training portion of the session ended and the lights were turned off (Fig. 15.7). During the training sessions in which the light was off part of the time, PVC frequency was as low or lower when the light was off as when it was on (Fig. 15.5).

Ward Cardiac activity on the ward generally paralleled events in the laboratory. Heart rate (Table 15.3) was highest during speeding and slowing, intermediate during the second slowing block (not shown in Tables 15.2 or 15.3), and lowest during the differential conditioning sessions. The PVC pattern was the same as that for HR (Table 15.2). Their lowest average frequency was about 12/min during the differential contingency. At the end of the study, they averaged about 19/min.

Pharmacologic Studies Both edrophonium (1–10 mg) and propranolol (0.5 mg every 3 minutes for eight times) separately slowed the heart from about 80 to about 73 beats/min. Neither had any effect on PVC frequency which remained at about 20/min. When administered together (edrophonium, 10 mg at the end of the above administration of propranolol),

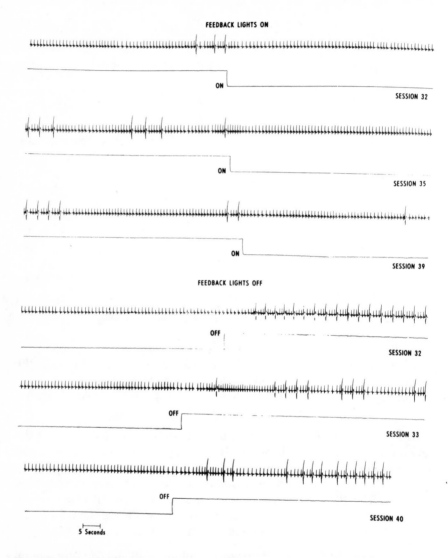

Fig. 15.7. Patient 3. EKG rhythm strips at onset and offset of feedback during HR slowing. These tracings show that patient was able to stop having PVCs when feedback began, and PVCs returned at end of sessions.

they slowed the heart from 75 to 60 beats/min and abolished PVCs from a prior level of 20/min. Phenylephrine (7–28 μg/min) increased the blood pressure from 104/70 to 138/76, slowed the HR from 77 to 54 beats/min, and abolished PVCs from a prior level of 12/min. Isoproterenol (0.5–1.0 μg/min) speeded the HR from 78 to 95 beats/min and stopped PVCs, the prior level being 25/min. Atropine (1.5 mg) speeded the HR from 75 to 97 beats/min and PVCs increased from 19/min to a bigeminal rhythm with 48/min. Phentolamine (5 mg), given at a time when PVC frequency was low (1/min), had no obvious effect on PVCs. It decreased the blood pressure from 108/68 to 90/62, and increased the HR from 75 to 82 beats/min.

These findings suggest that in this patient strong vagal tone inhibits PVCs, regardless of sympathetic input. Weaker vagal tone associated with β-sympathetic inhibition also inhibits PVCs. Vagal blockade leads to frequent PVCs.

Followup   The patient has been followed for 3 months since the study. PVCs have continued to be frequent on EKG during clinic visits, averaging 17.1/min on three EKGs. However, the patient says that she is able to stop them at home using the HR slowing technic learned in the laboratory. She has not been able to do so in the clinic. She has had no dizziness or syncope since the study.

Patient 4

RL was a 68-year-old Caucasian male with a history of an MI 4 months prior to study. Three months prior to study and after discharge from the hospital, the patient began to have PVCs. These were typically bigeminal or trigeminal, with a frequency of over 20/min, and were unifocal. The PVC occurred well after the preceding T wave, and after exercise, it occurred even later. Also, the PVCs did not increase with exercise; and the patient was unaware of their occurrence. For these reasons, no medications were given to control them.

Laboratory   The patient did not perform reliably during the slowing and speeding training sessions (Fig. 15.8 and Table 15.1), and his PVC frequency was highly variable throughout these sessions. He did differentiate consistently, however. Furthermore, he speeded from baseline during the speeding blocks in six of the sessions, and slowed from baseline in seven of them. He said that he moved his shoulders to increase his HR, and lay still and stared at the light to slow his HR. PVC

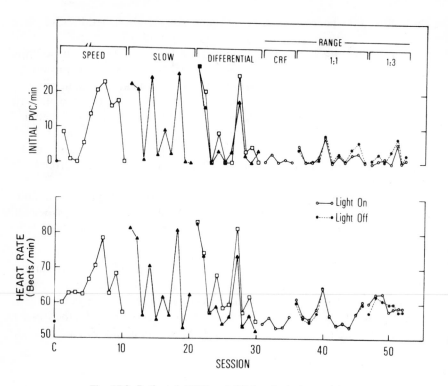

Fig. 15.8. Patient 4. PVC and HR levels during training.

frequency was variable, but was under 10/min in seven of the ten sessions. The PVCs were more frequent in the speeding blocks in seven of the ten sessions.

During the range sessions, the patient said that he generally just watched the light to keep PVCs infrequent. He said that sometimes he also moved his shoulders. PVC frequency was low, under 8/min throughout. During the first five sessions of the range contingency, when the feedback was on during the entire training period, the patient had 2.1 PVCs/min or less (Fig. 15.8). As the feedback was phased out, PVCs became somewhat more frequent. It is of note that the patient could not tell when he was having PVCs except when the feedback lights were on or when he took his pulse.

Ward   Ward data paralleled the laboratory data. Heart rates (Table 15.3) were highest during speeding and slowing and lowest during the range training. Similarly, PVCs (Table 15.2) were most frequent during speeding and slowing and least frequent during the range contingency.

Pharmacologic Studies No drug studies were performed on this patient.

Followup Because PVCs were noted to come from two foci (Fig. 15.9), the patient was started on quinidine at the time of discharge. PVC frequency has been low on followup visits, averaging 3.2/min on 5 EKGs. Because the patient was unable to detect PVCs except by taking his pulse, he was given twenty-four further training sessions to learn PVC detection. This was done 1 month after the first study. Whereas the patient initially was unable to detect any of his PVCs except by taking his pulse, by the end of the second study, he was able to detect them accurately 35–40% of the time without the light feedback. He said that he felt a sensation of warmth across the precordium when PVCs were occurring. When PVCs were frequent—e.g., 15/min—he also noted diaphoresis.

In one additional followup visit after the second study, there were no PVCs on EKG. During the clinic visit, the patient was able to sense that he was having infrequent PVCs (6/min). He reported that at home he also could sense his PVCs by the precordial warmth—verified by taking his pulse—and by sitting quietly, he could abolish them in half an hour. They stayed away for variable periods of time thereafter, usually for about an hour.

Patient 5

CA was a 73-year-old Caucasian male with a 19-month history of documented PVCs.

On thirteen visits to his private physician during the 19 months prior to our study, the patient was described as having no ectopic beats on five occasions, few to moderate ectopic beats ("few," "occasional," "slight irregularity of pulse," "irregularity of heart rate") on six occasions, and many ectopic beats on two occasions. The patient said that he could not sense the PVCs.

Laboratory The patient was unable to speed his heart during the speeding sessions; however, he was consistently successful at slowing his heart (Table 15.1). The patient differentiated well (Fig. 15.10). He slowed from baseline during all sessions, and he speeded from baseline in five of

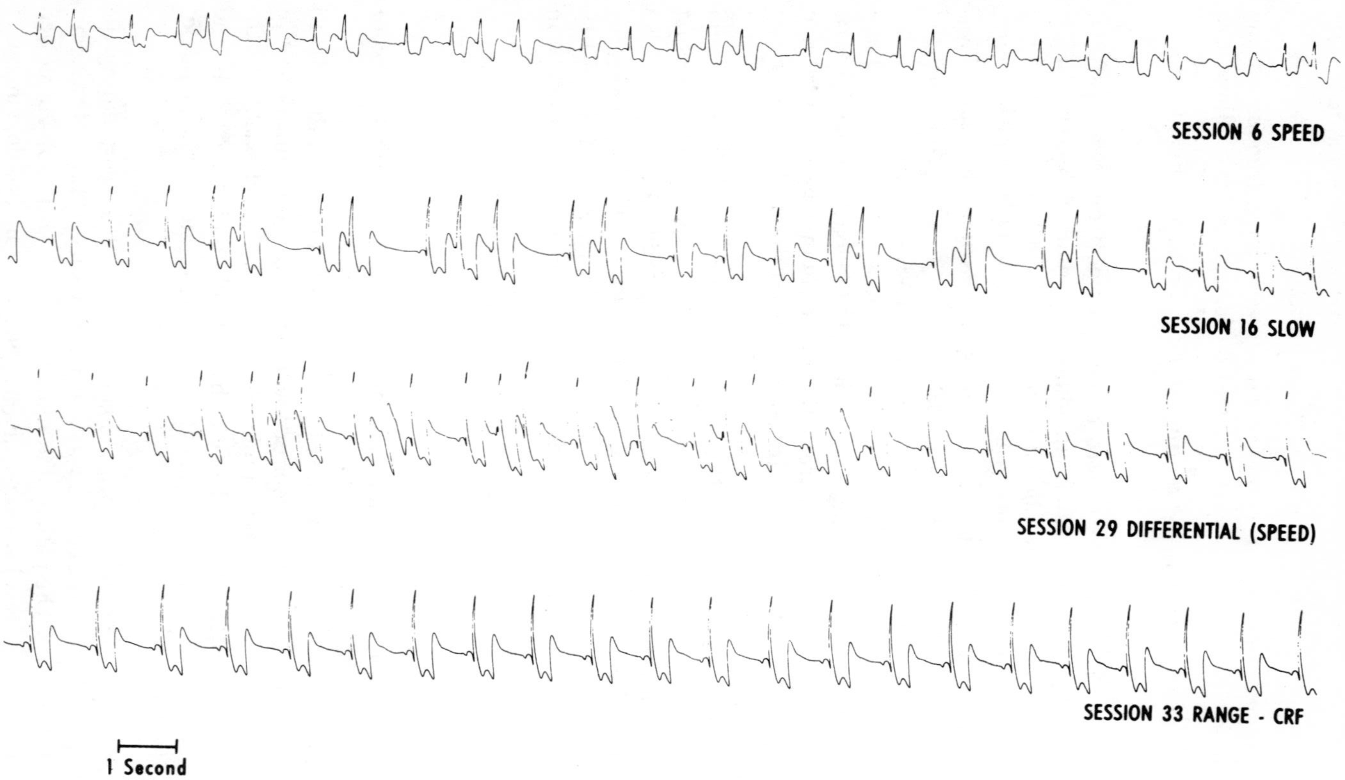

SESSION 6 SPEED

SESSION 16 SLOW

SESSION 29 DIFFERENTIAL (SPEED)

SESSION 33 RANGE - CRF

1 Second

Fig. 15.9. Patient 4. EKG rhythm strips during conditioning.

214

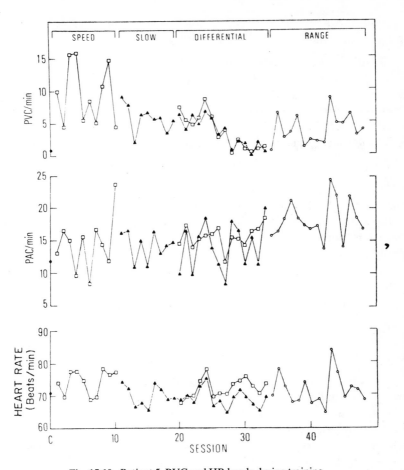

Fig. 15.10. Patient 5. PVC and HR levels during training.

the sessions, including four of the last seven. In order to speed his heart, the patient said that he thought about bouncing a rubber ball. To slow his heart, the patient said that he counted the amount of time the reinforcement light was on.

PVC frequency was highly variable during the speeding sessions (Fig. 15.10). During slowing, PVC frequency declined to about 5/min, and during the differentiation sessions, they fell still further so that there were fewer than three PVCs/min during the last six of these sessions. During the range sessions, PVC frequency remained low, averaging 4/min.

PACs increased slightly during the study, from about 14/min during speeding to about 18/min during the range condition (Fig. 15.10). The patient said that he still could not tell when the PVCs occurred.

Ward   There was little fluctuation in HR on the ward (Table 15.3). As in the laboratory, PVCs (Table 15.2) were most frequent during speeding and were fewest during the later range and differential contingencies. PACs on telemetry also paralleled their behavior in the laboratory, being least frequent early (9.5/min during speeding) and more frequent later (17.1/min during the range contingency).

Pharmacologic Studies   Drug studies were not done in this patient.

Followup   During 5 months of followup, the patient has been seen three times by his private physician. He was described as having no ectopic beats on two occasions, few to moderate ectopic beats on one occasion, and many ectopic beats on no occasions. An EKG taken 5 months after the study revealed 0.3 PVC/min and 22 PACs/min.

Patients 6, 7 and 8 all failed to learn to control their PVCs. Brief summaries of their cases are included in this report because they highlight important aspects about the limitations of operant training in the control of PVCs.

Patient 6

LS was a 60-year-old Negro male with a 5-year history of cardiac disease, including five hospitalizations for congestive heart failure.

His activities were severely limited by exertional dyspnea and palpitations, and less frequently by angina. He has paroxysmal nocturnal dyspnea about two nights per week. Chest X-ray revealed massive cardiomegaly, with a cardiac/thoracic ratio of 20/27.5. For almost 4 years prior to study, he had had premature atrial and ventricular contractions. Either or both of these were present on eight of nine EKGs during the 4 years prior to study. PVCs averaged 3.7/min and PAC, 1.6/min.

Laboratory   This patient was unable consistently to slow or speed his heart rate; however, he was quite successful at maintaining his rate within a ten-beat range (Table 15.1). His absolute heart rate declined from about 90 beats/min in the early sessions to about 65 beats/min by the end of speeding (slow training was given first in his case). The most likely explanations for this decline in HR are that during his period of hospitalization, he took his medications more regularly, and he reduced his alcohol consumption substantially.

During all training conditions, the frequency of his premature beats was highly variable, ranging from 1/min to 15/min. EKG tracings in the laboratory and on the ward were such that PVCs could not be differentiated from PACs; thus, all are listed together as premature beats.

It should also be noted that the patient drank heavily while on weekend passes so that he was too inebriated to return on Sunday evening as requested, and had to be fetched the next morning.

Followup   In 4 months of clinic followup, the patient continued to have many premature beats. On two EKGs, PVCs averaged 5.9/min and PACs, 9.7/min. His clinical status was unchanged. Thereafter, he was lost to followup. It was learned later that he died at home 10 months after the study.

Patient 7

EC was a 48-year-old Negro male with a history of hypertension for 27 years and cardiomegaly for 5 years, with hospitalization for congestive heart failure 4 years prior to study. After discharge from the hospital, the patient returned to work (manual labor) but he was so limited by dyspnea on exertion, that he was forced to quit. He proved to be little motivated to take a less strenuous job, and despite several professional attempts at rehabilitation, he has not worked since. At the time of study, he was functional Class II-B. The patient had had PVCs for 18 months prior to study, these being consistently present on physical examinations and on EKGs during that time. Their average frequency on three EKGs during that period was 9.0/min. The patient was an active Baptist, attending services twice a week.

Laboratory   The patient did not consistently speed his heart from baseline (Table 15.1); however, he did raise his absolute heart rate throughout the speeding sessions from 61 beats/min at the beginning to 78 beats/min by the end. He said he prayed to speed his heart. Although the patient did consistently slow his heart from baseline during the slowing sessions, his absolute heart rate did not change, remaining at 75 beats/min throughout these sessions. He said he tried to manipulate his breathing, and he prayed to slow his heart.

During the speeding sessions, PVC frequency increased from 6/min to 24/min. During the slowing sessions, PVC frequency was variable, ranging from 10/min to 20/min.

In an effort to enable this patient to gain control over his PVCs, he was given four sessions of training in the range contingency, and nine sessions of training in a PVC avoidance contingency in which a soft tone sounded whenever he had a PVC; his task was to silence the tone. However, PVCs persisted generally between 7 and 20/min, with an average of 12.4/min. HR averaged 76.2. The patient said that he tried mild exercise in bed, as well as praying and changing his breathing to decrease his PVCs.

Ward   Telemetry data (Tables 15.2 and 15.3) indicated that HR did not change throughout the study. However, the incidence of PVCs decreased during the slowing conditioning and then returned to prestudy levels during the range and PVC avoidance training.

Pharmacologic Studies   No drug studies were done in this patient.

Followup   During 17 months of followup, he has continued consistently to have PVCs, averaging 6.1/min. His clinical status is unchanged. The patient subsequently revealed that he was afraid that if his PVCs improved, he might lose his disability benefits and have to return to work. It is possible that this concern affected his performance during the study.

Patient 8

JF was a 77-year-old Caucasian male with a history of two probable MIs, the second one being 3 years prior to admission. He was not hospitalized on either occasion, and subsequent EKGs did not reveal definite evidence of an old MI. He also had had diabetes mellitus for 7 years. Shortly after the second probable MI, the patient developed CHF, and was hospitalized. PVCs were noted then for the first time. They did not respond to amelioration of the CHF (digoxin, chlorothiasize and potassium chloride), procaine amide, dilantin, or discontinuing digoxin for several months. They were consistently present thereafter, being seen on all of the nine EKGs taken from that time until the study. They were multifocal in origin, and their average frequency was 12.4/min. The patient said that he could not tell when they occurred.

Laboratory   Although there was evidence of heart rate control (Table 15.1) and a fall in absolute HR from an initial 90 beats/min to 76/min during slowing training, PVC frequency did not decrease. It should be noted that this patient had PVCs of at least four different configurations. Sometimes certain ones were more frequent; sometimes others were. This posed severe difficulties for our HR and PVC detection system. It also made it quite difficult to provide accurate feedback to the patient.

Ward   Telemetry data paralleled events in the laboratory in that HR was lower during the slowing periods (Table 15.3), and PVCs remained frequent (Table 15.2).

Pharmacologic Studies   No drug studies were performed in this patient.

Followup   Followup for 8 months revealed no significant changes in the patient's cardiovascular status. PVCs were present on all of four EKGs taken during these visits, with an average frequency of 10.0/min. The patient died suddenly at home 2 weeks after his last clinic visit.

DISCUSSION

This study shows that patients can be taught to control the prevalence of their PVCs. Patients 1–4 showed clear evidence of PVC control in the laboratory, and evidence of transfer of the learned effect to the ward. Patient 1 has sustained her low PVC rate for 21 months, and each of these other 3 patients who have been followed for shorter periods of time reports that he is able to detect and modify his PVCs while at home. Also, Patient 5 has maintained a low PVC frequency for 5 months after the study.

The presence of PVCs is associated with an increased probability of sudden death[28]. Corday *et al.* have demonstrated experimentally that PVCs can diminish coronary artery blood flow[29] and cerebral blood flow[30]. The fact that Patient 1 has had no further myocardial infarctions in the 21 months of followup, as contrasted with three in the 11 months preceding the study, may be related to her decreased PVC frequency.

In the patients in this study, at least two different mechanisms of PVC control appear to have been involved. The drug studies in Patient 1 suggested that reduced sympathetic tone to the heart was responsible for the decreased incidence of PVCs. As the cardiac sympathetic nerves are known to influence the ventricle strongly[31, 32], this effect probably occurred directly at the ventricular level. In Patient 3, the drug studies suggested that increased vagal tone decreased her PVC frequency. This may have represented a direct vagal effect on the ventricle, as there is anatomic evidence for vagal innervation of the ventricle in mammals[33, 34], and physiologic evidence for vagal effects on the mammalian ventricle[35, 36].

The flexibility of operant conditioning is demonstrated by the fact that

PVCs were reduced whether they were mediated primarily by the sympathetic or by the parasympathetic nervous system. This underscores the fact that operant conditioning can be used to alter pathologic conditions mediated by different mechanisms.

Heart rate per se does not determine the presence or absence of PVCs. Similar HRs in Patient 2 were associated with different PVC frequencies depending on the experimental contingency under which they occurred. Also, in Patient 1, HRs between 90 and 100 beats/min induced by isoproterenol were associated with PVCs, whereas similar HRs induced by atropine were not. In Patient 3, the opposite occurred. Atropine-induced HRs above 90 beats/min were associated with PVCs, while similar HRs induced by isoproterenol were not. This also suggests that extensive, short-term, experimental drug studies—of the type carried out in Patient 3—might be useful in clarifying the mechanisms of PVCs in different patients.

The imagery which patients reported while controlling their heart rates has been presented. However, the reports are highly idiosyncratic, and no consistent pattern is apparent.

There seem to be six elements that are important for successful learning of PVC control. These are: (a) peripheral receptors which are stimulated by the PVC; (b) afferents which carry the information to the CNS; (c) CNS processing to enable the patient to recognize the PVC and to provide the motivation and flexibility necessary to enable learning to occur; (d) efferents to an effector organ which can bring about the desired change in the pathologically functioning heart; (e) a heart which is not too diseased to beat more regularly; (f) a homeostatic system in the patient which will tolerate the more normal functioning of the heart.

Patient 4 illustrates the role of the afferent system. He did well at controlling his PVCs when he had continuous feedback in the range portion of Study 1, but did more poorly as the feedback was phased out. After Study 2, he was able to detect his PVCs, and then to reduce their frequency.

Patient 1 illustrates the importance of CNS processing. She had to learn to be comfortable with infrequent PVCs, whereas early in the study, she had been interpreting frequent PVCs as comfortable. This underscores the fact that physicians cannot always rely on the naive patient's interpretation of his physiologic state. The concern which Patient 7 expressed regarding his disability benefits suggests that motivation is also an important, CNS-mediated factor.

The grossly enlarged heart of Patient 6 and the electrically very unstable one of Patient 8 illustrate the importance of the heart itself.

These hearts may have been too diseased to beat regularly for prolonged periods of time.

Early intervention may facilitate the learning of PVC control—e.g., during convalescence from an infarction as in Patient 4. (The severity of the arrhythmias which the patients were able to generate in the course of conditioning was striking. Therefore, it would seem advisable not to attempt to condition patients during the acute, postinfarction period.)

This study was not concerned with optimization of technics. It should be possible to accomplish comparable results in much shorter periods of time, as more nearly optimal conditioning technics are employed. For example, studies should be feasible on an outpatient basis; and pretesting with autonomically active drugs such as those used in this study should suggest whether the patient will benefit more from being taught to slow or to speed.

REFERENCES

1. Skinner, B. F. *The Behavior of Organisms.* New York: Appleton-Century-Crofts, 1938.
2. Kimmel, H. D. Instrumental conditioning of autonomically mediated behavior. *Psychol. Bull.,* 1967, **67**, 337–345.
3. Miller, N. E. Learning of visceral and glandular responses. *Science,* 1969, **163**, 434–445.
4. Shearn, D. W. Operant conditioning of heart rate. *Science,* 1962, **137**, 530–531.
5. Hnatiow, M. and Lang, P. J. Learned stabilization of heart rate. *Psychophysiol.,* 1965, **1**, 330–336.
6. Engel, B. T. and Hansen, S. P. Operant conditioning of heart rate slowing. *Psychophysiol.,* 1966, **3**, 176–187.
7. Levene, H. I., Engel, B. T., and Pearson, J. A. Differential operant conditioning of heart rate. *Psychosom. Med.,* 1968, **30**, 837–845.
8. DiCara, L. V. and Miller, N. E. Instrumental learning of systolic blood pressure responses by curarized rats: dissociation of cardiac and vascular changes. *Psychosom. Med.,* 1968, **30**, 489–494.
9. Shapiro, D., Tursky, B., Gershon, E., *et al.* Effects of feedback and reinforcement on the control of human systolic blood pressure. *Science,* 1969, **163**, 588–590.
10. Miller, N. E. and DiCara, L. V. Instrumental learning of urine formation by rats: Changes in renal blood flow. *Amer. J. Physiol.,* 1968, **215**, 677–683.
11. DiCara, L. V. and Miller, N. E. Instrumental learning of vasomotor responses by rats: learning to respond differentially in the two ears. *Science,* 1968, **159**, 1485–1486.
12. Snyder, C. and Noble, M. Operant conditioning of vasoconstriction. *J. Exp. Psychol.,* 1968, **77**, 263–268.
13. Fowler, R. L. and Kimmel, H. D. Operant conditioning of the GSR. *Psychol. Rep.,* 1960, **7**, 555–562.
14. Kimmel, H. D. and Baxter, R. Avoidance conditioning of the GSR. *J. Exp. Psychol.,* 1964, **65**, 212–213.
15. Shapiro, D. and Crider, A. Operant electrodermal conditioning under multiple schedules of reinforcement. *Psychophysiol.,* 1967, **4**, 168–175.

16. Engel, B. T. and Melmon, K. L. Operant conditioning of heart rate in patients with cardiac arrhythmias. *Conditional Reflex*, 1968, **3**, 130.

17. White, J. D. and Taylor, D. Noxious conditioning as a treatment for rumination. *Ment. Retard.*, 1967, **5**, 30–33.

18. Lang, P. J. and Melamed, B. G. Case report: avoidance conditioning therapy of an infant with chronic ruminative vomiting. *J. Abn. Psychol.*, 1969, **74**, 1–8.

19. Scherf, D. and Schott, A. *Extrasystoles and Allied Arrhythmias*. New York, Grune and Stratton, Inc., 1953. Pp. 253–274.

20. Korth, C. The production of extrasystoles by means of the central nervous system. *Ann. Intern. Med.*, 1937, **11**, 492–498.

21. Weinberg, S. J. and Fuster, J. M. Electrocardiographic changes produced by localized hypothalamic stimulations. *Ann. Intern. Med.*, 1960, **53**, 332–341.

22. Attar, H. J., Gutierrex, M. T., Bellet, S. *et al.* Effect of stimulation of hypothalamus and reticular activating system on production of cardiac arrhythmia. *Circ. Res.*, 1963, **12**, 14–21.

23. Scherf, D., Blumenfeld, S., and Yildiz, M. Experimental study on ventricular extrasystoles provoked by vagal stimulation. *Amer. Heart J.*, 1961, **62**, 670–675.

24. Gillis, R. A. Cardiac sympathetic nerve activity: changes induced by ouabain and propranolol. *Science*, 1969, **166**, 508–510.

25. Estes, E. H., Jr. and Izlar, H. L., Jr. Recurrent ventricular tachycardia: a case successfully treated by bilateral sympathectomy. *Amer. J. Med.*, 1961, **31**, 493–497.

26. Peimer, I. A. Conditioned reflex extrasystole in man. *Fiziol. Zh. SSSR Sechenov.*, 1953, **39**, 286–292.

27. Perez-Cruet, J. Conditioning of extrasystoles in humans with respiratory maneuvers as unconditional stimulus. *Science*, 1962, **137**, 1060–1061.

28. Chiang, B. N., Perlman, L. V., Ostander, L. D., Jr. *et al.* Relationship of premature systoles to coronary heart disease and sudden death in the Tecumseh epidemiologic study. *Ann. Intern. Med.*, 1969, **70**, 1159–1166.

29. Corday, E., Gold, H., DeVera, L. B. *et al.* Effect of the cardiac arrhythmias on the coronary circulation. *Ann. Intern. Med.*, 1959, **50**, 535–553.

30. Corday, E. and Irving, D. W. Effect of cardiac arrhythmias on the cerebral circulation. *Amer. J. Cardiol.*, 1960, **6**, 803–807.

31. Rushmer, R. F. Autonomic balance in cardiac control. *Amer. J. Physiol.*, 1958, **192**, 631–634.

32. Sarnoff, S. J., Brockman, S. K., Gilmore, J. P. *et al.* Regulation of ventricular contraction: influence of cardiac sympathetic and vagal nerve stimulation on atrial and ventricular dynamics. *Circ. Res.*, 1960, **8**, 1108–1122.

33. Mitchell, G. A. G. *Cardiovascular Innervation.* Edinburgh and London: Livingstone, Ltd, 1956.

34. Hirsch, E. F., Kaiser, G. C., and Cooper, T. Experimental heart block in the dog. III. Distribution of the vagus and sympathetic nerves in the septum. *Arch. Path.*, 1965, **79**, 441–451.

35. Wildenthal, K., Mierzwiak, D. S., Wyatt, H. L. *et al.* Influence of efferent vagal stimulation on left ventricular function in dogs. *Amer. J. Physiol.*, 1969, **215**, 577–581.

36. Daggett, W. M., Nugent, G. C., Carr, P. W. *et al.* Influence of vagal stimulation on ventricular contractibility, O_2 consumption and coronary flow. *Amer. J. Physiol.*, 1967, **212**, 8–18.

Decreased Systolic Blood Pressure Through Operant Conditioning Techniques in Patients with Essential Hypertension*

HERBERT BENSON

Harvard Medical Unit, Boston City Hospital, Boston, Massachusetts 02118 *and*
Department of Medicine, Harvard Medical School, Boston 02115

and

DAVID SHAPIRO, BERNARD TURSKY, and GARY E. SCHWARTZ

Massachusetts Mental Health Center, Harvard Medical School

Abstract: Operant conditioning–feedback techniques were employed to lower systolic blood pressure in seven patients with essential hypertension. In five of the patients, meaningful decreases of systolic blood pressure were obtained in the laboratory, ranging from 16 to 34 millimeters of mercury. The therapeutic value of such techniques remains to be established.

Arterial blood pressure in animals can be made to rise and fall predictably when environmental stimuli are scheduled according to variations in blood pressure [1, 2]. Further, unanesthetized squirrel monkeys with behaviorally induced hypertension can be trained by operant conditioning techniques to lower their mean arterial blood pressure to control levels [2]. Normotensive human subjects can also be trained to raise and lower arterial systolic and diastolic blood pressure by the use of similar procedures [3]. The present report describes the lowering of systolic arterial blood pressure through operant conditioning–feedback techniques in seven patients with essential hypertension.

The diagnosis of essential hypertension was established by exclusion of the known causes of hypertension. The patients had moderate or severe

*Reprinted from *Science*, **173**, 740–742, 20 August 1971. Copyright © 1971 by the American Association for the Advancement of Science. With permission from the American Association for the Advancement of Science and Herbert Benson.

hypertension. All had complete medical evaluations, including renal arteriography in patients Nos. 2 and 6. The patients were ambulatory and were attending the Hypertension Clinic of the Boston City Hospital. The average age of the patients was 47.9 years (Table 16.1). There were five males and two females. Six of the seven were taking antihypertensive medications. Medications were not altered during the experimental sessions, and all patients had maintained constant medication regimens for at least 2 weeks prior to any laboratory sessions. Informed consent was obtained from each patient. They were told they would be paid $5.00 per session to come to the behavioral laboratory and have their blood pressure measured automatically for approximately 1 hour while they sat quietly. They were also informed that no other medications or invasive techniques would be employed and that the procedures might be of value in lowering their blood pressure.

Median systolic blood pressure was recorded by use of an automated constant cuff-pressure system[3]. A standard, 13-cm wide blood pressure cuff was wrapped around the left arm and inflated to a given pressure by a regulated, low-pressure, compressed-air source. The cuff was connected by plastic tubing to the air-filled chamber of a Statham P23Db strain gauge pressure transducer. The electrical output of the strain gauge was recorded on one channel of a Beckman type RM polygraph. The output of a crystal microphone, placed under the cuff and over the brachial artery, recorded Korotkoff sounds on a second channel of the polygraph. The electrocardiogram was recorded on a third channel. By setting the cuff at a constant pressure, close to systolic blood pressure, increases or decreases in systolic pressure with each heart beat relative to the cuff pressure could be ascertained. When cuff pressure exceeded brachial artery systolic pressure, no Korotkoff sound was produced; when cuff pressure was less than brachial artery systolic pressure, a Korotkoff sound was present. During each trial, the cuff was inflated for 50 consecutive heart beats (recorded automatically from the electrocardiogram) and then deflated. The presence or absence of a Korotkoff sound was noted within 300 msec after the R-wave of the electrocardiogram. Median systolic blood pressure during the trial was equal to cuff pressure when 14 to 36 Korotkoff sounds per cycle of 50 heart beats were present[3, 4]. If less than 14 Korotkoff sounds were present, indicating cuff pressure exceeded systolic arterial pressure for most of the trial, the cuff pressure was decreased by 4 mm-Hg for the next cycle. If more than 36 Korotkoff sounds were present, indicating cuff pressure was lower than arterial pressure for most of the trial, the cuff pressure was increased

Table 16.1. Patient Characteristics and Effects of Operant Conditioning on Systolic Blood Pressure.

Patient No.	Age (yr)	Sex	Antihypertensive medications administered throughout the study		No. of control sessions	No. of conditioning sessions	Median systolic blood pressure (mm-Hg)		
			Medication	Amount (mg/day)			Last five control sessions	Last five conditioning sessions	Conditioning minus control
1	30	M	None		5	8	139.6	136.1	−3.5
2	49	F	Spironolactone Methyl dopa Guanethidine	100 1500 30	5	33	213.3	179.5	−33.8
3	52	M	Methyl dopa	500	5	22	162.3	133.1	−29.2
4	54	M	Chlorothiazide Spironolactone Methyl dopa	1000 100 1500	16	34	166.9	150.4	−16.5
5	44	M	Chlorothiazide	1000	15	31	157.8	141.7	−16.1
6	53	F	Chlorothiazide Spironolactone Methyl dopa	1000 100 1000	15	12	165.7	166.6	+0.9
7	53	M	Hydrochloro- thiazide Spironolactone Methyl dopa	100 100 1000	15	12	149.0	131.7	−17.3
Mean	47.9				10.9	21.7	164.9	148.4	−16.5

by 4 mm-Hg. Thus, median systolic pressure was tracked throughout each session.

The patients were studied on consecutive weekdays. During all sessions, median systolic blood pressure was measured for 30 trials. Between trials, the cuff was deflated for 30 to 45 seconds. There were 5 to 16 control sessions for each patient during which median systolic blood pressure was recorded with no feedback or reinforcement of lowered systolic pressure. Thus, the control pressures represented median systolic blood pressure of between 7,500 and 22,500 heart beats.

In each of the following conditioning sessions, the first five trials had no reinforcement presented. However, in the subsequent 25 conditioning trials, relatively lowered systolic pressure, indicated by the absence of a Korotkoff sound, was fed back to the patient by presentation of a 100-msec flash of light and a simultaneous 100-msec tone of moderate intensity. The patients were told that the tone and light were desirable and they should try to make them appear. As a reward, after each 20 presentations of tones and lights, a photographic slide, equivalent to $0.05, was shown for 5 seconds. The slides consisted of scenic pictures and reminders of the amount of money earned. The conditioning sessions continued until no reductions in blood pressure occurred in five consecutive sessions.

Blood pressures did not change within the first five control sessions. In the four patients with 15 or 16 control sessions, no decreases in blood pressure were noted after the initial five control sessions[5]. Average median systolic blood pressure during the last five control sessions in the seven patients was 164.9 mm-Hg (Table 16.1). Pressures in the last five conditioning sessions were used as an index of the effectiveness of training. During these sessions, average median systolic blood pressure was 148.4 mm-Hg ($P < 0.02$)[6]. In the individual patients, systolic blood pressure decreased 3.5, 33.8, 29.2, 16.5, 16.1, 0, and 17.3 mm-Hg.

Systolic blood pressure did not change significantly within each control session. However, it decreased an average of 4.8 mm-Hg ($P < 0.001$)[6] within each conditioning session. This within-session decrease is equivalent to that observed in normotensive subjects with similar training[3]. In the two patients with little or no decrease in systolic blood pressure, patient No. 1 did not have elevated systolic blood pressure, while patient No. 6 had renal artery stenosis. No consistent changes in heart rate were present in any of the patients during the blood pressure changes.

Elevated arterial blood pressure increases the risk of coronary artery disease and cerebrovascular accidents[7]. This increased risk is lessened by lowering blood pressure[8]. At the present time, the means of lowering blood pressure are pharmacological or surgical or both. In the present experiments, systolic blood pressure could be decreased by operant conditioning techniques in six of seven patients with essential hypertension. Since the decrease in systolic pressure was measured only in the laboratory and no consistent measurements were made outside the laboratory, the usefulness of such methods in the therapeutic management of hypertension remains to be evaluated [9–12].

REFERENCES AND NOTES

1. L. V. DiCara and N. E. Miller, *Psychosomat. Med.*, 1968, **30**, 489.
2. H. Benson, J. A. Herd, W. H. Morse, and R. T. Kelleher, *Am. J. Physiol.*, 1969, **217**, 30.
3. D. Shapiro, B. Tursky, E. Gershon, and M. Stern, *Science*, 1969, **163**, 588; D. Shapiro, B. Tursky, and G. E. Schwartz, *Circ. Res.*, 1970, **26** and **27**, Suppl. I, I–27; D. Shapiro, G. E. Schwartz, and B. Tursky, unpublished data.
4. Simultaneous intraarterial studies have confirmed that median systolic blood pressure measured by this cuff system is equal to median intraarterial systolic blood pressure (unpublished data from our laboratory).
5. Separate analyses of variance were computed for the initial five control sessions in all patients and for differences between the initial five and final five control sessions in four patients. Although possible, it is unlikely that more than 15 or 16 control sessions would yield significantly lower systolic blood pressures.
6. The data were treated as a three-factor repeated measures experiment with two levels of the first factor (control-conditioning); five levels of the second factor (sessions); and 25 levels of the third factor (trials). For the significant main effect of control-conditioning, d.f. = 1/6; for the significant control-conditioning × trial interaction, d.f. = 24/144. Computed by the Biomed 08V Analysis of Variance Program on an IBM 360 computer.
7. W. B. Kannel, T. R. Dawber, A. Kagen, N. Revotskie, and J. Stokes, *Ann. Intern. Med.*, 1961, **55**, 33; W. B. Kannel, M. J. Schwart, and P. M. McNamara, *Dis. Chest*, 1969, **56**, 43.
8. E. D. Freis and the Veterans Administration Cooperative Study Group on Antihypertensive Agents, *J. Am. Med. Assoc.*, 1967, **202**, 1028; *ibid.*, 1970, **213**, 1143.
9. Since completion of this investigation on systolic blood pressure, a method for determining diastolic blood pressure by using the constant cuff-pressure technique has been developed. Studies are now under way with hypertensive patients to attempt to lower diastolic blood pressure through similar conditioning techniques.
10. We acknowledge the competent technical contributions of Miss Barbara R. Marzetta.
11. Supported in part by NIH (HE 10539-04, SF 57-111, SF 57-135, and grant RR-76 from the General Clinical Research Centers Program of the Division of Research Resources); Hoffmann-LaRoche, Inc., Nutley, N.J. 07110; the Council for Tobacco Research; National Institute of Mental Health (MH-08853; Research Scientist Award K5-MH-20,476; and MH-04172); and Office of Naval Research (Physiological Psychology Branch) N00014-67-A-0298-0024.
12. A preliminary report of these experiments was presented at the May 1971 meeting of the American Society for Clinical Investigation.

CHAPTER 5

The Musculoskeletal System: Tics, Spasmodic Torticollis, Postural Disorders, Stuttering

Disorders of the musculoskeletal system are usually associated with some form of observable psychomotor impairment, such as spasms, tics, tremors, paralysis, or limitations in range of motion. In many cases these disorders result from known organic conditions; for example, brain injury, infection, degenerative bone and muscle disease, and metabolic disturbances. However, for some patients it is not always possible to establish an organic etiology, nor to control their symptoms by medical or surgical means. These patients include tiqueurs, chronic stutterers, and individuals with other psychomotor conditions that can be defined behaviorally in terms of specific responses occurring at abnormal rates.

Although differential diagnosis of functionally and organically caused symptoms is of prime importance because of its implications for appropriate treatment selection, the knowledge that the causes are not organic may be of little comfort to the patient who seeks medical assistance. Whether due to organic factors or not, difficulties controlling motor function can be highly disabling and a continuous source of social embarrassment. To diagnose and dismiss these problems as *hysterical,* or to assume that they can only be treated effectively by in depth psychotherapy, is not only of little practical benefit to the patient, but also disregards the alternative approaches to treatment that have emphasized the modification of symptoms directly by behavioral techniques (Agras & Marshall, 1965; Barrett, 1962; Flanagan, Goldiamond, & Azrin, 1958).

The behavioral treatment of tics, spasmodic torticollis, postural disorders, and stuttering are described in this chapter. While these selections contain many useful therapeutic suggestions, they are not meant to be exhaustive of the kinds of motor disturbances that have been treated by behavior therapists (e.g., see Meichenbaum, 1966; Yates, 1970). Nor should they be construed as applicable only to nonorganically caused abnormalities. MacPherson's (1967) behavioral treatment of a patient suffering from Huntington's chorea demonstrates the utility of behavior therapy in achieving at least temporary symptomatic relief resulting from a progressive physical disease. Similarly, Meyerson *et al.* (1967) used relatively uncomplicated reinforcement operations to quickly shape up and maintain walking in a young "congenitally mentally retarded" child who many had felt was incapable of learning how to walk.

It should be noted that some of the papers in this chapter are closely related to articles in a later chapter on the modification of chronic pain and physical rehabilitation. Together this body of research should yield better methods for understanding and treating patients whose motor activity has been impaired but whose physiological potential for behavioral change is still intact.

The papers by Rafi (Article 17) and Thomas *et al.* (Article 18) describe several behavioral techniques used to reduce tics in three psychiatric patients. In each case these patients had previously received drugs and other forms of therapy with little if any noticeable improvement. Rafi's treatment is based on Yates' (1958) earlier study of tic reduction by *massed practice.* In the Yates' experiment, multiple tics of a young female patient were decreased by instructing her to reproduce them voluntarily until fatigue set in. At this point the patient was told to rest and not to perform the tic. Basically, the theory behind Yates' treatment is that a fatigue state is aversive and that other responses incompatible with the tic will be reinforced during the rest period by the avoidance of fatigue. Yates also predicted that a greater reduction of tics would occur under conditions of prolonged massed practice followed by prolonged rest. Rafi's results lend only partial support to Yates' predictions. In one patient who did not improve using the "standard procedure" of massed practice, Rafi later showed that her tics were susceptible to control by an alternative respondent conditioning technique. Although both of Rafi's patients improved considerably, in neither case was remission complete. Furthermore, the lack of objective information on the generalization and maintenance of tic free behavior outside of the hospital should serve as a warning that while the results are encouraging, they are by no means conclusive.

Thomas *et al.* treated a young male patient whose multiple tics and spasmodic vocalizations are characteristic of a peculiar tic syndrome referred to as Gilles de la Tourette's Syndrome. As with many other tiqueurs, this patient's symptoms had proven refractory to conventional medical and psychiatric procedures, with the possible exception of the drug haloperidol. The careful assessment of tic rate in various environmental settings and the use of multiple baseline techniques to demonstrate the efficacy of treatment are noticeable features of this research. Early assessment observations revealed that the rate of the patient's tics varied considerably according to the situation he was in. Moreover, when the patient was told to record the number of times his tics occurred, the rate of tics declined. This unexpected finding on the potential utility of self-monitoring served as the basis for later treatment plans. Regarding the choice of experimental design, it was indicated earlier (see Chapter 1) that multiple baselines provide a useful alternative to reversal techniques as a means of demonstrating behavioral control. Since this design involves the sequential introduction of treatment variables for different behaviors, or for the same behavior in different settings, it offers the practical advantage of not having to temporarily discontinue therapy and risk reinstating problem behaviors. Another advantage is that functional relationships can be established when dealing with several behaviors simultaneously. As suggested by Thomas *et al.*, both of these factors were important considerations in their research. Although the long-term effectiveness of the treatment used by Thomas *et al.* is unknown, the results are encouraging and deserve continued exploration.

Brierley (Article 19) describes an aversive conditioning procedure used to treat two patients with spasmodic torticollis. Often referred to as "wry neck," this condition is produced by spasms of the cervical muscles and results in abnormal movements and positioning of the head. In Brierley's study, the patients were equipped with a headgear apparatus that had been specifically designed to deliver a brief but unpleasant electric shock contingent on neck spasms. Operationally the technique involves both punishment and avoidance learning components. In both patients substantial improvement was reported. Unfortunately, however, neither quantifiable baseline nor post-treatment data are reported.

Like Brierley, Azrin *et al.* (Article 20) and Brady (Article 21) also make use of portable behavioral control devices, the former to modify postural problems and the latter to reduce speech disfluencies in chronic stutterers. From the standpoint of multiple subject replication of treatment effectiveness, both of these studies are impressive. The procedure described by Azrin *et al.* is conceptually similar to Brierley's except that a continuous noise stimulus rather than shock was made contingent on the target behavior, slouching. A resumption of erect posture immediately terminated the noise and was thus negatively reinforced. The results of the study are based on 25 subjects. All showed improvements in posture during the time that the apparatus was worn. In describing the apparatus, Azrin *et al.* refer to six requirements of behavioral engineering by means of portable equipment, and suggest that similar devices might also be used to treat other types of health problems that can be defined in terms of body movement or orientation.

In Brady's study a miniaturized metronome, which was worn unobtrusively behind the ear, was used to facilitate fluent speech among 23 chronic stutterers. The flexible design of this apparatus was well suited for shaping increasingly faster rates of fluent speech, and allowed it to be easily operated or disconnected depending on the degree of difficulty associated with particular speaking situations. Although as Brady points out, the means by which the metronome or other pacing devices produce greater speech fluency is not adequately understood, his results clearly demonstrate the usefulness of the procedure. Not only were speech patterns and general psychological adjustment improved in over 90% of the subjects, but equally important these changes endured for extended followup periods.

Points of key importance in this chapter include:

1. The treatment of tics by massed practice appears promising, but more extensive research with followups conducted in the patient's natural environment are needed before the efficacy of this procedure can be established. One variable that determines the appropriateness of this procedure is the patient's ability to reproduce the tic voluntarily.
2. Aversive conditioning has application for treating some functional motor disorders, however the results of Thomas *et al.* and of Azrin *et al.* suggest that other innocuous procedures might be equally effective. The common element of each of these studies is the manipulation of response produced consequences, whether carried out by the patient himself or dispensed automatically.
3. Behavioral techniques such as self-monitoring and relaxation training may be used to supplement conventional medical treatment of psychomotor disorders. Since these techniques can be administered inexpensively and with little risk of injury to the patient, they may also be used to achieve symptomatic relief among patients who have organically based motor disabilities. How much improvement to expect under these conditions is a question deserving additional research.

4. The research by Brady clearly shows the utility of behavioral approaches in the treatment of chronic stutterers. Together with the investigation by Azrin *et al.* this study also demonstrates the potential fruitfulness of combining behavioral and engineering technology to treat other health problems for which prolonged behavioral retraining is required. One advantage of this approach is that it allows for continuous therapy to be given in the patient's natural surroundings, presumably with a savings in professional man-hours.

REFERENCES

Agras, S. and Marshall, C. The application of negative practice to spasmodic torticollis. *American Journal of Psychiatry*, 1965, **122**, 579–582.

Barrett, B. Reduction in rate of multiple tics by free operant conditioning methods. *Journal of Nervous and Mental Disease*, 1962, **135**, 187–195.

Flanagan, B., Goldiamond, I., and Azrin, N. Operant stuttering: The control of stuttering behavior through response-contingent consequences. *Journal of the Experimental Analysis of Behavior*, 1958, **1**, 173–178.

MacPherson, E. Control of involuntary movement. *Behaviour Research and Therapy*, 1967, **5**, 143–145.

Meichenbaum, D. Sequential strategies in two cases of hysteria. *Behaviour Research and Therapy*, 1966, **4**, 89–94.

Meyerson, L., Kerr, N., and Michael, J. Behavior modification in rehabilitation. In S. Bijou and D. Baer (eds.) *Child Development: Readings in Experimental Analysis*. New York: Appleton-Century-Crofts, 1967.

Yates, A. The application of learning theory to the treatment of tics. *Journal of Abnormal and Social Psychology*, 1958, **56**, 175–182.

Yates, A. *Behavior Therapy*. New York: John Wiley & Sons, 1970.

ARTICLE 17

Learning Theory and the Treatment of Tics*

A. ABI RAFI

St. Andrew's Hospital, Thorpe, Norwich, England

Yates[1] reported a successful experiment on the extinction of four tics in a female psychiatric patient of high average intelligence. He based his method of treatment on a theoretical model treating the tic as a simple learned response which has attained its maximum habit strength. His general hypothesis was that massed practice in the tic leads to a significant decrement in the ability of the subject to respond voluntarily, and eventually leads to extinction of the tic by the process of building up a negative habit of not performing it. His results confirmed this hypothesis, i.e., the number of repeated voluntary evocations of the tic per minute declined significantly, and there was an improvement in his patient's involuntary tics. As Yates was attempting to produce maximal conditioned inhibition ($_sI_R$), he varied the conditions of practice systematically but always used a "standard procedure," by which each tic was given five one-minute periods of massed practice with one minute's rest between each period, as a control. He describes several experiments in detail but the main outcome was that very prolonged periods of massed practice, followed by prolonged rest periods, produced the largest declines.

This paper reports the outcome of similar experiments on two psychiatric patients with tics. One was given the "standard procedure" of Yates and the other the procedure of prolonged massed practice followed by prolonged rest.

SUBJECTS

The two patients were referred to the psychology department with a view to treatment based on learning theory constructs. Before the

---

*Reprinted from *Journal of Psychosomatic Research*, 1962, **6**, 71–76. Copyright © 1962. With permission from Pergamon Press and A. Abi Rafi.

235

experiments began, each patient underwent the usual neurological investigations and the possibility of an organic basis to the tics has been adequately excluded. Both patients were of high average intelligence (Wechsler Adult Intelligence Scale). One, a female, patient A, was 63 years old, and the other, a male, patient B, was 57 years old. The Maudsley Personality Inventory showed patient A to be very neurotic and slightly introverted, and patient B to be very extraverted but not neurotic.

Patient A suffered from a right foot tapping tic which appeared about two years before referral. The tapping, a see-saw-like movement of toe and heel, was continuous and forceful while she was standing up or sitting down. She was admitted to hospital on several occasions after the appearance of the tic complaining of depression and restlessness. She was treated with chlorpromazine and had modified electroconvulsive treatment. On every occasion she was discharged "relieved" but neither out-patient nor in-patient treatment, including ECT, had any influence on the tic. The tapping caused much annoyance to those who happened to be in her company. Her public life became considerably restricted because of the censure her tic evoked. She remained on chlorpromazine throughout the experiments.

Patient B was seen as an out-patient and remained one. His main complaint was a spasmodic movement of his head to the left. This began early in 1958, and gradually increased in conjunction with facial grimacing. He came to the out-patient clinic, had some physiotherapy, was given dexamphetamine and sodium amytal, also a series of pentothal abreactions, with no material progress. He continued on drugs but these were stopped with the consent of his psychiatrist after the fourth session of intensive practice.

METHOD

The tics were considered as symptoms which had developed originally as conditioned avoidance responses, became reinforced through satisfying temporary needs and thereafter existed as learned responses separated from the original circumstances which first occasioned them. The method of treatment by massed practice was adopted.

Both patients were treated separately. Patient A was given Yates' "standard procedure," two sessions a day, one in the morning and one in the afternoon under supervision. Patient B was given very prolonged massed practice sessions, each of two hours continuous practice, followed by prolonged rest periods (one week). The instructions were the same for both subjects, namely, to produce the tic as accurately as possible, to repeat it without pause during the practice period, and to pay attention to the tic. No stress was laid on speed.

Each voluntary evocation of the tic was recorded by the author for about 70 per cent of the records of patient A, and for all the records of patient B. Patient A carried out about 30 per cent of the total number of sessions at her home. These were performed under the supervision of her husband who has been adequately trained by the author in the strict procedure to be followed. He also recorded the voluntary tics. An instructions form and record sheets were provided. Patient B attended regularly at the hospital once a week. A stop watch was used.

RESULTS

The score recorded was the number of tics per minute as counted from the record sheets.

Table 17.1 shows the results. In the case of patient A, the frequency of occurrence of the tic per minute (under test conditions) did not show any appreciable decline either within single sessions or between sets of 50 sessions. The mean score for any one set of 50 sessions is not significantly lower than the mean score for any other set of 50 sessions (the highest value of t was 1.16; the lowest, 0.46). The results of this experiment do not support the general theory propounded by Yates.

The "standard procedure" was discontinued after the 280th session and

Table 17.1. Changes in Mean Frequency of Two Tics Under Condition of Voluntary Evocation.

Tapping						Head		
5 one-min sessions			5 five-min sessions			Two-hour sessions		
Sessions	M	σ	Sessions	M	σ	Sessions	M	σ
1–50	87.68	11.39	1–10	40.75	4.35	1–5	33.50	2.49
51–100	77.81	5.60	11–20	41.50	3.52	6–10	17.80	2.78
101–150	82.36	6.84	21–30	47.75	4.07	11–15	4.86	3.32
151–200	80.44	5.23	31–40	45.25	3.77	16–20	2.68	4.11
201–250	82.40	7.89	41–50	40.75	3.63	21–25	2.51	3.13
251–280	75.47	9.84						

another introduced with sessions of five five-minute trials under conditions of massed practice, with one minute's rest between each period. Fifty such sessions were completed. The results of this experiment are reported in Table 17.1. Here again the mean score for any one set of 10 sessions is not significantly lower than the mean score for any other set of ten sessions. In neither of these two experiments was Yates' general hypothesis that massed practice leads to a significant decrement in the ability of the subject to respond voluntarily, confirmed.

Yates[2] suggests that very prolonged sessions of massed practice in terms of 6–7 hr continuous practice in one session followed by very prolonged rest, 2–3 weeks at least, could be very effective. Could it be that patient A has shown very little decline because of a simple lack of foot-pounds work? To test this, very prolonged massed practice in terms of 2 hr continuous practice in one session was introduced. Patient A was unable to tolerate this kind of stress and refused to take another session. An apparatus was therefore devised (see Fig. 17.1)* with a foot treadle freely pivoted on two No. 12 screws. Under the foot treadle at the front and back, are two bell push switches. Each time the foot treadle is pressed downwards, whether by toe or by heel, a buzzer is sounded. There is a $\frac{2}{10}$ of an inch free play between the foot treadle and the bell push switches. Any slight pressure beyond that is enough to cause the buzzer to sound.

By the conditioned-response principle, it was hypothesized that a strong connection would be expected to develop between the stimulation arising from the desire to tap the foot and the response of hearing the buzzer and withholding the foot from tapping. Gradually this connection should become sufficiently well established to cause withholding of the foot from tapping in advance of the onset of the tapping, instead of afterwards. Patient A was given daily practice sessions each lasting one hour. She was instructed to sit comfortably, put her right foot on the foot treadle, pay attention to the buzzers and try to balance the foot treadle and not to cause the sounding of the buzzers. There were 70 sessions in all (see Fig. 17.2, curve 3). The results confirm the hypothesis. The frequency of occurrence of the tic almost invariably showed steady decline. A stage was reached where she was able to keep her foot still throughout any one practice session. At the termination of the experiment she felt much improved. The foot tapping became very faint and intermittent and ceased to be a source of annoyance to her or to those around her.

---

*Thanks are due to Mr. G. H. Tarlton, Chief Engineer, for building the apparatus to specifications.

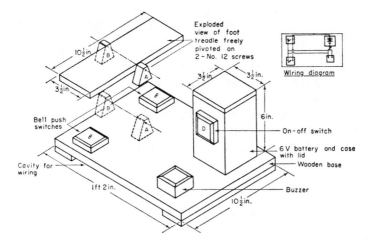

Fig. 17.1.

In the case of patient B, the procedure of intensive practice for 2-hr periods with one week's rest between sessions, led to significant decrement in his ability to respond voluntarily, (see Table 17.1). The frequency of occurrence of the tic per minute (under test conditions) showed a steady decline. The mean score for the second set of five sessions was significantly below that for the first set of five sessions ($t = 31.37$,

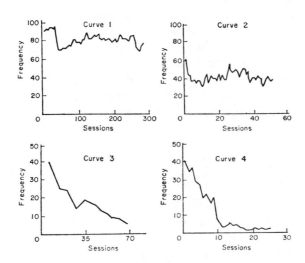

Fig. 17.2.

$P = 0.001$). Similarly, the mean for sessions 11–15 was significantly lower than that for sessions 6–10 ($t = 18.81$, $P = 0.001$); the mean for sessions 16–20 was significantly lower than that for sessions 11–15 ($t = 3.10$, $P = 0.01$). The mean score for sessions 21–25 was not significantly below that for sessions 16–20 (value of t here was 0.37). The results of this experiment conform to the general hypothesis of Yates.

The course of decline in the frequency of voluntary responding for each tic, using the different procedures, is shown in Fig. 17.2. Each point on curves 1 and 2 represents the average of five sessions (i.e., 25 one-minute trials for curve 1; 5 five-minute trials for curve 2). Each point on curve 3 represents the total number of tics (buzzes) of seven sessions (i.e., 7 one-hour trials). Each point on curve 4, represents the average of one session (i.e., one trial of 120 minutes).

CHANGES IN INVOLUNTARY TICS

Both patients reported improvement outside the test situation. Patient A felt more cheerful, started going out more frequently, and resumed her attendance at church which she stopped previously because of the annoyances her tapping caused to others; at one stage she used to put a cushion under her foot during church service, in order to make the continuous tapping inaudible. She reported total absence of the tic over three consecutive days, otherwise the frequency was sharply reduced, but complete cessation of involuntary tapping was not reported.

The condition of patient B did improve but not as dramatically as curve 4 appears to convey. The facial grimacings, which were very severely conspicuous in the early stages of treatment, completely vanished. He reported sleeping much better, whereas before treatment he used to lose a lot of sleep through the interference of the tic with any sleeping position he took. He feels much better generally, and although his head still has a tendency to move to the left, it is not so pronounced and so forceful as previously. He can now keep his head in a normal, facing-forward, position, for fairly long periods. The tic is much less frequent and very much less severe.

Towards the end of the experiment patient B was trained in the technique of systematic relaxation of muscles, with emphasis on the neck muscles. He was asked to maintain the relaxation exercises at home by devoting between fifteen and thirty minutes every day to this. He was also encouraged to try to cultivate the habit of general muscle relaxation whenever possible in the course of his every day life. A follow-up after three months showed that he felt more relaxed and that he believed his tic had diminished.

DISCUSSION

The results outlined above suggest that the procedure of very prolonged massed practice which was applied to patient B supports the theory proposed by Yates[1] to explain the origin of certain tics. The other two procedures applied to patient A, did not support that theory. The data further suggest that the rate of decline was steady in that tic which received the largest amount of massed practice. There is no evidence in curve 4 (see Fig. 17.2) of a cessation of the rate of decline in the frequency of voluntary responding to the tic, or by an initial rise in frequency, following the very prolonged rest periods. This probably indicates that the growth of the negative habit of "not doing the tic" did actually proceed at a rapid rate and contributed towards the growth of conditioned inhibition ($_sI_R$) rather than $_sH_R$.

In the case of patient A, the lack of response to repeated massed extinction trials may be ascribed to a variety of factors. Her age may very materially have increased the difficulty of development of conditioned inhibition. Yates' patient was 25 years old. She was also receiving chlorpromazine throughout the experiments. Still another factor is her position on the introversion-extraversion continuum. However, she responded favorably to the alternative method of treatment, i.e., the strengthening of one incompatible response opposite to the one to be eliminated. The foot treadle exercises resulted in the inhibition of the muscular response, the tapping of the foot, by the progressive strengthening of the connection between the buzzer, the warning stimulus, and the withholding the foot from tapping, the response. Tapping responses become spontaneously inhibited on hearing the warning, and this inhibition, by a conditioning process, ultimately occurred spontaneously without the warning and without sounding the buzzer.

SUMMARY

An attempt was made to treat two psychiatric patients suffering from tics by the method of treatment, proposed by Yates, based on the theoretical model that some tics may be conceptualized as drive-reducing conditioned avoidance responses, originally evoked in a traumatic situation.

Three procedures of massed practice were applied in order to build up a negative habit of "not doing the tic." Yates' "standard procedure" and a modification of this, did not confirm the hypothesis that massed practice leads to a significant decrement in the ability to respond voluntarily. His procedure of very prolonged periods of massed practice followed by very prolonged rest, supported the validity of the theory.

The patient who failed to respond favorably to Yates' method, improved significantly by exercises on an apparatus built on the basis of the classical conditioned-response principle.

Acknowledgments—The author wishes to acknowledge his indebtedness to Dr. W. J. McCulley, Medical Superintendent, St. Andrew's Hospital, for permission to publish and for making it possible for the investigation to be carried out.

REFERENCES

1. Yates, A. J. The application of learning theory to the treatment of tics. *J. Abnorm. Soc. Psychol.*, 1958, **56**, 175–182.
2. Yates, A. J. Personal communication, 1959.

ARTICLE 18

Self-Monitoring and Reciprocal Inhibition in the Modification of Multiple Tics of *Gilles de la Tourette's Syndrome**†

EDWIN J. THOMAS‡

School of Social Work and Department of Psychology, University of Michigan

KATHLEEN SHEA ABRAMS

Parkview Rehabilitation Unit, and Department of Psychology, University of Michigan

and

JAMES B. JOHNSON§

University of Michigan Medical School

Abstract: An 18-year-old male with multiple tics, including a bark-like vocalization and jerking neck movements, as components of the syndrome of *Gilles de la Tourette*, was treated using an empirically based practice procedure in an investigation that employed a modified multiple-baseline design. In the assessment, instigating and inhibiting stimulus conditions were identified by collecting observational data on the tics in many life situations in and outside of the rehabilitation unit where the therapy was undertaken. Self-monitoring was found to be tic-inhibiting and when it was introduced in the modification for the vocal tic, the rate dropped immediately and dramatically on the first day. Self-monitoring and reciprocal

*Reprinted from *Journal of Behavior Therapy and Experimental Psychiatry*, 1971, **2**, 159–171, Pergamon Press. Copyright © 1971. With permission from Pergamon Press and Edwin J. Thomas.

†Portions of the first author's work on this project were supported by a grant from the Social and Rehabilitation Service, Department of Health, Education and Welfare, Grant CRD-529-0. Portions of the second author's work on this project were supported by the State of Michigan Division of Vocational Rehabilitation and by Rehabilitation Services Administration, Grant No. 2-75-04.

‡Requests for reprints should be addressed to Edwin J. Thomas, The University of Michigan School of Social Work, 1065 Frieze Building, Ann Arbor, Michigan 48104.

§Present address: Christ Hospital, Cincinnati, Ohio.

inhibition procedures were subsequently associated with gradual reduction to nearly zero of a newly emerged minor vocal sound and of the neck tic. Evidence also suggested that the haloperidol the patient had taken previous to treatment and took throughout all but 1 week of the treatment period may have helped to reduce the tics.

INTRODUCTION

The strange syndrome of multiple tics that originates in childhood and consists of compulsive jerking of the voluntary musculature in the face, neck, or extremities combined with coprolalia, echolalia or of other spasmodic involuntary noises is widely known as the *maladie de Gilles de la Tourette* (Gilles de la Tourette, 1885). Many investigators have observed that these multiple tics are very frequently accompanied by so-called emotional disturbances, such as enuresis, phobias, and aggressiveness (e.g. see Corbett *et al.*, 1969; Lucas, 1967; and Morphew and Sim, 1969). The prognosis was originally thought to be poor and many writers still describe pessimistic prospects. However, recent studies by Corbett *et al.* (1969) and Lucas *et al.* (1969), in which this type of tiqueur was followed-up over long periods, now suggest a more favorable prognosis.

The causal basis for the syndrome is unknown. Although particular organic abnormalities have been found in some studies (e.g. see Balthazar, 1957; Eriksson, 1965; and Field *et al.*, 1966), other studies involving a relatively large number of subjects have failed to discover any consistent organic problem or history (Corbett *et al.*, 1969; Morphew and Sim, 1969). In addition to functional theories of origin (Ascher, 1948; Mahler, 1944 and 1945; Morphew and Sim, 1969), there are explanations in terms of both functional and organic factors. A clear case for the latter view is presented by Stevens and Blachly (1966) in whose study there was the successful treatment of the malady with a specific drug, haloperidol. This antipsychotic appears to be the most consistently effective drug, although success with it varies from complete, almost immediate relief of symptoms, to no discernible effect (e.g. see Abuzzahab, 1970; Challas and Brauer, 1963; Connell *et al.*, 1967; Ford and Gottlieb, 1969; Healy, 1970; Lucas, 1967; Shapiro and Shapiro, 1968; Stevens and Blachly, 1966).

CASE HISTORY

The patient is an 18-year-old male whose tics consisted of spasmodic, involuntary jerks of the neck, convulsive-like movements of his hands, and of plosive bursts of air that sounded like a sharp, loud bark. There were many other frequent, minor movements of the extremities, but these were less clearly discernible as discrete, convulsive-like movements. The patient came to our attention 10 days after he was admitted to the Parkview Rehabilitation Unit for an appraisal relating to his vocational potential. His tics were judged by the vocational evaluation staff as sufficiently severe to be a significant vocational and social handicap for mechanical work, his vocational choice. Although his tics did not cause physical interference with his ability to perform manual tasks, the vocal tic was noted to be distracting to co-workers.

Interviews with the parents disclosed that a tic consisting of a muscular movement in the face and mouth was first observed at age 5, 3 months after the patient began school. Before that, the patient was said to be a "high-strung baby" who didn't sleep much, cried and laughed more readily than his brothers, and was "fussy." The noise was first noticed at age 10 or 11 but the parents could not remember when his neck and hand tics developed. They recalled that the patient's tics had been much improved from about age 13 to 14 during which time he and his family lived in a different town where he did not go to school. At that time, the patient had a tutor assigned to him by the school and helped his father take care of the small grocery store and gas station that the father then owned. The year after, the family moved back to the community in which the patient was born. The patient returned to school, and once again the tics became worse. He missed a lot of school during the last 4 years that he attended because of what his parents alleged to be the strain on him to try to keep quiet at school. One teacher had become irritated by his noises and reprimanded him, making him sit in front of the class. That same year, in the eleventh grade, the patient dropped out of school because his tics had increased there and made him very nervous about school.

The family history disclosed that the mother had developed a tic at about the age of 13, following an attack of scarlet fever and the birth of her brother. Her tic was a neck jerk and she occasionally had a vocal tic which was neither as loud nor the same as the patient's. The husband, who had known her at the time, said that he had not noticed any tics. The mother said that her neck movement was worst between the ages of 13 to 16 after which it improved because, she said, she learned to relax and eventually "grew out of it." However, when she gets nervous, she still has a neck and an eyelid twitch, both of which were observed by the interviewer.

The patient's parents claim that they are relatively indulgent with the patient and their other five children although they appear to have strict moral standards. They say that they have not expected as much from the patient as they have of the other children, have tried to keep him calm, have not reprimanded him for his tics and have referred to him as a "handicapped child." He has been unemployed since he left school and has remained at home where he occupies himself with a variety of activities. Although the patient seems to get along well with people and says he likes to meet them, he has not dated and has had relatively few friends.

The patient received a variety of treatments for his condition since medical advice was first sought for him at the age of 5. At various times he has received psychotherapy, milieu therapy and hypnosis in addition to a variety of drugs, such as phenobarbital, meprobamate and haloperidol. The only form of treatment that had produced any benefit was halo-peridol. For most of the time since 1968, when he was hospitalized for several months at a child psychiatric facility, the patient had been taking $1\frac{1}{2}$ mg two times a day and he said this had a calming effect and reduced the tics somewhat. Larger doses made the patient drowsy and reduced his ability to function normally. Although earlier the patient's condition was given a variety of diagnoses (e.g. Huntington's Chorea), the most recent and authoritative is *Gilles de la Tourette.* Electroencephalograms had been done on two occasions and were found to be within normal limits. On the Wechsler Intelligence Scale for Children, he performed at age 15 within the average range of intellectual functioning, with a Verbal I.Q. of 106, a Performance I.Q. of 96, and a Full Scale I.Q. of 101.

ASSESSMENT PROCEDURE AND RESULTS

In Yates' (1970) appraisal of prior behavioral therapy and research on tics, he observed that most if not all behavioral assessment of tics has been undertaken in laboratory contexts, that the researchers had failed to obtain base rate and assessment data in situations approximating those of real life, and that modification had been mainly experimental rather than therapeutic. In this study, all behavioral assessment and modification were performed in a non-laboratory environment that included the rehabilitation unit and the city in which it is located.

The goal of modification was primarily therapeutic and an empirically-based behavioral practice procedure was followed (Thomas *et al.*, 1970; Gambrill *et al.*, 1971). The steps of the procedure followed here were the specification of the focal behavior, baselining, determination of the controlling conditions associated with the focal behavior, determination of environmental and behavioral resources, specification of behavioral objectives, the formulation of the modification plan, the implementation of the plan, and the monitoring of outcomes.

Specification

Identification of the component behaviors of the tic syndrome was accomplished by observing the patient for several hours through a one-way mirror while he engaged in different activities. The vocal tic was the most frequent and conspicuous, the neck tic second and the hand movements third. All these had convulsive, involuntary qualities and thus were different from other frequent and repetitive movements of the extremities. At this point, the separate tics appeared to be independent of one another inasmuch as they were not chained together nor were their rates related. It was possible for the patient voluntarily to suppress the tics only to a very minor degree and only for brief periods.

Baselines

The procedure used to record the tics involved counting and recording every tic in order of occurrence, using a separate row of the record sheet for each 5 sec interval. Major activities of the patient were also recorded for each interval. A cue sound, occurring at 5 sec intervals, which had earlier been recorded on a cassette tape, was listened to during observation with an inconspicuous ear attachment that made it possible for the observer alone to hear the cue sound. Reliability training was accomplished by having two or more observers code the patient's tics while observing him through a one-way mirror and being cued by interval sounds which, in this instance, were made audible to all observers. The practice sessions served to increase the reliability of coding. We learned from these sessions that only one tic at a time could be counted reliably in 5 sec intervals and that activity recording could include only major activities.

Reliability checks were based upon four 5 min samples of observation, using two observers, with the patient engaged in various, voluntary activities in real-life situations. Of a total of 106 judgments, 80 per cent fell within the same 5 sec intervals and 98 per cent within the same or adjacent intervals. Ninety-eight per cent agreement was achieved on the number of judgments in the total time period. Two 5 min periods were used to check on the coding reliability for the neck tics. Here the percentages of agreement were 34 for coding in the same 5 sec intervals, 69 for coding in the same or adjacent 5 sec intervals, and 90 for agreement on the total number counted. Clearly, the vocal tics could be coded more reliably than the neck tics.

Because it was impossible for an observer to record reliably more than one tic at a time, a modified multiple baseline design was used. First, the vocal tic was baselined and modified, then a newly developed minor vocal sound and the neck tic were baselined and each modified, beginning with the minor vocal sound.

Observations were taken of the tics in two types of real-life situations. The first consisted of those to which the patient voluntarily exposed himself and that occurred mainly in the institution. This was referred to as Tagalong observation because the observer, following a period of adaptation to his presence by the patient and others in the rehabilitation unit, followed the patient as unobtrusively as possible everywhere he went. For the most part, the patient was observed in Tagalong situations for 15 min, followed by 15 min rest for the observer. Table 18.1 shows the types of situations in which the patient was observed for the first day of baseline observation. The table also indicates that there were eight 15 min

Table 18.1 Barks per Minute for Eight Tagalong Observation Periods for One Day Before Intervention (2 November).

Time	Tics	Tics per minute	Activity
4:22–4:37	30	2.0	Reading aloud in own hospital room.
4:52–5:07	52	3.5	Playing guitar and singing intermittently.
5:23–5:38	102	6.8	Finishing meal in dining room, laughing, joking and talking with five other patients.
5:55–6:10	37	2.5	Typing in O.T. room; girl later sits next to patient.
6:25–6:40	79	5.3	Talking, laughing, joking in female friend's room.
6:56–7:11	57	3.8	Talking with female in her room.
7:28–7:43	52	3.5	Talking with female, combing her hair, in her room.
7:58–8:13	40	2.7	Entering own room, greets new roommate, reads magazine on mechanics.
All periods for 2 November	449	3.7	

observational periods beginning in the late afternoon and continuing into the early evening. For the time involved, a total daily rate of 449 vocal tics was recorded, yielding 3.7 as the daily rate of tics per min. It is this daily rate for the first day of baselining that is plotted on Fig. 18.1. The analogous rate for Tagalong observation periods two days later was 4.5. Figure 18.1 also indicates that the neck tic occurred at a lower rate than the vocal tic and was more variable; and that prior to modification the minor vocal sounds never attained a very high rate and were somewhat variable.

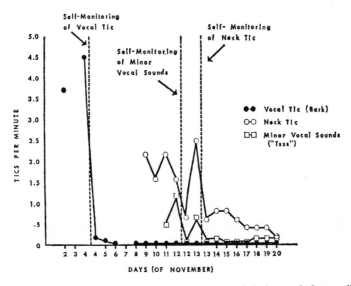

Fig. 18.1. Tics per min for daily Tagalong observation periods before and after modification by self-monitoring of vocal tic, minor vocal sounds, and neck tic. The number of daily observation sessions had a range from 1 to 13, the average being about 3–4 per day. Almost all observation sessions lasted 15 min. The number of min of observation per day had a range from 15 to 186, with an average of approximately 51.

The second type of observation was undertaken in connection with planned exposure by the therapist of the patient to different real-life situations, most of which were common to life outside an institution (Fig. 18.2 a–g). The cleaners and drug store, church, high school, restaurant, public library and supermarket were selected because the rate of tic behavior in these situations was either judged by the observer to be higher or was thought by the patient to be elevated. The patient's hospital room and the observation room were included because the patient thought that his tics occurred less frequently in these places. The itinerary for these so-called Exposure Tours was selected by the therapists and required the patient to enter the situation in question for about 10 min. In most cases, they were situations that the patient would not necessarily enter in the normal course of events while in the rehabilitation unit.

Figures 18.2a, b and c indicate that for the vocal tic, the cleaners and the drug store yielded the highest rate (5.8), that the church yielded a relatively high rate (4.1), and that the patient's hospital room yielded a relatively low rate (1.8). In these situations, comparable rates were found

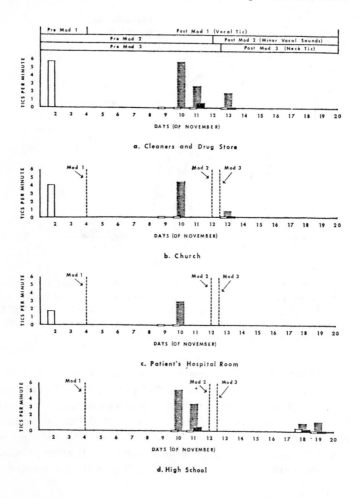

a. Cleaners and Drug Store

b. Church

c. Patient's Hospital Room

d. High School

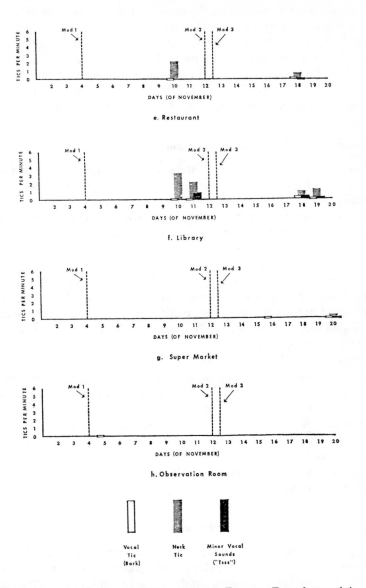

e. Restaurant

f. Library

g. Super Market

h. Observation Room

Vocal
Tic
(Bark)

Neck
Tic

Minor Vocal
Sounds
("Tsss")

Fig. 18.2. Tics per min for places patient was taken on Exposure Tours for vocal tic, minor vocal sounds, and neck tic. Rates based upon 10-min observation periods up to and including 11 November, except for 11–5 which was 45 min. From 11 November, the periods were 15 min each.

for the neck tic and, altogether, the rates for the neck tic ranged from 2.2, for the restaurant, to 5.8 for the cleaners and drug store. However, it should be noted that the neck tic diminished in all those situations in which observations were taken on at least two occasions prior to its planned modification. The rates for the minor vocal sound were less than 1 per min and were about the same in the three situations in which they were sampled prior to modification (see Figs. 18.2a, d and f).

Determination of Controlling Condition

Instigators as well as possible inhibitors of the tics were sought in the assessment of the stimulus conditions associated with the problem behavior. Information about stimulus conditions was obtained from Tagalong observation of the patient's behavior in hospital situations to which he had daily, voluntary exposure. Examples of these are given in Table 18.1 where it may be seen that the lowest rate was 2 for the vocal tic, obtained when the patient was reading aloud in his own hospital room, and that the highest rate of 6.8 occurred when he was laughing, joking and talking with other patients during and after a meal. Exposure Tours consisted of more systematic, planned exposure to stimulus conditions and yielded moderate to large differences in rates for the vocal and neck tic (see Fig. 18.2).

Probes were undertaken to observe whether conditions thought to be important in controlling the tics actually caused variation in the rate. The results are given in Fig. 18.3. When the patient was working alone in the observation room, the rates were among the lowest obtained in the entire assessment. Likewise, it may be seen that talking to a stranger greatly increased the rate as compared with talking to a familiar person, the therapist. The lowest rate of all (less than 1 per min) was obtained when the patient was asked to count his own tics for a period of 20 min, using a simple wrist counter.

Environmental and Behavioral Resources

The patient came from a small, remote community in the northern part of the state and because of the distance and lack of time, it was not possible to complete an assessment there nor to introduce modification in the patient's natural environment, as would have been ideal. Furthermore, there was a limited amount of time authorized for work on the tic and this precluded the use of behavioral modification techniques that involve long periods of time. The entire period actually embraced 25 days.

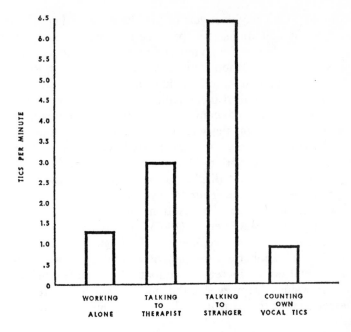

Fig. 18.3. Vocal tics per min for probes conducted in observation room. Length of observation periods were 60 min for working alone and 9, 10, and 20 min for the others, respectively.

Behavioral Objectives

On the basis of information collected up to this point, the objectives were, first, to reduce the rate for the vocal tic, which was clearly most socially stigmatic, and, if time permitted, to begin work on the neck tic.

MODIFICATION

Plan

The assessment had indicated that self-monitoring produced the lowest rate for the vocal tic and that it was the most certain technique to serve as a possible inhibitor of tics. Thus, the plan called for instituting self-monitoring as the first part of modification.

The assessment also provided information concerning the relative degrees to which other stimulus conditions served to elicit differential rates of the tics. One way to endeavor to reduce the instigating capability of such stimulus conditions is to produce responses incompatible with tics. To the extent that profound muscular relaxation is incompatible with the convulsive and spasmodic muscular contractions of the tics, the principle of reciprocal inhibition would be applicable (Wolpe, 1958). (It is this presumed physiological incompatibility of muscular relaxation and tics that justifies the use of reciprocal inhibition procedures in this case, not the assumption that the tics were based on anxiety, for the assessment did not disclose that anxiety alone was related to the rate of tic behavior.) To our knowledge, little work has been done on the use of relaxation with tics. Although Stevens and Blachly (1966) employed relaxation without success in a case with the *Tourette* syndrome, Clark (1963) reported modest success in the use of relaxation with a muscular spasm of an hysterical nature and MacPherson (1967) found that relaxation helped in reducing the involuntary movements of Huntington's Chorea.

Concerning the haloperidol the patient was taking, it was known that the dosage could not be increased without adverse side effects, such as excessive drowsiness. However, if the modification plan were successful, it was hoped to take the patient off the drug, assuming this to be feasible medically.

Implementation

Self-monitoring for the vocal tic was undertaken in mid-morning of the third day after the beginning of baseline observation (November 4). It was explained to the patient that we had observed the usefulness of self-monitoring from an earlier probe, undertaken during assessment, and that we believed this would be valuable for him to do in helping him to reduce his tics. He was provided with a quiet lever counter and asked to count all noises relating to the vocal tic, to do this all day and to continue the monitoring until instructed otherwise. He was to check the counter every 15 min, report the count to the observer who followed him around the first day, to reset the counter and resume recording. Brief practice was given in how to use the counter unobtrusively and to count a tic when it occurred. During the first day, the observer followed the patient, collected the information concerning the number of tics from the patient, and, observed the tics, as before, on a time-sampling basis. The next day the same procedure was followed except that the patient was instructed to record the counts of his tics when the observer was not present.

Whenever his rate was 0.5 or less, he was commended by the observer for the reduced rate. On the third day the patient was instructed to record any muffled sounds separately from those that were like the original vocal tic and, on the following day, the recording periods were lengthened from 15 min to 1 hr.

Self-monitoring of the minor vocal sounds and neck tic also consisted of an explanation, instructions, a practice session, frequent recording periods, surveillance by the observer, and verbal approval for low rates.

Following the procedure outlined by Wolpe (1969), relaxation training was undertaken for a period of 6 days (from 5 to 11 November). After this, scenes capable of making the patient tense were presented imaginally following a procedure directly comparable to that employed in systematic desensitization. The hierarchy of scenes capable of producing muscular tension was drawn up from observation of the patient in different situations as well as from the patient's self report. In order from the least to the most tension producing, the hierarchy was as follows: his room in the hospital, the drug store, the cleaners, the church, the library, the restaurant, the University High School, and the new city high school. In addition, there was periodic *in vivo* scene exposure during this period. During the last 3 days of the patient's tenure in the hospital (from 17 to 20 November), there was imaginal exposure to scenes from the home hierarchy which was based entirely on the patient's self report. The home hierarchy progressed from driving a car, being in the woods, patient's own house, brothers' houses, the local garage, a local food store, his church, any dance, his friend's house when family was there, the coffee shop, to the local school, the most tension producing.

Because of the evident success of the modification, the patient was taken off the drug beginning 11 November but placed back on it on 19 November after the rate of vocal and neck tics increased slightly and the patient complained of increased muscular tension.

All of the data produced by the patient from his recording of the frequency of vocal tics, minor vocal sounds and neck tics were examined. Unfortunately, the rates were all essentially less than one, even for the neck tics prior to modification, and there was a low relationship between the patient's counts and the observer's because of the patient's underrecording. Several sessions were undertaken expressly to improve the accuracy of the patient's recording by calling to his attention occasional tics that were observed. If there was any effect of the training sessions, it was minor and temporary.

Results

The self-monitoring reduced the vocal tic rapidly and markedly judging from the data presented in Fig. 18.1. Specifically, the rate was 4.5 in the morning of the day just before the introduction of self-monitoring and, following the introduction of self-monitoring later that day, the rate went essentially to zero. The rate actually attained zero 2 days later and remained there until 12 days later (18 November) at which time two of the original vocal tics were noted. Since arranging to have him stop taking the drug (on 11 November) we had observed an increasing excitability, tenseness and difficulty in achieving relaxation. Finally, the occurrence of two vocal tics caused us to arrange to have him placed back on the drug the following day (19 November), after which there were no more vocal tics.

The results presented in Fig. 18.2 generally indicate equally clear reductions in the vocal tic. We refer particularly to the difference in rates before and after modification for the situations of the cleaners and drug store, the church and the patient's hospital room (Figs. 18.2a, b, and c). The remaining rates are post-modification and are zero except for a very small increase on the last day that the patient was off the drug (18 November) for Exposure Tours of the high school (Fig. 18.2d), restaurant (Fig. 18.2e), and the library (Fig. 18.2f). All rates were zero again on the days after the patient resumed taking the drug (19 and 20 November).

Despite the reduction in the vocal tic proper, there were subtle aspects of response noted by us after the vocal tic essentially disappeared following modification. At first there appeared to be a muffled bark imbedded in laughing or talking, then there was sound that consisted of the passage of the air through the nose in a soft plosive manner. Both responses were observed just after modification started and evidently disappeared a few days after modification. The most noteworthy response, however, was what we have called the minor vocal sounds and these consisted of a *"tsss"* sound made by passing the air between the tongue and roof of the mouth. Although periodically repetitive, these sounds clearly lacked the convulsive, involuntary quality of the vocal tic.

Base rates were taken for these minor vocal sounds on 11 November and on the morning of the next day. Self-monitoring was undertaken on the afternoon of the second day, and, as Figure 18.1 indicates, there was an immediate reduction to zero, then resumption on the next day followed by a reduction to about zero for the remainder of the patient's stay in the hospital. Figure 18.2 indicates that all changes for the Exposure Tour data show a consistent decrease in the post-modification rates as compared with the pre-modification rates. Note the contrasts for the cleaners and drug store (Fig. 18.2a), the high school (Fig. 18.2d), and the library (Fig. 18.2f). Also, the rates are essentially zero for all data points obtained only after modification, namely, the rates for the church (Fig. 18.2b), the restaurant (Fig. 18.2e), the supermarket (Fig. 18.2g).

Concerning the neck tic, Fig. 18.1 indicates that following the introduction of self-monitoring there was a gradual and continuing reduction in the rate until it reached that of about one tic in 4 min on the last day prior to discharge from hospital. Results for the Exposure Tours indicate that all of the post-modification rates for the neck tic are less than those obtained prior to modification. These contrasts involve the cleaners and drug store, the church, the high school, the restaurant, and the library (Figs. 18.2a, b, d, e and f). Rates for the neck tic on the Exposure Tours never reached zero even just prior to discharge from hospital. The original intense, spasmodic character of the neck tic was replaced by a much less violent movement which was at times so slight as to be difficult to discern.

DISCUSSION

The effect of the self-monitoring was most evident for the vocal tic because the change was dramatic and occurred prior to the introduction of the relaxation and reciprocal inhibition regimen. Self-monitoring also probably served to reduce the minor vocal sounds and the neck tic. However, the changes in both instances were less dramatic than for the vocal tic and may be attributable in part or fully to the relaxation training or the reciprocal inhibition procedure, both of which had been introduced for the vocal tic before the self-monitoring was substituted for the other two tics. Because the results for the neck tic indicated a reduction in rate prior to the introduction of self-monitoring, it seems plausible to argue that the relaxation and the reciprocal inhibition procedure may have been effective to some extent. It seems probable, also, that the halperidol served to reduce somewhat the rate of tic behavior. As indicated, this drug has been the one found to be most successful to date with this particular syndrome. The drug inhibits motor activities in animals in open field tests and inhibits conditioned avoïdance responses in a manner similar to that of the phenothiazines.

The study provides information that may contribute to a greater understanding of self-monitoring. The direction of change here was clearly "positive," i.e., the self-monitoring evidently reduced the problem behavior. Studies have shown both positive and negative self-monitoring effects. For example, Rutner and Bugle (1969) reported that frequencies of self-recorded auditory hallucinations were greatly reduced when the patient kept counts under private conditions. Stollak (1967) found weight reductions associated with diary recording of the kinds and amounts of food eaten combined with frequent contacts with a graduate student who reviewed the diary data and praised moderate food intake. However, McFall (1970), in a classroom-based experiment, found an increase rather than a decrease in smoking for subjects asked to record the number of cigarettes smoked.

The rate of change in self-monitoring also may vary. In the case of the vocal tic, the decrease was almost instantaneous and precipitous whereas the changes for the minor vocal sound and neck tic, if due to self-monitoring, were more gradual. More gradual changes were observed in the studies cited above. Furthermore, the rate of change was found in this study to be approximately the same in different situations. That is, the amount by which the rate for the vocal tic, minor vocal sound, and neck tic were reduced in one stimulus context was similar to the amount of reduction in other situations (see Fig. 18.2). Such apparent pan-situational change clearly does not characterize all behavior changes.

In addition to the nature of the self-monitoring effect, considerable uncertainty attends the question of what its functional behavioral properties may be. In the case of rapid reduction of problem behavior following self-monitoring, as was the case for the vocal tic, the effects are largely a function of discrimination or eliciting antecedents for the problem behavior. In contrast, a gradual reduction allows response feedback to occur more readily and, hence, the effects of such factors as self-administered aversiveness or the withholding of self-reinforcement may then be operative. In either case, stimuli produced by the observation of one's own behavior may be crucial in mediating a self-monitoring effect. In the case of the vocal tic, the patient's own observations of the tics tended to underrepresent the rate; in other words, many tics occurred that were not attended to or tracked by him. Indeed, in the case of the minor vocal sound that emerged after the reduction of the vocal tic, the patient was totally unaware of the new sound until we called it to his attention as part of his self-monitoring. The vocal and neck tics were clearly known to the patient before self-monitoring and were a source of embarrassment. However, not every occurrence of these behaviors was attended to by the patient. Careful behavioral investigation of awareness phenomena and observation of one's own behavior as they affect changes in one's own behavior should contribute greatly to the understanding of self-monitoring.

There are several noteworthy features of the procedure employed in this study to guide the therapeutic activities. One is the essentially empirical nature of the assessment. The assessment of the tics by Tagalong observation, Exposure Tours in real-life situations and by tests based upon probes all served to highlight the remarkable extent to which the tics were differentially elicited by various stimulus conditions. Such information may allow the therapist to construct empirically based hierarchies of inhibiting and instigating stimulus conditions. The modification undertaken in this study was very much guided by the data yielded in the assessment, especially the information about self-monitoring as an inhibitor of tics. However, the data were collected in the hospital and in the city where the hospital was located. This meant that the data were not necessarily adequate to plan a maintenance procedure for the home situation, to which the patient returned.* As previously stated, it was not feasible to conduct the assessment and modification in the patient's home locale, but had they been undertaken, then this step-wise procedure would have been applicable. Different procedural guidelines need to be developed for the special circumstances in which assessment and modification cannot be undertaken in the patient's home environment.

The assessment and monitoring techniques yielded data relating to the phenomena of "symptom substitution," namely, to what happens to repertoire elements when one "problem" component is changed. The minor vocal sound did emerge after the vocal tic was reduced to zero. It was topographically very different from the bark of the vocal tic and, indeed, could not really be called a tic. Minor as it was, however, it was clearly a behavior that emerged following the reduction of the vocal tic. The only phenomenon known to us that is similar to this is the emergence of a hiss in the young patient with *Gilles de la Tourette* studied by Stevens and Blachly (1966). However, the hiss occurred after many *unsuccessful* attempts to alter the rate of the tics and before using haloperidol successfully. Other than the minor vocal sound, no other such behaviors were observed in our study following the introduction of modification for the sound itself or for the neck tic. Furthermore, the neck tic diminished

---

*Because of the distance to the patient's home, there was no way to assure the implementation of a modification plan after discharge. In recognition of this fact, this study was purposely restricted to what was undertaken and observed in the hospital context.

rather than increased after the modification was undertaken for the vocal tic and after the vocal tic diminished. Altogether, the results are not consistent with a literal doctrine of symptom substitution as applied here, i.e. another problem behavior did not appear following the modification of each of the target behaviors addressed in the modification. However, the results raise the possibility that the vocal tic may have been a member of the same operant class as the minor vocal sound. It is uncertain as to whether the neck tic could also have been a member of this class.

Acknowledgments—We wish to thank Marjorie Becker, Ph.D., Coordinator of the Parkview Rehabilitation Unit, and Robert Koski and Robert Stinson, DVR Coordinators who provided encouragement and support for this study.

REFERENCES

Abuzzahab, F. S. Some uses of haloperidol in the treatment of psychiatric conditions, *Psychosomatics*, 1970, **11**, 188–193.

Ascher, E. Psychodynamic considerations in *Gilles de la Tourette's* disease with a report of five cases and discussion of the literature, *Amer. J. Psychiat.*, 1948, **105**, 267.

Balthazar, K. Über das Anatomische Substrat der Generalisierten Tic-Krankheit. Entwicklungshemmung des corpus Striatum, *Archive Psychiat. Nervenkr.*, 1957, **195**, 531–549.

Challas, G. and Brauer, W. Tourette's disease; relief of symptoms with R1625, *Am. J. Psychiat.*, 1963, **120**, 283.

Clark, D. F. The treatment of hysterical spasm and agoraphobia by behavior therapy, *Behav. Res. & Therapy*, 1963, **1**, 245–250.

Connell, P. H., Corbett, J. A., Horne, D. J., and Mathews, A. M. Drug treatment of adolescent tiqueurs—a double blind trial of diazepam and haloperidol, *Brit. J. Psychiat.*, 1967, **113**, 375–381.

Corbett, J. A., Mathews, A. M., Connell, P. H., and Shapiro, D. A. Tics and *Gilles de la Tourette's Syndrome*: a follow-up study and critical review, *Brit. J. Psychiat.*, 1969, **115**, 1229–1241.

Eriksson, B. and Persson, T. *Gilles de la Tourette's Syndrome*: two cases with an organic brain injury, *Brit. J. Psychiat.*, 1969, **115**, 351–353.

Field, J. R., Corbin, K. B., Goldstein, N. P., and Klass, D. W. *Gilles de la Tourette's Syndrome. Neurology*, 1966, **16**, 453–462.

Ford, C. V. and Gottlieb, F. An objective evaluation of haloperidol in *Gilles de la Tourette's Syndrome, Dis. Nerv. System*, 1969, **30**, 328–332.

Gambrill, E. D., Thomas, E. J., and Carter, R. D. Procedure for sociobehavioral practice in open settings, *Social Work*, 1971, **16**, 51–62.

Gilles de la Tourette. Étude sur une affection nerveuse, caractérisée par de l'incoordination motrice, accompagnée d'écholalie et de coprolalie. *Archives de Neurologie*, 1885, **9**, 159.

Lucas, A. R. *Gilles de la Tourette's* disease in children: treatment with haloperidol, *Amer. J. Psychiat.*, 1967, **124**, 243–245.

Lucas, A. R., Kauffman P. E., and Morris E. M. *Gilles de la Tourette's* disease—a clinical study of fifteen cases. *J. Amer. Acad. Child Psychiat.*, 1969, **6**, 700–722.

MacPherson, E. Control of involuntary movement. *Behav. Res. & Therapy*, 1967, **5**, 143–145.

Mahler, M. S. Tics and impulsions in children: a study of motility, *Psychoanal. Quart.*, 1944, **13**, 430.

Mahler, M. S., Luke, J. A., and Dalttoff, W. Clinical follow-up study of the tic syndrome in children, *Am. J. Orthopsychiat.*, 1945, **15**, 631.

McFall, R. M. Effects of self-monitoring on normal smoking behavior, *J. Con. & Clin. Psych.*, 1970, **35**, 135–143.

Morphew, J. A. and Sim, M. *Gilles de la Tourette's Syndrome*—a clinical and psychopathological study, *Brit. J. Med. Psychol.*, 1969, **42**, 293–301.

Rutner, I. T. and Bugle, C. An experimental procedure for the modification of psychotic behavior, *J. Con. & Clin. Psych.*, 1969, **33**, 651–654.

Stevens, J. K. and Blachly, P. H. Successful treatment of *Maladie des Tics: Gilles de la Tourette's Syndrome*, *Amer. J. Dis. Child*, 1966, **112**, 541–545.

Shapiro, A. K. and Shapiro, E. Treatment of *Gilles de la Tourette's Syndrome* with haloperidol, *J. Psychiat.*, 1968, **114**, 345–350.

Stollak, G. Weight loss obtained under different experimental procedures, *Psychotherapy: Theory Res. & Prac.*, 1967, **4**, 61–64.

Thomas, E. J., Carter, R. D., and Gambrill, E. D. (eds.) *Utilization and appraisal of socio-behavioral techniques in social welfare—pilot phase.* Final report on research supported by the Department of Health, Education and Welfare, Social Rehabilitation Service, Grant SRS–CRD 425–C1–9, Ann Arbor, Michigan: University of Michigan School of Social Work, 1970.

Wolpe, J. *Psychotherapy by Reciprocal Inhibition.* Stanford, Calif.: Stanford Univ. Press, 1958.

Wolpe, J. *The Practice of Behavior Therapy.* New York: Pergamon Press, 1969.

Yates, A. J. *Behavior Therapy.* New York: Wiley, 1970.

ARTICLE 19

The Treatment of Hysterical Spasmodic Torticollis by Behavior Therapy*

H. BRIERLEY

Professorial Unit of Psychological Medicine, General Hospital, Newcastle-upon-Tyne, Northumberland

The condition of spasmodic torticollis is one in which there is a disorder of the cervical muscles, particularly the sternocleidomastoid muscle, resulting in abnormal movements or positioning of the head. Whilst the condition may be a symptom of disease of the extrapyramidal system, it may also have an hysterical origin. In torticollis of the hysterical type it is believed that the disorder follows an emotional trauma and presents with a relatively rapid onset. An insidiously developing condition is more usual in cases of organic etiology. In any event, attempts to treat this condition are generally "disappointing" (cf. Davidson, 1962). In popular usage the symptom is often termed "wry neck."

CASE HISTORIES

Case No. 1. A.M.

A married man, 32 yr old, who was employed as a draughtsman. His home environment showed no evidence of stress factors and his marital adjustment was normal. However, he came from a rather poor home and despite good intellectual endowment began his working life as a laborer. He succeeded in pulling himself up by his bootstraps to a post of some responsibility. Whilst he was generally happy at work he was ambitious for further promotion and was taking a management course at a college of advanced technology. This occupied most of his spare time. He was, however, manifestly unsuitable for management, being a shy retiring man of rather inadequate educational background. His ambition reflected a slightly paranoid aspect of his personality; he tended to ruminate over his lack of early opportunity. Whilst studying, the symptoms commenced fairly abruptly. He found he could not sit comfortably watching the blackboard but, curiously, had little difficulty at work over his drawing board in the early stages. The symptoms increased in severity until he had to discontinue the course and until there was a more general incapacity affecting his work. He also became unable to drive his car safely.

Over a period of 2 yr he was treated first by an orthopedic surgeon, then by a psychiatrist. Whilst under the care of the latter he made a very brief improvement but fully relapsed. At this stage he came for behavior therapy and his general practitioner reported, "He is worse than ever now and the condition of his neck is worrying him to a point where he can think of little else." When standing, his head appeared to be supported passively by his left shoulder but he was able to lift it and maintain a fairly normal posture for short periods. He found it difficult to turn his head from side to side. In all postures his head was steady and without stereotyped movements or jerking.

Case No. 2. M.C.

This lady was 32 yr old and the condition developed whilst she was a nun in a nursing order. Several members of her family had suffered from psychiatric illness and two sisters were currently under treatment, one suffering from a phobic state, the other from a bizarre personality disorder with marked religiosity. Until the present illness, however, although not a robust personality, the patient had shown no sign of psychiatric disorder.

After leaving school she had worked as a children's nurse until entering a convent at 20 years of age. Although she continued nursing children her symptoms began at about the time when she was transferred to nurse epileptic children. She denied that this change was at all important to her. Although she had taken her final vows there was an increasing unhappiness about them and doubts about her "worthiness" and so on. In this setting she began sleep-walking and had attacks of "shaking." She was treated at a psychiatric unit with an abreactive technique and improved sufficiently to return to work. Shortly afterwards she relapsed and the torticollis syndrome appeared. She was referred to a neurologist but became unable to continue working and she was recommended to seek a dispensation and leave the order.

She was referred for behavior therapy 2 years after the commencement of the symptom. Her head movements were very restricted so that she could only look over her left shoulder. Her head could not be turned forwards without its also tilting backwards so that she was looking almost vertically upwards. Her head was held with considerable rigidity but there were no jerking movements at this stage as apparently was the case at the onset of the illness.

METHOD OF TREATMENT

Accepting the diagnosis of a functional illness, the torticollis symptom was regarded as a learned maladaptive habit. In each case it could be postulated that the habit had been reinforced by the anxiety reduction which had occurred when the first patient had withdrawn from the promotion race and when the second patient had been temporarily released from her vows. In each case the symptoms had continued to be reinforced in so much as a return to the anxiety-provoking situation would have resulted if the symptoms were lost and also because of some generalization of the anxiety.

As Eysenck and Rachman (1965) have observed, aversion conditioning may be contra-indicated in patients with high anxiety or neuroticism scores on testing. In these cases the following results on the Eysenck Personality Inventory were obtained:

E.P.I. Form A.		
	Neuroticism	Extraversion
A.M.	6	8
M.C.	4	7

The low neuroticism scores and the clinical absence of strong anxiety symptoms indicated that an aversion method was applicable.

It was necessary to devise some technique where the occurrence of the undesirable habit of inclining the head could be associated with an aversive stimulus. The apparatus designed (Fig. 19.1) consisted of a

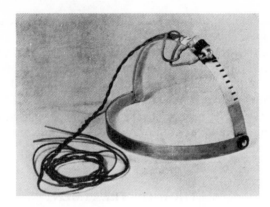

Fig. 19.1. Head-gear, showing sliding clip which mounts mercury switch on calibrated headband.

head-gear constructed on a spring steel band which could be positioned firmly over the top of the head. A clip slid along this band and carried a small mercury switch. This is substantially a glass tube with two electrodes spaced along one side, containing a quantity of mercury. As the tube tips the mercury runs down the tube to complete the circuit and administer a shock across the electrodes. Positioning the tube with the electrodes pointing to the back of the head and not at the bottom of the tube meant that the circuit could also be completed or broken by rotation of the tube or inclining the head backwards. Thus the switch controlled the shock circuit mostly by the inclination of the tube by tilting the head sideways but also to some extent by rotating the tube when the head tilted backwards. The position at which the shock would be switched on could be predetermined by the setting of the switch along the head band. The band was fitted to go vertically across from the apex of the ear to that of the other. By calibrating the band, conditions could be maintained from one session to another with a fair degree of accuracy.

There was one radical difference between the cases. In the female patient's case it was not physically possible for her to attain a normal position, nor could her head be moved to an upright position by the therapist. On the other hand the male patient could hold a normal position for several minutes if generally inactive. In the female patient's case the severe difficulty in overcoming the habit required special consideration. Obviously a posture far from normal, but better than the existing one, would have to be the first objective. Progress to the normal position would have to follow stage by stage as mobility and her general condition improved. The difficulty which the patient experiences in maintaining an improved posture must not be so great as to override a low aversive stimulus. On the other hand, the aversive stimulus should not be increased to the point where in the face of the subjective difficulty in maintaining the improved posture it might prove behaviorally disruptive and perhaps either exacerbate the symptom being treated or create new undesirable habits. Bearing the Yerkes–Dodson Law (Yerkes and Dodson, 1908) in mind in this way, the stimulus was never "unbearable" and the head-gear never adjusted to a point where the posture could not be maintained for several minutes. Errors in positioning the head-gear would produce after a few minutes a fatigue-like state where she would twist her head randomly but be unable to obtain any position where the shock was avoided. Errors of this kind early in treatment may have been a cause of the lack of progress in the early sessions in contrast to the response of the male patient.

If aversion therapy was to be carried out, it seemed that one of the major difficulties might be the production of an alternative form of rigid positioning. It was, therefore, necessary to occupy the subject in a task calling for a certain amount of controlled head movement. This was achieved by requiring the patient to read material projected on to a white wall in front of him. This called for a scanning movement both from side to side and from top to bottom of the screen. The degree and speed of movement could be controlled by the magnification of the print projected and also by re-adjusting the position of the patient in relation to the screen.

The shock was from a standard Faradic generator of the type used in physiotherapy departments. It was administered to the right wrist by wet electrodes. In fact it did not prove necessary to apply a highly noxious level of shock. Although there was always an implied threat of a painful shock, the applied shock was always small enough to allow the patient to avoid by conscious effort. The patients were not provoked into making impulsive sudden movements other than perhaps in the early stages of treating the female patient as mentioned above. The shocks were not detectable as such to the outside observer except in so much as the patient would alter the head position but in any event this frequently occurred without shock. Neither patient showed any dislike or fear of the treatment in any way.

Beech (1960) comments on the significance of secondary reinforcers in the treatment situation, e.g., the sound of the trembler on the Faradic stimulator. The present treatment also drew attention to this aspect of aversion regimes. Few people approach electric shock in an entirely naive way. Even before the *S* has experienced the shock itself, the electrical apparatus usually has an anxiety-provoking aversive value for the patient. The very low shock here, like the buzz of the machine in Beech's case, may well have functioned primarily as a secondary reinforcer. Whatever the explanation of the efficacy of an aversive stimulus (i.e. one which reduces the rate of production of a concomitant learned response) which could barely be called noxious, it contrasts rather significantly with the massively punitive aversive stimuli which have been employed with doubtful efficacy in some aversion regimes, e.g., with apomorphine.

RESULTS

Both patients were treated as out-patients on a weekly basis until improvement was observed. The attendances were then reduced to fortnightly. Progress varied between the two cases.

A.M. began with 10-min reading sessions divided by 5-min rest periods during which the apparatus was disconnected. There were three reading periods at each treatment session. After two sessions the reading periods were reduced to 3 min since the patient complained of eye strain.

At the second session A.M. showed marked improvement. At the fourth session he showed no definite inclination of the head. He was driving his car again and reported that the only residual trouble was stiffness in turning his head which he felt mostly whilst washing. From this point constant manipulation of his position in front of the screen was employed to increase his head movements. Despite the lack of noticeable symptoms, treatment was continued until the twelfth session. He was re-examined by the consultant psychiatrist almost 7 months after starting and about $2\frac{1}{2}$ months after finishing treatment. He reported, "He has responded extremely well to treatment. Not only has his torticollis as such disappeared but he has pretty free mobility in moving his head in both directions. He himself is extremely pleased with his progress. This is a really gratifying response."

At present the patient is still symptom-free over a year after starting treatment.

M.C. responded more slowly. The sessions consisted of three 5-min reading periods exactly as in the later stages of treating A.M. There was no observable improvement over the first four sessions but a definite increase in mobility was observed at the fifth session. At this stage she was referred to the D.R.O. to discuss employment although she was still loathe to consider it.

From this session onwards there was a distinct gradual improvement until at the tenth session she appeared substantially symptom-free. The consultant in charge of the cases reported at this stage, "She has responded extremely well and she is now symptom-free. She herself no longer makes any complaints and is very happy with her good recovery." Six months after conclusion of treatment and 10 months from starting she reported, "I am feeling very well now and will be starting work next week."

SUMMARY

The cases reported were suffering from a condition which had been diagnosed as of hysterical origin after prolonged observation. Both had been treated by established medical and psychiatric methods but according to usual expectation their response had been disappointing. Both were seriously incapacitated and becoming unemployable. Treating the symptom as a simple maladaptive learned habit according to learning theory principles the symptoms were extinguished. Follow-up has shown that both patients made a stable improvement and are now employed and leading normal lives.*

The difficulty which can be foreseen is that of differential diagnosis. There seems to be considerable danger in confusing organic and functional conditions. However, this danger is partly dispelled by the fact that the treatment did not employ conditions of very great discomfort. The aversive stimulus was not painful; providing this condition was maintained, the possibility of error in differential diagnosis need not contraindicate the use of a technique of this kind. Indeed it might be added that the whole treatment of these cases involved a great deal less discomfort to the patient that many routine investigations. However, attention is

---

*Since this paper was submitted, the patient M.C. has twice reverted for short periods to the torticollis symptom. She was, apparently, under severe stress on both occasions, e.g., when both her sister and mother developed gross psychiatric disorders. Thus, this patient remains liable to revert to the symptom. However, the severity of the stress she withstood may be some indication that behavior therapy substantially reduced the possibility of torticollis reappearing as a long-standing incapacity, as it was when she was first seen 18 months ago.

drawn to the fact that high neuroticism or overt anxiety are probably a strong contra-indication to treatment of this kind as they are to other forms of aversion conditioning.

Acknowledgment—This work was carried out whilst the author was Principal Psychologist at Queen's Park Hospital, Blackburn. The author wishes to record his gratitude to Dr. Maurice Silverman for referring these cases, and for his help and interest in the development of behavior therapy techniques in the Psychological Department at that hospital.

REFERENCES

Beech, H. R. Symptomatic treatment of writer's cramp. In *Behaviour Therapy and the Neuroses* (Ed. Eysenck, H. J.). Pergamon Press, London, 1960. P. 356.
Davidson, S. *Principles and Practice of Medicine*, Sixth Ed. Livingstone, London, 1962.
Eysenck, H. J. and Rachman, S. *The Causes and Cure of Neurosis*. Routledge & Kegan Paul, London, 1965.
Yerkes, R. M. and Dodson, J. D. The relation of strength of stimulus to rapidity of habit formation. *J. comp. Neurol.*, 1908, **18**, 455–482.

ARTICLE 20

Behavioral Engineering: Postural Control by a Portable Operant Apparatus*[1]

N. H. AZRIN, H. RUBIN, F. O'BRIEN, T. AYLLON,[2] and D. ROLL[3]

Anna State Hospital

Abstract: Recent studies suggested a general behavioral engineering approach to behavioral disorders by portable operant treatment instruments. The approach was applied to the problem of poor posture, specifically rounding of the back or slouching. An apparatus was developed that provided a warning stimulus followed by an aversive tone for the duration of slouching. Slouching was thereby punished by onset of the tone, and non-slouching was reinforced by tone termination and postponement. Twenty-five adults wore the apparatus during their normal working day during alternate periods in which the aversive tone was connected and disconnected experimentally. A miniature time-meter recorded the duration of slouching. The results showed that slouching decreased for each subject during each period in which slouching produced the aversive tone. For two subjects, a second control procedure was applied in which slouching terminated the tone. The result was an increase of slouching, demonstrating that the postural changes were controlled by the scheduled relation between the aversive tone and the response, and not by other factors such as simple response feedback. The substantial changes in posture indicate that the present procedure may prove to be an effective treatment alternative and suggests the general value of the behavioral engineering approach.

*Reprinted from *Journal of Applied Behavior Analysis*, 1968, **1**, 99–108. Copyright © 1968 by the Society for the Experimental Analysis of Behavior, Inc. With permission from the Society and N. H. Azrin.

[1]This investigation was supported by grants from the Mental Health Fund of the Illinois Department of Mental Health and NIMH Grant 4926. Grateful acknowledgment is given to the active assistance and cooperation of the staff members of Anna State Hospital who participated in developing and testing this method and especially to K. Henson, R.N., who contributed greatly to its final stages. Reprints may be obtained from N. Azrin, Behavior Research Laboratory, Anna State Hospital, 1000 N. Main St., Anna, Illinois 62906.

[2]Now at Department of Psychiatry, University of Pennsylvania, Philadelphia, Pa.

[3]Now at Florida State University, Tallahassee, Florida.

Psychological treatment of behavioral problems usually is given in a restricted locale, such as an office or hospital, and for restricted periods; the hope is that the desired behavioral changes will occur in the patient's normal environment. Recently, operant conditioning procedures have been used in this same manner to modify behavior problems (see examples, summaries, and reviews in Bijou and Baer, 1967; Ulrich, Stachnik, and Mabry, 1966; Ullmann and Krasner, 1965; Ayllon and Azrin, 1968. An alternative to this brief treatment approach is to have the treatment continuously operative in the patient's natural setting by apparatus that can be worn and which provides the stimuli known to be needed for the behavioral change. Several continuous treatment devices have been developed for behavior problems that can be treated by a simple rearrangement or introduction of sensory inputs such as eyeglasses, hearing aids, the cardiac Pacemaker, and watches. If this continuous approach is to be extended to treatment by operant conditioning procedures, something more than simple sensory inputs are needed. Since reinforcement (Holland and Skinner, 1961) and punishment (Azrin and Holz, 1966) are defined procedurally as a stimulus consequence of a response, an operant conditioning treatment device must also discriminate physically when responses occur and only then deliver the stimuli. Only one example of this approach seems to have been developed and proven. In treating bedwetting, Mowrer and Mowrer (1938) developed a special bed pad that sounded an annoying tone when urine caused an electrical current to flow through wires imbedded in the pad. The result was that bedwetting decreased. This technique has not resulted in the emergence of any general principles that suggested similar applications to other behavioral problems. Rather, the bedwetting device seems to be considered as an isolated technique for treating a very specific problem. The possible generality of this technique was suggested very recently in the course of developing an apparatus to eliminate cigarette-smoking behavior (Powell and Azrin, 1968). The apparatus was originally described by Whaley (personal communication) and later reported by Whaley, Rosenkranz, and Knowles (1968). A painful electric shock was delivered to the smoker when he opened a specially designed cigarette case. Analysis of the many behavior modification studies, especially those of bedwetting and smoking, revealed several common factors that in combination suggested a general rationale for treating undesired behaviors.

This general approach is designated here as behavioral engineering and seemed to involve the following requirements. (1) *Behavioral definition*:

define the undesired behavior in specific behavioral terms; (2) *Apparatus definition*: isolate some essential aspect of that behavior that can be physically sensed by an apparatus; (3) *Response precision*: the response output of the apparatus must be made selective so that it is activated by all instances of the undesired behavior (no false negatives) but by no instance of normal behaviors (no false positives); (4) *Effective stimulus consequence*: discover some stimulus event that is reinforcing or aversive and that can be delivered physically; (5) *Programming the stimulus consequence*: program that stimulus as a consequence for the undesired response; and (6) *Portable device*: construct a portable device that performs the response definition and stimulus delivery and which allows the patient to engage in his normal activities.

The present study attempted to apply this method of operant treatment aids to remedy poor posture, specifically "slouching." Slouching was selected because it is apparently socially undesirable and because many medical authorities consider it detrimental to health. Goldthwait, Brown, Swaim, and Kuhns (1945) are perhaps the strongest proponents of the causative relationship between good posture and good health, and their views are accepted in varying degrees by other medical authorities (see for example Burt, 1950) as well as physical therapists (Williams and Worthingham, 1957) and individuals interested in maximizing the performance of athletes (see Lowman, 1958). However, this view is not shared by all (see excellent review by Hellebrandt and Franseen, 1943).

A psychological or social need seems to exist for postural treatment aside from any medical need. Patients that have been hospitalized in institutions for the retarded or mentally ill frequently present a postural appearance that discourages social acceptability and discharge to the community. Similar social-aesthetic reasons seem to lead some non-institutionalized individuals to exercise and to use postural braces.

METHOD

Subjects

Twenty-five adults, 18 to 49 years of age, participated; 11 were male, 14 female. All were employees of the Anna State Hospital except for one mental patient and one chiropractor in private practice. All were selected on the basis of their availability and willingness to participate and without regard to their normal posture. Of the hospital employees, seven were attendants, three were speech therapists, one was a clerical worker, two were administrators, one was a psychologist, and the others were general assistants. All were studied at their place of employment and while they were engaged in their usual job activities. The patient was studied while she was engaged in her usual activities on the token-system ward environment described elsewhere (Ayllon and Azrin, 1965; Ayllon and Azrin, 1968).

Instructions   The subjects were asked to participate in a study of posture. None declined, although several spontaneously stated that they felt no great need for posture improvement. Three subjects stated without being asked that they desired to improve their posture and actively inquired about participating before being approached (S-10, S-22, S-23). The subjects were shown how the apparatus functioned and were told they would be wearing it for several hours. They were instructed to engage in all of their normal activities while wearing the apparatus and to report afterward on any problems, or inconveniences, resulting from its usage. They were informed on the developmental status of the apparatus, the experimenter's lack of knowledge regarding its possible efficacy, and the possibility that no change in posture might result. The instructions were in written form for six subjects.

Apparatus and Procedure

The procedure and apparatus will be described in terms of the six requirements listed above.

1. Behavioral Definition   Slouching was behaviorally defined as a sustained rounding of the shoulders or upper back while in a standing position. Medically, this condition is called "round shoulders" and is defined as a "faulty posture in which dropping of the shoulders and increased convexity of the thoracic spine are conspicuous" (Hoerr and Osol, 1956, p. 1053).

2. Apparatus Definition of Response   The apparatus defined slouching as an increased distance between two points on the back. A miniature snap action switch (Model 11SM1, Microswitch) was modified to operate upon being pulled rather than pushed. This posture switch was mounted on the back at about the level of the second thoracic vertebra (see Fig. 20.1). The switch was connected to an elastic cord and attached to the back such that rounding of the back caused the switch contacts to close.

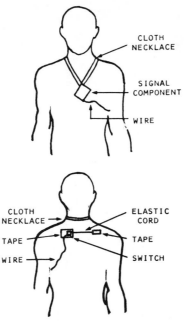

CLOTH
NECKLACE

SIGNAL
COMPONENT

WIRE

CLOTH
NECKLACE

ELASTIC
CORD

TAPE

TAPE

WIRE

SWITCH

Fig. 20.1. Front and rear view of a subject wearing the posture switch. The front view in the upper sketch shows the signal component worn around the neck. A wire runs from the component, under the arm, to the posture switch on the back which is shown in the lower sketch. The posture switch is attached to the back by two strips of adhesive tape. The subjects wore their outer garments over the assembly which was thereby concealed from view.

Two methods of attachment to the back were used: adhesive tape was used for most subjects to provide the more exact measure of the response for purposes of experimental evaluation (see Fig. 20.1). A second method was a harness (see Fig. 20.2) which allowed a slight error due to movement of the straps but was more convenient for the subject: it could be removed and attached by the subject himself once adjusted properly, whereas the adhesive mounting required assistance and readjustment for each wearing. Fifteen subjects used the adhesive mounting and 10 the harness. A small strip of tape was used to hold the harness strap in a fixed position on the shoulders for some of the subjects who wore the harness.

The amount of slouching needed to activate the switch was determined by the subject's own judgment. The subject was asked to assume a shoulder posture which he felt bordered on, but did not constitute, slouching and which he would like to maintain. The switch was adjusted

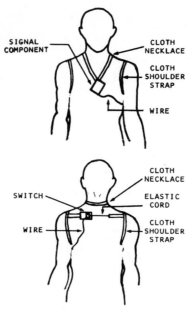

Fig. 20.2. Front and rear view of a subject wearing the posture switch. The front view in the upper sketch shows the signal component worn around the neck. A wire runs from the component, under the arm, and to the posture switch on the back which is shown in the lower sketch. The posture switch is attached by the shoulder straps which are adjusted for the desired posture for the individual subject. Outer garments are worn over the assembly and thereby conceal it from view.

via the adhesive tape or straps to be on the point of activation at that posture. The subject then returned to his usual activities for about 5 min after which the adhesive tape or straps were readjusted in compliance with the subject's request. These 5-min trial periods were repeated until satisfactory adjustment was found. All subjects achieved a satisfactory adjustment within three trial periods except for Subject 7. Measurement of Subject 7 revealed relatively little increase in distance between the shoulders when asked to slouch but a relatively large increase in spinal curvature. Accordingly, for Subject 7, the switch was taped along the spinal cord at its maximum convex dorsal curvature such that increased spinal curvature rather than the rounding of the back activated the posture switch. For other subjects, the switch was adjusted vertically after the first 5-min trial to the first or third thoracic vertebra if that location provided a greater distance change during slouching.

3. Response Precision The posture switch arrangement across the back was found to be effective in avoiding "false negatives"; i.e., the switch contacts closed whenever rounding of the back occurred. "False positives" did occur in the early development of this method; the switch contacts closed because of an incidental rounding of the back that was a part of normal activity. One type of false positive was a short-term rounding of the back such as occurred when the subject looked over his shoulder. This type of problem was solved by defining slouching as a sustained response. Therefore, slouching was defined as uninterrupted closure of the switch for at least 3 sec. A second type of false positive resulted from normal reaching movements that caused the switch contacts to close as a result of the associated shoulder blade movements. As described above, this problem was solved by mounting the switch at a level above the shoulder blades which for different subjects was the first, second, or third thoracic vertebra. A third type of false positive resulted when the torso was bent sharply forward as occurs during close reading while seated and when picking up an object from the floor. This problem was eliminated by a mercury tilt switch (Model: Gordo 1-220-L2) that blocked the output from the posture switch when the torso was tilted forward more than 10°.

4. Effective Stimulus Consequence A 500-cps tone at an intensity of 55 db was used as the stimulus consequence for slouching. The intensity was measured at a distance of 15 in. which was the approximate distance of the apparatus from the subject's ear when the apparatus was worn. Preliminary evidence indicated that this tone was aversive when it sounded while the subject was in his natural and usually social environment. (Experimental evidence regarding the aversiveness is presented below.) The tone was generated by a transistor circuit (see Fig. 15.9 in G. E. Transistor Manual, 1964) which included a hearing aid speaker (Audivox Model 8AA).

5. Programming the Stimulus Consequences Since slouching could occur at any time, it constituted a free operant response that should be amenable to treatment by free operant conditioning procedures. The present procedure programmed the onset of the tone as a punisher for the onset of slouching and the termination of the tone as escape reinforcement for the termination of slouching. A warning stimulus, consisting of a momentary click, occurred whenever the posture switch contact closed. The click sound was produced by the built-in snap action of the microswitch when the contacts opened or closed. The aversive stimulus tone sounded 3 sec later if the switch contacts remained closed. The termination of slouching opened the posture switch contacts and immediately terminated the tone.

6. Portable Apparatus   If the procedure was to operate in the subject's natural environment, the device had to be sufficiently small, light, and unobtrusive to be worn easily. The present study did not attempt to develop the ultimate in miniaturization but only to satisfy the requirements of portability to the extent needed to make this study possible. The posture switch arrangement described above was connected by a thin lead that passed loosely under the shirt to the programming device that was suspended by a necklace on the chest (see Figs. 20.1 and 20.2). Females usually wore the apparatus in their brassiere and males wore it under their shirt. The apparatus weighed 60 g, measured about 2 by 4 by 6 cm, and contained the mercury switch for measuring vertical tilt and the circuit and speaker for the tone.

Recording Response Duration in a Portable Apparatus   A major problem existed in objectively measuring the duration of slouching while the subject was in his natural environment. Previous studies had not developed such a method. The present use of a switch attached to the back offered an objective method but the problem remained as to how a record could be obtained of the posture switch output, since no fixed connection could be made from the posture switch to a stationary recording instrument. Even telemetry was impractical since the subjects could travel over a distance of several miles in their autos. A method was developed for recording the cumulative duration of slouching by arranging a miniature (2.8 by 0.5 by 0.5 cm) elapsed time meter (Curtis Instrument Co., Model 120-PC) in series with the posture switch. The measuring element of the meter consisted of a capillary tube filled with two columns of mercury separated by a gap of electrolyte. When current passed through the meter, the electrolyte gap moved at a rate determined by the amount of current flow. The speed of the timer was determined beforehand by the value of the fixed resistor in series with the time meter. Since slouching was defined as a maintained response, the current was allowed to pass through the time meter only after the posture switch was closed for 3 sec. The meter provided a silent, accurate method of recording the duration of slouching. It was necessary to magnify the timer in order to read the elapsed duration. A photograph was taken of the timer to provide a permanent and enlarged photographic record that could be measured at a later time. The time could be read with an accuracy of about one-fifth of 1% (about 30 sec) at the 4-hr time range used for almost all subjects.

Experimental Design   Two experimental conditions were imposed on each subject: (A) the normal condition in which the tone was disconnected but the timer continued to record slouching and the posture switch continued to click each time the switch contacts were opened or closed, and (B) the punishment of slouching condition in which the tone sounded during slouching. The change from one condition to the other required less than a minute and was made by disconnecting or connecting the speaker by a switch inside the programming apparatus. The sequence of conditions within each day was ABA for some subjects and BAB for the others; three subjects were BABA. The time spent in each period was 1 to 3 hr, with most subjects spending approximately equal durations in the two conditions. For three subjects, however, the conditions were changed between days in an ABA or BABA sequence; they wore the apparatus about 7 hr on each of the days. This design permitted a within-subjects and (except for three subjects) a within-session determination of whether the punishment of slouching by the tone reduced the duration of slouching. All features of the two conditions were comparable including the wearing of the apparatus, the presence of a warning stimulus click, the nature of the subject's activities, and the instructions to the subjects; the sole difference was the response contingency of sounding the tone during slouching.

Two subjects were given a second session during which the above procedure was changed in order to obtain additional evidence regarding the aversive properties of the tone. If the tone were simply providing information or feedback, slouching should be affected in the same way when the tone sounded only during slouching as when it sounded only during non-slouching. On the other hand, if the tone were aversive, slouching should be decreased when the tone was produced by slouching but increased when the tone was eliminated by slouching. The two subjects were given a second session about two weeks after the first, during which the same ABA design was used but in which slouching terminated, rather than produced, the tone. The tone sounded only when the subjects were not slouching. The same instructions were given as in the first session.

RESULTS

Table 20.1 shows the percentage of time spent slouching for each subject when slouching produced the tone and when the tone was disconnected. All subjects slouched less when the slouch produced the tone than when the tone was disconnected. Slouching increased each time the tone was disconnected and decreased each time it was connected. For a given subject no overlap between conditions can be seen: more slouching occurred during each period without the tone than during any period with the tone. The reduction of slouching occurred for the subjects

Table 20.1. Effect of a Tone Punishment for Slouching for 25 Subjects.

	Percentage of Time Spent Slouching					Per Cent Change of Slouching by Punishment
Subject	No Punishment	Punishment of Slouching	No Punishment	Punishment of Slouching	No Punishment	
1	34.4%	1.1%	51.1%	%	%	−97%
2	57.8	1.1	10.8			−97
3	25.8	0.9	18.1			−96
4	35.0	0.8	5.0			−96
5		0.4	7.8	0.4		−95
6	17.0	0.9	16.0			−95
7		0.5	8.1	0.5		−94
8		5.3	77.0	1.9	33.1	−94
9	93.1	4.4	57.7			−94
10		1.7	17.5	1.7		−90
11	8.0	0.9	9.8			−90
12	6.2	0.4	1.7			−90
13	32.2	4.4	49.8			−89
14	26.1	2.7	10.7			−86
15	57.3	8.0	30.6			−82
16	59.2	9.2	37.5			−81
17		2.1	6.2	0.4		−81
18	26.7	4.4	16.7			−80
19	2.9	1.4	10.8			−80
20		4.7	24.8	10.7	52.0	−80
21		6.3	16.3	1.2	21.3	−80
22	4.0	2.4	15.7			−76
23		4.2	20.0	6.7		−72
24		1.1	5.6	2.2		−71
25	2.5	0.8	1.7			−62

who had the conditions alternated within each day as well as those who had it alternated between days (S-8, S-19, S-22). Similarly, the reduction occurred for the subjects who wore the tape-mounted posture switch as well as those who wore the harness-mounted switch (S-3, S-6, S-9, S-11, S-12, S-13, S-14, S-15, S-20, S-21); for the normals as well as the mental patient (S-20); for the females as well as males; for those who slouched a high percentage of the time as well as those who slouched only rarely; for those who wore the posture switch across the back as well as the one subject who wore it along the spine (S-7).

The extent of the reduction for each subject can be described by the fraction B—A/B in which A is the percentage of time spent slouching when the slouch did not produce the tone and B when it did produce the tone. This fraction is expressed as a percentage in the column on the right of Table 20.1. This percentage change of slouching varied between -62% and -97% for different subjects with a mean reduction of 86% for all of the subjects.

For the 16 subjects given the ABA design, a comparison of the first and third periods indicated somewhat less slouching after exposure to the tone contingency than before it. Statistical analysis by the Wilcoxin Signed Ranks Test (Siegel, 1956) indicated that this residual effect of the tone contingency was not significant $(P > 0.05)$.

Table 20.2 shows the results of the procedure in which slouching terminated the tone rather than produced it. Both subjects showed an increase of slouching when the tone sounded and a decrease when the tone was again disconnected. The change in slouching was opposite in direction to that seen in Table 20.1 for the same two subjects.

Difficulties Encountered in Use of Apparatus   Although all subjects indicated the apparatus was usable, some problems were noted that suggest improvements. (1) Subjects in preliminary studies complained of the social distraction caused by the sounding of the tone in the presence

Table 20.2.   Effect of a Tone Punishment for Non-Slouching.

	Percentage of Time Spent Slouching			Per Cent Change of Slouching by Punishment
Subject	No Punishment	Punishment of Non-Slouching	No Punishment	
12	36	87	68	$+41$
13	61	93	61	$+53$

of another person, especially in relatively quiet surroundings. The present apparatus partly eliminated this problem by the 3-sec delay between the warning click and the tone; the subjects could correct their posture during this interval and avoid the tone. Several subjects stated that they would have preferred a longer delay or repeated warning clicks. These click sounds were not unusual and did not seem to draw the attention of others even in very quiet surroundings. (2) In a very noisy environment, such as exists near an air conditioner or fan or in some automobiles, some subjects stated that the tone was not loud enough to be heard. This problem seems to be of great importance only if the individual spends much of his time in such a noisy environment. (3) All subjects were asked about any inconvenience caused by the posture switch or the programming device. The programming switch could not be worn inconspicuously by one subject since it produced a bulge in his form-fitting shirt; his participation was postponed to the next day when he wore the more usual type of shirt. Three subjects stated that the weight of the programming apparatus on the neckline was annoying. This problem had been solved for females by resting the apparatus in the center of the brassiere and for the subjects who wore the posture harness by attaching the necklace to the two harness straps that passed in front of the arms. (4) In response to the question of interference with activities, several subjects stated there was some interference initially but none after they learned to discriminate how much slouching was permitted and how long the delay was between the warning click and the tone. (5) Several instances of apparent false positives were reported. One that permitted no general solution was sounding of the tone while one subject, an attendant, was physically separating two combative patients. A second instance was when the shoulders were rounded while pushing a shopping cart, driving a car, or reading. In each instance the subject could learn to avoid the tone by tilting the torso forward slightly, thereby activating the vertical tilt switch and permitting the rounding of the back that is often normal when engaging in these activities.

DISCUSSION

The present results showed the procedure was effective in reducing slouching for all subjects during every period in which it was worn. The magnitude of the reduction was considerable, averaging 86% for all subjects and almost 100% for some. A slight enduring effect of the procedure was seen from the lower duration of slouching after exposure to the punisher than before it. Possibly longer periods of wearing the apparatus might have decreased the slouching to an even greater extent. The large and consistent reduction of slouching by this procedure suggests the usefulness of this behavioral engineering approach for developing similar procedures for other behavior problems in which a body movement or orientation can be used to define the problem.

When slouching produced the tone, slouching decreased; when non-slouching produced the tone, non-slouching decreased. The results satisfy the definition of the tone as a punishing stimulus in that slouching was reduced when slouching produced the tone (Azrin and Holz, 1966). The tone also meets the definition of an aversive stimulus (Holland and Skinner, 1961) in that non-slouching increased in duration when non-slouching terminated the tone and similarly, slouching increased when that response terminated it. The present procedure represents a combination of punishment and escape conditioning of a free operant response. The click sound can be considered as a warning or discriminative stimulus for the tone. Previous findings of discriminated punishment show that a punished response will be suppressed by a warning stimulus that precedes the punisher (Dinsmoor, 1952; Azrin, 1956; Brethower and Reynolds, 1962; Hake and Azrin, 1965; and see review by Azrin and Holz, 1966); and an avoidance response will occur primarily during a warning stimulus that precedes the aversive stimulus in discriminated avoidance (Sidman, 1955; Ulrich, Holz, and Azrin, 1964; Azrin, Holz, Hake, and Ayllon, 1963; and see review by Hoffman, 1966). The click was included in the procedure to increase the control exerted by the tone. Unfortunately, the present method of recording posture did not permit independent evidence of this function, except for the verbal statements of several subjects that the click sound enabled them to correct their posture and to avoid the tone more easily.

The effectiveness of the tone as a punisher or aversive stimulus raises the question as to the reason for this aversiveness. One possibility is the inherent aversiveness of the tone because of its intensity, duration, or on-off pattern. Although the intensity of the sound was far below that found to be aversive in other studies with humans (Azrin, 1958), its long duration may have made it aversive (see Church, Raymond, and Beauchamp, 1967). A second possibility is that the aversiveness was acquired in the manner of a conditioned punisher (Hake and Azrin, 1965) or a conditioned aversive stimulus by association with existing aversive events. One such event was the social distraction or embarrassment that often resulted when the tone sounded in the presence of others. A second event was the aversiveness of the behavior being treated. Slouching was defined for each subject as the degree of rounding of the back that he wished to avoid. If this degree of slouching is considered an aversive event for a given subject, the tone would be a conditioned aversive stimulus because of its pairing with that undesired posture. This explanation seems identical to the description of the tone as response feedback: the tone providing a warning that an undesirable behavior has occurred. As noted above, however, this feedback explanation cannot account for the *increase* in slouching when the tone was scheduled as a punisher for non-slouching. In summary, the present data showed that the tone was a punisher and that these punishing properties did not derive simply from the information that the tone provided about slouching. Mowrer and Mowrer (1938) also found that noise was an effective punisher but apparently because it awakened the enuretic patient. The present results reveal that a fairly mild tone can serve as a punisher for the waking individual and suggest its use in other behavior applications as an easily programmed stimulus consequence that does not cause the apprehension caused by electric shock (Powell and Azrin, 1968).

Although the critical feature of the present procedure seems to have been the presence of the tone and its relation to the response, several other explanations of the results should be examined. A novelty effect of wearing the apparatus could not account for the response changes since the apparatus was worn when the tone was operative as well as when it was disconnected. The click that signaled that the back was rounded could not have caused the reduction simply by providing feedback, since the clicks sounded all of the time that the apparatus was worn. Differences between subjects were not relevant since all comparisons were done within subjects. Variations in the nature of the subjects' activities could not account for the reduction since the subjects' activities were predetermined by the responsibilities of their jobs. The effect of the simple passage of time was made comparable by the alternating sequence of the experimental conditions. The feedback or information function of the tone was not a critical factor, since the information was equivalent when the slouching produced the tone and when it terminated it; yet the slouching decreased in the former procedure and increased in the latter. This same reversal showed that the changes in slouching were not caused by a general suggestion effect of the instructions since they were identical for the two procedures. A simple "alerting" function of the tone also could not account for this reversal because the tone was present during both procedures but decreased slouching only when the slouching produced the tone. Thus, the click sound, the mere sounding of the tone, the wearing of the apparatus, the instructions, the identity of the subjects, and the passage of time were all comparable or controlled for between conditions by the within-subjects and within-sessions design; only the response-tone relation differed and would seem to be the principal reason to account for the postural change.

The practical applicability of the posture apparatus will depend on factors such as the need for treatment, convenience, effectiveness, interference with other activities, and characteristics of the patient. The apparatus seemed to be sufficiently convenient to wear during most everyday activities and did not interfere seriously with them. For long-term use, the harness arrangement would be more convenient than the tape arrangement: the patient would not require assistance each time the posture switch was removed, as in bathing and sleeping. The need for postural treatment is partly a medical question that can only be answered by the clinical practitioner for a given patient. In clinical practice, successive approximation to the desired degree of erect posture has been recommended for the treatment of severe slouchers (Williams and Worthington, 1957), a procedure to which this apparatus is well suited. The present technique appears to have some potential advantages over two of the major alternatives to postural control, which are postural braces and exercise periods. Unlike a fairly rigid back brace, the present apparatus permitted any type of posture or movement without discomfort. Additionally, the relevant muscles must be used by this method rather than being passively supported as with the postural support. Unlike the limited periods of exercise, the present apparatus motivated the subjects to use the relevant muscles continuously rather than to hope for possible transfer from the exercise period.

REFERENCES

Ayllon, T. and Azrin, N. H. The measurement and reinforcement of behavior of psychotics. *Journal of the Experimental Analysis of Behavior*, 1965, **8**, 357–383.

Ayllon, T. and Azrin, N. H. *The Token Economy: A Motivational System for Therapy and Rehabilitation.* New York: Appleton-Century-Crofts, 1968.

Azrin, N. H. Some effects of two intermittent schedules of immediate and non-immediate punishment. *Journal of Psychology*, 1956, **42**, 3–21.

Azrin, N. H. Some effects of noise on human behavior. *Journal of the Experimental Analysis of Behavior*, 1958, **1**, 183–199.

Azrin, N. H. and Holz, W. C. Punishment. In W. K. Honig (Ed.) *Operant Behavior: Areas of Research and Application.* New York: Appleton-Century-Crofts, 1966. Pp. 380–447.

Azrin, N. H., Holz, W. C., Hake, D. F., and Ayllon, T. Fixed-ratio escape reinforcement. *Journal of the Experimental Analysis of Behavior*, 1963, **6**, 449–456.

Bijou, S. W. and Baer, D. M. *Child Development: Readings in Experimental Analysis.* New York: Appleton-Century-Crofts, 1967.

Brethower, D. M. and Reynolds, G. S. A facilitative effect of punishment on unpunished behavior. *Journal of the Experimental Analysis of Behavior*, 1962, **5**, 191–199.

Burt, H. A. Section of physical medicine. *Proceedings of the Royal Society of Medicine*, 1950, **43**, 187–194.

Church, R. M., Raymond, G. A., and Beauchamp, R. D. Response suppression as a function of intensity and duration of a punishment. *Journal of Comparative and Physiological Psychology*, 1967, **63**, 39–44.

Dinsmoor, J. A. A discrimination based on punishment. *Quarterly Journal of Experimental Psychology*, 1952, **4**, 27–45.

General Electric. *G. E. Transistor Manual.* New York: General Electric, 1964.

Goldthwait, J. E., Brown, L. T., Swaim, L. T., and Kuhns, J. G. *Essentials of Body Mechanics in Health and Disease* (4th ed.). Philadelphia: J. B. Lippincott Co., 1945.

Hake, D. F. and Azrin, N. H. Conditioned punishment. *Journal of the Experimental Analysis of Behavior*, 1965, **8**, 279–293.

Hellebrandt, F. A. and Franseen, E. B. Physiological study of the vertical stance of man. *Physiological Review*, 1943, **22**, 220–256.

Hoerr, N. L. and Osol, A. (Eds.). *Blakiston's New Gould Medical Dictionary* (2nd ed.). New York: McGraw-Hill, 1956.

Hoffman, H. S. The analysis of discriminated avoidance. In W. K. Honig (Ed.) *Operant Behavior: Areas of Research and Application.* New York: Appleton-Century-Crofts, 1966. Pp. 499–530.

Holland, J. G. and Skinner, B. F. *The Analysis of Behavior: A Program for Self-Instruction.* New York: McGraw-Hill, 1961.

Lowman, C. L. Faulty posture in relation to performance. *Journal of Health, Physical Education and Recreation*, 1958, **29**, 14–15.

Mowrer, O. H. and Mowrer, W. M. Enuresis: a method for its study and treatment. *American Journal of Orthopsychiatry*, 1938, **8**, 436–459.

Powell, J. and Azrin, N. H. The effects of shock as a punisher on cigarette smoking. *Journal of Applied Behavior Analysis*, 1968, **1**, 63–71.

Sidman, M. Some properties of the warning stimulus in avoidance behavior. *Journal of Comparative and Physiological Psychology*, 1955, **48**, 444–450.

Siegel, S. *Nonparametric Statistics for the Behavioral Sciences.* New York: McGraw-Hill, 1956.

Ullmann, L. P. and Krasner, L. *Case Studies in Behavior Modification.* New York: Holt, Rinehart & Winston, Inc., 1965.

Ulrich, R. E., Holz, W. C., and Azrin, N. H. Stimulus control of avoidance behavior. *Journal of the Experimental Analysis of Behavior*, 1964, **7**, 129–133.

Ulrich, R. E., Stachnik, T., and Mabry, J. *Control of Human Behavior.* Glenview, Illinois: Scott, Foresman and Co., 1966.

Whaley, D. L. Personal communication.

Whaley, D. L., Rosenkranz, A., and Knowles, P. A. Automatic punishment of cigarette smoking by a portable electronic device. Unpublished manuscript, 1968.

Williams, M. and Worthington, C. *Therapeutic Exercise for Body Alignment and Function.* Philadelphia: W. B. Saunders Co., 1957.

ARTICLE 21

Metronome-Conditioned Speech Retraining for Stuttering*[1, 2]

JOHN PAUL BRADY[3]

University of Pennsylvania

Abstract: A new treatment for severe stuttering is described: metronome-conditioned speech retraining (MCSR). The procedure involves the use of a miniaturized, electronic metronome which is worn behind the ear like the hearing-aid it resembles. The treatment is derived from a behavioral analysis of the disorder of stuttering and experimental studies on the effects of a metronome on the speech of stutterers. The performance characteristics of a metronome suitable for this procedure are given along with a detailed description of the MCSR procedure itself. The application of this treatment approach to 26 severe stutterers who ranged in age from 12 to 53 years is also presented. Of the 23 patients who completed the treatment program, 21 (or over 90%) showed a marked increase in fluency and an improvement in their general adjustment as well. These clinical results have persisted for follow-up periods that range from 6 months to over 3 years. These results compare favorably with available data on treatment outcome with alternative methods of treatment. Common objections to this general approach to the treatment of stuttering are also discussed.

One of the most intriguing phenomena in the puzzling disorder of stuttering is the marked increase in fluency which usually occurs when a stutterer paces his speech with an iterated stimulus. The effect is especially striking if the stimuli are rhythmic and externally generated, as when a stutterer paces his speech with a metronome (Barber, 1940).

*Reprinted from *Behavior Therapy*, 1971, **2**, 129–150. Copyright © 1971 by Academic Press, Inc. With permission of Academic Press, Inc. and John Paul Brady.

[1] An abridged version of this paper was read at the 46th Annual Convention of the American Speech and Hearing Association, Nov. 20–23, 1970, New York City.

[2] This research was supported in part by a USPHS Research Scientist Award (K3-MH-22,682) from the National Institute of Mental Health. The author is indebted to Mrs. Jean F. Nadel, speech pathologist, for assistance with various aspects of this study.

[3] Requests for reprints should be addressed to John Paul Brady, Hospital of the University of Pennsylvania, Philadelphia, Pa. 19104.

Although efforts to use metronomes for the treatment of stuttering date back more than a century (Colombat De L'Isère, 1831), the principle has been of limited use therapeutically, mainly because of poor carry-over of fluency from speaking with a metronome to speaking without one. The problem of carry-over appears to be solvable, however, by virtue of two technical developments—one electronic and the other behavioral. Miniaturized, electronic metronomes have been developed which can be worn unobtrusively by the patient on his body. This makes the metronome available to the stutterer in a great variety of speaking situations, in particular, in the situations he encounters in his daily life in the natural environment. Equally important is the development of a behavioral program for extending the use of the metronome into these various situations and then systematically withdrawing its use while allowing the patient to remain fluent. This latter development proceeds from a behavioral analysis of stuttering and makes use of principles of conditioning and learning which form the basis of many behavior therapy procedures (Brady, 1970).

In this paper a procedure termed "metronome-conditioned speech retraining" (MCSR) for the treatment of severe stuttering is described. As this term implies, the metronome is not used passively as a prosthesis but is used to facilitate the acquisition of more fluent speech patterns. The results of its application to 26 severe adolescent and adult stutterers are also described.

Before proceeding with a detailed description of the treatment procedure, it will be helpful to outline the rationale for the treatment and the general behavioral principles involved.

EMPIRICAL AND THEORETICAL BASES OF PROCEDURE

There is a growing consensus among behaviorally oriented clinicians that it is therapeutically useful to view the disorder of stuttering in learning theory terms (e.g., Brutten & Shoemaker, 1967; Gray & England, 1969). A behavioral analysis published elsewhere by this author (Brady, 1968a) may be summarized as follows. The disorder of stuttering consists of two components which continuously interact; nonfluencies in speech generally recognized by the patient and his listeners as "stuttering" and anxiety and tension in a variety of speaking situations. The anxiety and tension are largely in anticipation of stuttering which, in fact, make stuttering all the more likely in that particular situation. This is the "vicious circle" aspect of stuttering which is well known to most stutterers and their therapists. Since the production of speech sounds is largely voluntary in nature, it is greatly influenced by operant (skeletal motor) conditioning. Since the anxiety and tension associated with speaking occasions are largely involuntary in nature, they are viewed as the product of Pavlovian (autonomic) conditioning.[4]

The first step in the metronome-conditioned speech retraining (MCSR) program is to find conditions under which the patient can be highly fluent with the aid of a desk metronome. For a severe, chronic stutterer this may require being alone with the therapist and pacing one syllable of his speech to each beat of a loud metronome set as slow as 40 beats per minute. Almost always conditions can be found under which the patient speaks in an easy, relaxed, and fluent manner. It is not known *why* pacing speech with a metronome has this effect. From a series of experiments, however, it is clear that the effect is not due merely to slowing the rate of speech or providing a distraction (Brady, 1969). Further, it is not merely a matter of "suggestion" or a "placebo response" since the effect is very reliable and does not "adapt out" over time.

Once fluent verbalizations can be made, albeit at a low rate and in very particular circumstances, the task is to gradually and systematically "shape" verbalizations to approximate the rate and cadence of normal speech and to help the patient extend this fluency to other situations to which anticipatory anxiety and tension have been conditioned. This involves the use of a general principle known as "reciprocal inhibition" which is inherent in several behavior therapy procedures (Wolpe, 1969). In brief, the principle is that one can usually reach a feared goal (or situations and circumstances previously associated with intense anxiety and tension) if the goal is approached through a series of very small steps and in a psychophysiological state that is inhibitory of anxiety (Brady, 1970). In MCSR the series of small steps corresponds to a hierarchy of speaking situations arranged from those associated with minimal stuttering to those associated with severe stuttering. For example, the first situation on the list might be "speaking with wife" and the last "giving an

---

[4]Of course, skeletal motor and autonomic responses interact in very complex ways, and recent experiments of Miller (1969) and others have shown that some of the classical distinctions between operant and Pavlovian conditioning do not hold. Nevertheless, it remains useful to conceptualize the disorder of stuttering in terms of the operant reinforcement of motor components and the Pavlovian conditioning of autonomic (emotional) components of the disorder.

impromptu after-dinner speech." The relaxed, self-confident, and reassured state of the patient brought about by speaking success (fluency) at each step provides the psychophysiological state inhibitory of anxiety and tension. That is, the patient must be successful in emitting relaxed, fluent speech with the aid of a metronome at each step before progressing to the next step of his hierarchy in the natural environment.

Another process is also operating. After the patient has experienced relaxed and fluent speech in the presence of the metronome's beats for a long time, the latter begin to serve as conditioned stimuli to elicit a relaxed state and the expectation of fluency. Put another way, after a time the metronomic beats are not only *instructional* stimuli telling the patient when to emit the next syllable or word, but become *discriminative* stimuli, inducing relaxation and fluency.

Once the patient has achieved fluency in virtually all speaking situations he encounters, he begins to discontinue the use of the metronome in the same order. That is, he discontinues its use in the first situation in the original hierarchy. If he remains fluent in that situation, he tries discontinuing its use in the second situation and so forth. Many patients find that the transition from metronome-aided to unaided speech is facilitated by pacing their speech to the beats of an imaginary metronome, at least for a while. This phase of treatment may be conceptualized as a gradual "fading out" of the unnatural cues of the metronome's beats as discriminative stimuli for fluency and hence allowing the cues naturally present in speaking situations to take their place. The latter can now serve this function since they are no longer associated with anxiety, tension, and nonfluency but with relaxed, fluent speech.

DESIGN OF A SUITABLE METRONOME

As described below, the initial phase of MCSR makes use of an ordinary desk metronome, such as might be used in piano practice. However, extending the retraining procedure into the natural environment requires a miniaturized metronome. Several such devices have been described in recent years (Meyer & Mair, 1963; Horan, 1968; Wohl, 1968). Most of these have limited usefulness, however, because of their bulk and lack of flexibility. The characteristics of an ideal metronome for the present purpose can be deduced from the requirements of the MCSR procedure itself and some additional systematic observation made by the present author (Brady, 1969) and others (e.g., Greenberg, 1970; Beech & Fransella, 1968) on the metronome effect.

First, the metronome should be small, light-weight, and able to be worn unobtrusively. A miniaturized, battery-operated metronome built into the housing of a flesh-colored hearing-aid of the behind-the-ear type is suitable. Such a device is assumed to be a hearing-aid by most observers and is not discernible at all on persons with sufficiently long hair.

Second, it should be possible to turn the device on and off without removing it from behind the ear. This adds flexibility. For example, a student might leave the metronome turned off but in place behind the ear during a classroom lecture, turning it on quickly and easily when the recitation portion of the class begins.

A third characteristic is an external volume control, i.e., a means by which the patient can vary the loudness of the beats, preferably without having to remove the device from behind the ear. This feature is essential because the level of ambient noise will vary from one speaking situation to the next. Thus, if the patient is in a noisy room he can set the volume sufficiently high to hear the beat. Then if he enters a quiet room he can turn the volume down so that, as before, he alone will hear the device. A practical volume range is from 10 decibels (just perceptible to most patients in a quiet room) to a maximum of 60 decibels. Another benefit of the loudness control is that it provides the patient with a means of gradually fading out the strength of the signals he is using to pace his speech to facilitate the transition from metronome-aided to unaided fluency. However, as will be described below, most patients prefer to accomplish this transition by varying the situations in which they use the device rather than varying the strength of the signals in a particular situation.

A fourth characteristic of a suitable metronome is an external control for the rate of the beats. This is essential because fluent speech may only be obtainable early in treatment by setting the device at a slow rate and generating slow speech. The rate of speech is then gradually increased, in part by gradually increasing the rate of the metronome. Also, in the course of retraining, the patient may find that he is having unexpected difficulty in a given speaking situation. It is important then for the patient to be able to reduce the rate of the metronome and hence reduce the rate of his own speech. Usually this will be accompanied by an increase in fluency. Often after having reestablished his fluency in that situation, and with it a return of self-confidence and composure, the patient is able to re-set the metronome at the previous higher rate in a short time. A practical range of rates is from 30 to 150 beats per minute.

Finally, a metronome with a pure tone should be avoided since this may prove to be irritating to the patient. Rather, a metronome which emits a complex sound (an admixture of frequencies), such as the ticks of an ordinary clock, is desirable.

The metronome used in the present research which meets these various requirements is shown in Fig. 21.1. It weighs 0.3 oz, measures 2 in. in length, contains an on/off switch, and knobs for controlling the rate and volume of the beats. It is powered by a tiny mercury battery of the hearing-aid type.

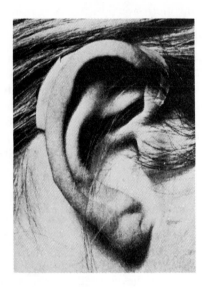

Fig. 21.1. This metronome, known as a Pacemaster, is made by Associated Auditory Instruments, Inc., 6796 Market Street, Upper Darby, Pa. 19082.

Other Kinds of Metronomes

The beats of the metronome described above are brief and equispaced. Jones and Azrin (1969) described experiments with stutterers in which the duration of the metronome's stimulus beats were systematically varied while the duration of the stimulus-off period was held constant at 1 sec. They reported that a metronome which emits beats about 1–3 sec in duration (with the stimulus-off periods of 1 sec) generates speech which is equally fluent but more "natural" than the speech generated by a metronome with beats of momentary duration. However, these studies involved only four patients treated for a brief period of time and no carry-over of fluency to unaided speech was noted. The present author has experimented with metronomes of this type and found them clinically unsatisfactory for the present program. The longer duration of the stimulus-on phase sets limits to the rate at which the metronome can be operated which, in turn, sets limits to the shaping procedure which is an important part of the MCSR procedure. "Naturalness" of speech is acquired in MCSR by carefully following a prescribed retraining procedure as is described in detail below.

Experiments in several laboratories have shown that nonauditory metronomes which emit stimuli in other sensory modalities are also effective in pacing the speech of stutterers (Brady, 1969; Azrin, Jones, & Flye, 1968). Indeed, some stutterers appear to be more fluent when pacing their speech with tactile pulses delivered to a fingertip or with brief and nonaversive flashes of light (Brady, 1969). However, we have not succeeded in developing a tactile or visual metronome of sufficiently small size and cosmetic acceptability to be of practical use clinically.

TREATMENT PROGRAM

The MCSR Procedure

Details of the procedure are tailored to the needs of each patient in accordance with the characteristics of his particular speech problem and his rate of progress. In general treatment proceeds along the five steps outlined below, the patient usually being seen at weekly intervals.

I. The first task is to demonstrate to the patient that he can speak with nearly 100% fluency with the aid of a desk metronome in the therapist's office. With a very severe stutterer this may mean pacing one syllable of speech to each beat of a metronome set as slow as 40 beats per minute while using easy reading material as the source of words. A much less severe stutterer might be able to begin with extemporaneous, conversational speech with the metronome set at 80 and pacing one word to each beat. In this first session the patient is usually given an overview of the total treatment program: the manner in which the fluency he is now demonstrating will gradually be modified to successively approximate speech of normal rate and cadence as well as the way in which this fluency will be extended to situations in the natural environment. He is instructed to practice speaking with a desk metronome at home in the same manner during the time before the next visit. Some of this is to be done while the patient is alone, even though most patients are almost totally fluent in this situation. This low-stress situation allows the patient to practice the technique of pacing his speech under ideal conditions. Assuming that he can remain fluent while doing so, he is instructed also to practice pacing his speech with the metronome in the presence of one other person with whom his stuttering is usually minimal; his spouse, a parent, roommate, girl friend, etc. Patients are usually expected to practice at least $\frac{3}{4}$ of an hour daily.

II. Usually the shaping of speech of more usual rate and cadence begins with the second session. The rate is increased by gradually and systematically increasing the rate at which the metronome is beating and by beginning to pace longer units of speech to each of the metronome's beats. A patient who previously paced one syllable to each beat might begin to pace two-syllable words to one beat on some occasions; a patient who was previously pacing whole words to one beat might begin to pace small groups or sequences of words to one beat, etc. This gradual increase in the rate of speaking is also done during the home practice. More normal cadence and juncturing of speech can be accomplished by allowing some beats to be voluntary pauses, varying the number of syllables fitted to each beat, etc. In addition the patient begins to extend the situational dimension in his practice by varying the person who is present during his home practice and by having more than one person present at a time. This phase of treatment is completed when the patient is able to speak with the metronome at a rate within the normal range (100–160 words/min) with no pronounced blocks in speech and a nonfluency rate that is no more than 20% of the nonfluency rate he exhibited before treatment without a metronome. During this phase of treatment many patients report that their speech in daily situations without the metronome is more fluent. However, failure of this to happen is not a cause for concern since this is still an early phase of the retraining program. Typically Phase II requires 2–4 weeks.

III. At this juncture, the desk metronome is replaced by a miniaturized, electronic metronome in all treatment and practice situations. Sometimes the transfer to the miniaturized metronome is associated with partial relapse, i.e., a decrease in metronome-aided fluency. This may be due to the unfamiliarity of the new sound, the fact that it is less loud, presented to one ear only, or other unrecognized factors. This is handled by reducing the rate of speaking and/or constricting the situational dimensions (kind and number of persons present while using the device) sufficiently to reestablish fluency. Then, as before, these are gradually and systematically extended at a rate determined by the patient's progress.

During this phase of treatment the patient constructs a list or hierarchy of speaking situations he is likely to encounter in his daily life, arranging them in increasing order of anticipated speaking difficulty. The patient then begins to use his metronome in the first situation, i.e., the situation associated with the least anticipatory anxiety and the least probability of severe stuttering. After he gains experience and self-confidence speaking fluently in this category of situation he is ready to begin using the metronome in the next, and so forth. This process corresponds to the behavior therapy procedure called systematic desensitization except that the desensitization is carried out encountering the actual situations in the "real world" rather than simply imagining them in the therapist's office. It can be seen that much of the retraining is accomplished by the patient while he is carrying out his usual daily activities. The therapy sessions are now largely devoted to coaching the patient in this process. If other therapeutic procedures are not needed, sessions may now be spaced out at fortnightly or 3-week intervals.

During this phase of treatment it is not uncommon for the patient to experience unexpected difficulty in some situations from time to time. If this occurs it is essential for the patient to regain fluency in the situation as soon as possible by the same means he has used before, viz., by reverting to a slower rate of speech and, if necessary, to more strict pacing (one syllable or one word per beat). When he becomes more fluent and regains the feeling of "control" of his speech he may gradually return to more rapid speech and less strict pacing on a trial basis. This is an important principle and sometimes requires much coaching by the thera-pist. Often it is helpful for the patient to rehearse this procedure in the therapist's office by simulating outside speaking situations.

The time required for this phase of treatment varies a great deal from patient to patient. The goal is being able to speak in a relaxed, fluent manner in virtually all speaking situations.

IV. In this phase the patient discontinues the use of the metronome. This is also done gradually and systematically, starting with the speaking situations in which the patient has the least amount of difficulty. During this phase many patients find it helpful to pace their speech to the beats of an "imaginary" metronome. If in any situation during this process the patient finds himself having appreciable speaking difficulty, he must again immediately return to stricter pacing of his speech even though the metronome is not present. Only a few sentences may be required before control is regained. If he continues to have difficulty in this and related situations, he may need to return to the use of the actual metronome again. Thus the withdrawal of the metronome proceeds in a cautious, trial-and-error manner until the patient is not using a metronome at all.

As will be described with the patients treated in this clinical study, the end point of this phase of treatment is variable. Some patients succeed in withdrawing the use of the metronome in all situations. A second category of end result is being able to speak in most situations without a metronome but continuing to use the device in situations of high anxiety and tension. For one patient this may mean continuing to use the metronome only while delivering lectures or conducting seminars. For another the only situation requiring the metronome might be talking over the telephone. Among the patients we have studied in this category the number of situations in which they require the metronome tends to diminish over time. It may be that eventually most of these patients will also not be using the metronome at all. However, several more years of follow-up will be required to answer this question. The final category of end result includes patients who continue to be fluent with the metronome but find that they still have appreciable speaking difficulty without it, except perhaps in the least stressful situations. Again it may be that in time these patients will evolve into the other two categories. However, with the limited period of follow-up to date we cannot say this will happen. Originally we were troubled by the prospect of these patients using a prosthesis for a prolonged or indefinite period. However, in reviewing our cases it became clear that only the most severe and intractable stutterers fall into this category. For them the use of the metronome has meant the difference between being able to communicate effectively in educational, occupational, and social situations and not being able to do so. All of these patients regard the burden of having to wear a metronome a very small price indeed for the substantial increase in verbal functioning and the attendant increase in self-esteem and self-confidence they experience. We now regard the use of the metronome by this category of patient quite analogous to the indefinite use of a hearing-aid by the person who is very hard of hearing or the permanent use of eyeglasses by the person who is functionally blind without them.

V. The primary treatment is complete with Phase IV. However, the strength of the tendency to stutter often waxes and wanes over time. For reasons that are not always apparent, a period of several weeks or months of high fluency may be interrupted by a period of greater speaking difficulty lasting days or weeks. Patients who have not been using a metronome are urged to use the device again at the earliest signs of such a relapse. The prompt return to metronome-paced speech seems to "abort" such episodes of nonfluency, usually within a few days. In our experience these brief periods of relapse become less frequent over time.

Additional Behavior Therapy Procedures

Earlier in our clinical studies we routinely combined MCSR with other behavior therapy procedures (Brady, 1968a). Now we find that it is not necessary to do so in most cases. Specifically, we now use systematic desensitization only if the patient has difficulty extending metronome-aided fluency into a particular situation, even though he may be quite fluent in closely related situations of equal difficulty. In brief, the patient is instructed to vividly imagine himself in the difficult speaking situation while he is, in fact, deeply relaxed with his eyes closed in the therapist's office. He is then instructed to speak out loud in this imagined scene and pace his speech with the metronome. It is assumed that the psycho-physiological state induced by the deep muscular relaxation will counter-condition the anxiety aroused by this scene which will in turn permit more fluent speech. Once the patient is able to speak in a relaxed and fluent manner in these imagined scenes he is usually able to speak more fluently in the corresponding real-life situation.

Other behavior therapy procedures, such as the use of delayed auditory feedback or the operant reinforcement of fluent responses, are not incompatible with MCSR and could be used in conjunction with it.

Speech Therapy Procedures

Many of the techniques commonly used in "traditional" speech therapy are not incompatible with the MCSR procedure but play an adjunctive or secondary role. For example, "secondary symptoms" such as facial grimaces, shoulder jerks, and eye blinking are especially sensitive to the metronome's effect and usually greatly diminish or disappear even before a marked decrease in nonfluency is seen. However, any that do persist may be treated by speech therapy techniques, such as making the details of the tic or abnormal movements better known to the patient to facilitate his bringing them under control. Erroneous beliefs and harmful attitudes are also corrected. For example, if the patient tends to regard his stuttering passively as something that happens to him, an effort is made to have him adopt the more realistic, active, and therapeutically useful view that stuttering is something he does, albeit involuntarily. However, there are other precepts and procedures which interfere with MCSR and are hence contraindicated. One of these is the procedure variously called "negative practice," "paradoxical intention," or "voluntary stuttering" in which the patient is instructed to stutter intentionally in some situations in order to gain more control over his speech in other situations. This practice tends to undermine the patient's confidence that by properly pacing his speech he is able to communicate verbally without stuttering. Common advice to stutterers is that they not avoid any speaking situation out of fear of stuttering. Although one of the ultimate goals of the present treatment program is avoiding no speaking situation, the patient must not prematurely place himself in a difficult speaking situation in which stuttering is likely despite the presence of the metronome. Such a "failure experience" in the early phases of treatment tends to reinforce the tension and anxiety associated with that situation and retards progress.

Psychotherapy

There is no adequate evidence that most cases of stuttering are caused by unconscious conflicts or repressed drives. Hence it is not surprising that the results of treatment of chronic, severe stutterers by psycho-therapy alone are generally poor (Glauber, 1968; Ostwald, 1970). It is also not surprising that patients who learn to speak fluently, whether by behavioral techniques or "speech therapy," do not develop substitute symptoms as a consequence (Brady, 1968a; Falck, 1969).

Many severe stutterers do have adjustment problems and personality difficulties, but the available clinical and experimental evidence favors the view that these are the result rather than the cause of stuttering (e.g., Yates, 1963). It is not surprising that the years of frustration, embarrass-ment, guilt, and shame associated with a persistent speech problem often lead to the development of a poor self-concept, a passive and retiring manner, inadequate social skills, or other problems. Many of these problems improve as the patient gains fluency but skillful psychothera-peutic handling is often necessary. It is unrealistic to expect a man in his early twenties who has few social contacts because of his fears of speaking to suddenly acquire the missing parts of his social repertoire when he can speak fluently. Patient counseling and supportive psycho-therapy are much needed. Thus psychotherapeutic procedures also play an adjunctive role in many cases. These are only started, however, after the patient already shows substantial improvement in his primary speech-problem.

CLINICAL STUDY

Characteristics of the Clinical Sample

The treatment sample consisted of 26 severe, chronic stutterers. About two-thirds were referred by psychiatrists, clinical psychologists, speech pathologists, or other professional workers and about one-third were referred by the patient himself, a friend, or a relative. In all cases the referral was made on the basis of the knowledge that we were developing new methods for the treatment of stuttering. The patients ranged in age from 12 to 53 years (mean 24.8 years) and all but five were male (see Table 21.1). Fourteen of the 26 were undergraduate or graduate students in universities in the Philadelphia area. All were continuously regarded as "stutterers" by themselves and others from early childhood (age 4–7) until the time of referral. All had some form of therapy for their speech in the past. The amount of therapy during the past 5 years ranged from 0 to 191 hr (mean 49.6 hr) and in most instances consisted of speech therapy. However, three patients had dynamically oriented psychotherapy alone (case numbers 4, 16, and 26), five had both speech therapy and psychotherapy (cases 6, 9, 10, 12, and 25), and two had both behavior therapy and speech therapy (cases 14 and 24). In one instance (case 14) the behavior therapy consisted of systematic desensitization and in the other (case 24) the use of a delayed auditory feedback (Goldiamond, 1966). No patient believed that his speech had improved substantially during the 2-year period prior to the present treatment program.

In summary, the sample consisted of 26 chronic stutterers, predominately late adolescent or adult in age, whose stuttering had proved to be refractory to a variety of treatment approaches, and whose severe speech problem had not changed substantially over the 2 years prior to the present treatment program.

Initial Evaluation

Assessment of Severity of Stuttering Three measures of the patient's speech were collected.

1. A tape recorder was used to collect a 3-min sample of the patient's reading and a 3-min sample of extemporaneous speaking (on an arbitrarily assigned topic without apparent high emotional content) in the presence of the therapist only. The total number of nonfluencies and the total

Table 21.1. Summary of Clinical Data.[a]

Case no.	Sex	Age	Total treatment (1-hr sessions)	Change in clinician's rating	Change in patient's rating	% Nonfluency before treatment	% Nonfluency after treatment	% Decrease in nonfluency	Pacemaster status	Follow-up months
1	F	28	14	3	2.2	8.3	0.2	97.6	N	6
2	F	22	14	2	1.0	6.2	1.5	75.8	N	44
3	M	20	22	2	0.8	6.7	1.6	76.1	N	24
4	M	26	5	3	0.9	18.2	2.0	89.0	S	9
5	M	19	9	3	0.8	42.5	11.4	73.2	S	13
6	M	24	21	1	0.9	3.1	1.7	45.1	S	6
7	M	21	6	1	-0.3	2.5	2.0	20.0	N	16
8	F	22	9	2	1.7	19.8	2.3	88.4	S	6
9	M	28	31	3	1.3	8.5	1.0	88.2	M	12
10	M	27	5	3	0.8	8.5	1.3	84.7	N	13
11	M	22	6	3	1.5	8.5	5.2	38.8	S	19
12	M	19	5	2	1.5	6.1	2.0	67.2	N	21
13	F	12	8	1	0.4	30.0	7.3	75.6	N	6
14	M	14	9	3	0.8	55.7	8.4	84.9	N	6
15	M	45	12	2	0.6	14.1	3.8	73.0	S	6
16	M	25	15	5	2.0	13.7	0.8	94.2	N	21
17	M	32	5	3	-0.5	43.0	6.4	85.1	M	11
18	M	37	13	1	0.2	9.5	2.4	74.7	N	11
19	M	53	8	3	1.3	44.5	6.0	86.5	S	14

20	M	21	17	2	1.1	10.6	4.4	58.5	N	19
21	M	16	10	4	2.6	10.5	2.2	79.1	M	21
22	M	24	11	0	0.3	8.5	10.3	−17.5	N	7
23	M	23	17	0	0.2	12.2	11.0	9.9	S	7
24[b]	M	12	3	—	—	8.4	—	—	—	—
25[b]	M	26	3	—	—	14.9	—	—	—	—
26[b]	F	26	9	—	—	50.5	—	—	—	—
Mean of all patients (N = 26)		24.8	11.0	2.3	0.96	17.9				
Mean of patients completing treatment (N = 23)		25.2	11.8	2.3	0.96	17.0	4.14	67.3	—	13.8

[a] The "Change in clinician's rating" is the difference between the Form 14 rating at initial interview and at follow-up assessment. The "Change in patient's rating" is the difference between the Form 16 rating at initial interview and at follow-up assessment. A minus sign indicates a poorer rating after treatment. The "% Decrease in nonfluency" is obtained as follows: $100 \times (1 - \%$ after treatment $\div \%$ before treatment). "Pacemaster status" indicates whether at follow-up patient was using the Pacemaster (electronic metronome) not at all (N), for some situations (S) or most of the time (M).

[b] These patients dropped out of treatment.

number of words spoken in this 6-min sample were counted. A nonfluency was defined simply as a clear hesitation or block, the repetition of a syllable, word or phrase, the prolongation of a sound, or the use of a "filler" ("ah," "er," etc.). No effort was made to assign different "weights" to nonfluencies of different duration or severity. From these data the patient's nonfluency rate was calculated: the percentage of nonfluencies in this 6-min sample. These rates are given for the 26 patients in Table 21.1. Although these percentages indicate a wide range of nonfluency (3.1–55.7), it can be seen that most of the patients were indeed severe stutterers (mean of 17.9%).

2. The therapist made a global rating of the patient's stuttering using the Scale for Rating Severity of Stuttering (Form 14) developed by Johnson, Darley, and Spriesterbach (1963). This scale ranges from 0 (no stuttering) to 7 (very severe). These scores ranged from 2 to 7 (mean of 4.6) again indicating the severity of the stuttering of most patients in the sample.

3. The patient completed the severity category of the Stutterer's Self-Rating of Reactions to Speech Situations (Form 16) also developed by Johnson *et al.* (1963). This inventory lists 40 common speaking situations and asks the patient to rate the severity of his stuttering in each on a 5-point scale ranging from "I don't stutter at all in this situation" (rated 1) to "I stutter severely in this situation" (rated 5). The patient's score was obtained by summing his responses to the individual items and dividing by the number rated (usually 40). These scores ranged from 1.7 to 4.1 (mean of 2.99).

Assessment of Psychological Adjustment   This was undertaken for two purposes. First it was felt to be important to exclude from the study any patient who in addition to stuttering suffered from a major, disabling psychiatric disorder such as schizophrenia or severe depression. It happened that only one patient referred for treatment had to be excluded on this basis. The second reason for this general assessment was to detect any major effect of the treatment program on the patient's adjustment in general. The assessment consisted of the following three parts.

1. A general psychiatric interview was conducted by the author. The emphasis here was on the quality of the patient's social relationships, his self-esteem, and his capacity to discharge his major current responsibilities (as student, employee, parent, spouse, etc.).

The clinical interviews revealed a variety of personality problems and neurotic traits in some of the patients. In almost all instances these were not disabling and were most parsimoniously accounted for as consequences of the patient's speech problem. Contrary to the generalization made by some clinicians (e.g., Sadoff & Collins, 1968), however, no consistent personality traits or patterns were seen in the sample. This is in keeping with a recent thorough and critical review by Sheehan (1970) who concluded that there is no evidence for personality differences between stutterers and nonstutterers.

2. The patient completed the Symptom Check List, a self-administered 64-item list of common psychoneurotic complaints adapted from the Johns Hopkins Distress List (Lipman, Cole, Park, & Rickels, 1965). The patient indicates how much each symptom has bothered him during the past week on a 4-point scale: 1. not at all; 2. a little; 3. quite a bit; and 4. extremely. The patient's score is obtained by summing his responses to the individual items and dividing by 64. The range of scores of the patients in the present study before treatment was 1.12–2.70 (mean of 1.55). Most of the scores fell above those obtained from a large normative (non-patient) sample but below those obtained from several samples of neurotic patients seen in private practice and psychiatric outpatient clinics (Uhlenhuth, Rickels, Fisher, Park, Lipman, & Mock, 1966; Rickels, Garcia, & Fisher, 1971).

3. The patient also completed the IPAT Anxiety Scale Questionnaire (Cattell, 1957). The patients' scores were converted to "sten scores" which in the present sample ranged from 3 to 10 with a mean of 6.82. Here again most scores were above those of a normative (nonpatient) sample but below those of most neurotic patients seen in a psychiatric outpatient clinic (Cattell & Rickels, 1965). The symptom Check List and IPAT Anxiety Scale are both suitable for repeated administration (e.g., before and after treatment) and together provide a broad measure of a patient's current psychological distress and neurotic symptomatology.

Treatment Results

The MCSR procedure as described above was initiated with all 26 patients. Table 21.1 shows the total number of treatment sessions for each patient. These figures include adjuvant psychotherapy which was employed in five cases (numbers 1, 6, 16, 23, and 26) and the adjuvant use of systematic desensitization during Phase III of MCSR in two cases (numbers 3 and 9).

Each patient's clinical status was assessed at the end of treatment and at follow-ups after varying periods of time by the same methods used in the initial evaluation. Some of these data are summarized in Table 21.1. For convenience the cases have been numbered in such a way that the treatment failures occur together at the end. Three patients (numbers 24, 25, and 26) terminated therapy after a few sessions. None gave a reason for dropping out of therapy and none was willing to be reevaluated. These patients as a group were not clearly different from the rest of the sample in severity of stuttering, the psychological test measures, or in most other respects. However, two of the three cases (numbers 24 and 25) had an unusual amount of unsuccessful therapy for their speech during the past five years (156 and 191 hours, respectively). They must be considered failures of a sort.

Two patients (numbers 22 and 23) must be considered treatment failures. Both terminated therapy in part because they were moving some distance from Philadelphia but they were willing to be reevaluated. Neither showed significant improvement in his speech at the time while speaking without the aid of a metronome (see Table 21.1). However, one of them (case 23) is able to speak much more fluently while wearing the metronome, is encouraged by this, and continues to use the device in his new school setting. He is more optimistic about the future and is avoiding difficult speech situations less. The other patient (case 22) was discouraged by his failure to progress and to our knowledge is not using a metronome at this time.

A discussion of the clinical results with the remaining 21 successfully treated patients follows.

Severity of Stuttering   As indicated in Table 21.1 the remaining 21 patients showed substantial improvement in speech. This is most striking in the percentage reductions in nonfluency (mean of 67.3%). These reassessments were made while the patient was not wearing a metronome. (The percentage of nonfluency for most of the patients while wearing a metronome is near zero.) In almost every instance these follow-up nonfluency rates are at least as low as those obtained immediately after treatment was completed. In other words, almost all patients continued to improve after termination of active therapy. No doubt one reason for this is that patients who continue to use the metronome, at least in some situations, are in effect continuing the treatment in the natural environment. The clinicians' ratings (Form 14) showed the same improvement. The patients' self-ratings (Form 16) showed less marked changes and in some cases near zero changes. Only two were in an unexpected (negative) direction. The reasons for this are not clear but may reflect the tendency of most patients to use the middle of the 5-point scale provided in Form 16. By inspection, all these measured changes are highly significant statistically. The Spearman Rank Correlation Coefficients among the three measures of improvement are as follows: between percentage reduction in nonfluency and Form 14, $+0.71$ ($p < 0.001$); between percentage reduction and Form 16, $+0.46$ ($p < 0.025$); and between Form 14 and Form 16, $+0.58$ ($p < 0.005$).

General Adjustment   The follow-up psychiatric interview revealed that all patients believed that they were speaking much more fluently in most situations and were pleased with this change. All were more self-confident and seemed better able to deal with the challenges provided by daily life in the social, school, and occupational areas. There was no evidence of "symptom substitution." The range of scores on the Symptom Check List was 1.09–2.00 (mean of 1.44). The decreases in Symptom Check List scores between initial evaluation and follow-up assessment proved to be statistically significant at the 0.005 level [Wilcoxon Matched-Pairs Signed-Ranks Test (Siegel, 1956)]. The range of IPAT Anxiety Scale scores was 2–10 (mean of 5.30). These scores are significantly different from the initial evaluation values at the 0.005 level (Wilcoxon test).

The decreases in the Symptom Check List and IPAT scores by themselves are not strong evidence that the patients experienced a decrease in psychological stress and neurotic symptomatology as a consequence of the treatment program. It is possible that a "halo effect" was operating, patients tending to *report* less distress and fewer symptoms when they are being reassessed at follow-up. The important point is that we observed no evidence that the patients' general adjustment suffered as a consequence of markedly improving their speech by a predominately behavioral approach. The clinical evidence strongly suggests that every patient's general adjustment was significantly improved. This is in keeping with the observations of other investigators who have used behavioral approaches to stuttering (Goldiamond, 1966; Curlee, 1968).

It will be noted (Table 21.1) that three of the patients are still using a miniaturized metronome "most of the time" and eight are using it "some of the time." We do not know if these patients will evolve into the other large group of 11 patients (excluding the treatment failures) who no longer need to use the metronome at all. In the meantime, however, all feel that the "burden" of wearing the device is well worth the continuing fluency they experience. In addition, most report that with continued use of the metronome the carry-over to fluency without the device is greater and greater.

DISCUSSION

Efficacy of the MCSR Program

Of the 26 chronic, severe stutterers referred for treatment, 21 showed substantial improvement in their speech and general adjustment by several criteria. If the three patients who dropped out of treatment are excluded, this is an improvement rate of over 90%. This required a mean of 11.8 treatment sessions over a period of several months. Although a longer follow-up period is essential to fully evaluate the program, the mean follow-up period of 13.8 months suggests that the clinical results are indeed lasting. In fact, several clinical studies indicate that if relapse is going to occur it will occur within 6 months or so (Van Riper, 1958; Prins, 1970). However, the significance of these results has to be examined against the "spontaneous remission rate" for this disorder and against the results of treatment by other methods.

Several studies indicate that about 80% of persons who stutter significantly in childhood and adolescence show spontaneous remission (Sheehan & Martyn, 1966, 1970). Most of these remissions occur before age 18 and it is generally a gradual process (Shearer & Williams, 1965). Comparable studies do not exist for the prognosis of severe stuttering in adults without treatment but most clinicians concur that the likelihood of recovery is much less, even over a period of many years. Hence it is very unlikely that the marked improvement of severe stutterers observed in the present treatment program can be attributed to "spontaneous remission."

It is very difficult to assess the efficacy of other programs for the treatment of stuttering for several reasons. First, descriptions of treatment procedures and programs far outnumber reports of treatment results in the speech therapy literature. Second, most reports of treatment results in the psychiatric, psychological, and speech pathology literature tend to involve only a small number of cases (often one case)! It is impossible to estimate the general effectiveness of treatment procedures without knowing the number of treatment failures in the same sample treated. Third, treatment results are often stated in vague, subjective, or impressionistic terms. Some of the more experimentally oriented studies, especially those of a behavioral nature, often do define an experimental sample and present more objective data. However, the clinical results reported tend to be limited to assessments of the patients' fluency in the laboratory setting or immediately after treatment is completed but without follow-up data (Shames, Egolf, & Rhodes, 1969; Goldiamond, 1966). The practical, clinical effectiveness of these procedures cannot be judged from these kinds of data because fluency obtained in a laboratory setting often does not carry-over to the natural environment and the relapse rate following treatment-induced improvement is often very high.

Those clinical studies in which a number of cases are followed-up after treatment-induced improvement tend to disclose rather high rates of relapse (e.g., Van Riper, 1958; Prins, 1970). The treatment results of the present program, a 90% improvement rate with a minimum follow-up period of 6 months, are encouraging indeed.

Objections to the Use of a Metronome in Stuttering

The use of a metronome in the treatment of stuttering is criticized by some traditionally oriented therapists. In view of the power of the technique and the apparent success of the programs related or similar to the present program (Brady, 1968a; Rothman, 1969), these criticisms seem difficult to justify. Wingate (1969) recently listed several possible bases for their reservations and the present author has encountered several more. Principal among these are the following:

1. The means by which the metronome brings about fluency are not understood. This is true but is not a valid basis for rejecting treatment procedures which make use of the principle. Some of the most useful therapeutic agents and procedures in medicine were once in this category and some still are. For example, penicillin had been used to save millions of lives before its biochemical modus operandi was understood. The use of lithium salts in the treatment of severe manic-depressive psychosis is a current example.

2. The past association of the use of metronomes to treat stuttering with the "commercial schools" and practitioners who were considered charlatans. Of course, this is no reason for rejecting an effective treatment at this time.

3. The use of a metronome does not get at the stutterer's "underlying problem." There is no convincing evidence of an "underlying problem" in stutterers and, even if there were, its existence would be irrelevant to a program of treatment which is effective in correcting the speech problem and facilitating general improvement in the patient's adjustment.

4. The belief that the metronome works by "distraction" and that the beneficial effect does not last. Recent experimental evidence indicates that the metronome effect cannot be attributed to distraction (Fransella,

1967; Brady, 1969). In addition, there is no evidence that "adaptation" to the metronome effect occurs and, if used in a systematic program of speech retraining, there is good carry-over of fluency for most patients to metronome-unaided speech.

5. A metronome treatment places the focus on an impersonal, mechanical device rather than on the patient as a person. Related to this is the criticism that such treatment is technique oriented rather than patient oriented. Both of these are non sequiturs. An apt analog in medicine would be to criticize the orthopedist's prescription of a brace for a back ailment for the reason that it precludes his responding to the patient as a unique human being. Of course a good clinician is always mindful of and concerned with the entire person.

6. Finally, there is the concern that the use of a metronome fosters "dependency" on a "crutch" rather than the development of self-reliance. This criticism reflects a misunderstanding of the treatment procedure. The metronome is not a substitute for learning to speak fluently but an aid in learning to speak fluently. For most patients the appropriate orthopedic analog is the *temporary* use of a crutch after a leg fracture to aid the retraining of muscles and to facilitate rapid recovery. There is a minority of severe stutterers who appear to require the continued use of the metronome to maintain fluency. As mentioned earlier, this use of the device is analogous to the continued use of eyeglasses by those with poor eyesight.

In sum, the only relevant question is whether the use of a metronome in a systematic program of treatment as described in this paper impedes or facilitates recovery from stuttering and associated adjustment problems. The clinical evidence to date strongly recommends this approach to the treatment of the disorder of stuttering.

REFERENCES

Azrin, N. M., Jones, R. J., and Flye, B. A synchronization effect and its application to stuttering by a portable apparatus. *Journal of Applied Behavior Analysis*, 1968, **4**, 283–295.

Barber, V. B. Studies in the psychology of stuttering—XVI: rhythm as a distraction in stuttering. *Journal of Speech Disorders*, 1940, **5**, 29–42.

Beech, H. R. and Fransella, F. *Research and Experiment in Stuttering*. London: Pergamon Press, 1968.

Brady, J. P. A behavioral approach to the treatment of stuttering. *American Journal of Psychiatry*, 1968, **125**, 843–848. (a)

Brady, J. P. Psychotherapy by a combined behavioral and dynamic approach. *Comprehensive Psychiatry*, 1968, **9**, 536–543. (b)

Brady, J. P. Studies on the metronome effect on stuttering. *Behaviour Research and Therapy*, 1969, **7**, 197–204.

Brady, J. P. Behavior therapy. In J. H. Price (Ed.) *Modern Trends in Psychological Medicine*, Vol. II. London: Butterworths, 1970. Pp. 256–276.

Brutten, E. J. and Shoemaker, D. J. *The Modification of Stuttering*. Englewood Cliffs, N.J.: Prentice-Hall, 1967.

Cattell, R. B. *Handbook for the IPAT Anxiety Scale*. Champaign, Ill.: Institute for Personality and Ability Testing, 1957.

Cattell, R. B. and Rickels, K. Diagnostic power of IPAT objective anxiety neuroticism tests. *Archives of General Psychiatry*, 1965, **11**, 459–465.

Colombat De L'Isère, M. *Du Bégaiement et de Tous les Autres Vices de la Parole Traites par de Nouvelles Méthodes*. (2nd ed.) Paris: Mansut, 1831.

Curlee, R. F. Personality factors in stuttering: effects of behavioral modification of stuttering on selected measures of personality and anxiety. Paper read at the 44th Annual Convention of the American Speech and Hearing Association, Denver, Colo., 1968.

Falck, F. J. *Stuttering, Learned and Unlearned*. Springfield, Ill.: Thomas, 1969.

Fransella, F. Rhythm as a distractor in the modification of stuttering. *Behaviour Research and Therapy*, 1967, **5**, 253–255.

Glauber, P. Dysautomatization: a disorder of the preconscious ego functioning. *International Journal of Psychoanalysis*, 1968, **49**, 89–99.

Goldiamond, I. Stuttering and fluency as manipulatable operant response classes. In L. Krasner and L. P. Ullmann (Eds.), *Research in Behavior Modification*. New York: Holt, Rinehart, & Winston, 1966. Pp. 106–156.

Gray, B. B. and England, G. (Eds.) *Stuttering and the Conditioning Therapies*. Monterey, Calif.: The Monterey Institute for Speech and Hearing, 1969.

Greenberg, J. B. The effect of a metronome on the speech of young stutterers. *Behavior Therapy*, 1970, **1**, 240–244.

Horan, M. C. An improved device for inducing rhythmic speech in stutterers. *Australian Psychologist*, 1968, **3**, 19–25.

Johnson, W., Darley, F. L., and Spriesterbach, D. C. *Diagnostic Methods in Speech Pathology*. New York: Harper & Row, 1963.

Jones, R. J. and Azrin, N. H. Behavioral engineering: stuttering as a function of stimulus duration during speech synchronization. *Journal of Applied Behavior Analysis*, 1969, **2**, 223–229.

Lipman, R. S., Cole, J. O., Park, L. C., and Rickels, K. Sensitivity of symptom and nonsymptom-focused criteria of outpatient drug efficacy. *American Journal of Psychiatry*, 1965, **122**, 24–27.

Meyer V. and Mair, J. M. A new technique to control stammering: a preliminary report. *Behaviour Research and Therapy*, 1963, **1**, 251–254.

Miller, N. E. Learning of visceral and glandular responses. *Science*, 1969, **163**, 434–445.

Ostwald, P. F. The psychiatrist and the patient who stutters. *Journal of Nervous and Mental Disease*, 1970, **150**, 317–324.

Prins, D. Improvement and regression in stutterers following short-term intensive therapy. *Journal of Speech and Hearing Disorders*, 1970, **35**, 123–135.

Rickels, K., Garcia, C. R., and Fisher, E. A measure of emotional symptom distress in private gynecological practice. *Obstetrics and Gynecology*, 1971, **38**, 139–146.

Rothman, I. Stuttering: theory and treatment. *Experimental Medicine and Surgery*, 1969, **27**, 336–349.

Sadoff, R. L. and Collins, D. J. Passive dependency in stutterers. *American Journal of Psychiatry*, 1968, **124**, 1126–1127.

Shames, G. H., Egolf, D. B., and Rhodes, R. C. Experimental programs in stuttering therapy. *Journal of Speech and Hearing Disorders*, 1969, **34**, 30–47.

Shearer, W. M. and Williams, J. D. Self-recovery from stuttering. *Journal of Speech and Hearing Disorders*, 1965, **30**, 288–290.

Sheehan, J. G. *Stuttering: Research and Therapy*. New York: Harper & Row, 1970.

Sheehan, J. G. and Martyn, M. M. Spontaneous recovery from stuttering. *Journal of Speech and Hearing Research*, 1966, **9**, 121–135.

Sheehan, J. G. and Martyn, M. M. Stuttering and its disappearance. *Journal of Speech and Hearing Research*, 1970, **13**, 279–289.

Siegel, S. *Nonparametric Statistics*. New York: McGraw-Hill, 1956.

Uhlenhuth, E. H., Rickels, K., Fisher, S., Park, L. C., Lipman, R. S., and Mock, J. Drug, doctor's verbal attitude and clinic setting in the symptomatic response to psychotherapy. *Psychopharmacologia (Berlin)*, 1966, **9**, 392–418.

Van Riper, C. Experiments in stuttering therapy. In J. Eisenson (Ed.) *Stuttering: a Symposium*. New York: Harper & Row, 1958. Pp. 273–390.

Wingate, M. E. Sound and pattern in "artificial" fluency. *Journal of Speech and Hearing Research*, 1969, **12**, 677–686.

Wohl, M. T. The electronic metronome—an evaluative study. *British Journal of Disorders of Communication*, 1968, **3**, 89–98.

Wolpe, J. *The Practice of Behavior Therapy*. New York: Pergamon Press, 1969.

Yates, A. J. Recent empirical and theoretical approaches to the experimental manipulation of speech in normal subjects and in stammerers. *Behaviour Research and Therapy*, 1963, **1**, 95–119.

CHAPTER 6

The Nervous System: Epilepsy and Migraine Headaches

No two disorders of the nervous system have been more frequently associated with psychological variables than migraine headaches and epilepsy. Psychiatric consultations are often requested for both disturbances since a relationship to psychological factors such as emotional stress, anger, and manipulativeness is commonly observed. The prevalence of epilepsy in the general population has been difficult to ascertain since few statistics are available. Nevertheless, Kurland (1959) conservatively estimated the incidence of epilepsy to be around 365 per 100,000, while other estimates have run as high as 500 per 100,000 adults (Lennox, 1960). Cooper (1965), in a longitudinal study of children, reported an alarming rate of 2270 per 100,000 based on one or more convulsive seizures among those who survived to the age of two years. The number of people who experience migraine headaches is also quite high, with estimates ranging from between five and ten percent of the general population (British Medical Journal, 1963).

In many cases, the causes of these common clinical syndromes are not entirely understood. Although epilepsy may often result from such diverse factors as lesions, trauma, perinatal injuries, infections, and metabolic disorders (Schmidt & Wilder, 1968), an equal number of cases are of unknown etiology, that is, *idiopathic* in nature. Similarly, although many divergent theories of migraine have been proposed (Pearce, 1969; Sacks, 1970), its exact etiology remains to be determined. One set of factors that these syndromes seem to have in common, however, is that individuals in both categories display a heightened sensitivity to stress eliciting variables. This relationship between seizure occurrence and psychological upset has been clearly elucidated by Efron (1957). Other investigators have addressed themselves to the interaction between psychological variables and migraine attacks (Maxwell, 1966; Pearce, 1969; Sacks, 1970).

Apart from the immediate physical consequences of epilepsy and migraine, the patient may also experience other social consequences which can prove to be equally if not more distressing. For example, the epileptic frequently finds himself the victim of job discrimination, vehicle operation restrictions, and social ostracism. In a similar fashion, the migraine sufferer may be unable to participate in desired social activities because of migraine attacks which disable him for varying periods of time.

Although chemotherapeutic advances have greatly aided in the treatment of epilepsy and migraine, the fact remains that the condition of many individuals remains somewhat intractable. Carter and Gold (1968) report that 25% of children suffering from seizure disorders benefit only partially from anticonvulsant medication, while an additional 25% do not respond at all. In other words, about 50% of all epileptic children experience at least occasional seizures despite chemical efforts to control them. Schmidt and Wilder (1968) are more optimistic, reporting significant chemotherapeutic control in 70–80% of all patients with recurring seizures. Statistics on the treatment of migraine are even more difficult to evaluate since conflicting outcome data have been reported in the literature (Pearce, 1969).

Prompted by experimental research on conditioning of autonomic processes (Kimmel, 1967; Miller, 1969), a number of investigators have begun to develop therapeutic strategies based on learning principles. The four selections included in the present chapter describe applications of both operant and respondent conditioning procedures to the treatment of epileptic disorders and migraine headaches. A common theme of many of the articles, particularly the papers related to epilepsy, is the emphasis on the experimental analysis of symptomatic complaints. The ongoing collection of precise data on the frequency of symptom occurrence, associated, or related response consequences, and antecedent stimulus conditions represents an important contribution of behavioral science to the field of medicine, for this information may be used to supplement patient's medical history, physical data, and laboratory findings in order to determine more accurately appropriate treatment plans. The utility of selecting treatments based upon careful behavioral assessment should become increasingly evident in this and succeeding chapters.

Zlutnick, Mayville, and Moffat (Article 22) propose a treatment strategy for major and minor motor seizures based upon the principle of response chaining. The authors conceptualize seizures as a terminal link in a chain of behaviors and propose intervention at earlier occurring links. These investigators first identify behaviors that reliably precede seizures. Once predictability has been established, the chain is interrupted by applying contingencies to the preseizure behaviors. In this case, the target behaviors were modified by punishment and the differential reinforcement of incompatible behavior. Zlutnick *et al.* found that reductions in patients' seizure frequency ranged from 40 to 100%. A reversal procedure was used in all cases, further strengthening the credibility of the authors' conclusions.

The papers by Parrino (Article 23) and by Forster (Article 24) describe two alternative approaches to seizure control derived from respondent conditioning paradigms. Parrino, noting the relationship between seizure frequency and emotional arousal to specific stimulus conditions, trained an epileptic patient in deep muscle relaxation. Having devised a hierarchy of anxiety provoking stimuli that appeared to trigger the patient's grand mal attacks, Parrino instituted a desensitization program that resulted in the elimination of all seizure activity.

Forster has proposed other respondent conditioning techniques for the *reflex* epilepsies. These are seizure disorders that can be precisely attributed to environmental stimuli, such as stroboscopically (flickering light) induced seizures, audiogenic (sound) seizures, or reading induced seizures. Assuming that seizures elicited in this manner are conditioned responses to conditioned stimuli, Forster describes a treatment strategy utilizing extinction procedures in which the conditioned stimulus (e.g., light, sound, etc.) is presented in massed trials until extinction occurs. A variant of this procedure involves the gradual encroachment upon sensitive stimulus intensity ranges such that seizures are never elicited. Although not mentioned specifically by the author, elements of fading (see Chapter 1) appear to be instrumental in producing therapeutic results.

The final papers in this chapter describe two behavioral approaches to the treatment of migraine headaches. Mitchell and Mitchell (Article 25) present a well-designed research effort to investigate the effects of desensitization, relaxation techniques, and assertion therapy on patients with recurrent migraine headaches. In their article a relationship between stress eliciting environmental stimuli and migraine episodes is again suggested. Desensitization was carried out both individually and in combination with other techniques to modify patient reactions to these stimuli. The results showed that headache frequency and hours duration were reduced in several migraine sufferers. Significantly greater reductions occurred when using combined behavior methods rather than a single method approach.

Sargent *et al.* (Article 26) describe a technique they call *autogenic-feedback training* that also appears promising in the treatment of migraine patients. As explained by the authors, autogenic feedback is basically a combination of the biofeedback procedures discussed in Chapters 1 and 4, and autogenic training, which involves the alteration ·of somatic responses by intense concentration on certain words and phrases (Schultz & Luthe, 1969). In this case, Sargent *et al.* found that by having patients increase the temperature of their hands, migraine attacks could often be reduced if not avoided in some cases. The procedure involves training the patient to concentrate on relaxing phrases while viewing a temperature meter that continuously monitors hand warmth as reflected by the amount of blood flow to this area. Patients are purported to associate subjective feelings with objective changes in hand temperature. With practice, the patient's subjective feelings presumably replace the temperature meter as the source of biofeedback reinforcement. The theory behind the success of this procedure is not clearly understood, although as Sargent *et al.* point out it is probably related to vascular dysfunction associated with migraine attacks.

Points of key importance in this chapter include:

1. Epileptic seizures and migraine headaches can be controlled in some patients by environmental, nonchemotherapeutic manipulations.
2. Some epileptic seizures are more reliably predicted than was previously assumed. This greater predictability provides opportunities for direct intervention prior to the seizure climax.
3. Accurate, representative, and reliable data on the frequency of symptom occurrence are of great importance in the effective treatment of physiological as well as psychological disorders.
4. Many of the therapeutic techniques discussed in this chapter are simple in design and could easily be mastered by health professionals, especially if psychological training and consultation are available to them.
5. A wide variety of learning principles and techniques from both major learning paradigms (operant and respondent) have applicability to the treatment of nervous system disorders. Nevertheless, it is important to realize that many of these techniques are in an experimental stage of development. Although preliminary results look promising, additional

controlled research is needed. This is especially true in considering the Sargent *et al.* paper, for the authors have relied heavily on anecdotal evidence to substantiate their claims.

REFERENCES

British Medical Journal. Drug treatment of migraine. *British Medical Journal*, 1963, 1, 661.

Carter, S. and Gold, A. Convulsions in children. *New England Journal of Medicine*, 1968, **278**, 315–317.

Cooper, J. Epilepsy in a longitudinal survey of 5,000 children. *British Medical Journal*, 1965, 1, 1020–1022.

Efron, R. Conditioned inhibition of uncinate fits. *Brain*, 1957, **80**, 251–262.

Kimmel, H. Instrumental conditioning of autonomically mediated behavior. *Psychological Bulletin*, 1967, **5**, 337–345.

Kurland, L. The incidence and prevalence of convulsive disorders in a small urban community. *Epilepsia*, 1959, 1, 143–161.

Lennox, W. *Epilepsy and Related Disorders*. Boston: Little, Brown, and Company, 1960.

Maxwell, H. *Migraine: Background and Treatment*. Bristol: John Wright and Sons Ltd., 1966.

Miller, N. Learning of visceral and glandular responses. *Science*, 1969, **163**, 434–445.

Pearce, J. *Migraine*. Springfield: Charles C. Thomas, 1969.

Sacks, O. *Migraine*. Berkeley: University of California Press, 1970.

Schmidt, R. and Wilder, B. *Epilepsy*. Philadelphia: F. A. Davis, 1968.

Schultz, J. and Luthe, W. *Autogenic Therapy*, Vol. 1. New York: Grune and Stratton, 1969.

ARTICLE 22

Behavioral Control of Seizure Disorders: The Interruption of Chained Behavior[1]

STEVEN ZLUTNICK,[2] WILLIAM J. MAYVILLE, and SCOTT MOFFAT

University of Utah College of Medicine, Rural Clinics, Reno, Nevada, and Garfield School, Salt Lake City, Utah

Recent laboratory advances in the operant control of autonomic functioning (Kimmel, 1967; Miller, 1969) have lent credence to anecdotal clinical reports on the success of environmental manipulations in modifying behaviors previously thought to be beyond voluntary control. Other case reports frequently emanate from neurological sources, specifically in the area of seizure control, e.g., the inhibition of focal seizures by various forms of distraction (Efron, 1957a, 1957b). More recently, a number of other investigators have begun to explore the use of conditioning techniques for controlling seizure disorders.

Forster (1969), dealing exclusively with the reflex epilepsies (e.g., seizures elicited by stroboscopic, musicogenic, and pattern stimuli), has described a treatment strategy based upon respondent extinction. Essentially, Forster's procedures have consisted of either repeated presentations of the eliciting stimulus until extinction occurs, or gradual stimulus shifting from noneliciting to eliciting values.

Gardner (1967) reported one of the first explicit applications of operant conditioning techniques to the control of seizures. In his report, psychogenic seizures were eliminated in a 10-year-old girl by means of a differential reinforcement procedure, i.e. extinction contingent upon any approximations to or instances of seizure behavior, and reinforcement for incompatible behaviors, such as appropriate play with siblings.

[1]Portions of this research were supported by the University of Utah Biomedical Research Grant 6139-365. The authors thank Drs. Donald P. Hartmann and Roger C. Katz for their comments and suggestions.

[2]Reprints may be obtained from Steven Zlutnick, Ph.D., Department of Psychiatry, University of Utah College of Medicine, Salt Lake City, Utah 84132.

The cases presented below represent a further attempt at controlling seizures of both organic and nonorganic etiology with operant conditioning techniques by applying consequences to behaviors that reliably *precede* the seizure itself. Reliably occurring preseizure behaviors (prodromal behavior, or premonitory symptoms) such as headaches, tinnitus, polydipsia and localized spasms have been described by Henner (1962), and in some cases these behaviors precede the seizure by as long as ten days.

Basic research data support the notion that chained behavior can be disrupted, particularly if earlier components are involved (Findley, 1962; Kelleher & Fry, 1962; Skinner, 1934; Thomas, 1964). If seizures are viewed as the terminal link in a chain of behaviors, these data suggest the feasibility of preventing seizure occurrence by interfering with preseizure behaviors.

Clinical applications of this chaining strategy are rare. Efron (1957a, 1957b) was able to abort grand mal seizures in a 46-year-old woman by the presentation of what might be described as an aversive stimulus (odor of hydrogen sulfide) contingent upon behaviors occurring prior to the grand mal climax. The subject in his study had described quite clearly a sequence of behaviors that reliably preceded the grand mal climax. Similarly, Kohlenberg (1970) successfully eliminated vomiting in a 21-year-old retarded girl by applying electric shock contingent upon stomach contractions that reliably preceded vomiting episodes.

The purpose of the present study was an attempt to eliminate or decrease the rate of seizures in children by the identification and modification of reliable preseizure behaviors. The effects of two operant procedures were examined: contingent punishment and the reinforcement of behavior incompatible with seizures. Concomitantly, an effort was made to investigate the predictability of seizures as well as confirm the feasibility of employing nonprofessionals in the environment of seizure prone children as primary change agents. That parents can be employed successfully as therapists for their children has been amply demonstrated (Johnson & Katz, 1973). The high rate of interaction between the young epileptic child and his family should presumably enable the parents to function effectively in a therapeutic role.

GENERAL METHOD

The pool of 19 subjects from which five were selected for this study was obtained from a variety of sources including referrals from local neurologists, public schools, and occasionally, word-of-mouth from physicians and psychologists. The criteria for selection were that they show: (1) a behaviorally observable seizure, such that a percent agreement reliability figure of at least 90% could be established between two observers (this excluded such forms of epilepsy as petit mal, where it is often difficult, if not impossible, to determine the occurrence of a seizure without corresponding electroencephalographic data); (2) a seizure frequency of at least one per day in order to facilitate data collection and more easily assess the effects of experimental manipulations; and, when possible, (3) a formal diagnosis of epilepsy based upon EEG and/or clinical observation by a neurologist. In general, subjects were eliminated from the pool when either reliable data could not be acquired (eight children) or the seizure could not be operationalized for accurate measurement (five children).

Reliability checks were obtained for all dependent measures and consisted of two observers (or one observer and a parent, depending upon the treatment setting) watching the subject in question for one hour or more from physically separate vantage points, noting the time and occurrence of each seizure. Reliability was computed as percent agreement by dividing the total number of seizures recorded identically by the observers by agreements plus disagreements. The same procedure was employed for determining reliability figures on preseizure behaviors. Absolute frequencies were used due to the relative low frequency of the behaviors in question. Once satisfactory reliability was established subsequent reliability checks were made at the rate of one per experimental phase.

A punishment contingency for preseizure behavior was the same for Subjects 1–4. Essentially it consisted of the following procedure to be implemented by the change agent: (1) Shout, "No!" loudly and sharply; and (2) grasp the subject by the shoulders with both hands and shake him once, vigorously.

For Subject 5, a differential reinforcement procedure was implemented contingent upon the preseizure behavior of arm raising. It consisted of: (1) Placing the subject's hands down to her side (or lap if she were sitting); (2) waiting approximately five seconds; and (3) delivering a combination of primary and social reinforcement contingent upon "arms down."

SUBJECT 1

This subject was a seven-year-old male Caucasian enrolled in a behavior modification program for emotionally disturbed children. He had been alternately diagnosed as autistic, brain damaged, and as having a learning disability. He had a history of seizures from the time that he was two years old. No recent EEG testing results were available, and earlier testing had evidently revealed no abnormalities. Although these seizures were not at any time described as functional, a formal diagnosis of epilepsy was never specifically made. Medication notwithstanding ($8\frac{1}{4}$ grain tablets of dilantin per day), the frequency of seizures remained relatively high and averaged 12 per day.

The seizure itself consisted of at least three distinguishable component behaviors: (1) Fixed gaze at a flat surface (either a table top or wall); followed by (2) the body becoming rigid; followed by (3) myoclonic spasms (violent shaking); and (4) terminating with a fall to the floor. No seizures were ever observed that were not preceded by the fixed stare. As a result, the staring behavior was chosen as the target for modification.

With the discrete nature of these behavioral components, interobserver reliabilities obtained on the seizure and preseizure response were 100%.

Subject 1 was treated within the setting of a local public school behavior modification unit. With few exceptions, all procedures were carried out in the regular classroom, which consisted of a group of 10–12 children who were involved in a developmental curriculum. Since the child occasionally seizured in the washroom, this area was also included in the treatment setting.

Procedure

Baseline   The child was observed continuously from 9:00 a.m. until 3:00 p.m. for a period of three weeks by an assigned staff member who worked in his classroom and recorded the total number of seizures per day. Further data were also obtained in order to determine whether the seizures were discriminated on time, activity, or person(s). Once a seizure occurred, the reaction of the school staff was that of general inattention, which approximated the conditions in effect prior to baseline.

Punishment Phase   When baseline data had stabilized, the staff were instructed to implement the punishment procedure described above contingent upon the occurrence of visual fixation. No consequences were applied once the seizure itself had commenced.

Reversal Phase   During this condition a multiple baseline strategy was instituted to determine if the reduction in seizure rate was a function of the independent variables. From 9:00 a.m. to 12:00 p.m., the punishment contingency was removed, and fixated staring was no longer followed by aversive consequences. From 12:00 p.m. until 3:00 p.m., however, the punishment contingency remained in effect. The reversal was implemented for one day only, due to the reluctance of the investigators to employ reversal procedures for a behavior as severe as seizures. Parental permission was obtained prior to the implementation of this phase.

Punishment Phase At this point, the punishment contingency was reinstated in all conditions.

Results and Discussion

Figure 22.1 shows the number of seizures plotted per week. During baseline, seizures occurred with a frequency of just under 60 per five-day school week, or about 12 per day. Data from prebaseline conditions revealed no apparent discrimination of these seizures on person, place, time, or activity. With the introduction of the punishment contingency, the frequency quickly fell to 5–10 per week, or about one or two per day.

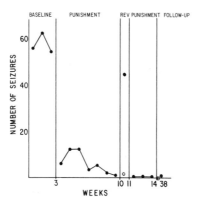

Fig. 22.1. The number of minor motor seizures per week for Subject 1. The reversal is prorated for a 5-day week. During reversal, ● = A.M. and ○ = P.M. Follow-up data represent the absolute number of seizures for the next six months.

The seizures were completely eliminated by the 10th week (seven weeks of treatment). During reversal, when the punishment contingency was removed in the morning, seizures began reoccurring only during the hours when the punishment contingency was not in effect. Prior to this time, seizures had been distributed unsystematically throughout the day. With the reintroduction of the punishment contingency, the seizure frequency quickly dropped to zero where it remained for the duration of the study.

Two additional points merit discussion. First, the preseizure behavior of fixed staring decreased in direct proportion to the decline in rate of the seizures themselves (since this was the case for all subjects, only the seizure data will be presented in the figures). Secondly, following the introduction of punishment, seizures occurred only when staff members were unable to apply the contingency in time, i.e., within 10–15 seconds after the onset of staring. About two weeks into the first punishment phase, the subject was observed to suddenly terminate the visual fixation in order to see if anyone were approaching.

Further, the subject's anticonvulsant medication was systematically reduced by one tablet every two weeks. Thus, at the termination of treatment, the seizure frequency was zero, and no medication was being administered.

Although therapy plans originally called for parental involvement, almost complete spontaneous generalization from the school setting to the home eliminated the need to do so. Although no data were formally collected in the home environment, the parents reported an immediate reduction in both staring and seizures that coincided with the introduction of the punishment contingency at school.

At the end of the first six-month follow-up only one seizure had been observed, which occurred while the subject was on the playground. No other instances of seizures have been reported.

SUBJECT 2

Subject 2 was a four-year-old male Caucasian, diagnosed as moderately retarded with undetermined brain damage. Seizures began at the age of 18 months. A diagnosis of epilepsy, minor motor type, had been made by a neurologist on the basis of seizure history and corroborative abnormal EEG findings. A wide spectrum of anticonvulsant medications had been tried with slight or no success.

Behaviorally, the most prominent seizure pattern consisted of (1) a lowered activity level, followed by (2) the minor motor seizure that was characterized by a sudden flexion of the arms and head. A second, less serious form of seizure, referred to neurologically as an "absence," was characterized by 20–30 seconds of vacant staring which terminated with brief vomiting.

Reliabilities of 100% agreement between observers were obtained on both variants of seizures, and reliabilities of 92% were obtained between two observers and the subject's mother for the lowered activity level. The predictability of this response ranged between 50 and 80% (i.e. the lowered activity level preceded 50–80% of the seizures). No preseizure behaviors were observed for the absence seizure.

Since this study was initiated during the summer months prior to the subject's enrollment in a behavior modification school program, the minor motor seizures were treated in the home environment. The absence seizure pattern commenced in the fall and was treated at school.

Procedure

Baseline—Minor Motor Seizures   The child's parents were interviewed in order to informally determine the number of seizures per day, relevant stimulus conditions, possible consequences, and the existence of preseizure behaviors (i.e. predictability). Next, a running description of behavior (Bijou, Peterson & Ault, 1968) was collected on the child in his home environment in order to verify the accuracy of this information. Finally, in conjunction with the subject's parents, data collection procedures were developed which included the recording of (1) the total seizure frequency per day, and (2) the percent of seizures per day that were predictable.

Punishment—Minor Motor Seizures   Once baseline data had stabilized, the same punishment procedure that was employed for Subject 1 was instituted for this subject contingent upon the occurrence of the lowered activity level. The subject's mother was successfully utilized as the therapeutic agent and no difficulties were encountered.

Baseline—Absence Seizures   In the fall, the "absences" with vomiting began. In this instance, periods of "absences" as well as episodes of vomiting were recorded each day, along with relevant information regarding the stimulus conditions under which they occurred. Parents and staff were instructed not to give excessive attention over and above that previously given to these behaviors, other than to take the steps necessary to clean up after the vomiting, in order to get accurate baseline data and reduce the chance of reinforcing the seizures.

Punishment—Absence Seizures   During this phase, the standard punishment procedure was instituted as close to the onset of the absence (and prior to the vomiting) as possible. No consequences were delivered contingent upon the vomiting. Contingencies were delivered according to a multiple baseline design, i.e. absence seizures were punished at school but not at home.

Reversal—Absence Seizures   At this point, the punishment contingency was removed to determine the effectiveness of the procedures. Thus, when the "absence" began, no consequences were programmed at any time in either stimulus condition.

Punishment—Absence Seizures   At this point, the punishment contingency was reinstated for the absence seizures during school hours (9:00 a.m. to 3:00 p.m. only).

Results and Discussion

Figure 22.2 shows the number of minor motor seizures plotted daily for Subject 2. During baseline, minor motor seizures averaged six per day. With the introduction of the punishment contingency, the number dropped to an average of three per day. The effect proved only transitory, however, and eventually seizure frequency recovered to approximately five per day. Eight months later, the frequency had reduced gradually to an average of two per day. However, this effect was independent of experimental operations. Thus, although approximately 60% of the minor motor seizures were predictable, they were only immediately reducible by 50%, and terminally by 17%.

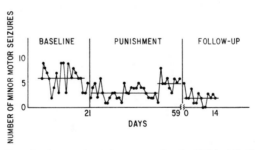

Fig. 22.2. The number of minor motor seizures per day for Subject 2. The horizontal lines represent the mean rate for each condition.

Figure 22.3 shows the frequency of absence and vomiting episodes for Subject 2 plotted daily. During baseline conditions (Part B) the frequency of absences and subsequent vomiting covaried exactly and continued to increase. Because the vomiting caused the subject's family a great deal of discomfort, baseline conditions were terminated before stability was achieved. Part B of Fig. 22.3 shows the total number of vomiting episodes (open circles). With the introduction of the punishment contingency, the vomiting was reduced to a near-zero frequency. However, the number of absences increased over baseline.

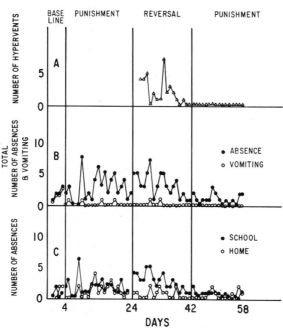

Fig. 22.3. The number of absence seizures, hyperventilations, and vomiting episodes per day for Subject 2.

The effects of the reversal are not immediately apparent until the data are scrutinized carefully. Although vomiting did not recur during this phase, on the third day of the reversal, Subject 2 began hyperventilating both at home and school (Part A of Fig. 22.3) and continued to do so until the punishment contingency was reinstated. Further, when the absences are viewed separately by stimulus conditions (i.e. home and school as in Part C of Fig. 22.3), it can be seen that relative to the number during punishment, the frequency of absences during reversal increased temporarily at school (closed circles) where the punishment was originally introduced, and declined further with reintroduction of the punishment procedure.

Absence seizures differ markedly from those of the minor motor variant, however, and these differences might account somewhat for the relative ineffectiveness of the procedure in this case. Although vomiting decreased while the frequency of "absences" remained unaffected, it should be remembered that the "absence" is a seizure in and of itself, and not a preseizure behavior. This may well serve to support the notion that organic seizures must be modified by the manipulation of antecedents rather than consequences.

At the end of a one-year followup, minor motor seizure frequency remained at approximately two per day. Absence seizures were no longer occurring.

SUBJECT 3

Subject 3 was a four-year-old Caucasian male diagnosed as brain damaged with reduced dexterity on the left side (both arm and leg). Seizure onset began at 20 months and EEG testing revealed distinct abnormalities, confirming a diagnosis of epilepsy: minor motor type. Anticonvulsant medication had reduced seizure activity by 10%, but the rate remained high, averaging about 12% per day.

Behaviorally, the seizure pattern consisted of (1) subtle behavioral change from which the subject's mother could reliably predict 45–50% of his seizures, yet which proved impossible to define and yielded an interobserver reliability of only 15%; and (2) the seizure, characterized by a sudden flexion of the arms and head.

Reliabilities of 100% were obtained between two observers and the subject's mother for seizures. Subject 3 was treated in his home environment during the summer months prior to his enrollment in a formal special education program.

Procedure

The procedure for Subject 3 was identical to that described for Subjects 1 and 2. Data were collected by the subject's mother throughout the study. As with the two previous subjects, a nonprofessional (a parent) served as the therapeutic agent.

Results and Discussion

Figure 22.4 shows the number of minor motor seizures for Subject 3 plotted weekly. During baseline, the rate averaged about 75 seizures per week, or 10–12 per day. Prebaseline and baseline observations yielded no indication that seizures were discriminated on people, time, or activity. With the introduction of the punishment contingency, the frequency quickly decreased and stabilized at about 45–50 per week, or six to seven per day. Reversal conditions produced a frequency equal to slightly over 94% of that observed during baseline. Reintroduction of the punishment procedure resulted in a decrease of seizures nearly equal to that noted in the first punishment phase, although it took a longer period of time to achieve this effect.

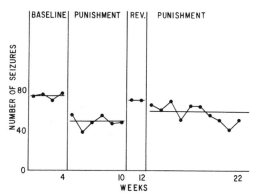

Fig. 22.4. The number of minor motor seizures per week for Subject 3. The horizontal lines represent the mean rate for each condition.

Preseizure behavior, as identified by the subject's mother, covaried exactly with seizure occurrence. At no time did the mother predict a seizure that did not subsequently occur. Thus, the drop in number from the baseline of 12 per day to the punished frequency of about seven per day represents the elimination of all predicted seizures (about five per day). In other words, the reduction of frequency occurred as a function of the abortion of predicted seizures. No change in the frequency of the preseizure behavior occurred throughout the study.

Why only 42% of the seizures were predictable remains unexplained. The fact that the investigator and other observers were unable to identify the preseizure behavior compounds the problem since it is difficult to control a behavior that cannot be identified. Close-up videotaping of the child might have proved more effective in increasing the predictability, and subsequently, control of seizures.

Followup data for Subject 3 are not yet available at this time.

SUBJECT 4

Subject 4 was a 14-year-old Caucasian female with a seizure history dating to the age of 18 months. EEG results were abnormal, confirming a diagnosis of epilepsy: minor motor and focal types. Even with anticonvulsant medication, seizure activity remained relatively high, averaging slightly less than two per day.

Behaviorally, this subject's seizure pattern was characterized by (1) the right arm slowly raised to a position parallel to the head, followed by (2) the seizure (about 60 seconds in duration) consisting of myoclonic jerking and vacant staring. Predictability of the seizure from arm-raising was 100% with obtained observer reliabilities of 100% on the seizure itself.

Subject 4 was treated at home, since the severity and regularity of seizures prohibited her attending school. A home-visiting teacher from the local school district visited the house twice weekly. The girl's mother was used as the therapist and other siblings were frequently employed as ancillary data collectors.

Procedure

The procedure was identical to that described previously for Subjects 1, 2, and 3. Data were collected throughout the study by the subject's mother, who was instructed to note each seizure occurrence, when it occurred, who was present, and the activity in which the child was engaged. She was further instructed to respond to any seizure occurrence in the same manner in which she had in the past, that is to ignore it.

Results and Discussion

Figure 22.5 shows the number of minor motor seizures plotted weekly for Subject 4. During baseline, seizures occurred on an average of 11 per week, or one to two per day. Prebaseline and baseline observations yielded no indication that seizures were discriminated on people, location, time, or activity. With the introduction of the punishment contingency, the frequency was quickly reduced and eventually stabilized, averaging two-and-one-half per week, or one every three days. With the introduction of reversal procedures, the frequency gradually increased to a peak of eight per week, at which time punishment was reintroduced. With this change in procedure, the number decreased to approximately three per week, or one seizure every two days. The occurrence of the preseizure behavior (arm-raising) covaried exactly with the seizure occurrence, and decreased in direct proportion to the seizure activity.

The only deviation from the downward trend of the data during punishment was the one near recovery of baseline frequency (arrow on Fig. 22.5). During this week the subject began her menstrual period and this may serve to explain this unusually high number of seizures. As reported by her mother, the subject's menstrual periods were highly unpredictable and were occasionally accompanied by an abnormally high number of seizures.

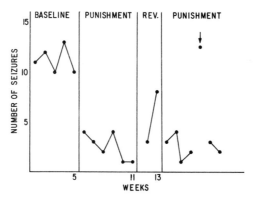

Fig. 22.5. The number of minor motor seizures per week for Subject 4.

The subject's mother reported that a further reduction in seizures might have been possible, but the other children in the family were too young to employ the procedure, and the father was reluctant to become involved in the treatment.

At the end of six months, followup data indicated that while seizure frequency had increased by one or two per week, it still remained far below the initial baseline level.

SUBJECT 5

Subject 5 was a 17-year-old Caucasian female diagnosed as mentally retarded with major motor epilepsy. She presented with a life-long seizure history, and at the time of this research was exhibiting multiple seizures daily despite large doses of dilantin and phenobarbitol.

Behaviorally, her seizures were comprised of the following chain of behaviors: (1) Her body became tense and rigid; (2) she clenched her fists and raised her arms at a 90 degree angle from her body; (3) her head snapped back and a grimace appeared on her face; and (4) the major motor seizure ensued. Reliabilities of 100% were obtained on the seizure and preseizure target behavior of arm-raising.

Subject 5 was treated at a training center for adolescent retarded children. This experiment was conducted by the second author concurrent to, but not in conjunction with the treatment of Subject 1. Because the strategy was so strikingly similar in concept to that used by the first and third authors, it is included here.

Procedure

Data collection, observations, and reliability measures were identical to those described earlier. However, in place of the punishment procedure used with Subjects 1–4, a differential reinforcement procedure was implemented in an attempt to suppress seizure frequency. Essentially, this procedure consisted of the following steps: (1) As soon as the subject raised her arms into the air (component 2 described above) they were placed back down to her side, or in her lap if she were sitting; (2) a delay of five seconds was interposed; (3) she was praised effusively for having her arms lowered; and (4) she was given a piece of M&M candy. The time delay was used to insure that reinforcement was not contingent upon an undesired chain of behaviors, e.g., hands up, followed by hands down.

This procedure was initially implemented by the second author and other teaching staff. Eventually, however, control was faded to other students at the training center.

Results and Discussion

Figure 22.6 shows the number of major motor seizures plotted daily for Subject 5. During baseline, seizures occurred on the average of 16 per day. Commensurate with the introduction of the differential reinforce-

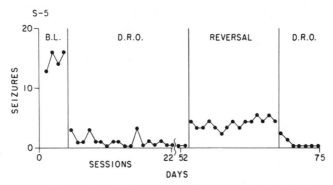

Fig. 22.6. The number of minor motor seizures per day for Subject 5.

ment procedure, the frequency of seizures diminished rapidly to a near-zero frequency. During the reversal phase, this contingency was removed and seizure frequency increased to about six per day. When the differential reinforcement procedure was reintroduced, seizure frequency again dropped to a near-zero level.

The occurrence of arm-raising was observed consistently prior to the seizure climax. As with Subjects 1 and 4, the frequency of the preseizure target behavior decreased as a function of the experimental manipulation, in this case differential reinforcement. No seizures were observed that were not preceded by this behavior. Only when staff were unable to reach the subject in time to lower her arms did seizures occur during the DRO phase.

A nine-month followup indicated that the subject's seizure frequency remained at a near-zero level. One instance of marked seizure increase occurred during a three- or four-day period about six months after the termination of treatment. The DRO procedure was again introduced and seizures were rapidly eliminated.

GENERAL DISCUSSION

The data in the present study lend support to a number of conclusions concerning the control of seizures with conditioning techniques. First, it seems clear that some variants of seizures, particularly those involving gross motor movements, are modifiable by systematic environmental manipulations introduced prior to the seizure climax. With the possible exception of Subject 2, some degree of control was exerted over the seizures of all five subjects. Further, contrary to traditional clinical impressions (Gibbs & Stamp, 1958), identifiable behaviors frequently occur reliably prior to a minor motor seizure climax. In some cases, these preseizure behaviors were quite obvious, as in arm-raising for Subjects 4 and 5. In other cases, they were less obvious as in the lowered activity level for Subject 2. In still another (Subject 3) it was so subtle as to be discriminable only by the child's mother. With the single exception of the "absence" seizures of Subject 2, a high degree of seizure predictability was possible in all cases.

In one sense, the degree of predictability of a behavior is as important to its subsequent control as the development of the technology needed to eliminate it. Frequently childhood seizures, particularly the minor motor variant, are described as unpredictable and occurring without warning. This was clearly not the case in the present series of experiments. The concept of predictability is crucial to the control of seizure behavior, and its verification is significant in and of itself.

The notion of chaining as a conceptual framework within which to develop treatment methods for seizure control appears to be both practical and efficacious. Furthermore, the data presented here are generally consistent with outcomes of similar treatment strategies described by Efron (1957a,b) and Kohlenberg (1970).

Clearly, the more components of the seizure chain that can be identified, the more latitude one has in planning strategies of intervention. Theoretically, any component could be selected as the target behavior. While the present study has dealt primarily with seizures preceded by one behavior, further research and observation are needed to determine if multiple behaviors occur prior to the seizure which could increase the number of therapeutic options.

Although the interruption of preseizure components reliably altered seizure frequency in most cases, the specific behavioral effects of this procedure are unclear. Azrin and Holz (1966) have defined punishment as a decrease in the occurrence of a response following the contingent application of an aversive stimulus. In some instances described earlier, the frequency of preseizure behavior decreased (Subjects 1 and 4) while in others it remained unaffected (Subjects 2 and 3).

Assuming that the interruption procedure was aversive for some subjects, two parameters of punishment are relevant to this discussion: (1) The intensity of the aversive stimulus and (2) the schedule with which it is delivered. The "startle and shake" procedure used in this study is relatively mild compared to other unconditioned aversive stimuli such as electric shock. Numerous studies on the intensity of punishment have shown that the greater the intensity of the aversive stimulus, the greater the magnitude of suppression (Appel, 1963; Azrin, Holz & Hake, 1963). These data suggest that a more intense aversive stimulus might have produced greater suppression of preseizure behaviors. The schedule with which aversive stimuli are delivered depends upon seizure predictability and may also affect seizure suppression. For example, only 42% of Subject 3's seizures were predictable. Assuming that every predicted seizure were punished, the ratio of punishment to response would be an intermittent one, i.e. about 2.5 to 1. Intermittent punishment schedules have consistently been less successful in suppressing behavior than continuous schedules of punishment (Azrin, Holz & Hake, 1963; Estes, 1944).

The partial effectiveness of the "startle and shake" procedure as punishment is in some ways consistent with findings reported by other investigators (Azrin, 1968; Hollenberg & Sperry, 1951; Karsh & Williams, 1964) who have shown that loud noise and verbal punishment can suppress behavior. One limitation of this procedure is that it may vary in intensity and duration and cannot be applied as uniformly as other stimuli, such as electric shock. In this respect other forms of aversive control, such as timeout or shock, might prove to be more effective and should be investigated. Conversely, the effective use of differential reinforcement also suggests the feasibility of more innocuous approaches.

Precise data on the number of times the punishment procedure were used are not available. In general, however, this number remained constant in cases where the overall frequency of the preseizure behavior was unaffected, and decreased proportionally in those where the preseizure rate declined. Nonetheless, the absence of these data presents problems in analyzing the results. For example, according to the data presented for Subject 1, seizure frequency and preseizure frequency (fixed staring) dropped immediately after the introduction of the punishment contingency. The only occurrence of seizures from that point on was if the subject emitted the fixed staring and school staff were unable to reach him in time to apply the punishment procedure. In other words, from weeks four to ten, *no aversive consequences were administered.* If this were the case, the increase of seizures during the reversal is somewhat perplexing, since for all practical purposes no discriminable change in the subject's environment occurred. One explanation for this phenomenon is that although the shaking component of the punishment procedure was no longer in effect, occasionally a staff member might still shout, "No!" if he were too far away from the subject to shake him. Subjective recall by staff and parents indicates that this may have occurred.

The focus of this study has been placed on preseizure behavior and its relationship to seizure occurrence. Nevertheless, the importance of the consequences of seizures per se should not be overlooked. If reinforcing consequences could be identified, treatment strategies might be enhanced by the use of straightforward extinction operations. In this study, the effects of consequences upon seizure occurrence were investigated only for the "absence" seizures exhibited by Subject 2. Based on this single case,[3] the punishment procedure, though effective in reducing the vomiting associated with the termination of the seizure, did not reduce the overall rate of absences.

A decided advantage of the procedure used in this study is that it can be carried out by appropriately trained parents and other nonprofessionals in the child's natural environment. These procedures are straightforward and require little knowledge of behavioral principles, as contrasted with the relatively high requisite skill levels of parent-therapists for general behavior change. In this respect the investment of time for training parents and staff in the intervention techniques was minimal. Each parent was seen for a total of four to six hours, which included the initial history-taking and assessment (two hours), preliminary observations (two hours), and the explanation (one-half hour), and initial implementation (one hour) of the punishment procedure. Beyond this, the investigator made one to three phone calls per week to each parent for the purpose of data collection and monitoring of progress.

A final point concerns the neurological distinction between seizures of organic versus functional etiology. Although clinical and EEG findings are the usual basis for this distinction, the fact that environmental events may affect seizures of organic etiology highlights the importance of improved communication between neurology and the behavioral sciences. This particular area of medicine has a sound understanding of the neurophysiology processes as well as appropriate chemotherapeutic treatments. On the other hand, behavioral science offers the technology for precise assessment and data collection, together with promising environmental interventions.

In summary, the results of this study lend support to the following

---

[3]Behaviorally, the absence does not resemble the minor motor seizure, thus making generalizations from this case extremely difficult.

conclusions: (1) Seizures of both organic and functional etiology appear to be sensitive to environmental manipulations. (2) Seizures, particularly those of the minor motor variant, are more predictable than was previously assumed. (3) A strategy of seizure control based on the interruption of preseizure behaviors is effective in some cases. (4) Improved communication and cooperation between neurology and the behavioral sciences might improve the efficiency of treatment strategies.

REFERENCES

Appel, J. Punishment and shock intensity. *Science*, 1963, **141**, 528–529.

Azrin, N. Some effects of noise on human behavior. *Journal of the Experimental Analysis of Behavior*, 1968, **1**, 183–200.

Azrin, N. and Holz, W. Punishment. In W. K. Honig (ed.) *Operant Behavior: Areas of Research and Application*. New York: Appleton-Century-Crofts, 1966.

Azrin, N., Holz, W., and Hake, D. Fixed-ratio punishment. *Journal of the Experimental Analysis of Behavior*, 1963, **6**, 141–148.

Bijou, S., Peterson, R., and Ault, M. A method to integrate descriptive and experimental field studies at the level of data and empirical concepts. *Journal of Applied Behavior Analysis*, 1968, **1**, 175–191.

Efron, R. The effect of olfactory stimuli in arresting uncinate fits. *Brain*, 1957, **79**, 267–281. (a)

Efron, R. The conditioned inhibition of uncinate fits. *Brain*, 1957, **80**, 251–262. (b)

Estes, W. An experimental study of punishment. *Psychological Monographs*, 1944, **57** (3, Whole No. 263).

Findley, J. An experimental outline for building and exploring multioperant behavior repertoire. *Journal of the Experimental Analysis of Behavior*, 1962, **5**, 113–166.

Forster, F. Clinical therapeutic conditioning in epilepsy. *Wisconsin Medical Journal*, 1969, **68**, 289–291.

Gardner, J. Behavior therapy treatment approach to a psychogenic seizure case. *Journal of Consulting Psychology*, 1967, **31**, 209–212.

Gibbs, F. and Stamp, F. *Epilepsy Handbook*. Illinois: Charles C. Thomas, 1958.

Henner, K. Aurae and their role in reflex mechanisms of epileptic seizures. *Epilepsia*, 1962, **3**, 391–401.

Hollenberg, E. and Sperry, M. Some antecedents of aggression and the effects of frustration in doll play. *Personality*, 1951, **1**, 31–42.

Johnson, C. and Katz, R. Using parents as change agents for their children: A review. *Journal of Child Psychology and Psychiatry*, 1973, **14**, 181–200.

Karsh, E. and Williams, J. Punishment and reward in instrumental learning. *Psychonomic Science*, 1964, **1**, 359–360.

Kelleher, R. and Fry, W. Stimulus functions in chained fixed-interval schedules. *Journal of the Experimental Analysis of Behavior*, 1962, **5**, 167–173.

Kimmel, H. Instrumental conditioning of autonomically mediated behavior. *Psychological Bulletin*, 1967, **5**, 337–345.

Kohlenberg, R. The punishment of persistent vomiting: A case study. *Journal of Applied Behavior Analysis*, 1970, **3**, 241–246.

Miller, N. Learning of visceral and glandular responses. *Science*, 1969, **163**, 434–445.

Skinner, B. The extinction of chained reflexes. *Proceedings of the National Academy of Sciences*, 1934, **20**, 234–237. Cited by A. C. Catania (ed.) *Contemporary Research in Operant Behavior*. Illinois: Scott Foresman, 1968.

Thomas, J. Multiple baseline of stimulus functions in an FR chained schedule. *Journal of the Experimental Analysis of Behavior*, 1964, **7**, 241–245.

ARTICLE 23

Reduction of Seizures by Desensitization*

JOHN J. PARRINO†

Georgia Regional Hospital at Atlanta

Abstract: Desensitization of several anxiety hierarchies reduced seizure activity associated with the presence of anxiety-provoking stimuli. The seizures progressively decreased during 3 months of inpatient treatment, and ceased after continuation of the treatment on an outpatient basis.

The precipitation of seizures through conditioning has been studied by Efron (1957). In his review of the clinical literature he provided evidence to show that pathological neural responses (fits, as he called them) could be conditioned to specific stimuli such as music and light. He described cases in which seizures were precipitated in patients by touching them, particularly if there was an element of surprise in the touch. The studies reviewed in his paper indicate that seizures can be triggered by a variety of neutral environmental events.

The precipitation of seizures by emotionally-laden stimuli has been studied by several investigators. Wilson (1928) first applied the term "affective epilepsy" to those seizures in which the exciting agent was of emotional significance. Temporal-lobe epilepsy is often associated with personality disorder and psychosis (Gibbs, Gibbs and Fuster, 1948; Hill, 1953). In these cases emotional tension often precedes and leads up to a seizure. Mitchell, Falconer and Hill (1954) report the case of a fetishist with temporal lobe epilepsy who could precipitate fits voluntarily. The epileptogenic stimulus was the sexually charged object of the fetish, which in this instance was a safety pin. In addition, seizure activity

---

*Reprinted from *Journal of Behavior Therapy and Experimental Psychiatry*, 1971, **2**, 215–218, Pergamon Press. Copyright © 1971. With permission from Pergamon Press and John J. Parrino.

†Requests for reprints should be addressed to John J. Parrino, Georgia Regional Hospital at Atlanta, 3073 Panthersville Road, Decatur, Georgia 30032.

without demonstrable neurological cause has been observed among institutionalized patients with a variety of emotional disorders (Revitch and Zallanski, 1969). The stimulus conditions surrounding the elicitation of seizures were not studied in these cases. The present case history specifically pinpoints the stimuli triggering the emotional antecedents of the seizures in a hospitalized psychiatric patient.

The customary treatment for psychiatric patients who exhibit seizures is to administer anti-convulsant medication. In Efron's (1957) paper, a case is cited of the arrest of uncinate seizures by the use of a conditioning procedure. The case presented here illustrates the efficacy of desenitization in extinguishing seizures due to anxiety provoked by environmental stimuli.

CASE HISTORY

Mr. S was a 36-year-old male, a well-known personality in his community. He began having serious difficulties in April, 1969, when he experienced his first grand mal seizure. He had been diagnosed at a reputable medical center as having Jakob Creutzfeldt Syndrome, a progressive neurological disorder characterized by dementia and violent episodes of bizarre muscular movements. The diagnosis was based on the following factors: (1) complaints of failure of recent memory, (2) several grand mal seizures, (3) right-sided twitches and transient loss of balance, and (4) an electroencephalogram which showed diffuse abnormality with questionable temperoparietal spikes. A pneumoencephalogram, lumber puncture and biopsy of nerve and muscle revealed no abnormality. All other medical and neurological findings were normal.

Following this, the patient resided in two other general hospitals before his admission to the present psychiatric institution in September, 1969. He was seen as a serious management problem who required constant supervision for his own safety. His sudden uncontrollable movements often left him unable to balance himself. He had been placed on anticonvulsant medication during his first hospitalization which had been continued except for small changes in dosage. There were, however, no significant changes in the patient's condition or seizure activity.

Several months after his admission to our hospital, Mr. S's general mood, attention span and physical appearance improved. The change in his behavior led the staff to question the accuracy of the neurological diagnosis. For the first time, he was well oriented enough to be placed on the general token system on the unit. Extensive behavioral observations were initiated, which provided further evidence of emotional triggers to the episodes of bizarre muscular movements.

At this time, Mr. S began to participate in a work adjustment program run by the vocational rehabilitation counselor. There was further improvement during the next 4 months of hospitalization, but the seizures continued at very high frequency. The staff felt that behavior therapy might help reduce them and also accelerate the improvement in his general condition. They referred him for behavior therapy on 4 June, 1970.

Mr. S was informed of the impending change in therapy, and was asked to count his seizures for 13 days before it began. Staff members were asked to observe the seizures in order to check the reliability of his seizure count. During these 13 days, the seizures ranged from a low point of 22 to a high point of 95 on 16 June, 1970, the day before therapy began (see Fig. 23.1). The average rate for this period was 58 per day. The variability in seizure activity during this period seemed to be related to Mr. S's activity: the seizures would diminish at work and increase upon his return to the unit. Also, seizure activity would decrease during visits on weekends to close friends and relatives. In general, Mr. S's level of anxiety was a good positive predictor of daily rate of seizure activity.

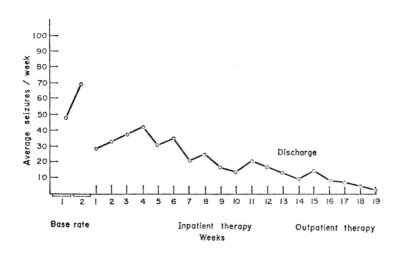

Fig. 23.1. Weekly seizure activity (average).

TREATMENT

From the behavioral observations of the staff and the reports provided by the patient, it appeared that Mr. S's seizures were triggered by particular anxiety-provoking stimuli in the ward and at work. The following are some of the anxiety-provoking situations which triggered seizures:

1. Socializing with fellow patients in the unit, particularly when Mr. S was the focus of attention.
2. Meeting someone in authority, friend or stranger (e.g. the director of the unit).
3. Initiating conversation with an acquaintance during visiting hours.
4. Dealing with a particularly difficult female patient in the unit who constantly harassed Mr. S.
5. The mention of family-related material (e.g. wife's name, children's names).

Deep muscle relaxation is routinely taught to all patients in the unit. Mr. S learned to relax during this routine and continued practicing throughout his stay at the hospital. Anxiety hierarchies were derived from each of the anxiety-provoking situations mentioned above. Items from the hierarchies were presented twice a week during individual sessions. In addition, Mr. S was taught self-desensitization to enable him to use desensitization when the therapist was absent. All hierarchies were completed during a 3 month period. The following items (beginning with the least disturbing) made up the hierarchy on the topic of initiating a conversation with a visitor:

1. A person you recognize appears in the unit.
2. The acquaintance is having a conversation with a staff member.
3. The acquaintance looks in your direction.
4. The acquaintance and you make eye contact.
5. The acquaintance smiles at you from across the room.
6. The acquaintance starts walking towards you.
7. The acquaintance is getting very close to you.
8. The acquaintance extends his hand to you.
9. You shake hands with the acquaintance.
10. You engage in conversation with the acquaintance.

Figure 23.1 represents the seizure data collected during desensitization therapy. It indicates a great deal of improvement in Mr. S's condition during the 15 weeks of therapy. During this time, the seizure count dropped from a high point of 43 per day (4th week) to 10 per day in the 14th week. Mr. S was discharged to outpatient status in the 15th week (September, 1970). The figure shows an increase in seizure activity during Mr. S's first week back to fulltime employment (15th week) and a reduction to nine, six and three daily seizures on the following weeks. Self-desensitization hierarchies which focused on the work situation were completed during outpatient treatment and accompanied by a gradual reduction of the seizures to zero.

The form of the seizures also changed significantly during therapy— from gross motor movements at the beginning to tic-like mannerisms at the termination of inpatient treatment. The response was then minimal and restricted to the facial region. The few seizures that did then occur usually went unnoticed by the casual observer.

Marital and vocational stresses had apparently precipitated Mr. S's illness. He had been relieved of certain responsibilities at work, which he had perceived as a demotion. Also, he had become painfully aware of difficulties developing with his wife whom he had suspected of an affair with one of his best friends. As the stresses surrounding these situations were alleviated (by divorce and termination of employment), Mr. S's general disposition had improved; but, seizure activity had continued to be elicited by conditioned stimuli in the environment.

At the present time, Mr. S is continuing with outpatient treatment and is doing very well in adjusting to life outside the hospital. He is engaged to be married and has returned to fulltime employment at the job held before hospitalization. All medication has been withdrawn and he has remained seizure-free for approximately 5 months.

REFERENCES

Efron, R. Conditioned inhibition of uncinate fits, *Brain*, 1957, **80**, 251–262.

Gibbs, E. L., Gibbs, F. A., and Fuster, B. Psychomotor epilepsy, *Archs Neurol. Psychiat.*, 1948, **60**, 331.

Hill, D. Discussion on the surgery of temporal lobe epilepsy, *Proc. R. Soc. Med.*, 1953, **46**, 965.

Mitchell, W., Falconer, M. H., and Hill, D. Epilepsy with fetishism relieved by temporal lobectomy, *Lancet*, 1954, **2**, 626.

Revitch, R. and Zallanski, Z. Slow anterior temporal foci in a mental hospital population, *Behav. Neuropsychiat.*, 1969, **1**, 8–10.

Wilson, S. A. K. *Neurology, Lond.*, 1928, **2**, 1504.

ARTICLE 24

Conditioning in Sensory Evoked Seizures*†

FRANCIS M. FORSTER, M.D.

Department of Neurology, University of Wisconsin School of Medicine, Madison, Wisconsin

Abstract: This paper presents the results of conditioning studies in animals and in patients with epilepsy. In animals it was not possible to produce sensory evoked seizures by conditioning unless an epileptogenic lesion was produced. Patients with stroboscopic induced, startle, pattern and musicogenic epilepsy were treated by conditioning techniques.

It was at first felt that the nature of this was an extinction process, but certain factors such as the need for reinforcement suggest that the therapy is actually a conditioning process. Changes in the electroencephalogram occur during this conditioning therapy as do changes in galvanic skin resistance.

The original hypothesis by the author was that sensory evoked seizures might be conditioned reflex responses and that sensory stimuli, for example, music or flashing lights, which to most people are neutral, somehow had acquired the factor of a conditioning stimulus, thus evoking clinical seizures as a conditioned response. This hypothesis was evolved by the author while serving as chairman of the First Medical Exchange Mission to the U.S.S.R. in 1958. During this tour of duty the author was impressed by the careful and diligent approach to the central nervous system by our Soviet scientific colleagues, employing the mechanism of study of conditional responses.

To test the hypothesis, beginning in January of 1959, a series of studies was carried out on animals. After three years of intensive study, it was

---

*Reprinted from *Conditional Reflex*, 1966, Vol. 1, No. 4. Copyright © 1966. With permission from J. B. Lippincott Company and Francis M. Forster, M.D.

†Presented at the Symposium on "Higher Nervous Activity" at the IV World Congress of Psychiatry, Madrid, Spain, Sept. 9, 1966.

Supported by USPHS grant # B 3360, awarded by the National Institute of Neurological Diseases and Blindness.

found that it was not possible, if the brain of the animal was intact, to evoke seizures in animals by intermittent light or startling noises. These studies consisted of the presentation of the CS (intermittent light or raucous sound) for four seconds alone and for two seconds coupled with the US (stimulation of the motor cortex of one hemisphere evoking a focal motor seizure on the opposite side of the body). While these studies failed to produce a conditioned seizure, there were significant electroencephalographic changes and behavioral responses to the CS. The electroencephalographic changes consisted primarily of a generalization of the evoked potential from the primary cortical analyzer to all areas of cortex and, in the case of sound stimulation, to a subsequent depression or decrease of electrical activity for the duration of the conditioning stimulus. These electrographic and behavioral changes could be removed by the process of extinction, that is, the repeated presentation of the CS without reinforcement.

It was, therefore, decided that while behavioral and EEG changes could be elicited, it was not possible by conditioning to produce sensory evoked seizures in an animal with an intact brain (Forster *et al.*, 1963).

A series of experiments was then carried out, combining the conditioning process with the induction of epileptogenic lesions of the cortex. For this latter purpose a number of various techniques were employed, including the acute application of epileptogenic drugs (for example, Metrazol, strychnine, picrotoxin, penicillin, acetylcholine) and the production of an epileptogenic subacute or chronic lesion using lead or freezing of the cortex for the chronic lesion, and tetanus toxin intracerebral injection for the subacute lesions. For these purposes the tetanus toxin was found to be the most feasible since in time it presented the ideal situation of a lesion not so acute as to disturb the conditioning process, yet not so chronic that the conditioning had to be carried on over an indefinite period of time, awaiting the determination of whether or not a "take" had occurred.

In the epileptogenic studies, the cats were prepared with imbedded electrodes for stimulation and recording and also a plastic tube was inserted, open to the dura on one end and sealed to the exterior on the other end. The cats were then conditioned to the presentation of light or sound stimulus as a CS, using the electrical stimulation of the motor cortex for the US. When the conditioning had been well established with the development of both electroencephalographic and behavioral changes as noted above, the plastic tube was opened from the outside so as to allow the direct injection intracerebrally of the epileptogenic substance.

Under these conditions it was possible to produce the electroencephalographic and clinical seizure by the presentation of the CS alone. This could be best developed when the lesion was placed in the primary cortical analyzer, for example, the visual cortex for a CS of light, or acoustic cortex for CS of sound. However, the converse could be obtained, namely, that intermittent light could elicit seizure discharge from the acoustic cortex after rendering the conditioned acoustic cortex epileptogenic. These studies were controlled with animals without conditioning and with an equivalent number of unconditioned stimulations and in animals without conditioning and without unconditional stimulations (Forster *et al.*, in press).

In view of the experience obtained from the animal studies, the author and colleagues concluded that they had sufficient evidence to begin applying their studies to human clinical material. Early in 1962, a university student who had had her first convulsion while fixing her television for "flop-over" the night before, presented herself in the Neurology Clinic. During the course of studying her in the laboratory, 76 myoclonic seizures were elicited over the course of the afternoon when intermittent light was administered between the range of 15 and 38 cycles per second with both eyes open or closed and with or without various kinds of filters interposed.

The serendipitous observation was made that by occluding the vision of one eye with a soft, black, cloth patch, no dysrhythmia could be obtained. Subsequent studies on this patient showed that the repeated presentation of monocular stimulations rendered her less sensitive to binocular stimulation, and this was specific for the approximate range of frequencies at which the monocular presentations were made (Forster, 1964).

The discovery of photosensitivity in a patient with monocular vision forced the investigators to find another technique for conditioning, and thus the method of differential light intensity was developed. This consisted in the placing of the stroboscope behind an opaque screen together with two photoflood lamps. The photofloods received their power through a rheostat and by varying the amount of current passing to the photofloods through the rheostat, the room light intensity could be controlled and varied from illumination so bright that the stroboscope became virtually imperceptible, (600 foot candles) to room darkness where the stroboscope was at maximum intensity. The presentation of stroboscopic stimulations, beginning with high room light intensity, was innocuous and by the repeated photic stimulation and gradual diminution of ambient light it was possible to render the patient less sensitive.

These observations of monocular insensitivity of the efficacy of differential light intensity were continued on a series of nine patients and proved to be reliable. There is, however, the difficulty that while the sensitivity to light could be ameliorated by this process, there was an early regression and redevelopment of sensitivity to the previous level.

A patient was chosen for periodic study over a long period of time. She was treated intensively by the differential light intensity method while in the hospital and discharged to her home, then brought in every Sunday morning for two hours of intensive stimulations using the differential light intensity technique. This procedure was employed for a period of six months, yet her daily seizure incidence of 4–40 per day was not altered.

In order to protect her in her daily environment from intermittent light and also to give her an opportunity to maintain reinforcement in her day to day environment, studies were undertaken to associate the decrease in sensitivity to light obtained by the differential light intensity technique with auditory clicks administered simultaneously with stroboscopic stimulation. A pilot study was made, using a pair of earphones with a brush set activated by a photoelectric cell. It was found after repeated innocuous stimulations with light, and each light stimulus being associated with auditory clicks, the auditory clicks could be employed to block seizures in a light range which was otherwise sensitive. A special pair of glasses were then designed for this patient, with a photoelectric cell over the nose bridge which activated a hearing aid device over the mastoid process. She was treated intensively for ten days in the hospital with innocuous stroboscopic stimulations associated with auditory clicks and discharged to her normal home environment with the admonition to daily pass her hands, with fingers spread, before her eyes ten times while looking at a light and to repeat this process four times daily. With this reinforcement, and protection against light changes in the environment, the seizure incidence fell remarkably. Whereas she had previously experienced from four to forty seizures per day, she had a very occasional seizure when not wearing her glasses and her academic achievement had remarkably changed. She had been scheduled for admission into a retarded students' class and instead is now attending the regular classes and achieving well. This would indicate that she probably had more seizures during the day than were apparent (Forster *et al.*, 1964).

This process, productive as it is for the individual patient, is time-consuming and the patient herself spent 300 hours in the laboratory. Most of these hours were monitored by at least one, and usually two, staff physicians of the Department of Neurology. This obviously is too time-consuming to be practical in view of the number of patients so afflicted. However, since the efficacy had been demonstrated, a method was sought to make this technique more practical.

For this purpose, a computer automation program was designed whereby a data phone was employed to transmit the patient's brain waves directly from the research EEG laboratory in the Epilepsy Center to the Behavioral Cybernetics Laboratory of the University. The computer was programmed to monitor the stroboscopic stimulus and to decrease the room light by sending a signal every minute. The computer was "taught" to identify the dysrhythmia elicited by stroboscopic stimulation in a particular patient and to return a signal upon the appearance of the dysrhythmia. This second signal was employed to (a) turn off the stroboscope and (b) increase room light intensity by one logarithmic step. A third of a second after the signal had been sent carrying out these two missions, the computer again sampled the brain waves and if they were now normal, the program of stroboscopic stimulations was again presented and re-programmed. If however, the dysrhythmia still persisted, the room light intensity was again increased before the stroboscope was activated. Originally, periods of one minute each were employed in each of the various logarithmic steps of the room light intensity. It was found later that the entire programming seemed more effective if shorter time intervals were used. The interval was therefore reduced to 15 seconds for each of the eleven logarithmic steps in the room light intensity. Using this procedure and employing a pair of the specially designed glasses, the patient was successfully treated in a period of 60 hours. This was, therefore, a significant reduction in the time involved. The feeling of the authors is that this time can be still further decreased after further experience with this technique (Forster *et al.*, 1965).

Limited experience has been obtained in two patients with pattern epilepsy, that is, seizure discharges and minor seizures occurring upon presentation of specific patterns. The same techniques of light intensity were employed in these patients, viewing the pattern with a dim light and then gradually increasing the room light in these cases to make the pattern more and more evident. Our preliminary studies would indicate that the same type of technique can be employed in pattern epilepsy as in stroboscopic induced seizures.

Startle epilepsy, the evocation of seizures by sudden loud noises, is also susceptible to the conditioning procedures. Monaural insensitivity occurred in both patients studied in our laboratory. It is important, however, in monaural presentations that the earphone be carefully buffered and that the sound level be kept below 60 decibels, so that there is no inadvertent binaural stimulation. Repeated presentation of monaural stimulations rendered binaural stimulations innocuous. This is specific for a particular noise, for example, rifle shots versus bells versus buzzers, and the process has to be repeated for each particular type of noise. It is somewhat faster and simpler if stereophonic earphones are used and the noise volumes in each ear, for example, 40 decibels into one ear and 5 decibels in the other, with a gradual increase in decibels to equal or greater than the level which originally produced seizures (Booker *et al.*, 1965). We have not yet devised a technique for reinforcing the conditioning of startle epilepsy similar to the device of the special glasses in stroboscopic induced seizures.

Probably the most intriguing type of sensory evoked seizures is the musicogenic. This apparently can vary from evocation by a single note or chord to the very complex types evoked by groups of musical numbers. This occurs in the very sophisticated musician with self-induction, or may occur in someone with virtually no musical ability or sophistication.

Three patients with musicogenic epilepsy have been studied in our laboratory and successfully treated. All had psychomotor seizures. They varied from relatively simple through moderately complex to extremely complex. In all three patients, all presentations of music were monitored by EEG. None of the three had their seizures evoked by notes or chords or sequences of notes. This was carefully checked to be certain that there was no particular part of the noxious number which always evoked the seizure discharge. The simplest instance was the lady who was sensitive to western type music and this when recorded in a rather amateurish style. The western folk songs obtainable in the usual albums were not noxious, only those played on her local radio station and in a raucous manner. Repeated presentation of the same melodies decreased the seizure discharges and rendered the music innocuous.

A patient of intermediate complexity was a lady of 48 who had had musicogenic seizures since childhood. She was a pianist, and quite accomplished as an amateur. She had induced her own seizures beginning in childhood. Only one seizure was evoked in the laboratory this by a melody known as "People Will Say We're in Love." This music was immediately repeated while she was in the postictal confusional state and a period of relative refractoriness of her cortex. Repetitions were continued through the alert and awake phase and again the following day. No seizure discharges were subsequently elicited by this music and it was taped and given to her to listen to in her own room. No other music evoked a seizure in the laboratory, but a number of varying types of musical numbers evoked right temporal spiking discharges. With the repeated playing of the same number consecutively the discharges decreased and disappeared entirely. When this occurred, the number was taped for the patient to audit in her room to maintain her reinforcement. Occasionally, when the repetition of a number failed to continue the decrease in the spiking discharges, monaural stimulations were employed for a time, and then binaural.

The third patient was the most complex (Forster *et al.*, 1965A, 1965B). Seizures were elicited by a class of music derived from Debussy and Sibelius, but only when these numbers were played by a combination of instruments and a combination of instrument and voice. The repeated playing of innocuous music did not render him insensitive. Musical numbers which evoked seizures would do so repeatedly, so that, for example, he had six seizures on six consecutive days to the playing of the same number. Unfortunately, we did not attempt the postictal stimulations in this patient. The technique employed in the conditioning of this patient was the repeated presentation of the organ rendition of a particular commercial number. The organ, being of course a single instrument, provided a rendition to which he was not sensitive. When this had been played repeatedly he was still sensitive to the full orchestration. He was, therefore, presented with 98 measures of organ music and two measures of orchestral. This was repeated over and over and then the increments of orchestration gradually increased so that after 50 hours of presentation he was able to audit the full orchestration without a seizure. By a very laborious technique, this particular full orchestration was then modified synthetically in the laboratory with the addition of piano accompaniment, male voice, female voice, the various combinations of male and female voice and piano accompaniment, and finally a synthetic syncopated number made by speeding up the standard presentation. These synthetic parameters were then presented in combination with commercially available numbers closely resembling them. The commercial numbers had all been noxious. By presenting him with mixtures of both the noxious commercial and the synthetic numbers, it was possible to remove the sensitivity to the various commercial numbers.

The exact nature of the process by which the desensitization to noxious special sensory stimulation occurs is not clear. The members of our research team have some semantic difficulties in arriving at the exact nomenclature for this. In our earlier reports we employed the term extinction. This was based on the original hypothesis that the evoked seizure was a conditional response. Some credence was given to this theory by the observation that it was possible to make the patients more sensitive. In patients being subjected to monocular stimulation, it was noted that when light leaks occurred in the eye of presumably occluded vision these patients could become monocularly sensitive. It was also shown that it was possible to make a patient sensitive at a light intensity frequency where he had not been previously sensitive (Forster *et al.*, 1964). Moreover, one of my colleagues transferred a startle patient to be photosensitive and then extinguished this by the repeated non-reinforced presentation of photic stimulation (Booker *et al.*, 1965). In this latter study, discrimination could be induced between light frequencies, one frequency being the CS and the other a neutral stimulus. These observations lent credence, therefore, to the possibility that the sensory evoked seizures can be conditioned reflexes.

However, if the process of therapy were a true extinction, then reinforcement should not be necessary. Inadvertently, the first patient— the student in whom the monocular insensitivity was noted—was advised to repeat the television "flopover" stimulations at home and her husband, being an engineer, was able to simulate the original frequency quite well. These were administered nightly and monocularly, with patching of the vision of one eye. When this was done she became insensitive binocularly. However, when she received binocular stimulations at home her sensitivity returned. The role of the specially designed glasses which administer the auditory clicks with flickering light have already been noted as a means for reinforcement at home. All three musicogenic patients were given music to continue the reinforcement. In the two more complex patients with musicogenic epilepsy, controls were built into the process. They were given tapes of music to which they had been rendered insensitive and these they listened to twice a day in their own rooms in the hospital and later, at home. In both patients, certain music which had been rendered insensitive was deliberately withheld for variable periods of time and re-presented at a later date and found to be noxious in both patients. This, therefore, was construed as evidence that it was necessary for the patients to maintain reinforcement. The need for reinforcement suggests that this was a conditional reflex rather than an extinction process. The possibility is further enhanced by the observation in the musicogenic patients that music to which they have become insensitive by generalization need not be reinforced. This is especially evident in the third patient, in whom a particular number was especially noxious. This number was withheld for three months, during the period in which the conditioning process was employed. When it was played, it was innocuous. When it was again withheld for three months and re-presented to him, it was still innocuous despite the fact that he had not heard it in the intervening period of time. Reinforcement, as one might expect, was not necessary for the beneficial effects of generalization, but only for those in the conditioning process.

The various scientists involved in this series of studies are loath to come up with a clear, sharp definition of the type of conditioning that this should be called. It is certainly not true Pavlovian, although allied to it. It is not truly operant, and certainly not avoidance conditioning. It is, in fact, a kind of negative rather than positive conditioning. Probably the nearest related type of conditioning is that described by Wolpe and his colleagues in the conditioning of the phobias.

One of the advantages of studying this conditioning process in epilepsy is that neurophysiological changes are evident which give a definitive measure of the efficacy of the process. This leads us to the considerations of the mechanisms by which this conditioning may be effective. There is evidence that the process of conditioning was effective in the primary cortical analyzer or in other words, in that area of cortex from which the seizure discharge was evoked. This was best evidenced in the cases of musicogenic epilepsy with specific anterior temporal evoked spiking dysrhythmias. In the course of conditioning to a particular musical number, there was a change in the focal cortical dysrhythmia. The sharp, clearly evident spike gradually became lower in voltage and assumed more of a slow wave component until it was often difficult to differentiate from a theta-like dysrhythmia. Not only was the focally elicited spike different, but the spread of the spike to adjacent areas of the cortex became less and less evident and finally the spike remained defined only in the anterior temporal lead. In two of the musicogenic patients there was a well defined change in the GSR occurring within one second after the elicitation of the anterior temporal spike. This, too, disappeared in approximately the time in which the spread of the discharge to other temporal areas disappeared. The degradation of the spike in the anterior temporal lead and the decrease in the GSR responses upon repeated rendition of the same musical number in the process of conditioning was not a step-by-step procedure, for there were some variations. The change in dysrhythmia also occurred in patients with stroboscopic seizures. We were made aware of this when the computer, which had been so carefully taught to discriminate between movement artifacts (yawning, coughing, etc.) and the spiking dysrhythmia elicited by the stroboscope and could turn off the stroboscope within a fifth of a second after the appearance of the discharges, became less reliable during the process of conditioning. It was discovered that this was because of the alteration in the spiking dysrhythmia elicited by stroboscopic stimulation. The sensitivity of the computer had to be reset in order to recognize the discharges, now less sharp, but equally dangerous if allowed to continue. Therefore, the degradation of the evoked dysrhythmia was not only apparent to the eye, but was indicated by the change in the computer automation response.

The spread from cortex to subcortical structures in musicogenic epilepsies was a fascinating process. In all three of our patients, there was a lapse of a period from one to forty seconds between the first appearance of the anterior temporal spike and the subsequent progression into the temporal lobe seizure. Despite nasopharyngeal and sphenoid electrodes we were never able to determine the sequence of the dysrhythmia in this intervening clear period. The orchestration of the popular number which served as a base of operations in the most complex of our musicogenic seizure patients, after several thousand renditions of having been used as the structure upon which the other parameters of music were grafted, became so innocuous that if the spiking dysrhythmia occurred in the anterior temporal lead and the noxious music was stopped and this now basic conditioning number played within $\frac{3}{5}$ of a second, no seizure occurred. This would seem to indicate that the conditioning process could definitely inhibit the spread to other structures. This, of course, was also suggested by the changes in GSR responses and the decrease in spread from the anterior temporal spike to the other leads.

While it is obvious, therefore, that alterations of the cortical evoked spiking discharge are possible, it is also obvious that the subcortical structure discharges can be ameliorated. In the photosensitive patient, frequently the discharge was first seen in one occipital lead. If the paper records were run at extremely rapid speeds, a slight takeoff could be seen in one occipital lead prior to the generalized dysrhythmia. However, this was not always so, and the stroboscopic discharges which have a heavy centrencephalic component can obviously be altered by this conditioning process. Even more evident of subcortical alterations is the study on the startle epilepsy. Both patients studied in our laboratory had myoclonic jerking seizures due to sudden loud noise. One of these patients was curarized; when he was in this condition the presentation of sudden loud noise evoked no EEG dysrhythmia. This was construed as evidence that what appeared to be a dysrhythmia was actually pseudodysrhythmia due to the movement artifact. However, by conditioning of the subcortical analyzer, myoclonic spasms could be ameliorated.

In conclusion, the work of my colleagues and myself indicates that while it is possible to condition animals and probably patients to have evoked seizures, this requires careful conditioning processes and probably properly placed epileptogenic lesions. That this happens in the actual history of the sensory evoked seizures in patients is quite unlikely. This concept is further evidenced and enhanced by the fact that simple extinction processes will not alleviate the sensory evoked seizures, but when due care is taken to maintain a conditioning type of therapeutic process, the seizures can be ameliorated. The process consists of the careful and repeated presentation of stimuli using various mechanisms for altering and rendering the stimuli innocuous and gradually approaching the noxious stage, or by the repetitive presentation in periods of relative cortical refractoriness. However, reinforcement is necessary in order to maintain the amelioration, for this process is a conditioning process.

REFERENCES

Booker, H. E., Forster, F. M., and Klove, H. Extinction factors in startle (acousticomotor) seizures. *Neurology*, 1965, **15**, 1095–1103.

Forster, F. M., Chun, R. W. M., and Forster, M. B. Conditioned changes in focal epilepsy—I. In animals with intact central nervous system. *Arch. Neurol.*, 1963, **9**, 188–193.

Forster, F. M. and Chun, R. W. M. Conditioned changes in focal epilepsy—II—(In animals with damaged central nervous system). In preparation.

Forster, F. M. and Campos, G. B. Conditioning factors in stroboscopic induced seizures. *Epilepsia*, 1964, **5**, 156–165.

Forster, F. M., Ptacek, L. J., Peterson, W. G., Chun, R. W. M., Bengzon, A. R. A., and Campos, G. B. Stroboscopic-induced seizure discharges. *Arch. Neurol.*, 1964, **11**, 603–608.

Forster, F. M., Ptacek, L. J., and Peterson, W. G. Auditory clicks in extinction of stroboscope-induced seizures. *Epilepsia*, 1965, **6**, 217–225.

Forster, F. M., Klove, H., Peterson, W. G., and Bengzon, A. R. A. Modification of Musicogenic Epilepsy by Extinction Technique. *8th International Congress of Neurology*, Vienna, 1965A.

Forster, F. M., Klove, H., Peterson, W. G., and Bengzon, A. R. A. Modification of Musicogenic Epilepsy by Extinction Technique. *Transactions of the American Neurological Association*, 1965B.

ARTICLE 25

Migraine: An Exploratory Treatment Application of Programmed Behavior Therapy Techniques*†

KENNETH R. MITCHELL‡ and DAPHNE M. MITCHELL

University of New South Wales, New South Wales, Australia§

The classical concept of migraine is that of a paroxysmal, episodic disturbance of cerebral function associated with unilateral headache and vomiting. Although headache is the most prominent feature of migraine the diagnosis is made on the basis of the occurrence in an individual of several of the following symptoms as described by Frazier[1]: (1) Recurrent throbbing headaches, usually unilateral at onset. (2) Nausea, vomiting, and irritability commonly occurring at the height of the attack. (3) Temporary visual disorders preceding the headache. (4) History of migraine in the immediate family. (5) Dizziness, sweating, and other vasomotor disorders during an attack. (6) Response to ergotamine tartrate if administered early. (7) Duration variable, but commonly 2–8 hr.

The importance of *psychological* factors in the etiology of migraine is well documented. Kolb[2], Selinsky[3] and Wolff[4] have reported that migraine sufferers are usually sensitive, worrisome and perfectionistic individuals, often chronically tense, apprehensive, and preoccupied with achievement and success. The migraine sufferer's behavior was also reported as being characterized by superficial interpersonal relationships, sexual maladjustments, and obsessive preoccupation with moral and

*Reprinted from *Journal of Psychosomatic Research*, 1971, **15**, 137–157, Pergamon Press. Copyright © 1971. With permission from Pergamon Press and Kenneth R. Mitchell.

†The authors wish to acknowledge the continued assistance of G. G. Gray, Head, Student Counseling and Research Unit.

‡Research psychologist, Student Counseling and Research Unit, University of New South Wales.

§School of Applied Psychology.

ethical issues. Maxwell[5] further reported that migraine patients were significantly more neurotic than nonmigraine patients. In the past the psychological treatment of migraine has relied upon the application of psychoanalytic and psychodynamic therapeutic methods. The traditional viewpoint being that anxiety stemming from early unconscious conflicts is the major cause of migraine. Only limited success has been claimed using such methods.

Physiological procedures such as dieting, tranquilizers, antidepressant drugs, relaxation exercises, histamine desensitization and manipulative and surgical operations have been tried, but the results have been inconsistent and invariably disappointing. At present the management of migraine still depends on pharmacotherapy. Preparations such as ergotamine tartrate and its derivatives afford most migraine sufferers relief from the intensity of the acute attack, but are by no means preventative. Daily prophylactic pharmacotherapy (interval medication) in the period between migraine attacks is perhaps the most effective medication available for the treatment of migraine.

Jaspers[6] suggested that certain types of psychosomatic illness can be acquired by learning, as responses conditioned to anxiety. If such were the case then it may be appropriate to treat migraine along the lines indicated by behavior therapy. Walton[7], Cooper[8] and Moore[9] successfully employed Wolpe's[10] behavior therapy technique of reciprocal inhibition (desensitization) procedure to extinguish disruptive anxiety in the treatment of a number of chronic bronchial asthmatics. With this type of treatment, the unadaptive conditioned reflex of bronchospasm was extinguished by conditioning an incompatible response, such as relaxation, to the conditioned stimulus. Subsequently, whenever the conditioned stimulus presented, the response was relaxation instead of bronchospasm. Paul[11] also showed that while traditional psychotherapeutic methods produced subjective change, only reciprocal inhibition improved physical indices of anxiety, e.g. pulse rate and palmar sweat index. These findings confirmed those reported by Moore[9] and suggest that reciprocal inhibition may be particularly useful in changing the physical aspects of psychosomatic disorders. The foregoing suggests that conditional behavior is sensitive to internal changes associated with endocrine and other autonomic nervous system factors. Hence, any type of therapy or diagnostic procedures concerned with shaping, molding, modifying, altering, or changing complex nervous system functioning, whether or not it is based on learning theory or psychodynamic principles, should be consistent and integrated with current neurobiological data.

Gelder and Marks[12] however, have demonstrated in long-term follow-ups the restricted improvement obtained when a target symptom (e.g. a phobia) is treated by desensitization while other maladaptive behaviors are ignored. By an overly narrow restriction of the definition of behavior therapy to desensitization, they illustrated the hazards of single-model procedures which exists when other behavioral approaches relevant to these socially maladaptive behaviors are discarded. Recently, Kanfer and Phillips[13] stated that a treatment program should include not only conditioning methods (desensitization) but also educative, environmental manipulative, chemotherapeutic, socioeconomic, and any other types of procedures necessary to bring about a change in the patients' disturbing life patterns.

Mitchell[14] independently arriving at the same conclusion as Kanfer and Phillips treated ten migraine Ss diagnosed as suffering one to eight migraine episodes each month using the behavior therapy techniques of applied relaxation training, desensitization and assertive therapy (combined desensitization). Migraine episodes subsequently decreased by an average of 66.8 per cent in the treatment Ss but no change in migraine frequency was reported by three no-treatment control Ss.

A further study was later carried out by Mitchell[15] designed to assess the consistency of migraine frequency changes by obtaining objective follow-up measures, and to control and standardize the treatment presentation to each S [16]. Six Ss diagnosed as suffering two to eight migraine attacks each month were treated using the same combined desensitization treatment procedures as the earlier study. Significant differences were obtained between the treatment and no-treatment controls in migraine frequency reduction both for the 8-week treatment period ($p < 0.01$) and for the 8-week posttreatment period ($p < 0.01$). Migraine episodes for the treatment Ss were found to decrease by an average of 89.5 per cent when compared with their pretreatment migraine base rate. The results were seen as providing some support for the efficacy of a comprehensive behavior therapy approach in obtaining a reduction in migraine episodes and for maintaining that reduction over a limited period of time.

The present investigation consists of two further exploratory studies designed to replicate previous findings and test the relative effectiveness of the separate component behavior therapy techniques to the treatment of migraine. A new treatment must be shown to be not only effective but that it is effective by virtue of the factors in which it differs from other treatments. In behavior therapy by "combined desensitization," a therapeutic effect may occur from applied relaxation training (relaxation application); contact with a supportive agency; desensitization (reciprocal inhibition); and assertive therapy; as well as by a combination of these referred to as combined desensitization.

First, conceiving migraine reduction as a function of increased ability to control emotional reactivity that is, reduced sympathetic nervous system activity to events perceived as stressful in the environment (see Discussion) it was decided (Study I) to compare the specific therapeutic effectiveness of applied relaxation training with that of combined desensitization (relaxation application, desensitization and assertive therapy). The hypothesis that the application of relaxation training alone is therapeutic follows the conclusion of Cautela[17] who stated, "...that relaxation can be considered a self-control technique in its own right: first, when it is used to reduce the overall anxiety level, and second, as a means of decreasing anxiety or tension whenever the patient is either involved in a readily identifiable anxiety-provoking situation, or is experiencing anxiety without being able to discern the antecedent conditions (p. 328)."

In Study II, relaxation application plus desensitization (systematic desensitization) were compared with combined desensitization. Following the successful results obtained by other investigators on psychosomatic disorders it was hypothesized that the separate behavior therapy techniques of relaxation application and systematic desensitization would reduce the frequency of migraine episodes. On the basis of Gelder and Marks' conclusion[12] it was further hypothesized that a significant difference in treatment outcome would exist between combined desensitization, systematic desensitization and relaxation application. It was predicted that the comprehensive approach of combined desensitization would be more effective, than either of the single-model behavior therapy procedures.

STUDY I

Method

*S*s were 17 male and female volunteer university staff and students, ranging in age from 17 to 44 yr (mean = 22.8), each having been diagnosed as suffering migraine episodes. Pretreatment frequency of migraine attacks ranged from 3 to 56 (mean = 11.1) per 8-week period, the first attack having occurred from 3 to 19 yr previously (mean = 8.0). All *S*s took medication for acute migraine attacks, 13 *S*s, were in addition taking either sleeping pills or tranquilizers. The latter drugs were eliminated or reduced under medical supervision. No drug intake changes were made with the no-treatment controls regarding acute migraine medications or of other medications prescribed to ease emotional tensions. The effect of not doing so, if any at all, was expected to operate against hypotheses predicting treatment effects.

All *S*s attended an individual 30 min introductory session where they were presented with a simple standardized explanation of the pathogenesis of migraine as a psychosomatic disease with psychological mechanisms of the learned type. At the end of this interview all *S*s were asked to take away and complete a biographical questionnaire containing among others; items related to familial migraine incidence and previous treatment programs. Prior to a second interview each *S* was randomly allocated to one of the three experimental conditions of no-treatment, relaxation application, or combined desensitization.* At a second individual session all *S*s completed a pretreatment test battery which included scales to assess (1) relatively stable personal-social characteristics such as, general anxiety (Cattell[18]) and neuroticism (Willoughby [19]); these measures were obtained primarily to provide descriptive data on the experimental population; (2) anxiety in interpersonal-evaluative situations such as, test-anxiety (Alpert and Haber[20]), and social anxiety (Watson and Friend[21]); and, (3) distressing "minor type" target behaviors such as sex, family life, academic activities, vocation, morals, religion, health, etc.

Data on "major" target behaviors were also taken from each *S* for the 8-week period preceding treatment for migraine frequency, hours duration, pre- and postmedication pain intensity, along with a detailed description of neurofocal and other symptoms experienced during a migraine episode. The duration of the migraine attack was recorded to the nearest half hr, and the pain intensity was scored on a 10 point scale, where 2 represented "very slight" pain, and 10—"very intense pain." The premedication pain intensity levels represented the *S*s' report prior to the intake of medications prescribed by a physician (usually ergotamine tartrate or compounds containing it such as "Cafergot" and "Migral").

---

*The exception to the randomization procedure was the patient who reported 56 migraine episodes during the pretreatment 8-week period, who was placed in the no-treatment group to control for the possibility of either a treatment effect confounded by statistical regression, or measurement error resulting from the inclusion of muscular-contraction headaches in his report.

None of the *S*s was taking "interval" medication such as methysergide during the 32 weeks of the study. A detailed account of everyday behavior patterns, and the nature of typical interpersonal relationships with family, friends and work-mates were also recorded. The pretreatment test battery was again administered to all *S*s posttreatment (Week 16), and at two, 8-week follow-up sessions (weeks 24 and 32 respectively). The *major* target behaviors, that is, actual migraine attacks, were recorded and symptoms listed on a standard questionnaire by the subjects at the time they occurred. Additional screening procedures were used to exclude *S*s with evidence of psychotic behavior, low motivation, or of participation in other treatment programs either of a psychological or chemotherapeutic nature. No *S* was excluded for any of these reasons.

All treatment conditions were time-limited to 15 sessions of 50–60 min duration given at rate of two per week, with at least 2 days between sessions. All treatment sessions were conducted by the first author who had previous clinical experience with migraine *S*s and who was experienced in the behavior therapy techniques used in the study. Treatment was terminated at the conclusion of the fifteenth session regardless of therapeutic progress. The treatment procedure for each of the three experimental conditions was as follows:

No-Treatment Control (C)   To this group ($N = 3$) an explanation was given of the episodic nature of migraine. It was explained that effective treatment decisions depended to a large extent upon an accurate description of events preceding and accompanying the migraine attacks, for this reason it was suggested that treatment be delayed for several months. They were given migraine symptom questionnaires and asked to record in detail every migraine and headache they experienced together with a report of events preceding the attack and to report back for further interviews every 8 weeks.

Relaxation Application (RA)   Three sessions spread over 2 weeks were devoted to progressive relaxation training which followed the accelerated procedure and rules of timing developed by Jacobson[22] and Paul[11] and further modified by Mitchell[16].* With this technique, the subject reclined with eyes closed and was taught to relax by successively tensing and releasing gross muscle groups throughout the body on instruction from the therapist. Attention was focused upon identification

---

*The modified procedures for relaxation training and reciprocal inhibition exist in standardized manual form and can be obtained upon application to the senior author.

of localized tension and relaxation, commencing with the dominant arm. Care was taken to limit competing stimuli and responses by using a dimly illuminated room furnished with carpet and curtains to minimize distracting sounds. Each *S* was asked to practice relaxation for three, 10 min periods per day, mid-day, early evening and before going to sleep. The remaining sessions were devoted to a combination of illustration and discussion of the appropriate use of relaxation particularly in situations perceived as anxiety-arousing or tension-producing and further relaxation practice in the therapy session itself. Each *S* was also given migraine symptom questionnaires and instructed to complete each week in the same manner as the *C* group.

Combined Desensitization (CD) The treatment program for this group involved the simultaneous application (concurrent within each treatment session) of applied relaxation, desensitization, and assertive therapy. Wolpe's[10] desensitization, based on relaxation, was used to detach or remove anxiety and hostility. Systematic desensitization, or simply desensitization, is limited to a treatment "package" which systematically includes: (1) Training in deep muscular relaxation—the same procedure for the first three sessions of the *R.A.* group was followed; (2) Construction of anxiety hierarchies; and, (3) Desensitization proper—the graduated pairing, through imagery of anxiety-eliciting stimuli from the hierarchies, with the relaxed state. Anxiety hierarchies are graded lists of anxiety-eliciting stimuli, constructed to form subjective, equal-intervals of just noticeable differences in the degree of anxiety elicited, ranging from the weakest elicitation of anxiety to the strongest. Construction typically began at about the same time as relaxation training, items being drawn from initial interviews, psychological measures, and the *S*s' reported lists of distressing feelings and situations.

The procedure for desensitization was as follows: A relatively deep state of relaxation was induced and instructions given to signal even the slightest degrees of tension, discomfort, or anxiety, by raising a finger. The weakest anxiety hierarchy item was then presented by the therapist and the subject asked to visualize it as vividly as possible. After an appropriate exposure period (usually 10 sec) the subject was instructed to stop visualizing the item and to continue relaxing. When desensitization was unimpeded by the subject indicating the presence of anxiety, each hierarchy item was repeated for a further two presentations in the same manner (10 sec and 30 sec respectively), moving from the weakest to the strongest anxiety-eliciting items. When any given item aroused an anxiety reaction the S was immediately instructed to stop visualizing the scene, and relaxation was again induced—aided by instructions to visualize a calm and pleasant scene. The same item was then presented once again for a few sec and if anxiety was again experienced a weaker item from the same hierarchy was re-presented.

Following the procedures of Salter[23], Jackson[24], and Stevenson[25] which can be loosely grouped under *assertive therapy*, daily tasks were jointly planned for each S where problems existed in sexual, interpersonal, vocational, occupational, academic, marital or recreational areas. The procedure was similar to the following. Firstly, the S gives a verbal report of difficulties experienced in some area of his environment, in this case, inability to approach an attractive girl and make a date. (The verbal report of the S is invariably accepted by the therapist as a description of outside events.) There followed an intra-session demonstration of an initiating social approach by the therapist and several "rehearsals" by the S during which the therapist used verbal reinforcers such as approval, praise, specific approval for compliance with instructions, and selective attention. A specific and systematic program was then planned jointly with "tasks" ranging from smiling at the girl in passing, through introducing oneself over coffee, to actually asking for a date. The actual program covered 3 weeks with several tasks to be completed per week. After each task, the S reported his experience, the next task was rehearsed in specific detail down to actual conversation topics, and the S sent out for "real-life" practice. Programs of this type covering several problem areas may be operating concomitantly, and where possible, designed to maximize the probability of payoffs. Particular emphasis is placed upon reinforcing frank verbalizations and spontaneous expression of basic feelings and emotions such as love, affection and hostility. Where necessary the expression of these was "reshaped" into more socially appropriate and acceptable forms. Where it was felt necessary, daily routines were periodically restructured to match, ease, or accelerate therapeutic progress. With sexual problems additional use was made of factual material on anatomy, physiology, sexual responsibility, differences between the sexes, techniques, "arousal" signs and any other data of relevance to the particular problem. In summary, four activities took place: (1) Detailed descriptions of daily routine and problems experienced, (2) Intra-session rehearsal of procedures designed to cope more effectively with the problems and the joint planning of an execution program, (3) Reports of the Ss execution of assignments, and discussion of results, followed by further rehearsals, and, (4) Verbal reinforcement of positive changes in the Ss behavior.

Results

Consistent with recent research by Johnson and Spielberger[26], Spielberger[27], and Mitchell and Ingham[28], no significant changes occurred over the 32 weeks in the level of general anxiety manifested by the Ss in any of the three experimental groups. Significant improvements on presenting "minor" target problems occurred only in the combined desensitization group, particularly problems related to hypochondria, sex, morals, academic and vocation. Some improvements, in particular sex, were shown at the 32 week follow-up stage with the relaxation application group. No significant changes occurred in the no-treatment control group.

A Two-Factor with repeated measures analysis of covariance, using the pre-score as the covariate (Winer[29]) was carried out on the two major target behaviors of migraine frequency and hours duration.

The main effect for Type of Treatment for both migraine frequency and hours duration was found to be significant ($F = 9.33$, 1, 11 $d.f.$, $p < 0.01$; $F = 6.65$, 1, 11 $d.f.$, $p < 0.05$). That is, Ss in the combined desensitization group showed a significant reduction in both the number and duration of migraine episodes over the 32 week period of the study whereas no significant changes occurred for the relaxation application group. The *eta* correlations of 0.678 for migraine frequency and 0.614 for hours duration indicated that the size of the effect due to differences in treatment were large, permitting reliable generalizations to similar samples using the same treatment.

A comparison of means between the two treatment groups and the no-treatment controls showed a significant difference for both migraine frequency and hours duration between the combined desensitization and no-treatment controls ($t = 2.87$, $p < 0.01$; and 1.89, $p < 0.05$) but no significant differences between the relaxation-application group and the no-treatment controls ($t = 0.76$, and 0.15 respectively).

The trends of migraine frequency and hours duration change produced by the three experimental conditions are represented in Fig. 25.1.

Table 25.1 presents the mean change in migraine frequency and hours duration for all experimental groups.

Mean and percentage reduction changes were computed for each S by subtracting migraine frequency and hours duration scores at the 32 week

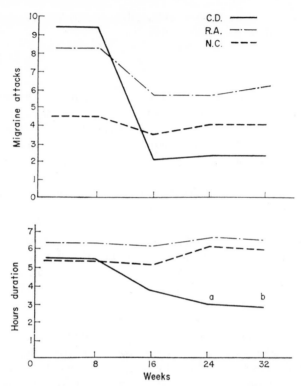

a, b   Two Ss in this group did not experience any migraine attacks at these
            stages. The mean hours duration for the remaining five Ss was 4.4
            and 4.0 respectively.
C.D.   Combined desensitization group.
R.A.   Relaxation application group.
N.C.   No-treatment control group.

Fig. 25.1. Frequency and duration changes during treatments.

follow-up stage from scores reported for the 8 weeks preceding treatment. Also presented in Table 25.1 are the percentages of Ss in the
experimental and control groups who evidenced improvement following
the treatment period. Noting the percentage of Ss within each therapy
group whose migraine symptoms improved following treatment, it is
evident that the combined desensitization treatment was beneficial to all
Ss and that the results are not due to dramatic changes in only a few Ss.
Furthermore, it is evident that as far as "target" symptoms are concerned,
that is, migraine symptoms *per se*, there existed no significant mean

Table 25.1. Summary of Mean Changes in Migraine Frequency and Hours Duration for Treatment and Control Groups over 32 Weeks.

Group	N	Migraine frequency			Hours duration		
		Mean change	Mean % reduction	% Improved	Mean change	Mean % reduction	% Improved
Combined desensitization	7	−7.1	76	100	−2.8	50	71
Relaxation application	7	−2.0	24	71	0	0	43
No-treatment controls	3	−0.5* (−4.6)	2* (21)	33	+0.4	0	33

*This score represents the results of the two control Ss with moderate migraine frequency. The high frequency S (56 migraine attacks per 8 weeks) was removed to eliminate regression effects due probably to measurement error.

differences between the relaxation application and no-treatment groups either on migraine frequency reduction or hours duration.

STUDY II

Method

20 male and female volunteer university staff, students, and others served as Ss. Age ranged from 18 to 55 yr (mean = 27.9), each having been diagnosed as suffering migraine episodes. At the commencement of treatment the frequency of migraine attacks ranged from 6 to 30 (mean = 12.8) per 8-week period, the first attack having occurred from 2 to 18 yr previously (mean = 9.2). All Ss took medication for acute attacks, 15 Ss were currently taking either sleeping pills, tranquilizers or antidepressants, and in addition, 5 Ss had had previous prophylactic pharmaco-therapy treatment for a period of 1–2 yr without success. At the time of treatment no S was actively engaged on a program of pharmacotherapy.

All introductory interviews, pretreatment measures and group allocations were the same as those employed in Study I except for the five pharmacotherapy failure Ss who were all placed in the same experimental group. Four experimental conditions existed: (1) no-treatment; (2) desensitization; (3) combined desensitization (previous pharmacotherapy treatment); and (4) combined desensitization (no previous pharmacotherapy treatment). Wherever possible drug reduction for treatment Ss was implemented (other than the usual medications for acute attacks) with medical supervision. No drug intake changes were attempted with the no-treatment controls.

The treatment procedures for the no-treatment and combined desensitization groups were the same as those in Study I. The remaining group received a combination of relaxation application and systematic desensitization (see also procedure for Study I). All treatments were again time-limited to 15 sessions of 50–60 min duration.

Results

A Two-Factor with repeated measures analysis of covariance using the pre-score as the covariate[29] was again carried out on the migraine frequency and hours duration scores. The analyses revealed that significant reductions in both migraine frequency and hours duration had occurred over the 32 weeks of the study.

Furthermore, with both the migraine frequency and hours duration the decreases were due to the existence of significant treatment effects ($F = 17.93$, 3, 15 *d.f.*, $p < 0.01$; and $F = 3.679$, 3, 15 *d.f.*, $p < 0.05$ respec-

Table 25.2. Analysis of Covariance for Four Types of Treatment* and Three Measures of Migraine Frequency and Hours Duration for Study II.

		Symptom					
		Frequency				Duration	
Source	*d.f.*	MS	F	*n*†	MS	F	*n*
Type of treatment	3	196	17.93‡	0.738	65	3.679§	0.443
Error	15	10.93			17.67		
Post–F/UP I—F/UP II	2	52	6.83‡	0.424	9.5	15.57‡	0.57
Treatment × Post–F/UP							
I—F/UP II	6	17.5	2.29‖	0.262	5.5	9.02‡	0.47
Error	31	7.61			0.61		

*Treatments were combined desensitization, combined desensitization for pharmacotherapy failures, systematic desensitization and no-treatment controls.

†Eta correlation.

‡$p < 0.01$.

§$p < 0.05$.

‖$p < 0.06$.

tively). The *eta* correlations of 0.738 for migraine frequency and 0.443 for hours duration again indicated that the size of the effect due to differences in treatment was large enough to permit reliable generalizations to similar *S* samples.

An analysis of group contrasts of migraine frequency treatment condition means at the final follow-up stage using Scheffe's[30] test of *post-hoc* comparisons showed that both combined desensitization groups displayed a significantly greater reduction in migraine frequency than either the systematic desensitization ($F = 13.92$, 3, 15 *d.f.*, $p < 0.05$) or the

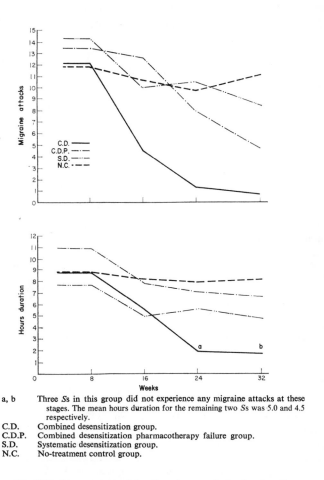

a, b   Three *S*s in this group did not experience any migraine attacks at these stages. The mean hours duration for the remaining two *S*s was 5.0 and 4.5 respectively.

C.D.   Combined desensitization group.
C.D.P. Combined desensitization pharmacotherapy failure group.
S.D.   Systematic desensitization group.
N.C.   No-treatment control group.

Fig. 25.2. Frequency and duration changes during treatments.

no-treatment control groups ($F = 24.75$, 3, 15 *d.f.*, $p < 0.01$) but no significant mean differences were found between the systematic desensitization and no-treatment control groups ($F = 1.55$).

The significant interaction among treatment groups was due to the combined desensitization group (no previous pharmacotherapy treatment) displaying a greater migraine frequency reduction over time than any of the remaining three groups ($F = 5.78$, 19.97, 35.39; 6, 31 *d.f.*, $p < 0.05$, < 0.01 and < 0.001 respectively). Both combined desensitization groups reported a significantly greater reduction in migraine frequency than the systematic desensitization and no-treatment controls ($F = 128.9$, 6, 31 *d.f.*, $p < 0.001$). No difference was found between the two latter groups ($F = 2.22$).

A comparison of treatment conditions means for hours duration of migraine attacks showed that only the combined desensitization group (no previous pharmacotherapy treatment experience) significantly differed from the no-treatment controls ($F = 7.47$, 3, 15 *d.f.*, $p < 0.05$).

The trends of migraine frequency and hours duration changes within each treatment condition are shown in Fig. 25.2.

Mean and percentage reduction changes were computed for each *S* after the manner of Study I and are set out in Table 25.3.

The change in number of hr in which *S*s actually experienced headache,

Table 25.3. Summary of Mean Changes in Migraine Frequency and Hours Duration for Treatment and Control Groups over 32 Weeks.

Group	N	Migraine frequency			Hours duration		
		Mean change	Mean % reduction	% Improved	Mean change	Mean % reduction	% Improved
Combined desensitization	5	−11.4	95	100	−7.2	80*	100
Combined desensitization (pharmacotherapy failures)	5	−8.6	64	80	−4.2	38*	60
Systematic desensitization	5	−5.8	41	80	−3.0	38	100
No-treatment controls	5	−0.8	7	20	−0.8	9	40

*Three *S*s in this group did not experience any migraine attacks at this stage. The mean percentage reduction for the remaining two *S*s was 50 per cent.

that is migraine frequency x hours duration for Studies I and II separately and combined, is shown in Fig. 25.3. This outcome index is perhaps the most meaningful in terms of actual distress reported by Ss.

DISCUSSION

The results of both studies clearly indicate that migrainous Ss completing a short-term program of comprehensive behavior therapy, namely,

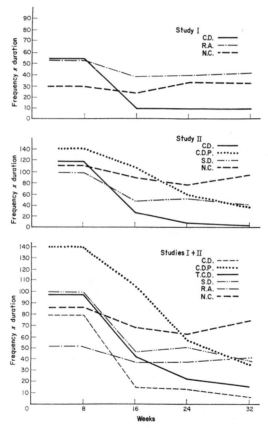

T.C.D.   All Ss treated by combined desensitization.

Fig. 25.3. Average trends of change from a combination of number of migraine attacks × duration of attack for each treatment condition.

combined desensitization, report a significantly greater reduction in migraine episodes and hours duration of headache than single-model treatment programs, such as systematic desensitization and relaxation application, or no-treatment control Ss with comparable pretreatment migraine severity. It was found that whilst Ss in the relaxation application group reported some reduction in migraine frequency, this reduction was neither significant nor significantly different to that of the no-treatment controls. The systematic desensitization group reported a somewhat greater reduction in both migraine frequency and hours duration than the relaxation application group but the reductions were neither large enough to reach significance ($p < 0.25$) nor significantly different from those of the no-treatment controls.

It was also found that significant improvements on presenting "minor" target problems occurred only in the combined desensitization group, particularly problems related to sex, interpersonal relationships, anxiety in assessment and social situations and hypochondria. The failure to obtain any significant improvements in these problems with the relaxation application treatment was to be expected since although the treatment focused on environmental problem areas it did not provide the S with any method of controlling or modifying his environment. The systematic desensitization group on the other hand, did achieve some significant improvements particularly those specific aspects of problems focused upon during therapy, e.g. test anxiety. It did not however, provide the S with techniques for modifying his behavior or performance in actual problem situations, e.g. learning and examination skills for use preceding or during the actual examination situation.

One further analysis (principal components) of the data was carried out. This was done because it permitted a multivariate analysis of change of all migraine symptoms for both Studies I and II simultaneously. The pretreatment, posttreatment, and two follow-up scores for the four migraine symptom variables were presented as 4 separate Ss, reducing a 4 (variables) × 4 (repeated measures) × 36 (subjects) data matrix to a 4 (variables) × 144 (subject × repeated measures) data matrix.

The principle components analysis* revealed one factor with an eigenvalue of 2.54, accounting for 64 per cent of the variance. The loadings of variables on this unrotated component (migraine syndrome

---

*Acknowledgment is made to Kevin Bird of the School of Applied Psychology, University of New South Wales for advice on this procedure.

factor) were: migraine frequency 0.65; hours duration 0.76; premedication pain intensity 0.87; and, postmedication pain intensity 0.87.

Component scores for each S were computed on this factor and the mean factor scores for each treatment group over the four testing occasions are presented in graphic form in Fig. 25.4.

The marked reduction of scores on the migraine syndrome component for the combined desensitization group (1.98 S.D.'s) supports the results of the independent univariate covariance analyses reported elsewhere. The other two groups revealing reductions of greater than 1.0 standard deviation were the systematic desensitization group (1.02 S.D.'s) and the combined desensitization pharmacotherapy failure group (1.60 S.D.'s). The relaxation application and no-treatment control groups displayed reductions of less than 0.5 of a standard deviation. It is important to note that zero on Fig. 25.4 represents the mean of all Ss in terms of the severity of the migraine syndrome component, and that increasing negative scores represent decreasing migraine severity or increasing improvement relative to the total sample of migraine Ss. It follows then that although the pharmacotherapy failure Ss displayed, in relative terms, a reduction of 1.30 standard deviations in migraine severity their final level of improvement (0.17) was very much less than that of the other

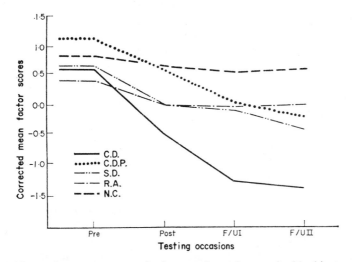

Fig. 25.4. Means of component scores for five experimental groups for 36 subjects over four testing occasions. Component scores are based on the Migraine Syndrome Component and represent a linear combination of subject scores on four variables (migraine frequency, hours duration, pre- and postmedication pain intensity).

combined desensitization group (1.98 S.D.'s reduction and -1.37 final mean score). A Two-Factor with repeated measures analysis of covariance on unequal groups using the pretreatment factor score as the covariate was then carried out. In summary, the combined desensitization group displayed significantly fewer headaches at the second follow-up phase ($F = 111.21$, 4, 26 $d.f.$, $p < 0.001$) and a significantly greater reduction over time than the other four experimental groups ($F = 12.65$, 2, 54 $d.f.$, $p < 0.01$).

The restricted improvement obtained by the use of relaxation application and systematic desensitization is in agreement with the findings of Gelder and Marks[12] who found that single-model procedures are only partially effective when applied to relatively complex behavioral problems. In retrospect, it is apparent that both the single-model procedures of relaxation application and systematic desensitization focused on by-products of larger behavior patterns that were only the consequences of other more important problems in the Ss' lives. The treatment goals of these procedures emphasized a change in feelings, anxieties and moods (or at least the Ss' report about them), rather than modifying the perceptual and interpersonal behavioral patterns and other environmental factors which were precipitating and maintaining the habitual response of migraine. Furthermore, it is more plausible to interpret the presence of disruptive emotionality as a product of perceptual reactivity to ongoing environmental stresses. The present authors believe that the success of the combined desensitization treatment program was due to the fact that it included not only a conditioning technique (desensitization) but also re-educative and environmental manipulative procedures individually designed to bring about changes in the Ss' disturbing life patterns.

Lance[31] has asserted that the management of migraine still depends on prophylactic pharmacotherapy, the aim being to prevent painful dilation of cranial vessels, particularly the scalp arteries which appear to be the main sources of headache. Methysergide (Methyl-D-lysergic acid and butanolamide) a semi-synthetic ergot derivative was suggested for such prophylactic treatment as it is the most effective preparation at present available for the control of migraine. The basis for the foregoing rests upon the description of migraine as a low serotonin syndrome and evidence which has shown methysergide to have many actions simulating those of serotonin. Thus it is said to provide some protection against a sudden fall in the blood serotonin level.

A comparison of the outcomes between behavior therapy and methysergide prophylactic pharmacotherapy treatment proves interesting.

Lance [31] reported that regular medication with methysergide suppresses migraine completely in about 20 per cent of patients and improves substantially another 40 per cent. The data on which this success rate was based appears to be that of Curran and Lance [32]. A review of the clinical trials that have used methysergide (Curran *et al.* [45]), revealed only one other study where complete migraine suppression occurred namely, a study by Sicuteri [33] who obtained a suppression rate of 50 per cent with 18 migrainous *S*s. It is known that Lance now pursues a treatment policy that includes training his patients to relax in addition to the administration of methysergide,* but it is not known whether relaxation training or other forms of treatment occurred in the two studies mentioned. In the light of the results obtained in Study I, a combination of relaxation training and methysergide would partially explain the disparity in reported suppression rates. Table 25.4 shows the methysergide suppression rate to be about 3.1 per cent when averaged over the studies reviewed.

Table 25.4. Summary of Results of Methysergide Trials* and Behavior Therapy Treatment of Migraine from 1959 to 1969.

Treatment	No. of patients	% Withdrew treatment	% Headache free	% Substantially improved†	% Unimproved‡
Methysergide†	2329	13.8	3.1	52.1	31.0
Behavior Therapy‖	27	0	22.2	70.4	7.4

*The majority of trials were obtained from Curran, Hinterberger and Lance [36].
†Approximately 40–60 per cent reduction in migraine attacks.
‡Less than 20 per cent reduction in migraine attacks. Placebo effect appeared to vary between 5–20 per cent in studies reporting the use of placebo procedures.
§Accumulated results from 25 clinical trials.
‖Combined desensitization results from four separate studies.

In contrast, the suppression rate for behavior therapy using combined desensitization was about 22.2 per cent (Table 25.4) over four studies (0 per cent, 33.34 per cent, 28 per cent, and 30 per cent respectively). The initial pilot study (0 per cent suppression rate) was included to provide an unbiased comparison. The significant differences between the two approaches to treatment appear to be more related to comparisons of the number who withdraw from treatment (13.8 per cent and 0 per cent

---

*Personal communication (1969).

respectively) and those who remain unimproved despite treatment (31.0 per cent and 7.4 per cent) rather than to comparisons of suppression and improvement rates. Problems relating to different methods of S selection in the different studies using methysergide, suggest caution in making inferences from these comparisons.

There remains two important areas for discussion, namely, the behavioral and biochemical correlates associated with the genesis and site of migraine. Both are important as far as treatment rationale and procedures are concerned, but for the sake of clarity they will be discussed independently.

1. Behavioral Correlates and Treatment Rationale

Following the conclusions reached by Maxwell[5], Wolff[34] and Whitty[35], supported by clinical observations of the Ss in the four studies reported by the authors, it was tentatively concluded that the person prone to persistent migraine headaches is subject to chronic anxiety. In terms of behavior, the anxiety was seen as being manifested in "overcontrolled" or "defensive" behavioral patterns to selectively perceived events in the environment whilst, experiencing emotional arousal and its concomitant activation of the sympathetic aspects of the autonomic nervous system. The existence of the foregoing behavioral-anxiety/somatic dichotomy is postulated firstly, on the observation of behavioral patterns and characteristic verbal communication responses of migrainous Ss, and secondly, on the basis of anxiety (emotional)—somatic links in the chain of events seen by the authors as being related to both the causation and maintenance of migraine episodes.

Research findings (Spielberger[27]), suggest that it is meaningful to distinguish between anxiety as a *transitory* state and as a relatively stable personality *trait*, and to differentiate between anxiety states, the stimulus conditions that evoke them, and the defenses that serve to avoid them. There exists considerable agreement that "A-state" anxiety is characterized by subjective, consciously perceived feelings of apprehension, uncertainty and tension, accompanied by or associated with activation or arousal of the autonomic nervous system. General or "A-trait" anxiety on the other hand is seen as a personality trait, referring to the degree to which individuals are disposed to manifest A-state reactions disproportionate in intensity to the magnitude of the objective danger. The level of A-trait anxiety is not expected to influence A-state reactions to all stimuli, only to particular classes of stimuli. Stimuli that have little or no threat value obviously would not be expected to elicit an A-state response. Additionally, A-state reactions vary as a function of acquired behavioral dispositions. Generally, the arousal of A-states involves a sequence of temporally ordered events in which a stimulus that is cognitively appraised as dangerous evokes an A-state reaction. This A-state reaction then initiates a behavior sequence designed to avoid the danger situation, or to evoke protective tactics which alter the cognitive appraisal of the situation. In the case of migrainous individuals, perfectionistic cautious patterns are employed to reduce "danger" and defensive maneuvers, expressed usually as hostility, to alter cognitive appraisal.

The environmental "life style" pattern of the 47 or so migrainous Ss treated in the four studies already reported could, almost without exception, be categorized as defensive with characteristic anxiety-hostility interaction patterns. Situationally-anxious, achievement-oriented, perfectionistic, overcontrolled and routine-regimented behavior patterns were seen as supporting evidence for such a description. It is probable that during periods of perceived threat where the consequences of the threat are uncertain (increased ego-involvement) the migraine susceptible individual becomes increasingly defensive behaviorally, and anxious and hostile emotionally, resulting in the placement of more emphasis upon established routine even when inappropriate to changed circumstances. Defensive behavior was operantly defined here as "uncertainty-reactive behavior," and was seen as being indexed by an anxiety-laden, high frequency emission of "clarification-type" verbal responses. The expression of hostility was generally observed as being dependent upon the perceptual-correlation between threat and its control or resolution.

In summary, chronic migraine sufferers seem to be characterized by firstly, a *"low uncertainty threshold."* The selective perception of uncertainty it is suggested leads to an increase in uncertainty-reactive or defensive behavior, anxiety-hostility covariance and subjective but conscious feelings of insecurity which result in continued compensatory efforts to "reduce" uncertainty by overcontrolling the environment. It is further suggested that failure to control or perceptually resolve uncertainty results in a concomitant increasing arousal of the sympathetic aspects of the autonomic nervous system. Secondly, *"cognitive inflexibility"* in the migrainous person's approach to and handling of changing environmental circumstances. Appropriate coping behaviors learned and established in childhood and later developmental phases of life, which, though adequate at the time they were established, are maintained despite changes in the kinds of gratifications necessary to satisfy changing emotional needs and radical changes in environmental life space. That is, there seems to be an avoidance of activities oriented towards appraising in a realistic fashion present circumstances and the satisfaction of existing needs in relation to those circumstances.

The general therapeutic position taken for the combined desensitization treatment program reported in this paper was that migraine is a symptom representing the interactive effect of constricted overt emotional *expression* and chronic covert emotional over-reactivity with its somatic concomitant, excessive sympathetic nervous system activity, manifested via hypersensitive cranial arteries which are presumed to be an inherited physiological reactivity pattern. Individual differences in A-trait probably determines the particular stimuli that are cognitively appraised as threatening because it is assumed that A-trait reflects the residues of past experience that in some way determine individual differences in anxiety-proneness, that is, in the disposition to see certain types of situations as dangerous and to respond to them with A-states. The apparent contradiction of significant reductions in anxiety occurring to specific situations like assessment, and social situations whilst no changes were reported in the general level of anxiety is substantially resolved through such a clarification of the meaning of anxiety.

The disparity or incongruence between overt and covert behavioral patterns was seen as a learned response, occurring to "signals" (conditioned stimuli) that have in the past been followed by situations of injury or pain (unconditioned stimuli). Covert emotionality, it was postulated, has become "attached" (for a variety of reasons) to general and specific situations resulting in learned patterns of defensive behavior which, though idiosyncratically inflexible, and hence maladaptive, are not necessarily maladaptive in terms of observable behavior and cultural norms. Additionally, anxiety may have resulted in both specific and generalized forms of avoidance conditioning which further obstructs the migrainous individual in the learning of efficient methods of adaptation to his environment.

Treatment consequently took the form of "detaching" or reducing the level of disruptive and chronic anxiety-laden emotionality associated with general and specific environmental situations. That is, the treatment aimed at increasing the migrainous individual's capacity to control emotional reactivity to events perceived as stressful in his environment thus, stabilizing sympathetic nervous system activity and reducing its "triggering" effect upon cranial arteries. Concurrently, treatment procedures also emphasized the perceptual-reduction of nonreality based threats and the modification of threat or uncertainty-resolution behavior by the conditioning of new responses which were seen to be more adaptive. According to this rationale the potential of given stimuli to evoke disruptive chronic emotionality and hence disruptive fluctuations in sympathetic nervous system reactivity will be permanently weakened and eventually extinguished.

The treatment techniques used and referred to in this paper as *combined desensitization* were selected purely on the basis of their appearing to be the "best fit" procedures for the comprehensive behavioral change implied by a rationale of migraine frequency being conceptualized in terms of ". . . . increased capacity to control emotional reactivity, that is, reduced sympathetic nervous system activity, to events perceived as stressful in the environment."

2. Biochemical Correlates and Migraine Schema

The importance of a reduced or stabilized sympathetic nervous system activity is related to the emotional-somatic links in the chain of events postulated by the present authors as being crucial to the explanation of migraine in terms of both *genesis* and *location*. It is suggested that the organic location is the end result of a psycho-functional genesis involving constant or periodically-recurring chronic emotional states and the concomitant innervation of the sympathetic aspects of the autonomic nervous system manifested in individuals with hypersensitive cranial arteries as migraine.

Biochemical investigations preceding, during and following an attack of migraine have accumulated sufficient evidence to suggest that changes in serotonin metabolism are not only associated with the migraine syndrome but may play a part in its causation. Curran, Hinterberger and Lance[36] in a study of plasma serotonin levels of migrainous *S*'s during attacks of migraine as well as headache-free periods found that in 80 per cent of *S*s serotonin levels were lower during headache.

The fall was found to occur at the onset of the migraine attack and persisted for most of the duration of the headache of *S*s studied. This finding was later confirmed in a study carried out by Anthony, Hinterberger and Lance[37], who estimated total plasma serotonin in 15 migrainous *S*s during 21 migraine headaches and found that serotonin levels fell in 20 out of 21 headaches, by an average of 60 per cent when the first headache specimen was compared with the last before headache, and by an average of 45 per cent when the mean value during headache was compared with the mean for the 24 hr before headache. They concluded that a fall in total plasma serotonin is a specific feature of the migraine attack, and probably one of the humoral mechanisms in the production of migraine headache.

Lance, Anthony and Hinterberger[38] further found that migraine is precipitated when serotonin levels are lowered artificially by the injection of reserpine and was relieved by increasing plasma serotonin level through the injection of serotonin. They concluded that the precipitation of a migraine attack appears to be specifically related to a fall of plasma serotonin. They further speculated that some endogenous substance with a reserpine-like action (serotonin-releasing action) is liberated at the onset of the migraine attack and that the consequent lowering of plasma serotonin initiates the vascular changes responsible for migraine headache.

Early indications of the involvement of a serotonin-releasing factor present in the blood plasma came out of work carried out by Blaschko and Philpot[39] who showed that serotonin was oxidatively deaminated by monoamine oxidase (MAO). Kimball, Friedman and Vallejo[40] further showed that when the MAO inhibitor phenelzine was given to some migrainous Ss to increase endogenous serotonin, in all cases but one, the headaches decreased in severity and frequency. Lance[31] reported a further use of the MAO inhibitor phenelzine given three times daily to 19 migrainous Ss. Fourteen Ss became either headache-free or showed a substantially reduced frequency of headache. In all 14 Ss plasma serotonin increased more than 20 per cent above pretreatment initial resting levels. It is known that MAO governs the oxidative deamination of many simple primary and secondary amines including that of serotonin. The alleviation of migraine through administration of MAO inhibitors suggests the involvement of MAO activity perhaps accounting for or contributing towards the release of plasma serotonin immediately preceding a migraine episode. Since both MAO and serotonin are released through sympathetic nervous system activity (SNSA), it seems reasonable to speculate that chronic SNSA can lead to an imbalance of fluctuations in the distribution of MAO in relation to serotonin.

It is thus hypothesized that migraine may be precipitated in response to:

1. The production of variable distributions of MAO and excess serotonin in response to SNSA; together with
2. The existence of hypersensitive cranial arteries either to increased

absolute levels of serotonin or to general fluctuations in serotonin level.

Some support for the latter point is seen in work carried out by Dalessio[41] who concluded that unstable central vasomotor functions might play a role in the pathophysiology of migraine.

Whatever the serotonin-releasing mechanism involved, SNSA is seen as crucial in the long chain of events leading to migraine. In summary the issue is one of *genesis* and *location*. Figure 25.5 is representative of a conception of migraine as a psychogenic organic disorder innervated by the autonomic nervous system. The authors suggest that its genesis can be appreciated only when emotional disturbances associated with psychological or behavioral events are investigated, in addition to the biochemical events arising out of the concomitance between sympathetic nervous system activity and emotional arousal (Lacey[42]). The psychological or behavioral events are seen as primary antecedents of migraine episodes and the site of migraine as secondary. Present evidence regarding migraine location points to individuals with certain inherited patterns of physiological reactivity which, as Lance has already proposed, may well be manifested in hypersensitive cranial arteries. The existence of inherited patterns of physiological reactivity is the most feasible and commonsense answer to the question as to why some individuals with similar perceptual-behavioral correlates develop migraine and others not. Figure 25.5 then represents a tentative attempt to show the postulated concomitant and interactive relationships between behavioral and biochemical events.

The authors are aware that the scheme is simplistic in concept, however, the indicated interactions between behavioral and biochemical events are only intended to represent a first-stage approximation of what is happening to the *total* organism. It remains for further research to test the hypotheses arising out of the interactions.

In contrast to the rationale proposed and the results reported in this paper Lance[31] stated that, "At present, the unpalatable fact has to be accepted that psychological readjustment . . . . do little to alter the natural history of migraine." The conclusion to be reached from the comparison of prophylactic pharmacotherapy and behavior therapy treatment programs is that they do not at this stage, appear to significantly differ in their success or substantial improvement rates. However, behavior therapy may claim the advantages of having no apparent adverse side effects, a much lower failure rate and being an *active* modifier of disruptive

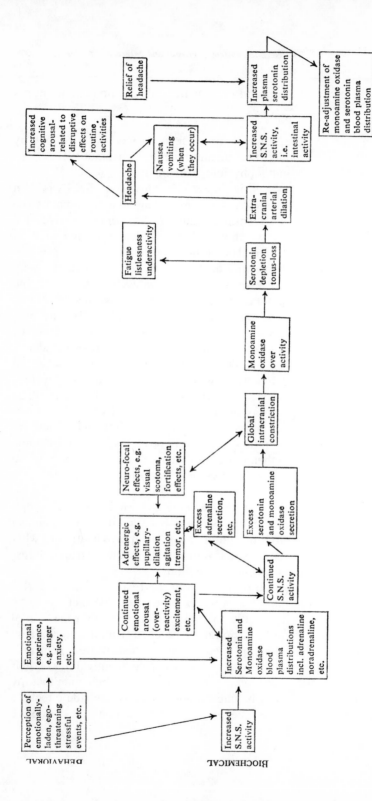

Fig. 25.5. Postulated concomitant and interactive relationships between behavioral and biochemical events preceding and during the migraine attack.

behavioral patterns. Consequently, there appears to be little justification in dismissing the applicability of comprehensive psychological programs to the treatment of migraine. Furthermore, whereas pharmacotherapy treatment of the prophylactic type has in the past decade been the object of intensive investigation, the psychological program reported in this paper has only been superficially examined and possibly retains the potential for further refinement.

Clearly, the line of research which the present investigations have followed has broader implications for the field of psychosomatic research. More specifically, research is required into the comparable therapeutic effectiveness of massed versus spaced treatment or periodic treatment phases; the possibility of group programs at the behavioral rather than biochemical level; a combination of pharmacotherapy and behavior therapy programming approaches; success prognoses including such factors as age and age of onset stress and perceptual-response specificity (e.g., the five pharmacotherapy failure Ss had a mean age of 38.6 yr and age of onset of 27.4 yr compared with 24.8 and 16.2 yr respectively for the remaining Ss); and finally, familial-behavioral patterns and their relationship to constructs such as uncertainty threshold and cognitive inflexibility hypothesized by the present authors as central to the understanding and treatment of migraine.

In conclusion, it is important to bear in mind, that essentially the prophylactic aims of pharmacotherapy and behavior therapy are similar, namely, the regulation or control of certain vascular events postulated as being central to the causation of the migraine attack. However, differences between the two are evident. Pharmacotherapy directs its resources to biochemical changes relating to or underlying neurovascular changes. On the other hand, behavior therapy by manipulating features in the external environment perceived as stressful by the migrainous person, seeks to stabilize and control his emotional reactions to these, thus raising his "stress threshold" and reducing the impact of disruptive emotions on the physiological organs related to or underlying vascular events in the body. Perhaps the most effective treatment program will prove to be some combination of prophylactic pharmacotherapy and behavior therapy approaches. The former aiming for a quick initial organic impact and the latter for progressive perceptual-behavioral changes designed to reinforce and further reduce, firstly the decreased frequency of migraine episodes resulting from pharmacotherapy and secondly, to stabilize such reduction in the face of pharmacotherapy withdrawal.

It is not suggested that the treatment reported in this paper has effected either a permanent cure or improvement but rather that the combined desensitization program has enabled the *S*s to adapt more effectively and thus remain reasonably composed in certain situations previously perceived as stressful. Severe psychological trauma could still evoke sufficient anxiety or disruptive emotional arousal to precipitate a migraine attack. Spaced or booster treatment programs are a feasible alternative and could be easily implemented should it prove necessary.

SUMMARY

Two investigations were made into the efficacy of certain single-model and combined behavior therapy programs in the treatment of migraine. Thirty-six migrainous subjects participated, each having been diagnosed by a physician as suffering migraine episodes. Results indicated that the combined program was superior to single-model approaches, obtaining significant reductions in migraine attacks in both investigations.

An explanation, in terms of learning theory, is given concerning the precipitation and maintenance of the migraine attacks. A rationale for treatment is presented, the psychogenesis of migraine discussed and a comparison made with prophylactic pharmacotherapy treatment.

REFERENCES

1. Frazier, S. H. The psychotherapy of headache. In *Research and Clinical Studies in Headache. An International Review.* (Edited by Friedman, A. P.), Vol. 2, Williams & Wilkins, Baltimore, 1969.
2. Kolb, L. C. Psychiatric aspects of the treatment of migraine. *Neurology*, 1963, **13**, 34.
3. Selinsky, H. Psychological study of the migraine syndrome. *Bull. N.Y. Acad. Med.,* 1939, **15**, 757.
4. Wolff, H. G. Personality features and reactions of subjects with migraine. *Arch. Neurol.,* 1937, **37**, 895.
5. Maxwell, H. *Migraine: Background and Treatment.* Wright, Bristol, 1960.
6. Jaspers, K. *Allgemeine Psychopathologic.* Springer-Verlag, Berlin, 1948.
7. Walton, D. The application of learning theory to the treatment of a case of bronchial asthma. In *Behaviour Therapy and the Neuroses.* (Edited by Eysenck, H. J.), Pergamon Press, Oxford, 1960.
8. Cooper, A. J. A case of bronchial asthma treated by behaviour therapy. *Behav. Res. Ther.,* 1964, **1**, 351.
9. Moore, N. Behaviour therapy in bronchial asthma: a controlled study. *J. Psychosomatic Res.,* 1965, **9**, 257.
10. Wolpe, J. *Psychotherapy by Reciprocal Inhibition.* Stanford University Press, Stanford, 1958.

11. Paul, G. L. *Insight versus Desensitization in Psychotherapy: An Experiment in Anxiety Reduction.* Stanford University Press, Stanford, 1966.
12. Gelder, M. G. and Marks, I. M. Severe agoraphobia: a controlled prospective trial of behaviour therapy. *Br. J. Psychiat.*, 1966, **112**, 309–319.
13. Kanfer, F. H. and Phillips, J. S. A survey of current behavior therapies and a proposal for classification. In *Behaviour Therapy: Appraisal and Status.* (Edited by Franks, C. M.), McGraw-Hill, New York, 1969.
14. Mitchell, K. R. The treatment of migraine: an exploratory application of time limited behaviour therapy, *Technology*, 1969, **14**, 50.
15. Mitchell, K. R. Behaviour therapy treatment of migraine: A further pilot study. Unpublished manuscript, University of N.S.W., 1969.
16. Mitchell, K. R. Therapist manual for relaxation and desensitization. Unpublished manuscript, University of N.S.W., 1969.
17. Cautela, J. R. Behaviour therapy and self-control: techniques and implications. In *Behaviour Therapy: Appraisal and Status.* (Edited by Franks, C. M.), McGraw-Hill, New York, 1969.
18. Cattell, R. B. *Handbook for the IPAT Anxiety Scale.* A.C.E.R., Melbourne, 1957.
19. Willoughby, R. R. Norms for the Clark-Thurstone Inventory. *J. Social Psychol.*, 1934, **5**, 91.
20. Alpert, R. and Haber, R. M. Anxiety in academic achievement situations. *J. Abnor. Soc. Psychol.*, 1960, **61**, 207.
21. Watson, D. and Friend, R. Measurement of social-evaluative anxiety. *J. of Consulting Clin. Psychol.*, 1969, **30**, 448.
22. Jacobson, E. *Progressive Relaxation.* University of Chicago Press, Chicago, 1938.
23. Salter, A. *Conditioned Reflex Therapy.* Capricorn, New York, 1961.
24. Jackson, D. D. *Etiology of Schizophrenia.* Basic Books, New York, 1960.
25. Stevenson, I. Direct instigation of behavioural changes in psychotherapy. *Arch. Gen. Psychiat.*, 1959, **1**, 99.
26. Johnson, D. T. and Spielberger C. D. The effects of relaxation training and the passage of time on measures of state—and trait-anxiety. *J. Clin. Psychol.*, 1968, **24**, 20.
27. Spielberger, C. D. (Editor) *Anxiety and Behaviour.* Academic Press, New York, 1966.
28. Mitchell, K. R. and Ingham, R. J. The effects of general anxiety on group desensitization of test anxiety. *Behav. Res. Ther.*, 1970, **8**, 69.
29. Winer, B. J. *Statistical Principles in Experimental Design.* Harper, New York, 1962.
30. Scheffe, H. A. *The Analysis of Variance.* McGraw-Hill, New York, 1960.
31. Lance, J. W. *The Mechanism and Management of Headache.* Butterworths, London, 1969.
32. Curran, D. A. and Lance, J. W. Clinical trial of Methysergide and other preparations in the management of migraine. *J. Neurol. Neurosurg. Psychiat.*, 1964, **27**, 463.
33. Sicuteri, F. Prophylactic and therapeutic properties of 1-methyl-lysergic acid butanolamide in migraine: preliminary report. *Int. Arch. Allergy*, 1959, **15**, 300.
34. Wolff, H. G. *Headache and Other Head Pains.* 2nd Edn. Oxford University Press, New York, 1963.
35. Whitty, C. W. The management of migraine. *The Practitioner*, 1964, **192**, 82.
36. Curran, D. A., Hinterberger, H., and Lance, J. W. Methysergide. In *Research and Clinical Studies in Headache: An International Review.* (Edited by Friedman, A. P.), Vol. 1, pp. 74–122. Karger, New York, 1967.
37. Anthony, M., Hinterberger, H., and Lance, J. W. Plasma serotonin in migraine and stress. *Arch. of Neurol.*, 1967, **16**, 544.

38. Lance, J. W., Anthony, M., and Hinterberger, H. The control of cranial arteries by humoral mechanisms and its relation to the migraine syndrome. *Headache*, 1967, **7**, 93.
39. Blaschko, H. and Philpot, F. J. Enzymic oxidation of tryptamine derivations. *J. Physiol.*, 1953, **122**, 403.
40. Kimball, R. W., Friedman, A. P., and Vallejo, E. Effect of serotonin in migraine patients. *Neurology*, 1960, **10**, 107.
41. Dalessio, D. J. Recent experimental studies on headache. *Neurology*, 1963, **13**, 7.
42. Lacey, J. I. Psychophysiological approaches to the evaluation of psychotherapeutic process and outcome. In *Research in Psychotherapy*. (Edited by Rubinstein E. A. and Parloff M. B.), American Psychotherapy Association, Washington, 1959.

ARTICLE 26

Psychosomatic Self-Regulation of Migraine Headaches*

JOSEPH D. SARGENT,† M.D., E. DALE WALTERS, M.A., and
ELMER E. GREEN, Ph.D.

Abstract: A historical perspective regarding research and treatment of the migraine syndrome and the studies in animals and humans relating to control of the autonomic nervous system is given. Pilot experience with 75 subjects is presented, and a detailed clinical account of one successful subject with pertinent research records is given. Reference is made to the implications of this clinical research to psychosomatic medicine.

Migraine headaches have been described in the literature for the past 2000 yr, but it has been only in the past three to four decades that this affliction has been subjected to scientific scrutiny, beginning with Wolff and his colleagues. Since then many investigators have intensely studied this disorder; however, its pathophysiology still remains poorly understood.

It is estimated that as much as 5%–10% of the U.S. population suffers from migraine attacks. As yet, no effective treatment has been developed that does not have significant side effects and risks that seriously affect patients' acceptance. The plethora of recommended treatment methods is evidence of the lack of a truly successful treatment for migraine.

For the most part, migraine attacks, although intensely disabling at times, are a benign disorder for which patients are often overly medicated and are frequently given potentially addicting drugs. Because this type of

*Reprinted from *Seminars in Psychiatry*, Vol. 5, No. 4 (November), 1973, 415–428. Copyright © 1973 by Grune & Stratton, Inc. With permission from Grune & Stratton, Inc. and Joseph D. Sargent, M.D.

†Reprint requests should be addressed to Dr. Joseph D. Sargent, Department of Neurology, Neurosurgery and Internal Medicine, Menninger Foundation, Topeka, Kans. 66601.

headache poses such a difficult problem, any possible approach that can safely answer this enigma merits study, and such an approach is the use of autogenic feedback training to control blood flow dysfunction in migraine.

BACKGROUND

Possible Mechanisms for Migraine Attacks

Graham and Wolff were the first to show that the pulsation of the temporal artery during the headache phase was increased[8]. Their work was based on observations of ergotamine tartrate effects on extracranial vessels in relief of migraine attacks. Ergotamine tartrate diminished the increased amplitude of the arterial pulsation with corresponding relief of the headache. These results seemed reasonable in view of the previous work with histamine, which had clearly shown that stretched extracranial arteries were capable of producing pain[3, 19].

Schumacher and Wolff, working further with methods to increase intracranial pressure and the administration of amyl nitrite, reached the following conclusions: "The essential migraine phenomena result from dysfunction of cranial arteries and represent contrasts in vascular mechanisms and vascular beds. Preheadache disturbances follow occlusive vasoconstriction of cerebral arteries, where the headache results from dilation and distension chiefly of branches of external carotid arteries"[26]. Thus, the vascular theory of migraine was born.

A chance cerebral angiogram done on a patient while in a classic migraine attack showed a diminution in the size of the internal carotid system with reflux into the vertebral vessels during the prodromal phase. At the beginning of the headache phase, blood flow returned to normal[4]. O'Brien has shown a profound reduction in blood flow in the cerebral cortex with the changes lasting much longer than the aura. This change may even occur without symptoms and is generalized and bilateral in distribution. From this evidence it can be concluded that each attack of migraine is biphasic with the occurrence of the aura being "an accidental expression of a more generalized process"[14].

Wolff proposed in his neurogenic theory of migraine headache that vasodilation of the cerebral circulation occurred whenever adequate blood supply to the brain is endangered. If cerebrovascular dilation is great enough, the extracranial arteries will dilate and release a number of chemical factors with production of edema and a lowering of pain threshold. What initiates vasoconstriction is not clearly delineated[30].

In recent years, investigators have postulated that an agent (or agents) causing vasoconstriction may be released to start the headache sequence. Sicuteri has proposed that such liberated chemical substances are amines such as norepinephrine, epinephrine, or serotonin, all powerful vasoconstrictors[28]. Other biochemical agents implicated in the headache sequence are acetylcholine, adenosine, triphosphate, bradykinin, and histamine[15]. Of these, serotonin may be the most important one, since under some circumstances it can also be a vasodilator substance[16]. In the migraine attack, some migrainous subjects have excreted increased amounts of catecholamine end-products, particularly, 5HIAA from serotonin and VMA from norepinephrine and epinephrine[28]. Lance, Anthony, and Hinterberger have shown a corresponding reduction in blood serotonin levels[12].

According to Friedman and Elkind, "Methysergide maleate (Sansert) has proven to be the most useful prophylactic agent in migraine"[6]. Interestingly, this medicine is an anti-serotonin agent and has two actions—inhibition of central vasomotor reflex effects and accentuation of peripheral vasoconstriction produced by catecholamines. Also ergotamine tartrate has significant central effects, in addition to its well-known peripheral vasoconstrictor effect, as demonstrated in man and animals[8, 21, 22, 30]. Thus, Friedman concludes that the "traditional view that migraine consists of phases of vasoconstriction and vasodilation is far too simplified, and it is apparent that migraine is a complex vasomotor disturbance"[7].

Because the migraine syndrome is a multi-faceted clinical disorder, some investigators have postulated a dysfunction in the hypothalamus as the provoking element in the attack. Thus, Graham has suggested that the hypothalamus can profoundly influence the autonomic control of the peripheral vasculature and has postulated a periodic central disturbance of hypothalamic activity or labile threshold accounting for the periodicity of the migraine attack and providing a mechanism whereby emotional disturbances could be mediated by pathways from the limbic system to the hypothalamus[18]. From three groups of clinical observations, Herburg has proposed an etiologic role in migraine headaches for the variation of hypothalamic activity. These groups of clinical observations are as follows: (1) the peripheral vasomotor involvement as seen in the temporal arteries, conjunctiva, and skin; (2) metabolic and vegetative disturbance, such as variations in water balance, food intake, mood, and sleep; and (3) the "accentuated secondary drives" of the migraine personality, which have been related to hypothalamic activity[11]. Rao and Pearce failed to demonstrate in migraine subjects a disturbance in the hypothalamic–pituitary–adrenal axis using metyrapone and insulin hypoglycemia tests. However, a consistently observed pattern of "hypoglycemia unresponsiveness" suggested a possible hypothalamic dysfunction [20].

Treatment of Migraine

Friedman, commenting on drug therapy in migraine, found "that the results of drug prophylaxis were remarkably similar, irrespective of the drug, and only a few drugs were more effective than a placebo"[7]. Ergotamine tartrate is still the drug of choice for the migraine attack and methysergide maleate has proved to be the most useful prophylactic agent in migraine[7]. However, both of these medications have significant adverse side-effects that may decrease patient acceptance. "In general, the surgical therapy of migraine is not effective and should be discouraged"[7]. In a small, selected number of cases, psychotherapy and treatment of allergic factors precipitating migraine headaches can be beneficial.

In the U.S., there is a sizable segment of poorly controlled migraine sufferers who might welcome a totally new approach to the treatment of migraine.

Research Experience Leading to Pilot Study

Neal Miller recently performed research that challenges the concept that "learning" in the autonomic nervous system is a reflection of skeletal muscle activity. He has shown that heart rate, gastrointestinal contractions, blood pressure, and the rate of saliva and urine formation in animals can be directly controlled through "operant conditioning techniques" via the autonomic nervous system[13]. In humans, there is scientific evidence for voluntary control of the autonomic nervous system through the training techniques of yoga, biofeedback training[5, 10, 23, 24, 27, 29] and the work of Schultz and Luthe on "autogenic training"[25].

Autogenic training, according to Luthe, is a basic therapeutic method of a series of psychophysiologically oriented approaches that are in contrast to other medical or psychologic forms of treatment. It involves the simultaneous regulation of mental and somatic functions. The desired somatic responses are brought about by passive concentration upon phrases or preselected words. The first two specific somatic responses in preliminary training brought under voluntary control are heaviness in the limbs and warmth in the extremities.

In treating migraines, Schultz and Luthe reported that the majority of their patients responded with lessened frequency and intensity of headaches with autogenic training exercises. A number of patients reported a cure after several months of practice and learned to interrupt the onset of an attack by starting autogenic exercises as soon as prodromal symptoms appeared[25].

Biofeedback training, a recently developed technique, holds promise of accelerating psychosomatic self-regulation. This technique, when combined with autogenic phrases, is called autogenic–feedback training and uses visual and auditory devices to show the subject what is happening to normally unconscious bodily functions as he attempts to influence them by his use of mental, emotional, and somatic visualizations. Work in our laboratory has shown that skin temperature in the hands is directly related to blood flow in the hands[23], and an increase in skin temperature of the hand is used as an index of voluntary control of the sympathetic section of the autonomic nervous system.

The possibility of using autogenic–feedback training for migraine patients was suggested by the experience of a research subject who, during the spontaneous recovery from a migraine attack, demonstrated considerable flushing in her hands with an accompanying 10° F rise in 2 min. Knowledge of this event quickly spread throughout the laboratory and prompted two individuals with migraine to volunteer for training in hand temperature control. One was wholly successful and learned to eliminate migraine for the most part. The other had a partially beneficial result, and she was able to somewhat alleviate headache intensity and reduce frequency of headache. On the basis of this prepilot experience, it seemed useful to conduct further study with a number of headache patients in a clinical setting.

RATIONALE

Although considerable research must be conducted before we are certain about the neural mechanisms involved in "voluntary controls" training programs, it seems quite clear that the limbic–hypothalamic axis is an essential part. The classic paper of Papez[17], "A Proposed Mechanism of Emotion," has laid the groundwork for an understanding of bioemotional factors, and additional work has elaborated Papez's position[1]. It seems clear beyond reasonable doubt that the limbic system, the "visceral" or "emotional" brain, is the major responder to psychologic stress and that psychosomatic problems become chronic in somatic processes through numerous interconnections between the limbic system and autonomic control centers in hypothalamic sections of the midbrain. The chain of events might be hypothesized as follows: psychologic response (perception of stimuli) → limbic response → hypothalamic response → autonomic response → somatic response.

In the case of migraine, which seems to be a part of a stress-related syndrome, the somatic response is dysfunction of vascular behavior in the head, related to intense sympathetic dysfunction, if other parts of the syndrome (such as cold hands, due to vasoconstriction) can be used as indicators. Vasoconstriction in the hands is a function only of sympathetic activation and vasodilation is a one-variable indication of decrease of sympathetic outflow. The peripheral vascular structure does not have significant parasympathetic innervation.

With these concepts and facts in mind, it seems reasonable to hypothesize that autogenic–feedback training for hand-warming is effective in amelioration of migraine, because patients are learning to "turn off" excessive sympathetic outflow. Since the sympathetic control centers for vascular behavior are located in subcortical structures, it seems that the attack on vascular dysfunction in the head is linked to a general relaxation of sympathetic outflow, rather than through hydraulic maneuvering of blood in various portions of the body. This hypothesis of sympathetic relaxation rather than blood volume changes per se, as the effective agent in migraine amelioration, is supported by the fact that patients who put their hands in warm water in order to increase the blood volume in the hands usually do not obtain migraine relief. A couple of patients who have obtained a measure of relief in this way have, according to the sympathetic-control hypothesis, merely taught themselves to relax with the conditioned stimulus of warm water.

The limbic system is certainly brought into action by the interaction of patient and machine. Considerable emotion is involved in learning to control the temperature machine, and if this involvement increases the sympathetic activation, then the resultant vasoconstriction causes the hands to cool. In order to "make" the hands get warm, it is literally necessary to learn "passive volition." This includes a condition of relaxed detachment, in which the body is told what to do through autogenic imagery and then is allowed to do it without anxious introspection. Only under this condition, which seems to be opposite to the normal state preceding migraine attack, can the hands be made to become warmer at will. In other words, learning to control hand temperature is a good indicator of learning to control central processes that are associated with vascular dysfunction. It is voluntary control of this functional relationship, in the authors' opinion, that is responsible for migraine relief. It includes normalization of homeostatic balance in hypothalamic control centers.

METHODS

The initial 75 subjects out of a total of approximately 150 in the pilot study have been either self-referred or referred by physicians in the community. Each patient, before participating in the project, had a detailed history, complete physical examination, and laboratory studies (EEG, skull x-rays, echoencephalogram, chest x-ray, serology, CBC, and urinalysis). Subjects with severe psychologic and/or physical disorders were eliminated from the study. There were two with cluster headaches, five with combined headache, 11 with tension headaches, and 57 migraine sufferers.

Each patient received instructions in the use of a "temperature trainer," which indicated the differential temperature between the mid-forehead and the right index finger. He was also given a typewritten sheet containing autogenic phrases. The first group of phrases helped the subject achieve passive concentration and relaxation of the whole body. The second group of phrases focused on the achievement of warmth in the hands. After learning the phrases, the participant dispensed with the typewritten sheet and visualized the changes while watching the temperature trainer. A positive warmth response, as indicated by the trainer, was accomplished by increasing temperature of the hands in comparison to the forehead and helped the subject to learn to observe the change of feeling that occurred in his hands while practicing. Since absolute temperatures were not measured at either site, it was impossible to know whether a positive response indicated an actual increase in hand warmth or a decrease in forehead temperature. However, results from our laboratory with absolute temperature feedback have indicated that the specific change in temperature occurs in the hands rather than in the forehead. Also, most subjects reported that a positive response with the trainer was associated chiefly with the feeling of change in the hands rather than change in the forehead. The coordination between mind–body or psychosomatic responses is an important aspect of the training exercises, because it allows the subject to overcome his initial doubt with respect to the control of basic physiologic processes. A positive response on the trainer reinforces the patient's confidence in doing his exercises.

One month prior to training, a subject charted daily the type of headache, and if a headache was present, he rated headache severity, presence or absence of associated symptoms, degree of disability from the headache, and duration of headache. Also the type, strength, and total number of units taken in 24 hr for each medication used for headache and its associated symptoms were recorded (see Fig. 26.1).

After instruction in the use of the temperature trainer and hand temperature control each participant practiced daily at home and recorded presence or absence of relaxation and warmth in the hands, readings from the trainer at the start and end of each practice session, and the interval of time to detect warmth in the hands from the beginning of the session. Later in the training period, the subject tried to control his headache by warming his hands and estimated his success at doing it. The meticulous recording of all data was expected of each participant while in the study.

At first the subject was seen at weekly intervals until he had a consistent, positive response on the meter and an associated change of feeling in the hands. After mastering the hand-warming technique, he practiced on alternate days without the trainer and usually the trainer could be withdrawn within a month after starting. Subsequently, he was expected to continue daily practice sessions and was encouraged to use hand-warming to help control headache. After the trainer was withdrawn, the participant returned to the clinic every 1–3 mo. During the return visits, pertinent data that may have influenced the patient's headache and his response to the exercises were recorded, and he practiced voluntary relaxation on the warmth trainer. The expected follow-up period was a minimum of a year, preferably for 2–3 yr.

As the data were collected, they were scored, and graphs were plotted so that the subject's progress over 1 yr could be viewed at a glance. The variables evaluated to date are (1) headache intensity, (2) the total of individual analgesics used, and (3) total potency of analgesics used. The subjects rated on a 5-point scale the severity of the most intense period of its activity in each 24-hr period. Each analgesic was assigned a number, representing its potency, the extremes of which were aspirin[1] and morphine[7], and the potency scale represented the sum of strengths of analgesics used in 24 hr.

1. Date							
2. Type of Headache (check one or more) If headache is present check items 3 thru 6	[] Migraine [] Tension [] Sinus [] None	[] Migraine [] Tension [] Sinus [] None	[] Migraine [] Tension [] Sinus [] None	[] Migraine [] Tension [] Sinus [] None	[] Migraine [] Tension [] Sinus [] None	[] Migraine [] Tension [] Sinus [] None	[] Migraine [] Tension [] Sinus [] None
3. Intensity of headache*a *(circle one)*	1 2 3 4	1 2 3 4	1 2 3 4	1 2 3 4	1 2 3 4	1 2 3 4	1 2 3 4
4. Presence of associated symptoms *(circle one)*	YES NO	YES NO	YES NO	YES NO	YES NO	YES NO	YES NO
5. Rate degree of disability from headaches*b *(circle one)*	0 1 2 3 4	0 1 2 3 4	0 1 2 3 4	0 1 2 3 4	0 1 2 3 4	0 1 2 3 4	0 1 2 3 4
6. Length of headache *(In hours)*							
7. Name Strength of Tab., Cap. or No. in 1 Shot 24 hrs	1 2 3 4 5	1 2 3 4 5	1 2 3 4 5	1 2 3 4 5	1 2 3 4 5	1 2 3 4 5	1 2 3 4 5
8. Rate presence of warmth in hand*c *(circle one)*	0 1 2	0 1 2	0 1 2	0 1 2	0 1 2	0 1 2	0 1 2
9. Rate ability to bring warmth to hands*d *(circle one)*	0 1 2 3 4	0 1 2 3 4	0 1 2 3 4	0 1 2 3 4	0 1 2 3 4	0 1 2 3 4	0 1 2 3 4
10. Rate degree of relaxation*e	0 1 2	0 1 2	0 1 2	0 1 2	0 1 2	0 1 2	0 1 2
11. Change of temperature registered on meter							
12. Rate ability to control headaches with exercise*f *(circle one)*	0 1 2	0 1 2	0 1 2	0 1 2	0 1 2	0 1 2	0 1 2

*a 1-Slight
2-Moderate
3-Moderately Severe
4-Severe

*b 0-No interference with activities
1-Interferance with activities
2-Had to go to bed
3-Go to Emergency Room or Doctor's office for treatment
4-Need to be hospitalized

*c 0-None
1-Questionable
2-Present

*d 0-Absent
1-More than 5 minutes
2-Between 3 and 5 minutes
3-Between 1 and 3 minutes
4-Less than 1 minute

*e 0-None
1-Questionable
2-Present

*f 0-None
1-Partially successful
2-Successful

Fig. 26.1. Headache project data collection sheet.

Each patient's progress was evaluated as to degree of improvement, based on the senior author's global clinical judgment with benefit of the plotted data.

As an outgrowth of this work, it seemed necessary to determine the behavior of skin temperature in the forehead and hands as the patient tried to warm his hands. The Biomedical Electronics Laboratory of The Menninger Foundation built a temperature scanner, which measures in rapid sequence skin temperatures from four sites. A number of subjects were evaluated using this temperature scanner.

RESULTS

Work in the headache project, begun almost 4 yr ago, was initially reported after accumulating data on 28 subjects, of whom 19 were afflicted with migrane[23]. A later report was based on the data from 33 migrainous individuals. Of the 33, 32 had migraine attacks and 68%–90% of the patients were considered to be improved in the judgment of three raters[24].

Of the initial 75 subjects in the headache project, approximately 81% of the migraine patients followed for over 150 days were helped to a significant extent. The degree of improvement ranged from slight to very good (see Table 26.1).

Since the initial study with 75 patients, we have worked with approximately 75 additional patients using absolute temperature feedback. Those data have not been completely scored to date. To understand fully what we have done in this study, we feel that it will be particularly helpful to follow one participant from entrance until voluntary withdrawal from the project.

Illustrative Case

Mrs. L. O. was first seen by me in consultation in January, 1971, in a community hospital for a long, complex illness. As a result of this encounter, the patient was started on Tofranil at 10 mg t.i.d. for endogenous depression. Interestingly, the symptom of headache assumed little importance of its own at that time in the midst of other complaints. Eventually her personal physician increased the Tofranil to 100 mg daily with considerable improvement of her depression, but the headache problem continued unabated to the time of my next consultation in October, 1971.

Table 26.1. Classification of Degree and Type of Improvement and Evaluation of Treatment for the Initial 75 Headache Patients.*

Degree of improvement	Type of improvement	Number of migraine patients	
None	Headache activity continued at the same level with little or no reduction in medication	8	19% Not Improved
Slight	Shortened headache duration, for instance, from 24 hr to 12 hr, reduced severity of headache, for instance, from severe to moderate, and reduced frequency of headache, for instance, from 20 headache days/mo to 15/mo	9	
Moderate	All in the slight category and, in addition, aborting headache after its onset by voluntarily relaxing, and some reduction of drug use	9	
Good	All in the slight and moderate categories and, in addition, detection of preheadache symptoms and voluntarily relaxing to avoid headache, and considerable reduction of drug use	10	81% Improved
Very good	All in the slight, moderate and good categories and, in addition, almost complete elimination of drug use for headache relief except for a few brief, isolated episodes	6	
	Total	42	

*The data of the following groups of patients are not included in this table: (1) 15 migraine patients, eight with tension headache and one with cluster headache who did not participate in the project for a criterion of 150 days and (2) five patients with mixed headache (vascular and tension components), one with cluster and three with tension headache who participated for over 150 days, but represented too few cases for evaluation.

At the time of the second consultation the patient was 58 yr old and now complained principally of headaches that seemed typical of migraine and were located always on the right side of the head. A complete physical examination with emphasis on the nervous system and laboratory workup including an EEG, echoencephalogram, and skull x-rays revealed no other causes for headache except for an "abnormal EEG with photic sensitivity and a spike focus in the left temporal region." A repeat EEG in August, 1972, was normal.

She was accepted for participation in the headache project in October, 1971, and concluded her participation in January, 1973. Data were collected on this patient for just over 1 yr. Figure 26.2 shows the patient's progress as indicated by (1) ratings of headache severity, (2) number of analgesic drugs used, and (3) sum of the potency of analgesic drugs used. Base-line data for 1 mo prior to training is also shown. On visual inspection, it can be seen that steady improvement occurred in the control of headache. By the 20th week, mean severity of headache was reported as slight to none and remained at that level except for several slight episodes.

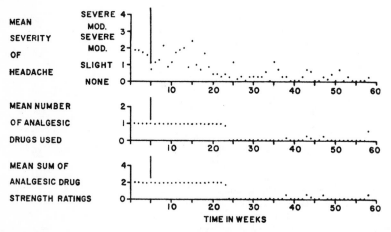

Fig. 26.2. Clinical progress for 1 yr of Mrs. L.O. in the reduction of severity of headache and analgesic drug use during baseline, training, and follow-up.

Figure 26.3 shows the skin temperature behavior of Mrs. L. O. from four body locations over time in a practice session "without headache" during a follow-up office visit. A similar record is shown in Fig. 26.4 of Mrs. L. O. during another follow-up session with a moderately severe frontotemporal migraine, which was partially relieved by hand-warming. Comparison of the headache and nonheadache sessions of Mrs. L. O. indicates some differences in skin temperature behavior: (1) During nonheadache, right-hand skin temperature is warmer throughout the session than left-hand skin temperature, but during headache, right-hand skin temperature is cooler through the session than left-hand skin temperature; (2) zero-time or starting right-hand skin temperature for the headache and nonheadache sessions are approximately the same, i.e., within $1\frac{1}{2}°$ F and (3) zero-time or starting left-hand skin temperature is

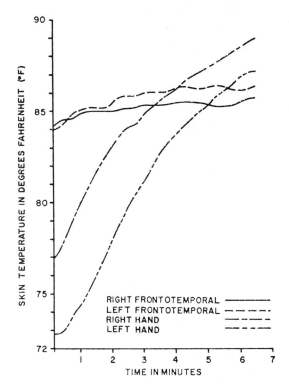

Fig. 26.3. Skin temperature behavior of Mrs. L.O. from four body locations over time in a practice session "without headache" during a follow-up office visit.

warmer by 6° F during headache than during nonheadache. What these observations may mean in terms of vascular behavior in migraine headache is, at present, not certain; however, they will be the subject of continuing research.

DISCUSSION

The results of the initial 75 patients, some of whom were discussed in a previous paper, were reevaluated according to degree of improvement defined by behavioral criteria. It is of interest that a significant degree of improvement was seen in 81% of the 42 migraine patients who were followed for more than 150 days. Furthermore, some individuals do not seem to be helped by using hand-warming to control migraine headache.

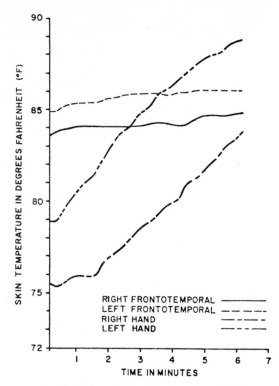

Fig. 26.4. Skin temperature behavior of Mrs. L.O. from four body locations over time in a practice session with right frontotemporal migraine during a follow-up office visit.

Nineteen per cent of the migraine patients received little or no reduction of headache activity and drug use in relief of headache.

Many patients who develop voluntary control of migraine headache progress through a hierarchical series of behaviors. Patients who exemplify headache control at the "good" level, for instance, demonstrate relatively consistent behaviors of detection of preheadache symptoms and voluntary relaxation to avoid migraine attacks; however, this does not exclude, at certain times, headaches that may become temporarily beyond an individual's immediate control, such as awakening from a sound sleep with a moderately severe headache.

From our clinical experience, it seems all normal individuals have the physiologic capability to produce warmth in their hands. Psychologic factors seem to be important in determining success or failure in learning to increase blood flow into hands. Persons who were comfortable with the hypothesis that thoughts and feelings have an influence over bodily processes seemed to learn much faster. Also it seems as though psychologic-mindedness is helpful in learning psychosomatic self-regulation of migraine headache. Younger persons seem to respond quicker to the training than older individuals. A possible explanation for this finding may be that a person's life values increase in rigidity with increasing age, a person may then adjust less readily to new situations. The issue of being in command of situations seems important in patients who could not give up their headache; symptom substitution was found in only one person out of approximately 150 that we have seen. Although the above psychologic factors may be important in learning hand blood flow control in management of migraine attacks, we have no systematic data to support these claims. This is an area in which we plan to do further research.

In our opinion, most of the clinical studies in headache research are carried out for too brief a period of time. In our project, we have a number of subjects who have been followed for 1–3 yr. These extensive follow-ups will help provide hypotheses concerning whether successful subjects can sustain their improvement over a long period of time and whether initially unsuccessful subjects can improve if followed long enough.

The absolute skin temperature scanner has given us flexibility by monitoring four different skin sites at a time and recording these on a paper strip. These permanent tracings are now obtained on all new patients accepted into the project, and therefore, data are available on skin temperature behavior in subjects while voluntarily relaxing.

Since many migraine patients also have tension headache at times, the work of Budzynski, Stoyva, and Adler should be cited here. They report that "in general the results seemed to indicate that chronic tension headache sufferers can be trained to voluntarily lower their striate muscle tension in the face of daily life stresses and to reduce the incidence of tension headaches"[2]. In their program, tension headache patients are given a thorough medical examination to confirm the diagnosis of tension headache. Then, patients received feedback for muscle action potentials or electromyographic activity (EMG) generated in the forehead area. Patients generally received two or three 30-min feedback training sessions per week from 4–8 wk and worked at reducing frontalis EMG to low levels. Patients were encouraged to practice relaxation training at home at least once a day. It was found that (1) both headache activity and EMG levels declined as training progressed and (2) patients reported changes in their day-to-day lives outside the laboratory such as a heightened awareness of maladaptive rising tension, an increasing ability to reduce such tension, and a decreasing tendency to overreact to stress.

Because headache poses such a difficult problem, any possible approach that can safely answer the headache problem merits study. Such an approach is the use of autogenic feedback training to increase hand blood flow for treatment of migraine and the use of frontalis EMG feedback training for tension headaches.

Biofeedback and voluntary control may have usefulness in the treatment of a great number of psychosomatic disorders and may provide new tools to explore the mind–body interface.

The authors think that an important trend is beginning to take place in the areas of psychosomatic disorders and medicine. This is the increasing involvement of the patient in his own treatment. The traditional doctor–patient relationship is giving way slowly to a shared responsibility in which the patient is helped to become aware of his problems, both physical and emotional, and can therefore become a responsible partner in going toward psychosomatic and physical health.

In summary, (1) most migraine patients, aided by Autogenic Feedback Training, learn to voluntarily regulate their headaches; (2) patients develop psychosomatic self-regulation of migraine headache by voluntarily relaxing the sympathetic section of the autonomic nervous system in the hand, thereby increasing the blood flow to that area; (3) the degree of improvement varies across migraine patients, as some patients' improvement is better than others; (4) there seems to be a hierarchy of behaviors through which the migraine patients progress toward regulating their headaches; and (5) during training sessions in the clinic, it has been observed that significant increases occur in hand skin temperatures, while only small changes occur in frontotemporal skin temperatures.

REFERENCES

1. Brady, J. V. The paleocortex and behavioral motivation. In Harlow, H. F. and Woolsey, C. N. (eds.) *Biological and Biochemical Bases of Behavior*, Madison: Univ of Wisconsin Press, 1958.
2. Budzynski, T., Stoyva, J., and Adler, C. Feedback-induced muscle relaxation: Application to tension headache. In Barber, T. X. *et al.* (eds.) *Biofeedback and Self-Control.* Chicago: Aldine-Atherton, 1971.
3. Clark, D., Hough, M., and Wolff, H. G. Experimental studies on headache observations on histamine headaches. *Arch. Neurol. Psychiatry*, 1932, **140**, 23.

4. Dukes, H. T. and Vieth, R. G. Cerebral arteriography during migraine prodrome and headache. *Neurology*, 1964, **14**, 636.
5. Engel, B. T. and Melmon, K. R. Operant conditioning of heart rate in patients with cardiac arrhythmias. *Cond. Reflex.*, 1968, **8**, 130.
6. Friedman, A. P. and Elkind, A. H. Appraisal of methysergide in the treatment of vascular headaches of the migraine type. *JAMA*, 1963, **184**, 125–128.
7. Friedman, A. P. Migraine headaches. *JAMA*, 1972, **222**, 1399–1402.
8. Graham, J. R. and Wolff, H. G. The mechanism of the migraine headache and the action of ergotamine tartrate. *Arch. Neurol. Psychiatry*, 1938, **39**, 737.
9. Green, E. E., Ferguson, D. W., Green, A. M. *et al. Preliminary Report on Voluntary Controls Project: Swami Rama.* Research Department, The Menninger Foundation, June 1970.
10. Green, E. E., Green, A. M., and Walters, E. D. Voluntary control of internal states: Psychological and physiological. In Barber, T. X. *et al.* (eds.) *Biofeedback and Self-Control.* Chicago: Aldine-Atherton, 1971.
11. Herburg, L. J. The hypothalamus and the aetiology of migraine. In Smith, R. (ed.) *Background to Migraine.* London: Heinemann, 1967.
12. Lance, J. W., Anthony, M., and Hinterberger, H. The control of cranial arteries by humoral mechanism and its relation to the migraine syndrome. *Headache*, 1967, **7**, 93–102.
13. Miller, N. E. Learning of visceral and glandular responses. *Science*, 1969, **163**, 434–445.
14. O'Brien, M. D. The relationship between aura symptoms and cerebral blood flow changes in the prodrome of migraine. In Dalessio, D. J., Dalsgaard-Nielsen, T., and Diamond, S. (eds.) *Proceedings of the International Headache Symposium*, May 16–18, 1971, Elsinore, Denmark. Basle, Switzerland, Sandoz, Ltd, 1971.
15. Ostfield, A. M. Migraine headache, its physiology and biochemistry. *JAMA*, 1960, **174**, 110–112.
16. Page, I. H. Serotonin (5 hydroxy tryptamine). *Physiol. Rev.*, 1954, **34**, 536–588.
17. Papez, J. W. A proposed mechanism of emotion. *Arch. Neurol. Psychiatry*, 1937, **38**, 725–743.
18. Pearce, J. *Migraine: Clinical Features, Mechanisms and Management.* Springfield, Ill.: Thomas, 1969.
19. Pickering, G. W. and Hess, W. Observations on the mechanism of headache produced by histamine. *Clin. Sci.*, 1933, **51**, 77.
20. Rao, L. W. and Pearce, J. Hypothalamic-pituitary-adrenal axis studies in migraine with special reference to insulin sensitivity. *Brain*, 1971, **94**, 289–298.
21. Rothlin, E. Recherches experimentales sur l'ergotamine, alcaloi de specifique de l'ergot de seigle. *Arch. Int. Pharmacodyn. Ther.*, 1923, **27**, 459.
22. Rothlin, E. and Cerlitti, A. Untersucmumgere uber die kreislauf wirkumg des ergotamine. *Helv. Physiol. Pharmacol. Acta*, 1941, **7**, 333.
23. Sargent, J. D., Green, E. E., and Walters, E. D. The use of autogenic feedback training in a pilot study of migraine and tension headaches. *Headache*, 1972, **12**, 120–124.
24. Sargent, J. D., Green, E. E., and Walters, E. D. Preliminary report on the use of autogenic feedback training in the treatment of migraine and tension headaches. *Psychosom. Med.*, 1973, **35**, 129–135.
25. Schultz, J. H. and Luthe, W. *Autogenic Therapy*, vol 1. New York: Grune & Stratton, 1969.

26. Schumacher, G. A. and Wolff, H. G. Experimental studies of headache. *Arch. Neurol. Psychiatry*, 1941, **45**, 199.

27. Schwartz, G. E., Shapiro, D., and Trusky, B. Learned control of cardiovascular integration in man through operant conditioning. *Psychosom. Med.*, 1971, **33**, 57–62.

28. Sicuteri, F. Vasoneuroreactive substances and their implications in vascular pain. In Friedman, A. P. (ed.) *Research and Clinical Studies of Headache.* Baltimore: Williams & Wilkins, 1967.

29. Weiss, T. and Engel, B. T. Operant conditioning of heart rate in patients with premature ventricular contractions. *Psychosom. Med.*, 1971, **38**, 301–321.

30. Wolff, G. H. *Headache and Other Head Pain* (2nd ed.) New York: Oxford Univ. Press, 1963.

CHAPTER 7

The Respiratory System: Asthma

Bronchial asthma is a widespread, potentially serious respiratory problem affecting over four million individuals in this country alone (Rowe & Rowe, 1963). Often beginning in childhood, this disease may require continued medical treatment throughout the patient's life. Asthmatic attacks typically manifest themselves by periods of labored breathing, shortness of breath, coughing, and wheezing. The etiology of asthma is unclear and may include such factors as allergy (Rowe & Rowe, 1963), respiratory infection (Forman, 1951), and psychophysiological reactions to life stress (Schneer, 1963). Traditional psychological formulations of asthmatic individuals have discussed faulty maternal relationships (French & Alexander, 1941; Miller & Baruch, 1951), and a higher degree of hostile and dependent behavior (Fine, 1963).

In many instances remission is achieved quickly by chemical compounds such as epinephrine and cortical steroids, or diet restrictions for allergenic substances (Rowe & Rowe, 1963). However, because of the overt nature of its predominant symptoms, asthmatic episodes are susceptible to environmental control and may persist in spite of traditional treatment regimens. Consciously or unconsciously, some patients may learn that attacks are followed by predictable consequences—alarmed reactions on the part of family members, sympathy, medication, or the avoidance of routine responsibilities. These consequences, despite their intended helpful effect, may be reinforcing to the patient and so increase the frequency, severity, or duration with which the attacks occur. For other patients, attacks may be elicited by specific emotional situations, and occur independently of the consequences they produce. In short, we are again presented with a disease entity which, independent of its origin or physiological underpinnings, seems to be influenced by environmental factors. Because these factors may affect the patient's well being, careful attention should be directed to their identification and control.

The implications of these observations should be clear. Individuals who provide care to asthmatic patients may require instruction in behavior therapy techniques. An increased sensitivity to the social aspects of this disease should allow for greater utilization of these individuals in a manner that will facilitate rather than retard the patient's progress.

Four behavioral approaches to the treatment of asthma are described in this chapter. In the first two selections, asthmatic symptoms are viewed as operant behavior and treatments designed within the framework of operant conditioning. Neisworth and Moore (Article 27) taught parents the techniques of extinction and reinforcement of incompatible behavior to reduce the duration of coughing, wheezing, and gasping in a 7-year-old asthmatic boy who had not responded favorably to medication regimens. Treatment procedures involved the discontinuation of parental attention (including administration of medication) when bedtime asthmatic attacks occurred. Concurrently, the child was reinforced with money for attack-free nights. With these simple procedures, the parents were able to reduce the duration of attacks from a baseline average of 70 minutes per night to approximately five minutes per night. The effectiveness of changing the parents' behavior toward their child was demonstrated by a reversal design.

Creer (Article 28) used a timeout procedure to reduce the frequency and duration of hospitalization in two 10-year-old asthmatic boys. Both of these children were suspected of exaggerating attacks and inventing new symptoms to prolong their hospital stay. Prior to the initiation of therapy, these children spent a majority of their time in the hospital rather than participating in a program at an asthmatic research center. After a six-week baseline, Creer implemented a timeout procedure, which in this instance entailed hospitalizing each child in a private room, reducing visitation rights, and restricting such privileges as television and comic books, as well as the opportunity to dine with other children. Subsequently, the duration of hospitalization was reduced from 67% to 7% in one child, and from 55% to 5% in the other. Interestingly, neither of the children attributed much significance to the use of the timeout procedure, despite the fact that the incidence of rehospitalization increased when timeout was temporarily discontinued.

Cooper (Article 29) and Alexander *et al.* (Article 30) described two treatment procedures based upon a respondent conditioning paradigm.

Cooper describes a 24-year-old woman whose asthmatic attacks appeared to be related to specific areas of emotional stress. This patient had suffered from asthma for over seven years, with a striking increase in the frequency of attacks during the two years prior to the initiation of therapy. During this time, any minor emotional upset was capable of eliciting attacks. Furthermore, the onset of frigidity during the year prior to therapy compounded her problems, since intercourse became an additional source of anxiety. Desensitizing the patient to conditions of anger, excitement, and other forms of stress proved remarkably successful in eliminating the asthma as well as the frigidity.

Alexander *et al.* pursued a slightly different approach that involved instructing asthmatic children in relaxation procedures. Investigating the utility of the customary admonition to have asthmatic patients sit quietly and relax during acute attacks, they compared the relative effectiveness of systematic relaxation training with sitting quietly, in two groups of asthmatic children. One group of subjects received three sessions of relaxation training, while the other was simply instructed to sit quietly for the same period of time. Using peak expiratory flow rates (PEFR) as a dependent measure, the authors demonstrated that relaxation training significantly increased respiratory function as measured by PEFR. Surprisingly, children who had been instructed to sit quietly showed a slight decrease in PEFR.

Points of key importance in this chapter include:

1. Predominant asthmatic symptoms such as shortness of breath, coughing, and wheezing are susceptible to environmental control. Environmental factors that influence these symptoms deserve careful attention in developing therapy plans.
2. Behavioral techniques shown to be effective in reducing asthmatic disturbances include extinction, timeout from positive reinforcement, and differential reinforcement of incompatible behavior, as well as systematic desensitization and relaxation training. These techniques may be used independently, where a predominant psychogenic origin is clearly indicated, or in conjunction with traditional medical treatments to supplement patient care plans.
3. The therapeutic use of behavioral methods by members of the patient's immediate family, or other significant individuals in the patient's natural environment, is demonstrated by the results reported here and shows great promise as an effective, practical and economic strategy for improving patient care.

4. Although it seems clear that asthma is etiologically related to allergies and other physiologic causes, the significance of the interaction between physiologic factors and environmental maintenance cannot be overemphasized.

REFERENCES

Fine, R. The personality of the asthmatic child. In Schneer, H. (ed.) *The Asthmatic Child: Psychosomatic Approach to Problems.* New York: Harper & Row, 1963.

Forman, J. The differential diagnosis of asthma. In Abramson, H. (ed.) *Treatment of Asthma.* Baltimore: Williams & Wilkins, 1951.

French, T. and Alexander, F. Psychogenic factors in bronchial asthma (Part I). *Psychosomatic Medicine Monograph IV.* Washington: National Research Council, 1941.

Miller, H. and Baruch, D. Maternal rejection in the treatment of bronchial asthma. In Abramson, H. (ed.) *Treatment of Asthma.* Baltimore: Williams & Wilkins, 1951.

Rowe, A. and Rowe, A. *Bronchial Asthma: Its Diagnosis and Treatment.* Springfield: Charles C. Thomas, 1963.

Schneer, H. (ed.). *The Asthmatic Child: Psychosomatic Approach to Problems and Treatment.* New York: Harper & Row, 1963.

ARTICLE 27

Operant Treatment of Asthmatic Responding with the Parent as Therapist*

JOHN T. NEISWORTH†

Pennsylvania State University

and

FLORESE MOORE

Wilmington Special School District, Delaware

Abstract: Pronounced reduction of chronic asthmatic responding in a 7-year-old boy was achieved through parental management of "therapeutic" contingencies. Treatment was begun with professional guidance by the mother after she had attended several instructional sessions in operant conditioning. Reinstatement of original consequences and return to treatment contingencies produced corresponding changes in the duration of asthmatic behavior. An 11-month follow-up confirmed the stability of the therapeutic changes, general improvement in the child's health, and the absence of any demonstrable deleterious side-effects. The results suggest closer and extended scrutiny of operant techniques in the treatment of asthma and other allergic responses.

Applying empirically based principles and strategies, behavior therapies are increasingly promoting the feasibility and desirability of using the home as the setting and parents as the agents for child therapy. This is in contradistinction to traditional approaches that employ hypothetical models, clinical settings, and highly trained personnel.

A growing number of successful studies dealing with various child problems is demonstrating the economy of time and professional effort of behaviorally based therapies. Representative of such studies are those of

---

*Reprinted from *Behavior Therapy*, 1972, **3**, 95–99. Copyright © 1972 by Academic Press, Inc. With permission from Academic Press, Inc. and John T. Neisworth.

†Requests for reprints should be addressed to John T. Neisworth, S-24 Human Development Building, University Park, PA 16802.

Williams (1959), O'Leary, O'Leary, and Becker (1967), and Zeilberger, Sampen, and Sloane (1968) dealing generally with parental treatment of disruptive or aggressive child behaviors. Lal and Lindsley (1968), and Conger (1970) provide examples of somatic problems responsive to therapy conducted by mothers. Results and descriptions of training groups of mothers as reinforcement therapists are reported by Lindsley (1966), and Hirsch (1968).

The problem of interest in this study, asthma, has received much attention from psychoanalytic perspectives but rarely has asthma been conceived of as an operant (see review by Hirt, 1965). Turnbull (1962) has summarized previous research that views asthma as a learned response. Most of this research, however, has employed a respondent rather than operant paradigm. While asthma-like responses can be respondently conditioned, extinction rapidly occurs in the absence of UCS, and it is suggested that operant reinforcement could account for maintenance and amplification of respondently or organically produced asthmatic responses. While this study does not investigate the origin of asthmatic responses in a child, it does report successful treatment through operant procedures.

HISTORY AND DIAGNOSIS

The patient, a 7-year-old boy, was the oldest of two sons of American parents who resided in Japan until the patient was 18 months old. At the age of 6 months, the boy was diagnosed as asthmatic; he was frequently hospitalized for periods of 1–4 weeks. Doctors stated that his condition would probably improve upon the family's return to the United States. However, by the age of two the patient continued to display repeated asthmatic attacks (coughing, wheezing, abrupt inspiration) which required frequent visits to the hospital emergency room for immediate relief. From the ages of 2 to 7 years, the boy was seen almost monthly by a specialist due to continued severity of the problem. Various medications were administered and dietary restrictions imposed in an effort to ameliorate the condition.

Results of the various medical attempts were questionable; the child still had frequent attacks and visits to hospital emergency rooms remained necessary.

By the time it was suggested that the child might be helped by behavior therapy, a pattern of parental concern and continued attention to the problem had been well established. Typically, the mother would caution the child not to overexert himself, not to eat certain foods, and to be sure to take his medicine. She described the child as "nervous" and reported that emotional upsets or excitement precipitated the child's attacks. Of particular concern were the child's prolonged wheezing and coughing at bedtime. Further investigation revealed that both medicine and sympathetic attention were given especially during the bedtime asthmatic episodes.

After exposure to operant conditioning rationale and treatment procedures, the mother herself suggested that the child's problem might well be conceived of in operant terms and treated accordingly. She analyzed her own behavior towards the child and suggested that it might be supporting or aggravating the problem. Specifically, it was hypothesized first, that asthmatic responding was being maintained or amplified by the presentation of verbal and tactile attention (as well as medicine) during or immediately after a seizure, and second, that behavior incompatible with coughing, wheezing, and generally "being sick" was not being reinforced. A schedule of differential reinforcement for being "sick" as opposed to being well seemed to be operating.

INTERVENTION AND RESULTS

In addition to the case history, and prior to any systematic changes in the contingencies related to asthmatic behaviors, data were collected for 10 days to provide a baseline (Fig. 27.1). It was decided to record only nighttime in-bed responding since this was the occasion of most intense behavior; further, it was not possible to obtain accurate daytime data. Due to the nature of the responses and data collection restrictions, duration rather than frequency was chosen as the response measure. Coughing, wheezing, gasping, and similar responses lacking in discreteness and often overlapping in occurrence made frequency counts difficult. Response time, however, was relatively easy to record. All data were collected each evening in the home of the child by the junior author.

Immediately following the baseline phase, two systematic treatment strategies were initiated. First, based on the hypothesis that parental attention to the problem was reinforcing the behavior, an extinction procedure was employed. The parents agreed to discontinue all attention and administrations of medicines during bedtime asthmatic attacks. The child was put to bed with the usual affectionate interactions between

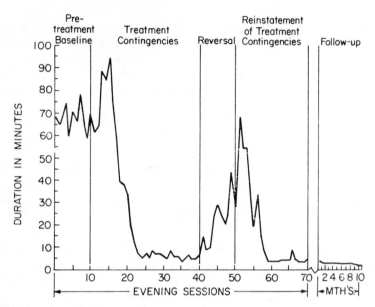

Fig. 27.1. Duration of bedtime asthmatic responding as a function of contingency changes.

parents and child. Once the bedroom door was closed, however, no further interaction occurred until morning.

Because extinction procedures often require extended use, it was decided to implement an additional strategy; reinforcement of incompatible behavior. Specifically, the child was told he could have lunch money (instead of taking his lunch to school) if he coughed less frequently on a given night than the night before. This contingency permitted reinforcement for even slight improvements in the behavior, making reinforcement highly probable and progress easy.

It can be seen from Fig. 27.1 that the initial effect of the intervention program was to increase the duration of coughing and wheezing. (We have frequently found this initial inflation of behavior on an extinction schedule). However, after 7 days the effects of treatment became noticeable; by Day 23 the behavior reached a low that remained somewhat stable.

To provide further evidence of the efficacy of the treatment contingencies, the parents reluctantly agreed to reversal procedures. Specifically, attention and medication again were given during the brief asthmatic episodes. (Lunch money, however, was not withdrawn, i.e., the child received money on a noncontingent basis.) As Fig. 27.1 shows, response duration increased quickly and climbed towards baseline intensity. At this point, the parents urged a return to the treatment contingencies. This was done, resulting again in an initial increase in response duration followed by a drop to a stable new low of about 5 min. As a follow-up, the parents periodically were requested to time bedtime coughing. This reminded the parents of the need to continue the new contingency arrangements and provided follow-up data. During 11 months of such follow-up inquiries and data, the problem remained at essentially the treatment low (between 2–7 min).

DISCUSSION

The systematic management of two simple contingencies resulted in a drastic reduction in the duration of nighttime asthmatic responding in a 7-year-old boy. Withholding of attention during coughing and wheezing and "payment" for reduction of such responding successfully and quickly effected changes that years of medical treatment alone could not. Reinstatement of the original cough-attention contingency relationship produced a return to prolonged asthmatic episodes. Minimal responding was again established upon restoration of treatment contingencies. An 11-month follow-up failed to reveal any appreciable increment in the child's nighttime asthmatic attacks. Indeed, the parents reported that daytime coughing also sharply declined and pediatrician's reports indicated a general improvement in health. This study, which adds to the growing literature that stresses the crucial role of "therapy" conducted by parents, does not purport to obviate "organic" factors in the etiology or maintenance of asthmatic responses. Rather, it pinpoints the dramatic role that environmental contingencies may have in the amplification and attenuation of the problem.

REFERENCES

Conger, J. C. The treatment of encopresis by the management of social consequences. *Behavior Therapy*, 1970, **1**, 386–390.

Hirt, M. L. *Psychological and Allergic Aspects of Asthma.* Springfield, Il.: Charles C. Thomas, 1965.

Hirsch, I. S. Training mothers in groups as reinforcement therapists for their own children. *Dissertation Abstracts*, 1968, **28** (11-B), 4–156.

Lal, H. and Lindsley, O. R. Therapy of chronic constipation in a young child by rearranging social contingencies. *Behaviour Research and Therapy*, 1968, **6**, 484–485.

Lindsley, O. R. Parents handling behavior at home. *Johnstone Bulletin*, 1966, **9**, 27–36.

O'Leary, K. D., O'Leary, S., and Becker, W. C. Modification of a deviant sibling interaction pattern in the home. *Behaviour Research and Therapy*, 1967, **5**, 113–120.

Turnbull, J. W. Asthma conceived as a learned response. *Journal of Psychosomatic Research*, 1962, **6**, 59–70.

Williams, C. D. The elimination of tantrum behavior by extinction procedures. *Journal of Abnormal and Social Psychology*, 1959, **59**, 269.

Zeilberger, J., Sampen, S., and Sloane, H. N. Modification of a child's problem behaviors in the home with the mother as therapist. *Journal of Applied Behavior Analysis*, 1968, **1**, 47–53.

The Use of a Time-Out from Positive Reinforcement Procedure with Asthmatic Children*

THOMAS L. CREER

Children's Asthma Research Institute and Hospital, Denver, Colorado

The practice of systematically modifying inappropriate behavior by withdrawing a situation where reinforcement occurs (the "time-out" procedure) has increased in recent years. An example of the use of this technique is the study of Wolf, Risley, and Mees[1]. These investigators found that they were able to eliminate tantrums and self-destructive responses in a 3-yr-old boy by making placement alone in a room contingent upon such behaviors.

The present study analyzed the effect of the time-out procedure in modifying the behavior of two asthmatic boys.

Subjects and Setting

The subjects were two, 10-yr-old boys who were residents at the Children's Asthma Research Institute and Hospital (CARIH) in Denver, Colorado. This is a residential treatment center for approximately 160 children with intractable asthma. While here, the children attend public schools, participate in a wide variety of recreational and social activities and, except during attacks of asthma, are managed as if they were asthma-free. One subject, Jack had been a resident at CARIH for 18 months at the beginning of the study. During this period, he was admitted to the institute's hospital on 49 separate occasions for a total of 137 days. Don, the other subject, had been at CARIH for 16 months when the study

---

*Reprinted from *Journal of Psychosomatic Research*, 1970, **14**, 117–120, Pergamon Press. Copyright © 1970. With permission from Pergamon Press and Thomas L. Creer.

was initiated. In this span, however, he was hospitalized 88 times for a total of 248 days. While the Ss were primarily admitted because of asthma, they were frequently hospitalized when other children would be treated medically and released. The reason the Ss received this special treatment was that they appeared capable of exaggerating their asthma attacks by hyperventilating, failing to heed early warnings of asthma and seeking medical attention while the attacks were relatively mild, etc. Once admitted, furthermore, the Ss would sometimes remain hospitalized long after all symptoms or indications of asthma had disappeared. This occurred because each S had a series of physical complaints they would present to the medical staff. Jack, for example, frequently reported that he was experiencing stomach pains. This invariably would initiate a series of examinations and tests, all of which would delay Jack's release from the hospital. Don, on the other hand, sometimes complained of chest pains. Such comments always elicited a complete mobilization of the medical staff because Don had a history of at least two cardiac arrests. After several episodes where their complaints were medically unverified and after observing that the Ss were spending an increasing amount of time in the hospital, the medical staff were becoming perplexed as to how they should manage the Ss. While they were convinced that the pair malingered a great deal of the time, they were reluctant to completely ignore the Ss' complaints for fear that these reports might, at times, prove to be valid. It was at this time that the present study was initiated.

Dependent Variables

The two measures employed in this study were frequency and duration of hospitalizations. Both of these variables were under the sole control of a staff physician who, based on a number of criteria, decided whether the Ss should be admitted to or discharged from the hospital. The criteria for hospital admittance most frequently followed in this study, for example, was to hospitalize either S when the physician had prescribed two or more inhalations of isoproternol within a 24 hr period. The Ss were most commonly discharged, on the other hand, when they exhibited a relative decrease in such asthmatic responses as wheezing, coughing up mucus, etc. The nursing staff at CARIH determine, after consultation with members of the Behavior Science Division, how a child will be treated behaviorally while he or she is in the hospital. This meant that the nurses and their aides were primarily responsible for the implementation of the experimental conditions utilized in the study. They were never involved, however, in making the decisions as to when the Ss would be admitted to or discharged from the hospital.

Since knowledge of the experiment may have modified the attitudes of the medical personnel with regard to the two Ss and, in turn, have contaminated the findings of the study, several precautions were taken. First, the physician responsible for admitting and discharging the Ss from the hospital was not informed that a study was taking place. Secondly, only the E was aware of the nature of the experimental design employed in the study. Finally, only the nursing staff was notified by the E as to which experimental condition was to be in operation at any one time. No instructions about the sequence of conditions was given to the nurses, nor was *a priori* information issued about the duration of each experimental phase. Post-study discussions with the physician responsible for the care of the Ss revealed that he had been unaware that a study was being conducted with the two boys. Conversations with members of the nursing staff, on the other hand, indicated that they had not been concerned with the overall nature of the experimental design employed in the investigation, but had merely attempted to comply with the specific instructions provided them by the E.

EXPERIMENTAL CONDITIONS

Baseline

For 6 weeks, a record was taken of both the number and duration of hospitalizations for each S. It was noted that once admitted, the Ss remained at least 24 hr for purposes of observation.

Time-Out

During this 6 week period, the nursing staff and their aides were given the following instructions to be used whenever either of the two Ss was admitted:

1. Each boy will be placed in a room by himself whenever he is hospitalized.
2. The Ss can receive no visitors other than medical or nursing personnel.
3. Both boys are not allowed to visit with other patients while in the hospital.

4. Only books related to school work are allowed to be in the Ss' possession. Comic books and television sets are forbidden.
5. The Ss can leave their room only to go to the restroom. The nursing staff will prevent the Ss from visiting with other patients on their way to and from the restroom.
6. The boys will eat all of their meals in their room by themselves rather than joining the other children in the hospital dining room. These instructions were strictly adhered to at all times during this phase of the study.

Reversal

The above instructions were rescinded during this segment of the experiment. Thus, each time the Ss were hospitalized in this three week period, they were treated like other patients in that they could socialize with others, they could view TV or read comic books, and they were allowed to have visitors.

Time-Out

The instructions noted in the first time-out phase were reinstated for 8 weeks. This part of the experiment was terminated simultaneously with the ending of the school year.

RESULTS

The time-out procedure was effective in reducing both the mean number of hospitalizations and days hospitalized for both Ss. As can be seen in Table 28.1, Don was admitted on 16 separate occasions during the baseline period for a total of 28 days. This amounted to his spending an average of 4.67 days in the hospital each week. During the first time-out phase of experiment, on the other hand, Don was admitted 6 times for a total of 8 days or for an average of 1.33 days per week. Table 28.2 shows that Jack exhibited similar behavior. Whereas he was admitted ten times for a total of 23 days during the baseline period, he was hospitalized for only one 3 day period when the time-out was introduced. The average number of days hospitalized each week during these two periods was, respectively, 3.83 and 0.50 days.

In the reversal segment of the study, there was an increase in both the

Table 28.1. The Frequency and Duration of Hospitalizations for Don.

Conditions	No. of weeks	No. of hospitalizations	No. of days hospitalized	x̄ no. of hospitalizations per week	x̄ no. of days per hospitalization	x̄ no. of days hospitalized per week	Percentage of time hospitalized
Pre-study	69	88	248	1.28	2.82	3.59	51
Baseline	6	16	28	2.67	1.75	4.67	67
Time-out	6	6	8	1.00	1.33	1.33	19
Reversal	3	4	8	1.33	2.00	2.67	38
Time-out	8	2	4	0.25	2.00	0.50	7

Table 28.2. The Frequency and Duration of Hospitalizations for Jack.

Conditions	No. of weeks	No. of hospitalizations	No. of days hospitalized	x̄ no. of hospitalizations per week	x̄ no. of days per hospitalization	x̄ no. of days hospitalized per week	Percentage of time hospitalized
Pre-study	78	49	137	0.63	2.80	1.76	25
Baseline	6	10	23	1.67	2.30	3.83	55
Time-out	6	1	3	0.17	3.00	0.50	7
Reversal	3	2	5	0.67	2.50	1.67	24
Time-out	8	2	3	0.25	1.50	0.38	5

frequency and duration of admittances per week for both Ss. In considering only duration, for example, Don was admitted an average of 2.67 days each week while, for the same period, Jack was hospitalized an average of 1.67 days. The reinstatement of the time-out procedure again brought this behavior under control, however, with the mean weekly hospitalizations dropping to 0.50 days for Don and to 0.38 days for Jack.

The percentage of time each of the Ss was hospitalized is worthy of note. Whereas Don spent 67 per cent of his time in the hospital during the baseline period, this dropped to 7 per cent during the final phase of the study. Similar findings were obtained with Jack. The percentage of time hospitalized decreased from 55 per cent during the baseline period to 5 per cent during the second time-out phase of the study.

For each S, a One-Way Analysis of Variance was performed on both the number of hospital admittances and days hospitalized each week that occurred during the course of the study. As is shown in Table 28.3, the analyses were all significant at beyond the 0.01 level of significance.

Table 28.3.   Statistical Treatment of Frequency and Duration of Hospitalizations for Both Ss.

| | One way analysis of variance | | Orthogonal comparisons | |
	Frequency	Duration	Frequency	Duration
Don	12.99	7.96	11.71	14.20
Jack	8.34	7.96	13.13	20.44
	df = 3/19		df = 1/19	

All values significant beyond the 0.01 level of significance.

Orthogonal comparisons of the two time periods against the baseline and reversal phases of the study are also shown in Table 28.3. These comparisons were also significant beyond the 0.01 level of significance. These statistical results indicate that the modification of the hospital behavior of the Ss occurred because of the experimental conditions employed in the study and not because of random variation in the Ss' behavior.

DISCUSSION

This study demonstrated that time-out from positive reinforcement was effective in reducing both the frequency and duration of hospital admittances in two asthmatic children. The experimental procedure did not, however, prevent the Ss from seeking medical attention or from being hospitalized when they experienced valid attacks of asthma or other physical ailments.

Not all asthmatic children display the same behaviors with regard to hospitalization as those shown by the Ss. Frequently, some asthmatic children will postpone treatment until they become cyanotic and have to be brought to the hospital by others. Once admitted, furthermore, they are apt to bombard attending nurses and other medical personnel with questions as to when they will be released. This behavior, when considered along with the responses of the Ss in this study, suggest that how a child reacts to his or her asthma attacks may be, to a large degree, a function of his or her reinforcement history. The histories of the two Ss, for example, appear to be similar. According to comments in their records, each boy had been considered in hospitalizations prior to their arriving at CARIH, the "darlings of the nursing staff." In the case of one of the Ss, Don, it had been necessary to transfer one of his nurses because she displayed undue consideration and attention to her patient, even when she was supposedly off-duty. Such treatment, however, was in sharp contrast to that accorded the Ss by their parents. Both have mothers who were asthmatic as children and who were, according to their statements, personally aware of how a child can use asthma to manipulate others. To insure that this did not occur, the Ss' parents reported that they had attempted to take a firmer approach in managing the Ss than was the case with their other children. It is possible that the contrasting behaviors exhibited toward them at home and in the hospital may account for the responses exhibited by the Ss at the beginning of the study.

The Ss were never informed that they were participating in a study. In a post-investigation interview, however, Jack was able to verbalize some awareness of the time-out procedure used in the study. Don, on the other hand, never seemed to have grasped the contingencies of the investigation. Rather, he dismissed the time-out procedure with the complaint that "the hospital is no fun no more."

SUMMARY

This study demonstrated the use of the time-out from positive reinforcement in effectively curtailing the frequency and duration of hospitalizations in two asthmatic children.

REFERENCE

A Case of Bronchial Asthma Treated by Behavior Therapy*

A. J. COOPER

Barrow Hospital, Barrow Gurney, Bristol

Abstract: Desensitization employing the reciprocal inhibition principle was applied to a case of intractable bronchial asthma. Therapy has resulted in dramatic and maintained improvement. An explanation, in terms of learning theory, is given on the development of the psychosomatic symptom, and the rationale of the treatment explained. It is suggested that should relapse occur, booster treatments administered on an out-patient basis would be a feasible proposition.

INTRODUCTION

Psychosomatic medicine in the broadest sense, is concerned with the inter-relationship between psychological and physical manifestations of illness. A patient of Pinel's once said: "The source of all my sickness is in my stomach. It's so sensitive that sorrow, pain, pleasure, and in fact any kind of spiritual affliction has its origins there. I think with my stomach if one can say that." This statement, and similar ones heard every day in the clinic, indicate in the clearest possible way the origins of this branch of medicine. A formal definition of psychosomatic disorder is difficult and Weiss and English (1943) adopted a different procedure, defining the concept by description. They recognized three groups of psychosomatic illnesses.

Group 1 Comprises a large borderline group of patients who have subjective somatic symptoms but no evidence of organic illness and who are not psychotic. These constitute approximately one third of the

---

*Reprinted from *Behaviour Research and Therapy*, 1964, **1**, 351–356, Pergamon Press. Copyright © 1964. With permission from Pergamon Press and A. J. Cooper.

patients who consult any doctor, and represent the so-called functional illnesses of ordinary medical practice.

Group 2   Comprises patients whose symptoms are in part due to emotional factors, although organic changes can be demonstrated. They form approximately another third of the patients reaching the doctor.

Group 3   Includes those illnesses which bear an intimate relation to the autonomic nervous system, such as migraine, essential hypertension and asthma. This group is perhaps the most interesting, since it is often possible to demonstrate a clear, causal relationship between psychological factors and the development of the somatic symptoms.

It has been suggested by Jaspers (1948) that certain types of psychosomatic illness can be acquired by learning, as responses conditioned to anxiety. If this postulate is accepted as valid, it would seem appropriate to treat such disorders along the lines indicated by learning theory. Although the literature is sparse on the subject, Walton (1960) employing therapy based on reciprocal inhibition successfully treated a case of long-standing bronchial asthma. This present paper reports a further case which responded favorably to behavior therapy.

Case History

The patient was a married woman, aged 24, who had been referred to the Psychiatric Outpatient Dept. following discharge from a general hospital where she had been admitted in status asthmaticus.

At the age of 8 she had developed pneumonia and radiological investigation revealed that she was suffering from tuberculosis. Since then she had been treated regularly at the chest clinic, being finally discharged one year ago as cured. In spite of constant reassurance however, she had been left with the impression that her "chest was weak" and that she was prone to respiratory disease.

Her first asthmatic attack occurred seven years ago; subsequently they recurred about once a month and were usually related to some stressful situation. On the average these attacks lasted about half an hour and invariably responded to broncho-dilator drugs. Five years ago she had become pregnant and following delivery of her daugher had remained free of symptoms for three years.

In the last two years she had become increasingly "nervous" and discovered that any minor upset had become capable of precipitating an asthmatic attack. During the last year she had become frigid. This she ascribed to developing a bout of asthma during intercourse with her husband. This attack had been of undue severity, she had experienced marked feelings of panic and thought that she was going to die. Following this she had experienced a good deal of anxiety in the sexual situation and had been unable to relax sufficiently to engage in coitus. Considerable stimulus generalization had occurred and she was even afraid of digital insertion, in case this should provoke a further attack.

In the three months preceding admission to mental hospital her condition had markedly deteriorated. She was having several attacks daily, resulting in a complete disruption of her life. To make matters worse, these attacks were proving resistant to drug therapy, and it was frequently necessary to call in the G.P. in order to administer an injection of adrenaline to abort the attack. Her mental state paralleled her physical deterioration; she had become tense, anxious, prone to panic attacks and intolerant of the slightest stress. She was admitted from Outpatient's in an acute anxiety state.

Physical examination in hospital revealed no abnormality. Chest X-ray was normal and sinus X-rays showed opacities of both frontal sinuses and both antra. It was thought that these changes were probably long standing and not relevant to her present illness. Psychometric testing revealed an anxiety-prone hysterical personality of below average intelligence.

TREATMENT

Theoretical Considerations

The following considerations were considered relevant in designing a treatment program.

1. The psychosomatic symptom (asthma) had been acquired as a conditioned response to anxiety.
2. Considerable stimulus generalization had occurred and practically any stressful situation had become capable of evoking an attack.
3. The patient did not relate her asthma to any specific stimulus, but stated that the anxiety she experienced accompanying emotional states (particularly anger and excitement) could trigger off a bout of asthma.
4. Because of the diversity of the stimuli involved it was decided that constructing an object or situation hierarchy for desensitization was impracticable.

The treatment was designed to reciprocally inhibit (by deep relaxation) the anxiety evoked by the emotional states of anger and excitement induced by the use of appropriate direct verbal suggestion. The aim was to eventually extinguish the conditioned psychosomatic symptom. Successful completion of this program would weaken the bond between the stimuli (excitement and anger) and the anxiety responses, and thus lead to extinction of the psychosomatic symptom (asthma).

Method

Stage 1   To ensure an optimum environment, treatment was carried out in a darkened single room, the patient lying on a couch. Initially, deep relaxation was taught. The patient received up to a 0.5 g of sodium amytal intravenously, administered at a rate of 1 ml every 3 min. She was then instructed to concentrate on her toes and it was suggested to her that they were becoming heavy, loose, and relaxing. This and similar suggestions were repeated several times, until it was thought that muscular relaxation was proceeding. The same suggestions were made in turn for other parts of her body. (For therapeutic purposes the body was arbitrarily divided into toes, calves, thighs, fingers, arms, shoulders, eyes, head, neck and chest.) Great emphasis was placed on the chest and she was instructed to concentrate on my suggestions that her chest muscles were relaxing completely and that her breathing was slow and regular. This procedure was continued until complete muscular relaxation was obtained, as determined by slow steady pulse, steady B.P. and by the patient indicating that subjectively she felt calm and tranquil.

The first session produced rather an interesting result. On the day prior to commencing treatment she had been interviewed and the form of the treatment had been explained. It had been suggested that this might involve hypnosis, and a full and frank explanation as to what this entailed, had been given. During the evening she had been told by the other patients that hypnosis was a sinister business and that the hypnotist could make people do things against their will. This had frightened her a good deal, but she had put on a show of bravado and laughed off the whole issue. The next day, following the injection of sodium amytal and during the preliminary suggestions, she had experienced severe anxiety which provoked an asthmatic attack. This was quickly aborted by anxiety-allaying suggestions. She was told that she was feeling relaxed and drowsy, that her anxiety was lessening and that she was feeling calm and tranquil. It was suggested that her breathing was becoming slow and regular and that her chest muscles were losing their tenseness. She responded to these suggestions after about 5 min. Following this incident it required a further two sessions to desensitize her to the therapeutic situation. This initial phase was spread over two weeks and comprised six 45 min sessions during which deep muscular relaxation and slow regular breathing were taught. Additionally, during this period the patient practiced relaxation on her bed for one hour daily.

Stage 2   This consisted of introducing increasing doses of stress when the patient was fully relaxed. Direct verbal suggestion was employed and followed the pattern laid down by Wolpe (1958) of commencing with easy stimuli and, as inhibition of anxiety proceeds, introducing progressively more difficult ones.

In practice, deep muscular relaxation was first induced, and then verbal suggestions were made to the patient that she was becoming emotional. It was suggested that she was feeling uneasy, worried and apprehensive, and that these feelings of anxiety and agitation would worsen into fear and even panic. During the treatment she was carefully observed for signs of anxiety and if such signs appeared the suggestions were immediately stopped. (The criteria for anxiety were purely physiological manifestions, being, increased pulse rate, sweating, and of most significance, any irregularity or increase in the rate of respiration. In the past this had always heralded an attack of asthma.) The session was invariably concluded by further deep relaxation.

In succeeding sessions the pressure was progressively stepped up, until she was able to remain relaxed and comfortable even under the most anxiety-evoking suggestions.

PROGRESS

Except for the attack during the first treatment session, the patient remained free from asthma during the remainder of her hospital stay. She was convinced that the relaxation exercises had accomplished much, and stated that she felt calmer and more relaxed than she had for years past.

Prior to discharge the problem of her frigidity was broached. It was explained that in a purely fortuitous manner her asthma had become conditioned to the sexual act and more specifically to intercourse. She was advised to practice deep relaxation during the intimate side of marriage, lying nude in close physical proximity to her husband but not to attempt intercourse until she felt completely calm and relaxed, and likely to succeed. It was explained that observation of these principles would bring about a progressive diminution of anxiety, restore confidence and responsiveness and suppress her asthma. The patient was successful at the first attempt. She had experienced no anxiety during coitus, which had been entirely satisfactory. She has never since felt anxious during sexual intercourse, and has had no further asthmatic attacks in this situation.

Following discharge she attended Outpatients a total of 12 times at approximately three weekly intervals, when the desensitization program outlined above was carried out. (Two sessions were devoted to allaying the anxiety of fear responses and five each to the desensitization of states of "excitement" and "anger.")

The results so far have been most encouraging. Since being discharged from hospital 16 months ago she has suffered only four attacks. One of these followed the self administration of a patent medicine, another occurred when her mother was seriously ill, and the other two were associated with strong feelings of anger and frustration following quarrels with neighbors.

At our last meeting 8 weeks ago, she described herself as feeling fine, much better able to control her feelings, particularly her temper. She stated that she was more tolerant, easier to get along with, and found it easier to relax in situations that used to upset her.

DISCUSSION

Bronchial asthma can be defined as a condition characterized by recurrent bouts of wheezing, mainly or entirely expiratory with an associated variable difficulty in breathing (Ogilvie, 1962). Functionally, asthma results from constriction of the smooth muscle of the bronchial wall, with swelling of the mucosa, and the hypersecretion of mucus. Traditionally, from the therapeutic standpoint, asthma can be divided into two groups.

Extrinsic Asthma

In this type there is aggravation of symptoms after contact with an environmental allergen and/or a strong positive skin reaction with wealing and erythema after intradermal administration of extracts of allergens.

This type frequently starts in childhood, but may develop for the first time in adults or even late in life.

Intrinsic Asthma

This characteristically starts in adults, especially women between the ages of 40 and 60. No allergen can be identified either from the history or from the skin testing. This type is frequently complicated by bacterial bronchitis. In addition to these purely organic factors there is an increasing awareness of the role of psychological determinants as precipitants in asthma and other psychosomatic disorders.

In the case under discussion it was thought that the factors concerned in the genesis of her illness were probably multiple and interwoven, but there was little doubt that the anxiety evoked in certain emotional states was playing a central role in the precipitation of attacks. In the absence of any demonstrable allergic or pathological cause it was thought likely that her asthma had been acquired as a learned response to anxiety (i.e. as a neurotic symptom). Turnbull (1962) commented that asthma-like behavior can be learned and will persist as a means of resolving an approach—avoidance conflict. This is well demonstrated in this case, the asthmatic attacks being precipitated by anxiety engendered in situations in which a state of conflict was present. In view of the psychopathology, it seemed logical to apply behavior therapy, and desensitization based on relaxation (Wolpe, 1958) was considered appropriate. In view of the wide diversity in the nature of the provoking stimuli it appeared inappropriate to construct an object or situation hierarchy and accordingly the patient was desensitized, employing reciprocal inhibition, to emotional states, particularly excitement and anger. Technically this proved a fairly simple procedure and was accomplished by direct verbal suggestions. This method, when applicable, would appear to have advantages over "hierarchy desensitization" as described by Wolpe (1958), in which it is essential that the patient be able to visualize the anxiety-evoking object or scene in order that desensitization might proceed.

Jacobson (1938) demonstrated that intense muscle relaxation is accompanied by autonomic effects that are antagonistic to the characteristic effects of anxiety. In this patient, it was considered that muscle relaxation and breathing exercises, whilst playing an important role in the treatment was subordinate to the desensitization program, as previously she had practiced relaxation without much benefit. Mention must be made of the earlier spontaneous remission which followed her pregnancy.

Amelioration, or exacerbation of psychosomatic symptoms, is observed to occur fairly commonly following such events. Although in our present state of knowledge it remains speculative, it is not unlikely that these may be due to physiological or endocrine changes occurring within the organism. It is obviously impossible to state categorically that the patient's remission was due to the therapy, but the evidence would tend to support this contention rather than a spontaneous cure. There had been nothing to account for a major physiological change in the patient, neither had the circumstances operating in her external environment altered. It is likely that this treatment program by training the patient to relax in traumatic situations has effectively raised her "stress threshold" and rendered her relatively immune to asthmatic attacks precipitated by anxiety.

CONCLUSIONS

It is not suggested that the treatment has effected a complete and permanent cure, but rather that the desensitization program has enabled the patient to relax and remain composed in situations of stress. Severe psychological trauma can still evoke sufficient anxiety to precipitate an asthmatic attack, but in spite of this, there has been dramatic and maintained improvement in this case. Booster treatments are a feasible proposition and could be easily applied on an outpatient basis should the patient relapse.

REFERENCES

Jacobson, E. *Progressive Relaxation.* University of Chicago Press, Chicago, 1938.
Jaspers, K. *Allgemeine Psychopathologie* (4th Ed.). Springer-Verlag, Berlin, 1948.
Ogilvie, A. G. *Thorax,* 1962, **17**, 183.
Turnbull, J. W. Asthma conceived as a learned response. *J. Psychosom. Res.,* 1962, **6**, 59–71.
Walton, D. The application of learning theory to the treatment of a case of bronchial asthma, in *Behavior Therapy and the Neuroses* (Ed. H. J. Eysenck). Pergamon Press, Oxford, 1960.
Weiss, E. and English, S. O. *Psychosomatic Medicine.* W. B. Saunders, Philadelphia, 1943.
Wolpe, J. *Psychotherapy by Reciprocal Inhibition.* Stanford University Press, Stanford, 1958.

ARTICLE 30

The Immediate Effects of Systematic Relaxation Training on Peak Expiratory Flow Rates in Asthmatic Children*†

A. BARNEY ALEXANDER, PhD,‡ DONALD R. MIKLICH, PhD,
and HELEN HERSHKOFF

Children's Asthma Research Institute and Hospital Denver, Colo. and Harvard
College, Cambridge, Mass.

Abstract: Clinical experience has often suggested that having asthmatic patients sit quietly and/or relax during asthma attacks is helpful. The present study was an attempt to provide a controlled experimental demonstration of the effect of systematic relaxation on peak expiratory flow rate in asthmatic children. Eighteen male and 18 female asthmatic children were divided into two groups matched for mean age, sex composition and asthma severity. One group of subjects underwent three sessions of modified Jacobsonian systematic relaxation training, while the second group sat quietly for three sessions. Peak expiratory flow rate measures were obtained prior to and following each session. It was found that relaxation subjects manifested a significant mean increase in peak expiratory flow rate over sessions compared to a nonsignificant mean peak expiratory flow decrease for control subjects. It was suggested that these results have important implications both for the clinical treatment and the understanding of bronchial asthma.

Physicians often ask asthmatic patients to rest or to sit quietly at the onset of and/or during an asthma attack. Patient report and clinical evidence both indicate that such a procedure often helps to mollify or alleviate wheezing. Experience at the Children's Asthma Research

*Reprinted from *Psychosomatic Medicine*, Vol. 34, No. 5 (September–October 1972), 388–394. With permission from the American Psychosomatic Society, Inc. and A. Barney Alexander.

†Supported in part by National Institute of Child Health and Human Development Grant HD 01529.

‡Address for reprint requests: A. Barney Alexander, PhD, CARIH, Behavior Science Division, 3401 W. 19th Ave. Denver, Colo. 80204.

Institute and Hospital (CARIH) suggests that some asthmatic children do benefit from purposeful nonexertion during attacks. Likewise, clinical observations at CARIH suggest that many asthmatics suffer disadvantages from the reciprocal situation—i.e., that exertion can sometimes precipitate or aggravate asthma attacks. These observations suggest that training in purposeful relaxation, such as the systematic relaxation procedure introduced by Jacobson[1] for the treatment of psychosomatic and psychoneurotic syndromes, may be of benefit to some asthmatics during attacks. However, none of the above clinical observations appears to have been investigated systematically.

Little empirical data exist concerning the effect of relaxation on pulmonary functioning in asthmatics. In a study comparing relaxation alone against Wolpe's technique of relaxation plus systematic desensitization[2], a psychotherapy designed to reduce anxiety, Moore[3] found greater peak expiratory flow rate (PEFR) changes in the latter condition. There was, however, some PEFR increase noted in the relaxation-only condition. Unfortunately, Moore used only one PEFR measurement per week, a frequency which allows no reliable conclusions to be drawn regarding either the immediate or long-term effects of relaxation on pulmonary functioning[4]. Van Lith *et al.*[5] studied the effect of deep hypnotic relaxation upon total respiratory compliance in 24 subjects with obstructive lung disease. They found no significant differences in compliance between the trance and normal awake states. The relationship between hypnosis and relaxation, however, has not been extensively studied. Paul[6] found that while both hypnotic relaxation and systematic relaxation training produced significantly more physiologic changes than a control procedure, the effects were not as pronounced for hypnotic relaxation as for the training method. This suggests that the Van Lith *et al.* results cannot be safely generalized to systematic relaxation training. Moreover, Van Lith and associates used an esophageal balloon in the measurement of compliance. It is doubtful that any considerable degree of relaxation can be achieved under such circumstances.

While there are several studies of nonpulmonary physiologic responses to relaxation, their data are contradictory and provide little information from which to infer the probable effect of systematic relaxation training upon the pulmonary functioning of asthmatics. Grossberg[7] compared a group trained in systematic relaxation with a control group instructed only to rest. Employing three physiologic measures, EMG from forearm and forehead, skin conductance and heart rate, no significant differences were found between groups. Similarly, Edelman[8] failed to find any unique effects on autonomic functioning due to relaxation. However, two other studies have found differences. In the investigation cited above[6], Paul compared systematic relaxation, hypnotic relaxation and a control procedure. He found that heart rate and EMG, and to a lesser extent respiration rate, were lower for the two experimental groups than for controls. These effects were more pronounced in the relaxation than in the hypnosis group. No differences were found in galvanic skin response (GSR). Matthews and Gelder[9] compared systematically relaxed subjects with controls. They found that EMG and GSR were lower in the relaxation groups. There were no differences between groups for heart or respiration rates.

The present investigation was an attempt to provide a controlled, experimental demonstration of the effects of systematic relaxation training on air exchange in asthmatic children.

METHOD

Subjects

The subjects, 24 males and 20 females, were children 10 to 15 years of age who were patients at CARIH, a residential treatment home for children with chronic, intractable asthma. Specifically excluded from this population and, hence, from the study were suspected mental retardates, children with organic brain pathology and those children showing evidence of serious psychopathology (e.g., psychosis). Represented in the sample were children whose asthma ranged in severity from moderate to very severe. During the actual experimental sessions, subjects participated in any particular session if they were not experiencing audible wheezing at the time. However, on any particular day, individual subjects displayed degrees of airflow impairment, as measured by PEFR, ranging from moderate airway obstruction to minimal obstruction.

Procedure

The subjects were randomly divided into experimental and control groups, with the restriction that, as near as was possible, the groups were matched for mean age, sex composition and asthma severity. Approximate severity matching between groups was accomplished by attaining in each group an equal proportion of children who were receiving maintenance steroid medications and children who were not.

Six control and six experimental sessions were held. Because of scheduling conflicts, visits with parents or hospital unit admissions for acute asthma episodes or other illnesses, etc., all subjects did not participate in each of the six sessions appropriate to their groups. However, all subjects who completed a minimum of three sessions were retained in the study for purposes of analysis. The minimum requirement of three sessions was chosen on the basis of experience at CARIH which indicated that children can readily learn systematic relaxation in three training sessions[10]. Of the initial number of 44, two subjects were lost from the experimental group and six from the control group. The resultant groups contained 20 and 16 children, respectively. The mean age was 11.9 years in both groups, and the mean number of sessions attended was 4.1 for the experimental group and 4.7 for the control group. These latter means were not significantly different statistically. The experimental group had 11 males and 9 females and the control group had 7 males and 9 females. The percentage of subjects receiving corticosteroid therapy was 40% for experimental subjects and 31% for the controls; thus the chronicity of the disease was roughly equal between the two groups.

For purposes of systematic relaxation training, experimental subjects were randomly divided further into three training groups, each of which underwent the same training procedure. At the first session, experimental subjects were told that "we want to find out if relaxation effects your peak flows." Experimental subjects received a modified Jacobsonian relaxation training procedure like that used by Paul[11]. Each session lasted about 20 minutes, 15 minutes of which was occupied by relaxation training. Briefly, the training consisted of successively tensing and relaxing muscles in the following order: hands and forearms, biceps, upper face, calves and feet. Throughout each session, the experimenter emphasized feelings of no tension, relaxation and warmth.

Controls were also randomly divided into three groups, each receiving identical treatment. Again each session lasted about 20 minutes, 15 of which were occupied by rest. Control subjects were told that "we want to find out if inactivity affects your peak flows," and they were simply instructed to sit quietly for 15 minutes. Examples of permitted activities in the control sessions included quiet talking, reading and sewing.

Determination of flow rates was made by measuring PEFR with the Wright Peak Flow Meter.* The PEFR is the most conveniently obtained

---

*Air-Med Ltd, England.

measure of flow rate and it correlates well with FEV[4]. Because PEFR readings display some degree of variability even when taken in quick succession from the same individual, three readings were obtained at the beginning and end of each session. There are many errors of measurement which can make a PEFR inaccurately low, but none can make it inaccurately high. Hence, the highest PEFR obtained of the three taken was used as the best measurement in that series; however, it is still not impossible that in some cases this highest PEFR did not indicate a maximum subject effort. Since the study included subjects of greatly differing ages, sizes and airflow impairment at the time of any particular session, absolute PEFR scores are of little meaning. Accordingly, the data used in the analyses were post-PEFR minus pre-PEFR change scores. Immediately after the PEFR readings, subjects rated their feelings of relaxation on a "relaxation thermometer"; this is a scale from 1 to 10: 1 meaning "not relaxed at all," 10 meaning "very relaxed." The experimenter emphasized that subjects were to rate their feelings at the moment, rather than how they felt generally. At the end of each session, all subjects again rated their feelings of relaxation, and three more PEFR's were obtained for each subject.

During the experiment, subjects sat in comfortable chairs in one of three treatment rooms. When sessions were in progress, three groups were being run concurrently. There were two session times each day, the six sessions for each group being completed over an 8-day period. In order to control for experimenter effects, three trained experimenters were employed. The experimenters and the rooms were rotated on a regular basis, so that each group was in a different room and was handled by a different experimenter at each successive session.

RESULTS

The relaxation thermometer was intended to provide an assessment of how successful the training procedure was in producing relaxation in experimental subjects. The mean presession level of relaxation was 5.37 for experiment subjects and 5.81 for control subjects, a statistically nonsignificant difference. The mean post-PEFR minus pre-PEFR change for the relaxation thermometer over the last three sessions was 2.73 ($t = 7.03$, $df = 19$; $P < 0.005$, two-tail) for experimental subjects and 0.37 ($t = 1.86$, $df = 15$; ns, two-tail) for control subjects. The difference in mean pre-post change between experimental and control groups was significant ($t = 5.01$, $df = 34$; $P < 0.005$, two-tail). As measured by self-report, therefore, we may conclude that the relaxation training did increase relaxation in the experimental subjects, while the control procedure had little effect on self-reported feelings of relaxation.

The major experimental question was answered by analysis of the mean PEFR change scores over the last three sessions. For experimental subjects, the mean change was an increase in PEFR of 21.63 liters/min. This increase is significantly different from no change ($t = 2.64$, $df = 19$; $P < 0.01$, one-tail). The control group PEFR's showed a nonsignificant mean decrease of 6.14 liters/min ($t = 0.96$, $df = 15$; ns). The difference between the mean change scores for the two groups was also statistically significant ($t = 2.60$, $df = 34$; $P < 0.01$, one-tail).

Since subjects in the present study differed considerably in the degree of airflow impairment at the time of any given session, it is necessary to consider the possibility of a "law of initial values" (LIV) effect[12]. For example, subjects whose flow rates, at the time of a session, were considerably below maximum would conceivably have a greater opportunity to show improvement than subjects whose initial flow rates were more nearly normal. Two lines of evidence indicate that the present data were not affected by LIV. First, the mean presession percent predicted PEFR's, employing the norms from Murray and Cook[13], were not significantly different for the two groups: relaxation group = 75% predicted and control group = 72% predicted. Second, correlations between the presession PEFR's and the amount of change over each session were nonsignificant both for the experimental group ($r = 0.20$, $df = 18$; ns) and the control group ($r = 0.20$, $df = 14$; ns). Taken as a whole, then, there is no evidence that the significant effect of relaxation obtained in the present study can be accounted for by LIV. In fact, the control group had an initial mean percent predicted PEFR which was slightly lower than that of the relaxation group.

Yet another line of reasoning may be used to demonstrate that the PEFR change observed in the experimental group resulted from relaxation. Because the procedure employed was a relaxation training procedure, the relaxation subjects would be expected to be better able to relax during their last training session than in their first session. Therefore, if relaxation was the cause of the PEFR improvement in the relaxation group, the amount of PEFR change in the last session should be greater than that in the first session. The mean post-PEFR minus pre-PEFR change score for the first session was -14.25; the mean for the last session was 27.50. The difference between these means was statistically significant ($t = 2.39$, $df = 19$; $P < 0.025$, one-tail). On the other hand, as would be expected, the control group showed no such significant growth in PEFR change from first to last session (first trial mean change $= -12.50$; last trial mean change $= 4.37$; $t = 0.79$, $df = 15$; ns).

DISCUSSION

In the present experiment we sought to investigate systematically the effects of relaxation on the airflow rates of asthmatic children. In considering the present results it is important to recall that, while the mean increase in the relaxation group was highly reliable ($P < 0.01$), the corresponding P value for the decrease in the control group is approximately 0.40. Hence, the results are best understood as reflecting an increase in flow rates for subjects who received relaxation training as compared with no change in flow rates for subjects who simply sat quietly. However, since the study grew out of the observation that some asthmatics seem at times to benefit during asthma attacks by simply sitting quietly, it is of some interest to consider the fact that, overall, the control group did not show any improvement in pulmonary functioning.

The most parsimonious and probably the most likely explanation is that while both inactivity and trained relaxation can lead to increases in flow rates, systematically trained relaxation is by far the more effective procedure. A second possibility, related to the above, is that subjects in the control condition, while they were inactive, were making no efforts to relax. Control subjects were instructed only to remain inactive. Three control subjects did in fact manifest mean PEFR increases over the last three sessions in excess of the mean increase for relaxation subjects. These subjects may have actually attained some degree of relaxation either through noninstructed effort during the control sessions or an ability to relax acquired independently of the experiment. The preceding accounts suggest that in the control condition subjects probably responded in a variety of ways to the instructions to "sit quietly and remain inactive." In all likelihood, their behavior ranged from mere inactivity to some efforts to relax by whatever means they had at their disposal. That, on the whole, control subjects made little efforts to actually accomplish what they considered to be a relaxed state is attested to by the very small pre–post change (0.37) in self-reported feelings of relaxation as compared to a large and highly significant mean change of 2.73 in the relaxation group. It is important to note, however, that both experimental and control subjects began the last three sessions with essentially identical, self-perceived levels of relaxation (5.37 and 5.81, respectively).

A third possibility to account for the relative ineffectiveness of inactivity would be that inactivity favorably promotes increases in air flow in only some asthmatics. As noted above, quiet sitting indeed produced beneficial effects in three control subjects, and these subjects may be representative of a susceptible subgroup of asthmatics.

Still a fourth possibility is that the effect of the relaxation procedure was due to an interaction with another factor—e.g., anxiety. For example, if relaxation is conceived of as a way of reducing tension, and if tension can lead to reduced pulmonary functioning, then it is possible that tension levels were being reduced less effectively in the control as compared to the relaxation condition. There is clearly need for further research to explore all of the above possibilities.

This study was undertaken only to determine if relaxation had an immediate beneficial effect on the pulmonary functioning of asthmatics. Replication is necessary before this proposition can be considered to be established. For example, it is desirable to measure pulmonary functioning with a technic less dependent on subject effort and cooperation than the PEFR. Nevertheless, it is not inappropriate to discuss briefly the potential value of the present results. The most important implication would appear to be the use of relaxation training in the symptomatic treatment of asthma. The mean PEFR improvement over sessions in the relaxed condition was about 11%. While this amount of improvement would probably not be sufficient to produce substantial relief of most moderate-to-severe asthma attacks, there are several reasons for believing that much greater improvement could be obtained. First, these subjects received only a few relaxation training sessions, and there is nothing in the present data to suggest that they had reached a maximal degree of ability to relax. Since increasing PEFR improvements were found from the first to the last training session, it is reasonable to expect that even greater improvements could be obtained with more training. Second, just as the control subjects manifested large individual differences in response to sitting quietly, so did experimental subjects show large differences in their responses to relaxation. This suggests that relaxation training, like the majority of other therapy techniques used in the treatment of asthma, may be effective only with some patients. In particular, if the 10 relaxation subjects who manifested the greatest PEFR improvement are viewed separately, the 11% mean PEFR improvement noted previously becomes 32%. The latter figure represents considerable symptomatic improvement in these subjects. Third, while training children in Jacobsonian relaxation for other purposes, there have been two instances involving separate children where a child reported to a training session evidencing audible wheezing. In both cases, the children (who were not subjects in the present study) experienced subjective relief from asthma and remission of the audible wheezing. These incidences were accompanied by 38% and 41% improvement in PEFR over sessions. Fourth, there have been several case history studies published in which psychotherapeutic techniques designed to reduce tension and anxiety have been successfully used in the treatment of asthma[14–17]. For all of the above reasons, it is suggested that relaxation training procedures be given close attention as potential treatment techniques for use in bronchial asthma.

Finally, the present findings may relate to the recent work of Mathe and Knapp[18]. These investigators have found that psychologic stress is associated with airway resistance decreases in normals but that airway resistance increases in asthmatics. Similarly, several investigations suggest that exercise leads to bronchodilation in normals but to bronchoconstriction in asthmatics[19–23]. As yet there appears to be no evidence regarding the effects of relaxation on the pulmonary physiology of nonasthmatics. Mathe and Knapp have suggested that these differences between normal and asthmatic subjects may be due to insufficient epinephrine secretion in asthmatics. If relaxation is conceived of as the opposite of emotional arousal or exercise, then the present findings can be considered to be congruent with the notions of Mathe and Knapp. While the tentativeness of these speculations must be emphasized, nevertheless, further study of the effects of relaxation on the pulmonary functioning of normal and asthmatic subjects would appear to offer a most fruitful opportunity for understanding the nature and treatment of bronchial asthma.

SUMMARY

Clinical experience suggests that having asthmatic patients sit quietly and/or relax during asthma attacks often helps to alleviate or mollify the wheezing. Conversely, exertion is often observed to precipitate or aggravate wheezing. The present investigation was designed to provide a controlled experimental demonstration of the immediate effects of systematic relaxation on the pulmonary functioning of asthmatic children.

Two groups of children, matched for sex, age and severity of asthma, were selected from the patient population at CARIH.

One group of children (N = 20) was given three to six training sessions in a modified form of Jacobson's systematic relaxation technique. The second group (N = 16) received an equivalent number of sessions in which they simply sat quietly. Measures of PEFR were obtained at the beginning and end of each session from all subjects.

The results indicated that relaxation subjects manifested a significant ($P < 0.01$) pre–post session, mean increase in PEFR, compared to a small nonsignificant mean PEFR decrease over sessions for control subjects. Two additional lines of evidence were presented in support of the conclusion that the PEFR increase in the relaxation group was due to relaxation. First, the relaxation group, but not the control group, manifested a significant increase in self-reported feelings of relaxation from beginning to end of session. Second, the amount of PEFR improvement in the relaxation group was significantly greater on the last as compared to the first session.

The implications of these results for the symptomatic treatment of asthma were discussed and further study of relaxation as a treatment technic was strongly recommended. Finally, the compatibility of the present results with the adrenal medulary insufficiency theory of asthma was noted.

REFERENCES

1. Jacobson, E. *Progressive Relaxation.* Chicago: University of Chicago Press, 1938.
2. Wolpe, J. *Psychotherapy by Reciprocal Inhibition.* Stanford: Stanford University Press, 1958.
3. Moore, N. Behavior therapy in bronchial asthma: a controlled study. *J. Psychosom. Res.,* 1965, **9**, 257.
4. Chai, H., Purcell, K., Brady, K. *et al.* Therapeutic and investigational evaluation of asthmatic children. *J. Allergy,* 1968, **41**, 23.
5. Van Lith, P., Barrocas, M., Nelson, R. A. *et al.* Effect of hypnosis on total respiratory compliance. *J. Appl. Physiol.,* 1969, **27**, 804.
6. Paul, G. L. Physiological effects of relaxation training and hypnotic suggestion. *J. Abnorm. Psychol.,* 1969, **74**, 425.
7. Grossberg, J. M. The physiological effectiveness of brief training in differential muscle relaxation. *Technical Report No. IX.* La Jolla: Western Behavioral Sciences, Inc, 1965.
8. Edelman, R. I. Effects of progressive relaxation on autonomic processes. *J. Clin. Psychol.,* 1970, **26**, 421.
9. Matthews, A. M. and Gelder, M. G. Psychophysiological investigations of brief relaxation training. *J. Psychosom. Res.,* 1969, **13**, 1.

10. Creer, T. L. Psychologic factors in allergic disease. Invited Address at the Twenty-Seventh Annual Meeting of the American Academy of Allergy, Chicago, Ill., 1971.
11. Paul, G. L. *Insight Versus Desensitization in Psychotherapy: An Experiment in Anxiety Reduction.* Stanford: Stanford University Press, 1966.
12. Hord, D. J., Johnson, L. C., and Lubin, A. Differential effect of the law of initial value (LIV) on autonomic variables. *Psychophysiology,* 1964, **1**, 79.
13. Murray, A. B. and Cook, C. D. Measurement of peak expiratory flow rates in 220 normal children from 4.5 to 18.5 years of age. *J. Pediatr.,* 1963, **62**, 186.
14. Cooper, A. J. A case of bronchial asthma treated by behavior therapy. *Behav. Res. Ther.,* 1964, **1**, 351.
15. Gardner, J. E. A blending of behavior therapy techniques in an approach to an asthmatic child. *Psychother: Theory, Res. & Prac.,* 1968, **5**, 46.
16. Sergeant, H. G. S. and Yorkston, N. J. Verbal desensitization in the treatment of bronchial asthma. *Lancet,* 1969, **2**, 1321.
17. Walton, D. The application of learning theory to the treatment of a case of bronchial asthma, in *Behavior Therapy and the Neuroses.* Edited by H. Eysenck. London: Pergamon Press, 1960. P. 188.
18. Mathe, A. A. and Knapp, P. H. Emotional and adrenal reactions to stress in bronchial asthma. *Psychosom. Med.,* 1971, **33**, 323.
19. Evler, U. S. Sympatho-adrenal activity and physical exercise. *Med. Sport,* 1969, **3**, 170.
20. Karki, N. T. The urinary excretion of noradrenaline and adrenaline in different age groups, its diurnal variation and the effect of muscular work on it. *Acta Physiol. Scand.* (*Suppl.*), 1956, **29**, 132.
21. Sly, R. M. *et al.* Exercise-induced bronchospasm: effect of adrenergic or cholinergic blockade. *J. Allergy,* 1967, **40**, 93.
22. Itkin, I. H. and Anand, S. C. The role of atropine as a mediator blocker of induced bronchial obstruction. *J. Allergy,* 1968, **41**, 88.
23. Zaid, G., Beau, G. N., and Heimlich, E. M. Bronchial response to exercise following beta-adrenergic blockade. *J. Allergy,* 1968, **42**, 177.

CHAPTER 8

Patient Management and Pain Control

Educating the patient to understand better and to collaborate actively in the management of his illness is an important component of health care. Frequently, the objectives of patient education include increasing or decreasing specific patient behaviors so that needed treatment plans can be successfully implemented. The diabetic patient, for example, must reduce his consumption of carbohydrates if diabetic acidosis is to be avoided. For the hypertensive patient, constraints may be placed on smoking as well as undue physical exertion and emotional stress. Similarly, patients recovering from stroke or spinal cord injury may require prolonged physical therapy if ambulation is to be achieved, self-care skills reacquired, and secondary disabilities prevented. Because patient compliance is of vital importance to treatment outcome, techniques to promote compliance and otherwise modify patient behavior should be of interest to those in the health care field.

Relief from discomfort and anticipation of improved functional capacity often provide sufficient motivation to produce adherence to recommended care plans. However for some patients corrective therapy may be experienced as highly painful, effortful, tedious, or frustrating. Largely because of their immediacy, these aversive consequences can precipitate the development of unwanted avoidance behaviors which in turn may interfere with continuing treatment efforts. To the extent that exaggerated pain complaints, forgetfulness, statements of "I can't or won't," or a consistently half-hearted performance are instrumental in avoiding unpleasant routines, they will most assuredly persist and probably increase in their frequency or intensity of occurrence. Subsequent attempts to improve cooperation by persuasion, cajoling, or counseling the patient to uncover hidden sources of resistance do not always succeed in producing needed behavioral change (Berni *et al.*, 1971; Fowler *et al.*, 1969). On the contrary, attention of this kind may be reinforcing and tend to exacerbate management problems, especially when comparable amounts of attention do not accompany desired activity (Ayllon & Michael, 1959; Meyerson *et al.*, 1967). For these reasons it may be necessary to alter the behavior of those involved in patient care before reliable changes in patient behavior can be expected to occur. Training hospital personnel to prompt and positively reinforce desired patient behavior, while concurrently withholding reinforcement for behaviors considered to be inappropriate, can increase compliance and by so doing improve the quality of patient care.

In previous chapters it was emphasized that therapeutic behavioral intervention requires (1) operational definitions of behaviors to be modified, and (2) careful analysis and manipulation of controlling environmental conditions. The papers in this chapter demonstrate how investigators have applied these same techniques to alter various activities that were either interfering with effective disease management, were impeding physical rehabilitation efforts, or that were indicative of existing illness for which there was not always a determinable organic basis. These latter behaviors include a broad class of verbal and physical activity associated with complaints of chronic pain.

Sand *et al.* (Article 31) describe how positive reinforcement and timeout operations were used to increase fluid intake and strengthen self-care skills in two paraplegic patients, as well as to reduce tantrums and noncompliance in a young brain-damaged child. The two paraplegic patients were asked to monitor and display graphic records of behaviors selected for modification. By clearly explaining expected performance criteria, as well as by conspicuously posting patient collected data to prompt positive attention from ward staff, the therapists produced an abrupt increase in desired activities. For the child, token economy procedures and timeout were used to reduce noncompliance that had previously prevented the subject from participating in a prescribed physical therapy program. That the authors' treatment was instrumental in controlling the child's behavior was shown by the use of reversal techniques.

Goodkin's paper (Article 32) provides additional support for the usefulness of operant conditioning in physical rehabilitation. Citing results obtained from four physically handicapped patients, he explains how targeted behaviors were carefully defined, a behavioral analysis performed, and therapeutic manipulations then methodically carried out.

In most cases improvement was quickly achieved by modeling desired responses and then reinforcing approximations to them, while simultaneously withholding attention for substandard or marginal performances. Katz *et al.* (Article 33) show a close correspondence between appropriate patient behavior and staff reinforcing activity, while also cautioning that simple instructions to ward personnel about behavior modification procedures may not suffice to maintain desired staff-to-patient interaction.

Chronic pain, that is associated with lower back problems and other conditions, is a common and potentially serious medical symptom. Although attempts to relieve pain often involve surgery or the long-term use of narcotic analgesics, both of these procedures confer predictable risks and may not be entirely effective. In their paper, Fordyce *et al.* (Article 34) analyze chronic pain from a learning standpoint and contend that two interrelated processes are operative. The first involves an internal physiological component elicited by stimulation of peripheral pain receptors. The second component is triggered by the first and consists of an overt behavioral response; that is the expression of pain is based inevitably on what the patient says or does. Furthermore, because these pain behaviors often produce reinforcing consequences (e.g., alarm, sympathetic attention, relief from unpleasant responsibilities, etc.), they are susceptible to learning and may persist even after the original cause of the pain has been treated. According to this model, therefore, no fundamental distinction exists between "real" pain complaints and so-called "imagined" ones for both are expressions of behavior that may be influenced by their environmental surroundings. Following this introduction, Fordyce *et al.* describe the operant conditioning approach they used to modify debilitating behaviors associated with chronic pain, such as excessive reliance on pain medications and decreased activity resulting from impinging pain stimuli. In discussing their results, the authors warn that while operant methods are not appropriate for all pain problems, the prospect that learning has exacerbated pain complaints should be considered when physical examination reveals no identifiable pain source and when opportunities for learning are both favorable and extended. Although not discussed extensively in this paper, followup of over 30 chronic pain patients treated by these methods have produced encouraging results (Fordyce *et al.*, 1973).

In the final selection, Gannon and Sternbach (Article 35) discuss an alternative operant conditioning technique for attenuating chronic pain. Hypothesizing that alpha rhythm brain wave activity and pain reception are incompatible behaviors, these investigators attempted to increase the former in order to reduce the latter in a patient who experienced recurrent and incapacitating headaches. Although their hypothesis was not supported, the results suggest that by learning to increase brain alpha the patient was able to prevent headaches in previously headache producing situations.

Points of key importance in this chapter include:

1. Increasing or decreasing specific patient behaviors is an integral component of patient education. Techniques to affect behavioral change should thus be useful to those involved in patient care.
2. In order to maintain compliance with prescribed care plans, it may be necessary to employ contingency management procedures.
3. Hospital staff may respond to patients in ways that maintain problem behaviors. Since staff behavior plays an important role in treatment, it deserves careful analysis and supervision. Training ward personnel in the appropriate use of reinforcement techniques represents one way to reduce patient management problems and increase quality of care.
4. Many behaviors associated with chronic pain are learned and may be modified by the manipulation of environmental consequences. To the extent that these behaviors interfere with daily living, such modification may enable the patient to function more effectively in spite of his pain.

REFERENCES

Ayllon, T. and Michael, J. The psychiatric nurse as a behavioral engineer. *Journal of the Experimental Analysis of Behavior*, 1959, **2**, 323–334.

Berni, R., Dressler, J., and Baxter, J. Reinforcing behavior. *American Journal of Nursing*, 1971, **71**, 2180–2183.

Fordyce, W., Fowler, R., Lehmann, J., DeLateur, B., Sand, P., and Trieschmann, R. Operant conditioning in the treatment of chronic pain. *Archives of Physical Medicine and Rehabilitation*, 1973, **54**, 399–408.

Fowler, R., Fordyce, W., and Berni, R. Operant conditioning in chronic illness. *American Journal of Nursing*, 1969, **69**, 1226–1228.

Meyerson, L., Kerr, N., and Michael, J. Behavior modification in rehabilitation. In S. Bijou and D. Baer (eds.) *Child Development: Readings in Experimental Analysis*. New York: Appleton-Century-Crofts, 1967.

ARTICLE 31

Behavior Modification in the Medical Rehabilitation Setting: Rationale and Some Applications[*][1]

PATRICIA L. SAND, ROBERTA B. TRIESCHMANN,
WILBERT E. FORDYCE, and ROY S. FOWLER

Department of Physical Medicine and Rehabilitation, University of Washington Medical
School

Abstract: A significant component of medical rehabilitation is the learning of behaviors appropriate to a specific physical disability. Learning of new self-care, ambulation, interpersonal, vocational and recreational behaviors may all be required. Marginal "motivation" on the part of the patient is frequently seen by rehabilitation workers as the principal impediment to the patient's functional improvement through rehabilitation efforts.

Behavior modification principles can provide direction and some practical strategies for improving response acquisition and "motivating" the patient. A rationale and some examples showing the use of behavioral tactics in a medical rehabilitation setting has been presented, based on the experiences of the authors as psychologists functioning within a medical rehabilitation center.

An increasing number of patients are now being seen who present rehabilitation problems resulting from chronic disease or accident. The patient newly paralyzed as a result of spinal cord injury, the stroke patient, the amputee, the patient who has incurred traumatic brain damage, the patient with a chronic disease such as multiple sclerosis or rheumatoid arthritis—these are representative patients in a medical rehabilitation setting. Previously many such patients died or were viewed as permanently disabled, with limited professional attention being directed toward producing functional improvement. Rehabilitation programs have changed that picture. The general objective of rehabilitation

*Reprinted from *Rehabilitation and Practice Review*, 1970, 1(2), 11–24. With permission from the journal and Patricia L. Sand.

[1]This research project was supported in part by Social and Rehabilitation Grant Number RT-3.

efforts is to reduce residual physical disabilities and to assist the patient toward an optimal level of total functioning, despite a pathology which cannot be totally reversed (Lehmann, 1968). The accomplishment of this objective will frequently require learning of some new behaviors on the part of the patient, and management of learning on the part of an interdisciplinary rehabilitation team which may include nurses, occupational therapists, physical therapists, speech therapists, vocational counselors, prosthetists, social workers, and psychologists, in addition to the physician.

Traditionally, the psychologist's role has been one of assessing the individual characteristics the patient brings to the rehabilitation effort. Is the recently paraplegic patient "motivated" to learn necessary self-care behaviors? Is he "mature" and "emotionally stable" so that he can be counted on to engage in self-care behaviors reliably, and to anticipate and practice necessary changes in social, recreational, and vocational behaviors? Or is he "overly dependent" or "passive-aggressive," and thus likely to avoid engaging in appropriate behaviors? We would see answers to the above questions as insufficient by themselves for psychological direction of the patient's rehabilitation programs.

Knowledge of how the patient's behavior can be influenced and modified through management of his environment is of at least equal importance. After all, even a "dependent" and "intellectually limited" paraplegic *can* reliably emit appropriate bowel and bladder care behaviors, skin care behaviors, recreational, work, and work-support behaviors. However, he may need a carefully programmed environment in order to acquire and maintain these behaviors. The rehabilitation psychologist with a thorough knowledge and practical experience in behavior modification is well prepared to specify management programs which may help produce specific, desired rehabilitation behaviors in the individual patient. His consultation with other rehabilitation team members can assist them in establishing appropriate environmental interactions in all areas, and helping to achieve rehabilitation objectives, even with the "difficult" patient.

BEHAVIOR MODIFICATION PRINCIPLES RELEVANT TO MEDICAL REHABILITATION

1. *Operant Behavior*   Most of the behaviors that are focused on during rehabilitative efforts can be classified as *operants*. This means that

they are behaviors which can be influenced by their consequences. What has happened following the occurrence of an operant response before determines the probability of the response occurring in the future. One may see, for example, the right hemiplegic with aphasia using unintelligible jargon as he attempts to make a request; he may only infrequently point or gesture to communicate his request. If it is clear over time that pointing and gesturing become more frequent as they are followed by favorable consequences (e.g., friendly smiles and appreciative nods from nurses, immediate response to his request) this is evidence that pointing and gesturing are indeed operants.

Some physiologic responses, referred to as *respondents*, are not controlled by their consequences, but only by antecedent stimuli. Changing respondent behaviors requires near-simultaneous presentation of stimuli which automatically elicit a response and new stimuli, which will, through classical conditioning, come to elicit the same response. There are no natural stimuli which automatically elicit the responses of using gestures rather than jargon, walking correctly on a newly-fitted prosthetic limb, drinking prescribed amounts of water, or driving a car using only hand controls. Rehabilitation behaviors such as these are operants, which will develop in accordance with phenomena observed in operant conditioning. There is a considerable amount of empirical data which describes in detail conditions which influence acquisition and maintenance of operant behaviors in animals and humans (Sidman, 1960; Skinner, 1938, 1953, 1961). This provides a foundation from which the behavioral psychologist in a rehabilitation setting may choose to work.

2. *Reinforcement*   Analysis of the patient's day while he is in a medical treatment setting reveals a variety of events which could function as strengthening consequences (reinforcement) for his operant behaviors. Often these events occur randomly; they may occur without staff's consideration of the influence that events such as rest, medication, or social signals showing attention, approval, sympathy, or indifference, could potentially have on the strengthening or weakening of the immediately preceding behaviors.

As Fordyce, Fowler, Lehmann, and DeLateur (1968) suggest, for example, some individuals may learn exaggerated "pain-expressive" behaviors (complaining, grimacing, lying down, refusing to attempt normal activities) because significant environmental events have been such that over a period of time "pain-expressive" behaviors may have been consequated with positive reinforcement and "normal" behavior has been

extinguished. Narcotics, rest, escape from dull or unrewarding responsibilities, and attention from physician and family members may immediately follow "pain" behavior. Talking about "non-pain" topics, doing
daily work, spending a busy and physically active day may be responded
to quite neutrally by the patient's family and physician.

Experience with selected patients having chronic pain disabilities in the
Department of Physical Medicine and Rehabilitation at the University of
Washington tends to support the interpretation that environmental events
may influence "pain."

By reversing the contingencies so that the patient receives rewards
such as rest, medication and attention from health care professionals and
family after or during "normal" behavior, and receives neutral, unexpres-
sive responses after "pain" behavior, a number of patients show diminution or resolution of "pain." The general importance of this is as an
illustration that the delivery of reinforcement in a health care setting may
indeed have powerful implications for the patient's learning of adaptive or
maladaptive behaviors.

3. *Effects of Physical Disability*   Physical disability is likely to disrupt
the behavioral repertoire of an individual. Responses acquired through
the patient's prior reinforcement history may be unavailable physically,
now maladaptive, or not likely to be consequated as they were prior to
disability. Extinction or punishment of old responses and a need for
relearning of alternative responses may occur more suddenly than is the
case in most populations. The high school dropout who becomes permanently paraplegic in a reckless automobile accident or the energetic
salesman left with some residual aphasia following a stroke face profound
disruption of their behavioral repertoires and typical patterns of reinforcement. Directed therapeutic learning, by which is meant careful
attention to the patient's access to new sources of reinforcement and to
his development of alternative behaviors that will lead to reinforcement,
is seen here as an important aspect of "adjustment" to disability.

4. *Techniques for Changing Operant Behaviors*   The rehabilitation
worker can choose from an ever-lengthening list of references to inform
himself regarding operant techniques for changing behavior. Some available sources are highly simplified and practical (Patterson and Gullion,
1968; Bensberg, 1962). Concise statements at an introductory level
(Reese, 1966; Schaefer and Martin, 1969; Holland and Skinner, 1961) can
be found, as well as basic references (Skinner, 1953, 1961). The reader
may find references specific to medical rehabilitation of special interest
(Fowler *et al.*, 1969; Meyerson *et al.*, 1960, 1967; Michael, 1970).

The above references can provide an introduction to operant techniques which is not possible within the scope of the present paper. However, the following points might be kept in mind for now.

The most fundamental principle is that immediate delivery of reinforcement, using cues that actually function as reinforcers for the individual patient, will tend to strengthen behavior. Engineering the relationship that exists between reinforcers in the environment and specific responses the patient makes will influence what may be referred to loosely as "motivation;" it will determine whether and how rapidly new behaviors are acquired.

The following points, adapted from Reese, summarize a general procedure for changing operant behaviors. We have found that discussion of this sequence with ward personnel and students, combined with illustration from ongoing case studies, gives participants an acceptable start toward understanding behavior modification tactics.

STEPS FOR PRODUCING BEHAVIOR CHANGE

1. *Specify desired terminal behavior.* Exactly what should occur; how frequently; under what conditions.
2. *Observe and record* present occurrence of behavior or closely evaluate effectiveness of your behavior change program. This also may reveal possible reinforcers, control stimuli, and response components already in the patient's repertoire.
3. *Structure a favorable situation for learning.* If possible, minimize distractions and cues patient will respond to with anxiety or confusion. Involve patient in developing program, as appropriate. Provide discriminative stimuli for appropriate behavior; remove discriminative stimuli or opportunity for incompatible behavior.
4. *Establish motivation.* Locate reinforcers effective for *this* individual; deprive, if necessary; locate and withhold reinforcers for incompatible behavior.
5. *Plan program using systematic reinforcement* to increase or decrease an occurring behavior; shape new behavior; produce discriminated behavior. Plan to reinforce successive approximations to final performance; raise criterion for reinforcement gradually; move from continuous to intermittent reinforcement.
6. *Implement program.* Remember communication within team so that program as being carried out actually coincides with program

planned. Make sure that correct response is visible (e.g., graphs, records patient keeps himself), so that staff can respond appropriately. Keep records so that you can revise program if it is not changing behavior.

7. *Plan toward maintenance of behavior,* once systematic reinforcement is gradually reduced or removed. Will events in natural environment reinforce new desirable behavior? If not, attempt to influence and rearrange environmental contingencies.

SOME REPRESENTATIVE APPLICATIONS OF BEHAVIOR MODIFICATION IN A MEDICAL REHABILITATION CENTER[2]

Changes in General Behavior Management

As various members of the rehabilitation staff observe and participate in the frequent effectiveness of behavioral techniques, changes in their management of other patient care problems might be anticipated. One would hope that clear behavioral observation becomes more frequent generally, and not just for patients on explicit "operant" programs. Similarly, *staff's awareness of the importance of reinforcement contingencies should improve quality of care for all patients.* We have no "hard" data on this score. But impressionistically, it does seem that many staff members have assimilated a behavioral approach and apply it with many of their patients.

From time to time one may still observe ward personnel busying themselves with *other* patients while a patient is engaging in appropriate behaviors, e.g., doing his exercises, working on his OT project, performing difficult new self-care activities, and becoming immediately available at the first sign of inappropriate behaviors, such as refusing to complete exercises, self-deprecatory comments, or ineffectual inability to complete a task. Frequently, though one hears staff comments, paired with appropriate behaviors along the following lines, "I plan to stay nearby . . . want to make sure I spend some extra time chatting with Mr ⎯⎯ while he is working as hard as he is today." "I have noticed that the OT praises ⎯⎯ more and comments more on specific improvement. He is learning well in

[2]The help and support of medical, nursing, occupational and physical therapy staffs in carrying out these programs is gratefully acknowledged.

her sessions now ... I'll plan on using the same approach." "All the nurses have been looking for something in self-care that ____ does well, so we can reinforce it. Maybe that will give him a better start toward all the other self-care skills he'll have to learn."

Operant techniques which have been tried with patients having special problems in learning rehabilitation behaviors may be adapted into routine management practice so that the psychologist no longer needs to consult with staff on management of recurring problems. Management of fluid intake behavior provides one example of such a problem.

Fluid Intake

Patients with spinal cord injury are advised to maintain daily fluid intake in excess of 3,000 cc's so that renal complications may be avoided. Often it is difficult for patients to develop habits around necessary fluid intake.

Figure 31.1 shows fluid intake for a 46-year old paraplegic, injured at age 16, who, according to medical records, had for years neglected adequate fluid intake. The importance of adequate fluid intake had been explained before and was re-explained by both nurses and physicians during the first two weeks of his hospitalization at the rehabilitation

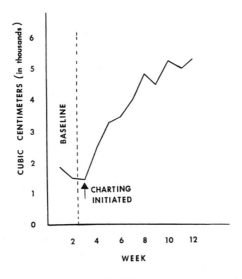

Fig. 31.1.

center. He "understood" why he was to drink, but yet the record shows that these attempts to inform and persuade him were not all effective in changing his behavior.

At the beginning of the third week of his hospitalization, bar graphs were posted in his room showing daily totals for fluid intake and output. The nurses instructed the patient on how to keep his own records. The graph provided immediate feedback for the patient on how adequate and consistent fluid intake was. This also gave visibility to the correct behaviors, so that physicians, nurses, and psychologists on rounds could comment favorably and praise the patient when he was drinking well. As is apparent in the graph, these very simple techniques were sufficient to increase fluid intake. This approach is now routine and is carried on by nurses, with the occasional help of a psychology research assistant.

CONSISTENCY OF SELF-CARE BEHAVIORS IN A YOUNG ADULT PARAPLEGIC

Background

The patient was a twenty-eight year old high school graduate whose paraplegia resulted from a bullet wound received under police fire while patient attempted to get away following a robbery. His history included variable general labor work and drug habituation. His performance in the rehabilitation program was inconsistent. He often omitted necessary self-care tasks or took so long in completing them that he missed scheduled therapies.

Procedure

Behaviors expected of the patient were defined and listed as illustrated in the copy of the patient's morning care schedule in Table 31.1. Records of the number of items he completed per day were kept for one week. Based on this performance quotas were set, starting slightly below the observed frequency. Expected daily totals were increased by one during each successive week. Meeting quotas was rewarded by a week-end pass to his home, with his wife and children, under personal recognizance as authorized by the Police Department.

Table 31.1.   Program for W. P.

The following is a list of activities that W. is expected to perform every day. Staff members will initial in the proper place to indicate whether W. has successfully performed the activities expected of him.

Morning	Staff Signatures												
	Mon		Tues		Wed		Thurs		Fri		Sat		Sun
	Yes	No	Y	N	Y	N	Y	N	Y	N	Y	N	Y	N
1. Record Ph														
2. Record intake-output														
3. Catheter irrigation														
4. Take medication														
5. Wash himself														
6. Dress himself														
7. Remove and clean leg bag														
8. Put braces on himself														
9. Be at OT by 10:00														
10. Be at PT by 11:00														

Results

Introduction of the list by itself, without additional reinforcement contingencies, produced improved behavior. With the list alone, satisfactory items per day ranged from thirteen to twenty-two, with twenty-two as the total possible. Once quotas were set, the patient started participating actively in all aspects of the rehabilitation program. By the end of the first week he was consistently at or above nineteen out of the twenty-two items. This performance was maintained for the following four weeks until his discharge to another medical service where he continued to show exemplary self-care, despite discontinuance of the formal operant program.

TEMPER TANTRUMS AND NON-COOPERATIVE BEHAVIOR IN A SEVEN YEAR OLD BRAIN DAMAGED CHILD

Background

C. incurred brain damage at the age of $4\frac{1}{2}$, after being thrown from a horse. During an initial rehabilitation effort six months after injury, he became able to walk with a wheeled walkerette and use a few words despite having been initially aphasic and functionally quadriplegic. Since then, he had made little progress in ambulation or self-care, where he continued to rely on others to dress and feed him completely. Speech had improved to meaningful eight and nine word sentences. He was working at a first grade reading level in special education classes. His re-admission to the rehabilitation center at the age of seven was planned to provide medical re-evaluation and intensive physical and occupational therapy for improved ambulation and self-care.

Problems

Temper tantrums had been reported as a frequent occurrence at home and school; they also became a problem at the rehabilitation center. C.'s tantrums were characterized by loud screaming, and spitting at, hitting, kicking, and biting treatment personnel who were nearby. Full tantrums, which included hitting, biting, and kicking, occurred as many as six times a day during the first $1\frac{1}{2}$ weeks of treatment. Situations in which he was to comply with some mildly uncomfortable treatment procedure (e.g., PT exercises) or was asked to try to do something new (e.g., feed himself) were especially likely to produce tantrum behavior.

Therapists indicated that on five of the first eight days in physical therapy and occupational therapy, one or more therapy sessions had to be cut short. Twice physical therapy had to be discontinued after ten minutes, though a full hour of treatment had been prescribed.

Refusal to work on rehabilitation tasks was also a problem. The child would indicate, "I *can't* do that!" and refuse to participate, despite attempts made by therapists to make the task appealing or game-like.

C. appeared to understand the general purpose for his exercise and therapies, and he appeared to like his therapists. Despite this, his refusal to comply with requests and his tantrums were interfering with all therapeutic efforts.

Procedure

It was decided that C. would need special behavioral management in order to benefit maximally from rehabilitation. It seemed that the attention C. was getting during tantrums might be helping to maintain their frequency. Also, it seemed likely that "progress," or signs of "progress" would not be as apparent or meaningful to this child as they were for our adult patients. Therefore, tangible extrinsic rewards should be made available when he was behaving appropriately.

Nurses and therapists were instructed to put C. in his room promptly and in a matter-of-fact manner as soon as he began a tantrum. Thus, he had little opportunity to scream, bite, hit, or kick in their immediate presence and they had little opportunity to respond to him attentively as he showed these inappropriate behaviors. After a fifteen-minute "time out" period, therapist entered his room pleasantly and returned with him to the treatment area.

To improve cooperative behavior and compliance with requests, nurses and therapists started giving C. tokens when he followed their requests or as he worked on difficult or new tasks (e.g., PT exercises). At the end of each day he could purchase with these tokens treats, such as small toys, extra fruit juice, candies, a picnic lunch with the nurse outside the hospital. During the fifth week of treatment, a reversal period was introduced during which C. continued to receive praise for good performance, but neither tokens nor "time out." Observations were made to see whether his behavior corresponded to his initial behavior in the hospital under reversal conditions. Following the eight day reversal period, use of "time out" following all tantrum and tokens for cooperation in physical therapy was resumed.

Results

Within the week that the program was instituted, C.'s behavior began improving. Figure 31.2, summarizes the occurrence of problem behaviors in PT. As is indicated in the figure, during C.'s pre-treatment period (Period A) refusal and verbal tantrum behavior is estimated by therapist to have occurred in all sessions. Physical tantrum behavior occurred in most sessions. With institution of the treatment plan (Period B), physical tantrum behavior and refusal became appreciably less frequent. Screaming and whining continued, but at a reduced rate. During the reversal period (Period C), when child continued to receive praise and social

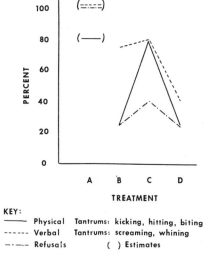

KEY:
——— Physical Tantrums: kicking, hitting, biting
------ Verbal Tantrums: screaming, whining
—·—·— Refusals   ( ) Estimates

Fig. 31.2.

attention for appropriate behavior, but no tokens or "time outs," a marked increase in physical tantrum behavior and some increase in refusal occurred. With resumption of the program (Period D), problem behaviors again declined.

His behavior in occupational therapy was demonstrably more cooperative, as is shown by Fig. 31.3. Here again it appears that the behavior program produced immediate improvement in his behavior. He has tended to show progressively less problem behavior over the course of treatment. The reversal period did not produce any increase in problem behavior. From this, one might assume that in this area his behavior had come under the control of social cues (attention and approval), and intrinsic reinforcement in OT activities. Together these were sufficient to maintain appropriate behavior, once it got started. Based on this data, it was decided that there was no need to continue the token program in OT during period D though tokens were continued in PT and use of "time outs" continued in all areas.

The influence of a token economy on staff behavior is illustrated in Fig. 31.4, which shows the average number of verbal reinforcers and tokens delivered per physical therapy session during the various intervals. With tokens no longer being dispensed, the therapist actually started giving *fewer* social reinforcers, though one might assume that she would compensate for loss of tangible reinforcers by praising the child and

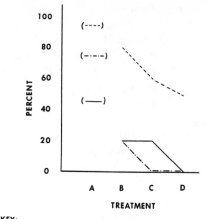

KEY:

—— Physical Tantrums : kicking, hitting, biting
---- Verbal Tantrums : screaming, whining
—·—·— Refusals ( ) Estimates

Fig. 31.3.

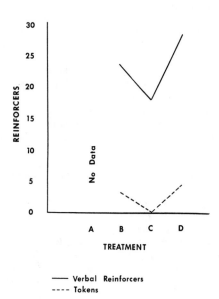

—— Verbal Reinforcers
---- Tokens

Fig. 31.4.

showing approval more frequently. This finding is consistent with the experience of other workers using token economies.

By the end of hospitalization, C. had made excellent progress. In physical therapy he was starting to use correct movement patterns in independent walking. He was feeding himself independently with assistive devices. He appeared as a cheerful, appealing child whom nurses and therapists worked with willingly. C. behaved well and thoroughly enjoyed frequent out-of-hospital passes that nursing staff members arranged for him on their own free time. The behavioral management program was seen as of assistance in promoting productivity and adjustment in the rehabilitation setting.

REFERENCES

Bensberg, G. *Teaching the Mentally Retarded: A Handbook for Ward Personnel.* Southern Regional Education Board, Atlanta, Georgia, 1962.

Fordyce, W. E., Fowler, R. S., Jr., Lehmann, J. F., and DeLateur, B. J. Some implications of learning in problems of chronic pain. *Journal of Chronic Diseases*, 1968, **21**, 179–190.

Fowler, R. S., Jr., Fordyce, W. E., and Berni, R. Operant conditioning in chronic illness. *American Journal of Nursing*, 1969, **69**, 1226–1228.

Holland, J. G. and Skinner, B. F. *The Analysis of Behavior.* New York: McGraw-Hill, 1961.

Lehmann, J. F. Patient care needs as a basis for development of objectives of physical medicine and rehabilitation teaching in undergraduate medical schools. *Journal of Chronic Diseases*, 1968, **21**, 3–12.

Meyerson, L., Kerr, N., and Michael, J. Behavior modification in rehabilitation. In *Child Development: Readings in Experimental Analysis.* Bijou, S. and Baer, D. (Eds.), New York: Appleton-Century-Crofts, 1967.

Meyerson, L., Michael, J., Mowrer, O. H., Osgood, C. E., and Staats, A. W. Learning, behavior, and rehabilitation. In *Psychological Research and Rehabilitation*, Lofquist, L. H. (Ed.), Conference Report, 68–111, Miami Beach, Florida, November 9–12, 1960.

Michael, J. Rehabilitation. In *Behavior Modification in Clinical Psychology*, Neuringer, Charles and Michael, Jack, (Eds.), New York: Appleton-Century-Crofts, 1970.

Patterson, G. R., and Gullion, M. E. *Living with Children: New Methods for Parents and Teachers.* Research Press, 1968.

Reese, E. P. *Analysis of Human Operant Behavior.* Wm. C. Brown Company, 1966.

Schaefer, H. H., and Martin, P. L. *Behavioral Therapy.* Blakiston Division, New York: McGraw-Hill Book Company, 1969.

Sidman, M. *Tactics of Scientific Research.* New York: Basic Books, 1960.

Skinner, B. F. *The Behavior of Organisms.* New York: Appleton-Century-Crofts, 1938.

Skinner, B. F. *Science and Human Behavior.* New York: Macmillan, 1953.

Skinner, B. F. *Cumulative Record.* New York: Appleton-Century-Crofts, 1961.

ARTICLE 32

Case Studies in Behavioral Research in Rehabilitation*[1]

ROBERT GOODKIN

Institute of Physical Medicine and Rehabilitation, New York University Medical Center

Abstract: Problems of four rehabilitation patients were approached with operant methodology. These problems included learning to write faster with the non-dominant hand, learning to increase speed on a key-punch machine, learning to push a wheelchair faster, increasing understandable and appropriate speech, and decreasing unintelligible and perseverative speech. Each study began by measuring the patients' performance on the task before treatment. Then, classes of desired and undesired responses were designated, and reinforcers and punishers capable of increasing and decreasing these responses were investigated. Such response classes as speed and frequency of desired and undesired responses were affected. Both verbal and perceptual-motor responses were modified. It was concluded that operant techniques may enable the psychologist to contribute to a variety of areas in the rehabilitation center which have, to date, received little attention. Such techniques provide a rational technology for training disabled people.

Psychology is frequently defined as the science of behavior, with the major goals of prediction and control of behavior. Prediction and control involve a concern with the processes that go into behavior modification (i.e., increasing, maintaining, and decreasing behaviors). Though the pure psychological researcher is concerned primarily with establishing general principles that operate in all behavior, the applied researcher involves himself with application of these principles to the particular situation. In recent years methods derived from the behavioral laboratory have been

*Reprinted from *Perceptual and Motor Skills*, 1966, **23**, 171–182. With permission from publisher and Robert Goodkin.

[1]This study was in part financed by the Vocational Rehabilitation Administration Grant No. 35-T-66, under the direction of Leonard Diller. The support of the VRA to the Institute of Physical Medicine and Rehabilitation, New York University Medical Center, as a research and training center also helped to facilitate this study.

applied to such settings as the classroom (Schramm, 1964), the mental institution (Ayllon & Michael, 1959), and the school counselor's office (Michael & Meyerson, 1962). One arena which lends itself to behavioral research but which has received very little attention in this regard is the rehabilitation center (Meyerson *et al.*, 1960). One of the major activities in the rehabilitation setting is increasing certain behaviors and decreasing others. The increasingly rich literature on practical means of modifying behavior (Ullmann & Krasner, 1965) indicates that the psychologist may have much to offer in the rehabilitation effort in ways which have been relatively unexplored.

Instances in the rehabilitation center that involve increasing or decreasing specific behaviors include: teaching ambulation and balance in physical therapy classes, teaching fine perceptual-motor skills such as writing and operating office machines in occupational therapy classes, teaching patients to push their wheelchairs and to transfer from wheelchairs to other furniture in activities of daily living classes, teaching aphasic patients to increase understandable and appropriate speech and to decrease unintelligible and inappropriate speech. In short, any section of rehabilitation that involves the teaching of motor or verbal skills can be broken down into units of behavior to be increased or decreased.

This article describes some applications of modern behavior theory, primarily operant conditioning methodology, to rehabilitation problems. These applications may be illustrated by the following case studies which have been conducted at the Institute of Physical Medicine and Rehabilitation.

CASE STUDIES

In the following cases the behavioral principles of reinforcement, punishment, extinction, and modeling were systematically introduced. The major approach to the patients involved: (1) observing and quantifying the patient's mode of responding to the task in question, (2) specifically defining a response class of behaviors to be accelerated and a class of behaviors to be decelerated, and (3) finding available reinforcers and punishers capable of altering these behaviors. The treatment methods employed in these cases are all available, and many have been employed to a degree by therapists in the various areas. The major difference in the present approach is the systematic nature of clearly defining responses and consistently treating them in a predetermined fashion.

Case Number One

Miss H. is a 41-yr.-old woman who suffered a cerebrovascular accident (CVA) following heart surgery, resulting in paralysis of her right extremities (hemiplegia) and moderate aphasia. Both her ability to speak and to understand speech were moderately affected. Prior to her disability she was employed in an office where she operated a number of business machines. Approximately one year after her CVA she was put on an occupational therapy program to relearn the operation of the key-punch machine with her left, non-dominant hand. She had manipulated this machine with two hands before her disability. The key-punch machine entailed punching holes correctly on IBM cards by means of an electronic keyboard. After working at this task approximately one-half hour a day for several months, she was making little progress in terms of speed of copying numbers. She copied numbers very slowly.

At this point E began to observe Miss H. and recorded the time it took her to punch each series of numbers on the IBM cards assigned to her. The average time to complete each card was calculated each day. She received ten trials per day. After a base rate of performance was obtained on Days 1 and 2, the training procedure began. This training consisted of: (1) telling the patient she was doing well, (2) telling her the number of seconds it took to complete a card, (3) telling her how much time she cut off her previous best time when she performed the task faster. These verbal responses by E were intended as reinforcing conditions. When she performed more slowly than her former best time, she was simply told to go on to the next card. This lack of responding by E was intended as an extinguishing condition. The first verbal reinforcement in a session came after Miss H. responded faster than her average time the previous day. At the end of the session she was told her average time on that day, and this time was compared with her performance on previous days.

It was observed that prior to this treatment, verbal reinforcement by the occupational therapist was not contingent upon actual performance but was merely given periodically on a subjective basis. By carefully recording performance on the task, verbal reinforcement could be systematically administered on the basis of objective data. This procedure functioned to shape closer approximations to the desired behavior, faster performance. By first obtaining a measure of performance prior to intervention by E and then measuring changes in key-punching speed while the treatment was in operation, the effects of the treatment could be objectively evaluated.

The results are indicated in Fig. 32.1. The patient's mean time to complete each card was reduced within ten sessions. Although she initially averaged 110.6 sec. per card, on Day 9 she had an average time of 71.0 sec. Sessions ranged from 15 to 30 min. each.

Approximately 4 mo. after Miss H. was seen in regard to key-punching, the occupational therapist told *E* that, although this patient had been practicing writing with her left hand for over a year, she appeared to be making little gain in speed of writing. Miss H. stated that she was frustrated because she felt she was not writing any faster than she did 6 mo. ago.

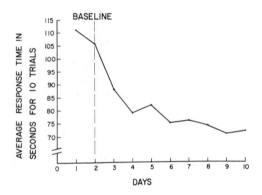

Fig. 32.1. Changes in average response time on a key-punching task.

This behavior was approached by recording *S*'s performance and reinforcing only better performance. An additional condition of making periodic suggestions was added in an effort to correct errors faster than shaping alone would. First, the number of letters copied from a paragraph during 1-min. trials was recorded. She was given 10 trials each session with a ½-min. rest interval between the trials. The average number of letters per trial was calculated at the end of each session.

After a base rate of performance was obtained (two sessions), the training procedure began. This training consisted of: (1) telling Miss H. that she was doing well, (2) telling her the number of letters she copied during the one-minute trial, (3) telling her how many letters she added to her previous best score when she copied more letters. When she copied fewer letters than her best previous performance, she was told nothing. The first verbal reinforcement each session came when the patient copied more letters than her average performance on the previous day. At the end of each session she was told the average number of letters she copied per trial that day, and this was compared with her performance in each previous session.

In addition to this treatment, which was in effect from the third session on, certain suggestions were made on given days. Since it was noted that she often lost her place, on Day 4 it was suggested that she use an underliner. On Day 5 she was encouraged to look at two or three words before writing them, rather than copying one word at a time as she had been doing. On Day 6 she was told to say two or three words aloud before copying them, since she still frequently copied only one word at a time.

The results are shown in Fig. 32.2. From *S*'s first day of treatment, she gradually improved her writing speed each day. She copied an average of approximately 27 letters per minute prior to the treatment conditions, but after five treatment days Miss H. averaged nearly 37 letters in the same period of time.

Further research would be necessary to evaluate the separate effects of the reinforcement and of the suggestions in this situation. However, since the primary aim was to facilitate the patient's performance to a maximum level and not to test the efficacy of different approaches, no specific data were gathered to clarify this question.

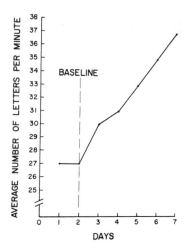

Fig. 32.2. Changes in number of words copied per minute.

Case Number Two

Mrs. B. is a 61-yr.-old woman with a 15-yr. history of Parkinson's disease. It was called to *E*'s attention by the psychologist working with Mrs. B. and by the activities of the daily living therapist working with her that Mrs. B. refused to push her wheelchair. Mrs. B. stated that it was no use trying because even very small children were able to propel their chairs much faster than she was. It was suggested by her physician that it would be advisable for Mrs. B. to propel her own chair because it would make her less dependent on others. Moreover, muscle tests suggested that she did have the strength and range of motion to perform the activity.

Observations of the patient in her regular activities in the daily living class suggested that she had put forth very little effort in propelling her wheelchair and that she spent nearly half of the session complaining to the therapist that she could not do it. Mrs. B. was seen by *E* in a classroom free from distractions of other people. Prior to the introduction of the experimental conditions, strips of red tape were placed on the floor to mark off each 5-ft. interval of a 20-ft. distance. Each trial consisted of having the patient move 5 ft. The time was recorded and used as a base rate. There were 1-min. rest intervals before starting each new trial. The average time to propel the chair 5 ft. was calculated at the end of each session. The patient was seen for approximately 20 min. each day.

Table 32.1. Response Time (in sec.) to Propel a Wheelchair a Distance of Five Feet.

Trials (5 ft.)	Day 1	Day 2	Day 3
1	32	25	17
2	20	19	15
3	25	17	22
4	29	23	20
5	24	15	20
6	19	17	16
7		20	15
8		15	17
9			16
10			21
11			17
Total	149	151	196
M	24.8	18.9	17.8

The treatment started on the second day. It consisted of: (1) telling Mrs. B. that she was doing well, (2) telling her the number of seconds it took her to go 5 ft., and (3) telling her how many seconds she cut off her previous record when she performed faster. When she performed more slowly, she was told nothing. Each day the patient received her initial verbal reinforcement after her first response that excelled her average time of the previous day.

At the end of the session the patient was told her average time for that day, and it was compared with that obtained on previous days. In this way she tended to speak more about her own performance and less of how she compared with others. She also complained very little during the second and third sessions.

The results are indicated in Table 32.1. Each day she spontaneously asked to do more trials. Mrs. B. wheeled her chair faster and further each day. Unfortunately she was unable to continue with this procedure because of her discharge from the Institute.

Case Number Three[2]

Mr. M. had a stroke resulting in right hemiplegia and moderate to severe receptive and expressive aphasia. His speech therapist regarded him as an aphasic patient who appeared to be making very little progress on the treatment program. He was also perseverating a great deal during speech therapy sessions so that he tended to repeat words that were inappropriate to stimuli being presented to him. *E* observed from brief attempts to communicate with the patient before regular speech therapy sessions that Mr. M. seemed to use more words in attempting to respond to general questions asked of him than he did to the highly structured stimuli presented in his speech therapy sessions. When asked where he had just come from, for example, he said, "class . . . walking around . . . cane." In his regular speech sessions he was working on a task that called for naming objects in pictures such as a comb, a pen, a house, and a car. After working on the same pictures on a daily basis for a period of 2 mo. there was little carry-over from session to session in responding correctly to these items.

Mr. M. was seen by *E* outside of his regular speech therapy class time. The goals were: (1) to increase the frequency of understandable words

[2]The author wishes to thank Leonard Krasner for his suggestions with regard to Mr. M.

and phrases that he would emit in response to a relatively unstructured question, (2) to decrease the frequency of unintelligible utterances, (3) to decrease the frequency of repeated verbal responses (perseverations). Each day the following questions were asked and responded to for 2 min.:

1. Tell me about this room. What are some of the things you see in the room?
2. Tell me about your clothes. Describe the clothes you are wearing.
3. Tell me about your classes here. What classes do you have and what are you doing in them?
4. What kinds of things do you do outside of your classes?
5. Tell me about where you live. Describe your home.
6. Tell me about your family. Tell me about some of the people in your family.
7. Name as many animals as you can.
8. Name as many cities and towns as you can.
9. Tell me a little about New York City.
10. Tell me a little about IPMR (The Institute of Physical Medicine and Rehabilitation).

During the first five sessions, no experimental treatment was introduced, and a base rate of responding was recorded. For the purpose of this study, good responses were defined as utterances that included at least one clearly distinguishable word following the stimulus question. Bad responses were defined as those continuous utterances that contained no new words but consisted of either repeated words or only indistinguishable sounds. As long as at least one new word was produced in a response, it was counted as a good response. These response classes were found to be appropriate for Mr. M. since he tended to speak in brief utterances with pauses of at least 3 sec. between responses. As seen in Fig. 32.3, Mr. M. responded fairly consistently from day to day, generally emitting slightly greater number of bad responses than good ones.

Starting on Day 6, Questions 1, 4, 5, 7, and 9 were treated in the following way: good responses were followed by E's (1) giving a verbal compliment or a comment on the item's correctness and (2) repeating the response (i.e., very good, it's a chair). Bad responses were followed by E's shaking his head and not responding verbally.

With Questions 2, 3, 6, 8, and 10, Mr. M. responded and E did not respond verbally or with any specific gesture. These questions will be referred to as non-treated questions. As seen in Figs. 32.3 and 32.4, this treatment had little influence on the patient's total performance, and he

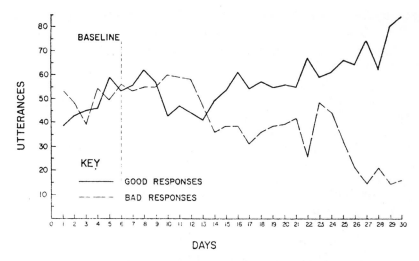

Fig. 32.3. Total frequency of good and bad utterances per session.

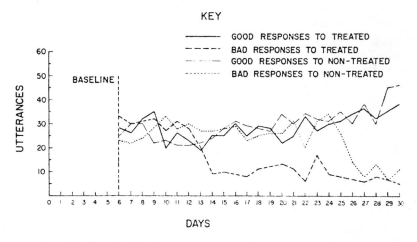

Fig. 32.4. Good and bad utterances to treated and non-treated questions.

did not perform very differently under the experimental and control conditions. Because adequate responses were neither increased nor decreased by these operations, although they were intended as reinforcers and punishers, they cannot accurately be so labeled.

Following this procedure numerous other conditions were systematically introduced on different days. The most effective changes in behavior were noted on Days 14, 22, and 26. On Day 14 the following procedure was in effect. After good responses E complimented Mr. M., repeated the good response, and pointed to a box of blue poker chips from which Mr. M. took one chip (introduced on Day 9). Following bad responses, E told the patient the nature of his error (repetition or unintelligible utterance) and pointed to a box of red poker chips from which the patient took a chip (introduced on Day 13). At the end of the session E added up the pile of good chips in front of the patient. The condition added this day was the patient's taking the red chip by himself rather than E's placing the chip in front of him as in previous sessions. The procedure had a considerable effect in reducing the frequency of bad responses to the experimentally treated questions.

On Day 22 a modeling procedure was introduced prior to the patient's responding to treated questions. This procedure consisted of E's responding to the question for 1 min. During each of the five modeling periods, E included several new good responses, two repeats, and one unintelligible response. Following E's good responses he rewarded himself with a compliment, a repetition of the response, and a blue poker chip, and following bad responses he punished himself by saying the kind of error he committed and by taking a red poker chip. Other than the introduction of modeling, the procedure was the same as on Day 14. When this procedure was introduced, Mr. M. made the most intelligible responses and the least errors up to that point.

In the beginning of Session 26, Mr. M. was instructed to take a blue chip after every good response and a red chip after every error without being told verbally or through gestures whether his responses were good or bad. Both boxes of chips were closed while responding to non-treated questions. During the 2-min. response period, Mr. M. independently reinforced or punished his own responses to each treated question. Then, E first responded to Mr. M. A blue chip was given for each good response tallied by E and a red chip was given for each bad response. As each red chip was placed down, E stated the reason for it. At the end of each treated question, the number of blue and red chips put down by Mr. M. was openly compared with the number of each put down by E. After only two questions were responded to, there was close agreement between Mr. M. and E in the number of red and blue chips given. This treatment resulted in a sharp reduction in the number of bad responses made to non-treated questions. Up to this session, the numbers of good and bad responses to non-treated questions were nearly the same. This resulted even though non-treated questions were not modeled.

New experimental conditions are still being introduced in an effort to: (1) produce more good responses, (2) decrease bad responses, (3) increase generalization to other situations, and (4) increase self-monitoring.

Case Number Four

Essentially the same approach employed with Mr. M. was used with Mrs. S., who, following a CVA, had also suffered a speech disturbance of 3 yr. duration when E first saw her. Unlike Mr. M., this patient used many words, but she tended to shift very quickly from one topic to another and spoke quite inappropriately in terms of questions asked of her. Rather than receiving reinforcement and punishment in connection with new words, perseverations, and unintelligible talk as in the case of Mr. M., a different response class was used with Mrs. S. Receiving the above-mentioned stimulus questions and responding for 2 min., this patient was reinforced verbally and with a blue poker chip for each 15-sec. period which included some material relevant to the question. She was told that she was off the topic and received a red chip after each 15-sec. period that failed to include any relevant material. In fewer than 15 sessions Mrs. S. had shown a marked reduction in irrelevant responses to the stimulus questions.

DISCUSSION

These cases are intended to illustrate a few of the situations within the rehabilitation setting which might profit from systematic behavioral research. Though the principles involved are not new, their systematic application in a context of staying close to observable responses to tasks which are rather common in a physical, medical and rehabilitation setting is novel.

In general, modeling and reinforcement in the form of tokens, verbal compliments, repetition of good responses, and objective feedback tended to increase desirable responses. Extinction (not responding) and punishment in the form of tokens and stating errors tended to decrease undesirable responses.

Many of the behaviors that form the criteria for admission and discharge to a rehabilitation program and constitute the heart of the treatment program can be broken down into quantifiable response classes which the therapist can manage. Behavioral techniques might well offer the psychologist a method for contributing to a wide range of rehabilitation activities which have been hitherto ignored.

The question of "the role of the psychologist" was raised by a few therapists who wondered what interest a psychologist had in physical therapy or occupational therapy treatment problems. However, a general explanation of the relevance and aims of the psychologist's recommendations generally sufficed to elicit cooperation and interest. Approaching patients in collaboration with, rather than independently of, the regular therapist proved to be most fruitful.

The preliminary research cited suggests that setting up typical rehabilitation situations in a manner which permits objective measurement and careful observation might be of considerable value in assessing more accurately the progress patients are making and the effects of new training techniques. Three response measures which seem to be applicable are: (1) speed, (2) frequency of desired responses, and (3) frequency of undesired responses. The above cases suggest that gross and fine perceptual-motor behaviors and the content of verbal behavior all lend themselves to operant study.

Pilot data are being collected in which an effort is being made to teach the wife of an aphasic patient to function as a continued speech therapist. The technique employed permits observations to be made on both the effects of E's feedback on the wife's verbal behavior and of her information on the patient's behavior. The wife observed E through a one-way vision screen. E asked the patient the 10 questions listed above. The patient responded for 2 min. and following each intelligible utterance E complimented and repeated it. After each unintelligible response or repetition of a previous good response, E stated the nature of the error.

After observing two sessions, the patient's wife was given a copy of the 10 questions and was told to permit the patient to respond for 2 min. before progressing to the next question. The patient and his wife then entered the experimental room where they could be observed by E. She was given a single earphone, through which she could hear E's voice. The patient could not hear comments made by E. During the session E said nothing and simply observed the operant behavior of the patient and his wife. It was observed that in dealing with the patient, the wife exhibited a number of behaviors cited by speech therapists as being undesirable (Taylor, 1958). (1) She strongly criticized his errors in speaking. (2) She neglected to show approval of successful efforts to produce words. (3) She rapidly supplied words he was searching for without giving him time to emit them himself.

In two following sessions *E* interceded every time the patient's wife made one of the above errors. She was verbally reinforced each time she showed approval of a good response and was told to ease up on the criticism or to delay in supplying words when she committed errors of this type. These comments by *E* were given at the time of occurrence of the error in an effort to decrease their frequency. It is too early to evaluate the effects of this technique.

A study will be carried out in which the relatives of aphasics will be taught by this method to categorize the patient's verbal behavior into appropriate response classes and to engage in speech training methods. The methods taught will closely approximate those procedures the patient had been receiving from *E* prior to the experimental participation of the relative.

Although the major concern of the author in the above cases was the application of generally accepted operant principles to rehabilitation problems, a number of basic research questions emerged. These include the following: (1) What are the definitions of response class, and what constitutes desired and undesired behaviors? (2) What are the effects of cues or suggestions given in addition to reinforcement as in Case Two? (3) Does self-punishment result in more effective deceleration of undesired behavior than punishment by others would? In the case of Mr. M. the introduction of self-punishment was accompanied by a marked decrease in undesirable responses. This finding agrees with some recent findings by Ogden Lindsley. (4) Are tokens, in themselves, sufficient to alter behavior in some populations? It is of some interest that poker chips aided in modifying behavior without being "cashed in" for material rewards as they are in many studies. Perhaps with populations of patients who indicate strong wishes to improve, tokens representing positive and negative feedback are sufficient to alter behavior. (5) Are undesired responses eliminated much more readily than desired responses are acquired in patients with aphasia? The cases of Mr. M. and Mrs. S. suggest that this may be true. This observation relates to the question, what does the patient learn in acquiring skills in rehabilitation (Diller & Weinberg, 1962; Diller, 1965).

REFERENCES

Ayllon, T. and Michael, J. The psychiatric nurse as a behavioral engineer. *J. exp. Anal. Behav.*, 1959, **2**, 323–334.

Diller, L. Rehabilitation and behavior pathology. *Bulletin of Division 22, APA*, 1965, **12**, 44–49.

Diller, L. and Weinberg, J. Learning in hemiplegia. Paper read at APA meetings in St. Louis, Missouri, 1962.

Meyerson, L., Michael, J., Mowrer, O. H., Osgood, C. E., and Staats, A. W. Learning, behavior, and rehabilitation. In L. H. Lofquist (Ed.), *Psychological Research and Rehabilitation*. Washington, D.C.: American Psychological Association, 1960. Pp. 68–111.

Michael, J. and Meyerson, L. A behavioral approach to counseling and guidance. *Harv. Educ. Rev.*, 1962, **32**, 382–402.

Schramm, W. *The Research on Programmed Instruction: An Annotated Bibliography.* Washington, D.C.: U.S. Govt. Printing Office, 1964. (No. FS5.234:34034)

Taylor, M. L. *Understanding aphasia.* New York: Inst. Phys. Med. & Rehabil., New York Univer. Med. Centr, 1958. (Publ. No. 2)

Ullmann, L. P. and Krasner, L., *Case Studies in Behavior Modification.* New York: Holt, Rinehart & Winston, 1965.

ARTICLE 33

Modifying the Dispensing of Reinforcers: Some Implications for Behavior Modification with Hospitalized Patients*

ROGER C. KATZ,[1] CLAUDIA A. JOHNSON, and SIDNEY GELFAND

University of Utah and Salt Lake City Veterans Administration Hospital

Abstract: This study systematically examined the effects of instructions, verbal prompts, and monetary reinforcement given to psychiatric aides for reinforcing patients within a token economy program. Baseline observations revealed that psychiatric aides dispensed low rates of reinforcement for appropriate patient behavior. Instructing the aides had no effect, verbal prompts produced a slight increase, and a monetary bonus resulted in a substantial increase in aide-dispensed reinforcement. This latter change in aide behavior was accompanied by improved functioning in two of the three patients selected for observation. When the monetary bonus was withdrawn, aide-dispensed reinforcement as well as task-oriented patient behavior declined to a near baseline level. Procedures for maintaining the reinforcing behavior of aides toward patients are briefly discussed.

Several studies have demonstrated the utility of psychiatric aides as behavioral engineers in a token reinforcement environment (Ayllon & Azrin, 1968; Schaefer & Martin, 1969). Conversely, other studies have shown that some psychiatric aides may unwittingly reinforce, and thus perpetuate, the inappropriate responding of hospitalized patients (Ayllon, 1965; Ayllon & Haughton, 1962).

Hospital personnel whose vocational roles are intended to be therapeutic do not necessarily perform according to these expectations (Gelfand,

---

*Reprinted from *Behavior Therapy*, 1972, **3**, 579–588. Copyright © 1972 by Academic Press, Inc. With permission from Academic Press, Inc. and Roger C. Katz.

[1]Special thanks are extended to Madge Elliot, R.N. and Charles Parsons for their helpfulness and cooperation in carrying out this study. Requests for reprints should be addressed to Roger C. Katz, Department of Community and Family Medicine, Medical Center, University of Utah, Salt Lake City, Utah 84112.

473

Gelfand, & Dobson, 1967). In a token reinforcement program, for example, it is important that psychiatric aides not only dispense a high density of reinforcement for appropriate patient behavior, but also that they withhold or remove reinforcement contingent upon inappropriate patient activity. Although it is assumed that instructions, demonstrations, and in-service training are usually sufficient to instill and maintain these therapeutic contingency dispensing behaviors, instruction alone, without accompanying reinforcement for the instructed activity, may exert weak or only temporary behavioral control (Ayllon & Azrin, 1964; Hopkins, 1968).

Data obtained by Buel (1972) and others (Patterson, 1971; Patterson, Ray, & Shaw, 1968) point to the value of actively prompting or systematically reinforcing the therapeutic responding of psychiatric aides toward patients in their care. Since behavior is primarily a function of the reinforcement it produces, programs to modify behavior should include reinforcing outcomes for those individuals who are the main dispensers of reinforcement. In a psychiatric hospital, these reinforcer dispensers are psychiatric aides, technicians, and nursing personnel.

The present study investigated the effects of three separate manipulations (instructions, verbal prompts, and monetary reinforcement) on the reinforcement dispensing behavior of several psychiatric aides in a token economy environment. The purpose of the research was to examine the relative efficacies of these procedures in modifying the reinforcing behavior of aides toward patients, and to determine the effects of these manipulations on selected classes of appropriate and inappropriate patient behavior.

METHOD

Setting and Subjects

The study was conducted in the occupational therapy (OT) workshop of the Salt Lake City Veterans Administration Hospital during a regularly scheduled 1-hr morning visit. The experimental area usually contained at least 20 male patients, an OT staff varying in number from three to five members, and from one to three psychiatric aides.

Each of the three patients selected for observation performed marginally to poorly in the token economy program, and each displayed predominant undesirable response patterns that were relatively discrete and observable. Patient #1 was a withdrawn 33-year-old male who had been hospitalized for 11 years. Two months prior to the study, this patient's frequently assumed squatting posture was believed to have caused a prolapsed rectum requiring surgical intervention. Patient #2 was a depressed, listless 53-year-old male who had been hospitalized for 7 months prior to the study. This patient showed low rates of both functional work and social behavior, and could usually be observed sleeping or gnawing on his hands, unresponsive to the activity that was going on around him. Patient #3 was a 23-year-old male who had also been hospitalized for 7 months prior to the study. Although at the time of the experiment this patient could be described as withdrawn and unsociable, his general level of functioning on various ward assignments exceeded that of either of the other two patients.

Each of the seven psychiatric aides observed during the study had completed a training program in the therapeutic application of reinforcement principles consisting of selected readings, didactic lectures, and shaping demonstrations conducted by the psychology staff. In addition, each had at least 1 year of experience on the token reinforcement ward. The criterion for the selection of the four aides who participated during the monetary reinforcement phase was that they were the ones who had been assigned to the OT area at the time.

Recording

Two male university undergraduates served as data collectors and prompt dispensers. Both were trained in behavior sampling procedures prior to the beginning of the study.

The patient and aide behaviors selected for observation are summarized in Table 33.1. These behaviors were defined, coded, and listed on a standard rating schedule. The rating schedule also contained the coded identities of the various psychiatric aides, thus providing information concerning the nature of the consequences dispensed by each aide to whom and for what behaviors.

The basic data of the study were the relative frequencies of the specified patient behaviors, as well as the frequency of the corresponding aide-dispensed consequences. An interaction was scored only if it occurred between one of the targeted patients and an aide from the token reinforcement ward. Data collection proceeded as follows: each patient

Table 33.1. Behaviors Selected for Observation.

Patient behaviors	Aide behaviors

1. *Task-oriented behavior* (T-O): occurrence scored if patient had hands on work materials at any time during the observation interval, or if patient was receiving assistance on a project from a staff member.
2. *Inappropriate behavior:*
  a. squatting: knees fully bent and patient stationary for the duration of the interval.
  b. sleeping: patient seated or lying on the floor with eyes closed for duration of the interval.
  c. hand chewing: hand in mouth with accompanying movement of the jaws occurring at any time during the interval.
  d. pacing: nongoal-directed walking characterized by two or more ambulatory circuits between any two points in the OT area. Occurrence scored if observed during the entire interval.
	1. *Positive interaction:* occurrence scored when patient either praised, congratulated, or reinforced with tokens, cigarettes, or candy for his performance.
	2. *Negative interaction:* patient scolded, reprimanded, threatened, given a command to "stop it," or fined by a loss of tokens for his behavior.
	3. *Neutral interaction:* indicated for interactions not characterized by either (1) or (2) above; e.g., aide questions the patient, attends to patient's verbalization, etc.

was observed for four consecutive 15-sec intervals during which the occurrence or nonoccurrence of the targeted patient behaviors were recorded. The aide-dispensed consequences correlated with these patient behaviors were simultaneously recorded during the intervals in which they occurred. Following 1 min of observation, the raters observed another patient whose behavior was similarly recorded for four consecutive 15-sec intervals. This procedure was continued for 30 min, thus providing a sample of 40 15-sec observations for each of the three patients.

Interrater reliability estimates, obtained by dividing the number of agreements by the number of agreements plus disagreements across the observation intervals, were computed on eight of the sessions scheduled throughout the study. The average interrater agreement was 95%, and at no time did any observer show less than 90% agreement. Because of the high incidence of agreement, a single observer was employed throughout most of the study.

Experimental Conditions and Procedures

Five different experimental conditions were scheduled. These conditions are described below under headings that correspond to the condition specifications in Table 33.2.

Table 33.2. Summary of the Mean Percentage of the Observation Intervals in Which the Target Behaviors Occurred.

		Baseline (%)	Instructions (%)	Verbal prompts (%)	Reinforcement (%)	Followup (%)
Positive	Pt. #1	5.6	1.25	8.0	70	23
interaction	Pt. #2	0	0	1.25	23.5	9
	Pt. #3	1.1	3.25	3.0	32	—
Neutral	Pt. #1	0.3	0	0	2.0	1.4
interaction	Pt. #2	0.4	0	0	50.5	9
	Pt. #3	0	0.25	0	11.5	—
Negative	Pt. #1	0.3	0.25	0	0	0
interaction	Pt. #2	1.66	0	1.35	0	0
	Pt. #3	0	0	0	0	—
T-O	Pt. #1	11	2	34	74	39
behavior	Pt. #2	0	0	1.0	67	46
	Pt. #3	76	66	74	60	—
Inappropriate	Pt. #1	5.3	8.5	2.5	0	0.2
behavior	Pt. #2	61.6	68.1	49.5	0	28
	Pt. #3	0	0.5	1.0	0	—

Baseline During the initial eight sessions, the raters simply observed the three patients, noting the occurrence or nonoccurrence of the behaviors in Table 33.1.

Instructions Prior to session 9, the aides were informed that two of the targeted patients were performing poorly in OT, and that even though patient #3 was displaying high rates of task-oriented behavior, he was receiving virtually no positive reinforcement for his efforts. Next, the aides were told that appropriate patient behavior could be strengthened if it produced more favorable consequences, such as praise, tokens, cigarettes, etc., all of which the aides were instructed to carry and could easily dispense. Also, the aides were told to weaken undesirable patient behaviors by reinforcing incompatible behavior. To insure that all aides were exposed to these instructions, the information was conspicuously posted in the nursing station.

Verbal Prompts   Prior to the nineteenth session, the aides were informed that, since instructions did not facilitate either task-oriented patient behavior or reinforcing contacts between the patients and staff, one of the undergraduates would now be prompting (or reminding) the aides to reinforce appropriate patient behavior whenever it occurred. Additionally, the undergraduate would encourage the aides themselves to prompt task-oriented activity in those patients who spent most of their OT time either sleeping or sitting idly. The undergraduate was told to dispense these reminders as often as possible in a pleasant but business-like manner.

Monetary Reinforcement   The reinforcement phase began on the twenty-ninth session and continued through session 33. Four of the aides were told that if they could increase the frequency of their reinforcing contacts with the targeted patients for at least 2 days to a level approximating 50% of the intervals in which appropriate patient behavior was observed, they would receive a $15 cash bonus. The only other instruction given was that the aides could receive daily feedback concerning their respective reinforcement rates if they so desired. Prompts were discontinued during the entire reinforcement period.

Followup   This condition, which was procedurally identical with the baseline phase, was incorporated to determine the durability of the changes obtained during the reinforcement period. Immediately prior to the initial followup session, aides who had received money contingent upon their reinforcing output were told that the cash bonus was no longer available.

RESULTS

Table 33.2 shows the mean percentage of the observation intervals in which target behaviors occurred. Figure 33.1 shows the percentage of intervals per session in which the attending aides reinforced those patients selected for observation, as well as the corresponding percentage of intervals in which task-oriented behavior occurred. The percentage of intervals in which aides interacted with the patients, positively or otherwise, is usually based on the total interactive output of two and frequently three aides who were present during the observation period. However, on session 4 of the prompting phase, as well as sessions 3 and 8 of the followup, one aide accompanied the patients to OT. The data for

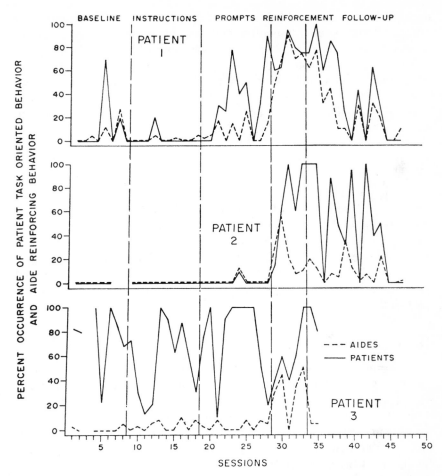

Fig. 33.1. The percentage of occurrence of patient task-oriented behavior and aide-reinforcing behavior during each of the experimental sessions.

these sessions thus reflect aide–patient interactions involving only a single aide.

Baseline

During baseline, the incidence of reinforcing contacts between patients and aides was extremely low. Similarly, neutral or negative interactions were rarely observed (Table 33.2). Although patients #1 and #2 rarely engaged in task-oriented behavior, thus providing few opportunities for reinforcement to occur, the infrequency of aide-dispensed reinforcement cannot be attributed solely to low rates of appropriate patient behavior. Figure 33.1, for example, shows that patient # 3 often engaged in various OT projects even though the rate of reinforcement for this activity failed to exceed 5% of the intervals throughout the baseline period. Inappropriate patient behavior also occurred primarily in the absence of aide attention.

Instructions

Instructing aides to reinforce patients for task-oriented behavior, or behaviors incompatible with those designated as undesirable, had little if any effect on the subsequent rate of aide-dispensed reinforcement. During the instruction condition, positive contacts between aides and patients decreased slightly to an average of less than 4% of the observation intervals for each of the targeted patients. In view of the unaltered reinforcement contingencies, it is by no means surprising that the behavior of patients showed little change.

Verbal Prompts

Prompting the aides to reinforce or initiate appropriate patient behavior produced a slight but variable increase in aide-dispensed reinforcement. The mean percentage of the intervals in which patient # 1 was observed in positive interaction increased from a baseline of 5.6 to 8%. This increase in reinforcement was accompanied by a gain in the occurrence of task-oriented behavior, especially on sessions 23, 25, and 28 (Fig. 33.1). Similarly, it was during the prompting phase that patient # 2 first displayed functional work activity. Nevertheless, this behavior was observed during only one of the sessions, while sleeping and hand chewing continued to occur at consistently high rates. Patient # 3 continued to display task-oriented behavior on the average of 74% of the intervals; as previously, however, aide-dispensed reinforcement for this activity rarely occurred.

The data obtained during the prompting condition may represent an underestimate of the actual incidence of interactions between aides and patients. Even though an average of five prompts were dispensed per session, some of the interactions that followed these prompts were so brief that they were initiated and completed before the patient was scheduled for observation.

Monetary Reinforcement

The introduction of the monetary incentive produced an abrupt increase in the reinforcement dispensed by each of the aides to whom the incentive was provided. The average percentage of the intervals in which aides reinforced the patients was 70, 23.5, and 32% for patients #1, #2, and #3, respectively. A corresponding increase in neutral aide–patient interactions shows the extent to which the aides were spending their time with the targeted patients rather than in activities unrelated to the patients (Table 33.2). This increase in both positive and neutral interactions coincidental with the incentive provision can be taken as evidence that the incentive itself was instrumental in facilitating the rate of reinforcement dispensed by the aides to these patients.

An inspection of Fig. 33.1 reveals that the increase in the dispensing behavior of the aides was correlated with an increase in task-oriented behavior displayed by patients #1 and #2. Patient #2 was observed in task oriented activity on the average of 67% of the intervals; this compares with a previous baseline of near 0%. Similarly, patient #1 showed task-oriented behavior 74% of the time. Concomitant with the increase in functional behavior displayed by these patients, there occurred a complete cessation of undesirable activity (Table 33.2).

Followup

Followup observations were conducted during the first, third, and fourth weeks after the reinforcement period. Patient #3 was discharged on the third day of the followup, thus data are presented for patients #1 and #2 only.

During the course of followup the occurrence of both aide-dispensed reinforcement and task-oriented patient behavior declined and eventually returned to near baseline level (Fig. 33.1). As appropriate behavior decreased, the incidence of inappropriate activity increased (Table 33.2). This reduction in the reinforcing output of the aides in the absence of the monetary contingency again underscores the functional role of that contingency in accelerating the reinforcing behavior of the aides.

The first two sessions of the followup are based on the performance of aides who participated during the reinforcement condition. The high incidence of aide-dispensed reinforcement during these sessions suggests that the improved functioning of the patients may have been a reinforcer that temporarily maintained continued aide interactions. Indeed, some of the aides expressed the desire to continue their involvement with the patients because of the behavior change they had observed while working closely with them. The reduction in the task-oriented activity of patient #2 on sessions 36, 39, and 41 occurred when the aides who had previously dispensed most of the reinforcement to him were not in attendance. Conceivably, these aides may have acquired a discriminative control function over the appropriate behavior displayed by this patient.

Notably, aides who were not reinforced with money for their reinforcing behavior failed to show an increase in the rate of reinforcement dispensed to patients. On sessions prior to the reinforcement condition, approximately 44% of the total intervals in which reinforcing interactions were observed involved aides who were not provided with the monetary incentive. During followup, however, less than 10% of these interactions were initiated by nonreinforced aides, even though at least one of these aides was present on 11 of the 14 sessions.

DISCUSSION

The results clearly indicate that psychiatric aides can be effective behavior modifiers when outcomes are contingent upon their own reinforcing behavior. Without reinforcement, the aides ignored most of the patients (whether they were selected for observation or not) a high percentage of the time. Rather than interact with patients, it was more typical to observe the aides engaged in such competing activities as conversation with other aides or "babysitting" particularly difficult patients. Following the provision of the monetary bonus, each of the aides who stood to earn money began to prompt and reinforce the targeted patients at a rate considerably higher than that observed during previous experimental periods. Furthermore, the patient subjects responded to the new contingencies by showing a substantial increase in appropriate, task-oriented activity. These results are consistent with the findings of Ayllon & Azrin (1964), Buel (1972), and Patterson (1971) on the utility of systematic reinforcement in affecting behavioral change.

One issue that emerges from the present research is how to maintain a reasonably high density of aide-dispensed reinforcement for specific patient behaviors that will facilitate institutional discharge rather than prolong institutional care. Taking into consideration the many routine, and often excessive, job demands expected of psychiatric aides, it is meaningful to ask what can be done to maximize the effectiveness of aides as therapeutic change agents rather than perpetuators of an "aide culture" which traditionally reinforces institutionally valued patient behavior (Ullmann & Krasner, 1969). The use of money as a reinforcer is all too often impractical and other available reinforcers should be considered, such as a choice of work shifts, bonus vacation time, special recognition, or promotions—each of which offer the administrative advantage of being usually controlled by Nursing Service directly.

Another possible means of changing aides' behavior is to redefine the aide job description to include the implementation of individual behavior modification programs. But this also poses several difficulties; for example, aides already have many responsibilities which realistically occupy much of their time. Requiring them to do their routine duties as well as being behavior modifiers seems unfair if aides on other wards have lesser job requirements. Nursing Service, despite being cooperative and sympathetic to a token reinforcement treatment program, might object to setting up different work standards for one ward.

If it is not feasible to provide adequate reinforcers for psychiatric aides, it might be desirable to restructure the ward team. A new set of personnel could be added whose only assignment would be the implementation of the ward behavior modification program. These people could be directly responsible to the ward administrator and trained specifically in behavior modification theory and practice. It would not be necessary to have full-time personnel but it would be desirable to have them serve regularly for several hours each day. These technicians could be undergraduates who are receiving independent study credit, or who are participating in a federally funded work-study program (see Johnson, Katz, & Gelfand, 1972).

REFERENCES

Ayllon, T. Some behavioral problems associated with eating in chronic schizophrenic patients. In L. P. Ullmann and L. Krasner (Eds.) *Case Studies in Behavior Modification.* New York: Holt, Rinehart, & Winston, 1965. Pp. 73–77.

Ayllon, T. and Azrin, N. Reinforcement and instructions with mental patients. *Journal of the Experimental Analysis of Behavior,* 1964, **7**, 327–331.

Ayllon, T. and Azrin, N. *The Token Economy: A Motivational System for Therapy and Rehabilitation.* New York: Appleton-Century-Crofts, 1968.

Ayllon, T. and Haughton, E. Control of the behavior of schizophrenic patients by food. *Journal of the Experimental Analysis of Behavior,* 1962, **5**, 343–352.

Buel, L. Effects of instructions, monetary bonus contingencies, and training on behavior modifying skills of a nursing staff. Unpublished manuscript, 1972.

Gelfand, D. M., Gelfand, S., and Dobson, W. Unprogrammed reinforcement of patients' behavior in a mental hospital. *Behaviour Research and Therapy,* 1967, **5**, 201–207.

Hopkins, B. L. Effects of candy and social reinforcement, instructions and reinforcement schedule leaning on the modification and maintenance of smiling. *Journal of Applied Behavior Analysis*, 1968, **1**, 121–130.

Johnson, C. A., Katz, R. C., and Gelfand, S. Undergraduates as behavioral technicians on an adult token economy ward. *Behavior Therapy*, 1972, **3**, 589–592.

Patterson, G. R., Behavioral intervention procedures in the classroom and in the home. In A. E. Bergin and S. L. Garfield (Eds.) *Handbook of Psychotherapy and Behavior Change.* New York: Wiley, 1971. Pp. 751–775.

Patterson, G. R., Ray, R. S., and Shaw, D. A. Direct intervention in families of deviant children. *Oregon Research Institute Research Bulletin*, 1968, **8**, No. 9.

Schaefer, H. H. and Martin, P. L. *Behavioral Therapy.* New York: McGraw-Hill, 1969.

Ullmann, L. P. and Krasner, L. *A Psychological Approach to Abnormal Behavior.* Englewood Cliffs, Prentice-Hall, 1969.

ARTICLE 34

Some Implications of Learning in Problems of Chronic Pain*†

WILBERT E. FORDYCE, Ph.D., ROY S. FOWLER, JR., Ph.D., JUSTUS F. LEHMANN, M.D., and BARBARA J. DeLATEUR, M.D.

Department of Physical Medicine and Rehabilitation, University of Washington School of Medicine, University of Washington, Seattle, Washington

INTRODUCTION

Pain may originate in many parts of the body. Causes of pain vary greatly, but signals of it are activated mainly by stimulation of peripheral receptors. When the phenomena of pain persist, either continuously or intermittently, over long periods of time, it is termed chronic. But chronic pain is not a unitary concept. The term implies only that pain has persisted over an unspecified period of time, regardless of cause. While recognizing this and many other vagaries to the concept of chronic pain, this paper will consider implications of viewing some chronic pain problems as learned behavior and will present supporting case data.

Chronic pain is a problem for which many different kinds of medical treatment may be used. From a medical point of view, sometimes the problem is a chronic problem with pain as but one aspect. In other instances, pain is the central feature. In either case, the complaint of pain tends to be viewed from the perspective of a "medical" or "disease" model[1]. That is, the inference is made that the pain is a symptom of some underlying pathology and that the strategy of treatment is to modify the underlying pathology in order that the symptom will disappear or be reduced. Where the underlying pathology cannot be influenced signifi-

*Reprinted from *Journal of Chronic Diseases*, 1968, **21**, 179–190, Pergamon Press. Copyright © 1968. With permission from Pergamon Press and Wilbert E. Fordyce.

†This study was supported in part by Vocational Rehabilitation Grant No. RT-3.

cantly, medical management may focus on symptomatic relief, e.g. via palliative medication or surgery. Such a conceptualization of chronic pain is so well established in medical practice that it is easy to overlook the fact it is based on a conceptual model or theory of disease—and dis-ease. While the model has much factual support, there is not enough to justify universal application to phenomena of chronic pain. It is a theoretical model or conceptual scheme, not a statement of facts.

Some aspects of chronic pain may also be conceptualized in learning terms. The observable phenomena of pain consist essentially of some kind of signal sent by the patient that he is in pain. He may verbalize complaints, moan audibly, grimace, recline to await the termination of pain, assume a special posture to minimize the pain, seek distraction, or, perhaps, request the help of others, as in asking for pain relieving medication. The combination of the visible or auditory pain signals sent by the patient and the immediately ensuing behavior in which he engages relating to the pain signal will be subsumed under the term, "pain behavior."

When pain behavior occurs, people in the presence of the patient are likely to make some kind of response to his pain signal. Their responses will vary according to who and where they are but are likely to be of a supportive or solicitous character. They may take action designed to relieve the patient's pain. The parent may console the pain-signaling child. The spouse may fetch water and palliative medication for the pain-signaling mate. The physician may express concern and prescribe pain relieving medication and the nurse may administer it. Such ministering behaviors may function as a kind of favorable consequence to the pain signal. They do so by reducing the pain, or by distracting the patient from his pain, or by evoking pleasant feelings associated with having the attention and regard of a valued or prestige figure.

When those around the patient engage in ministering behavior in response to pain signals, they may observe some favorable effects on his pain behavior by their actions. Various kinds of relief or gratitude signals may follow their efforts. These may be rewarding to them. That is, the consequences of ministering behavior to a person who is signaling pain may be of positive value to the person giving the help.

These relationships between pain behavior and environmental responses to it, lend themselves to analysis from the frame of reference of operant conditioning[1–5]. Some of the major components to operant conditioning will be described briefly before proceeding but more detailed accounts should be consulted for fuller understanding of the subject.

Operant conditioning is based on the premise that behavior is governed by its consequences. Consequences which strengthen behavior are called reinforcers. If behavior is followed by a positive reinforcer, that behavior is likely to increase in frequency. If behavior is followed by a negative or adverse consequence, that behavior is likely to decrease in frequency and behavior designed to remove the adverse consequence is likely to increase. When behavior is followed by neither positive reinforcement nor adverse consequences, the behavior will tend to decrease in frequency, a process termed extinction. Reinforcers are more effective if delivered immediately following the behavior to be reinforced. Reinforcers may be delivered each trial or intermittently. The former is preferred for initiating a behavior pattern. The latter is preferred for maintaining a behavior pattern; i.e. for building maximal resistance to extinction.

Application of an operant conditioning model to behavior associated with chronic pain results in a different set of premises and strategies from those derived from a medical model. The first premise is that pain behavior, though not necessarily the peripheral signal which originally led to the pain behavior, is subject to the same set of laws and systems for modification as other kinds of behavior. Stating that premise another way, treatment or management of a chronic pain problem may proceed by using learning or behavior modification principles rather than by relying exclusively on procedures derived from a medical model. This paper will illustrate examples of the use of an operant conditioning model in problems of chronic pain.

METHOD

To influence behavior through operant conditioning three essentials are needed. One is to identify the behavior to be produced or increased, to be maintained, and to be extinguished or diminished. A second is to determine what kinds of reinforcers are effective. What is a positive reinforcer for one person may not be for another. A third essential is to develop sufficient influence or control over the environment so as to be able to regulate consequences (i.e. the occurrence and non-occurrence of reinforcers) of the behavior to be influenced.

In the cases presented here the specific behaviors to be extinguished or diminished are mainly those of taking pain medication and responding to pain signals by a cessation or reduction of productive behavior; e.g. by reclining, by halting work until the pain abates. The behaviors to be produced or increased are activity responses incompatible with non-productive behavior.

The reinforcers under substantial control in the hospital environment which seem to have general applicability to patients complaining of chronic pain are: medication, rest, and social attention. Use of these reinforcers will be described in further detail below.

The final step is to develop sufficient control over the environment to be able to influence the consequences of the patient's behavior. This becomes feasible within the hospital rehabilitation setting in which these studies occurred because of an unusually well integrated rehabilitation team. The team encompasses a ward or nursing service, a series of specific treatment components (e.g. Occupational Therapy, Physical Therapy), and the coordinated efforts of physiatrists, social workers, rehabilitation counselors and psychologists.

Some control over the extra-hospital environment of the patient also needs to be gained in order to change responses to pain behavior. If that doesn't happen, gains in the hospital are likely to extinguish upon discharge.

PRESENTATION TO THE PATIENT

Patients are not admitted to the program until the general objectives and methods have been explained to patient and spouse. The process is described as a different kind of approach to problems of chronic pain in which an attempt is made to condition the individual's system to respond to pain differently than previously has been the case. It is pointed out that demands will be made upon the patient to perform, as well as upon the spouse to come in for regular sessions and to participate in various kinds of record keeping and related activities. Patients are told there will be times when the treatment staff will seem to be ignoring them and that it is part of the program.

The patient is told he will be expected to meet assignments given to him. Failure to perform is, so far as possible, ignored, following an initial therapist reminder of the assignment. The consequence to non-performance is the absence of social reinforcers. On rare occasions some patients have failed to meet individual treatment session quotas. No patient has failed systematically to meet quotas. Were he to do so he would be discharged from the program. That hasn't happened yet.

MEDICATION

Traditionally medication for pain is administered following expression of discomfort by the patient. Such a régime may reinforce pain behavior, both with chemotherapeutic relief and by social attention from the medical staff. To be consistent with an operant approach the medication prescription is therefore shifted from a pain contingency to a time contingency program. That is, medication is given after a specified time interval whether or not the patient is complaining of pain. Medication is never given following a pain complaint unless the complaint coincides with the elapse of the time interval. The analgesic components of the prescription are suspended in a masking vehicle which allows manipulation of dosage without the patient's awareness. Active analgesic components are gradually withdrawn and the time interval extended until a minimum maintenance dosage is reached, often just the vehicle.

SOCIAL REINFORCEMENT—STAFF ATTENTION

In a hospital, overt expressions or demonstrations of discomfort are usually followed by attention from medical personnel. Staff attention has been shown to be a rather potent reinforcer [5–7]. The typical medical setting would seem designed to reinforce sick complaints. To minimize this, all treatment staff are instructed to be as neutral and socially unresponsive as possible to complaints of pain and discomfort. When the patient is observed participating in any kind of desired activity the staff is instructed to make a positive effort to be friendly and socially responsive. Staff are instructed to be particularly responsive to increases in activity level. Pain behavior receives a minimum of social reinforcement while activity is maximally reinforced.

OCCUPATIONAL THERAPY

In occupational therapy an effort is made to capitalize upon the high value of rest to a patient with pain complaints. The patient is given a simple repetitive task such as a weaving project on a floor loom in which daily performance can be quantified; e.g. counting the number of threads per session. At the outset the patient is instructed to "work as long as you can." After several days a baseline in time and quantity of work is obtained. Leaving the therapy setting to rest is then made contingent upon meeting a quota set by the therapist.* Quotas are periodically increased. Daily records of quantity and duration of activity are kept. These are recorded in graph form and displayed to the patient. Under these conditions it is possible for both patient and staff to be continuously aware of and responsive to progress.

WALKING

Walking is an activity which demands significant physical exertion, can be done anywhere at any time, is very visible, and is incompatible with ceasing activity because of pain. The patient is instructed to walk a measured course both on the ward and in the treatment area. After several days, a baseline of walking activity is obtained. The patient is then assigned walking periods in the treatment area during the day and on the ward in the evening. He is assigned a distance quota during these walking periods which initially is within the limits of his demonstrated baseline. The distance quotas are periodically increased. Rest and social attention are the reinforcers for the walking behavior. The patient is instructed that returning to his room to rest is contingent upon completing the assigned quota. He is instructed to keep a distance and time record of his walking. In addition, he is instructed to report to his therapist or to the nursing station at the start and finish of his walking period. By reporting, he makes it easier for the staff personnel to check the reliability of distance and time records of his performance. The reporting also alerts the staff to provide social reinforcers during and following the walking. The records reflect increments in distance which the patient and others can observe and to which social reinforcers can be attached. All patients thus far studied have proved to be very reliable recorders and the recording has soon been turned entirely over to them.

---

*The converse of this example illustrates further the way treatment personnel more commonly react to complaints of pain. If a patient complains of pain, while, for example, engaging in a physically active Occupational Therapy task, his therapist is likely to suggest he stop and rest until he feels ready to continue. Such an approach makes rest contingent upon complaining of pain and activity contingent upon non-complaining of pain. From an operant conditioning point of view, that approach can be expected to increase the likelihood a patient will again complain of pain and will again cease activity in the presence of pain.

EXTRA SCHEDULED ACTIVITIES

The patient is also asked to record activities throughout the day in addition to those regularly scheduled in therapy. This is done by giving him a small notebook in which he is asked to keep a daily diary of his extra scheduled activities. Each activity is described and the duration recorded in minutes. A daily total is then calculated and a graphic record is kept. Increases in daily activity are then reinforced by positive comments from the staff at daily recording sessions.

OFF-WARD ACTIVITIES

Several steps are taken to increase the probability of generalization in the learning patterns of off-ward situations. Before a patient is accepted for the operant program a commitment is made by immediate family members to attend training sessions with the staff. These sessions occur once or twice a week and typically consist of hour long sessions in which the family members are taught behavior modification principles. The rationale for this program is freely discussed. The emphasis is on reward for desirable performance. Staff and family members are not issued a license to punish the patient for undesirable actions. Careful steps are taken to discover techniques for being socially rewarding to the patient. Selective praise need not be artificial. As soon as it is felt that family members sufficiently understand the program and are ready to reinforce appropriately, patients are allowed short home visits. Family members are instructed in techniques of being non-responsive to inactivity or pain behavior and being positively responsive to activity. They are also instructed to keep records of the patient's activities. Recording serves as a check on the patient's activity record and forces family members to attend to activities which might otherwise be overlooked. The records also give the family opportunity for more precise indications of patient improvement and give the therapist a basis for reinforcing the family's contributions[8]. All activity other than reclining is recorded and re-sponded to by family members. After each home visit the interactions are discussed with the family and suggestions made as to techniques for responding to desired and undesired behaviors. As family members become more adept and reliable in their response techniques, the duration of home visits is increased until the patient is placed on an outpatient schedule.

CASE SUMMARIES

The following cases illustrate how the operant methods were applied and give results through the in- and outpatient treatment phases.

Mrs. Y is a 37-yr-old white female high school graduate, with a teen-age son. Her husband is a school administrator. Since 1948, approximately 1 yr after her marriage, she had had virtually constant low-back pain, and had been decreasingly able to carry out normal homemaking activities. At time of admission to the hospital, she complained of a continuous pain which increased with any activity. She reported her maximum continuous period of activity without an interval of reclining rest as approximately 20 min. Her husband reported that she was active in the home an average of less than 2 hr daily. The remainder of her time was spent reclining; either reading, watching television, or sleeping. During Mrs. Y's 18 yr history of back pain, she had undergone four major surgical procedures including removal of a herniated disc and a lumbosacral spine fusion. At the time of admission, Mrs. Y was taking four or five habit-forming analgesic tablets per day when she experienced pain. Physical and radiologic examination revealed a stable spine at the fusion site, with no evidence of neurologic deficit.

Medication was placed on a time rather than pain contingency régime, utilizing a color and taste masking vehicle. The time interval initially was within her observed tolerance but was gradually extended. She was allowed to rest in occupational therapy only after the completion of a progressively increasing production schedule, a walking program was instituted, a diary of daily activities begun, and her husband attended weekly training sessions. She was seen daily for 10–15 min by a psychologist to construct graphs from her own records in order to document and to reinforce daily progress.

At the end of 7 weeks hospitalization, Mrs. Y was walking just under a mile in both morning and afternoon sessions as shown in Fig. 34.1. She had reached a walking speed approximately twice that of normal. By the thirteenth day of admission, Mrs. Y was working voluntarily during the full period of available occupational therapy time, slightly under 2 hr daily. Forty days after admission, the narcotic content of Mrs. Y's medication was deleted completely. One week later, doses of the vehicle were decreased to every 4 hr, deleting the night dosage. Figure 34.2 summarizes Mrs. Y's activity record. At the time of the preparation of this report, Mrs. Y's program had consisted of eight weeks of inpatient care, and 23 weeks of decreasingly frequent outpatient visits. She was

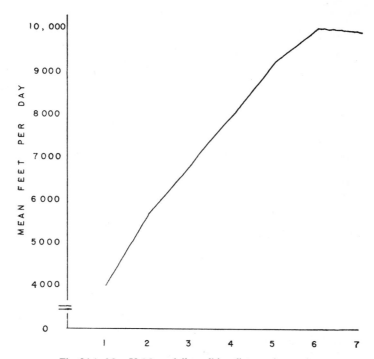

Fig. 34.1. Mrs. Y. Mean daily walking distance by week.

being seen for a brief recheck evaluation approximately once a month. The family has acquired a second car and she has become independently mobile in the community.

Mr. T. is a 46-yr-old white male high school graduate, with one year of junior college. He is married and has a teen-age son. He has long worked in specialized insurance underwriting and contracting. He was admitted with a 6 yr history of intractable back pain. The onset of chronic pain began with a herniated disc secondary to a twisting injury to his ankle and back, in 1959. Subsequently, among other procedures, he received:

    1960: Following flexion-extension injury in auto accident, laminectomy diskectomy and L5–S1 fusion, with right iliac bone graft.
    1961: Following another auto accident, an L4–5 fusion.
    1963: Refusion due to development of a pseudo-arthrosis at L4–5.
    1964: Multiple lumbosacral foraminectomies, freeing adhesions releasing sciatic sheath.
    1966: Bilateral lumbar sympathectomies.

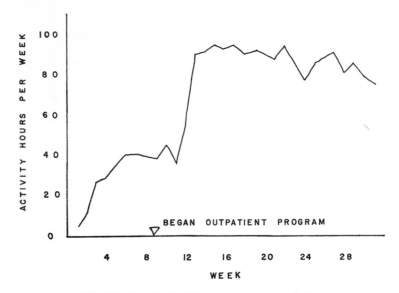

Fig. 34.2. Mrs. Y. Total hours of activity per week.

Mr. T. and his wife described separately a daily non-reclining activity pattern of approximately 2 hr/day, of several months duration. He reported virtually constant back pain. Examination provided minimal evidence of neurologic deficit (slight depressed ankle jerk on the left).

At the time of admission he had been taking 16–24 Percodan and 900 mg of Tuinal for sleep. Medication was immediately put on a time contingency basis, utilizing a color and taste masking vehicle. Demerol and Phenergan were contained in the analgesic solution. A long acting barbiturate was put in the sedative solution. This was necessary in order to prevent withdrawal symptoms. By the 10th week following admission and the 2nd week following moving to outpatient status, medication had been reduced to the masking vehicle only.

Mr. T. made rapid progress in the walking program, as shown in Fig. 34.3. During the first 4 days after admission, he was given no schedule and was simply observed to determine baselines. After his walking reached one mile in Physical Therapy sessions (the 25th day of formal treatment) no further additions were made in walking quotas because his daily activity schedule, as shown in Fig. 34.4, was showing maintenance of approximately 14 hr of activity. The data shown in Figs. 34.3–34.4 are based on 9 weeks of inpatient and 5 weeks of outpatient care at which

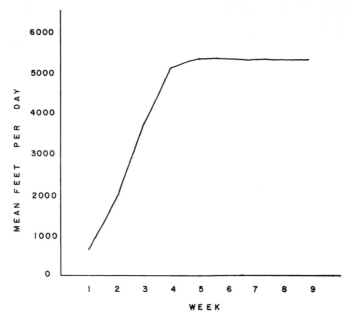

Fig. 34.3. Mr. T. Mean daily walking distance by week.

time he was discharged. During the last 2 weeks of the program, he had reached a schedule of 2 days per week, while he explored re-establishing himself vocationally the balance of the time. Activity was maintained throughout the week-ends, as confirmed by his reports and those of his wife.

The third case, Mrs. W was of a somewhat different order. Mrs. W is a 66-yr-old white female who had had chronic back trouble since 1942. Her diagnosis is post-menopause osteoporosis with multiple compression fractures of the vertebral column. She is a high school graduate and worked as a bookkeeper until 1959, when a laminectomy was done. She had been treated with a long series of pain medications without appreciable relief of pain. At the time of hospitalization, she had resigned almost all housekeeping tasks to her housekeeper and her husband. Mrs. W had been repeatedly encouraged in the past to walk, wear a back brace, and increase her activity level, so as to avoid many of the secondary problems associated with physical inactivity. At the time of hospitalization, she steadfastly refused to walk without medication, had relegated her back brace to her dresser drawer, and would dress with great reluctance.

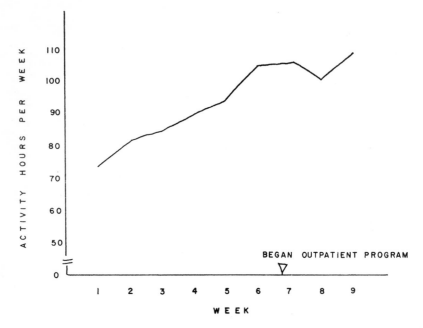

Fig. 34.4. Mr. T. Total hours of activity per week.

Radiographs confirmed the compression and anterior wedging of the thoracic vertebrae; symptomatology was compatible with occasional root compression on coughing or sudden movements. Her program involved the time contingency medication régime plus recording of walking and brace wearing. Daily records were kept of these activities and plotted in graphic form. Her walking, her brace wearing, and the records she kept of these received much social reinforcement from the staff. In addition, treatment included use of appropriate fluoride and hormonal preparations in the attempt to arrest progression of the disease. After a very short period of hospitalization, she was discharged and asked to return once a week for a brief recheck. She was given graph paper and instructed to continue her graphic record. Her husband and a public health nurse who made routine home visits were contacted and asked to reinforce these activities. Figures 34.5–34.6 contain summaries of her records. At the time of writing, outpatient visits had been extended to once every 2 weeks. She was expressing a great deal of enjoyment in walking and described herself as the pride of the neighborhood children who join her in her daily excursions. She still claimed to find her brace uncomfortable but appar-

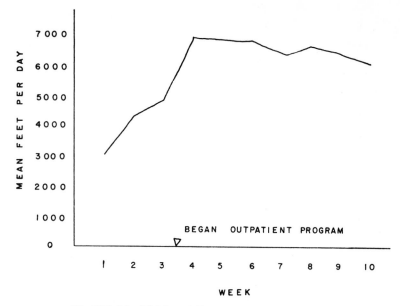

Fig. 34.5. Mrs. W. Mean daily walking distance by week.

ently was wearing it faithfully. Her grooming and physical appearance had improved noticeably and she had become quite active in church affairs.

DISCUSSION

The thesis of this paper is *not* that pain is originally produced by operant conditioning (i.e. that pain originates from its consequences in the environment) but that much of the behavior occurring subsequent to presentation of a presumed noxious stimulus may be accounted for and modified by principles of learning, whatever the original cause of pain.

The issue of whether the pain a patient reports is "real" or otherwise is simply not relevant. In this context "real" means approximately that some neurophysiological defect or pathology can be demonstrated (or reasonably inferred), from which competent observers can account for the reported pain experiences of the patient. Characteristically, from the medical model, the alternative to an explanation of reported pain as being "real" is to attribute pain to so-called mental or psychic processes.

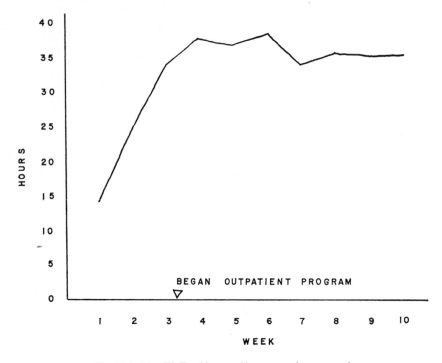

Fig. 34.6. Mrs. W. Total hours of brace wearing per week.

Examples are represented by labels such as "hysterical," "suggestion," "imaginary," "hypochondriacal," or "secondary gain." In essence, these alternative labels reflect but another application of a medical or disease model, though now referring to presumed underlying psychic processes. The sign or symptom of pain is conceptualized as an overt or surface representation of some underlying state of affairs (e.g. conflict in a hysterical personality, dependency needs in a hypochondriacal personality). The strategy for treatment or management is conceptually the same as in other medical approaches in that it is directed toward modifying the inferred underlying state so that the surface symptom, in this example, pain, may be ameliorated. In contrast, the approach described in this paper focuses on modifying the pain behavior itself, however much or little "real" its origins were.

It is not suggested here that all pain problems should be dealt with from a learning model frame of reference or that operant conditioning approaches to problems of chronic pain should proceed without regard for medical factors in the picture. Where a problem of chronic pain is said to exist, as was true with each case described here, there is presumptive evidence that the pain problem has not been entirely resolved by medical approaches. Where the problem has existed for an extended time, the opportunities for learning pain behavior patterns by operant mechanisms are increased. Those pain behavior patterns are the point of attack. Even then, careful determinations are needed as to the medical feasibility of some of the behaviors which are to be generated by the methods used. Patients entering the program described here are given a thorough medical evaluation. They are followed closely by physiatrists throughout the program. The activity schedules, walking quotas, etc., are always held within limits of medical prudence defined by attending physicians. Comprehensive management of chronic pain problems is furthered by using both medical and learning models in planning treatment strategies. These models complement each other.

REFERENCES

1. Ullmann, L. P. and Krasner, L. (Eds). *Case Studies in Behavior Modification*. Holt, Rinehart and Winston, New York, 1965.
2. Staats, A. W. *Human Learning*. Holt, Rinehart and Winston, New York, 1964.
3. Reese, E. P. *The Analysis of Human Operant Behavior*. William C. Brown, Dubuque, Iowa, 1966.
4. Krasner, L. and Ullmann, L. P. *Research in Behavior Modification*. Holt, Rinehart and Winston, New York, 1966.
5. Haughton, E. Shaping participation in occupational therapy. Paper given at the *Third International Congress World Federation of Occupational Therapists*. Boston, Massachusetts, November 1962, mimeo.
6. Ayllon, T. and Michael, J. The psychiatric nurse as a behavioral engineer, *J. exp. Anal. Behav.*, 1959, **2**, 323.
7. Meichenbaum, D. H. Sequential strategies in two cases of hysteria, *Behav. Res. & Therapy*, 1966, **4**, 89.
8. Birnbrauer, J. Exploration of operant conditioning in physical therapy. Address given at Workshop for Physical Therapists. Chicago, Illinois, May 9–10, 1966.

Alpha Enhancement as a Treatment for Pain: A Case Study*

LINDA GANNON† and RICHARD A. STERNBACH

Department of Psychiatry, University of Wisconsin Medical School, and Wisconsin Psychiatric Institute

Abstract: Drawing on past reports of raised pain thresholds of yogis in a meditative state, the high alpha content during meditation, and reports of operant alpha wave conditioning, a hypothesis was formulated that a high alpha state and pain are incompatible behaviors, and thus the production of alpha could be used for symptomatic treatment of pain. A patient, who suffered from severe headaches resulting from head injuries, went through 67 alpha conditioning sessions and increased his alpha activity from 20 per cent time alpha with eyes closed to 92 per cent time alpha with eyes closed and 50 per cent with eyes open. Although the patient was not able to rid himself of pain by achieving a high alpha state, he was in some instances able to prevent pain by going into a high alpha state before the headache began.

Anand, Chhina and Singh (1961) observed that in some instances yoga meditators were able to raise their pain thresholds. In their study, 2 yogis, while in meditation, were able to keep their hands in water at 4°C for up to 55 minutes without subjective pain sensation and without alpha blocking. EEG recordings were taken before and during meditation. Before meditation, the subjects showed prominent alpha activity and alpha blocking when stimulated. However, when the yogis were meditating, their EEG records showed no blocking during stimulation.

In our laboratory, we have conducted some pilot research on alpha feedback training. The subjects' description of the high alpha state was

---

*Reprinted from *Journal of Behavior Therapy and Experimental Psychiatry*, 1971, **2**, 209–213, Pergamon Press. Copyright © 1971. With permission from Pergamon Press and Linda Gannon.

†Requests for reprints to: Linda Gannon, Department of Psychology, University of Wisconsin, Madison, Wisconsin 53706.

similar to that reported by Kamiya (1969). Our results in alpha conditioning were not as dramatic as those reported by Kamiya, but they were in the same direction. The procedure for alpha conditioning that we developed in the pilot research was used in the present study.

The yoga study implies that the meditative state and pain are incompatible behaviors and that one component of the meditative state is a high alpha content. In light of this research and our own observations, we decided to investigate the possibility of utilizing the ability to achieve a high alpha state as symptomatic treatment for intractable pain. To test this hypothesis, we used a patient who was suffering from recurrent pain for which orthodox medicine had given little or no relief.

MEDICAL HISTORY OF THE PATIENT

The patient's problem began in the fall of 1964 when he suffered a head injury. Six weeks after the injury, he began having headaches. The diagnosis was that he had had a concussion resulting from the head injury. Pain medication was prescribed and the headache disappeared in 3–4 weeks. In January, 1965, the patient suffered a second head injury and 4 weeks later the headache returned. The diagnosis was that he had had a relapse of the concussion and the patient took pain medication for 6–7 weeks. In May, 1965, the headache returned, possibly caused by a third slight head injury 3 weeks previous. This time the patient required pain medication for 6 months. In June, 1966, the patient hit his head a fourth time and 2 weeks later the headaches recurred. This time he took medication to control the dilation of blood vessels. This enabled him to function better, but the pain persisted for almost 2 years. In May of 1968, the patient suffered a fifth head injury, and 6 weeks later the headaches reappeared. In January, 1970, he still had headaches and at that time, we began our treatment. Usually, each series of headaches was most intense and of longest duration when it started, gradually decreasing in intensity and duration and finally disappearing. From 1966 to 1969, the patient had three neurological examinations and a psychiatric evaluation—the results of which were essentially negative. The final diagnosis was inadequate control of dilation and constriction of blood vessels as a result of the head injuries.

At the time the patient started treatment in our laboratory, his headaches had abated somewhat, but were still fairly constant and prevented him from exerting himself physically or mentally. Usually after about 15 minutes of exertion, a headache would either begin or, if he already had one, would become more intense to the point of being incapacitating.

PROCEDURE

EEG recordings were taken from two occipital leads on the right side of the head with a ground electrode on the ear. We used Grass Type E–1A Durable Disc Silver electrodes which were filled with Redux Electrode Paste, and after Redux had been rubbed into the scalp, they were applied with Collodion. The brain waves were amplified by a Grass EEG preamplifier, model 5P5B, calibrated at $30 \mu V$ equal to 0.5 cm and recorded on a Grass polygraph, model 5A running at 5 mm/sec. At the same time, the signals were passed through a Krohn-Hite electronic band pass filter, model 330BR set at 9–11 cycles/sec, and this filtered output was recorded on a separate channel of the polygraph. From the band pass filter the data went to a Schmitt trigger which was set at 0.5 cm (later at 0.6 cm). When the alpha amplitude reached $30 \mu V$, the Schmitt trigger set off a timer to record the seconds of alpha, a Magnecord tape recorder to supply feedback to the patient in the form of a tone or music, a counter to record the number of alpha bursts, and a third channel on the polygraph which recorded the *on–off* of alpha.

The patient was in a dimly-lighted room seated in a comfortable chair. Instructions were given through a speaker situated behind him. He was told to keep the tone or music on as much as possible during the learning periods, and simply to rest during the rest periods.

Each session lasted 29 minutes and consisted of five 2-minute learning periods (later changed to four 3-minute learning periods) with one minute of rest between learning periods and a 5-minute rest period at the beginning and end. During the rest periods the patient received no feedback. During the learning periods, he received instant feedback consisting of either tones or music, and at the end of each learning period was told the number of seconds he had had alpha. The amount of alpha was recorded for both the learning and rest periods.

We started with five 2-minute learning periods with the triggering amplitude at $30 \mu V$. When the patient's EEG showed the specified frequency (9–11 cycles/sec) and amplitude, he heard a low tone; at other times he heard a high tone. This procedure was used for four sessions. We then changed to four 3-minute learning periods at the patient's request.

After three more sessions, we substituted organ music for the low tone and eliminated any sound for the non-alpha state. This was done because the patient reported that he often used organ music as a background for studying—he enjoyed it, but it did not distract him. He also reported that the high tone irritated him.

We continued in this manner for 30 sessions. At this point we changed the procedure so that during part of the session, the patient would have his eyes open. We felt it necessary for him to be able to achieve a high alpha state with his eyes open, so that it might be possible for him to get rid of his pain and, at the same time, function normally.

After 4 sessions, the patient increased eyes closed alpha time to the point where it was no longer challenging; so we raised the required amplitude to 36 μV and conducted 19 more sessions in this way. In the last 4 sessions we eliminated the music and the patient's only feedback was a report to him on the amount of alpha during each learning period. We did this to encourage him to attempt a high alpha state outside the laboratory where he would not have instant feedback. This concluded the conditioning procedure. In the next few months, the patient returned 3 times for follow-up sessions.

In Fig. 35.1, the obvious change in the patient's resting EEG can be seen. In the upper portion is a sample of the patient's EEG record during the first 5-minute rest period of session 1. In the lower portion is a sample of the patient's EEG record during the first 5-minute rest period of session 50. There is a marked increase in alpha time and amplitude.

Figure 35.2 summarizes the procedures used and the results obtained over all sessions. For the first 41 sessions, alpha was defined as a frequency of 9–11 cycles/sec and a minimum amplitude of 30 μV. For the remaining sessions, the minimum amplitude was raised to 36 μV. As can be seen in the graph, the introduction of music in place of the tones seemed to help the patient increase his per cent alpha time.* Also, when we changed to eyes open during part of the session, the eyes closed alpha time showed a very large increase—during one session as high as 92 per cent.† After we increased the amplitude requirement, there was a sharp

---

*The rest periods and learning periods were combined to form these percentages because, as his ability to produce alpha increased, his resting alpha increased also. Since our purpose was not only to provide the patient with a means of treating his pain, but also to raise his pain threshold by increasing the amount of alpha in his resting EEG, we thought it best to represent his progress by total per cent alpha.

†It should be noted that there was a great deal of variability in the total per cent alpha. Some days, usually when the patient had a headache or was tired, he had very little alpha—as little as 12 per cent.

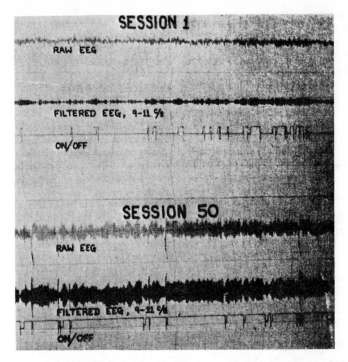

Fig. 35.1. Sample EEG during first 5-minute rest period for sessions 1 and 50.

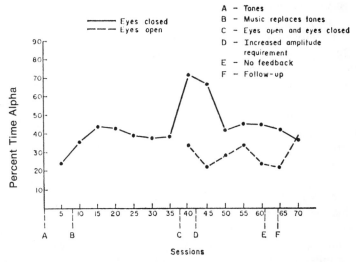

Fig. 35.2. Percentage time alpha averaged over successive series of 5 sessions. The letters A, B, etc., mark the points at which changes of procedure were introduced.

drop after which eyes open and eyes closed per cent alpha time tended to converge.

DISCUSSION

Our original hypothesis was that pain and a high alpha state are incompatible behaviors. Therefore, if a person suffering from pain were able to achieve a high alpha state, he would have no pain, or at least report feeling no pain. We found this not to be true with our patient. He often reported having a headache when he came to the laboratory, and although he never had much alpha when he had a headache, he always had some alpha. When he had a headache, he was not able to concentrate enough to achieve a high alpha state. But when he did not have a headache, and was able to achieve a high alpha state, he always reported that he felt much better after the session. So it seemed that all we were able to do was to make him feel better when he felt normal, but that we had no effect when he was already experiencing pain.

The intensity and duration of the patient's headaches did decrease gradually during the course of treatment but this result was confounded with spontaneous improvement. Because of the patient's previous experience, one would expect the headaches to improve without any treatment. We therefore cannot determine to what extent improvement occurred spontaneously and to what extent it occurred as a result of our treatment. The patient, however, did benefit from our treatment in two ways.

1. After 20 sessions, he reported that his attention span had lengthened, and that he was able to read without getting a headache for about 30 minutes—as opposed to 15 minutes before treatment. There are, as far as we can determine, two possible explanations for this. The first is that his pain threshold was actually raised. The alpha conditioning sessions were 29 minutes long, and he may have trained himself to achieve a high alpha state for that period of time, consequently being able to avoid a headache for 30 minutes. The fact that in the first few sessions his per cent alpha was much higher during the first 15 minutes than during the last 15 minutes tends to substantiate this explanation. He gradually learned to extend his high alpha state to include all 29 minutes.

The other explanation is that we trained him to increase his attention span by putting him in a situation in which it was necessary to concentrate for 30 minutes. It is possible that we could have asked him to read for 30 minutes every day, and he would have gradually learned to do the task without a headache. In other words, his increased attention span may have been due to concentration training rather than alpha training.

2. The other beneficial result of our treatment was noticed by the patient after about 50 sessions. He reported that when he participated in certain activities, such as swimming or attending a rock concert, he always had a headache afterward. Generally, he would avoid these activities but when he did engage in them, he expected the resulting headache. After about 50 treatment sessions, the patient attended a rock concert. When the concert was over, he realized that he had been in a sort of trance during the concert. He described this state of mind as being very similar to a high alpha state during a treatment session with the added dimension of a condensed time perception. When the concert was over he had no headache. He had a similar experience when he was swimming a few days later. He had no headache afterward and felt that he had been in a sort of trance similar to a high alpha state. Neither of these experiences was planned by the patient beforehand, but when he reported them to us, we encouraged him to try to achieve a high alpha state whenever he was in a potentially headache-producing situation. He tried this and was quite often, though not always, successful. He may have been more successful after fewer sessions had we begun with this goal in mind. As it was, we only discovered it because of the perceptiveness of our patient.

Although we had not expected the phenomenon discussed above, it is compatible with the yogi's raised pain threshold. The yoga meditators were not in pain when they began meditation, but were exposed to a painful stimulus after they were in a meditative state. Our subject's experience was similar in that he could prevent the onset of pain, although he could not get rid of pain already present.

There is obviously much more research to do in this area before arriving at even tentative conclusions. Not only do we need a larger sample and adequate controls, but also a procedure requiring fewer sessions. One hypothesis in this area which merits future research is the possibility that psychophysiological variables other than EEG exhibit marked changes during the yoga meditative state. If this is so, simulation of the meditative state might be achieved more completely and in a shorter period of time by conditioning more of the relevant physiological functions. With all its limitations, however, this single case study does provide some evidence that it is possible for a patient to learn to prevent the onset of pain by means of operant alpha conditioning techniques.

Acknowledgments—The authors wish to thank Jan Martinson for designing the equipment, and Burt Kaplan and David Rice for their helpful comments. The study was supported in part by USPHS Grant No. MH12858-01, NIMH, and by University of Wisconsin Medical School Research Committee Grant No. M-321-24 to David Rice.

REFERENCES

Anand, B. K., Chhina, G. S., and Singh, B. Some aspects of electroencephalographic studies in Yogis, *Electroenceph. clin. neurophysiol.*, 1961, **13**, 452–456.

Kamiya, J. Operant control of the EEG alpha rhythm and some of its reported effects on consciousness. In *Altered States of Consciousness* (Edited by C. T. Tart), John Wiley, New York, 1969.

CHAPTER 9

Two Common Health Problems: Alcoholism and Obesity

Two of the most common public health problems affecting people today are obesity and alcoholism. According to Wilkinson (1970), alcoholics in the United States currently number around 10 million. Similarly, statistics compiled by the U.S. Department of Health, Education, and Welfare (1967) suggest that as many as 50 million Americans are significantly overweight.

The seriousness of both alcoholism and obesity is magnified considerably when one considers the many medical, social, and economic problems associated with them. Both of these major health problems are associated with a high incidence of morbidity and mortality. Problems resulting from alcoholism include half of all fatal accidents in this country (Wilkinson, 1970) while one-third to one-half of the country's criminal arrests are partially attributed to drinking (Hayman, 1972). Cirrhosis of the liver, heart disease, brain damage and nutritional deficits (Harrison *et al.*, 1966) are but a few of the secondary physical disabilities associated with the alcoholic patient. Obesity likewise has been linked to cardiovascular disease (Stallones, 1969), diabetes (Bruch, 1957), respiratory difficulties (Mayer, 1968), and problems of self-image (Berlinger, 1969).

Although etiologically some aspects of obesity may be organic, as in endocrine or metabolic disease, these disorders account for only a small percentage of cases. For the vast majority of overweight people, however, the nature of their problem is primarily behavioral: the overweight individual tends to consume unnecessary quantities of high caloric and carbohydrate foods. Similarly, the alcoholic may be differentiated from the social drinker on the basis of magnitude of consumption, preference for "straight" liquor, and drinking rate (Schaefer *et al.*, 1971). The discrete nature of the symptomatology of obesity and alcoholism has made these two health problems obvious targets for behavior therapy techniques.

At present, the available treatments for alcoholism and obesity vary greatly in substance and kind. Therapeutic strategies for the obese patient have stressed diet (e.g., low calorie, low carbohydrate, ketogenic, and rice), appetite suppressors, surgical removal of parts of the intestine, and intensive group and individual psychotherapy (including Weight Watchers). While some approaches produce temporary success, in general the long-term prognosis for the obese patient has not been favorable since most patients who do lose weight quickly regain it (Stunkard, 1958). Similarly, a poor prognosis exists for many alcoholic patients irrespective of the type of treatment they receive. Therapeutic success in excess of 30–50% of treated cases is virtually unheard of when followups from six months to one year are conducted (Moore & Buchanan, 1966; Pattison, 1966). A wide assortment of strategies including Alcoholics Anonymous, traditional psychotherapy, antibuse blocking, some forms of aversive conditioning, and broad spectrum rehabilitation programs have shown some promise. However, none has been consistently effective.

The articles in this chapter include a cross section of behavioral approaches to the treatment of alcoholism and obesity that may represent an improvement over alternative treatment methods. The first three papers pertain to alcoholism and incorporate the techniques of high density reinforcement of behaviors incompatible with drinking, controlled drinking by means of avoidance conditioning, and behavioral contracting.

Hunt and Azrin (Article 36) describe a broad spectrum approach to the treatment of alcoholism based upon an abstinence model. Essentially, their procedure was designed to make nondrinking activities produce an extremely high density of reinforcers. In this way any recurrence of drinking would interrupt the ability to earn reinforcement and produce a period of timeout. Attempts to increase the density of reinforcement for abstinence included vocational counseling, marital counseling, and planned exposure to potentially reinforcing events. The authors report significant increases in employment, income, time at home and decreases in drinking and rehospitalization for their experimentally treated patients relative to a group of similar patients who had been treated by more traditional means. A six-month followup indicated continued success.

Until recently, the concept of total abstinence in the treatment of alcoholism has been rigidly propounded as a necessary condition for successful rehabilitation. In the second paper (Article 37) by Sobell and

Sobell, the feasibility of controlled drinking as a radical, yet viable alternative to abstinence, is proposed and experimentally supported. Employing an avoidance conditioning paradigm, they devised a treatment regimen whereby alcoholic patients avoided shock by not exceeding a specified alcohol intake during simulated barroom training sessions. In addition, the authors attempted to identify the conditions under which alcohol consumption was most likely to occur (stimulus control), in order to train patients in more appropriate alternatives to drinking. Although followup by the Sobells is relatively brief, a more recent report (Sobell & Sobell, 1973) indicates an 85% success rate based upon numerous variables one year after the termination of treatment. The Sobells' views on abstinence follow from a careful analysis of the conditions to which an alcoholic must return; namely, a society that tends to reinforce moderate alcohol consumption. Only a very small segment of the population (AA, various religious groups, etc.) supports abstinence. Thus, in many instances an attempt to place a totally abstinent alcoholic in a society that reinforces drinking is to add to his stress, not decrease it. It should be noted, however, that Sobell and Sobell found equally successful results with an abstinence behavior therapy group; thus, the combination of avoidance and the acquisition of alternative responses to drinking cues appear to be the key therapeutic variables.

The third paper (Article 38) by Miller describes the treatment of an alcoholic patient by behavioral contracting, a procedure derived from the early work of Homme *et al.* (1967). Essentially behavioral contracting entails the specification in writing of behaviors expected from two or more individuals and the ways in which they will provide reinforcement for the emission of desired behavior. Once the contingencies have been explicitly stated, the contract is signed by both parties. Utilizing this reciprocal reinforcement technique with an alcoholic and his wife, Miller was able to reduce alcohol consumption to mutually acceptable limits. A six-month followup revealed maintenance of an acceptable drinking level. Like the previous work of Sobell and Sobell, treatment goals were aimed at producing a *socially acceptable* level of alcohol consumption rather than total abstinence.

The three papers on obesity parallel in many ways procedures for the control of alcoholism. Mann (Article 39) describes the use of contingency contracting to produce weight loss in obese patients, literally requiring them to put their money (or other valuables) where their mouths were. His treatment strategy involves the use of positive reinforcement (money or valuables returned contingent upon weight loss) as well as response cost (loss of reinforcers) for weight gain. The use of reversal procedures strengthens considerably his conclusion that contracting can be an effective means of weight loss, although the absence of followup data mitigates against its possible long-term usefulness. Nevertheless, the design of the study demonstrates the power of the procedures, however long the contingencies are in effect.

Because of his emphasis on stimulus control and response definition, the paper by Stuart (Article 40) resembles the approach used by Sobell and Sobell with alcoholics. Stuart stresses the stimulus control of overeating, believing that for the obese patient eating has generalized to a variety of inappropriate stimulus conditions (e.g., watching television, socializing, and reading in bed). Considerable attention is also directed toward planned exercise programs and training patients in specific ways to modify ineffective eating habits. As the author explains, the purpose of this training is to help the obese patient gradually achieve a more equitable balance between energy consumed and energy expended. The utility of Stuart's approach is reflected by the positive results he obtained from six overweight patients. Importantly, these patients showed continued weight loss up to six months after formal treatment had ceased.

The final paper (Article 41) by Jeffrey, while not striking in the magnitude of weight loss achieved and lacking in long-term followup, is included because of its unique demonstration of the potential significance of self-control procedures in weight loss. By shifting the locus of control from the therapist to the patient, Jeffrey has possibly discovered an effective practical solution to the problem that has long plagued obesity research: the lack of long-term maintenance of weight loss without an external contingency system.

Points of key importance in this chapter include:

1. A variety of behavioral techniques have been used successfully in the treatment of alcoholism and obesity.
2. Successful treatment of some alcoholics does not appear to require total abstinence as traditionally assumed. A potentially fruitful, albeit controversial approach lies in the acquisition of social drinking skills together with other alternative responses to drinking situations.
3. A careful analysis of stimulus control characteristics of both alcoholism and obesity may lead to successful therapeutic strategies involving the acquisition of more appropriate responses to stressful situations.
4. Long-term psychotherapy for overeating or alcoholism does not

appear to be a significant prerequisite to the successful treatment of these disorders.
5. With the possible exception of the treatment of alcoholism involving avoidance conditioning, most of the procedures described in this chapter could easily be implemented in clinical practice.

REFERENCES

Berlinger, K. Obesity and psychological stress. In Nancy L. Wilson (ed.) *Obesity.* Philadelphia: F. A. Davis, 1969.

Bruch, H. *The Importance of Overweight.* New York: W. H. Norton, 1957.

Harrison, T., Adams, R., Bennett, I., Resnik, W., Thorn G., and Wintrobe, M. (eds.). *Principles of Internal Medicine.* New York: McGraw-Hill, 1966.

Hayman, M. Warning! Social drinking may be hazardous to your health and welfare. *Report,* 1972, **30**, 1–22.

Homme, L., Attila, T., and Csanyi, A. P. *Contingency Contracting: A System for Motivating Change in Education.* Albuquerque, New Mexico: Westinghouse Learning Corporation, 1967.

Mayer, J. *Overweight: Causes, Cost and Control.* Englewood Cliffs, New Jersey: Prentice-Hall, 1968.

Moore, R. A. and Buchanan, T. K. State hospitals and alcoholism: A nation-wide survey of treatment techniques and results. *Quarterly Journal of Studies on Alcoholism,* 1966, **27**, 459–468.

Pattison, E. M. A critique of alcoholism treatment concepts with special reference to abstinence. *Quarterly Journal of Studies on Alcoholism,* 1966, **27**, 49–71.

Schaefer, H., Sobell, M., and Mills, K. Baseline drinking behaviors in alcoholics and social drinkers: Kinds of drinks and sip magnitude. *Behaviour Research & Therapy,* 1971, **9**, 23–27.

Sobell, M. and Sobell, L. Alcoholics treated by individualized behavior therapy: one year treatment outcome. *Behaviour Research and Therapy,* 1973, **11**, 599–618.

Stallones, R. Population patterns of disease and body weight. In Nancy L. Wilson (ed.) *Obesity.* Philadelphia: F. A. Davis, 1969.

Stunkard, A. The results of treatment for obesity. *New York State Journal of Medicine,* 1958, **58**, 79.

United States Department of Health, Education, and Welfare. Obesity and health: A sourcebook of current information for professional health personnel. Arlington, Va.: 1967.

Wilkinson, R. *The Prevention of Drinking Problems.* New York: Oxford University Press, 1970.

ARTICLE 36

A Community-Reinforcement Approach to Alcoholism*†

GEORGE M. HUNT and N. H. AZRIN

Southern Illinois University and Anna State Hospital, Anna, Illinois, U.S.A.

Abstract: Several theoretical approaches to alcoholism exist. An operant reinforcement approach was used in the present study to develop a new procedure that rearranged community reinforcers such as the job, family and social relations of the alcoholic such that drinking produced a time-out from a high density of reinforcement. The results showed that the alcoholics who received this Community-Reinforcement counseling drank less, worked more, spent more time with their families and out of institutions than did a matched control group of alcoholics who did not receive these procedures. This new approach appears to be an effective method of reducing alcoholism. An analysis in reinforcement terms is presented of the etiology, epidemiology, and treatment of alcoholism.

Alcoholism is perhaps the number one public health problem in the United States: alcoholics number approximately 10 million (Wilkinson, 1970); half of all fatal accidents involve a drunken driver (Wilkinson, 1970); cirrhosis of the liver, heart disease and suicide have been linked to alcoholism (Wallgren and Barry, 1970). Yet, as two recent reviews have concluded (Hill and Blane, 1967; Wallgren and Barry, 1970) alcoholism continues to be a major problem for which even a partial solution is being sought. A variety of approaches for treating alcoholism have been

*Reprinted from *Behaviour Research and Therapy*, 1973, **11**, 91–104, Pergamon Press. Copyright © 1973. With permission from Pergamon Press and George M..Hunt.

†This paper is based in part on the first author's dissertation submitted to the Department of Guidance and Educational Psychology, Southern Illinois University. The work was supported by the Illinois Department of Mental Health and Grant MH-17981 from the National Institute of Mental Health. Special appreciation is extended to Bill Anderson, Earl Kiphart, Ken Lawler, John Meskenas and Ernest Sauerbrunn of the Alcoholic Treatment Program Staff of Anna State Hospital. Reprints may be obtained from either author, Behavior Research Laboratory, Anna State Hospital, Anna, Illinois 62906.

developed including the psychodynamic and psychoanalytic model (Freytag, 1967), transactional analysis (Steiner, 1969), the medical and physiological approach (see review by Jellinek, 1960; Wallgren and Barry, 1970), the anxiety model (Vogel-Sprott, 1967) and the peer-friendship model of Alcoholics Anonymous (Alcoholics Anonymous, 1960). A fairly recent emphasis has been the learning theory approach which used the Pavlovian reinforcement model (see review by Rachman and Teasdale, 1969).

Another learning theory approach is the operant reinforcement approach (Skinner, 1938). The operant approach stresses the interaction between behavior and the environment whereas classical conditioning stresses the associations between different environmental events. With the exception of a case study by Sulzer (1965), an operant approach to alcoholism treatment has not been evaluated.

One method of developing an operant method of deterring alcoholism is to examine the natural deterrents of alcoholism and conceptualize them in operant terms. The principles of operant conditioning might then be used to alter these natural deterrents to maximize their effectiveness. It appears that individuals are deterred from drinking because of the interference that drinking produces with other sources of satisfaction. In the alcoholic state, one may incur social censure from friends as well as from one's family. Discharge from one's employment is likely. Pleasant social interactions and individual recreational activities cannot be performed as satisfactorily, if at all, when one is alcoholic. Conceptually, this state of affairs may be characterized in learning terms as a postponement or omission of positive reinforcers as a result of alcohol intake. This statement suggests that deterrents will be maximized if the postponed reinforcers are of maximum quality, frequency, varied in nature and regularly occurring. The general process seems to be that of time-out from positive reinforcement (Leitenberg, 1965; Ferster, 1958; Holz and Azrin, 1963) which has been studied extensively and has been applied to a variety of clinical situations including classroom disorders (Wahler, 1969), tantrums (Wolf, Risley and Mees, 1964) and self-injurious behavior (Bucher and Lovaas, 1967). An additional major factor is the distribution of these reinforcers in time. Time-out from positive reinforcement cannot be a new event if the natural distribution of reinforcers is such that extended interruptions normally occur. Consequently, for maximum effectiveness of this time-out dimension, the normal reinforcers should be grouped closely together in time, as well as being of qualitatively great value.

This type of operant reinforcement approach to alcoholism incorporates essential features of the recent emphasis in mental health programs known as the community mental health approach (Bindman and Spiegel, 1969; Caplan, 1964, 1970; Klein, 1968). This approach may be characterized by a realization that mental disorders result from forces operating in and by the community on the individual and suggests that treatment be conducted by rearranging these community influences on the patient in the community rather than in a hospital. Examples of community based treatments include the home care program for schizophrenics (Pasaminick, Scarpitti and Denitz, 1967), the home based reinforcement program for school aged children (Tharp and Wetzel, 1969), the community located business owned and operated by former mental patients (Fairweather, Sanders, Maynard and Cressler, 1969) and an open facility for skid-row alcoholics (Meyerson and Mayer, 1967). Since the operant based model described above deals with the rearrangement of the alcoholic's vocational, social, recreational and familial satisfactions, most of which are found in the community, this approach is in accord with the general community treatment approach and may be designated therefore, as a Community-Reinforcement approach to alcoholism.

The present study developed a method of treating alcoholics and evaluated the effectiveness of this Community-Reinforcement procedure with hospitalized alcoholics, a group which is known to have an extremely poor prognosis. A matched control group was included since recent reviews (Hill and Blane, 1967; and Wallgren and Barry, 1970) have concluded that virtually no treatment procedure can be stated to have been effective because of the lack of a suitable control group against which to evaluate that procedure.

METHOD

Subjects

The population consisted of those patients admitted to a State Hospital for treatment of alcoholism who suffered withdrawal symptoms and were diagnosed alcoholic. This institution was responsible for the hospital treatment of all alcoholics and mental patients in a sparsely populated rural Midwestern region. Sixteen males were selected from this population. Patients were excluded who had serious medical ailments which precluded employment.

Design for Evaluation

Eight available alcoholics were selected arbitrarily and then matched individually with eight others on the basis of employment history, family stability, previous drinking history, age and education (see Table 36.1). The rationale for the matching according to these characteristics is based on studies by Gerard and Saenger (1966) and Schmidt, Smart and Moss (1968). A coin flip determined which member of each pair received the Community-Reinforcement counseling. The other pair member did not receive the Community-Reinforcement counseling procedures. Both groups received the same housing, didactic program and other services of the hospital.

Table 36.1.   Patient Characteristics.

	Control (Mean)	Reinforcement (Mean)
Age	36.75	39.87
Education	11	10.2
Number of hospitalizations	2.5	2.6
Marital status	5 M—3 S	5 M—3 S
Recent job	5 yes—3 no	5 yes—3 no

The Community-Reinforcement Program

The Community-Reinforcement program was designed to rearrange the vocational, family and social reinforcers of the alcoholic such that time-out from these reinforcers would occur if he began to drink. On the first day, a brief description of the nature of the procedures and the reasons for them were presented to the alcoholic. For example, he was told by the counselor that extensive research and experience have shown that the alcoholic's chances of staying sober are improved if he has a satisfying steady job. Therefore, one part of this counseling program involved helping him achieve a satisfactory job. The family and social adjustment procedures were introduced to the alcoholic in a similar manner. Also, on the first day, the alcoholic was asked if he had any pressing problems. If he had a legal problem, he would be referred to a lawyer. If his major problem was financial, then the job-finding procedures would begin immediately. The client's reluctance to attempt these large scale changes was overcome by assuring him that such changes were possible and that the counselor would be accompanying him at every step of the way.

The specific manner and sequence in which these procedures were carried out varied somewhat from patient to patient depending on the specifics of his situation. For example, if he stated that he was happy with his job, and it seemed that he did not drink at work, the family counseling procedures were begun. Typically there was continued overlap in the procedures.

Vocational Counseling

Those patients without jobs were instructed to (1) prepare a resumé, (2) read the pamphlet "How to get the job" (Dreese, 1960), (3) call all friends and relatives on the phone to inform them of the need for employment and ask them for job leads, (4) call the major factories and plants in the area, (5) place a "Situations-Wanted" advertisement in the local papers, (6) rehearse the job interview and (7) place applications and interview for the jobs which are available. While the alcoholic was following the above procedures, the counselor was physically present and actively assisted the client. He stood by while phone calls were made, role-played interviews with the client and arranged for typing of the resumé. Also, he escorted the alcoholic to the job interviews and immediately following the interview discussed the results. These procedures are based on recent studies concerning the relevant considerations in successful job-finding (Jones and Azrin, 1973; Sheppard and Belitsky, 1966). As soon as the patient acquired a job, which he said would be satisfactory to him, he was released from the hospital. The counselor typically accompanied the client to the job on the first day. The counselor arranged for transportation to work by friends when necessary. In some cases employer–employee situations were role-played.

Marital and Family Counseling

The marital counseling attempted to (1) provide reinforcement for the alcoholic to be a functioning marital partner, (2) provide reinforcement for the spouse for maintaining the marital relation and (3) to make the drinking of alcohol incompatible with this improved marital relation. The first sessions usually took place in the hospital, the remainder in the home after discharge. The alcoholic and his wife were given the Marriage Adjustment Inventory (Manson and Lerner, 1962) which identified twelve specific problem areas in the marriage, including money management, family relations, sex problems, children, social life, attention, neurotic tendencies, immaturity, grooming, ideological difficulties, general incompatibility and dominance. The husband and wife met jointly with the counselor who assisted them in listing specific activities which each spouse agreed to perform to make the other spouse happy in the identified problem area, thereby providing reciprocal benefits to each other. This list typically included preparing meals, listening to the partner with undivided attention, picking up the children from school, redistributing the finances, engaging in sexual activities of a particular type or at a minimal frequency, visiting relatives together and spending a night out together. To facilitate communication about sexual interaction, a marriage manual with specific instructions on sex (Ellis, 1966) was given to the partners. Absolute sobriety was a stipulation by all of the wives as one of the agreements. The rationale for this general approach to marital counseling has been described by Stuart (1969).

For unmarried patients living with their families, a similar procedure was used of providing reciprocal benefits between the patient and his parents, to be maintained only when the patient was sober. For patients with neither a marital nor parental family attempts were made to arrange a "synthetic" or foster family. The synthetic family consisted of those persons who might have some natural reason for maintaining regular interactions with the patient: relatives, or an employer or a minister. These synthetic families were encouraged to invite the ex-patient over for dinner on a regular basis, and to expect him to help with chores or offer his services in some other way. Again, sobriety was made a condition for maintaining these "family" benefits.

Several major problems arose in attempting to carry out the marital and family counseling procedures. A list of the major problems and the attempted strategy for solution is presented as follows: (1) Both the client and his wife often refused to engage in marital counseling on the grounds that the marital situation was so distressful that neither of them had a desire to return to it. The strategy for overcoming this objective was to strongly assure both the client and his spouse that no attempt would be made to return to the marital situation until the spouse had given convincing assurance that the distressful problems would be eliminated. (2) Great difficulty was often experienced by the patient and his wife in designating activities that would make their marriage a pleasant one, often because of their lack of verbal articulation and often because of general reticence and skepticism. The strategy used in overcoming these problems was for the counselor to suggest satisfactions that other married persons enjoyed, to phrase possible satisfactions in specifiable terms, to have the clients imagine what an ideal marriage would consist of, and to ask what satisfactions they might have received in the past or had expected to receive when first married. (3) They often expressed doubt that they could discontinue providing the agreed upon satisfactions when the client began drinking. The strategy for solving this problem was to advise the wife to discontinue physical and social contact with the client as much as possible during that time; in the extreme case she was advised to move out of the house into a motel or with a relative until the client in a sober state requested her return. (4) The client sometimes refused to initiate any unaccustomed activity that had been requested by the spouse such as different type of sexual behavior, the visiting of a particular relative or attending a social club together. The strategy for solving this was the principle of Reinforcer Sampling (Ayllon and Azrin, 1968) in which the clients were asked to "just try it for one week and then we will decide after that whether to continue it." (5) Even after agreements had been made and the couple was following them, a frequent difficulty was that new problems arose that were not covered by the agreements or some of the old agreements were found to be distasteful. The solution was to teach the couple how to draw up these reciprocated agreements on their own.

About five marital and family counseling sessions were conducted in drawing up the complete set of agreements between the spouses or between the patient and his parental or synthetic family.

Social Counseling

Most social interaction of the alcoholic had been reduced to a small circle of friends who also had a severe drinking problem. Consequently, drinking became a behavioral prerequisite for maintaining those social relationships. A social counseling procedure was developed which attempted to restore and improve the client's social relationships and to make continuation of these improved relationships dependent upon sobriety rather than upon drinking. The clients were counseled to schedule social interactions with friends, relatives and community groups with whom alcoholic drinking was not tolerated. At the same time they were discouraged from interacting with those friends known to have a drinking problem. In many instances the client's circle of friends had become circumscribed because of his drinking problem. Hence, a more structured method of creating these incompatible social reinforcers was devised. A former tavern was converted into a self-supporting social club for the clients. This organization provided a band, jukebox, card games, dances, invited female companions, picnics, fish fries, bingo games, movies and other types of social activities. The wives of the clients were strongly advised to attend and often did. Each client was given paid membership to the club for a period of one month, after which he paid his own membership dues. Each member was encouraged to invite personal friends to the club as guests. The club's principal meeting was on Saturday night. For those members without transportation, the other club members made a deliberate effort to provide transportation. Alcoholic beverages were strictly forbidden at the club and any member who arrived at the club with any indication of drinking was turned away. In this manner the clients experienced a greatly improved social life which was incompatible with alcoholic drinking.

Reinforcer-Access Counseling

An improved adjustment in the aforementioned three areas of the family, the job and the social life was often hindered by the absence of facilities that are commonly available to the non-alcoholic. For example, one might find it difficult to obtain employment without a telephone or newspaper. Successful social adjustment was also often hindered by this inability to call and speak with friends, by the absence of transportation facilities (no public transportation was available in this rural area) and by the absence of timely topics of conversation (some of the clients did not read newspapers, listen to the radio or watch television). The attractiveness of the home or family situation was also diminished by the absence of these facilities. In order to make the home a more attractive place, to facilitate communication with potential employers, and to increase access to friends and social occasions, the counselor encouraged and arranged for the clients to obtain a radio and/or television set in their home, to subscribe to the area newspaper, to subscribe to magazines, to obtain an automobile or driving license and to have a telephone installed in their home. If necessary, the counselor arranged for payment of the initial costs in order to prime the activity. So, for example, the required installation charge by the telephone company was paid by the counselor but not the monthly payments thereafter; likewise the first month's payment on the newspaper but not the succeeding months. The rationale for priming these activities was to increase the ease with which the alcoholic could engage in the areas of vocational, marital, and social activities, these three areas of activities already being incompatible with drinking. A second reason why these "access" activities would be expected to be incompatible with drinking is that most of these activites required continued payments and thereby provided an additional incentive for the client to maintain his remunerative employment. Also it might be expected that these activities would reduce the need for obtaining reinforcement from drinking by providing alternative sources of reinforcement.   ·

Existing Hospital Program

Both the reinforcement and control groups received the counseling and instruction that was standard at the institution. This consisted of approximately 25 one-hour didactic sessions which presented by means of lectures and audio-visual aids: (1) a description of the basic workings of Alcoholics Anonymous, (2) information regarding the statistics on drinking and the problems of alcoholics, (3) examples of alcoholics' behavior, (4) examples of physiological pathologies resulting from alcoholism, (5) examples of sex problems caused by alcohol and the means of overcoming the problems and (6) other related topics.

Community Maintenance

For the first month after discharge, the alcoholic was visited by the counselor once or twice a week. During these visits he was reminded of the reinforcers which existed for family, job, and social life participation. Also, any problems which might have arisen in following the procedures were discussed and several alternative solutions were offered. The visits also functioned as a means of following up the progress of the ex-patient in terms of his sobriety, employment, and social life. After the first month, these visits continued on the average of twice a month, then decreased thereafter to once a month. If the alcoholic attended the social club, contact was made on a more frequent, although more informal basis.

Recording and Reliability

On every visit, the counselor obtained information about the days unemployed, days drinking occurred and days spent away from home. In most cases, a member of the family was present for the purpose of helping the ex-patients to remember the exact situation. In addition, an assistant who was in no way connected with the counseling, and was unaware that the patients were treated differently, called on the ex-patients after the 6 month period and explained that he was collecting information for the purpose of better understanding alcoholism. The information he collected correlated with that of the counselor at greater than 0.95 using the Pearson *r* (Edwards, 1969).

RESULTS

Figure 36.1 shows that the mean per cent of time spent drinking, unemployed, away from home, and institutionalized was more than twice as high for the control group as for the Community-Reinforcement group. The mean per cent of time spent (1) drinking was 14 per cent for the reinforcement group and 79 per cent for the control group; (2) unemployed was 5 per cent for the reinforcement group and 62 per cent for the control group; (3) away from family or synthetic family was 16 per cent for the reinforcement group and 66 per cent for the control group; (4) institutionalized was 2 per cent for the reinforcement group and 27 per cent

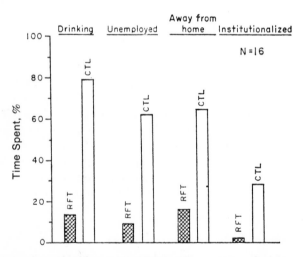

Fig. 36.1. A comparison of the key dependent measures for the reinforcement and control groups since discharge: mean percentages of time spent drinking, unemployed, away from home and institutionalized.

for the control group. The *t* test of differences for paired comparisons (Edwards, 1969) yielded significant differences ($p < 0.005$) for all measures. The dependent measures were calculated by dividing the number of days the patient was drinking, unemployed, away from home, and institutionalized by the total number of days since discharge. For the drinking measure, time spent in an institution was not included. If a person had a job but did not work because of temporary weather conditions, illness, being on vacation or weekends or holidays, he was still considered to be employed full-time.

Figure 36.2 shows that the mean per cent of time spent for all measures computed monthly remained stable over the 6 month period. In no month was there a major fluctuation in any of the measures. For every month and for every measure, the *t* test of differences yielded significant

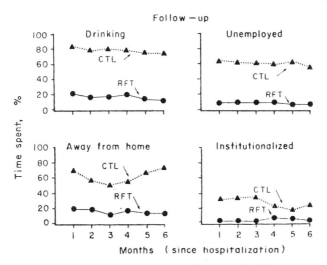

Fig. 36.2. The stable difference between groups over the 6 months after discharge of the key dependent measures: mean percentages of time spent drinking, unemployed, away from home and institutionalized.

differences between the control group and the Community-Reinforcement group ($p < 0.005$). Analysis of the earnings of the patients revealed that the reinforcement group, having a mean income of $355 per month per patient, made more money than did the control group which had a mean income of $190 per month. Analysis of the patients' social activities showed that the Community-Reinforcement patients spent a mean of 13 weekends per patient in a structured social activity out of the home whereas the mean of the control patients was 4 such weekend activities.

Figure 36.3 shows the per cent time spent drinking for each of the matched pairs. For 6 of the 8 pairs, the counseled group differed radically from the control group. However, both members of pair 7 remained sober and neither member of pair 5 remained sober. The counseled member of pair 5 was the only patient for whom counseling produced only minimal changes. He was retarded (IQ = 70), remained single, lived with his alcoholic father, had a low status job, did not attend the social club, and even though a synthetic family was arranged, they lived eight miles away and lack of transportation seemed to prohibit active involvement with them. This patient had the least resources of all patients in this study prior to counseling, and seemed to change the least. Also, he was accidentally discharged from the hospital without the counselor's consent and before the initial hospital-based portion of the counseling was completed. The control member of pair 7 was the highest functioning member in the control group. He returned from the hospital to his well-established family and job situation. Not only did he express satisfaction with his well-paid job as manager of a dairy business, but he also seemed happy with his family and regularly participated in Alcoholics Anonymous.

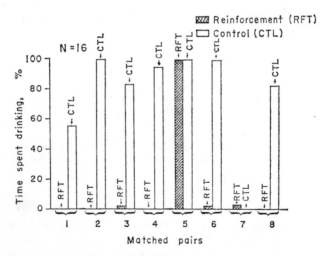

Fig. 36.3. Sobriety: a comparison of the matched pairs—one receiving the Community-Reinforcement procedures, the other the control—in terms of mean percentage of time spent sober since discharge.

The job-finding procedures led to satisfactory employment for 4 of the 8 counseled alcoholics. Two were located by systematically checking with the major places of employment. The other 2 were located through advertisement. One job proved unsatisfactory because it was too far from the alcoholic's home and after 2 weeks the job hunt procedures were resumed until a closer job was obtained. For one patient, the "Situations-Wanted" procedure located a variety of what seemed to be acceptable job leads. However, this alcoholic turned down every job offer since he was satisfied with his former job as a trade union construction worker. The remaining 4 counseled patients returned to former jobs. All jobs were located within 10 days after the procedures were started.

All 5 of the married couples in the Community-Reinforcement group initially suggested the possibility of divorce. Two had already separated by the time the husband was admitted to the hospital. Within a short time after counseling had begun, the couples decided to remain married for a while longer. It seemed that counseling was particularly valuable in pointing out the reinforcers which existed for remaining married. All 5 couples in the Community-Reinforcement group eventually remained together while 2 of the 4 control couples permanently separated or divorced.

The counseled group participated actively in the social club. Three of the 8 held offices in the club and attended over 80 per cent of the Saturday night meetings; 4 attended about 25 per cent; only 1 failed to attend. The club had been equally available to the control group alcoholics but without the special encouragement and structuring. Yet, only 2 members of the control group ever attended, and neither came more than 3 times.

DISCUSSION

Although the present procedure was tested in a hospital, the procedure does not require hospitalization except as a means of helping the patient through his withdrawal symptoms and physical debility, if any. The present results show that the patients who received the Community-Reinforcement procedures remained more sober than their matched controls. This improvement did not diminish over the 6 month period. The Community-Reinforcement patients also spent greater percentages of time gainfully employed, with their families, and out of institutions. Their average earnings were twice as great as the control group and they spent more time during weekends in acceptable social activities. These positive results for treating alcoholism are unusual in that no controlled study with state hospital patients has reported such general success (Chafetz, Hill and Blane, 1971; Hill and Blane, 1967; Mayer and Meyerson, 1971; Pittman and Tate, 1969).

To evaluate meaningfully the large benefits produced by the present procedure, it is necessary to compare the effects of the present procedure with the effects obtained by previous methods of treating alcoholism. In making such comparisons, a major problem is assuring that comparable populations were used since the rate of spontaneous recovery from alcoholism after hospitalization is often extremely high even among otherwise untreated patients. Improvement rates as high as 100 per cent have been reported for particular sub-groups of alcoholics after simple hospitalization, such as the control group whose members refused treatment in one study (Voegtlin, Lemere, Broz and O'Hallaren, 1941), whereas improvement or cure rates have been as low as 20 per cent for other sub-groups, even with treatment (Pittman and Tate, 1969). A reported effectiveness of 90 per cent with a given treatment procedure may, therefore, reflect no improvement by that procedure, since that percentage may have been even less than the spontaneous rate of improvement. Conversely, a reported rate of improvement of only 20 per cent by a given treatment method may represent a substantial effect if the spontaneous rate would have been only 10 per cent. Thus, judgment of the effectiveness of a given treatment procedure requires a comparison with a comparable group of controls. Yet, as recent reviews of alcoholism treatment programs and related studies (Hill and Blane, 1967; Chafetz, Hill and Blane, 1971; Wallgren and Barry, 1970) have concluded, only a handful of studies have been conducted containing a comparable control group. Among this handful are the studies by Madill, Campbell, Laverty, Sanderson and Vandewater (1966); Pittman and Tate (1969) and Waller-stein (1957). Although their measure of sobriety and related social behaviors are presented in terms different from the present study, a general comparison indicates that the present Community-Reinforcement procedure was at least as effective.

Examination of the post-hospital conduct of the control group reveals what the spontaneous rate of improvement would have been without the special Community-Reinforcement procedure. The results show that in the absence of this treatment the patients spent most of their time drinking, worked very rarely, had few acceptable social activities and did not form stable family relationships. Correlational studies have demonstrated that patients exhibiting this type of life style have extremely poor prognosis under virtually all treatment procedures (Gerard and Saenger, 1966).

A question to be raised is whether the present results can be accounted for in terms of the time-out explanation. Did the procedure raise the actual reinforcement density and thereby make the time-out produced by drinking especially aversive? Two lines of evidence support an affirmative answer. First the density of reinforcement of the Community-Reinforcement group was definitely higher than that of the control group as seen by the increased amount of time at work, increased time spent with families, increased salaries and increased social life. Second, the Community-Reinforcement patients often reported spontaneously that they were now more satisfied with their life. Actually, time-out did not occur in many cases since drinking never occurred. However, the patients all stated that time-out would occur if they did take a drink and this knowledge of the consequence seemed to be the deterrent.

The present study was concerned with specific variables such as time-out and immediacy of reinforcement. In a larger sense, the present results can be considered to offer support for a general Community-Reinforcement model for describing (1) the etiology of alcoholism, (2) the basis of effectiveness of current treatment methods, (3) the direction in which future treatment methods may have the greatest likelihood of success and (4) the epidemiological facts about alcoholism.

Consider first a reinforcement conceptualization of the etiology of alcoholism. Alcohol can be considered as a reinforcer. One source of reinforcement for drinking alcohol is probably the pleasant and relaxing subjective state which it produces. Purely taste factors seem to constitute another basis for the reinforcing value as seen in preferences for one specific type of alcoholic beverage. A third basis for the reinforcement value is the social reinforcement that is given by one's family, friends and peers directly for drinking as at a cocktail party or for drinking as part of a desired group activity, such as at a poker game. Or the social reaction may be that of social tolerance (non-punishment) of otherwise disapproved activities. A fourth source of reinforcement arises after prolonged drinking, namely, the individual becomes addicted to the alcohol and requires ever-increasing amounts to maintain the same subjective sensations and to avoid withdrawal symptoms. At this state the individual is usually characterized as being an alcoholic. In the absence of any inhibitory influences, these four combined sources of subjective, physical, social and addictive reinforcement could be expected to maintain drinking indefinitely, depending on the accumulated strength of these factors for a given individual.

Opposed to these factors that facilitate drinking are various influences that serve to inhibit drinking and which can be conceptualized as negative reinforcers. The major types of negative reinforcers correspond roughly to the major types of positive reinforcers. Under excessive alcohol consumption many of the subjective sensations become unpleasurable such as nausea, dizziness, incoordination and sexual impotence. Unpleasant social reactions rather than approval may result from one's friends, family, legal authorities and employers who then reject the alcoholic. The deterrent value of these negative reinforcers on a given individual will depend on whether they are operative on him (does he have a family or job), on the magnitude of the negative reinforcer (how much is lost when losing a given job or family) and the immediacy with which the negative reinforcer follows the act of drinking (how much does the employer tolerate drinking).

Current treatment methods may be conceptualized as emphasizing one or more of the above reinforcement influences. Shock-aversion therapy emphasizes the physical negative reinforcers and the importance of immediacy by arranging for very painful electric shocks to be delivered in an immediate association with the act or thought of drinking. Antabuse therapy emphasizes the importance of frequency of negative reinforcement by insuring that a painful, nauseous reaction will result shortly after each act of drinking. The Alcoholics Anonymous program emphasizes the social types of negative reinforcement by providing a social peer group which reacts negatively to drinking but arranges social positive reinforcement for non-drinking. Treatment approaches which include vocational and general counseling can be considered to be emphasizing the negative reinforcement influences in that by providing regular gainful employment to the alcoholic, he will be assured of a time-out from positive reinforcement resulting from drinking. The detoxification procedure that has become standard in hospitals emphasizes the elimination of the withdrawal symptom as a source of reinforcement in that once the alcoholic individual has been forcibly kept sober for a period of time he no longer has the same want to keep drinking in order to avoid the withdrawal symptoms. Efforts to discover a central nervous system center for alcoholism can be considered to be an emphasis on discovering the neurological basis for the pleasurable subjective sensations caused by drinking (St. Laurent and Olds, 1967).

This Community-Reinforcement model of alcoholism also appears capable of conceptualizing some of the major findings concerning the epidemiology of alcoholism. As noted below, the major association of alcoholism is with cultural factors (Bales, 1946; DeLint and Schmidt, 1971) which can be taken to mean that particular sub-cultures, such as the French and Italian, reinforce drinking whereas other sub-cultures, such as the Scandinavians, Jews and Moslems, give negative reinforcers for drinking. The lower rate of alcoholism among married individuals and those with stable families (Gerard and Saenger, 1966) is taken to show that negative reinforcers will be encountered to a greater extent by the time-out from positive family reinforcers. The finding that alcohol consumption decreases when the cost of alcohol is increased (DeLint and Schmidt, 1971) follows directly from the inhibitory properties of monetary cost as a negative reinforcer. Similarly, the lower rate of alcoholism among the regularly employed (Gerard and Saenger, 1966; Trice, 1962) is taken to be the result of the negative reinforcer of job dismissal that results only when one is regularly employed. The relatively high rate of alcoholism among the self-employed (Gerard and Saenger, 1966; Trice, 1962) can be explained on the basis of this negative reinforcer not being as immediate as when one is employed by others. The general observation of a higher rate of alcoholism during the "off-seasons" for various employment categories shows that in the absence of regular vocational reinforcement, a time-out from reinforcement will not occur for drinking. The varying susceptibility to alcohol by different individuals (Jellinek, 1960) is taken to indicate varying degrees of positive reinforcement and varying degrees of unpleasant medical reaction, i.e. negative reinforcement such as is normally encountered with all drugs (Wallgren and Barry, 1970). The common observation that some persons have a high level of social, economic and family satisfactions and yet become alcoholic can be analyzed by examining whether their drinking is immediately followed by loss of these satisfactions or whether a long delay occurs such as by the alcoholic's circumventing detection.

The relationship between the present model and the theory of tension reduction is especially relevant because of the general acceptance of that tension-reduction theory as an explanation of alcoholic drinking. The tension-reduction theory considers that alcohol is consumed primarily because it reduces anxiety or tension: the proposed model also assumes that alcohol is a reinforcer but not necessarily because of its ability to reduce tension. The Community-Reinforcement model assumes that alcohol is pleasant to drink (a reinforcer), that this reinforcement value will be great at moments of pleasure as well as stress, and that alcohol consumption will be governed by social, economic and other such reactions to the drinking. Only with respect to the stress of the withdrawal

532   Behavior Therapy and Health Care

symptoms do the two theoretical statements necessarily coincide. Evidence in favor of the Community-Reinforcement theory over the tension-reduction theory can be seen from two major sources: (1) As a very recent review has concluded, laboratory studies show that the evidence for the tension-reduction theory "is negative, equivocal and often contradictory" (Coppell and Herman, 1972). (2) As noted previously, epidemiological studies such as by DeLint and Schmidt (1971) show alcoholic consumption to be associated primarily with social and cultural factors and not with factors that might be considered as stressful such as low income level (Schmidt *et al.*, 1968) and neurotic or anxious personality (Lisansky, 1967).

The promise of different alcohol treatment approaches may be estimated on the basis of the known correlates of alcoholism. In general, the search for genetic, personality and economic correlates of alcoholism have shown little association (Wallgren and Barry, 1970; Schmidt *et al.*, 1968). The major factors associated with alcoholism have been the social–cultural and familial factors (Gerard and Saenger, 1966; Schmidt *et al.*, 1968; Wallgren and Barry, 1970). These findings may be taken to indicate that the greatest progress in future treatment research will come from treatments that alter these social–cultural influences and that community-based treatment procedures therefore hold great promise.

REFERENCES

Alcoholics Anonymous. *The Story of how Many Thousands of Men and Women Have Recovered from Alcoholism.* Alcoholics Anonymous Publishing, New York, 1960.

Ayllon, T. and Azrin, N. H. Reinforcer sampling: A technique for increasing the behavior of mental patients. *J. appl. Behav. Anal.*, 1968, **1**, 13–20.

Bales, R. F. Cultural differences in rates of alcoholism. *Q.J. Stud. Alcohol.*, 1949, **6**, 480–499.

Bindman, A. J. and Spiegel, A. D. (Eds.). *Perspectives in Community Mental Health.* Aldine Publishing Co., Chicago, 1969.

Bucher, B. and Lovaas, O. I. Use of aversive stimulation in behavior modification. In *Miami Symposium on the Prediction of Behavior* 1967: *Aversive Stimulation* (Ed. M. R. Jones). University of Miami Press, Coral Gables, Florida, 1968.

Caplan, G. *Principles of Preventive Psychiatry.* Basic Books, New York, 1964.

Caplan, G. *The Theory and Practice of Mental Health Consultation.* Basic Books, New York, 1970.

Chafetz, M. E., Blane, H. T., and Hill, M. J. (Eds.). *Frontiers of Alcoholism.* Science House, New York, 1971.

Coppell, H. and Herman, C. P. Alcohol and tension reduction. *Q.J. Stud. Alcohol.*, 1972, **33**, 33–64.

DeLint, J. and Schmidt, W. Consumption averages and alcoholism prevalence: A brief review of epidemiological investigations. *Br. J. Addict.*, 1971, **66**, 97–107.

Dreese, M. *How to Get the Job.* (Rev. Edn). Science Research Associates, Chicago, 1960.

Edwards, A. L. *Statistical Analysis.* Holt, Rinehart & Winston Inc., New York, 1969.

Ellis, A. *The Art and Science of Love.* Bantam Books, New York, 1966.

Fairweather, G. W., Sanders, D. H., Maynard, H., and Cressler, D. L. 1966. *Community Life for the Mentally Ill.* Aldine Publishing Co., Chicago, 1969.

Ferster, C. B. Control of behavior in chimpanzees and pigeons by time-out from positive reinforcement. *Psychol. Monogr.*, 1958, **72**, No. 8 (Whole No. 461).

Freytag, Fredericka. Psychodynamisms with special reference to the alcoholic. In *Alcoholism: Behavioral Research, Therapeutic Approaches* (Ed. Ruth Fox). Springer Publishing Co., New York, 1967.

Gerard, D. L. and Saenger, G. *Outpatient Treatment of Alcoholism.* University of Toronto Press, Toronto, Monograph No. 4, 1966.

Hill, M. J. and Blane, H. T. Evaluation of psychotherapy with alcoholics: A critical review. *Q.J. Stud. Alcohol.*, 1967, **28**, 76–204.

Holz, W. C. and Azrin, N. H. A comparison of several procedures for eliminating behavior. *J. exp. Anal. Behav.*, 1963, **6**, 399–406.

Jellinek, E. M. *The Disease Concept of Alcoholism.* College and University Press, New Haven, 1960.

Jones, R. J. and Azrin, N. H. An experimental application of social reinforcement approach to the problem of job finding. *J. appl. Behav. Anal.*, 1973, **6**, 345–354.

Klein, D. C. *Community Dynamics and Mental Health.* Wiley, New York, 1968.

Leitenberg, H. Is time-out from positive reinforcement an aversive event? *Psychol. Bull.*, 1965, **64**, 428–441.

Lisansky, E. S. Clinical research in alcoholism and the use of psychological tests: A reevaluation. In *Alcoholism: Behavioral Research, Therapeutic Approaches* (Ed. Ruth Fox). Springer Publishing Co., New York, 1967.

Madill, M., Campbell, D., Laverty, S. G., Sanderson, R. E., and Vandewater, S. L. Aversion treatment of alcoholics by Succinylcholine-induced apneic paralysis. *Q.J. Stud. Alcohol.*, 1966, **27**, 483–510.

Manson, M. P. and Lerner, A. *The Marriage Adjustment Inventory.* Western Psychological Services, Los Angeles, 1962.

Mayer, J. and Meyerson, D. J. Outpatient treatment of alcoholics. *Q.J. Stud. Alcohol.*, 1971, **32**, 620–627.

Meyerson, D. J. and Mayer, J. The origins, treatments and density of skid row alcoholic men. In *Alcoholism: Behavioral Research, Therapeutic Approaches* (Ed. Ruth Fox). Springer Publishing Co., New York, 1967.

Pasaminick, B., Scarpitti, F. R., and Denitz, S. *Schizophrenics in the Community.* Appleton-Century-Crofts, New York, 1967.

Pittman, D. J. and Tate, R. L. A comparison of two treatment programs for alcoholics. *Q.J. Stud. Alcohol.*, 1969, **30**, 888–899.

Rachman, S. and Teasdale, J. *Aversion Therapy and Behavior Disorders: An Analysis.* University of Miami Press, Coral Gables, Florida, 1969.

Schmidt, W. G., Smart, R. G., and Moss, M. K. *Social Class and the Treatment of Alcoholism.* University of Toronto Press, Toronto, Monograph No. 7, 1968.

Sheppard, H. L. and Belitsky, H. H. *The Job Hunt.* The Johns Hopkins Press, Baltimore, 1966.

Skinner, B. F. *The Behavior of Organisms.* Appleton-Century-Crofts, New York, 1938.

Steiner, C. M. The alcoholic game. *Q.J. Stud. Alcohol.*, 1969, **30**, 920–938.

St. Laurent, J. and Olds, J. Alcohol and brain centers of positive reinforcement. In *Alcoholism: Behavioral Research, Therapeutic Approaches* (Ed. Ruth Fox). Springer Publishing Co., New York, 1967.

Stuart, R. B. Token reinforcement in marital treatment. In *Advances in Behavior Therapy* (Eds. R. Rubin and C. Franks). Academic Press, New York, 1969.

Sulzer, E. S. Behavior modification in adult psychiatric patients. In *Case Studies in Behavior Modification* (Eds. L. Ullmann and L. Krasner). Holt, Rinehart and Winston, Inc., New York, 1965.

Tharp, R. G. and Wetzel, R. J. *Behavior Modification in the Natural Environment.* Academic Press, New York, 1969.

Trice, H. M. The job behaviors of problem drinkers. In *Society, Culture and Drinking Patterns* (Eds. D. Pittman and C. Snyder). John Wiley, New York, 1962.

Voegtlin, W. L., Lemere, F., Broz, W. R., and O'Hallaren, P. Conditioned reflex therapy of chronic alcoholism—IV. A preliminary report on the value of reinforcement. *Q.J. Stud. Alcohol.*, 1941, **2**, 505–511.

Vogel-Sprott, M. Alcoholism as learned behavior: Some hypotheses and research. In *Alcoholism: Behavioral Research, Therapeutic Approaches* (Ed. Ruth Fox). Springer Publishing Co., New York, 1967.

Wahler, R. G. Setting generality: Some specific and general effects of child behavior therapy. *J. appl. Behav. Anal.*, 1969, **2**, 239–246.

Wallerstein, R. S. (Ed.) *Hospital Treatment of Alcoholism: A Comparative Experimental Study.* Basic Books, New York, 1957.

Wallgren, H. and Barry, H. *Actions of Alcohol*, Vol. II. Elsevier Publishing Co., Amsterdam, 1970.

Wilkinson, R. *The Prevention of Drinking Problems.* Oxford University Press, New York, 1970.

Wolf, M., Risley, R., and Mees, H. Application of operant conditioning procedures to the behavior problems of an autistic child. *Behav. Res. & Therapy*, 1964, **1**, 305–312.

Individualized Behavior Therapy for Alcoholics*[1]

MARK B. SOBELL and LINDA C. SOBELL[2]

Patton State Hospital, California Department of Mental Hygiene

Abstract: A behavior therapy for alcoholism was designed based on the rationale that alcoholic drinking is a discriminated, operant response. Treatment emphasized determining setting events for each subject's drinking and training equally effective alternative responses to those situations. Seventy male, hospitalized, Gamma alcoholics were assigned to a treatment goal of either nondrinking ($N = 30$) or controlled drinking ($N = 40$). Subjects of each group were then randomly assigned to either an experimental group receiving 17 behavioral treatment sessions or a control group receiving only conventional treatment. Treatment of experimental groups differed only in drinking behaviors allowed during sessions and electric shock avoidance schedules. Nondrinker experimental subjects shaped to abstinence, while controlled drinker experimental subjects practiced appropriate drinking behaviors with little shaping, a result attributed to instructions. Follow-up measuring drinking and other behaviors found that experimental subjects functioned significantly better after discharge than control subjects, regardless of

*Reprinted from *Behavior Therapy*, 1973, **4**(1), 49–72. Copyright © 1973 by Academic Press, Inc. With permission from Academic Press, Inc. and Mark B. Sobell and Linda C. Sobell.

[1] This investigation was supported (in part) by Public Health Service Grant 1 RO 1 MH 16547-02 and California Department of Mental Hygiene Grant RP-69-11-15. The opinions or conclusions stated in this paper are those of the authors and are not to be construed as official or as necessarily reflecting the policy of the Department of Mental Hygiene.

The authors are considerably indebted to Halmuth H. Schaefer for assistance throughout all phases of the study and preparation of the manuscript and to Timothy Baker, David Bangsund, William Christelman, Kenneth C. Mills, Natalie Olsen, Robert Pilkington, Dee Schucker, and Donald Stern who constituted the research staff. Joseph V. Brady helped plan the study and Francis Tierney, Sebastian Casalaina, and the alcohol program staff of Patton State Hospital were instrumental in its accomplishment. A more detailed version of this manuscript is available from the authors upon request.

[2] Both authors are now with: Alcoholism Services, Orange County Department of Mental Health, 9842 West 13th St., Santa Ana, California 92703. Requests for reprints should be sent to this address.

treatment goal. Successful experimental subjects could apply treatment principles to setting events not considered during treatment, suggesting the occurrence of rule learning. Results are discussed as evidence that some "alcoholics" can acquire and maintain controlled drinking behaviors. Traditional treatment of alcoholics may be handicapped by unvalidated beliefs concerning the nature of the disorder.

Until recently, behavioral studies of alcoholism have emphasized classical aversive conditioning and neglected the instrumental nature of drinking. Rachman and Teasdale (1969) have thoroughly reviewed the aversive-conditioning literature and pointed out that the primary purpose of such techniques is to suppress drinking responses. Seldom have attempts been made concurrently to train socially acceptable behaviors in the place of heavy drinking. Lack of generalization has been perhaps the most severe problem plaguing such studies, but it is a problem not unexpected if heavy drinking is considered to be an operant, i.e., controlled by its consequences. These consequences are usually absent in a treatment environment but are an integral part of our society.

Cohen, Liebson, and Faillace (1971) have recently provided convincing demonstrations that the drinking of alcoholic beverages by alcoholics can be regarded as an operant response and manipulated according to the various laws of operant psychology. They also demonstrated that Gamma alcoholics could maintain a pattern of moderate drinking of 95-proof ethanol for extended periods, if reinforcement contingencies were appropriately arranged. In a very real sense, their results have shown that one can buy controlled drinking behavior from an alcoholic—if the price is right!

THE RATIONALE OF THE WORK REPORTED HERE

Several studies using both animal and human subjects have investigated the hypothesis that a voluntary increase in alcohol consumption is associated with increases in stress. Clark and Polish (1960) conducted a well-controlled baseline replication design study in which rhesus monkeys could drink either water, a solution of 20% alcohol in water, or both during initial baseline (no treatment) sessions, followed by electric shock avoidance sessions, and finally, baseline sessions once again. They reported that: "Alcohol consumption increased during, and decreased after, avoidance sessions. Water intake remained the same or decreased during avoidance sessions and stayed at this level after the sessions (p.

223)." In another animal study, Cicero, Myers, and Black (1968) found that hooded rats increased their intake of ethanol in the presence of cued unavoidable electric shock. More recently, von Wright, Pekanmäki, and Malin (1971) found that Wistar albino rats increased their alcohol intake significantly when subjected to an approach-avoidance conflict. They also present a critical review of additional experiments investigating the stress-reduction hypothesis.

Hershenson (1965), in a study based on self-reports by problem drinkers, concluded that their use of alcohol was stress induced. Also working with human alcoholic subjects, Schaefer, Sobell, and Mills (1971b) found substantial indirect evidence indicating that binge drinking could be stress induced. Bandura (1969) provided an excellent review of other studies supporting a stress-reduction hypothesis.

A behavioral approach to alcoholism which has been proposed by various investigators (Masserman & Yum, 1946; Conger, 1951; Bandura, 1969; Lundin, 1969) but never developed into a full treatment design, considers heavy drinking of alcoholic beverages as an alcoholic individual's predominant learned response to a stressful, anxiety-laden situation. The response of drinking is conceived as having been acquired because the problem drinker has been rewarded, consciously or not, for such drinking. Among the possible rewarding consequences which could result from heavy drinking in a stressful situation are:

1. Alcohol is an extremely effective sedative (Carpenter, 1957; Lienert & Traxel, 1959), and thus, by drinking, a person experiencing an aversive situation may significantly reduce the physiological components of that state. Once a drunken stupor is reached there is little doubt that a complete, although temporary, escape from the aversive situation has been attained.

2. Alcohol consumed in large quantities is physically debilitating. During a debilitated state the drinker can avoid participating in many situations which, for whatever reasons, he finds unpleasant. Knowledge of this means of avoidance could lead a person to initiate a binge. At the very least, if the person is made to go through the aversive situation, the sedative nature of intoxication would reduce the magnitude of the accompanying anxious state.

3. Alcohol intoxication is socially accepted as an excuse for engaging in certain otherwise inappropriate behaviors, such as extremes of flirtation, extremes of aggression, or homosexuality, which are generally considered socially unacceptable when engaged in by a sober individual, but are tolerated from a person who is drunk. Consequently, the oppor-

tunity to engage in these behaviors with minimal chastisement can act as a reinforcer for the drinking behavior.

While it is our contention that the alcoholic's primary use of alcohol is to escape from or avoid stressful or potentially stressful situations, other contingencies might also control the excessive drinking response to some extent. Cohen *et al.* (1971) have remarked that many powerful reinforcers, such as medical and psychiatric care, attention, money, welfare, rehabilitation programs, guidance and counseling are: ". . . sometimes dispensed when the alcoholic is sober, but they are often dispensed during or following excessive drinking."

It deserves mention that not all experimental studies have supported the stress-reduction hypothesis. Nathan, Titler, Lowenstein, Solomon, and Rossi (1970) reported that, although alcoholic subjects said they drank to decrease anxiety and depression, when put to the test of actual intoxication they behaved as though their anxiety and depression had increased. Likewise, McNamee, Mello, and Mendelson (1968) found that 9 of 12 alcoholic subjects who became inebriated as part of an experiment experienced an increase in anxiety and depression after the first day or two of drinking. In each of these studies, however, the subjects were volunteers from correctional institutions who probably: (1) had lower pre-experimental levels of stress and anxiety than the typical nonincarcerated alcoholic who is about to begin a drinking binge, and (2) were aware that they would eventually (at the designation of the experimenters) have to "dry out" and return to institutional life. Given these conditions, one might expect an increase in anxiety above pre-experimental levels as drinking progressed.

TREATMENT GOALS

Among professionals in the field of alcoholism there is a predominant belief that excessive drinking of alcoholic beverages signifies a progressive disease which can be arrested, but is irreversible (Williams, 1948; Jellinek, 1960; Knott & Beard, 1966). Many have considered the basis of this view as axiomatic (e.g., Lemere, 1963; Thimann, 1963), but contradictory evidence is mounting. There is an ever-increasing amount of reports demonstrating that persons who were at one time unquestionably "alcoholic" have been able to acquire, often without therapeutic intervention other than detoxification, a pattern of social, normal, or controlled drinking (Lemere, 1953; Selzer & Holloway, 1957; Pfeffer & Berger, 1957;

Davies, 1962; Mukasa, Ichihara, & Eto, 1964; Kendell, 1965; Bailey & Stewart, 1967; Mukasa & Arikawa, 1968; Reinert & Bowen, 1968; Anant, 1968; Quirk, 1968; Mills, Sobell, & Schaefer, 1971). Excellent reviews of this literature have been published by Pattison (1966) and Pattison, Headley, Gleser, and Gottschalk (1968). They, as well as Gerard, Saenger, and Wile (1962), also found no necessary association between abstinence and other criteria commonly accepted as indices of emotional adjustment. In short, while there is presently no evidence that controlled drinking by former alcoholics is impossible, there is extensive evidence to the contrary. Certainly the pattern of moderate drinking acquired by a former alcoholic is a special kind of drinking. Reinert and Bowen (1968) have suggested using the term "controlled drinker" to identify such persons. By their definition, the controlled drinker, unlike the normal or social drinker, ". . . must be on guard . . . must choose carefully and even compulsively the time, the place, and the circumstances of drinking, and he must rigidly limit the amount he drinks (p. 286)."

Persons working in the field of alcoholism, however, have been slow to accept these repeated findings of successful drinking by former alcoholics. For instance, when Davies innocently reported some positive results in a 1962 follow-up study, the report elicited a deluge of negative comments (see *Quarterly Journal of Studies on Alcohol*, 1963). The basis for much of the concern seemed to be a fear that the report might somehow mislead alcoholics the world over into beginning their own form of therapy aimed at controlled drinking. What some of the commentators (e.g., Lemere, 1963; Bell, 1963) overlooked, however, is that such a treatment goal should be the result of a treatment program and not merely acquired as a result of the patient's own initiative.

As long as the objections of traditionalists to controlled drinking had been mentioned, the other side of the issue should also be explored. The question asked is how many persons consistently deny that they have a drinking problem until they have truly become chronic alcoholics—and how much is such a denial based upon a resistance to being condemned to abstinence for life? Others have pondered this question as well (Gerard *et al.*, 1962; Brunner-Orne, 1963; Pattison, 1966; Reinert, 1968).

Any effective form of therapy must consider the kinds of behavior which our society reinforces. If the goal of therapy is to be abstinence, then the patient must be prepared to identify with certain social groups (e.g., AA, certain religious groups, etc.) which specifically reinforce nondrinking. If a patient cannot, or chooses not to identify with social groups supportive of abstinence, then the constraint of nondrinking might actually be a stressor for that patient rather than a support. The majority of our society reinforces a pattern of moderate drinking. If controlled drinking is the treatment goal which is most practical and potentially beneficial for a given individual, it should be the one pursued.

The experiment reported in the remainder of this paper was designed in accordance with the preceding rationale. Treatment sessions dealt directly with the inappropriate behavior of excessive drinking and emphasized a patient's learning alternative, more appropriate responses to stimulus conditions which had previously functioned as setting events for his heavy drinking. The treatment took into account the learning history of each individual patient and was specifically tailored to meet each patient's needs.

METHOD

Subjects

Seventy male patients who had voluntarily admitted themselves to Patton State Hospital for treatment of alcoholism and volunteered to serve in research studies were used as subjects. All subjects were screened for health problems and psychosis by a thorough medical and psychiatric examination. The staff then interviewed each subject for 45 min to determine his desire for treatment and which of the two treatment goals offered was most appropriate: nondrinking or controlled drinking. Those subjects who could socially identify with AA, requested abstinence, and/or lacked outside social support for controlled drinking were always assigned to nondrinking. Subjects who requested controlled drinking, had available significant outside social support for such behavior, and/or had successfully practiced social drinking at some time in the past were considered potential candidates for the controlled drinking goal. After a majority staff decision had determined a subject's treatment goal, the subject was then randomly assigned to either a control group receiving only the conventional hospital treatment (large therapy groups, AA meetings, drug, physio-, and industrial therapy), or an experimental group receiving 17 behavioral treatment sessions in addition to the conventional hospital treatment.

Statistics describing educational, demographic, and sociological characteristics of subjects in each of the four groups appear in Table 37.1. All subjects had experienced some withdrawal symptoms, damaged their

Table 37.1. Summary of Descriptive Statistics for Subjects in Four Experimental Conditions.

Descriptive variable	Experimental condition[a]			
	CD-E	CD-C	ND-E	ND-C
Age (years)				
Mean	40.30	41.25	40.40	43.27
SD	9.42	10.58	9.32	10.06
Education (years)				
Mean	12.60	12.45	13.03	11.27
SD	1.54	2.35	2.29	2.09
Drinking problem (years)				
Mean	9.70	8.65	11.33	11.86
SD	6.21	4.51	6.95	8.16
Alcohol-associated arrests (no.)				
Mean	6.25	5.70	8.85	9.86
SD	6.99	5.33	10.06	13.96
Prior hospitalization for alcoholism (no.)				
Mean	2.10	1.90	3.43	4.13
SD	2.83	1.29	4.97	2.83
Marital status				
Married	6	4	3	6
Single	4	5	3	2
Divorced, Separated	10	11	9	6
Widower	0	0	0	1
Religion				
Protestant	16	13	13	13
Catholic	2	5	1	1
L.D.S.	1	1	1	1
Agnostic	1	1	0	0
Occupation				
Blue collar	17	16	11	15
White collar	1	2	3	0
Retired	1	1	1	0
Student	1	1	0	0
Withdrawal symptoms				
Tremors, sweating	9	12	5	5
Convulsions, blackouts	4	4	3	2
Hallucinations, delirium tremens	7	4	7	8
N	20	20	15	15

[a]Experimental conditions were controlled drinker, experimental (CD-E), controlled drinker, control (CD-C), nondrinker, experimental (ND-E), and nondrinker, control (ND-C).

physical health, finances, and social standing as a result of excessive drinking. Thus, all subjects met the criteria of Jellinek's (1960) Gamma alcoholics. There were no statistically significant differences between respective experimental and control groups, with the exception that nondrinker, experimental subjects had a significantly ($p < 0.05$) higher level of education than nondrinker, control subjects.

Facilities

The research ward at Patton State Hospital contained the central research facilities, a simulated bar and cocktail lounge, and a simulated home environment. The bar environment, which has been fully described elsewhere (Schaefer *et al.*, 1971b), was equipped with a television camera which could be remotely controlled from an adjacent room which contained videorecording apparatus.

The simulated home environment was located immediately adjacent to the bar and separated from it by heavy, floor-length draperies. It was carpeted and included a sofa, a love seat, a soft chair, two end tables with lamps, two coffee tables, a pole lamp, a television set, and a phonograph.

Operant conditioning equipment which independently controlled two shock generators (1 BRS Foringer, 1 Grason-Stadler) was located behind the bar and could be operated by hand-held push button switches. The same shock equipment could be used in the home environment by attaching longer cables to the electrodes and switches. A large variety of confiscated alcoholic beverages were supplied by the California State Alcoholic Beverage Control Board.

Procedure

The 17 experimental treatment sessions emphasized specifically defining prior setting events for heavy drinking, and training the subject in alternative, socially acceptable responses to those situations. The treatment was designed so that each subject's sessions could be individually tailored for specific setting events and alternative responses appropriate to his case. Stimulus control variables, or setting events, for drinking were defined as those specific factors which had either immediately preceded or accompanied the onset of heavy drinking in the past. Intervening variables such as "depression" were not considered as stimulus controls for drinking unless the various defining situations could be precisely specified. A subject was always asked to generate a universe of possible alternative responses to each setting event and then evaluate each alternative for its appropriateness (effective as compared to self-destructive consequences) for the situation. To discriminate effective from ineffective responses, situations were constructed to practice various alternative responses. For each subject a cumulative treatment file of all delineated stimulus control variables and alternative responses was maintained.

In all except probe sessions (8, 12, and 16), inappropriate drinking behaviors (respective to treatment goal) were punished by electric shocks delivered on a variable ratio 2 (VR 2) avoidance schedule. An avoidance rather than escape schedule was used because of its potential for shaping self-control. A VR 2 ratio was used in order to increase resistance to extinction. A larger ratio schedule (e.g., VR 3, VR 10) was not used because it was suspected that the reinforcing effects of drinking might be sufficient to completely nullify the occasional receipt of shocks. Probe sessions during which drinks were available but shock contingencies absent made it possible to assess whether the drinking patterns demonstrated in shock sessions could be expected to generalize to situations not having immediate aversive consequences for inappropriate drinking.

The types of drinks available during sessions were: (1) mixed—1 oz liquor (43% alcohol content) with 2 oz mixer, (2) beer—12 oz (3–4% alcohol content), (3) wine—2½ oz (20% alcohol content) or 4 oz (12% alcohol content), and (4) straight—1 oz liquor (43% alcohol content) served in three one-third oz portions to guard against taking advantage of the variable shock schedule.

When shock contingencies were in effect, nondrinker subjects occasioned a 1-sec shock (delivered on a VR 2 schedule) by ordering any drink. The drink was then served and subjects occasioned a continuous shock from the time they touched the glass until the time they released it (the drink could be consumed). Rules for controlled drinking were derived from actual data collected from social drinkers who had participated in experimental baseline drinking studies conducted in the simulated bar (Sobell, Schaefer, & Mills, 1972; Schaefer, Sobell, & Mills, 1971a). Controlled drinker subjects occasioned a 1-sec shock (delivered on a VR 2 schedule) for the following inappropriate drinking behaviors: (1) ordering a straight drink, (2) taking a sip larger than one-sixth (mixed) or one-twelfth (beer) of the drink's total volume (glasses were demarcated), (3) ordering a drink within 20 min of previously ordering a drink, or (4) ordering any more than three total drinks. After consuming three drinks within a session, controlled drinker subjects were placed on the same shock contingencies as nondrinker subjects.

Table 37.2 presents a description of session characteristics, and the following describes the experimental procedures used in more detail:

Sessions 1 and 2, Drunk, Videotaped   Taking advantage of the sedative effects of alcohol, staff members probed each subject for stimulus controls for the drinking response, discussed fear-laden topics, and evaluated the subject's verbal and nonverbal reactions to potentially stressful situations. These sessions further served to demonstrate to each subject that he could become quite drunk and then sober up the next day without suffering from withdrawal symptoms or severe cravings for alcohol.

The majority of sessions 3 through 17 were conducted in either the home or bar environment, whichever most closely approximated the subject's usual drinking environment. In these sessions, subjects were run individually, with one staff member (determined on a rotating basis) assigned to each session.

Table 37.2.   Characteristics of Experimental Sessions.[a]

Session number	Type of session	Shock avoidance contingencies	Max. alcohol available (oz)[b]
1–2	Drunk, videotaped, 3 hr[c]	No	16
3	Education, 90 min	No	N.A.
4–5	Videotape replay, 90 min[d]	Yes	6
6	Failure experience, 90 min	Yes	6
7	Stimulus control, 90 min	Yes	6
8	Stimulus control, probe, 90 min	No	6
9–11	Stimulus control, 90 min	Yes	6
12	Stimulus control, probe, 90 min	No	6
13–15	Stimulus control, 90 min	Yes	6
16	Stimulus control, probe, videotaped, 90 min	No	6
17	Summary, videotape contrast, 90 min	N.A.	N.A.

[a]A more detailed description of experimental procedures is included in the expanded version of this manuscript, available from the authors upon request.

[b]An ounce was defined as 1 oz of 86-proof liquor or its equivalent in alcohol content.

[c]During these sessions only, subjects were run in pairs and allowed to consume up to 16 drinks during each session. Sessions were conducted in the experimental bar and were separated by 1 sober day. The final 90 min of each session were videotaped.

[d]Replay was of sessions 1 and 2, respectively. These sessions, as well as session 6, allowed an evaluation of each subject's responses to a novel stressful situation.

Session 3, Education   The subject, irrespective of treatment goal, was instructed about: (1) when and why various shock contingencies would apply, (2) the occurrence of probe (no shock) days, (3) the treatment rationale—emphasizing that drinking is considered to be a learned behavior which occurs in certain stimulus situations and not in others (discriminated response) and is controlled by its consequences, and (4) a response repertoire for refusing alcoholic beverages—structured situations where subjects could practice resisting social pressures to drink were used. Additionally, controlled drinker subjects were trained in a response repertoire for mixed drinks, as a previous study (Sobell, Sobell, & Schaefer, 1971) had demonstrated that many Gamma alcoholics had a gross deficiency in familiarity with types of mixed drinks.

During sessions 4 through 16, data were recorded for the following quantifiable drinking behaviors: drinks ordered, infractions of controlled or nondrinking rules (shocks occasioned), shocks actually received, sips per drink, kinds of drinks ordered, and time (sec) between successively ordered drinks.

Sessions 4 and 5, Videotape Replay   Videotape self-confrontation of drunken behavior was used because it had been found to be quite stress inducing for sober alcoholics and had seemed to increase a subject's spoken motivation for changing his drinking behavior (Schaefer *et al.*, 1971b). More importantly, it served to demonstrate various behavioral deficiencies (e.g., lack of overt emotional expression) as well as various setting events to a subject.

Session 6, Failure Experience   Twenty minutes before the session a series of plausible but impossible to complete tests were administered to the subject who was then informed of his poor test performance. The therapy session, conducted by a staff member other than the person who administered the tests, concentrated on the way the subject had responded to failure experiences, past and present. All subjects were debriefed after the session.

Sessions 7 through 16, Stimulus Control   An emphasis was placed on: (1) elucidating stimulus controls for heavy drinking, (2) generating a universe of possibly effective alternative responses to those situations, (3) evaluating the probable consequences of exercising each response, and (4) practicing the most beneficial alternative responses under simulated conditions. Thirty minutes of session 16 were videotaped.

When a nondrinker subject ordered no drink for two consecutive sessions during sessions 4 through 16, a priming prompt of a free drink was offered at the start of the next session. If the subject consumed the free drink, any applicable shock contingencies were then reinstated. If he chose not to consume the drink, he had to pour it down the sink and this procedure continued at 15-min intervals for the entire session.

Session 17, Summary, Videotape Contrast   Selected replays of drunken behavior which occurred during sessions 1 and 2 were contrasted with videotape of sober behavior during session 16. The subject's progress was discussed and he was presented with a wallet-sized research program card which included a list of *Do's* and *Do Not's* specific to his treatment. He was encouraged to extend the principles of self-behavioral analysis and exercising alternative responses to all phases of his life.

In almost all cases, subjects chose to discharge from the hospital within 2 weeks after session 17. An in-depth interview was conducted with each subject before discharge, and after discharge continuous phone and personal contact was maintained with all experimental and control subjects and their respective collateral sources. Formal follow-up intervals of 6 weeks, 6 months, and 1 year were scheduled. For each subject the following information was obtained over each follow-up interval:

1. Drinking disposition (1 oz defined as 1 oz of 86-proof liquor or its equivalent in alcohol content)—(a) drunk days defined as any days during which 10 or more oz were consumed or any days more than 2 consecutive days when between 7 and 9 oz were consumed, (b) controlled drinking days defined as any days during which 6 oz or less were consumed or any isolated 1- or 2-day sequence when between 7 and 9 oz were consumed, (c) abstinent days, and (d) abstinent days resulting from hospital or jail incarcerations for alcohol-related incidents (all incarcerations were verified through the holding facility and by inspecting the subject's rap sheet).

2. Vocational status as to improved, same as, or worse than prior to treatment.

3. Use or nonuse of therapeutic supports outside the hospital after treatment (e.g., AA, community counseling services, etc.).

4. Evaluation by a collateral of the subject's general adjustment to interpersonal relationships and stressful situations as compared to the year preceding his hospitalization (improved, same, or worse).

In all cases, both self-reports by the subject and collateral confirmation were sought in follow-up interviews.

RESULTS

Nondrinker Experimental Subjects

Nondrinker subjects who drank during treatment sessions 4–16 could minimize the number of electric shocks they received by ordering straight drinks (minimizing drink volume) and consuming those drinks in the smallest number of sips possible. The 11 subjects who ordered drinks during these sessions ordered a total of 59 drinks, the majority (74.57%) being straight drinks. No subject ordered drinks during more than six treatment sessions. Additionally, subjects consumed all but one of the 44 straight drinks ordered in the minimum number (three) of sips possible.

As a result of the VR 2 avoidance schedule, subjects received only 61 of the 120 total shocks occasioned. A shaping effect over sessions is evident in Fig. 37.1 which presents the total number of drinks ordered as a function of treatment sessions. Some subjects apparently formed a discrimination between shock contingency sessions and probe (no shock) sessions, but all four subjects who ordered drinks during session 12, and

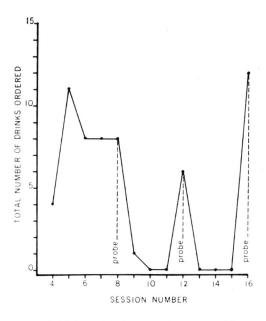

Fig. 37.1. Total number of drinks ordered per session by nondrinker subjects ($N = 15$) during experimental treatment sessions 4 through 16.

one of the three subjects who ordered drinks during session 16 ordered only one or two of the six total drinks available without penalty.

Drinks consumed as priming prompts (see Method) are not included in the data. Priming prompt drinks were offered to 11 subjects during a total of 17 sessions, but were consumed in only three cases. On each occasion when a priming prompt drink was consumed, the subject then proceeded to order and fully consume only one additional drink. Thus, there is no evidence that priming prompts were effective in producing increased drinking.

Controlled Drinker Experimental Subjects

All 20 controlled drinker experimental subjects ordered drinks at some time during sessions 4–16 with a mean of 27.80 drinks ordered per subject and a range from 9 to 43. Like the nondrinker subjects, controlled drinker subjects practiced drinking patterns which somewhat minimized the number of shocks they received. For instance, controlled drinker subjects never ordered straight drinks during any treatment session, and of the 556 total drinks ordered, 80.75% were mixed drinks, 13.48% were beer and 6.57% were wine. During only 14 total sessions did any subject order more than three drinks, with 11 of these occasions occurring on probe days and the remainder during session 6. During the 248 total sessions where drinks were ordered, the mean number of drinks ordered was 2.24 (SD = 0.92).

Table 37.3 displays the frequency with which drinking behaviors defined as inappropriate occurred during each treatment session and the number of subjects who engaged in those behaviors. Subjects received 30 total electric shocks for the total of 63 inappropriate behaviors in which they engaged. Fourteen subjects received two or fewer total shocks throughout the entire experiment, and the greatest number of shocks received by any single subject was six. Seven subjects never emitted an inappropriate drinking behavior. While receipt of electric shocks obviously was not important in controlling the subjects' drinking behaviors, there was evidence that the threat of shocks effectively suppressed inappropriate drinking behaviors. The number of inappropriate drinking behaviors emitted during probe sessions ($\bar{X} = 18.67$) was considerably greater than the number of those behaviors emitted during other treatment sessions ($\bar{X} = 2.20$). This difference is statistically significant ($t = 7.84$, $p < 0.01$). As in the case of the nondrinker subjects, this

Table 37.3. Number of Inappropriate Drinking Behaviors Emitted by Controlled Drinker Experimental Subjects During Treatment Sessions. Figures in Parentheses Indicate the Number of Subjects Who Emitted the Inappropriate Behavior at Least One Time During That Session.

	Inappropriate behavior[a]			
Session number	Ordering < 20 min apart	Ordering > three drinks	Sips > $\frac{1}{6}$ of drink volume	Total inappropriate drinking behaviors
4	0	0	3(3)	3(3)
5	1(1)	0	0	1(1)
6	2(2)	2(1)	4(2)	8(3)
7	1(1)	0	1(1)	2(1)
8-Pr[b]	3(3)	4(3)	8(4)[c]	15(6)
9	0	0	0	0
10	1(1)	1(1)	0	2(1)
11	2(2)	1(1)	1(1)	4(3)
12-Pr[b]	8(4)	8(4)	9(4)[c]	25(7)
13	1(1)	0	0	1(1)
14	1(1)	0	0	1(1)
15	0	0	0	0
16-Pr[b]	8(6)	5(4)	3(2)[c]	16(6)

[a]Each inappropriate drinking behavior which occurred was counted separately.

[b]Pr indicates probe session, no shock contingencies in effect.

[c]Known minimum value. Total number of occasions when a drink was consumed in fewer than six sips.

difference could not be attributed to any particular small group of subjects.

With the exception of subjects learning to drink with smaller sips, little or no shaping of drinking behavior was evident over sessions. This finding might be interpreted as reflecting a practice effect resulting from the instructions given subjects during session 3. The fact that no straight drink was ordered even during probe sessions also suggests that the subjects sincerely practiced controlled drinking patterns. This interpretation is additionally supported by Fig. 37.2 which presents the mean number of ounces of 86-proof alcohol or equivalent which were actually consumed during each treatment session by those subjects who ordered drinks. With the exception of probe sessions, the initial drinking pattern was one of exaggerated sipping (more than six sips per drink) with sip size then increasing to fulfill the minimum requirements necessary to avoid shocks.

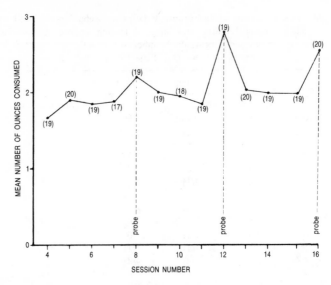

Fig. 37.2. Mean number of ounces of 86-proof alcohol (or the equivalent in alcohol content) consumed per session by controlled drinker subjects who ordered drinks during experimental treatment sessions 4 through 16. Numbers in parentheses indicate the number of subjects who ordered drinks during each session.

What Staff Members Learned

To the authors' knowledge, there is no reported precedent for the theoretical foundation of this experiment being as systematically applied to behavior therapy talk sessions as is here reported. This experiment, therefore, constituted a major learning experience for all of the staff members involved. The staff consisted of permanent, paid employees who were either upper division students at a local university, or research assistants who had already obtained their B.A. in psychology. Staff learning is documented in Fig. 37.3. A major stimulus control variable or alternative response was defined as meeting the criteria of specificity discussed in the Method section of this paper, as compared to vague descriptive terminology.

Follow-Up Results

All 70 of the subjects had been discharged from the hospital for at least 6 weeks prior to the preparation of this report, and 48 subjects had been

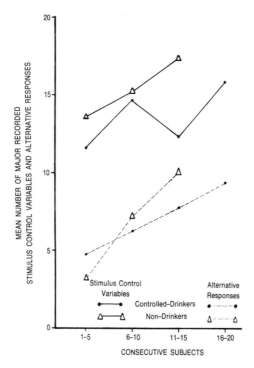

Fig. 37.3. Mean number of major stimulus control variables and alternative responses recorded by staff members in treatment notes for controlled drinker subjects ($N = 20$) and nondrinker subjects ($N = 15$) as a function of temporally consecutive groups of five subjects each.

discharged for longer than 6 months. Table 37.4 shows the number of subjects from each experimental condition who were due for follow-up, the percentage of subjects located, and the percentage of cases in which one or more collateral sources were interviewed.

The use of controlled drinking as a treatment goal made it necessary to obtain estimates of daily alcohol consumption. The criteria for different drinking dispositions have already been discussed (see Method). In most cases, there was little difficulty in obtaining reliable data, although the accuracy of reports based on memory is, of course, open to some question. However, reports by collaterals typically agreed well with reports by subjects. When there was reason to question the accuracy of a report, the data recorded were secured from the source who could best present evidence to substantiate the data. This method of follow-up data

Table 37.4. Summary of the Number of Subjects Due for Follow-up at 6-Week and 6-Month Intervals. Percentage of Subjects Found, and Percentage of Cases in Which One or More Collateral Sources Were Interviewed.

Experimental condition[a]	N due for follow-up at this time	Found (%)	One or more collateral sources interviewed (%)
Six-week follow-up			
CD-E	20	100	90.0
CD-C	20	100	90.0
ND-E	15	100	93.4
ND-C	15	100	93.4
Total	70	100	92.9
Six-month follow-up			
CD-E	18	100	94.4
CD-C	10	100	80.0
ND-E	8	100	87.5
ND-C	12	100	100.0
Total	48	100	91.6

[a]Experimental conditions were controlled drinker, experimental (CD-E), controlled drinker, control (CD-C), nondrinker, experimental (ND-E), and nondrinker, control (ND-C).

Table 37.5. Drinking Disposition During Majority of Follow-up Interval for Subjects from Each Experimental Condition.

Drinking disposition	Experimental condition[a]			
	CD-E	CD-C	ND-E	ND-C
Six-week follow-up				
Controlled drinking or abstinent, not incarcerated (%)	85.5	45.0	73.4	53.3
Drunk or incarcerated, alcohol-related (%)	15.0	55.0	26.6	46.7
Six-month follow-up[b]				
Controlled drinking or abstinent, not incarcerated (%)	77.8	30.0	75.0	16.7
Drunk or incarcerated, alcohol-related (%)	22.2	70.0	25.0	75.0
Deceased, alcohol or drug-related (%)	0.0	0.0	0.0	8.3

[a]Experimental conditions were controlled drinker, experimental (CD-E), controlled drinker, control (CD-C), nondrinker, experimental (ND-E), and nondrinker, control (ND-C).
[b]Not all subjects were due for 6-month follow-up. Data are presented for 18 CD-E, 10 CD-C, 8 ND-E, and 12 ND-C subjects.

collection was selected as being more representative of behavior occurring over the entire follow-up interval than more traditional probeday-status techniques.

Table 37.5 presents the drinking dispositions of subjects during a majority of the 6-week and 6-month follow-up intervals. Drinking dispositions were grouped according to whether the subject was functioning well (abstinent or controlled drinking days) or not functioning well (drunk or incarcerated, alcohol-related days). The one subject in the category of deceased, alcohol, or drug-related will be discussed later in this paper.

Fisher–Yates Exact Probability Tests (McNemar, 1962) were calculated comparing respective experimental and control groups by drinking dispositions (functioning well, not functioning well) at the two follow-up intervals. Differences between the controlled drinker experimental and control subjects were found to be statistically significant ($p < 0.05$) for each follow-up interval. At the time of this report, only 48 of the 70 total subjects were due for 6-month follow-up. However, continuing follow-up suggests that complete 6-month data will substantiate the data in Table 37.5. Differences between the nondrinker experimental and control subjects at the 6-week interval are not statistically significant, although in the predicted direction. At 6 months, the difference between these groups is significant ($p < 0.05$). For this computation, the one subject who had died in an automobile accident was included as not functioning well. Although this subject had remained abstinent until the time of his death (about 2 months after discharge), an autopsy found a heavy incidence (0.4 mgm) of barbiturates in his blood. Once again, continuing follow-up suggests that the 6-month differences between groups will still be significant when data are complete.

Table 37.6, which presents the mean percentage of days spent in each drinking disposition by subjects from different experimental conditions for 6-week and 6-month follow-up periods, supports the data of Table 37.5. It is interesting that the majority of incarcerations of experimental subjects were in hospitals, while control subjects were predominantly incarcerated in jails. This difference might have been the result of voluntary hospitalizations among the experimental subjects, either to curb the start of a binge or to avoid starting drinking at all. This particular behavior had frequently been discussed during sessions as an alternative favorable to starting or continuing to drink.

Three other indices of behavior change were obtained for all subjects in addition to drinking status. The measures of vocational status, use of therapeutic supports, and evaluation of subjects' general functioning by

Table 37.6.   Mean Percentage of Days Spent in Different Drinking Dispositions by Subjects in Four Experimental Groups for 6-Week and 6-Month Follow-up Intervals.

Drinking disposition	Experimental condition[a]			
	CD-E	CD-C	ND-E	ND-C
Six-week follow-up				
Controlled drinking[b]	41.80	10.70	7.20	12.93
Abstinent, not incarcerated	30.95	39.32	60.33	42.13
Drunk	17.55	42.70	23.20	41.60
Incarcerated, alcohol-related				
Hospital	9.15	2.00	6.94	3.20
Jail	0.55	5.35	2.33	0.14
Total	100.00	100.00	100.00	100.00
Six-month follow-up[c]				
Controlled drinking	27.33	9.10	2.87	14.54
Abstinent, not incarcerated	37.89	29.40	62.63	16.55[d]
Drunk	20.33	50.50	19.38	40.91
Incarcerated, alcohol-related				
Hospital	12.12	4.10	12.25	8.09
Jail	2.33	6.90	2.87	19.91
Total	100.00	100.00	100.00	100.00

[a]Experimental conditions were controlled drinker, experimental (CD-E), controlled drinker, control (CD-C), nondrinker, experimental (ND-E), and nondrinker, control (ND-C).

[b]Thirteen of the CD-E subjects successfully practiced substantial controlled drinking, eight of them doing so for an average of more than 50% of all days since discharge, and the remaining five to a lesser extent (an average of about 30% of all days since discharge). One subject in each of the other three groups also successfully practiced substantial controlled drinking. The ND-E subject doing so was not yet due for 6-month follow-up. A more detailed description of the incidence of controlled drinking among subjects is included in the expanded version of this manuscript which is available from the authors upon request.

[c]Not all subjects were due for 6-month follow-up. Data are presented for 18 CD-E, 10 CD-C, 8 ND-E, and 11 ND-C subjects. The one ND-C subject who died was not included in this presentation.

[d]Abstinent, not incarcerated days reported for ND-C subjects at 6 months include 26 days when one subject was not drinking but used other drugs heavily.

collateral sources have already been described (see Method). Table 37.7 presents 6-week and 6-month adjunctive measure follow-up data for subjects from each treatment group. As is evident in Table 37.7, these data support those reported earlier for drinking disposition. Continuing follow-up indicates that the figures reported in Table 37.7 will not change substantially when 6-month follow-up has been completed.

Table 37.7. Adjunctive Follow-up Measures for Subjects in Four Experimental Conditions.

Adjunctive measure[a]	Experimental condition[b]			
	CD-E	CD-C	ND-E	ND-C
Six-week follow-up				
Vocational status				
Improved (%)	20.0	20.0	33.3	33.3
Same (%)	80.0	75.0	60.0	53.3
Worse (%)	0.0	5.0	6.7	13.4
Use of therapeutic supports				
Yes (%)	35.0	20.0	60.0	33.3
No (%)	65.0	80.0	40.0	66.7
Evaluation of general adjustment				
by collaterals				
Improved (%)	80.0	30.0	73.3	46.7
Same (%)	20.0	55.0	20.0	53.3
Worse (%)	0.0	15.0	6.7	0.0
Six-month follow-up[c]				
Vocational status				
Improved (%)	55.6	20.0	62.5	9.1
Same (%)	44.4	70.0	37.5	72.7
Worse (%)	0.0	10.0	0.0	9.1
Use of therapeutic supports				
Yes (%)	66.7	10.0	87.5	18.2
No (%)	33.3	90.0	12.5	81.8
Evaluation of general adjustment				
by collaterals				
Improved (%)	88.9	30.0	75.0	18.2
Same (%)	11.0	60.0	25.0	72.7
Worse (%)	0.0	10.0	0.0	9.1

[a]See text for fuller explanation of adjunctive measures used.

[b]Experimental conditions were controlled drinker, experimental (CD-E), controlled drinker, control (CD-C), nondrinker, experimental (ND-E), and nondrinker, control (ND-C).

[c]Not all subjects were due for 6-month follow-up. Data are presented for 18 CD-E, 10 CD-C, 8 ND-E, and 11 ND-C subjects. The one ND-C subject who died was not included in this presentation.

DISCUSSION

The results of the present study can be succinctly summarized: Male Gamma alcoholics treated by the method of individualized behavior therapy described in this paper were found to function significantly better after discharge than respective control subjects treated by conventional techniques. Differences between experimental and control subjects were found not only for drinking behaviors, but for other adjunctive measures of functioning as well. Moreover, subjects who clearly met the criteria required by most experts for classification as "alcoholics" were able to acquire and maintain patterns of controlled drinking. These findings directly contradict the concept of irreversibility of alcoholic drinking which, lacking evidence, is but a *post hoc* tautology of little descriptive or predictive value.

A treatment goal of controlled drinking is uncommon and creates certain problems of data evaluation. The criteria used to distinguish controlled drinking days from drunk days were derived from data collected on actual social drinkers who had participated in baseline drinking behavior studies and, thus, were not completely arbitrary. The baseline data, however, were obtained from single drinking sessions. If a longitudinal baseline study were conducted, normal drinking patterns would probably be found to consist of a major proportion of abstinent days, a certain proportion of controlled drinking days, and a small proportion of drunk days. Thus, any appraisal of how well the controlled drinking patterns acquired by some of the subjects in this experiment approximated normal drinking behaviors must allow for a small proportion of drunk days. Furthermore, the extent of drunkenness which is typical among normal drinkers is probably greatly dependent upon socioeconomic status.

At times, many of the controlled drinker experimental subjects who were able to practice controlled drinking successfully after discharge from the hospital placed themselves on extended periods of abstinence. However, this self-imposed abstinence was not maintained by a fear of the supposedly unavoidable consequences of drinking. Instead, subjects reported they were abstinent either because drinking now served no useful purpose, or because they were dealing with stress-inducing situations and believed drinking might interfere with their effective handling of those problems. For instance, in all cases the extended periods of abstinence were occasionally interrupted by one or two days of controlled drinking. It is reasonable to suppose that the degree of self-respect associated with this sort of abstinence is much greater than that accompanying a period of abstinence which is maintained by fear, and this might help the individual to deal better with problem situations.

While reports of successful controlled drinking by a small proportion of control subjects may surprise some readers, as substantiated by numerous studies cited earlier in this paper such findings are not at all unusual. No doubt, the nature of the follow-up results one obtains are in large part a function of the measures used. Thus, if a category of controlled drinking is not included in a follow-up scale, an acquiescent subject may soon realize that this is not an expected behavior for an alcoholic and fail to report incidents which have occurred.

In many cases, an insistence upon abstinence as the only possible treatment goal for alcoholics may even be unrealistic or harmful. For instance, consider a heavy drinker who has greatly identified with social groups whose members are mostly normal drinkers. Such a person may well decide to continue drinking until he is physically debilitated, rather than risking the loss of most of his friends by being abstinent. The issue here is not the morality of such social consequences, but their reality. If, by definition, an alcoholic may never drink in a fashion even approximating normal drinking and must always be "different" from most other individuals, then abstinence will not make an alcoholic a functioning member of society *per se*, but only a member of a special society—a subculture which specifically reinforces nondrinking. If faced with this choice, many individuals may well decide to continue drinking rather than change their social identification.

The same is true for the problem drinker, as traditional beliefs about alcoholism leave such individuals little to gain from curtailing their drinking, and, in fact, may provide an incentive for them to repeatedly attempt to prove that they are not "alcoholics." One would expect problem drinkers to find the controlled drinker treatment described in this report to be both appealing and acceptable.

The effects of certain of the various treatment procedures used in this study have already been discussed to some extent. However, stimulus control sessions constituted the bulk of the experimental treatment. It became rapidly apparent in conducting follow-up that, for some subjects, the effects of stimulus control sessions had been much more than learning how to handle specific situations. In particular, subjects who were found to be functioning well after discharge seemed to have experienced a more general form of learning sometimes called rule learning, or learning to learn. Typically, the successful subject could apply what he had learned to novel situations. For example, approximately 1 month subsequent to discharge, nondrinker experimental subject J.A. was able to analyze an experienced desire to drink as resulting from the fact that his brother was living in his house, free-loading off of him, and attempting to seduce his wife. J.A. then generated a number of possible responses to this situation, including migrating to Chicago. After analyzing the various alternatives in terms of long-range consequences, he decided to confront his brother and demand that he move out of the house. To J.A.'s amazement, his brother did move out, and J.A.'s marital relationship improved considerably thereafter.

While the contribution of each component of the treatment procedure used must be evaluated experimentally, it is our contention that stimulus control sessions not only constituted the bulk of the treatment sessions, but were primarily responsible for the behavior changes which later occurred. In a refined treatment, it would seem logical to seek as a desired outcome the kind of rule learning which has just been described. Additionally, it would be desirable to conduct at least part of the treatment on an outpatient basis where the patient could deal with situations which were real, rather than simulated, setting events for drinking. If such a treatment approach continues to be successful as applied to drinking problems, it is possible that a modified version of the same treatment could be used for various of the neuroses, especially those which could be analyzed as involving escape and avoidance responses.

The generality of these results remains to be evaluated for other subject populations such as females and subjects from other types of socioeconomic backgrounds. The subjects who served in this study—male, voluntary Gamma alcoholic patients in a state hospital—may have been more deficient in a knowledge of appropriate alternative responses to setting events for drinking than subjects with a higher education or income. It is reasonable to expect that working with middle and upper class individuals will require dealing with different and perhaps more sophisticated alternative responses.

The findings of the present study are indeed highly encouraging, but only on the basis of continued investigation and outcome studies can one expect to develop an effective and efficient short-term treatment for alcoholism. The scientific method requires that statements of opinion, such as the supposed irreversibility of alcoholism, be evaluated by experimental test if at all possible. One such evaluative experiment is reported in this paper and clearly establishes that some alcoholic individuals can acquire and maintain controlled drinking patterns. Whether those patterns will persist over longer follow-up intervals can be determined only by continued follow-up.

REFERENCES

Anant, S. S. Former alcoholics and social drinking: an unexpected finding. *The Canadian Psychologist*, 1968, **9**, 35.

Bailey, M. B. and Stewart, J. Normal drinking by persons reporting previous problem drinking. *Quarterly Journal of Studies on Alcohol*, 1967, **28**, 305–315.

Bandura, A. *Principles of Behavior Modification.* New York: Holt, Rinehart & Winston, 1969.

Bell, R. G. Comment on "Normal drinking in recovered alcohol addicts." *Quarterly Journal of Studies on Alcohol*, 1963, **24**, 321–322.

Brunner-Orne, M. Comment on "Normal drinking in recovered alcohol addicts." *Quarterly Journal of Studies on Alcohol*, 1963, **24**, 730–733.

Carpenter, J. A. Effects of alcoholic beverages on skin conductance: an exploratory study. *Quarterly Journal of Studies on Alcohol*, 1957, **18**, 1–18.

Cicero, T. J., Myers, R. D., and Black, W. C. Increase in volitional ethanol consumption following interference with a learned avoidance response. *Physiology and Behavior*, 1968, **3**, 657–660.

Clark, R. and Polish, E. Avoidance conditioning and alcohol consumption in rhesus monkeys. *Science*, 1960, **132**, 223–224.

Cohen, M., Liebson, I., and Faillace, L. The modification of drinking of chronic alcoholics. In N. K. Mello and J. H. Mendelson (Eds.), *Recent Advances in Studies on Alcoholism.* Washington, D.C.: U.S. Government Printing Office, 1971, Pp. 745–766.

Conger, J. J. The effects of alcohol on conflict behavior in the albino rat. *Quarterly Journal on Studies of Alcohol*, 1951, **12**, 1–29.

Davies, D. L. Normal drinking in recovered alcohol addicts. *Quarterly Journal of Studies on Alcohol*, 1962, **23**, 94–104.

Gerard, D. L., Saenger, G., and Wile, R. The abstinent alcoholic. *Archives of General Psychiatry*, 1962, **6**, 99–111.

Hershenson, D. B. Stress-induced use of alcohol by problem drinkers as a function of their sense of identity. *Quarterly Journal of Studies on Alcohol*, 1965, **26**, 213–222.

Jellinek, E. M. *The Disease Concept of Alcoholism.* New Haven: Hillhouse Press, 1960.

Kendell, R. E. Normal drinking by former alcohol addicts. *Quarterly Journal of Studies on Alcohol*, 1965, **26**, 247–257.

Knott, D. H. and Beard, J. D. The disease concept of alcoholism. Paper presented at the 115th Annual Meeting of the American Medical Association, Chicago, 1966.

Lemere, F. What happens to alcoholics. *American Journal of Psychiatry*, 1953, **109**, 674–676.

Lemere, F. Comment on "Normal drinking in recovered alcohol addicts." *Quarterly Journal of Studies on Alcohol*, 1963, **24**, 727–728.

Lienert, G. A. and Traxel, W. The effects of meprobamate and alcohol on galvanic skin response. *Journal of Psychology*, 1959, **48**, 329–334.

Lundin, R. W. *Personality: A Behavioral Analysis.* London: MacMillan Company, 1969.

Masserman, J. H. and Yum, K. S. An analysis of the influence of alcohol on experimental neuroses in cats. *Psychosomatic Medicine*, 1946, **8**, 36–52.

McNamee, H. B., Mello, N. K., and Mendelson, J. H. Experimental analysis of drinking patterns of alcoholics: concurrent psychiatric observations. *American Journal of Psychiatry*, 1968, **124**, 81–87.

McNemar, Q. *Psychological Statistics.* New York: John Wiley & Sons, Inc., 1962.

Mills, K. C., Sobell, M. B., and Schaefer, H. H. Training social drinking as an alternative to abstinence for alcoholics. *Behavior Therapy*, 1971, **2**, 18–27.

Mukasa, H. and Arikawa, K. A new double medication method for the treatment of alcoholism using the drug cyanamide. *The Kurume Medical Journal*, 1968, **15**, 137–143.

Mukasa, H., Ichihara, and Eto, A. A new treatment of alcoholism with cyanamide (H_2NCN). *The Kurume Medical Journal*, 1964, **11**, 96–101.

Nathan, P. E., Titler, N. A., Lowenstein, L. M., Solomon, P., and Rossi, A. M. Behavioral analysis of chronic alcoholism. *Archives of General Psychiatry*, 1970, **22**, 419–430.

Pattison, E. M. A critique of alcoholism treatment concepts with special reference to abstinence. *Quarterly Journal of Studies on Alcohol*, 1966, **27**, 49–71.

Pattison, E. M., Headley, E. B., Gleser, G. C., and Gottschalk, L. A. Abstinence and normal drinking: an assessment of changes in drinking patterns in alcoholics after treatment. *Quarterly Journal of Studies on Alcohol*, 1968, **29**, 610–633.

Pfeffer, A. Z. and Berger, S. A follow-up study of treated alcoholics. *Quarterly Journal of Studies on Alcohol*, 1957, **18**, 624–648.

Quirk, D. A. Former alcoholics and social drinking: an additional observation. *The Canadian Psychologist*, 1968, **9**, 498–499.

Rachman, S. and Teasdale, J. *Aversion Therapy and Behavior Disorders: An Analysis.* Florida: University of Miami Press, 1969.

Reinert, R. E. The concept of alcoholism as a disease. *Bulletin of the Menninger Clinic*, 1968, **32**, 21–25.

Reinert, R. E. and Bowen, W. T. Social drinking following treatment for alcoholism. *Bulletin of the Menninger Clinic*, 1968, **32**, 280–290.

Schaefer, H. H., Sobell, M. B., and Mills, K. C. Baseline drinking behaviors in alcoholics and social drinkers: kinds of drinks and sip magnitude. *Behaviour Research and Therapy*, 1971a, **9**, 23–27.

Schaefer, H. H., Sobell, M. B., and Mills, K. C. Some sobering data on the use of self-confrontation with alcoholics. *Behavior Therapy*, 1971b, **2**, 28–39.

Selzer, M. L. and Holloway, W. H. A follow-up of alcoholics committed to a state hospital. *Quarterly Journal of Studies on Alcohol*, 1957, **18**, 98–120.

Sobell, M. B., Schaeffer, H. H., and Mills, K. C. Differences in baseline drinking behaviors between alcoholics and normal drinkers. *Behaviour Research and Therapy*, 1972, **10**, 257–268.

Sobell, L. C., Sobell, M. B., and Schaefer, H. H. Alcoholics name fewer mixed drinks than social drinkers. *Psychological Reports*, 1971, **28**, 493–494.

Thimann, J. Comment on "Normal drinking in recovered alcohol addicts." *Quarterly Journal of Studies on Alcohol*, 1963, **24**, 324–325.

von Wright, J. M., Pekanmäki, L., and Malin, S. Effects of conflict and stress on alcohol intake in rats. *Quarterly Journal of Studies on Alcohol*, 1971, **32**, 420–433.

Williams, R. J. Alcholics and metabolism. *Scientific American*, 1948, **179**, 50–53.

ARTICLE 38

The Use of Behavioral Contracting in the Treatment of Alcoholism: A Case Study*

PETER M. MILLER[1,2]

Veterans Administration Center, and University of Mississippi Medical Center, Jackson, Mississippi

Abstract: Behavioral contracting was applied to an alcoholic and his wife in order to change reinforcement contingencies maintaining drinking behavior. A moderate drinking pattern was established and was still being maintained after a 6-month followup. The study illustrates the value of altering social contingencies in the alcoholic's environment and questions the assumption that complete abstinence is a necessary treatment goal.

Applications of behavioral approaches to the treatment of alcoholism have been reported for many years (Franks, 1963). Although aversion therapy has been used most often, only about 50% of patients treated with this technique remain abstinent after at least a 1-year followup. Ullmann and Krasner (1969) note that these findings are not surprising since, upon return to their home environments, alcoholics are reexposed to stimulus cues and reinforcement contingencies that maintain drinking behavior. Studies aimed at altering these variables in the alcoholic's environment are rare. Sulzer (1965) utilized differential social reinforcement from peers to alter an alcoholic's drinking behavior and Cheek, Franks, Laucius, and Burtle (1971) trained wives of alcoholics to use a similar strategy to modify their husbands' behavior. Along these lines, behavioral contracting (Stuart, 1971) offers a systematic way of scheduling the mutual exchange of reinforcements between an alcoholic and his family or

*Reprinted from *Behavior Therapy*, 1972, **3**, 593–596. Copyright © 1972 by Academic Press, Inc. With permission from Academic Press, Inc. and Peter M. Miller.

[1]Requests for reprints should be sent to P. M. Miller, Psychology Service, Veterans Administration Center, Jackson, MS 39216.

[2]The author thanks Michel Hersen for his critical comments.

friends. The present case study illustrates the use of a behavioral contract with an alcoholic and his wife in modifying reinforcement contingencies maintaining drinking behavior.

CASE HISTORY

The subject was a 44-year-old, married male. He and his wife were referred for treatment by their family physician because of marital problems. A major source of conflict in the marriage appeared to be the husband's drinking behavior. The husband had previously used alcohol moderately, but during the past two years had increased his consumption to four to six pints per week. Prior to his excessive drinking the couple reported a much more enjoyable marital relationship. The husband could not specify any anxiety-producing situation preceding his drinking episodes. However, he revealed that his wife's frequent critical comments and disapproving glances in reference to his drinking had increased his consumption.

Treatment

For two weeks prior to treatment the husband was instructed to record number of alcoholic beverages consumed daily. A beverage was defined as $1\frac{1}{2}$ oz of alcohol either straight or mixed. His preferred alcoholic beverage was bourbon. During this baseline period mean consumption was seven to eight "drinks" a day. The wife corroborated these reports by her own observations and through observations made by friends.

A behavioral contract was established to change reinforcement contingencies maintaining drinking behavior. By mutual agreement the couple decided that between one and three drinks per day was an acceptable limit for the husband's drinking. Neither partner considered complete abstinence a necessary or desirable goal. Via the written contract the husband agreed to limit his drinking to this level. Unless the couple were invited for the evening or entertaining friends, these drinks were to be consumed in the presence of the wife before the evening meal. Drinking in any other situation (as determined by actual observation, liquor on his breath, or "drunken" behavior) was forbidden and resulted in a monetary fine ($20.00) payable to his wife (to be spent as frivolously as possible on a nonessential item) and withdrawal of attention by the wife (she would immediately leave his presence). Both partners were working independently, and the dispensation of money in this manner was reported to be highly aversive to the partner paying the fine. The behavioral contract also required the wife to refrain from negative verbal or nonverbal responses to her husband's drinking. A monetary fine ($20.00) payable to the husband in addition to withdrawal of attention by the husband were the consequences of this behavior. In addition, the husband agreed to increase his attentive behaviors toward his wife when she engaged in noncritical, nonalcohol related conversation. The wife also agreed to provide the husband with attention and affection whenever he voluntarily limited his drinking (i.e., stopped after one or two drinks) or when he refrained from drinking. The conditions of this agreement were written into a contract form and signed by both partners. Separate copies were kept by the husband and wife.

Daily records (corroborated by the wife and friends) were accumulated by the subject regarding number of alcoholic beverages consumed daily. Immediately after the contract was initiated the husband's drinking remained above the agreed upon level, but, after a few fines, rapidly dropped within acceptable limits (Fig. 38.1). His drinking behavior stabilized by the 30th day of the study, with some abstinent days apparent. As frequency of drinking decreased both partners reported a more enjoyable and less tense relationship. A 6-month followup revealed maintenance of both the moderate drinking pattern and improved marital

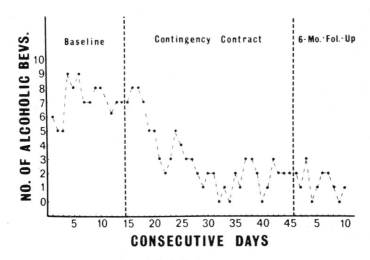

Fig. 38.1. Number of alcoholic beverages consumed daily.

relations. For comparative data at the 6-month followup the subject was requested to record his drinking for a 10-day period. As Fig. 38.1 illustrates, his drinking remained within a zero to three drink range per day.

DISCUSSION

This case study illustrates the successful use of behavioral contracting in changing reinforcement contingencies between an alcoholic and his wife. The husband's drinking behavior was subsequently decreased to a level acceptable to both partners. Establishment of moderate or social drinking as opposed to total abstinence has recently become a more acceptable therapeutic goal. For years total abstinence was considered the only acceptable goal for successful rehabilitation (Alcoholics Anonymous, 1955). Recent case study (Bailey & Stewart, 1967; Pattison, Headley, Gleser, & Gottschalk, 1968) and experimental evidence (Lovibond & Caddy, 1970; Mills, Sobell, & Schaefer, 1971) suggest that many alcoholics can maintain a pattern of limited social drinking. The present study has clinically substantiated this contention. It may be that alcoholics would be more willing to undergo treatment with *partial* abstinence as the goal. It must be noted that this subject's total disability resulting from excessive drinking was small (i.e., almost exclusively confined to his marriage) compared to some alcoholics. This may have been a factor in the rather rapid and stable behavior change after the use of only one treatment modality.

Nevertheless, the findings of this study illustrate the effectiveness of altering marital interactions in changing drinking behavior. In this regard, the behavioral contract may function to provide the commitment necessary to sustain the wife's total cooperation throughout the program. The contract also facilitates change by placing new contingencies on the behaviors of both partners. This is extremely important since Cheek *et al.* (1971) report that, due to the nature of their response styles (chronic, emotionally charged behavior patterns), the wives of alcoholics experience extreme difficulty in changing their typical behaviors toward their husbands. Those responses (e.g., negative and critical commentary) which are most relevant to the maintenance of their husband's drinking behavior may be the most resistant to change. The discovery of the relevant variables within behavioral contracting that most significantly alter these response patterns awaits further investigation.

REFERENCES

Alcoholics Anonymous. New York: Cornwall Press, 1955.

Bailey, M. B. and Stewart, J. Normal drinking reported by persons reporting previous problem drinking. *Quarterly Journal of Studies on Alcohol,* 1967, **28,** 305–315.

Cheek, F. E., Franks, C. M., Laucius, J., and Burtle, V. Behavior modification training for wives of alcoholics. *Quarterly Journal of Studies on Alcohol,* 1971, **32,** 456–461.

Franks, C. M. Behavior therapy, the principles of conditioning and the treatment of the alcoholic. *Quarterly Journal of Studies on Alcohol,* 1963, **24,** 511–529.

Lovibond, S. H. and Caddy, G. Discriminated aversive control in the moderation of alcoholics' drinking behavior. *Behavior Therapy,* 1970, **1,** 437–444.

Mills, K. C., Sobell, M. B., and Schaefer, H. H. Training social drinking as an alternative to abstinence for alcoholics. *Behavior Therapy,* 1971, **2,** 18–27.

Pattison, E. M., Headley, E. B., Gleser, G. C., and Gottschalk, L. A. Abstinence and normal drinking: An assessment of changes in drinking patterns in alcoholics after treatment. *Quarterly Journal of Studies on Alcohol,* 1968, **29,** 610–633.

Stuart, R. B. Behavioral contracting within the families of delinquents. *Journal of Behavior Therapy and Experimental Psychiatry,* 1971, **2,** 1–11.

Sulzer, E. S. Behavior modification in adult psychiatric patients. In L. P. Ullmann and L. Krasner (Eds.) *Case Studies in Behavior Modification.* New York: Holt, Rinehart, & Winston, 1965. Pp. 196–199.

Ullmann, L. P. and Krasner, L. *A Psychological Approach to Abnormal Behavior.* Englewood Cliffs, N.J.: Prentice-Hall, 1969. Pp. 489–512.

ARTICLE 39

The Behavior-Therapeutic Use of Contingency Contracting to Control an Adult Behavior Problem: Weight Control[*][1]

RONALD A. MANN

The University of California at Los Angeles

Abstract: Items considered valuable by the subject and originally his property were surrendered to the researcher and incorporated into a contractual system of prearranged contingencies. Each subject signed a legal contract that prescribed the manner in which he could earn back or permanently lose his valuables. Specifically, a portion of each subject's valuables were returned to him contingent upon both specified weight losses and losing weight at an agreed-upon rate. Furthermore, each subject permanently lost a portion of his valuables contingent upon both specified weight gains and losing weight at a rate below the agreed-upon rate. Single-subject reversal designs were employed to determine the effectiveness of the treatment contingencies. This study demonstrated that items considered valuable by the subject and originally his property, could be used successfully to modify the subject's weight when these items were used procedurally both as reinforcing and as punishing consequences. In addition, a systematic analysis of the contingencies indicated that punishing or aversive consequences presumably were a necessary component of the treatment procedure.

---

*Reprinted from *Journal of Applied Behavior Analysis*, 1972, **5**, 99–109. Copyright © 1972 by the Society for the Experimental Analysis of Behavior, Inc. With permission from the Society and Ronald A. Mann.

[1]This investigation was partially supported by PHS Training Grant 00183 from the National Institute of Child Health and Human Development to the Kansas Center for Research in Mental Retardation and Human Development. This study is based upon a dissertation submitted to the Department of Human Development, University of Kansas, in partial fulfillment of the requirements for the degree of Doctor of Philosophy. The author expresses deep appreciation and indebtedness to Dr. Donald M. Baer for his encouraging support, insightful advice, and helpful suggestions. Special thanks to Drs. L. Keith Miller and James A. Sherman for their critical evaluations and suggestions in preparing the manuscript. Reprints may be obtained from the author, Department of Psychology. University of California, Los Angeles, California 90024.

Comparatively few therapeutic techniques displaying generality in natural settings have been developed to deal with the behavior problems of normal non-institutionalized adults. Two major reasons for this are suggested. First, it is difficult for a therapist to discover and/or gain systematic control over relevant consequences of an adult's behavior in its natural settings. Second, even if a therapist did have such control, it would still be difficult to maintain reliable measurement of the behavior. Without reliable measurement, it would be difficult to deliver relevant consequences at appropriate times. Similarly, it would be difficult to assess any changes that might occur in the behavior. Thus, an applied demonstration of a therapeutic change in behavior could be made, but with difficulty.

A recently discussed procedure that may have potential as a technique to remediate adult behavior problems in their natural settings is that of contingency contracting (Homme, 1966; Homme, Csanyi, Gonzales, and Rechs, 1969; Tharp and Wetzel, 1969; Michael, 1970). Its applications as a therapeutic technique, however, have been suggested mainly for use in school settings with children (Homme *et al.*, 1969; Cantrell, Cantrell, Huddleston, and Woolridge, 1969) and in home settings to remediate the behavior problems of pre-delinquent adolescents (Tharp and Wetzel, 1969; Stuart, 1970).

The term "contingency contracting," as it has most commonly been used has meant an explicit statement of contingencies (i.e., a rule), usually agreed upon by two or more people. In other words, it has been a specification of a number of behaviors whose occurrence would produce specified consequences, presumably to be delivered by parents or teachers. It has been amply demonstrated that contingencies can, in fact, change behavior. Nevertheless, little evidence has been gathered to support the notion that the use of contingency contracts will facilitate the remediation of child or adult behavior problems.

The present study attempted to develop a therapeutic technique that would effectively remediate the behavior problems of normal noninstitutionalized adults. The basic technique used was that of contingency contracting. The contingency contract used in this study was similar to others that have been discussed, in that it too was an explicit statement of contingencies. However, this contract incorporated a number of additional techniques that were considered necessary to accomplish effectively an applied behavior analysis, and which were relevant to the problems both of gaining systematic control of effective consequences and of maintaining reliable measurement.

In brief, this study attempted to test the applicability of contingency contracting with adult subjects, and to assess the effects of various treatment contingencies on weight reduction. Weight was used as the dependent variable for two reasons: (1) It is a convenient and reliably measurable "behavior," and (2) weight control is a socially important behavior problem.

METHOD

Subjects

Seven women and one man, 18 to 33 yr old, had responded to an advertisement for a "behavior therapy research program of weight reduction." Each subject was required to give to the researcher a signed physician's statement indicating that it would be medically safe for him or her to lose the specified weight agreed upon for this research over the agreed-upon time and at the agreed-upon rate. Furthermore, the physician's statement included an entry indicating whether the subject's physician had prescribed a diet for him. It was made clear to every subject, both verbally and as a written clause included in each contract, that any diet or foods that the subject selected or his physician prescribed would be ultimately the subject's responsibility. With one exception, only those individuals agreeing to lose 25 pounds or more and who had their physician's approval were accepted as subjects. (The one exception was a subject who agreed to lose 16 pounds.)

The Contingency Contract

The Contingency Contract was a legal document that incorporated as separate clauses all of the procedures in the weight control program. First, the contract required each subject to surrender a large number of items considered to be valuable to himself. These items were retained by the researcher (a similar technique has been discussed by Tighe and Elliot, 1968). Secondly, the contract prescribed the manner in which the subject could earn back or permanently lose his valuables (i.e., the statement of contingencies). Third, the contract required the subject to be weighed by the researcher at regular intervals. Fourth, the contract stipulated that the researcher, at his discretion, would change the procedures from baseline, to treatment, to reversal, and back to treatment conditions. Thus, the contingencies of the contract could be either continued or temporarily discontinued in order to assess experimentally the causal variables and the efficacy of the contract itself. The details of the experimental conditions were also specified in the contingency contract.

In brief, the contract was a guarantee to the subject that valuables supplied by him would be returned contingent upon meeting the specified requirements, or would be permanently lost if those requirements were not met. It was also a guarantee to the researcher that the subject would be available for measurements and the delivery of consequences at specified intervals.

All individuals interested in losing weight were shown a copy of a contingency contract and given a detailed description of the procedures to be used. The procedures were explicitly characterized as being extremely rigid and severe. The researcher then answered any questions raised by the prospective subjects. Each subject was encouraged to take as much time as he needed to consider whether he should sign the contract. When an individual decided to be a subject in the program, he was asked to nominate a number of objects he considered valuable to himself, either in the form of money and/or personal items (e.g., medals and trophies, clothes, jewelry, etc.). It was emphasized to all subjects that the items should be as valuable as possible. The contract was then tailored to each subject's personal specifications, with reference to intermediate and terminal requirements of the program: (1) the minimum number of pounds to be lost cumulatively by the end of each succeeding two-week period (i.e., the minimum rate for losing weight), and (2) the terminal weight requirement. The number of valuables obtained from each subject to be used as consequences depended in part upon the amount of weight that the subject agreed to lose, and the minimum rate at which he agreed to lose it. Finally, the researcher, subject, and one witness signed two copies of the contract. The researcher and the subject retained one copy each.

Three sets of contingencies were specified in the contract: (1) Immediate Contingencies; (2) Two-week Contingencies; and (3) Terminal Contingencies.

The Immediate Contingencies were applied to each cumulative two-pound gain or loss of weight that occurred during the treatment conditions. Any time the subject cumulatively lost two pounds with reference to the final weight measurement of baseline, he received one valuable from the researcher. Each additional two-pound weight loss below the previous weight loss was rewarded with one more valuable, and so on. On the other hand, each cumulative two-pound weight gain (above the subject's lowest recorded weight) was punished by the loss of one valuable. The weight of each subject was always recorded to the nearest half-pound.

The Two-Week Contingencies required the subject to lose a minimum number of pounds by the end of each successive two-week period during the treatment conditions. The two-week periods and their associated minimum weight losses were calculated from the last baseline weight measurement and date. Every two weeks, if this requirement was met, the researcher delivered a bonus valuable. If this requirement was not met, the subject lost that valuable as a punishing consequence. The Immediate and the Two-Week Contingencies were each a single valuable selected unsystematically by the researcher. Subjects never knew in advance which valuable would be used as a consequence.

The Terminal Contingency was a portion of the valuables (or money) delivered to the subject *only* if and when his terminal weight requirement was met. These particular valuables were itemized in the contract as specifically for this purpose, and consequently were never in jeopardy of being lost as penalties (i.e., for weight gains or for not meeting a Two-Week Contingency) nor available to be regained before reaching terminal weight. In addition, the researcher agreed to deliver to the subject all of the other remaining valuables that had not been regained or lost as penalties, whenever the subject reached his terminal weight. However, if at any time the subject decided to terminate the program, then all remaining valuables in the possession of the researcher, including the Terminal Contingency, became the property of the researcher. Thus, the Terminal Contingency helped to ensure that the subject would remain in the program until his terminal weight requirement was met.[2] A clause in the contract stipulated that all items that became the property of the researcher would be disposed of in a manner not personally profitable or beneficial to the researcher. These items were subsequently donated to various charities.

It should be stressed that the Terminal Contingencies were always in effect during every phase of the program (i.e., during baseline, treatment, and reversal conditions). In other words, they were long-term consequences that presumably would operate against the usual outcome of a reversal.

---

[2]Although the contingency contract did not specify the possibility, the researcher, in fact, would dissolve the contract with the mutual agreement of the subject for special circumstances, and return to the subject the remainder of his valuables.

Measurement and Reliability

The contract stipulated that the subject be weighed at a specific time and place every Monday, Wednesday, and Friday of each successive week until his terminal weight was reached. The subjects were weighed on the same medical-type scale throughout the experiment. Both the subject and the researcher independently recorded the subject's weight to the nearest half pound. However, the consequences were delivered in accordance with the researcher's weight determinations.

Reliability determinations were made on each of the days that the subject was weighed by subtracting the subject's notation of his own weight from the researcher's notation. The range of differences of weight occurring throughout the program was the measure of reliability.

The differences between the subject's and the researcher's weight determinations ranged from plus or minus half a pound. Both the subject and the researcher were in agreement on 95% of the weight determinations.

Procedures

The procedures followed a single-subject reversal design (cf., Baer, Wolf, and Risley, 1968). The design included sequential baseline, treatment, reversal, and treatment conditions (i.e., an ABAB design).

During the baseline condition, the subject's weight was regularly measured; there were no scheduled consequences for weight, except the Terminal Contingency. Baseline data were recorded for approximately two to five weeks, depending upon the stability of the subject's weight. The criterion for stability was a two-week period in which either a subject gained weight, remained stable, or lost no more than one pound per week. The final two-week criterion period was considered baseline.[3] At a time unknown in advance to the subject, the researcher notified the subject that the treatment procedure was beginning. The weight of the subject and the date at the time of this notification were considered the final weight measurement and date of the baseline condition.

During the treatment condition, all three contingencies were in effect: The Immediate, Two-Week, and Terminal Contingencies. Both the Immediate and the Two-Week Contingencies were calculated from the final

---

[3]Use of the last 14 days of baseline gives each subject a uniform baseline to facilitate comparisons to other subjects. Fourteen days was the shortest baseline of any subject.

weight measurement and date of the baseline condition. The treatment condition was maintained at least for four weeks, and often longer, depending upon the stability of the subject's rate of losing weight. At a time unknown in advance to the subject, the researcher notified the subject that the reversal procedure was beginning and that until told otherwise, he could continue losing weight but he would neither receive back valuables for losing weight nor lose valuables for gaining. He was also told that whenever he reached terminal weight, the remaining valuables would be returned. The weight of the subject at the time of this notification was considered the final weight measurement of the treatment condition.

During the reversal condition, the subject continued to be weighed regularly, but there were no scheduled consequences, except the Terminal Contingency, regardless of whether the subject lost weight, gained weight, or remained stable. The reversal condition was maintained for approximately two to four weeks. At a time unknown in advance to the subject, the researcher notified the subject that the second treatment procedure was beginning. The weight of the subject and the date at the time of this notification were considered the final weight measurement and date of the reversal condition.

The second and first treatment procedures were identical. During the second treatment condition, however, both the Immediate and the Two-Week Contingencies were calculated from the final weight measurement and date of the reversal condition.

In summary, items considered valuable by the subject and originally his property were surrendered to the researcher and incorporated into a contractual system of prearranged contingencies. The contract prescribed the manner in which the subject could earn back or permanently lose these items. This complex of contingencies, presumably both of reinforcing and of punishing consequences, was in effect during the treatment conditions. Experiment I assessed the effects of the whole complex of treatment contingencies on weight reduction.

RESULTS AND DISCUSSION

Experiment I

Six of the eight subjects who were in the weight-reduction program participated in Experiment I. The data of one of these subjects have been selected to exemplify the procedures and are presented in Figs. 39.1a and 39.1b. In these figures, each open circle (connected by the thin solid line) represents a two-week minimum weight loss requirement. Each of the solid dots (connected by the thick solid line) represents the subject's weight on each of the days that he was measured. Each triangle indicates the point at which the subject was penalized by a loss of valuables, either for gaining weight, or for not meeting a two-week minimum weight loss requirement. Only the data of the first four conditions (i.e., baseline,

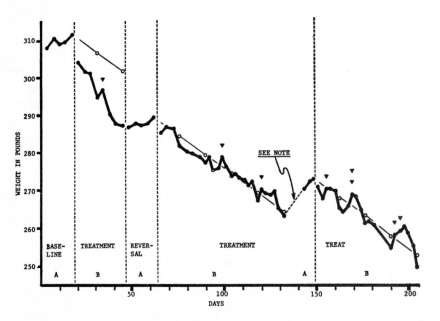

Fig. 39.1a. A record of the weight of Subject 1 during all conditions. The first four conditions (*i.e.*, Baseline, Treatment, Reversal, and Treatment) were considered as Experiment I. During the Baseline and Reversal conditions, the subject's weight was regularly measured; there were no scheduled consequences. During both Treatment conditions the contingencies of the contract, presumably both of reinforcing and of punishing consequences, were in effect. Each open circle (connected by the thin solid line) represents a two-week minimum weight loss requirement. Each of the solid dots (connected by the thick solid lines) represents the subject's weight on each of the days that he was measured. Each triangle indicates the point at which the subject was penalized by a loss of valuables, either for gaining weight or for not meeting a two-week minimum weight loss requirement. Experiment II begins with the third Treatment condition (continued in Fig. 39.1b). NOTE: the subject was ordered by his physician to consume at least 2500 calories per day for 10 days, in preparation for medical tests.

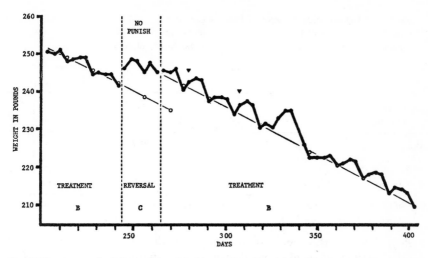

Fig. 39.1b. A record of the weight of Subject 1 (continued from Fig. 39.1a). The last three conditions (*i.e.*, Treatment, No Punishment Reversal, and Treatment) were considered as Experiment II. The Treatment conditions of Experiment II were procedurally identical to those of Experiment I. The No Punishment Reversal condition was identical to the Treatment conditions with the following exception: the punishing consequences were removed; only the reinforcing consequences continued to remain in effect.

treatment, reversal, and treatment) are considered as Experiment I (Fig. 39.1a). A subsequent experimental manipulation was made with this subject (Fig. 39.1b) and those data were considered as part of Experiment II. This is discussed later. As the data of Fig. 39.1a indicate, this subject gained weight (slightly) during baseline, lost weight during treatment conditions, and gained weight during reversal.

Although the data of this subject were selected as the most orderly to exemplify the procedures, it was representative to the extent that the data of the other subjects, similarly, suggested that the researcher's control of the treatment contingencies were responsible for all losses in weight. That is, most of the subjects gained weight or remained stable during baseline, lost weight during treatment conditions, and gained weight or remained stable during reversal.

A comparison of each subject's rate of losing or gaining weight during each of the first four conditions (i.e., baseline, treatment, reversal, and treatment conditions) is presented in Table 39.1. These data were calculated for each specified condition (except baseline) by subtracting the final weight measurement of the preceding condition from the final weight

Table 39.1. The Average Number of Pounds Lost or Gained Per Week by Each Subject During Each Condition of Experiment I (i.e., Baseline, Treatment, Reversal, and Treatment), and Experiment II (i.e., Treatment, No Punishment Reversal, and Treatment).

Experimental condition	Experiment I							Experiment II			
	S-1	S-2	S-3	S-4	S-5	S-6	$\bar{X}$	S-7	S-8	S-1	$\bar{X}$
Baseline A	1.4	0.0	−1.0	0.0	1.0	3.2	0.9	1.5	1.2	—	—
Treatments B	−6.1	−1.7	−2.0	−1.6	−1.3	−1.1	−2.1	−1.5	−1.4	−2.2	−1.7
Reversal A-C	0.8	2.1	4.1	0.4	*	*	1.9	0.4	2.6	1.2	1.4
Treatment B	−2.6	−0.2	−0.5	−1.4	*	*	−1.2	−1.4	−1.5	−1.8	−1.6

*Subjects 5 and 6 were terminated from the program before a Reversal and second Treatment condition.

measurement of the specified condition. The difference was then divided by the number of weeks that the specified condition was in effect. The baseline data were calculated by subtracting the first weight measurement from the final weight measurement of baseline. This difference was then divided by the two weeks considered as baseline. These calculations yielded an average estimate of the number of pounds lost or gained per week by each subject during each of the four conditions. Only the data from baseline and the first treatment condition are presented for Subjects 5 and 6. Subjects 5 and 6 each initially lost approximately 20 pounds during treatment. However, a continuation of scheduled consequences seemed to have no effect on decreasing their weight further. Therefore, both of these subjects were terminated from the program, by mutual agreement.

In all cases except one, the subjects either gained weight or remained stable during the baseline condition. The exception, Subject 3, lost weight during baseline. All of the subjects gained weight during the reversal condition and lost weight during the treatment conditions. Subject 3 lost weight at a greater rate during each of the treatment conditions than during the baseline condition.

A summary assessment of the functions of each of the first four conditions of the program are presented in Fig. 39.2. These data represent the mean weight change in pounds per week that were gained or lost during each of the four conditions. They were calculated by averaging the rates of each subject as listed in Table 39.1. The baseline and first treatment condition data of Subjects 7 and 8 (Experiment II subjects) were included in these calculations because the baseline and first treat-

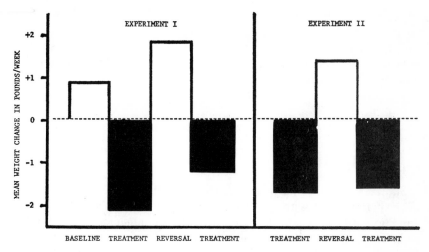

Fig. 39.2. Summary assessment of the functions of each condition of Experiment I and Experiment II for all subjects. These data represent the mean weight change in pounds per week gained (+) or lost (−) by all subjects during each of the conditions. They were calculated by taking the means of the average number of pounds lost or gained per week by each subject during each of the conditions of Experiments I and II.

ment condition procedures of these subjects were identical to those of Experiment I subjects. The reversal and second treatment condition data of Subjects 7 and 8 were not included, because the reversal condition of Experiment II differed from that of Experiment I. As Fig. 39.2 shows graphically, the mean weight change during baseline and reversal conditions was +0.9 and +1.9 pounds per week, respectively. Figure 39.2 also shows the mean weight change during the two treatment conditions was −2.1 and −1.2 pounds per week, respectively.

In summary, Experiment I investigated the applicability of contingency contracting with adult subjects, and assessed experimentally the effects of a complex of contingencies on weight reduction. A single-subject reversal design was used. Almost all of the subjects gained weight or remained stable during the baseline condition, lost weight during treatment conditions, and gained weight or remained stable during the reversal condition. The results suggest that items considered valuable by the subject and originally his property, can be used successfully to modify the subject's weight when these items are surrendered to the researcher and incorporated into a contractual system of prearranged contingencies. Both intra- and inter-subject replications support the generality of these findings. However, Experiment I did not analyze whether the reinforcing consequences, the punishing consequences, or both, were necessary components of the treatment procedure.

Experiment II was an attempt to ascertain whether the presumptive punishing consequences were, in fact, functional as a component of the treatment procedure.

METHOD

Experiment II

Subjects 1, 7, and 8 participated. The procedures were identical to those of Experiment I, with the following exception: during the reversal condition of Experiment II, the reinforcing components of the Immediate and the Two-Week Contingencies continued to remain in effect. The punishing components of the Immediate and the Two-Week Contingencies, however, were removed. In other words, during the reversal condition of Experiment II, the researcher continued to deliver to the subject one valuable contingent upon each cumulative two-pound weight loss. However, if the subject gained weight, he did not lose any of his valuables as a punishing consequence. In addition, the subject continued to receive a bonus valuable contingent upon meeting each two-week minimum weight loss requirement. Nevertheless, no valuables were lost by the subject if he did not meet this requirement. At a time unknown in advance to the subject, the researcher notified the subject that the second treatment procedure was beginning. The weight of the subject and the date at the time of this notification were considered the final weight measurement and date of the reversal condition. During the second treatment condition, both the Immediate and the Two-Week Contingencies were calculated from the final weight measurement and date of the reversal condition.

It should be noted that Subject 1 was used in both Experiments I and II, and consequently was exposed to both types of reversals.

RESULTS AND DISCUSSION

Only the treatment-reversal-treatment portions of the data were considered as Experiment II. The last reversal condition in which Subject 1 participated was procedurally identical to those of Subjects 7 and 8 (see

Figs. 39.1a and 39.1b). Therefore, the last treatment-reversal-treatment condition data of this subject were similarly included in the analysis of this experiment.

During the first and second treatment conditions, all of the subjects lost weight with reference to the final weight measurement of the preceding conditions (i.e., baseline and reversal). During the reversal condition, all of the subjects gained weight with reference to the final weight measurement of the preceding condition.

A comparison of each subject's rate of losing or gaining weight during each of the three conditions (i.e., treatment, reversal, treatment) is presented in Table 39.1. These data were calculated (in the same manner as for Experiment I) for each specified condition by subtracting the final weight measurement of the preceding condition from the final weight measurement of the specified condition. The difference was then divided by the number of weeks that the specified condition was in effect. These calculations yielded an average estimate of the number of pounds lost or gained per week by each subject during each of the three conditions. In all cases, the subjects lost weight during both treatment conditions and gained weight during the reversal condition.

A summary assessment of the functions of each condition are presented in Fig. 39.2. These data represent the mean weight change in pounds per week gained or lost during each of the three conditions. They were calculated (in the same manner as for Experiment I) by averaging the rates of each subject (i.e., Subjects 1, 7, and 8) as listed in Table 39.1. As Fig. 39.2 shows graphically, the mean weight change during the reversal condition was +1.4 pounds per week. The mean weight change during each treatment condition was −1.7 and −1.6 pounds per week, respectively. As can be seen in Fig. 39.2, the functions of the reversals in Experiment I and in Experiment II were almost identical.

In summary, Experiment II attempted to ascertain whether the permanent loss of a subject's valuables contingent upon either specified weight gains or losing weight at a rate lower than an agreed-upon rate, was a punishing or aversive consequence. Subjects 1, 7, and 8 lost weight during the two treatment conditions and gained weight during the reversal condition. When the presumably punishing consequences were removed from the procedure (i.e., during reversal), the subjects gained weight even though positive contingencies for losing weight remained in effect (Table 39.1). The data suggest that the permanent loss of the subject's valuables, when used as consequences are a necessary component of the treatment procedure.

GENERAL DISCUSSION AND SUMMARY

The present research investigated the applicability of contingency contracting with adult subjects, and the effects of a complex of treatment contingencies on weight reduction.

The results suggest that properly designed contingency contracts may be an effective means to control some behavior problems of normal non-institutionalized adults. In this case, being overweight was treated as the behavior problem.

This study demonstrated that items considered valuable by the subject and originally his property, could be used successfully to modify the subject's weight when used as reinforcing and as punishing consequences. Furthermore, a systematic analysis of the contingencies indicated that punishing consequences were a necessary component of the treatment procedure for the three subjects of Experiment II.

The contingency contract used differed from those previously discussed by other investigators (Homme *et al.*, 1969; Cantrell *et al.*, 1969; Tharp and Wetzel, 1970). Those contracts were essentially an explicit statement of contingencies, usually agreed upon by two or more people. The contingency contract used in this study was also an explicit statement of contingencies, but it incorporated a number of additional features considered salient to its effectiveness.

First, the contract required each subject to surrender a large number of his valuables to the researcher. The subject then could earn back portions of those valuables contingent upon meeting the specified behavioral requirements (i.e., weight losses), or lose valuables if those requirements were not met.

Second, the subject signed the contract in front of witnesses, thus further legalizing the researcher's authority to control the delivery of those valuables as consequences. The researcher also signed the contract, thus obligating him to abide by the terms of the contract.

Third, the contract required the subject to be available for behavioral measurement and the delivery of consequences at specified intervals.

Fourth, the contract included a clause stipulating that the researcher could, at his discretion, experimentally manipulate the treatment variables. Thus, the contingencies of the contract could be continued or temporarily discontinued in order to assess experimentally the casual variables.

Last, the contract was designed as a "behavior trap." A behavior trap, as discussed by Baer and Wolf (1970, p. 321) and Baer, Rowbury, and

Goetz (1971), is basically a situation in which "only a relatively simple response is necessary to enter the trap, yet once entered, the trap cannot be resisted in creating general behavioral change."

In this study, the subject's surrendering of his valuables to the researcher and signing the contract can be conceptualized as the "relatively simple response" required of the subject to enter the behavior trap. Once these responses were made, the subject was in the program (i.e., in the behavior trap), and was required to lose weight steadily (at the agreed-upon rate) or be penalized by the permanent loss of portions of his valuables. Furthermore, the subject could terminate the program, before reaching his terminal weight, only if he forfeited all of his remaining valuables. Thus, the contingencies of this contract presumably acted as a behavior trap by facilitating the subject both to lose weight steadily and to remain in the program until his terminal weight was reached. Still, it should be emphasized that the behavior trap principle was functional only to the extent that the subject did, in fact, surrender items of value.

Although each subject verbally reported which items he considered valuable before surrendering them to the researcher, the definition of valuable in this procedure was still in terms of the effects those items had on the subject's weight. In other words, the items surrendered to the researcher by some of the subjects, could have been valuable (i.e., reinforcing) with respect to affecting some behaviors, but not necessarily as effective with respect to losing weight. This may account, in part, for the variability in the effectiveness of this procedure.

Variability in the effectiveness of this type of procedure may have other sources as well. For example, as a subject steadily loses weight, presumably because of dieting, the probability of consuming larger quantities of food may increase. This increase in probability can then compete with the aversive effects of losing valuables. This type of effect may be facilitated further because the reinforcing effects of eating are immediate while the aversive effects of losing valuables are minimized by the delay in time imposed by this type of procedure.

Before concluding, it should be pointed out that this procedure had some problems, especially as it related to weight control. Unsolicited anecdotal reports from some of the subjects indicated that they had used extreme measures at various times to lose weight rapidly and temporarily in order to avoid aversive consequences. These measures, reportedly, included taking laxatives, diuretics, and doing vigorous exercises just before being weighed. This problem may have occurred because the contract specified that the treatment contingencies be delivered contingent upon specified weight changes rather than the behaviors that can produce those changes. Weight, as a measure, is the result of various other behaviors. The contract neither specified, controlled, nor prescribed the manner in which the subject could arrive at changes in his weight. Therefore, any one of a number of behaviors could have resulted in a reduction of weight. These included appropriate dieting, an increase in exercise, or both, as well as extreme measures such as taking laxatives or diuretics which could avoid aversive consequences, at least on a temporary basis.

Consequently, contingency contracting and other techniques should be used with caution to the extent that these techniques place effective contingencies on the outcomes of various behaviors. It is difficult for a researcher or therapist to anticipate all of the behaviors that can produce a specified outcome or result. And some of the behaviors that can produce such an outcome may be socially undesirable or even dangerous in some cases.

In summary, properly designed contingency contracts may be an effective technique to facilitate remediation of some behavior problems of non-institutionalized adults. The probability of this is increased to the extent that such techniques can facilitate a therapist both in gaining systematic control of effective consequences and in maintaining reliable measurement of the behavior to be changed. The present study met these two criteria and thereby demonstrated the application of contingency contracting with adult subjects. The dependent variable of this study was both a convenient and reliably measureable "behavior." Other behavior problems do not lend themselves as readily to reliable measurement. Smoking, drinking, and stealing, are examples of behaviors that are much more difficult to measure reliably. Nevertheless, as better methods of surveillance and monitoring of these types of behaviors develop, so may an increase in the use of contingency contracting with adult subjects.

REFERENCES

Baer, D. M., Wolf, M. M., and Risley, T. R. Some current dimensions of applied behavior analysis. *Journal of Applied Behavior Analysis*, 1968, **1**, 91–97.

Baer, D. M. and Wolf, M. M. The entry into natural communities of reinforcement. In R. Ulrich, T. Stachnick, and J. Mabry (Eds.), *Control of Human Behavior*. Glenview, Illinois: Scott, Foresman and Company, 1970. Pp. 319–324.

Baer, D. M., Rowbury, T., and Goetz, E. The preschool as a behavioral trap: a proposal for research. In C. Lavatelli (Ed.), *The Natural Curriculum of the Child.* Washington, D.C.: National Association for the Education of Young Children, 1971.

Cantrell, R. P., Cantrell, M. L., Huddleston, C. M., and Woolridge, R. L. Contingency contracting with school problems. *Journal of Applied Behavior Analysis,* 1969, **2**, 215–220.

Homme, L. Human motivation and the environment. In N. Haring and R. Whelan (Eds.), *The Learning Environment: Relationship to Behavior Modification and Implications for Special Education.* Lawrence: University of Kansas Press, 1966.

Homme, L., Csanyi, A. P., Gonzales, M. A., and Rechs, J. R. *How to Use Contingency Contracting in the Classroom.* Champaign, Ill.: Research Press, 1969.

Michael, J. L. Principles of behavior usage. In R. Ulrich, T. Stachnik, and J. Mabry (Eds.), *Control of Human Behavior.* Glenview, Illinois: Scott, Foresman and Company, 1970. Pp. 28–35.

Stuart, R. B. *Behavioral Contracting Within the Families of Delinquents.* Paper delivered at the American Psychological Association Convention, Miami Beach, 1970.

Tharp, R. G. and Wetzel, R. J. *Behavior Modification in the Natural Environment.* New York: Academic Press, 1969.

Tighe, T. J. and Elliot, R. A technique for controlling behavior in natural life settings. *Journal of Applied Behavior Analysis,* 1968, **1**, 263–266.

ARTICLE 40

A Three-Dimensional Program for the Treatment of Obesity*†

RICHARD B. STUART‡

The University of Michigan, Ann Arbor, Michigan, U.S.A.

Abstract: Obesity is seen as a consequence of a positive balance of energy consumed over energy expended. The reduction of obesity is accordingly sought through the reduction in the amount of food eaten coupled with an increase in the rate at which energy is expended. Both the reduction in the rate of eating and the increase in the rate of exercise are sought through management of critical aspects of the environment. Specific recommendations are made for the behavioral treatment of obesity, with the success of the treatment seeming to depend upon the effectiveness with which environmental stimuli are brought under control rather than depending upon motivational or other personal characteristics of the overeater. Pre-test data generated by the use of this procedure, coupled with the results of several recent studies appear to indicate uniquely positive results for the behavioral control of overeating.

Whether overweight is determined by gross body weight (Metropolitan Life Insurance Company, 1969) or skin-fold measurement (Seltzer and Mayer, 1965) even when differences in fat as a proportion of body weight are controlled (Durnin and Passmore, undated, p. 137), at least one in five

*Reprinted from *Behaviour Research and Therapy*, 1971, **9**, 177–186, Pergamon Press. Copyright © 1971. With permission from Pergamon Press and Richard B. Stuart.

†Portions of this paper were presented at the annual meeting of the American Bariatrics Society, Washington, D.C., November 1969, and at the Fourth Annual Meeting of the Association for the Advancement of Behavior Therapy, Miami, Florida, 6 September, 1970. The author wishes to express his gratitude to Barbara Davis, Judith Braver and Merrilee Oakes who contributed significantly to the development and testing of the approach which is described, and to Lynn Nilles for editorial assistance in the preparation of this manuscript. A more detailed description of the procedures may be found elsewhere (Stuart and Davis, 1972).

‡Requests for reprints should be sent to Richard B. Stuart, School of Social Work, University of Michigan, 1065 Frieze Building, Ann Arbor, Michigan 48104.

Americans is found to be overweight (United States Public Health Service, undated). The social and economic costs of being overweight are staggering and are complicated by greatly increased vulnerability to a broad range of physical diseases, including cardiovascular and renal diseases, maturity-onset diabetes, cirrhosis of the liver, and gall bladder diseases, among many others (Mayer, 1968).§ Despite the history of concern with obesity and the magnitude of the problem, little uncontested knowledge has been accumulated with respect to its etiology and treatment. Mayer (1968) has suggested that genetic factors may contribute to the onset of a small number of cases, while an additional small number of cases can be explained on the basis of injury to the hypothalamus, hormonal imbalance and other threats to normal metabolism. The exact role of genetic and physiological factors has, however, remained a mystery, and there has been little evidence to countermand an early observation by Newburgh and Johnston (1930) that most cases of obesity are:

> . . . never directly caused by abnormal metabolism but (are) always due to food habits not adjusted to the metabolic requirement—either the ingestion of more food than is normally needed or the failure to reduce the intake in response to a lowered requirement (p. 212).

Therefore most obesities can be attributed to an excess of food intake beyond the demands of energy expenditure, and a major objective in treating obesity is a reduction in the amount of excess food consumed.

Just as there is uncertainty concerning the etiology of obesity, there is great confusion over the role of psychological factors in overeating and its management. Some authors have contributed various useful typologies; for example, Stunkard (1959a) classified eating patterns as night eating, binge eating and eating without satiation, while Hamburger (1951) classified the triggers of excessive eating as either external or intrapsychic. Despite Suczek's (1957) observation that "single psychologic factors may not relate to either degree of obesity or ability to lose weight (p. 201)," other authors have sought to identify specific psychological mechanisms associated with obesity. For example, Conrad (1954) postulates that specific intrapsychic factors, such as efforts to prevent loss of love and to express hostility or efforts to symbolically undergo pregnancy and to ward off

---

§It has been argued that the relationship between obesity and such illnesses as cardiovascular diseases depends in part on the way in which fat is accumulated. For example, "People who become fat on a high carbohydrate, low fat diet are much less prone to develop atherosclerotic and thrombotic complications than those on a high fat diet (Cornell Conferences on Therapy, 1958, p. 87)."

sexual temptations, underlie obesity. In a similar vein, while eating has been seen as a means of warding off anxiety (Kaplan and Kaplan, 1957), it has also been seen as a depressive equivalent (Simon, 1963). Furthermore, while writers have suggested that "depression, psychosis . . . suicide (Cappon, 1958, p. 573)" and other stress reactions have accompanied weight loss (Cornell Conferences on Therapy, 1958; Glucksman *et al.*, 1968), other studies have shown that: (a) the so-called "depression" associated with weight loss by some people is actually just a function of lowered energy due to reduced food consumption (Bray, 1969); (b) negative psychological reactions are frequently not found (Cauffman and Pauley, 1961; Mees and Keutzer, 1967); and (c) a reduction in anxiety and depression may actually accompany weight loss (Shipman and Plesset, 1963). Despite this evidence, Bruch's (1954) admonition that treatment of overeating which does not give "psychologic factors . . . due consideration (can lead) at best to a temporary weight reduction (while being) considered dangerous from the point of view of mental health (p. 49)" is still influential in dissuading experimenters and therapists from undertaking parsimonious treatment of overeating.

While the research pertaining to physiological and psychological con-comitants of obesity has led to some paradoxical conclusions, Stunkard's (1968) review of environmental factors related to obesity has demonstrated a clear-cut connection between obesity and socioeconomic status, social mobility and ethnic variables. It is interesting to note, however, that where comparative data are available, the differences ascribed to each of these factors are stronger for women than men. One explanation of this sex difference may be that the physical expenditure of energy in work may reduce the tendency toward adiposity of lower class, socially nonmobile men while the women, faced with relative inactivity, may show a more direct effect of high carbohydrate, low protein diets common at lower socioeconomic strata (Select Committee on Nutrition and Human Needs, 1970).

The literature describing the treatment of obesity is dismal and confus-ing. One authoritative group noted:

> . . . most obese patients will not remain in treatment. Of those who do remain in treatment, most will not lose significant poundage, and of those who do lose weight, most will regain it promptly. In a careful follow-up study only 8 per cent of obese patients seen in a nutrition clinic actually maintained a satisfactory weight loss (Cornell Conferences on Therapy, 1958, p. 87).

Failure has been reported following some of the most ambitious and sophisticated treatments (e.g. Mayer, 1968, pp. 1–2; Stunkard and McLaren-Hume, 1959), while success has been claimed for some of the more superficial "diet-clinic"-type approaches (e.g. Franklin and Rynearson, 1960). The role of drugs has been extolled by many writers, while others have cautioned that their side effects strongly contraindicate their use (American Academy of Pediatrics, 1967; Gordon, 1969; Modell, 1960). Fasting has been shown to have a profound effect upon weight loss (e.g. Bortz, 1969; Stokes, 1969), but the results have been shown to be short-lived as the patient is likely to quickly regain lost weight when he leaves the hospital setting (MacCuish *et al.*, 1968). Claims of success have also been advanced for individual and group psychotherapy (e.g. Kornhaber, 1968; Mees and Keutzer, 1967; Stanley *et al.*, 1970; Stunkard *et al.*, 1970; Wagonfield and Wolowitz, 1968) and hypnosis (Hanley, 1967; Kroger, 1970), although these reports are typically not supported by controlled investigation. Finally, positive outcomes have been reported for behavior therapy techniques ranging from token reinforcement (Bernard, 1968), aversion therapy (Meyer and Crisp, 1964) and covert sensitization (Cautela, 1967) through complex contingency management procedures. Illustrative of the latter approaches are the work of Stuart (1967), which has been replicated in controlled studies by Ramsay (1968) and Penick and his associates (Penick *et al.*, 1970), and the work of Harris (1969), which included control-group comparisons in the original research.

It is probably true that behavior therapy has offered greater promise of positive results than any other type of treatment. This paper will present a rationale of and description for the treatment of overeating based upon behavioral principles.

RATIONALE

The treatment of obesity has typically attempted to stress the development of "self-control" by the overeater whose self-control deficit is often regarded as a personal fault. Conceding that behavior modifiers recognize first that self-control is merely the emission of one set of responses designed to alter the probability of occurrence of another set of responses (Bijou and Baer, 1961, p. 81; Ferster, 1965, p. 21; Holland and Skinner, 1961, Chapter 47; Homme, 1965, p. 504), and second, that self-controlling responses are acquired through social learning (e.g. Bandura and Kupers, 1964; Kanfer and Marston, 1963), most behaviorists still appear to regard self-control as a personal virtue and its absence a personal deficit (Stuart,

1971). For example, Cautela (1969, p. 324) is concerned with the individual's ability to manipulate the contingencies of his own behavior while Kanfer (1970) offers among other explanations for the breakdown of self-control "the patient's commitment to change," a presumed index of the patient's degree of motivation, or "the patient's prior skill in use of self-reward or self-punishment responses for changing behavior," a presumed index of the patient's capacity to utilize treatment.

In any event, the relevance of the concept of self-control to the management of overeating may be questioned in the light of many recent studies. The most basic of these is the work of Stunkard (1959b) who demonstrated that in comparison with nonobese subjects, obese subjects are far less likely to report hunger in association with "gastric motility." Thus the cues for hunger experiences of the obese may be tied to external events. Several ingenious studies have contributed to this possibility. First, Schacter and his associates demonstrated that obese subjects are less influenced than nonobese subjects by manipulated fear and deprivation of food (Schacter *et al.*, 1968), while they are more influenced by the time they think it is than by the actual time (Schacter and Gross, 1968). In addition it was shown that when the cues of eating are absent, as on religious fast days, obese subjects are more likely to observe dietary restrictions than nonobese subjects (Schacter, 1968). In a similar vein, Nisbett (1968) and Hashim and Van Itallie (1965) showed that obese subjects are more influenced by the taste of food than are nonobese subjects when the duration of food deprivation is controlled. These varied studies and others suggested that the first of two requirements for the treatment of overeating must stress environmental management rather than self-control because the cues of overeating are environmental rather than intrapersonal.

The second requirement for the management of obesity must be a manipulation of the energy balance—the balance between the consumption of energy as food and the expenditure of energy through exercise. If all of the energy which is derived from the consumed food is expended in exercise, then gross body weight will remain constant. Any excess of food energy consumption over energy expenditure, however, is stored as adiposity at the rate of approximately one pound of body fat for each excessive 3500 kcal (Gordon, 1969, p. 148; Mayer, 1968, p. 158). Weight can therefore be lost through: (1) an increase in the amount of exercise, holding food intake constant; (2) a decrease in the amount of food intake, holding exercise constant; or (3) both an increase in exercise and a decrease in food intake.

It has been well-demonstrated that the rising problem of obesity is associated with decreasing demands for exercise. Mayer (1968) suggested that "inactivity is the most important factor explaining the frequency of 'creeping' overweight in modern societies (p. 821)," while Durnin and Passmore (undated, p. 143) revealed that food intake is typically not adjusted to reduced exercise. Recent evidence adduced by the Agricultural Research Service (1969, pp. 22–24) demonstrated that the diets of young men in higher-income brackets include 20 per cent more kcal than the diets of those with smaller incomes and presumably more physically taxing occupations, and this is most likely to result in some measure of obesity among middle-class males. Increase in the rate of exercise can, however, have a profound effect upon body weight although the amount of exercise necessary is greater than generally expected.* Furthermore, given the fact that an obese person actually expends *less* energy than a nonobese person doing the same amount of work (e.g. a 250-pound man walking 1.5 mph expends 5.34 kcal per min, while a 150-pound man walking at the same rate and carrying a 100-pound load expends 5.75 kcal per min [Bloom and Eidex, 1967, p. 687]), planned programs for exercise are particularly important. In addition to aiding in the management of gross body weight, exercise programs for the thin as well as the obese seem definitely to reduce the risk of certain cardiovascular diseases (Mayer, 1967).

Just as it is important systematically to increase the amount of exercise, so too is it important to reduce the amount of food or change the nature of foods eaten. Mayer (1968) recommends:

> A balanced diet, containing no less than 14 per cent of protein, no more than 30 per cent of fat (with saturated fats cut down), and the rest carbohydrates (with sucrose—ordinary sugar—cut down to a low level) ... (p. 160).

Apart from its nutritional advantages, it is important to include a substantial amount of protein in the diet because smaller amounts of protein as opposed to carbohydrates produce satiety and because a portion of the caloric content of protein is used in its own metabolism (Gordon, 1969, p. 149), leaving a smaller proportion as a possible

---

*Stuart (unpublished data) asked a group of obese women to estimate the amount of exercise required to work off the weight gain attributable to such common foods as donuts, ice cream sodas and potato chips. Comparing their answers with the estimates based upon Konishi's (1965) figures for a 150-pound man walking at the rate of 3.5 miles per hr (29, 49 and 21 min respectively), they were found to underestimate the true work required by from 200 to 300 per cent.

contributor to adiposity. Conversely, it is important to reduce the amount of carbohydrates consumed because a higher proportion of its caloric content is available for adiposity, because at least certain carbohydrates—e.g. sucrose (Yudkin, 1969)—are associated with increased incidence of certain cardiovascular diseases to which obese persons are vulnerable, and because "carbohydrate food causes the storage of unusually large amounts of water (Gordon, 1969, p. 148)"— typically a special problem faced by obese individuals.

The foregoing observations lead to several basic considerations for weight reduction programs. First, it is essential to design an environment in which food-relevant cues are conducive to the maximal practice of prudent eating habits. This is required by the fact that overeating among obese persons appears to be under environmental control. Also, training the patient in the techniques of environmental control will probably reduce the gradual loss of therapeutic effect found in certain (e.g. Silverstone and Solomon, 1965) but not all (Penick *et al.*, 1970) other programs. Second, it is essential to plan toward a negative energy balance. In doing this, however, it is essential to avoid exercise or dietary excesses. They are unlikely to be followed, and if they are followed each may result in iatrogenic complications. Excessive exercise might lead to overexertion or serious cardiovascular illness. Unbalanced diets might lead to physiological disease, while insufficient diets might lead to enervation and physiologically produced depression. It is therefore essential to plan gradual weight-loss programs associated with progressive changes in the energy balance, as these are both safer and more likely to meet with success (Wang and Sandoval, 1969, p. 220). The exact determination of these levels must be empirically determined for each patient, beginning with tables of recommended dietary allowance (e.g. Mayer, 1968, pp. 168–169), adjusting these for the amount of exercise, carefully monitoring weight and mood changes as time on the program progresses, and being careful to make certain that the degree of weight loss provides sufficient motivation for the patient to continue using the program.

TREATMENT

Translation of the above rationale into a set of specific treatment procedures sometimes requires an arbitrary selection of intervention alternatives derived from contrary or contradictory conclusions in the basic research literature. For example, while Gordon, (1969) repudiated his earlier contention that a patient's eating several smaller meals each day would necessarily result in greater weight loss than his eating only the three traditional meals, others (e.g. Debry *et al.*, 1968) have shown that *with caloric intake held constant* patients who eat three meals daily may not only maintain their weight but may actually gain weight, while the same patients dividing their caloric allowance into seven meals lose weight precipitously. As another example, Nisbett and Kanouse (1969) demonstrated that obese food shoppers actually buy less the more deprived of food they are while nonobese shoppers increase their food buying as a function of the extent of food deprivation. In contrast, Stuart (unpublished data) demonstrated that when a group of obese women confined their food shopping to the hours of 3:30–5:00 p.m., they purchased 20 per cent more food than when they postponed their food shopping until 6:30–8:00 p.m. Thus the therapist reading the Gordon and Nisbett studies would have his patients eat three meals and delay their food shopping until they were at least moderately deprived of food, while the therapist familiar with the work of Debry *et al.* and Stuart would do just the reverse. The therapist familiar with both must decide which recommendations to follow, framing his decision as a reversible hypothesis which can be invalidated in response to patient-produced data.

The treatment procedures which have been used in this investigation fall into three broad categories. First, an effort is made to establish firm control over the eating environment. This requires: (a) the elimination or suppression of cues associated with problematic eating while strengthening the cues associated with desirable eating patterns; (b) planned manipulation of the actual response of eating to accelerate desirable elements of the response while decelerating undesirable aspects; and (c) the manipulation of the contingencies associated with problematic and desirable eating patterns. A sample of the procedures used in the service of each of these objectives is presented in Table 40.1.

Second, an effort is made to establish a dietary program for each patient on an individual basis. The first step in the development of a diet is completion by the patient of a self-monitoring food intake form. Because patients frequently claim to exist on unbelievably small quantities of food, only to lose weight rapidly when their diet is regulated at amounts two or three times greater than originally claimed, it is helpful to provide some social monitoring of the use of the monitoring sheets to ensure accuracy. Procedures such as those employed by Powell and Azrin (1968) have proven helpful. When validated eating records have been obtained

Table 40.1. Sample Procedures Used to Strengthen Appropriate Eating and to Weaken Inappropriate Eating.

Cue elimination	Cue suppression	Cue strengthening
1. Eat in one room only 2. Do nothing while eating 3. Make available proper foods only: (a) shop from a list; (b) shop only after full meal 4. Clear dishes directly into garbage 5. Allow children to take own sweets	1. Have company while eating 2. Prepare and serve small quantities only 3. Eat slowly 4. Save one item from meal to eat later 5. If high-calorie foods are eaten, they must require preparation	1. Keep food, weight chart 2. Use food exchange diet 3. Allow extra money for proper foods 4. Experiment with attractive preparation of diet foods 5. Keep available pictures of desired clothes, list of desirable activities

↓ Reduce strength of undesirable responses	↓ Increase strength of desirable responses
1. Swallow food already in mouth before adding more 2. Eat with utensils 3. Drink as little as possible during meals	1. Introduce planned delays during meal 2. Chew food slowly, thoroughly 3. Concentrate on what is being eaten

↓ Provide decelerating consequences	↓ Provide accelerating consequences
1. Develop means for display of caloric value of food eaten daily, weight changes 2. Arrange to have deviations from program ignored by others except for professionals 3. Arrange to have overeater re-read program when items have not been followed and to write techniques which might have succeeded	1. Develop means for display of caloric value of food eaten daily, weight changes 2. Develop means of providing social feedback for all success by: (a) family; (b) friends; (c) co-workers; (d) other weight losers; and/or (e) professionals 3. Program material and/or social consequences to follow: (a) the attainment of weight loss subgoals; (b) completion of specific daily behavioral control objectives

for a 14-day period, adjustments in food intake can be planned based upon recommended caloric levels, balanced diet planning and adjustments for the level of food intake in light of the patient's exercise. In dietary planning, "food exchange" recommendations are made (Stuart and Davis, 1972) rather than recommendations for specific food choices. In food exchange dieting, foods in each of six food categories (e.g. milk, fruit, meat, etc.) are grouped according to similar caloric levels (e.g. one egg has approximately the same caloric value as one slice of bread). Selections are made according to food exchanges and this greatly increases the ease and precision of meal planning. Furthermore, when this is done as a means of increasing the probability that the diet will be followed, the unavailability of specific foods frequently leads to a termination of the entire dietary program.   ·

Third, an effort is made to develop an individualized aerobics exercise program based upon walking in most cases (Cooper, 1968). In introducing the need for exercise, the patient is offered a choice between adherence to a punishing diet which may lead to chronic discomfort throughout the day and a more permissive diet coupled with exercise which may lead to discomfort for an hour or less per day. When an exercise program is developed, an effort is made to weave the exercise activity into the normal fabric of the patient's day to increase the likelihood that it will be followed. For example, a patient might be asked to park his car 10 blocks from the home of friends he is about to visit, to avoid elevators and walk up to his destinations, and to carry each item upstairs as needed—rather than allowing several items to accumulate—as a means of increasing the number of steps necessary.

RESULTS

The pilot investigation reported here reflects the treatment of six overweight, married, middle-class women (171–212 pounds) between the ages of 27 and 41. Each woman requested treatment on a self-referred basis. Treatment was offered on an individual basis, but women were randomly assigned to one of two cohorts. Both groups of three patients were asked to complete the Sixteen Personality Factor Questionnaire (Cattell and Eber, 1967) and to keep a 5-week baseline of their weight and food intake. The first group was then offered treatment twice weekly (average 40 min per session) for a 15-week period, while the second group was asked to practice "self-control" of eating behavior. The self-control subjects were given the same diet planning materials and exercise program that the treatment group was offered. They were not, however, given instruction for the management of food in the environment. At the conclusion of the 15-week period, the treated group was asked to continue the treatment program and the second group was offered 15 weeks of the same treatment. Approximately 6 months following the termination of treatment of Group 1 and 3 months following the termination of treatment of Group 2, follow-up data were collected including weight, eating patterns and the readministration of the Cattell 16 P.F. The results including follow-up data are presented in Fig. 40.1. It will be seen that patients in Group 1 lost an average of 35 pounds while those in Group 2 lost an average of 21 pounds. These results are consistent with the objective set for gradual weight loss approximating one pound per week. It will also be seen that the mere collection of baseline self-monitoring

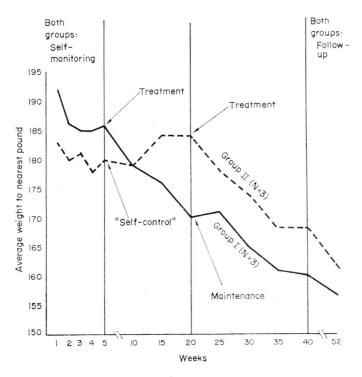

Fig. 40.1. Weight changes in two groups of women undergoing behavior therapy for overeating.

data was associated with mild weight loss in both groups, although these gains were dissipated as time progressed for the second group. Finally, comparison of the pre- and post-test personality test results reveal little change other than small improvement in "ego stability" and tension (Factors C and Q4) of the 16 P.F.

The results provide suggestive evidence for the usefulness of a threefold treatment of obesity stressing environmental control of overeating, nutritional planning and regulated increase in energy expenditure. The sample size was too small to permit generalization, and the superiority of the initially treated (Group 1) over the initially untreated (Group 2) patients may be due to an inclination among the latter group to be casual about weight reduction. To forestall this possibility, every effort was made to make the treatment appear "official" but no validation of the success of this effort was undertaken. Furthermore, it is perhaps noteworthy that the results were obtained with no evidence of psychological stress in a patient population which was regarded as "well-adjusted" at the start and termination of treatment.

To validate these procedures in any definitive manner, extensive replication is needed using careful experimental control procedures applied to a far more diverse population than was used in this pilot study. Research such as that recently completed by Penick *et al.* (1970) has made important strides in this direction. It is only through such experimentation that the vast amount of "faddism and quackery (Gordon, 1969, p. 148)" which characterizes the broad field of obesity control can be replaced by a scientifically validated set of procedures.

REFERENCES

Agricultural Research Service, U.S. Department of Agriculture. *Food Intake and Nutritive Value of Diets of Men, Women and Children in the United States, Spring* 1965: *A Preliminary Report.* (ARS 62-18), Washington, D.C.: United States Government Printing Office, 1969.

American Academy of Pediatrics, Committee on Nutrition. Obesity in childhood. *Pediatrics,* 1967, **40**, 455–465.

Bandura, A. and Kupers, C. J. Transmission of patterns of self-reinforcement through modeling. *J. abnorm. soc. Psychol.,* 1964, **69**, 1–9.

Bernard, J. L. Rapid treatment of gross obesity by operant techniques. *Psychol. Rep.,* 1968, **23**, 663–666.

Bijou, S. W. and Baer, D. M. *Child Development I: A Systematic and Empirical Theory.* Appleton-Century-Crofts, New York, 1961.

Bloom, W. L. and Eidex, M. F. The comparison of energy expenditure in the obese and lean. *Metabolism,* 1967, **16**, 685–692.

Bortz, W. A 500 pound weight loss. *Am. J. Med.*, 1969, **47**, 325–331.

Bray, G. A. Effect of caloric restriction on energy expenditure in obese patients. *Lancet*, 1969, **2**, 397–398.

Bruch, H. The psychosomatic aspects of obesity. *Am. Practnr. Dig. Treat.*, 1954, **5**, 48–49.

Cappon, D. Obesity. *Can. Med. Assoc. Jl*, 1958, **79**, 568–573.

Cattell, R. B. and Eber, H. W. *Handbook for the Sixteen Personality Factor Questionnaire*. The Institute for Personality and Ability Testing, Champaign, Ill., 1957.

Cauffman, W. J. and Pauley, W. G. Obesity and emotional status. *Penn. Med. Jl*, 1961, **64**, 505–507.

Cautela, J. R. Covert sensitization. *Psychol. Rep.*, 1967, **20**, 459–468.

Cautela, J. R. Behavior therapy and self-control: Techniques and implications. In *Behavior Therapy: Appraisal and Status* (Ed. C. M. Franks). McGraw-Hill, New York, 1969.

Conrad, S. W. The problem of weight reduction in the obese woman. *Am. Practnr. Dig. Treat.*, 1954, **5**, 38–47.

Cooper, K. H. *Aerobics*. Bantam Books, New York, 1968.

Cornell Conferences on Therapy. The management of obesity. *N.Y.S.J. Med.*, 1958, **58**, 79–87.

Debry, G., Rohr, R., Azouaou, G., Vassilitch, I., and Mottaz, G. Study of the effect of dividing the daily caloric intake into seven meals on weight loss in obese subjects. *Nutritio Dieta*, 1968, **10**, 288–296.

Durnin, J. V. G. A. and Passmore, R. (undated) The relation between the intake and expenditure of energy and body weight. *Problemes Actuels D'Endocrinologie et de Nutrition* (Serie No. 9), 136–149.

Ferster, C. B. Classification of behavior pathology. In *Research in Behavior Modification* (Eds. L. Krasner and L. P. Ullmann). Holt, Rinehart & Winston, New York, 1965.

Franklin, R. E. and Rynearson, E. H. An evaluation of the effectiveness of diet instruction for the obese. *Staff Meet. Mayo Clin.* 1960, **35**, 123–124.

Glucksman, M. L., Hirsch, J., McCully, R. S., Barron, B. A., and Knittle, J. L. The response of obese patients to weight reduction: A quantitative evaluation of behavior. *Psychosom. Med.*, 1968, **30**, 359–373.

Gordon, E. S. The present concept of obesity: Etiological factors and treatment. *Med. Times*, 1969, **97**, 142–155.

Hamburger, W. W. Emotional aspects of obesity. *Med. Clin. N. Am.*, 1951, **35**, 483–499.

Hanley, F. W. The treatment of obesity by individual and group hypnosis. *Can. Psychiat. Assoc. J.*, 1967, **12**, 549–551.

Harris, M. B. Self-directed program for weight control—A pilot study. *J. abnorm. Psychol.*, 1969, **74**, 263–270.

Hashim, S. A. and Van Itallie, T. B. Studies in normal and obese subjects with a monitored food dispensary device. *Ann. N.Y. Acad. Sci.*, 1965, **131**, 654–661.

Holland, J. G. and Skinner, B. F. *The Analysis of Behavior*. McGraw-Hill, New York, 1961.

Homme, L. E. Perspectives in psychology: XXIV. Control of coverants, the operants of the mind. *Psychol. Rec.*, 1965, **15**, 501–511.

Kanfer, F. H. Self-monitoring: Methodological limitations and clinical applications. *J. consult. clin. Psychol.*, 1970, **35**, 148–152.

Kanfer, F. H. and Marston, A. R. Conditioning of self-reinforcement responses: An analogue to self-confidence training. *Psychol. Rep.*, 1963, **13**, 63–70.

Kaplan, H. I. and Kaplan, H. S. The psychosomatic concept of obesity. *J. nerv. ment. Dis.*, 1957, **125**, 181–201.

Konishi, F. Food energy equivalents of various activities. *J. Am. Diet. Assoc.* 1965, **46**, 186–188.

Kornhaber, A. Group treatment of obesity. *G.P.*, 1968, **5**, 116–120.

Kroger, W. S. Comprehensive management of obesity. *Am. J. clin. Hypnosis*, 1970, **12**, 165–176.

MacCuish, A. C., Munro, J. F., and Duncan, L. J. P. Follow-up study of refractory obesity treated by fasting. *Br. Med. J.*, 1968, **1**, 91–92.

Mayer, J. Inactivity, an etiological factor in obesity and heart disease. In *Symposia of the Swedish Nutrition Foundation, V: Symposium on Nutrition and Physical Activity* (Ed. G. Blix). Almqvist & Wiksells, Uppsala, Sweden, 1967.

Mayer, J. *Overweight: Causes, Cost and Control.* Prentice-Hall, Englewood Cliffs, N.J., 1968.

Mees, H. L. and Keutzer, C. S. Short term group psychotherapy with obese women. *NW Med.*, 1967, **66**, 548–550.

Metropolitan Life Insurance Company. New weight standards for men and women. *Statistical Bulletin*, 1969, **40**, 1–8.

Meyer, V. and Crisp, A. H. Aversion therapy in two cases of obesity. *Behav. Res. & Therapy*, 1964, **2**, 143–147.

Modell, W. Status and prospect of drugs for overeating. *J. Am. Med. Assoc.*, 1960, **173**, 1131–1136.

Newburgh, L. H. and Johnston, M. W. The nature of obesity. *J. clin. Invest.*, 1930, **8**, 197–213.

Nisbett, R. E. Taste, deprivation, and weight determinants of eating behavior. *J. person. soc. Psychol.*, 1968, **10**, 107–116.

Nisbett, R. E. and Kanouse, D. E. Obesity, food deprivation, and supermarket shopping behavior. *J. person. soc. Psychol.*, 1969, **12**, 289–294.

Penick, S. B., Filion, R., Fox, S., and Stunkard, A. Behavior modification in the treatment of obesity. Paper presented at the annual meeting of the Psychosomatic Society, Washington, D.C., 1970.

Powell, J. and Azrin, N. The effects of shock as a punisher for cigarette smoking. *J. appl. Behav. Anal.*, 1968, **1**, 63–71.

Ramsay, R. W. Vermageringsexperiment, Psychologisch labratorium van de Universiteit van Amsterdam, *Researchpracticum*, **101**, voorjaar 1968.

Schacter, S. Obesity and eating. *Science*, 1968, **161**, 751–756.

Schacter, S., Goldman, R., and Gordon, A. Effects of fear, food deprivation, and obesity on eating. *J. person. soc. Psychol.*, 1968, **10**, 91–97.

Schacter, S. and Gross, L. P. Manipulated time and eating behavior. *J. person. soc. Psychol.*, 1968, **10**, 98–106.

Seltzer, C. C. and Mayer, J. A simple criterion of obesity. *Postgrad. Med.*, 1965, **38**, A101–A106.

Shipman, W. G. and Plesset, M. R. Anxiety and depression in obese dieters. *Archs. gen. Psychiat.*, 1963, **8**, 26–31.

Silverstone, J. T. and Solomon, T. The long-term management of obesity in general practice. *Br. J. clin. Pract.*, 1965, **19**, 395–398.

Simon R. I. Obesity as a depressive equivalent. *J. Am. Med. Assoc.*, 1963, **183**, 208–210.

Stanley, E. J., Glaser, H. H., Levin, D. G., Adams, P. A., and Cooley, I. C. Overcoming obesity in adolescents: A description of a promising endeavor to improve management. *Clin. Pediat.*, 1970, **9**, 29–36.

Stokes, S. A. Fasting for obesity. *Am. J. Nurs.*, 1969, **69**, 796–799.

Stuart, R. B. Behavioral control of overeating. *Behav. Res. & Therapy*, 1967, **5**, 357–365.

Stuart, R. B. Situational versus self control. In *Advances in Behavior Therapy* (Ed. R. D. Rubin). Academic Press, New York, 1971.

Stuart, R. B. and Davis, B. *Slim Chance in a Fat World: Behavioral Control of Obesity.* Research Press, Champaign, Ill., 1972.

Stunkard, A. Eating patterns and obesity. *Psychiat. Q.*, 1959a, **33**, 284–295.

Stunkard, A. Obesity and the denial of hunger. *Psychosom. Med.*, 1959b, **21**, 281–289.

Stunkard, A. Environment and obesity: Recent advances in our understanding of regulation of food intake in man. *Fed. Proc.*, 1968, **6**, 1367–1373.

Stunkard, A., Levine, H., and Fox, S. The management of obesity. *Archs. intern. Med.*, 1970, **125**, 1067–1072.

Stunkard, A. and McLaren-Hume, M. The results of treatment for obesity. *Archs. intern. Med.*, 1959, **103**, 79–85.

Suczek, R. F. The personality of obese women. *Am. J. Clin. Nutr.*, 1957, **5**, 197–202.

United States Public Health Service (undated) *Obesity and Health.* (Publication No. 1495), United States Department of Health, Education and Welfare, Washington, D.C.

United States Senate, Select Committee on Nutrition and Human Needs. *Nutrition and Human Needs—1970.* Parts I, II & III. U.S. Government Printing Office, Washington, D.C., 1970.

Wagonfield, S. and Wolowitz, H. M. Obesity and self-help group: A look at TOPS. *Am. J. Psychiat.*, 1968, **125**, 253–255.

Wang, R. I. H. and Sandoval, R. Current status of drug therapy in management of obesity. *Wis. Med. J.*, 1969, **68**, 219–220.

Yudkin, J. Sucrose and heart disease. *Nutrition Today*, 1969, **4**, 16–20.

ARTICLE 41

External vs. Self-Control in the Management and Maintenance of Weight Loss[1]

D. BALFOUR JEFFREY[2]

Emory University, Atlanta, Georgia

Obesity is a major health problem that affects over 50 million Americans (United States Department of Health, Education, and Welfare, 1967). The treatment of this problem by traditional medical and dietary methods, in general, has yielded poor results. In reviewing the literature, Stunkard and McLaren-Hume (1969) have concluded that most overweight people do not stay in treatment for obesity; of those who continue in treatment, most do not lose weight; of those who lose weight, most regain the weight they have lost after a short period of time. Since current work in reinforcement and attribution theory suggests promising leads for treating even the most refractory behavioral problems, these theories may have useful applications to the treatment of obesity.

Most human social behaviors are operant and under the control of their consequences (Skinner, 1938). Kanfer (1971) theorizes that these stimuli, when self-dispensed, have the capacity to control behavior in the absence of externally dispensed consequences. This proposition has been supported by laboratory and field studies that have reported equal behavioral

[1]This article is based in part on a Ph.D. dissertation submitted by the author to the University of Utah. Deep appreciation is expressed to Donald P. Hartmann, dissertation chairman, for his valuable suggestions and support. Gratitude is also extended to my other committee members, Donna M. Gelfand, Stewart Proctor, Howard N. Sloane, and David H. Dodd, for their helpful feedback. The author also thanks Rashel Jeffrey, Roger C. Katz, and Michael J. Mahoney for their assistance and suggestions. This study was partially supported by a Research Fellowship given to the author from the University of Utah Research Committee.

[2]Reprints, as well as the weight manual described in the article, may be obtained from the author, Department of Psychology, Emory University, Atlanta, Georgia 30322.

effects for external- and self-reinforcement (e.g., Bandura, 1971; Bolstad & Johnson, 1972; Kanfer, 1971).

An implicit aspect of training in self-reinforcement is that while the individual learns to dispense reinforcers to himself—reinforcers that in turn control his own behavior—he also learns that he is the controller of his behavior. This perception of the locus of control and its subsequent influence on behavior has been the major focus of attribution theory (e.g., de Charms, 1968; Rotter, 1966; Valins & Nisbett, 1972). de Charms (1968), for example, theorizes that if a person believes that he is the cause of his own behavior, he is more likely to maintain his behavior in the absence of external rewards. In support of this proposition, Davison and Valins (1969) found that subjects who attributed to themselves the ability to withstand electric shock maintained their toleration of shock longer than subjects who attributed their toleration to a drug that was actually a placebo.

Recent clinical studies of obesity, in which external- and self-reinforcement procedures were combined with other behavioral control techniques, have produced encouraging results (Hall, 1972; Harris, 1969; Mahoney, 1972; Mann, 1972; Penick *et al.*, 1971; Stuart, 1967, 1971). Unfortunately, however, none of these studies has compared the relative efficacy of external- and self-control procedures on both the production and maintenance of weight loss.[3]

Based on the speculations of Kanfer (1971) and de Charms (1968), self- and external-control procedures should be equally effective in producing weight loss during therapy, but self-control procedures should be more effective in promoting the maintenance of weight loss in typical posttreatment environments where external sources of reinforcement may not be available. In view of these considerations, the primary purpose of the present study was to compare the relative efficacy of external- and self-control procedures on both the production and maintenance of weight loss.

---

[3]To avoid confusion in the use of self- and external-hyphenated terms, definitions of these terms as presently used are as follows: Self-reinforcement consists of the individual's dispensing reinforcers to himself, while external reinforcement consists of someone other than the individual (e.g., therapist) dispensing reinforcers. Self-control procedures (i.e. self-reinforcement and self-attribution set) require that the individual be primarily responsible for managing his own behavior. External-control (i.e. external reinforcement and external-attribution set) occurs when other people are primarily responsible for managing an individual's behavior.

SIDE EFFECTS OF THERAPEUTIC INTERVENTIONS

In developing therapeutic techniques for behavioral and physical disorders, the potential adverse side effects of a "successful" treatment are often overlooked. Consider, for example, recent decisions by the federal government that now restrict, because of their dangerous side effects, the use of diet pills for the treatment of obesity. Behavioral interventions, like any treatment, can also have unwanted side effects. For example, while Mann's (1972) subjects achieved impressive weight losses as a result of external-reinforcement methods, many did so only after resorting to a variety of unhealthy techniques, including the use of diuretics, vomiting, starvation, and steam baths to meet their weight goals. In an investigation using self-reinforcement, Mahoney *et al.* (1973) instructed obese subjects to reward themselves with money each week that they achieved their weight goals. They were also told not to reward themselves when their weight goals were not achieved. These unearned rewards were permanently lost (a nonrefundable self-reward contingency). The authors reported that the nonrefundable self-reward contingency produced a high rate of cheating; that is, subjects took their money even though they had not made their weight goals. Another study (Jeffrey *et al.*, 1973) suggested that a nonrefundable contingency, when externally controlled, tended to increase absences at therapy sessions when goals were not met.

In view of these findings, the secondary purpose of this study was to investigate the differential effects of a nonrefundable and refundable contingency for weight loss on dropouts, absences, and cheating.

OVERVIEW

Obese adults were randomly assigned to three experimental treatment groups. A standard control group was not included because previous behavior studies employing a variety of control groups—no-treatment control, waiting-list control, attention-placebo control, information-only control, diet-only control—have consistently reported only small changes in weight ranging from +3.6 to −1.4 lb (e.g., Harris, 1969; Harris & Bruner, 1971; Jeffrey & Christensen, 1972; Mahoney *et al.*, 1973; Wollersheim, 1970). The three experimental groups were (1) an external-control group (EC), which combined external reinforcement with a nonrefundable contingency and an external-attribution set; (2) a self-control group

(SCN), which combined self-reinforcement with a nonrefundable contingency and an internal-attribution set; (3) a self-control group (SCR), which combined self-reinforcement with a refundable contingency and an internal-attribution set. The external- and self-control procedures were included to compare the relative efficacy of these procedures in producing and maintaining weight loss. The nonrefundable and refundable contingencies were used to test the hypothesis that the nonrefundable contingency condition would increase the rate of dropouts, absences, and cheating above that of the refundable contingency condition.

METHOD

Subjects

The subjects, who were solicited through newspaper and radio announcements, were told that the weight-control program was free; that it would require seven weekly meetings in addition to a six-week followup; that it would emphasize the alteration of eating habits; and that each person would need to deposit $35 at the first meeting, a portion of which he could then earn back each week by meeting a specified weight loss goal. They were then questioned to determine whether they met the following eligibility criteria: (1) between 10 and 80% overweight by the national standard of obesity (United States Department of Health, Education, and Welfare, 1967); (2) not pregnant; (3) not involved in any other current weight program; (4) not on any medication that might affect weight loss (e.g., "diet pills"); and (5) planning to remain in the immediate area during treatment and followup. Out of an initial pool of 148 potential subjects, 57 females and five males met these criteria and were randomly assigned to the three treatment groups.

In general, these subjects were typical of the "hard core" overweight (Young *et al.*, 1957). Most were middle-aged ($\bar{X}$ = 39 years old), considerably overweight (42% on the average), and all had experienced previous unsuccessful attempts to regulate their weight either through medical means (88%) or through commercial weight programs (61%).

Weight Control Therapists

Three undergraduate students, one male and two females, were the principal weight control therapists.[4] None of the therapists had previous

---

[4]Gratitude is extended to Scott Anderson, Vicky Harris, and Lesley Holloman, who served as therapists.

clinical experience working with obese patients. To insure proper administration of the treatments, all three were rehearsed prior to the beginning of the study and monitored while administering the individual sessions. They were not informed of the hypotheses of the investigation until after its completion. In addition, their appointment schedules were balanced to insure an equivalent amount of contact between therapists and subjects in all three treatment groups.

Standardized Treatment Procedures

The general sequence of treatment meetings consisted of an initial group orientation meeting, then seven individual weekly meetings, and finally a followup weigh-in six weeks after the end of treatment.

As the subjects arrived for their group's orientation meeting, they were told that the program would emphasize two aspects of weight control: reinforcement of appropriate weight-control behavior, and alteration of eating habits. The specific procedures that the subjects would use during the program were then explained.

Subjects were given a manual of weight-control procedures that provided (a) brief instructions on how to record one's own weight and eating habits, (b) basic facts of nutrition, (c) specific techniques of weight control, and (d) either an external-control or self-control orientation, depending on the subject's group assignment.[5] The weight-control techniques were divided into three classes: quantity control, quality control, and situation control. Quantity control techniques were designed to decrease the total quantity of food consumed by (1) reducing the amount of food purchased, prepared, and served, (2) leaving food on the plate, (3) eating slowly and taking small bites of food. Quality control techniques were designed to decrease the number of calories consumed by (1) eating low calorie foods, and (2) avoiding high calorie snacks. Situation control techniques were intended to restrict the range of situations in which food was formerly consumed by (1) separating eating from all other activities, (2) eating only when hungry, (3) delaying on-the-spot urges to nibble for progressively longer periods of time (e.g., 5 min., 8 min., etc.) before indulging, (4) buying food when not hungry, and (5) enlisting the help of family and friends to support dieting efforts.

The subjects were given a weight graph with the instruction to record

---

[5]The manual of weight control techniques and the eating habit recording system were modified versions of the ones developed by Mahoney (1972). Special thanks are extended to Michael Mahoney for his permission to use them in this investigation.

their daily weight at the same time, place and state of dress, and to bring the graph to each weekly meeting. Instead of being told to count calories, subjects were asked to keep a running diary of the quantity and quality of food they consumed as well as of the situation under which it was eaten. The subjects were instructed to record a plus each time they ate appropriately, such as eating a reduced serving of mashed potatoes or ice cream, and a minus each time they ate inappropriately, such as eating an extra serving of spaghetti. To insure that the subjects understood the scoring system, the eating diary contained examples of each eating category. In general, the subjects had little difficulty mastering the scoring system.

Two independent contingency systems, one for weight loss and one for eating habits, were applied to all subjects. The weekly criteria for the weight loss contingency required each subject to lose one or more pounds and to bring his completed daily weight graphs to the weekly meetings. The weekly eating habits contingency required each subject to make a ten-point improvement in desirable eating behavior (or when a subject reached 100 to remain above 100), to make a five-point decrement in undesirable eating habits (or maintain a score below 26), and to bring his completed eating diary to the weekly meeting. Each subject deposited $35 at the end of the orientation meeting; each subsequent week he could earn back $1.75 for achieving his weight goals and $2.50 for achieving his eating habit goals. To minimize absences and dropouts, all subjects were told that they would be fined $5 for each absence and would forfeit their entire deposit if they should drop out of the program. Money not earned back or forfeited was given to a nonprofit agency.

After the procedures were explained and questions answered, two copies of a behavioral contract were signed by the subject and the therapist. This contract simply summarized in writing the treatment procedures and the subject's commitment to follow the procedures to the best of his ability.

The weekly treatment meetings consisted of seven individual 15-minute sessions with a therapist. The standard format of these meetings consisted of the therapist weighing the subject, checking his weight graph, counting the number of desirable and undesirable eating habits, setting the weight loss and eating habit goals for the following week, answering questions related to the program, and then writing checks (if appropriate) for weight improvement and for eating habit improvement. Questions unrelated to the weight-control procedures were tactfully evaded.

Before the beginning of the last weekly meeting, the therapist scheduled an appointment for each subject six weeks later. He also reminded all the subjects that they would be paid $5.25, regardless of their weight at that time, for merely attending this final followup weigh-in.

Treatment Groups

External-Control Group (EC)   In addition to the standard procedures, which were explained during the orientation meeting, the therapist told the EC subjects that previous research has shown that weight loss is promoted if the therapist dispenses financial incentives (previously deposited by the subjects) for successful attainment of weight-control goals. The message emphasized the therapist's responsibility for weight loss by means of his control of rewards.

During the concluding portion of each weekly meeting, the therapist wrote two checks, one for $1.75 and the other for $2.50. If the subject brought his properly completed graph and met his weight-loss goal of one or more pounds, he was given the check for $1.75. If he failed to meet these criteria, the check was deposited into a cash box with the understanding that the money would not be refunded. Similarly, if the subject brought his properly completed eating diary and met his eating-habit improvement goal, he was given the check for $2.50. If he failed to meet these criteria, the check for $2.50 was deposited into the same cash box.

Self-Control/Nonrefundable Contingency Group (SCN)   In addition to the standard treatment instructions, SCN subjects were told that each person was responsible for his own weight management. The therapist told them that previous research has shown that weight loss is promoted if they learn to appropriately reward themselves for successful attainment of weight-control goals. They were asked to deposit money with the weight program and then to reward themselves a proportion of their deposit each time they met their weekly goals.

The therapist explained that the subjects should reward themselves $1.75 when they made their weight-loss goal and $2.50 when they made their eating-habit goal. Conversely, they should not reward themselves $1.75 when they did not make their weight-loss goal nor $2.50 when they did not make their eating-habit improvement goal. Although the therapist recommended the appropriate reward procedure, the subjects were reassured that they had complete discretion to pay or not to pay themselves, regardless of whether they had met their goals. To insure confidentiality and minimize any possible social pressure, the therapist wrote the checks to "cash," placed them on the table at the end of the weekly meeting, and then left the interviewing room and closed the door. The subject was left completely alone to decide whether to reward himself by simply picking up the checks and leaving the room, or not to reward himself by placing the check or checks in the cash box. The subject understood that once he deposited the check in the cash box, it would *not* be refunded.

Self-Control/Refundable Contingency Group (SCR)   The procedures in this group were exactly the same as in the other self-control group except for one important clause in the contingency system. The SCR subjects were told that any money they did not reward themselves during the weekly meetings would be refunded at the end of the program. Thus, there was no externally imposed response cost penalty if they did not reward themselves during any given week.

RESULTS

Changes in Weight within Treatments

The mean weights for the three groups across the three measurement periods—pretreatment, posttreatment, and followup—are presented in Fig. 41.1. The average weekly weight loss during treatment was 0.7 lb for the external-control group and 0.9 lb for the combined self-control groups.

Results of a repeated measures analysis of variance across the measurement periods for each of the three treatment groups are summarized in Table 41.1. The changes in weight across the three measurement periods are highly significant ($F > 8.5$, $p < 0.001$) for each treatment group. The Newman–Keuls multiple-range tests are also summarized in Table 41.1. These tests indicated that pretreatment weight was significantly greater than posttreatment and followup weight for all three groups (p's < 0.05). While there was no significant change from posttreatment to followup for subjects in the two self-control groups, subjects in the external-control group significantly increased in weight for posttreatment to followup.

Differences in Weight between Treatments

Feldt (1958) has argued that either blocking or covariance designs are preferred over designs using difference scores. Since previous research

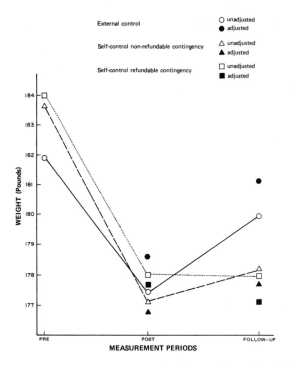

Fig. 41.1. Mean weights for the external-control, self-control nonrefundable contingency, and self-control refundable contingency groups across pretreatment, posttreatment and followup.

(Jeffrey & Christensen, 1972) has typically reported high correlations (r's > 0.9) between pre- and posttreatment weight—a condition that increases the relative power of a covariance analysis—analysis of covariance was used in assessing weight differences across groups.

Preliminary analyses of pretreatment weight differences across groups are not necessary with an analysis of covariance; however, these analyses indicated, as expected, that there were no significant differences among the three groups for actual weight, percentage overweight, or pounds overweight (F's < 1.2). Results of the analysis of covariance, with the pretreatment weight as the covariant and posttreatment and followup weights as the variants, are summarized in Table 41.2. The within-cell regressions were all above $r > 0.9$. The test of treatment differences between post-weights indicated no significant difference. The *a priori* planned comparisons of the followup data indicated a greater weight loss

Table 41.1. Analysis of Variance of Pretreatment, Posttreatment, and Followup Weights for Each Group.

Group/Source	df	MS	F	Newman–Keuls multiple-range test[a]
External-Control				
Within subject				
Treatment period	2	97.59	8.79*	
Error	35	11.08		Pre > Followup > Post
Self-Control/SCN				
Within subject				
Treatment period	2	192.02	13.51*	
Error	29	14.21		Pre > *Followup* > *Post*
Self-Control/SCR				
Within subject				
Treatment period	2	241.02	25.64*	
Error	37	9.40		Pre > *Post* > *Followup*

Note: Three subjects in the EC group and four subjects in the SCN group dropped out during treatment. Consequently, these subjects were excluded from all weight change analyses. One subject in each group attended meetings regularly during treatment, but did not come in for the followup weigh-in. The average weight change between posttreatment and followup for each group was assigned as the estimated weight change for the missing data cell in the respective groups. The smaller degrees of freedom were correspondingly used in the weight change analyses.

[a]Italicized time periods were *not* significantly different at $p < 0.05$.

*$p < 0.001$.

for both self-control groups as compared with the external-control group (p's < 0.05, one-tailed test). These differences between groups can be seen by examining the adjusted mean weights in Fig. 41.1.

Since therapists are usually more concerned with the percentage of individuals who improve rather than mean weight changes, and since treatment failures are more easily identified from individual data, further analyses were conducted on individual weight changes. A weight loss was operationally defined as a loss of 3.5 lb or more during the treatment period. Conversely, a weight gain was defined as a gain of 3.5 lb or more. A weight change of less than 3.5 lb was defined as no weight change.

Improvement rates for each treatment group from pre- to posttreatment and from pretreatment to followup are presented in Table 41.3. The percentage of subjects showing a weight loss from pre- to posttreatment was highly similar across groups and in the 60–69% range. The pretreat-

Table 41.2. Analysis of Covariance with Pretreatment Weight as the Covariant and Posttreatment and Followup Weights as the Variants for the Treatment Groups.

Test/Time	Analyses			
	Source	df	MS	F
Test of Equality of Regression in All Cells				
Posttreatment Weight	Regression	2	35.22	1.62
	Within-cell	49	21.74	
Followup Weight	Regression	2	11.19	0.34
	Within-cell	46[a]	33.11	
Test of Within-Cell Regression				
Posttreatment Weight	Regression	1	60722.73	2725.93†
	Within-cell	51	22.28	
Followup Weight	Regression	1	63172.43	1961.86†
	Within-cell	48[a]	32.20	
Test of Treatments				
Posttreatment Weight	Treatment	2	17.27	0.78
	Within-cell	51	22.28	
Followup Weight	Treatment	2	87.99	2.73*
	Within-cell	48[a]	32.20	

[a]Degrees of freedom for the within-cell has been reduced by 3 to adjust for the three subjects whose followup data were estimated.

*$p < 0.08$.

†$p < 0.001$.

Table 41.3. Percentage of Subjects Showing Changes in Weight from Pretreatment to Posttreatment and from Pretreatment to Followup.

Time	Weight change	Treatments		
		External-control ($n = 19$)	Self-control/ nonrefundable contingency ($n = 16$)	Self-control/ refundable contingency ($n = 20$)
Pretreatment to Posttreatment	Weight loss	63%	69%	60%
	No change	37%	31%	35%
	Weight gain	0%	0%	5%
Pretreatment to Followup	Weight loss	32%	56%	65%
	No change	42%	38%	35%
	Weight gain	26%	6%	0%

ment to followup percentages showed greater variation between groups and tended to support hypothesized differences. While 60% of the subjects in the two self-control groups showed weight losses from pretreatment to followup, only 32% of external-control subjects displayed a comparable weight loss; furthermore, 26% of EC subjects showed a weight gain at followup in comparison to 0 and 6% for the two self-control groups. A chi-square analysis indicated the combined self-control groups differed significantly from the external-control group ($X^2 = 8.57$, $df = 2$, $p < 0.01$, one-tailed test).

Side Effects of the Different Treatment Contingencies

The different contingencies appear to have predictable effects on such behaviors as dropouts, absences, and cheating (dispensing rewards inappropriately). The subjects experiencing the nonrefundable contingencies (EC and SCN subjects) showed a slightly higher dropout rate (16.7% vs. 0%; $X^2 = 2.28$, $df = 1$, $p < 0.08$) and substantially more absences (14.6% vs. 2.5%; $t = 2.18$, $p < 0.05$) than subjects in the SCR group who were on a refundable contingency.

Cheating could take two forms: overindulgence (taking undeserved rewards) and asceticism (not taking a deserved reward). All cases of cheating by self-control subjects, either reinforcement for weight loss (SCN = 15.1%, SCR = 4.4%) or reinforcement for eating-habit improvement (SCN = 3.9%, SCR = 1.8%), consisted of taking undeserved rewards. As expected, subjects in the self-control group with the nonrefundable contingency rewarded themselves undeservedly for weight loss significantly more often than did subjects in the self-control group with the refundable contingency ($t = 1.96$, $p < 0.05$, one-tailed test). In the EC group, there naturally was no cheating since the therapist controlled the dispensing of the monetary rewards.

Eating Habits

A two-way analysis of variance of undesirable eating habits with repeated measures (between pretreatment and posttreatment) for the three groups showed a significant reduction in undesirable eating habits ($F = 151.65$, $df = 1/52$, $p < 0.001$) between the beginning of treatment (mean = 48.9) and the end of treatment (mean = 20.5); however, neither the Treatment nor the Treatment × Time interaction was significant (F's < 1.0). Opposite results were found in the analysis of *desirable* eating habits, which was not surprising in view of the substantial negative correlation between desirable and undesirable eating habits ($r = -0.70$). Since every subject reported better eating habits, neither a decrease in undesirable eating habits nor an increase in desirable eating habits was significantly correlated with weight loss ($0.13 > r > -0.05$).

DISCUSSION

The results show that the self-control and external-control treatment conditions were equally effective in producing weight reduction and improvement in eating habits. The average weekly weight loss during treatment of 0.9 lb for the combined self-control groups and 0.7 lb for the external-control group was consistent with a widely recommended goal of a gradual weight loss of approximately one pound per week (Stuart & Davis, 1972). Furthermore, this rate was comparable to the average weekly weight losses ranging from 0.7 to 1.1 lb reported in previous behavioral studies (e.g., Hall, 1972; Harris, 1969; Mahoney, 1972; Mahoney *et al.*, 1973; Manno & Marston, 1972; Stuart, 1967, 1971; Wollersheim, 1970).

An even more important finding was that both self-control treatments were more effective than the external-control treatment in promoting maintenance of weight loss. Subjects in the self-control conditions maintained their posttreatment weight loss, while subjects in the external-control condition gained back approximately 55% of their weight during the followup period.

Only speculative inferences can be drawn about the specific mechanisms involved in the superior maintenance displayed by subjects in the self-control groups, since the primary purpose of the present study was to contrast self-regulatory procedures with external-control procedures, and not to conduct a component analysis of all treatment ingredients. There are, however, some obvious similarities and some differences among the various treatments used.

All subjects were (1) given the same instructions for recording daily their weight and eating habits (self-monitoring), (2) given the same weekly performance goals and procedures for determining whether they had met their goals (standard setting and evaluation), and (3) provided the same monetary rewards (consequences). In addition, all subjects attended similar individual weigh-ins and were given copies of the same instruction booklet for improving their eating habits. In terms of the results during treatment, all three groups achieved similar weight losses, improvement in eating habits, and attainment of weekly goals. Consequently, it seems unlikely that these factors could have accounted for the superior maintenance of the self-control groups. Instead, it would seem that these differences in maintenance resulted specifically from the manipulated treatment components—locus of reinforcement control and attribution set.

Subjects in the self-control condition were trained to rely upon themselves for consequent control (self-reinforcement) and were implicitly as well as explicitly trained in self-attribution of control. In contrast, subjects in the external-control condition were trained to rely upon others for consequent control and were implicitly as well as explicitly trained in external-attribution of control.

According to Kanfer (1971) and Thoresen and Mahoney (1973), training in the use of self-rewards increases the probability of continued maintenance of a behavior in the virtual absence of external reinforcement. While there was no independent verification of the posttreatment use of self-reinforcement, the present findings suggest that the superior maintenance of weight loss in the self-control groups was due in part to self-dispensed incentives for appropriate weight-control efforts.

Side Effects of the Different Treatment Contingencies

For most obesity studies reference is made to the problem of subjects missing meetings and dropping out of treatment. The 11% dropout rate of the present study compares favorably with the 30–66% dropout rates of traditional medical treatment studies (e.g., Shipman & Plesset, 1963; Silverstone & Solomon, 1965; Stunkard & McLaren-Hume, 1959) as well as with the 4–38% dropout rates of behavioral studies (e.g., Harris, 1969; Harris & Bruner, 1971; Mahoney, 1972; Manno & Marston, 1972; Stuart, 1967; Wollersheim, 1970). Notably, all dropouts and most absences in the present study came exclusively from the nonrefundable contingency groups and were typically people who were not losing weight. Because of these problems associated with the nonrefundable contingency, it would seem prudent to use the nonrefundable contingency very carefully, if at all, in clinical practice.

Eating Habits

An unexpected finding in this study was the lack of a relationship between change in eating habits, as reflected in the subjects' eating diaries, and weight loss. Anecdotal data indicated that when patients did not achieve their weight-loss goal, they tended to inflate the improvement in their eating habits so they would achieve at least one of their performance goals. Unreliability of the eating diary may also have resulted from the subjects not remembering exactly what they had eaten as they sometimes waited a day or longer before filling in the eating diary. Because the reliability of any self-monitoring system must be established before it can be said to be a useful procedure in weight-control programs (Jeffrey, 1974), additional improvements in the eating diary used in this study are needed before it can be recommended for clinical practice.

Recommendations

The findings of the present study demonstrated that the self-control treatments were as effective as the external-control treatment in producing weight loss during therapy and more effective in promoting maintenance of weight loss during followup. These findings suggest that behavioral self-control treatments offer a promising approach to the problem of obesity.

While the effectiveness of self-control interventions offer promise for the treatment of obesity, additional information would be helpful to researchers and clinicians alike. The following topics warrant investigation. First, replication of the self-control interventions using longer treatment and followup periods is needed before definitive conclusions can be made about the long-term efficacy of these procedures. Second, additional studies are required to separate the relative contribution of the self-reinforcement and attribution set manipulations. In the present study, these two components were intentionally combined; however, future studies should attempt to isolate them and assess their individual effects on weight loss. Third, investigations of the degree to which self-reinforcement is maintained over long periods of time are needed to understand more fully the mechanisms involved in the regulation of weight.

Finally, the subjects in this study made the following recommendations for improving future weight programs: (1) continue after the seven weekly meetings the weigh-in on a less frequent basis until the person achieves his weight goal; (2) include maintenance followup meetings after achievement of weight goals; (3) provide additional treatment programs for other problem behaviors that affect overeating (e.g., developing responses to depression other than eating); (4) individualize the monetary contingency system rather than using a standard $35 deposit for everyone. These recommendations deserve careful attention in future experimental research and clinical applications.

CONCLUDING REMARKS: TREATMENT FACTORS IN OBESITY

In applying behavioral principles to clinical settings it is important to keep in mind the complexity of obesity problems and the unique needs of each individual patient. The following overview of a three factor model for the treatment of obesity may serve as a helpful reminder of the many facets that a therapist should consider in implementing weight-control programs. The first factor consists of three intervention components— behavioral control of eating, nutrition management and exercise management. These interventions were initially proposed by Stuart (1971) and are described in Article 40 of this book. The second factor consists of comprehensive treatment planning, from assessment to therapeutic intervention, to followup planning. The present experiment focused primarily on the intervention phase. However, in clinical practice it is also important to first undertake a thorough behavioral assessment (see Chapter 1), and after formal treatment has ended, to hold routine followup meetings to ensure that weight loss is maintained. The third factor is the human factor. It is important that weight-control therapists not only be skilled in principles of behavior therapy, but also that they be skilled in interpersonal relations and be genuinely concerned about the well-being of their patients.

Behavioral approaches to obesity are not a panacea for this complex problem; however, the growing number of controlled experimental studies demonstrate that behaviorally based therapies are an effective approach to weight reduction.

REFERENCES

Bandura, A. Vicarious and self-reinforcement processes. In R. Glaser (ed.) *The Nature of Reinforcement.* Columbus: Merrill, 1971. Pp. 228–278.

Bolstad, O. O. and Johnson, S. M. Self-regulation in the modification of disruptive behavior. *Journal of Applied Behavior Analysis,* 1972, **5**, 443–454.

Davison, G. C. and Valins, S. Maintenance of self-attributed and drug-attributed behavior change. *Journal of Personality and Social Psychology,* 1969, **11**, 25–33.

de Charms, R. *Personal Causation.* New York: Academic Press, 1968.

Feldt, L. S. A comparison of the precision of three experimental designs employing a concomitant variable. *Psychometrika,* 1958, **23**, 335–353.

Hall, S. M. Self-control and therapist control in the behavioral treatment of overweight women. *Behaviour Research and Therapy,* 1972, **10**, 59–68.

Harris, M. B. Self-directed program for weight control—A pilot study. *Journal of Abnormal Psychology,* 1969, **74**, 263–270.

Harris, M. B. and Bruner, C. G. A comparison of a self-control and a contract procedure for weight control. *Behaviour Research and Therapy,* 1971, **9**, 347–354.

Jeffrey, D. B. Self-control: Methodological issues and research trends. In M. J. Mahoney and C. E. Thoresen (eds.) *Self-Control: Power to the Person.* Belmont, Calif.: Brooks/Cole, 1974.

Jeffrey, D. B. and Christensen, E. R. The relative efficacy of behavior therapy, will power, and no-treatment control procedures in the modification of obesity. In A. Stunkard (Chm.), Behavior modification approaches to the treatment of obesity. Symposium presented at the meeting of the Association for Advancement of Behavior Therapy, New York, October 1972.

Jeffrey, D. B., Christensen, E. R., and Pappas, J. P. Developing a behavioral program and therapist manual for the treatment of obesity. *Journal of the American College Health Association,* 1973, **21**, 455–459.

Kanfer, F. D. The maintenance of behavior by self-generated stimuli and reinforcement. In A. Jacobs and L. B. Sachs (eds.) *Psychology of Private Events.* New York: Academic Press, 1971. Pp. 39–57.

Mahoney, M. J. Self-reward and self-monitoring techniques for weight control. Unpublished doctoral dissertation, Stanford University, 1972.

Mahoney, M. J., Moura, N., and Wade, T. The relative efficacy of self-reward, self-punishment, and self-monitoring techniques for weight loss. *Journal of Consulting and Clinical Psychology,* 1973, **40**, 404–407.

Mann, R. A. The behavior-therapeutic use of contingency contracting to control an adult behavior problem: Weight control. *Journal of Applied Behavior Analysis,* 1972, **5**, 99–109.

Manno, B. and Marston, A. R. Weight reduction as a function of negative covert reinforcement (sensitization) versus positive covert reinforcement. *Behaviour Research and Therapy,* 1972, **10**, 201–207.

Penick, S. B., Filion, R., Fox, S., and Stunkard, A. Behavior modification in the treatment of obesity. *Psychosomatic Medicine,* 1971, **33**, 49–55.

Rotter, J. B. Generalized expectancies for internal vs. external control of reinforcement. *Psychological Monographs,* 1966, **80**, 28 pp.

Shipman, W. G. and Plesset, M. R. Anxiety and depression in obese dieters. *Archives of General Psychiatry,* 1963, **8**, 530–535.

Silverstone, J. T. and Solomon, T. The long-term management of obesity in general practice. *British Journal of Clinical Practice,* 1965, **19**, 395–398.

Skinner, B. F. *The Behavior of Organisms.* New York: Appleton-Century-Crofts, 1938.

Stuart, R. B. Behavioral control of overeating. *Behaviour Research and Therapy,* 1967, **5**, 357–365.

Stuart, R. B. A three-dimensional program for the treatment of obesity. *Behaviour Research and Therapy,* 1971, **9**, 177–186.

Stuart, R. B. and Davis, B. *Slim Chance in a Fat World: Behavioral Control of Obesity.* Champaign, Ill.: Research Press, 1972.

Stunkard, A. and McLaren-Hume, M. The results of treatment for obesity. *Archives of Internal Medicine,* 1969, **103**, 79–85.

Thoresen, C. E. and Mahoney, M. J. *Behavioral Self-Control.* New York: Holt, Rinehart & Winston, 1973.

United States Department of Health, Education, and Welfare. *Obesity and Health: A Sourcebook of Current Information for Professional Health Personnel.* Arlington, Va.: United States Department of Health, Education, and Welfare, 1967.

Valins, S. and Nisbett, R. E. Attribution processes in the development and treatment of emotional disorders. In. E. E. Jones, D. E. Kanouse, H. E. Kelley, R. E. Nisbett, S. Valins, and B. Weiner (eds.) *Attribution: Perceiving the Causes of Behavior.* Morristown, N.J.: General Learning Press, 1972. Pp. 137–150.

Wollersheim, J. P. Effectiveness of group therapy based upon learning principles in the treatment of overweight women. *Journal of Abnormal Psychology,* 1970, **76**, 462–474.

Young, C. M., Berresford, K., and Moore, N. S. Psychological factors in weight control. *American Journal of Clinical Nutrition,* 1957, **5**, 186–191.

Epilogue

History contains many examples of revolutionary technologies that promised to solve important human problems. From alchemy in chemistry to megavitamin therapy in medicine, these technologies have frequently succeeded only in raising false hopes and expectations. In light of this experience, how are we to evaluate and place in proper perspective the role of behavior therapy in health care? To accomplish this it is necessary to amplify the important difference between behavior therapy as an extension of the two major learning paradigms, and as *the experimental analysis of behavior*. Although behaviorists extol the virtues of operant and respondent conditioning techniques, it is their adherence to experimental rigor that has proven to be the greatest strength of behavior therapy. The central tenet of this investigative strategy is experimental manipulation, by which functional relationships between behavior and the environment are established. Behavior therapy research, and operant conditioning strategies in particular, has long been characterized by the collection of experimental data. Thus, it is not the anecdotal data surrounding a popular fad that have been presented in this book, but rather some early, experimental findings derived from the application of a well-established behavioral technology to problems of health and illness. Nevertheless, Agras' admonition in the foreword of this book to put these findings in their proper perspective should be taken seriously. New frontiers have merely been probed, and while preliminary reports and discoveries have been encouraging, overzealousness and premature conclusions could prove to be misleading.

In any event, we feel strongly that the strategy of an experimental analysis of behavior has much to offer any systematic study of the effects of the environment on physiologic disease. The collection of precise, reliable data, together with a careful analysis of the conditions under which symptoms occur and the consequences that they produce, are useful guidelines with which few behaviorists would disagree. Furthermore, the use of powerful experimental designs with reversals or multiple baselines, coupled with replications by other investigators, are important criteria by which to accept experimental findings with any degree of confidence.

With regard to specific health problems that have been shown to be amenable to behavior therapy techniques, global statements about effectiveness or utility should be made with great care. In many cases, behavioral methods may eventually become a useful adjunct to traditional medical treatments. Such would be the case for cardiovascular disease, where chemotherapy as well as surgical techniques have already greatly improved patient prognoses. A similar application seems likely for such diverse problems as epilepsy, migraine headaches, chronic pain, and asthma, where behavior therapy might be used to supplement existing treatment methods.

In some instances, however, behavior therapy techniques may prove to be the most effective approach in a combination of treatment modalities, if not the treatment of choice. These areas, where the results of behavioral treatments have been especially encouraging, include enuresis, encopresis, alcoholism, obesity, and anorexia nervosa.

Potential areas for research should not, however, be restricted to the ones described above. Other problems deserving further investigation include gastric dysfunction, palsies, neural functioning, habit disorders such as drug addiction, and the management of chronic dialysis and diabetic patients. Indeed, researchers seem bound only by the limits that technology places upon them in relation to the selection and measurement of appropriate dependent variables.

It is hoped that the material presented in this book will serve a number of purposes. First, we feel that it offers the practicing clinician new ways of conceptualizing and dealing with some common health problems. Second, these data may serve to stimulate interest and research in the application of behavioral technology to health care in general. And finally, we believe that this material highlights the need for closer communication and collaborative efforts between medical and behavioral scientists.

In summary, the application of behavior therapy techniques to health care represents a promising and exciting area for future research. Certainly, the optimism generated by these preliminary findings will be either tempered or fueled by carefully replicated experimentation. We encourage investigators in all health related disciplines to pursue this potentially powerful research strategy.

R.C.K.
S.I.Z.

Index

621

TITLES IN THE PERGAMON GENERAL PSYCHOLOGY SERIES